INSIGHTS INTO
PERSONAL COMPUTERS

INSIGHTS INTO PERSONAL COMPUTERS

Edited by **Amar Gupta** and **Hoo-min D. Toong**

Sloan School of Management
Massachusetts Institute of Technology

With valuable contributions from

J. F. Bucy,
President and Chief Executive Officer, Texas Instruments

P. D. Estridge,
President, IBM Entry Systems Division

B. O. Evans,
Senior Investment Partner, Hambrecht & Quist (formerly IBM Corporate Vice President of Engineering Programs and Technology)

W. R. Hewlett,
Vice Chairman, Board of Directors, Hewlett-Packard

M. Hsu,
Assistant Professor, Harvard University

K. Kobayashi,
Chairman of the Board and Chief Executive Officer, NEC Corporation

S. E. Madnick,
Associate Professor, M I T

R. C. Miller,
Senior Vice President, Data General Corporation

R. N. Noyce,
Vice-Chairman, Board of Directors, Intel Corporation

K. H. Olsen,
President, Digital Equipment Corporation

S. E. Pratt,
President, Venture Economics

J. V. Roach,
Chairman of the Board, President, and Chief Executive Officer, Tandy Corporation

F. A. Wang,
Executive Vice-President and Chief Development Officer, Wang Laboratories, Inc.

and others

IEEE PRESS

The Institute of Electrical and Electronics Engineers, Inc., New York

Copyright © 1985 by

THE INSTITUTE OF ELECTRICAL
AND ELECTRONICS ENGINEERS, INC.
345 East 47th Street
New York, NY 10017
All rights reserved.

PRINTED IN THE UNITED STATES OF AMERICA

IEEE Order Number PC01826

Library of Congress Cataloging in Publication Data
Main entry under title:

Insights into personal computers.

Includes indexes.
1. Microcomputers.   I. Gupta, Amar.   II. Toong,
Hoo-min D.   III. Bucy, J. F.   IV. Title: Personal
computers.
QA76.5.I486   1985   001.64   84-29707
ISBN 0-87942-188-6

The Contributors

Wallace W. Anderson
Texas Instruments

David J. Bradley
IBM

J. Fred Bucy
Texas Instruments

Robert E. Childs, Jr.
Intel Corporation

John D. Clarke
Digital Equipment Corporation

John Crawford
Intel Corporation

Bruce Daniels
Apple Computer Inc.

Amhed H. M. El-Sherbini
Wang Laboratories, Inc.

Phillip D. Estridge
IBM

Bob O. Evans
Hambrecht & Quist (Formerly IBM)

Barry James Folsom
Digital Equipment Corporation

Stan Fry
Wang Laboratories, Inc.

Amar Gupta
MIT—Sloan School of Management

Ronald J. Ham
Digital Equipment Corporation

William R. Hewlett
Hewlett-Packard Company

David L. House
Intel Corporation

Meichun Hsu
Harvard University

Ryohei Ichikawa
NEC Corporation

Sundaresan Jayaraman
Software Arts Products Corporation

Akira Kato
NEC Corporation

Roubina Khoylian
Venture Economics

Koji Kobayashi
NEC Corporation

Milos Konopasek
Software Arts Products Corporation

David A. Kummer
IBM

Steven W. Leininger
Tandy Corporation

Stuart E. Madnick
MIT—Sloan School of Management

Michael L. McMahan
Texas Instruments

Robert C. Miller
Data General Corporation

Gerald E. Nelson
Hewlett-Packard Company

Robert N. Noyce
Intel Corporation

Kenneth H. Olsen
Digital Equipment Corporation

Stanley E. Pratt
Venture Economics

John V. Roach
Tandy Corporation

Richard A. Ross
Metatron, Inc.

Mike Smutek
Wang Laboratories, Inc.

Richard T. Tarrant
Texas Instruments

Harry R. Tennant
Texas Instruments

Hoo-min D. Toong
MIT—Sloan School of Management

Donald A. Wade
Data General Corporation

Christine Wallis
Data General Corporation

William T. Walters
Tandy Corporation

Frederick A. Wang
Wang Laboratories, Inc.

Kazuya Watanabe
NEC Corporation

Nancy Webb
Wang Laboratories, Inc.

Dedicated to

<table>
<tr><td>

my father, Kanti Saran,
my mother, Urmila,
and
my wife, Poonam

Amar

</td><td>

and

</td><td>

my father, Peter,
my mother, Jessie,
and
my friends and colleagues
Stu, John, Mark, and Mei

Hoo-min

</td></tr>
</table>

CONTENTS

Preface   ***xii***

1   **Bringing Everyman into the Computer Age**   1

H. D. TOONG AND A. GUPTA

Introduction · Anatomy of a Computer · Characteristics of the Personal Computer · Hardware · Software · The Industry · Networks · Conclusion

2   **The First Decade of Personal Computers**   17

A. GUPTA AND H. D. TOONG

Introduction · Hardware · Software · Architectures · Markets · Conclusion

3   **The Design and Development of a Family of Personal Computers for Engineers and Scientists**   37

G. E. NELSON AND W. R. HEWLETT

Introduction · Design Objectives · Design Implementation · Future Trends · Conclusion

4   **Ease-of-Use Features in the Texas Instruments Professional Computer**   55

J. F. BUCY, W. W. ANDERSON, M. L. MCMAHAN, R. T. TARRANT, AND H. R. TENNANT

Introduction · TIPC Design · System Architecture · NaturalLink · Speech Command System · Summary

5 Digital's Personal Computers 78

K. H. OLSEN, B. J. FOLSOM, R. J. HAM, AND J. D. CLARKE

Introduction • Professional Personal Computers • Rainbow Personal Computers • DECmate II Personal Computer • Basic Configurations • Conclusion

6 The Wang Professional Image Computer: A New Dimension to Personal and Office Computing 103

F. A. WANG, A. H. M. EL-SHERBINI, S. FRY, M. SMUTEK, AND N. WEBB

Introduction • Wang Personal Computer • Overview of the PIC • PIC Hardware • PIC Software • Image Communications • Conclusion

7 Data General Desktop Generation Model 10: Architecture and Implementation 120

R. C. MILLER, D. A. WADE, AND C. WALLIS

Introduction • Design Alternatives • MicroECLIPSE Microprocessor • Product Implementation: System Processing Unit • Product Implementation: Bit-Mapped Color Graphics • Product Implementation: Software • Product Implementation: Packaging • Final Product • System Performance • Conclusion

8 The IBM PCjr 135

P. D. ESTRIDGE, D. J. BRADLEY, AND D. A. KUMMER

Introduction • The PCjr • Compatibility • Summary

9 The Anatomy of a Portable Computer 150

J. V. ROACH, S. W. LEININGER, AND W. T. WALTERS

Introduction • The Model 100 • Software • Hardware • Conclusion

10 Microprocessors — The First Twelve Years 167

A. GUPTA AND H. D. TOONG

Introduction • 4-Bit Microprocessors • 8-Bit Microprocessors • 16-Bit Microprocessors • 32-Bit Microprocessors • System Issues • Multiprocessor Capabilities • Special-Purpose Processors • Conclusion • Glossary

11 A Processor Family for Personal Computers 201

R. E. CHILDS, JR., J. CRAWFORD, D. L. HOUSE, AND R. N. NOYCE

Introduction • Software Structures • Secure Systems • Hardware Implementation • Future Directions • Conclusion

12 Structure and Capabilities of Key Personal Computer Operating Systems 222

M. HSU AND S. E. MADNICK

Introduction • DOS 2.0 • Concurrent CP/M • UNIX • Concluding Remarks

13 Graphics — The New Direction in Personal Computer Software 247

H. D. TOONG AND A. GUPTA

Introduction • Software • Office Environment • Graphics • Presentation Graphics Software • Applications • Frameworks for Analyzing Trends

14 The Architecture of the Lisa™ Personal Computer 266

B. DANIELS

Background • The Lisa Hardware • The Lisa Software • Summary

x / CONTENTS

15   Design of Personal Computer Software   282

R. A. ROSS

Introduction · Technical Issues · Conclusion

16   Expert Systems for Personal Computers: The TK!Solver Approach   301

M. KONOPASEK AND S. JAYARAMAN

Historical Note · Overview of TK!Solver · TK!Solver and Expert Systems · Conclusion and Further Developments

17   The Personal Computer in "C & C"   315

K. KOBAYASHI, K. WATANABE, R. ICHIKAWA, AND A. KATO

Introduction · PC-100 Specifications · System Block Diagram · Detailed Description of Design · Conclusion

18   Communications and Personal Computers   331

B. O. EVANS

Introduction · The Age of Personal Computers · Communications Facilities · Overall Trends · Conclusion

19   The Role of Venture Capital in the Growth of the Personal Computer Industry   347

S. E. PRATT AND R. KHOYLIAN

Introduction · Venture Capital · Role of the Venture Capitalist · Venture Capital Investment Criteria · Investment Patterns by Industry · Personal Computer Industry · Expected Future Developments

20 Epilogue 353

A. GUPTA AND H. D. TOONG

Introduction • Hardware • Software • Vendor Considerations • Conclusion

Authors' Biographies 363

Author Index 372

Subject Index 373

Preface

Insights Into Personal Computers is unique in several regards. *First,* it focuses on a topic that is relevant to everyone including computer professionals as well as persons with other specialties. *Second,* it highlights the efforts involved in translating innovative technical ideas into personal systems for widespread individual use. *Third,* this book carries the distinction of assimilating contributions by a number of individuals who are actively influencing and shaping the field of personal computing.

The personal computer revolution is no doubt fueled by technological advances. But the nature of this revolution is shaped even more strongly by another force: the decisions made by key executives of major manufacturers in this field. Just as the development of the color television is attributed to the zeal of RCA's David Sarnoff and the development of the pocket calculator to HP's David Packard, the flow of the personal computer revolution is modulated by the opinions of a relatively small set of persons. In this book we have encapsulated their thoughts.

IEEE has always placed a heavy emphasis on technical depth and clarity. Most of the chapters of this book have been coauthored by the chief technical designers of the respective systems. In a field where each day is critical, we are indeed fortunate that these designers consented to take time off from their pressing endeavors to contribute to this effort.

Reprint and multiauthored books frequently make a disjointed impression on the reader. To mitigate this problem, we took the approach of being very liberal at the editing stage. We feel privileged that the authors graciously concurred with these changes. It has indeed been a fascinating experience working closely with so many key contributors to the personal computer revolution to generate an interconnected archipelago of invaluable information.

No set of words can convey our sense of gratitude to the contributors to this volume. The success of this book is truly their success and an affirmation of our faith in this project. We also acknowledge the help of a number of persons at IEEE—David Staiger, Reed Crone, David Boulanger, and many others who worked in the shadows to assemble this book in record time. All of us shared the enthusiasm to develop a book befitting the commencement of the second century of IEEE.

Amar Gupta and Hoo-min D. Toong

Cambridge, January 1985

1
Bringing Everyman into the Computer Age

AMAR GUPTA AND HOO-MIN D. TOONG

The number of personal computers in use has increased by two orders of magnitude within the last six years. This rapid proliferation has been catalyzed by several factors including increased computing power and functionality of personal computers at steadily decreasing costs. Significantly less expensive than their harbingers (mainframes and minicomputers), personal computers of today are finding widespread use in nontraditional application areas. By making computational power accessible to untrained people, they promise to bring about the long heralded computer revolution. This chapter presents the salient highlights of this ubiquitous aid to mankind.

I. INTRODUCTION

By the turn of this century, the population of computers on this planet will exceed the population of human beings. A large number of these computers will be devoted to dedicated tasks such as in automobiles, household appliances, and industrial control. At the other end of the spectrum general-purpose computers, capable of performing one or several tasks from a virtually infinite range of functions, will be even more popular than calculators are today. In fact, by 1990 the number of personal computers in use worldwide will most likely exceed the population of the U.S.

The pace of the electronic revolution has been unparalleled by any other revolution. In a world of surging inflation, it is amazing to note that the cost of computer logic devices falls at the rate of 25 percent per year and the cost of computer memory at the rate of 40 percent per year. Computational speed has increased by a factor of 200 in 25 years. In the same period the cost, the energy consumption, and the size of computers of comparable power have decreased by a factor of 10 000. *If the aircraft industry had evolved as spectacularly as the computer industry over the past 25 years, a Boeing 767 would cost $500 today, and it would circle the globe in 20 minutes on five gallons of fuel.* Such performance would represent a rough analog of the reduction in cost, the increase in speed of operation and the decrease in energy consumption of computers.

The result is the advent of the personal computer, which for less than $500 can put at the disposal of an individual about the same basic computing power as a mainframe computer did in the early 1960s and as a minicomputer did in the early 1970s. Twenty years ago the cost of a computer could be justified only if the machine met the needs of a large organization. The minicomputers introduced in the 1970s are appropriate for a department or a working group within such an organization. Today the personal computer can serve as a work station for the individual. Moreover, just as it has become financially feasible to provide a computer for the individual worker, so also technical developments have made the interface between man and

---

The authors are with the Sloan School of Management, Massachusetts Institute of Technology, Cambridge, MA 02139, USA.

machine increasingly "friendly," so that a wide array of computer functions are now accessible to people with no technical background.

The first personal computer was put on the market in 1975. Sales are expected to surpass $6 billion in 1985. There has been talk of a "computer revolution" ever since the electronics industry learned in the late 1950s to inscribe miniature electronic circuits on a chip of silicon. What has been witnessed so far has been a steady, albeit remarkably speedy, evolution. With the proliferation of personal computers, however, the way may indeed be open for a true revolution in how business is conducted, in how people organize their personal affairs and, perhaps, even in how people think.

II. ANATOMY OF A COMPUTER

A computer is essentially a machine that receives, stores, manipulates, and communicates information. It does so by breaking a task down into logical operations that can be carried out on binary numbers—strings of 0s and 1s—and doing hundreds of thousands or millions of such operations per second. At the heart of the computer is the central processing unit, which performs the basic arithmetic and logic functions and supervises the operation of the entire system. In a personal computer the central processing unit is a microprocessor: a single integrated circuit on a chip of silicon that is typically about a quarter of an inch on a side. Other silicon chips constitute the computer's primary memory, where both instructions and data can be stored. Still other chips govern the input and output of data and carry out control operations. The chips are mounted on a heavy plastic circuit board; a printed pattern of conductors interconnects the chips and supplies them with power. The board is enclosed in a cabinet; in some instances there are several boards.

Information is entered into the computer by means of a keyboard or is transferred into it from secondary storage on magnetic tapes or disks. The computer's output is displayed on a screen, either the computer's own cathode-ray tube, called a monitor, or an ordinary television screen. The output can also be printed on paper by a separate printer unit. The device called a modem (for modulator–demodulator) can be attached to convert the computer's digital signals into signals for transmission over telephone lines.

The chips and other electronic elements and the various peripheral devices constitute the computer's hardware. The hardware can do nothing by itself; it requires the array of programs, or instructions, collectively called software. The core of the software is an "operating system" that controls the computer's operations and manages the flow of information. The operating system mediates between the machine and the human operator and between the machine and an "application" program that enables the computer to perform a specific task: solving a differential equation, calculating a payroll, or editing a letter. Programs are ordinarily stored in secondary-memory media and are read into the primary memory as they are needed for a particular application.

III. CHARACTERISTICS OF THE PERSONAL COMPUTER

A personal computer is a small computer based on a microprocessor; it is a microcomputer. Not all microcomputers, however, are personal computers. A microcomputer can be dedicated to a single task such as controlling a machine tool or metering the injection of fuel into an automobile engine; it can be a word processor, a video game, or a "pocket computer" that is not quite a computer. A personal computer is something different: a stand-alone computer that puts a wide array of capabilities at the disposal of an individual. We define a personal computer as a system that has all the following characteristics:

1) The price of a complete system is less than $5000.
2) The system either includes or can be linked to secondary memory in the form of cassette tapes or disks.

3)   The microprocessor can support a primary-memory capacity of 64 kilobytes or more. (A kilobyte is equal to 2^{10}, or 1024 bytes. A byte is a string of eight bits, or binary digits. One byte can represent one alphabetic character or one or two decimal digits. A 64-kilobyte memory can store 65 536 characters, or some 10 000 words of English text.)

4)   The computer can handle at least one high-level language, such as BASIC, Fortran, or Cobol. In a language of this kind instructions can be formulated at a fairly high level of abstraction and without taking into account the detailed operations of the hardware.

5)   The user is expected to interact with the system continuously, not only at the beginning and end of a problem. This interactive dialogue is facilitated by the operating system; the computer responds immediately (or at least quickly) to the user's actions and requests.

6)   Distribution is largely through mass-marketing channels, with emphasis on sales to people who have not worked with a computer before.

7)   The system is flexible enough to accept a wide range of programs serving varied applications; it is not designed for a single purpose or a single category of purchasers.

As shown in Fig. 1, the hardware of a personal computer includes devices for processing and storing information and for communicating with the user and with other electronic devices. A set of parallel conductors called a bus connects the main components. The processing unit, which generally includes not only the microprocessor chip itself but also various auxiliary chips, carries out essentially all calculations and controls the entire system. Information can be entered into the system through a keyboard. Pressing a key generates a coded signal unique to that key; the code is stored in the display memory and so appears on the cathode-ray-tube display. The primary memory, which consists of semiconductor memory chips, holds programs and data currently in use; it is a random-access memory, meaning that the content of any cell can be examined or changed independently of all the other cells. Disk storage generally has a larger capacity than the primary memory, but it is slower and its information is recovered in larger blocks. The interfaces connect the computer to other devices, such as a printer or a modem (which gives access to other computers through the telephone system). In a serial interface information is transferred one bit at a time; in a parallel interface multiple conductors carry several bits (in most instances eight) at a time. These interfaces are used to interconnect an array of personal computers into a single local-area network (LAN).

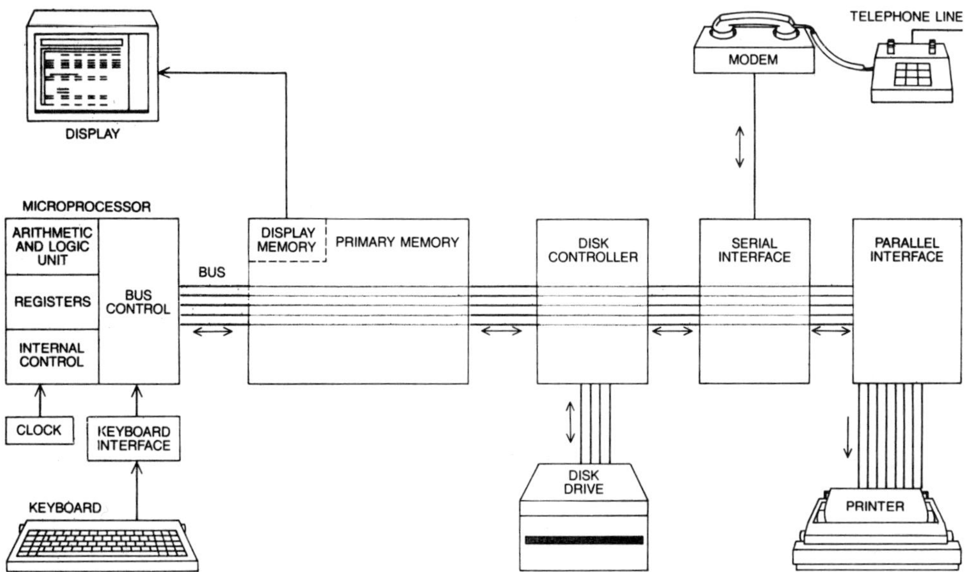

Fig. 1.   Anatomy of a personal computer.

IV. HARDWARE

Microprocessor

Two major determinants of the computational power of a microprocessor are its word size, which governs the "width" of the computer's data path, and the frequency of its electronic clock, which synchronizes the computer's operations. The trend in microprocessors is toward a larger word size and a higher frequency. As the word size increases, an operation can be completed in fewer machine cycles; as the frequency increases, there are more cycles per second. In general a larger word size also brings the ability to access a larger volume of memory. The first generation of true personal computers, which came on the market between 1977 and 1981, had eight-bit microprocessors. The next generation relied on 16-bit microprocessors. Now 32-bit microprocessor chips are used in most new designs of personal computers.

Primary Memory

There are two kinds of primary memory: read-only memory (ROM) and random-access memory (RAM). Read-only memory is for information that is "written in" at the factory and is to be stored permanently. It cannot be altered. For a single-application computer such as a word processor the information in ROM might include the application program. In the case of a versatile personal computer it would include at least the most fundamental of the "system programs," those that get a computer going when it is turned on or interpret a keystroke on the keyboard or cause a file stored in the computer to be printed. As the cost of ROM drops there has been a tendency among manufacturers to include more and more system programs in ROM rather than on secondary-storage media.

Random-access memory is also called read/write memory: new information can be written in and read out as often as it is needed. RAM chips store information that is changed from time to time, including both programs and data. For example, a program for a particular application is read into RAM from a secondary-storage disk; once the program is in RAM its instructions are available to the microprocessor. A RAM chip holds information in a repetitive array of microelectronic "cells," each cell storing one bit. The density of commercially available memory chips, that is, the number of bits per chip, has increased by a factor of 64 over the past decade, with a resulting 50-fold reduction in the cost per bit. At the dawn of the personal computer revolution, a single RAM chip stored no more than 16 kilobits (16 384 bits); now the 256-kilobit chip is widely available.

Even though the individual memory chip is an array of bits, information is generally transferred into and out of primary memory in the form of bytes, and the memory capacity of the computer is measured in bytes. A typical personal computer comes with a RAM capacity of between 16 and 512 kilobytes, which can be expanded by the addition of extra memory boards, or modules. In general it is a good rule to buy a system that has at least enough memory to accommodate the largest application program one expects to execute. Most off-the-shelf program packages carry an indication of the minimum memory required.

Secondary Memory

The standard medium for secondary storage is the floppy disk. A floppy-disk system (see Fig. 2) records large quantities of information on a flexible plastic disk coated with a ferromagnetic material. The disk rotates at 300 revolutions per minute in a lubricated plastic jacket. An electromagnetic head is moved radially across the surface of the disk by a stepper motor to a position over one of the concentric tracks where data are stored as a series of reversals in the direction of magnetization. The head can read or write: sense the reversals to retrieve information or impose magnetization to store information. An index mark, whose passage is sensed by a photoelectric device, synchronizes the recording or reading with the rotation of the disk. Around 1 megabyte of information can be stored in 40–100 concentric tracks on a disk.

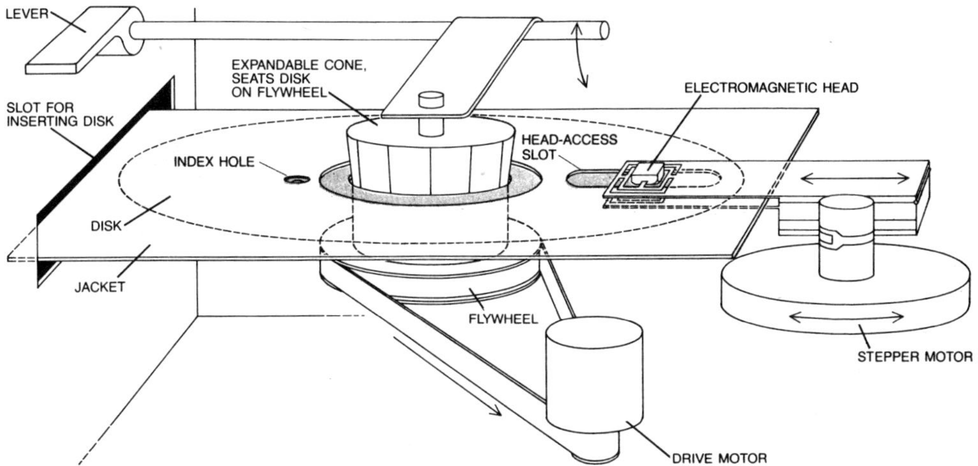

Fig. 2. Floppy disk system.

Double-sided disk drives offer twice the capacity using two gimballed heads, one on each side of the disk. More sophisticated secondary storage devices are described in Chapter 2.

A simpler, less expensive secondary-memory medium is the audio magnetic-tape cassette. One cassette can store about as much information as a relatively low-capacity floppy disk. The access time to a particular address, or storage location, is much longer for tape than it is for a disk because the speed of the tape is much lower than that of a disk and because the information is arrayed in a single linear sequence. An important feature of all the magnetic secondary-storage mediums is that information is maintained even when the computer is turned off.

Output Devices

The primary output medium for a personal computer is a visual display, usually on a cathode-ray tube: either a monitor supplied with the computer or the purchaser's own television screen. Flat-panel displays that exploit liquid-crystal or gas-discharge technology are beginning to be competitive, particularly for small, portable systems. The character images needed for the display of text are stored as patterns of dots in a special ROM called a character generator. The clarity of the text depends on the number of dots employed in forming each character. A typical monitor can display 24 lines of text, each line of which has a maximum of 80 characters.

The display of graphic images, whether they are engineering drawings, graphs, or moving targets in a video game, calls for complex software and for large amounts of memory. A detailed drawing or a smooth curve on a graph requires a high-resolution image. Resolution is determined by the number of pixels (picture elements) that can be addressed by the computer. A 280-by-192-pixel image in black and white fills more than 50 kilobits of RAM capacity, whereas a 128-by-48 image needs only about 6 kilobits. Many personal computers can generate images in color, which can raise the memory requirement by a factor of four or more. A high-resolution image, particularly one in color, can be displayed clearly only on a monitor.

For many purposes a printed copy of the computer's output is desirable. There are a number of different kinds of printers, which vary widely in price, speed, and the quality of the text they turn out. A dot-matrix printer is relatively inexpensive, fast (up to 200 characters per second), and flexible; it can generate compressed, expanded, or bold characters (or even graphic images), depending on the commands it receives from the computer. The printing head is a vertical array of pins that are fired selectively, as the head is swept across the paper, to press an inked ribbon

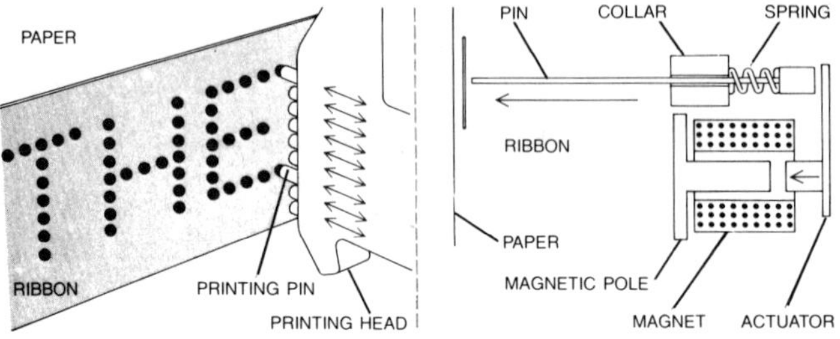

Fig. 3. Mechanism of a dot-matrix printer.

against the paper and thereby form a pattern of dots. In the example shown in Fig. 3, each capital letter is a subset of a matrix seven dots high and five dots wide; two more pins are available to form the descenders of lowercase letters such as *p*. The pins are fired by individual solenoids. Signals from the computer drive the wires against an inked ribbon, leaving a pattern of dots on the paper. The quality of the characters thus formed depends largely on the size of the dot matrix available for each character; the array of dots is commonly either five by seven or seven by nine. With suitable control programs and enough memory capacity the dot-matrix printer can generate graphic images in black and white or in color. Another class of inexpensive printers, called thermal printers, burn an image into a special paper at a rate of 50 characters per second.

Most thermal and dot-matrix printers generate text that is readable but hardly elegant. "Letter quality" printing calls for more expensive devices more closely related to a typewriter. One such device is the daisy-wheel printer, which costs at least $750 and can print up to 100 characters per second. As shown in Fig. 4, the printing wheel has a plastic hub around which are arrayed 96 (or more) radial spokes; a letter, number, or other symbol is molded into the end of each spoke. In response to signals from the computer the wheel is rotated either clockwise or counterclockwise to bring the proper symbol into position and is stopped; the hammer strikes

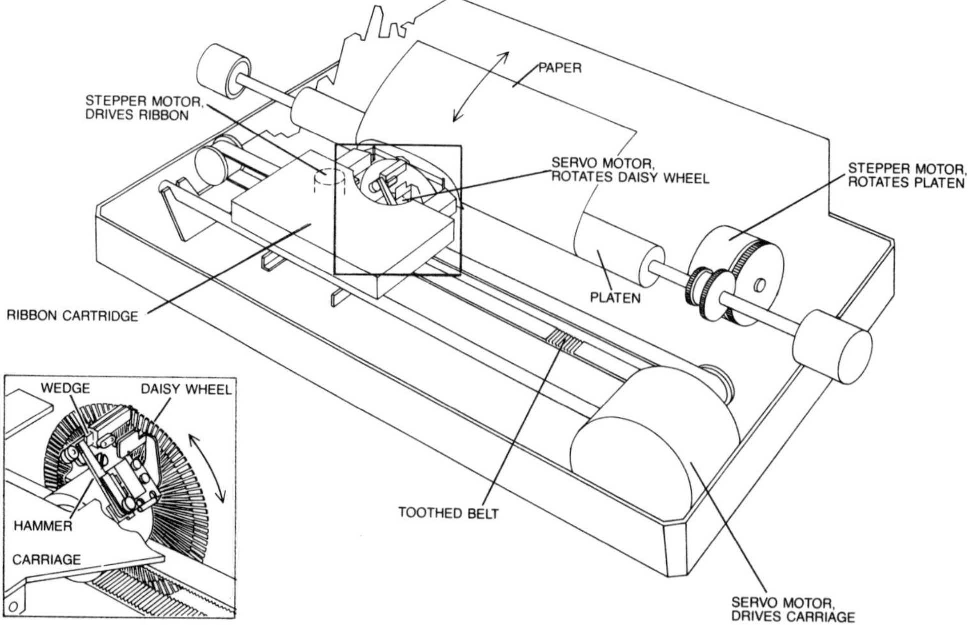

Fig. 4. Daisy wheel printer.

(with an energy proportionate to the area of the symbol: much harder, say, for a *W* than for a comma), driving the sliding wedge against the end of the radial arm to press the inked ribbon against the paper; the carriage and ribbon advance as the wheel is spun to bring the next symbol into position.

V. Software

Although the hardware of a computer ultimately determines its capacity for storing and processing information, the user seldom has occasion to deal with the hardware directly. A hierarchy of programs, which together constitute the software of the computer, intervenes between the user and the hardware.

Operating Systems

The part of the software that is most closely associated with the hardware is the operating system. To understand the kind of tasks done by the operating system, consider the sequence of steps that must be taken to transfer a file of data from the primary memory to disk storage. It is first necessary to make certain there is enough space available on the disk to hold the entire file. Other files might have to be deleted in order to assemble enough contiguous blank sectors. For the transfer itself sequential portions of the file must be called up from the primary memory and combined with "housekeeping" information to form a block of data that will exactly fill a sector. Each block must be assigned a sector address and transmitted to the disk. Numbers called checksums that allow errors in storage or transmission to be detected and sometimes corrected must be calculated. Finally, some record must be kept of where the file of information has been stored.

If all these tasks had to be done under the direct supervision of the user, the storage of information in a computer would not be worth the trouble. Actually the entire procedure can be handled by the operating system; the user merely issues a single command, such as "Save file." When the information in the file is needed again, an analogous command (perhaps "Load file") begins a sequence of events in which the operating system recovers the file from the disk and restores it to the primary memory. In Fig. 5 the functions of the operating system are illustrated by the successive events required to load an application program. Switching the computer on (Step 1) actuates a bootstrap program that loads the operating system into the primary memory. The operating system transfers a file directly from the disk memory to the primary memory; in the file directory is listed the address, or position, of every program and data file recorded on the disk. In response to the next instruction (Step 2) the operating system finds the BASIC interpreter on the disk and, after making certain there is enough space for it, loads it into the primary memory; the user is notified that the interpreter is ready. (Some personal computers perform Step 2 automatically as part of the switching-on sequence.) The operating system is called on to load the application program itself (Step 3). Now, with the interpreter again in control, the application program can be run. Output will be a new data file in primary memory, which can be transferred to disk storage.

In most instances an application program is written to be executed in conjunction with a particular operating system. On the other hand, there may be versions of an operating system for several different computers. Ideally, then, the same application program could be run on various computers, provided they all had the same operating system: in practice some modification is often necessary.

Levels of Software

The microprocessor recognizes only a limited repertory of instructions, each of which must be presented as a pattern of binary digits. For example, one pattern might tell the processor to load a value from the primary memory into the internal register called an accumulator, and another pattern might tell the machine to add two numbers already present in the accumulator.

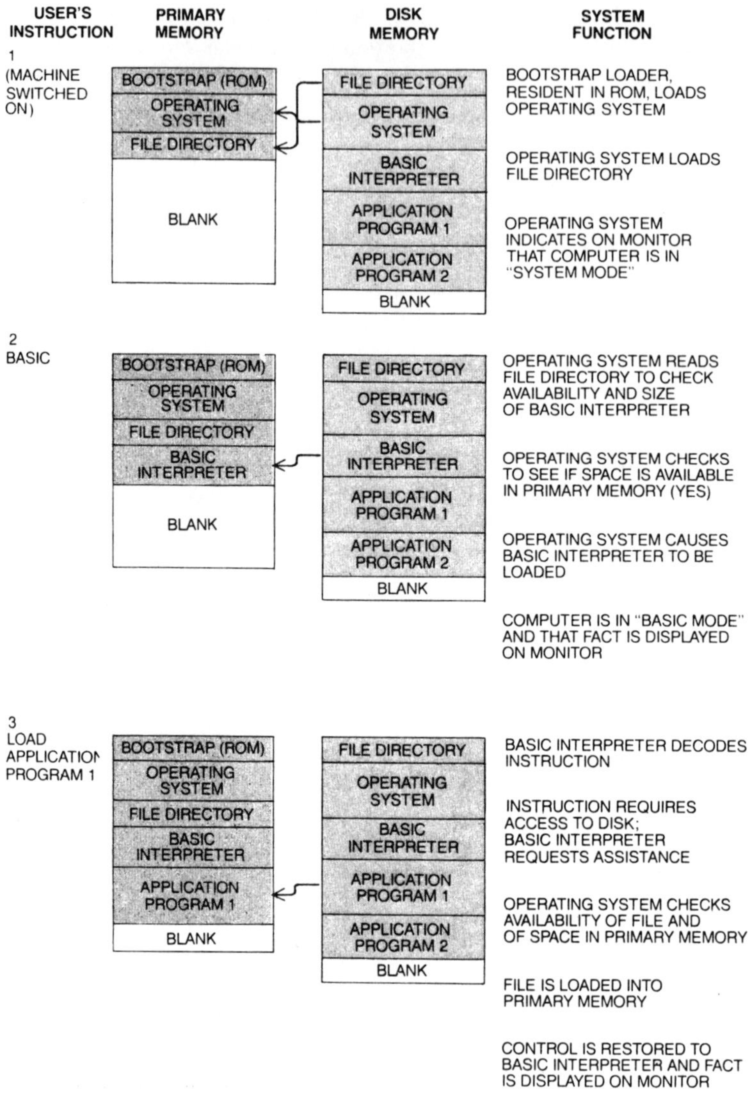

Fig. 5. Functions of the operating system.

It is possible to write a program in this "machine language," but the process is tedious and likely to result in many errors.

The next-higher level of abstraction is an "assembly" language, in which symbols and words that are more easily remembered replace the patterns of binary digits. The instruction to load the accumulator might be represented LOADA and the instruction to add the contents of the accumulator might be simply ADD. A program called an assembler recognizes each such mnemonic instruction and translates it into the corresponding binary pattern. In some assembly languages an entire sequence of instructions can be defined and called up by name. A program written in assembly language, however, must still specify individually each operation to be carried out by the processor; furthermore, the programmer may also have to keep track of where in the machine each instruction and each item of data is stored.

A high-level language relieves the programmer of having to adapt a procedure to the instruction set of the processor and to take into account the detailed configuration of the hardware. Two quantities to be added can simply be given names, such as X and Y. Instead of telling the processor where in primary memory to find the values to be added, the programmer specifies the operation itself, perhaps in the form $X + Y$. The program, having kept a record of the location of the two named variables, generates a sequence of instructions in machine language that causes the values to be loaded into the accumulator and added.

There are two broad classes of programs, called interpreters and compilers, that translate into machine code a program written in a higher language. A program written in an interpreted language is stored as a sequence of high-level commands. When the program is run, a second program (the interpreter itself) translates each command in turn into the appropriate sequence of machine-language instructions, which are executed immediately. With a compiler the entire translation is completed before execution begins. An interpreter has the advantage that the result of each operation can be seen individually. A compiled program, on the other hand, generally runs much faster since the translation into machine language has already been done.

Fortran was one of the earliest high-level languages and is now available in several versions (or dialects). Fortran programs are compiled; their main applications are in the sciences and mathematics. The most widely employed high-level language for personal computers is BASIC, which was developed in the 1960s by workers at Dartmouth College. BASIC was originally intended as an introductory language for students of computer programming, but it is now employed for applications of all kinds. Most versions of BASIC are interpreted. There are dozens of other high-level languages that can be executed by a microcomputer. The choice of a language for a particular program is often based on the nature of the problem being addressed; the language called Lisp, for example, is favored by many investigators of artificial intelligence. Considerations of personal programming style also have an influence: the language Pascal has been gaining popularity in recent years because it encourages writing of structured programs that can be readily understood.

Application Programs

Application programs are the ones that ultimately determine how effective a computer is in meeting human needs. For this reason it is likely that the owner of a personal computer will eventually invest more in software than in hardware. The investment can be made either by buying programs or by spending the substantial amount of time needed to write them. Unless one wants to do intensive programming, the breadth of a system's software base (the number of applications supported) and its depth (the number of different programs available for each application) should be significant considerations in the selection of hardware.

A thriving cottage industry supplying application programs has evolved. Many programs are highly specialized. There are programs for example, for generating a Federal income-tax return or (in conjunction with the necessary instrumentation) for analyzing thousands of blood samples per hour or for designing a bridge. Other programs have more general applications. Word-processing software is a prime example: it facilitates the writing and editing of documents of any kind, from letters and memorandums to book chapters such as this one.

The most popular single program for personal computers is called VisiCalc. It is an "electronic worksheet." The program lays out in the computer's memory and displays on its screen a table 63 columns wide and 254 rows deep. The user "scrolls" the worksheet right and left or up and down to bring different parts of it into view. Each position (that is, each intersection of a column and a row) on the screen corresponds to a record in memory. The user sets up his own matrix by assigning to each record either a label, an item of data, or a formula; the corresponding position on the screen displays the assigned label, the entered datum, or the result of applying the formula.

Consider a simple example. A company comptroller might enter the label *Cash* in the record corresponding to Column *B*, Row 1 (position *B*1), *Reserves* at *C*1 and *Total* at *D*1. He might then enter \$300 000 at *B*2, \$500 000 at *C*2 and the formula *B*2 + *C*2 at position *D*2. The screen will show \$800 000 at *D*2. If the comptroller changes the *B*2 entry to \$200 000 the program will reduce the total displayed at $D2$ to \$700 000. Moreover, what is entered in records $B2$ and $C2$ need not be primary data; it can be a function of data held in other records.

VisiCalc is an example of a *fourth-generation programming language*. It is a generic tool that offers greater programming functionality and a higher level of portability than available with any third-generation, high-level language such as Fortran or Cobol. VisiCalc offers a means of manipulating arrays of numbers with ease. Such generic tools are now available to perform many different functions: for example, plotting packages such as VisiPlot, Chartman, and Chartmaster are used to plot charts and graphs; business presentation packages such as VCN ExecuVision are used for generating business graphics and for assembling business presentations; and word-processing packages such as WordStar and EasyWriter are used to enter text and to edit it. The endeavor continues towards integrating different sets of facilities into the same package and to allow efficient manipulation on different types of information—numbers, text, graphs, and pictures.

VI. THE INDUSTRY

Evolution

The evolution of the small personal computer followed, perhaps inevitably, from the advent of the microprocessor. It was in 1971 that the Intel Corporation succeeded in inscribing all the elements of a central processing unit on a single integrated-circuit chip. The first microprocessor had only a four-bit word size, but within a year Intel produced an eight-bit processor and in 1974 there was an improved version, the Intel 8080. Small companies soon combined the 8080 with memory chips and other components to produce the first programmable microcomputers for industrial control and similar specialized applications. In 1975 a device flexible enough to be considered the first commercially available personal computer was developed by MITS, Inc. It was called the Altair 8800, and the basic system sold, primarily to hobbyists, for \$395 in kit form and for \$621 assembled. At the time the least expensive minicomputer cost about \$6000.

The Altair is no longer made. As a matter of fact, one irony of the personal computer industry, whose annual sales have increased by a factor of 100 in just six years, is that pioneering firms such as MITS, the IMSAI Manufacturing Corporation, and the Processor Technology Corporation failed to survive the initial phase. Their products were bought primarily by hobbyists: people with deep curiosity about computers and in most cases with some previous knowledge of electronics, who were willing—indeed eager—to grapple with the hardware. The companies that supplanted the pioneers and captured a major share of the market by 1978 were Radio Shack, Commodore Business Machines, and Apple Computer Inc. They saw the potential of a wider market in business and in the home; they offered "plug in" systems that were more accessible to people without computer training. The success of the second-generation companies alerted established mainframe manufacturers such as the International Business Machines Corporation and the Burroughs Corporation and makers of minicomputers such as the Digital Equipment Corporation and the Hewlett-Packard Company to the fact that their traditional markets might be eroded by the personal computer; the established companies then came into the field. New companies continue to be attracted to the industry.

Market Leaders

IBM, the world's largest supplier of data-processing equipment, has long dominated the market for mainframe computers but had not done as well with smaller computers before entering the personal computer field in mid-1981. It captured 14 percent of the market in 1981 itself. The strategy was to rely heavily on outside sources not only for software, distribution, and service, but also for hardware: the IBM personal computer's disk drive is supplied by the Tandon Corporation, the monitor is from Taiwan and the printer is from Japan. The keyboard is supplied by IBM—and so is the brand name. In the case of the IBM PCjr, even the keyboard is purchased from an outside vendor. IBM has become the undisputed leader of the personal computer industry, and many manufacturers—including giants like AT & T and Olivetti—have developed computers that are compatible with IBM computers. These look-alike computers are marketed at lower costs in order to compete against systems made by IBM.

IBM has a reputation of letting other companies experiment and open up a new field. It then uses its marketing and financial strength to become the leader and to reduce the original market leaders to insignificant positions. IBM's success has interesting implications for the future of the personal computer business. The industry is volatile. American companies such as the Xerox Corporation and Atari, Inc., and a number of Japanese manufacturers (notably the Nippon Electric Co., Ltd.) are in a position to overtake the leaders. New entrants are in the wings. In evaluating their prospects one must consider what the requirements are for commercial success. What is clearly not mandatory, to judge from IBM's strategy, is established manufacturing capability. Rather, the fundamental requirements would seem to be the financial resources to buy the necessary components and the ability to market a product successfully and distribute it rapidly over a wide area. Many organizations, including some whose present business has nothing to do with electronics, have such capabilities and will be able to acquire technical expertise as it is needed. Organizations as disparate as CBS and Coca Cola, as Time-Life and the Prudential Insurance Co., have the resources and the access to marketing and distribution facilities that could enable them to enter the personal computer market in a short period of time.

Distribution Channels

Strategies for marketing mainframe computers are not appropriate for marketing personal computers—profit margins are not large enough to justify hiring internal sales forces to sell directly to end users. As a result, producers are now experimenting with a wide variety of distribution strategies:

Franchised retail chains such as Computerland, MicroAge, and Software Center constitute a major distribution channel. These stores distribute the products of many vendors, and their volume is large enough to support a technical and maintenance staff.

Manufacturer-owned retail stores have been used successfully by Radio Shack. IBM, Digital, and Xerox have also opened such stores but only to supplement existing distribution channels. Except for Xerox, each manufacturer's stores sell only that manufacturer's products, and a prospective buyer is thus obliged to visit several stores to compare equipment of different makes.

Department-store outlets have generally been unsuccessful. Mass merchandisers depend for profits on fast-selling commodities. According to computer-industry data, personal-computer buyers make four shopping trips, totaling as much as seven hours, when selecting their machines. These buyers also expect sustained support and maintenance services that department stores are unaccustomed to providing.

Office-equipment stores specializing in copiers, typewriters, word processors, and other office equipment are well positioned to reach the most promising future market for personal computers and auxiliary equipment. If these stores can provide adequate servicing, they will become very popular.

Consumer-electronics stores such as Tech Hi-Fi have been marketing personal computers with some success, but the lack of expertise at the store level has been a constraint. Japanese manufacturers have also established ties with such stores as distributors of Japanese products. These channels will become a major factor as the Japanese increase their share of the personal-computer market.

Independent retailers often lack the capital required to compete vigorously and are therefore not gaining in numbers and importance as quickly as other retail channels.

Catalog showrooms have been used by Texas Instruments, but personal computers require follow-up support that such showrooms have been unable to provide.

Mail-order firms offering discounts ranging up to 50 percent appeal to price-sensitive customers, but their total lack of continuing support disenchants users. Price cutting penalizes the full-service dealers on which manufacturers want to rely as major sales outlets. Accordingly, major companies are trying to discourage sales through mail-order firms.

Direct-sales staffs are used for large-volume sales to government, educational institutions, and major corporations who prefer dealing directly with the manufacturer. But such direct sales tend to antagonize dealers by depriving them of some of their most profitable opportunities, and profit margins are inadequate to support direct sales to small-volume and individual buyers.

Value-added houses serve specialized users with coordinated hardware and software, such as printing companies that need word-processing and typesetting capabilities but have little or no internal computing expertise.

Though franchised retail outlets are the largest sellers of personal computers in the U.S., the one compelling characteristic of personal computer distribution today is diversity. No one form of vendor or market approach is dominant.

Market Segments

The personal computer market can be divided into four segments: business, home, science, and education. The business segment has already become by far the largest one, accounting for one-half of the total market in terms of unit sales and two-thirds of the total value of personal computers sold nowadays. There are 14 million businesses in the U.S., even the smallest of which is a potential buyer of a personal computer. Perhaps more important, there are some 36 million white-collar workers in the U.S., and a large fraction of them may eventually be working with a small computer of some kind.

The personal computer is currently best suited to the needs of small companies and of independent professionals such as lawyers and physicians. Larger organizations, however, are slowly coming to the concept of individual computer-centered work stations, which can be linked to one another and to central facilities (large memory units and printers, for example) by local-area networks. Personal computers are already powerful enough to handle most work-station tasks, and networks are under development. Personal computer networks are now in operation in many business organizations.

The home computer segment is the most visible and well-publicized segment. Most of the units were bought for recreation (primarily for playing video games), but they also serve as powerful educational aids for children, as word processors, electronic message centers, and personal finance tools. A broad range of new applications will be made possible by software now under development. The average cost of a complete home system is expected to fall from about $1000 now to perhaps $750 in 1990.

Computers intended for scientific and other technical applications tend to be more powerful than other personal computers and to have components that facilitate their being linked to analytical and sensing instruments. The market is therefore characterized by products with specialized hardware and an array of specialized programs.

The education segment is potentially very large, but it is critically dependent on the availability of funds; currently money is scarce for public school systems. Computer-assisted instruction involves the student in a lively interaction with the subject matter in almost any field of study and allows the individual to proceed at his own pace. The ability to work with a computer is coming to be considered a necessary basic skill and even some programming ability may soon be required in many occupations; clearly the place to acquire such skills is in elementary and secondary school. Reasoning that a student trained with the computer of a particular manufacturer is likely someday to be a purchaser of that brand, a number of major manufacturers have been donating personal computers to U.S. primary and secondary schools.

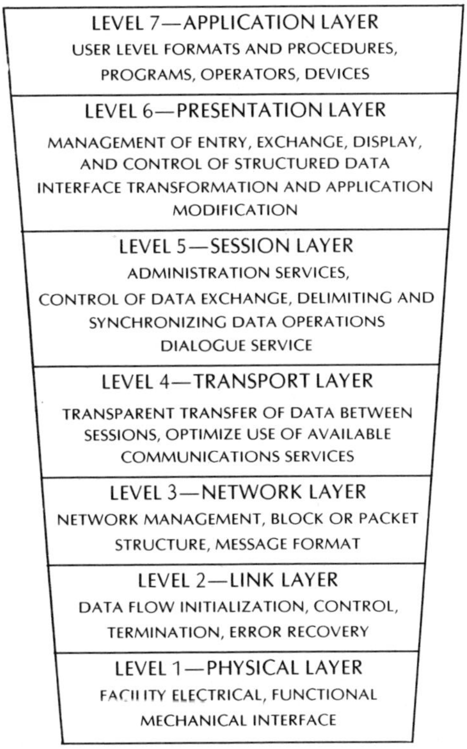

LEVEL 7—APPLICATION LAYER USER LEVEL FORMATS AND PROCEDURES, PROGRAMS, OPERATORS, DEVICES
LEVEL 6—PRESENTATION LAYER MANAGEMENT OF ENTRY, EXCHANGE, DISPLAY, AND CONTROL OF STRUCTURED DATA INTERFACE TRANSFORMATION AND APPLICATION MODIFICATION
LEVEL 5—SESSION LAYER ADMINISTRATION SERVICES, CONTROL OF DATA EXCHANGE, DELIMITING AND SYNCHRONIZING DATA OPERATIONS DIALOGUE SERVICE
LEVEL 4—TRANSPORT LAYER TRANSPARENT TRANSFER OF DATA BETWEEN SESSIONS, OPTIMIZE USE OF AVAILABLE COMMUNICATIONS SERVICES
LEVEL 3—NETWORK LAYER NETWORK MANAGEMENT, BLOCK OR PACKET STRUCTURE, MESSAGE FORMAT
LEVEL 2—LINK LAYER DATA FLOW INITIALIZATION, CONTROL, TERMINATION, ERROR RECOVERY
LEVEL 1—PHYSICAL LAYER FACILITY ELECTRICAL, FUNCTIONAL MECHANICAL INTERFACE

Fig. 6. OSI hierarchy; International Standards Organization (open systems interconnections).

VII. NETWORKS

The evolution of the personal computer market is generating a concurrent need for enhanced communication capabilities among personal computers as well as between personal computers and host computers. Network protocols refer to conventions that govern the transmission of information over a loosely coupled communication highway. The International Organization for Standardization has developed a reference model of open systems interconnection (OSI) comprised of seven layers as follow (Fig.6):

1) *Physical Layer:* this relates to transmission of raw bit streams and the electrical protocols. For example, RS 232 is a physical link protocol that specifies the required voltages, number of wires, and transmission speeds over a serial communication link.

2) *Data Link Layer:* this deals with issues such as converting unreliable transmission links into reliable ones.

3) *Network Layer:* this specifies conventions that govern the transmission of data messages over the communication highway.

4) *Transport Layer:* this is used to shield the customer's portion of the network from the carrier's portion.

5) *Session Layer:* this relates to setting up, managing, and splitting down process-to-process connections.

6) *Presentation Layer:* this deals with transformations (like data compression) on the data to be transmitted.

7) *Application Layer:* this refers to the ability of application programs involved in communication to freely exchange data and programs.

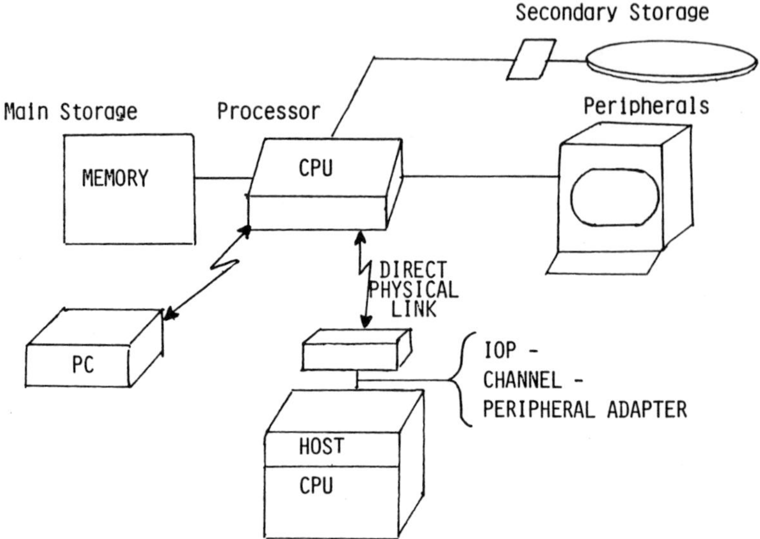

Fig. 7. Direct interconnection of personal computer to host computer.

The goal of supporting efficient communication at the application level involves efficient communication at all other levels as well. Efficient communication, especially between dissimilar systems, is critically dependent on the protocols and standards for interconnection.

There are several alternative ways of interconnecting computer systems. One is to establish a direct hard-wired physical link between the two personal computers or the personal computer and the host mainframe or minicomputer (Fig. 7). An alternative form is to substitute the direct physical link by a traditional remote access or dial-up service. The third mechanism is to interface the personal computer to a local area network. As shown in Fig. 8, this approach allows access to files and databases residing on the main computer, as well as access of centralized peripherals such as a high-speed printer. With proper coordination, distributed computing along with efficient local-area networks provide an ideal mechanism for automating decentralized functions in any large organization.

When multiple computing resources are interconnected with the same local area network, it is necessary to establish ground rules about who can use the network. If two or more computers become ready to transfer information at the same time, only one (or none) should be allowed to do so. Based on the strategy used to arbitrate in such situations, local-area networks are classified into two major categories: carrier-sense multiple access with collision detection (CSMA/CD) LANs and token-passing LANs.

In the case of a CSMA/CD network, each station wishing to transmit first senses the network state. If the network is already transmitting information, the station must wait. If the network is not transmitting, the station begins a test activity. It is possible that another station, having found the network "not busy," commences transmission at the same time resulting in a collision. If such a collision occurs, all stations cease transmission. Each station must retransmit the information. Different time delay strategies are used to avoid chances of collision during the next attempt by the stations.

In the case of a token bus, stations can be viewed as forming a logical ring around which a token is passed. A station receiving the token may transmit data. After its needs have been met, the station must pass the token to the next station in logical order. Although the token bus eliminates the overhead involved in collisions, it imposes the need to circulate the token around on a continuous basis.

Almost all leading personal computer vendors are striving to motivate use of their own network protocols. Although some standardization is beginning to occur, it is unlikely that a

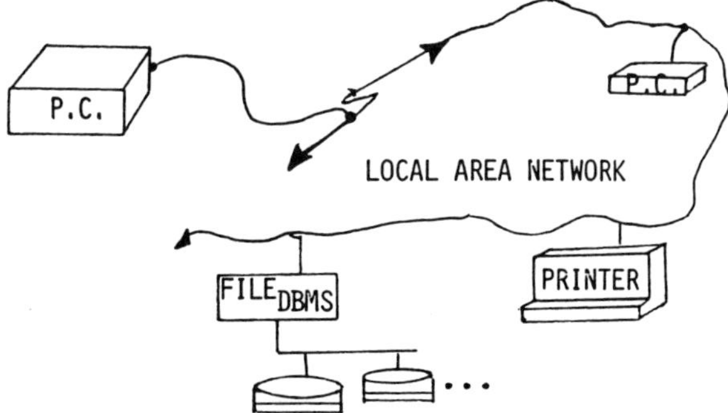

Fig. 8. Personal computer in a local-area network environment.

single standard will ever suffice for all sets of communication requirements. Meanwhile, businesses and organizations continue to forge ahead using the existing set of personal computers and local-area networks.

VII. Conclusion

In spite of the implications of the word "personal" and the popular image of family members gathered around the home computer to do schoolwork, balance the checkbook, and shoot down spacecraft, it is clear that most personal computers are being bought by businesses and other organizations. That does not necessarily make the computer any less personal; it may still be dedicated to the needs of one individual. More than a fifth of the U.S. labor force is engaged in office work; office costs constitute more than half of the total costs incurred by many companies, and those costs are increasing at a rate exceeding 7 percent per year. Personal computers can increase the productivity of the office and of white-collar workers. In an organization that already has a mainframe computer, personal computers can lighten the load on the central facility, which can spend more time on "batch" data-processing tasks such as payroll or inventory control. Personal computers make possible the mechanization of a wide range of office tasks that have been handled with typewriters, calculators, and photocopying devices.

Managers in business are said to devote more than 80 percent of their time to preparing for and attending meetings and "presentations," to collecting information, or to making decisions based on analysis of alternatives. Personal computers have impact on all three activities. New "business graphics" programs make it possible to quickly generate slides and printed material for meetings. Winchester disks and programs for the storing and management of large databases help the individual to examine a large body of information, discern trends, and detect problems. Data-manipulation programs such as VisiCalc enable the manager to evaluate alternative courses of action, to ask the kind of question that begins "what if" and to get an answer almost instantaneously. Such tasks can in principle be accomplished with a centralized mainframe computer, but they are done more efficiently with a personal computer, with far less expenditure of capital and by individuals who have had no technical training.

All of this having been said, the fact remains that the exact role to be filled by personal computers in an organization often cannot be foreseen. Many organizations have found that rather than meeting a known need, the presence of a personal computer identifies a previously unidentified need (much as the availability of a physician may bring to light a previously unrecognized health problem) and then meets that need.

Whether an individual needs or will profit from or enjoy his or her own personal computer is harder to say. For some professionals, to be sure, the advantage of having a computer always ready at hand is quite clear. Other people may buy one essentially because it is available and affordable, with the applications to be defined later. Specific applications will flow from the capabilities of the computer. A computer keeps track of things and sorts things. It calculates. It can marshal a large body of data, change one variable or more and see what happens. It can indeed balance a checkbook (rather, the owner can balance his checkbook with the help of the computer), list appointments or be linked to a home-security system. None of these applications by itself would justify the purchase of a computer. With curiosity and ingenuity, however, the owner of a personal computer will define his or her own applications, shaping the system to one's own personality and taste.

ACKNOWLEDGMENT

This chapter is based, in part, on our articles "Personal Computers" and "The Computer Age Gets Personal"; copyright © 1982, Scientific American, Inc. and the Alumni Association of M.I.T., respectively. All rights reserved.

2
The First Decade of Personal Computers

AMAR GUPTA AND HOO-MIN D. TOONG

The first decade of personal computers is characterized by three generations of these man-made devices. During the last six years alone, the number of personal computers purchased has increased by two orders of magnitude. This rapid growth has been catalyzed by innovations in computing and communication technology and by the advent of systems with friendlier human–machine interfaces geared towards individual needs. As the microelectronics revolution progresses and better software methodologies evolve, the personal computer will find widespread use in nontraditional application areas involving computing operations on information of many different types. The personal computer is becoming a ubiquitous aid for virtually all endeavors in life.

I. Introduction

Background

Since the dawn of the electronic computer era in the 1940s, there has been a sustained endeavor to minimize the human effort involved in communicating with the computer. The advent of higher level programming languages in the 1950s and the concepts of time sharing in the 1960s serve as evidence of this hypothesis. As computer logic and memory costs continued to decline by more than 20 percent every year, many corporations and individuals perceived that it was feasible to manufacture computers that were within the purchasing power of individuals. In 1968, Hewlett-Packard introduced the HP 9100A which was a hybrid between a calculator and a computer and was aptly described as a "computing calculator." Subsequently, in early 1973, Xerox designed the Alto personal computer "as an experiment to study how a small, low-cost machine could be used to replace facilities then provided only by much larger shared systems" [1]. The HP 9100A was geared primarily towards the computing needs of scientists and engineers. The Alto, too, was used more by persons with prior knowledge of computing techniques. The major thrust towards "personalization of computing" was provided by the widespread use of the microprocessor in the early 1970s. Microprocessors enabled personal computers to be built at lower costs than ever before.

Definition

Personal computers, like minicomputers, have no rigid definition. Today the term "personal computer" usually connotes a computer fulfilling *all* the following characteristics:

1) The price for the complete system is within the reach of individual buyers (usually under $5000).
2) The computing power is provided by using contemporary microprocessor technology.

The authors are with the Sloan School of Management, Massachusetts Institute of Technology, Cambridge, MA 02139.

3) The system is distributed through mass-marketing channels, with emphasis on sales to people with little or no prior experience with computers.
4) The system is flexible enough to accept a wide range of programs serving varied applications in industry, business, and at home; it is not designed for a single purpose or a single category of purchasers.
5) The operating system facilitates an interactive dialogue.
6) The computer can handle at least one high-level language, such as BASIC, Fortran, or Cobol.

In short, a personal computer is a stand-alone microprocessor-based, low-priced interactive system. The credit for designing the first personal computer is usually given to Micro Instrumentation and Telemetry Systems (MITS) Inc. for its Altair 8800 system designed during 1974 and advertized on the cover of the January 1975 issue of *Popular Electronics*. The basic system sold for $395 in kit form and $621 in assembled form. The Altair 8800 Advanced Accounting/Engineering System included sophisticated features and sold commercially for $10 500. The Altair 8800 is no longer manufactured. The next two years (1976–1977) witnessed the entry of Radio Shack, Apple, and Commodore into the market. The success of these companies convinced mainframe giants such as IBM and minicomputer leaders such as DEC to enter the fray. Unlike the Altair 8800, which was intended mainly for hobbyists, these larger companies emphasized fully assembled turnkey systems that were more user friendly. Intense competition has led to plummeting prices and increased performance at a hectic pace.

In terms of both hardware and software, mainframe computers were the harbingers of personal computers. The successive stages of the microelectronic revolution involving the inventions of vacuum tubes, transistors, integrated circuits, and large-scale integrated circuits have all contributed to the evolution of sophisticated computer hardware that permits large computing power to be generated in tiny wafers of silicon, and at minimal costs. Relative to hardware capabilities, the emergence of the personal computer is even more dependent on the development of better and more human-oriented program interfaces and methodologies. The historical trends are summarized in Table 1. Today's personal computers are equivalent in basic computing power to the mainframes of the 1960s and the minicomputers of the 1970s. However, unlike the 1960s and the 1970s when computers were principally used for well-structured jobs such as scientific calculations or payroll accounting, today's personal computers are primarily used for *ad hoc* analyses and for supporting the solution of nonstructured tasks.

At the heart of any personal computer there is a silicon-chip microprocessor capable of performing hundreds of thousands of calculations every second, complemented by memory

Table 1 Five Generations of Systems

Generation	Hardware		Software		Principal Kind of Data Handled
	Technology	Example Systems	Methodology	Examples	
1st Generation 1950s	vacuum tubes	ENIAC, WHIRLWIND	binary	0, 1 (machine specific)	binary numbers
2nd Generation Early 1960s	transistors	IBM 709	Assembly	Assembly (machine specific)	numbers
3rd Generation Late 1960s	integrated circuits	PDP 11	higher-level languages	Fortran, Pascal, PL/I	numbers and some text
4th Generation 1970s	large scale integration	IBM 370; AMDAHL 470	elementary information systems	IMS, SQL	numbers, text
5th Generation Mid-1980s	hardware implementation of traditional software functions, truly user-friendly systems	yet to come	high level decision support systems	yet to come	numbers, text, video

chips that provide the primary storage for instructions and data. External storage devices, such as cassette tapes or floppy disks, augment the memory capacity and provide a storage medium that can be physically transferred from one personal computer to another. Input is through a typewriterlike keyboard unit. Output can be in the form of printed paper; this requires attachment of a printer unit. More frequently, the output is displayed either on a normal television screen or on a specialized CRT screen called a monitor. Attachment of a modem (for modulator/demodulator) permits the computer to receive and transmit data over a conventional telephone line. The current trend is to share information stored on different systems by linking multiple personal computers in a network. In addition to the hardware components described so far, any personal computer requires software, especially an efficient operating system, which is comprised of a set of programs that manage the computer's resources, supervise the storage of programs and other information, and coordinate various tasks. Finally, there are application programs to carry out specific functions at the direction of the user.

Markets

Over the years, the use of personal computers has nucleated around four primary areas: in business, in science and engineering, at home, and in education. Business use is primarily structured around spreadsheets, word processing, elementary graphics, database, and communications for hookup to host computers and local area networks. The applications are somewhat similar in the scientific area. In addition, the personal computer is utilized for high-quality graphics, for communicating with scientific instruments and equipment, and for on-line analysis of data. At home, the personal computer is primarily used for entertainment purposes. Many personal computers are now finding their way into the home primarily to allow users to accomplish job-related tasks. This is consistent with the observed fact that tasks that require sustained work, attention, or reflection are usually done by managers at home [3]. In the education sector, personal computers are being used for classroom instruction, one-to-one tutorials, and self-paced computer-based training (CBT). Personal computers are fast taking over the role served by the calculator—in fact, several universities require entering students to either own or acquire a personal computer [2].

The analogy with calculators can be considered at another level. In recent years the prices of calculators have stabilized while the simple four-function calculator has almost disappeared. Even the low-priced calculator contains 15–20 functions and as technology improves more functionality in terms of timekeeping and games is being inserted. In the case of personal computers, prices for a full business system are expected to stabilize at around $1500 with increasing functionality over time. In order to predict specific areas of enhanced sophistication, it is necessary to study the different building blocks that constitute a personal computer.

II. Hardware

A personal computer consists of three different classes of hardware subsystems—the central processing unit (CPU), the memory subsystem, and the input–output subsystem. Trends in each of these three areas are described below.

Central Processing Unit (CPU)

The CPU of a personal computer consists of one or more microprocessors. Two parameters upon which to gauge the computing power of a microprocessor are its word size and the frequency of its clock. The word size reflects the basic unit of work. A larger word size implies more information can be processed in parallel; also, it enables access to a larger volume of memory. The first microprocessor, the Intel 4004, was only 4 bits wide. In their twelve years of existence (1971–1983) microprocessors have witnessed four generations characterized by different word sizes (see Table 2). Increased word size is made possible by implanting larger numbers of electronic elements on the same chip. This number has increased from 2300 in 1971 to

450 000 today. During this period, the clock frequency has increased by more than an order of magnitude. The first generation of personal computers used 8-bit microprocessors. Personal computers using 16-bit microprocessors were first introduced in 1981 [4]. The first use of a VLSI 32-bit microprocessor was in the Hewlett-Packard 9000 series of computers, which are currently too expensive to be classified as personal computers [5]. The 32-bit microprocessor is becoming the industry standard. Just as the mainframe computer industry has continued to use the 32-bit word size for the last two decades, it is expected that 32-bit microprocessors will be the most popular word size, at least until the end of the 1980s. Meanwhile, there is a growing trend to use more than one microprocessor within the same personal computer either for supporting multiple operating systems or for performing dedicated functions such as keyboard decoding, disk control, or graphics subsystems.

Table 2 Microprocessor Characteristics

	4-bit	8-bit	16-bit	32-bit	64-bit (projected)
Year of First Chip	1971	1972	1974	1981	1986
Number of Devices	2300	10 000	70 000	450 000	1 000 000
Function	calculator	dedicated controller	minicomputer	micro– mainframe	maximicro– mainframes
Clock Speed (in MHz)	0.4	0.5	1	10	50
Prices (1984)	$1	$5	$50	$250	$1250

Around the time of the introduction of the first personal computer, Moore had predicted that by the end of the decade the complexity of VLSI chips would double every two years [6]. One advantage of the increased device density has been the ability to implement larger and more powerful instruction repertoires enabling more compact programs. Single instructions now perform multiple functions. Also, contemporary instructions have a close resemblance to instructions of higher level languages thus facilitating compilation of such programs by performing, in hardware, an increasing number of functions traditionally done in software. In recent years, the focus has been on supporting instruction sets with an established base. The DEC F-11 microprocessor uses the PDP-11/34 instruction set, and the Data General microEclipse uses the DG-Eclipse instruction set; these chips have been used in the personal computers developed by these companies. IBM, on the other hand, has chosen to microcode Motorola 68000s to emulate its 360/370 instruction set; these microcoded chips are used in the IBM PC-XT/370. Such personal computers with direct software compatibility with popular mainframes and minicomputers can be used to off-load applications from a larger system and to run them in a local environment. Additionally, executives can be provided with personal computers that have greater potential of using existing software for accessing databases maintained on the central system. In coming years personal computers will offer greater flexibility in retrieving information from computers of widely different architectures and integrating such information in a cohesive manner.

Primary Storage

Primary memory is of two kinds: read-only memory (ROM) and random-access memory (RAM). In the former, information is "written in" at the factory and cannot be altered subsequently. Most manufacturers supply system programs on ROMs because such programs are secure against power failures, and users are less able to duplicate programs in this form. RAMs offer both read and write capability and are used for general program/data storage. RAMs are of two types—dynamic RAMs which are cheaper but need to be "refreshed" very often, and static RAMs which are less dense and costlier but need no refresh. Dynamic RAMs have higher bit densities per chip and are the device of choice for most personal computer program/data primary memory.

The size of memory refers to the amount of RAM installed in the personal computer. The upper limit is determined by two constraints. First, the maximum limit from a logical viewpoint is dependent on the memory address space of the particular microprocessor used in the personal computer. Most 8-bit microprocessor-based personal computers can deal with programs that are no larger than 64K bytes in size (16-bit address space). Most 16-bit personal computers offer native address space of 1M byte or more (20-bit or greater address space). The second constraint comes from physical packaging limitations, especially in the case of portable computers. Using the popular 64K-bit RAM chip, a 1M-byte (or 8M-bit) memory space implies a minimum of 128 chips, taking up substantial room inside the personal computer. For this reason, current personal computers rarely offer more than 4M bytes of memory capacity within the system unit. With the introduction of the 256K-bit RAM, these packaging constraints will now shift by a factor of four and by a further factor of four around the end of the 1980s when the megabit chip becomes popular. The speed of memory devices doubles every two to three years. Over the past decade, memory density increased by a factor of 64 with a simultaneous reduction in costs, on a per-bit basis, by a factor of 25. This trend should continue for several more years.

Secondary Storage

Secondary storage devices offer larger and relatively inexpensive (though slower) memory for long-term storage of programs and data files and a mechanism, via removable media, for physical transportation of programs and data from one system to another. The *cassette tape*, though inexpensive and widely supported on all systems, is unsuitable for serious applications because of its low speed, sequential access, and low reliability. Currently, the most popular personal computer secondary storage device is a *floppy disk* consisting of a disk of mylar with a coating of magnetic material on one or both sides. Data are stored on concentric magnetized tracks on the disk surface. Heads for reading or writing data are moved radially across the disk to access a specified segment of circular track. The storage capacity varies greatly depending on the formats used for the stored data, the quality of the surface media, and the head design. Formatting considerations include: the density of data stored along the tracks (bits per inch), the number and density of concentric tracks stored on the medium (tpi), the number of segments into which each track is subdivided for addressing purposes, and the software and hardware conventions used for interfacing with the disk. Floppy disks currently have capacities of between 125K bytes to 3M bytes. Floppy disks have standardized around two principal physical formats: one is the 5-1/4 inch which is the current *de facto* industry standard drive, and the other is the 8-in drive which is less popular and is not available on many current generation personal computers. New physical standards in small-sized floppy disks are also evolving. However, floppy disks from one personal computer vendor do not generally run in the disk drive of another vendor because of different data-formatting conventions. For most business applications, two drives are necessary since many software application programs (e.g., language compilers, spreadsheets, etc.) make use of two drives. With a one-drive system, even simple operations such as backup, compiling, and editing require multiple disk swappings. Frequently, two read/write heads are ganged together, one to access the top surface of the floppy disk and the other to access the bottom surface. Although only one head is active electronically at any one time, such a double-sided floppy unit doubles the amount of storage capacity and, as such, is preferred over a single-sided drive. Technological advances have enabled manufacturers to double the density of recorded information by doubling the number of tracks per inch. This has led to a new generation of double-density floppy units. Double-density, double-sided recording has become industry standard, yielding floppy capacities of 320K–1M bytes in the case of 5-1/4-in disks.

The primary performance characteristic of floppy disks is the response time to a read/write request which may range from 200 to 500 ms. For a single file request, this may not be a significant amount of time; however, during language compilation or word processing, an individual user command may involve twenty or more accesses to the floppy disks, and disk accesses may account for more than 80–90 percent of the total command execution time. Where better performance is required, a hard disk is used with access times ten times as fast as the floppy disk.

The *Winchester disk* was originally projected to contain 30M bytes and two disk units were ganged together. Consequently, the total capacity was 30/30 and hence the name Winchester, based on the Winchester rifle of the Old West. A Winchester is a rigid disk with a movable read/write head in a sealed module. The disk is not removable. Because it is in a sealed unit, the introduction of dirt and impurities from the external environment can be controlled more rigorously; consequently, the read/write heads can fly at heights that are orders of magnitude closer to the disk surface than in the case of a floppy read/write head. This enables higher density of recording and faster speeds of access. The rigid Winchester disk is rotated about ten times faster than a floppy. Typically, a Winchester disk unit costs between $1500 and $2500 whereas a 5-1/4-in floppy unit costs between $300 and $500. Further, Winchester disks are very sensitive to dirt and foreign substances since the low-flying disk head cannot tolerate small particles of smoke and pollen. Also, the Winchester cannot be taken out and put on the shelf like a floppy. Consequently, there is no backup copy of the data stored on the Winchester. Normal backup involves the use of many floppy disks or a "streaming tape," which is a cassette tape containing an image of the information stored on the entire Winchester disk.

A promising technology that will greatly impact the secondary storage capacities of personal computer systems is the *optical disk*. Optical disks have their roots in the laser video-disk technology with modifications and interfaces designed especially for processing digital data in a personal computer environment. Several manufacturers including DEC, Toshiba, IBM, Thomson/CSF, Phillips, and Sharp will be releasing such devices in the 1984–1985 timeframe. The advances represented by this device are large storage capacity per disk (approximately 200M bytes in a 5-1/4-in format) and low cost per bit ($25–$50 per 5-1/4-in optical-disk cartridge). The disks themselves are reliable, easily transportable, and not subject to as delicate handling constraints as magnetic media. Binary patterns of 1 and 0 are written on the disk using a laser and are read back from the disk by the same laser device at a lower intensity level. The first generation of optical disk units will allow information to be written once only. Access times will be a factor of 3–4 times faster than floppy speeds. The limitation of nonerasability implies that whenever a modified version of one's data is to be recorded, it must be written in a new area of the disk and the old copy marked as being not-the-current one. Such an archival storage procedure is desirable for many applications, for instance, financial records, medical records, tax returns, and other applications where an audit trail is desirable. Optical disks are likely to be most suited for two distinct sets of applications. First, as a permanent storage media for financial, educational, medical, and legal records. Second, as a low-cost media for widespread distribution of databases containing information that is updated regularly, e.g., for distributing

Table 3 Attributes of Storage Media (Updated and Expanded Version of Table from [7])

Attribute	Floppy Disk	Winchester Disk	Hard Disk	Audio Cassette	Digital Cassette	Cartridge Tape	Video Disk	Video Cassette	Bubble Memory
Storage (M byte)	0.3–3	3–30	3–20	0.1	0.5	2.5	10K	20K	0.5–10
Access Time	200–500 ms	20–80 ms	20–80 ms	40 in/s	300 in/s	30–90 in/s	2.5 s	4.5 min	0.5–5 ms
Transfer Rate (K bit/s)	60	5000	5000	75	2–8	70	750	750	100
Replaceable or Fixed (R/F)	R	F	F	R	R	R	R	R	F
Read/Write	R–W	R–W	R–W	R–W	R–W	R–W	R	R–W	R–W
Drive-Unit Cost	250–500	1000–6000	1000–6000	50–80	500–900	1000–1500	400–750	700–1200	1000–2000
Media Cost	5–10	n/a	n/a	2–10	10	15	15–25	10–15	n/a
Cost/Byte (cents)	0.01	0.01	0.04	0.05	0.1	0.04	0.00001	0.000005	0.5

product catalogs and airline timetables. Subsequent generations of optical disks will offer full read/write capability and pose a challenge to Winchester capacities.

A comparison of different storage devices along with their relative costs is presented in Table 3. An overview of memory requirements for various applications is shown in Fig. 1. A portfolio of several different types of storage devices provides the desired storage space and retrieval speed at an acceptable price.

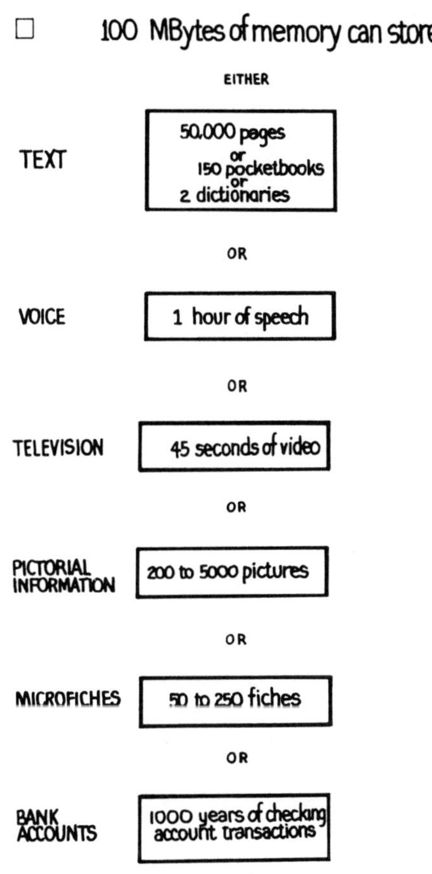

Fig. 1. Memory requirements for various applications.

Input/Output Devices

All personal computers contain a keyboard as the standard input device. Although almost all computers use the qwert... keyboard layout pattern, the number of keys varies from system to system. In the minimum case, the number of keys is around 50. Additional keys are used as "function keys" and enable an operation (such as PRINT or INSERT) to be initiated by a single key depression instead of having to type in the entire word. Such function keys help in increasing speed of inputs by users and reducing the probability of typing errors. The disadvantage, however, is that the user must be aware of the function performed by each key. Since manufacturers have designed keyboards based on their own ergonomic studies and with no mutual consultation with other manufacturers, the task initiated by a particular function key differs from system to system. Keyboard designs often have individual idiosyncrasies. For example, on the IBM Personal Computer the RETURN key, the LEFT-ARROW cursor key, and the BACKSPACE key, each performing vastly different functions, have all been clustered in near proximity—further, the key-top markings are also similar causing confusion to first-time users. In personal computers, the keyboard may be an integral part of the computer or a movable self-contained unit connected to the computer by a cable or through an infrared link as in the case of the IBM PCjr.

The primary output display device used in all personal computers is a television screen, or a monitor. In both these raster-scan devices, an electron beam is swept across the screen from left to right. The brightness of the screen is determined by the energy of the electron beam and controlling this energy allows display of a horizontal line with varying intensities along the line. During the return sweep from right to left, the electron beam is turned off and hence leaves no trail. The electron beam is again swept from left to right at a position slightly lower than the previous time, and this process of "raster scan" is continued until the entire screen is complete. The process is again repeated from top to bottom thirty times each second. Each scan line is comprised of several hundred sample points called picture elements or *pixels*. The difference between high- and low-resolution displays lies in the number of pixels that can be addressed by the computer. A typical low-resolution number is 128 × 48 (6144 pixels) while high-resolution displays may contain more than 1000 × 1000 distinct pixels on the screen. In such high-resolution displays, more than a million bits of information must be transferred to the CRT every thirtieth of a second, thus involving significant overhead. To reduce this overhead several options are possible. One option is to reduce the frequency of refresh—this causes a "flicker" effect which is irritating to the eye. Another option is to reduce the number of scan lines and scan points—this results in a relatively "coarse" picture being generated. A third option is to use a storage CRT (a CRT which retains brightness levels). Such CRTs are costlier and introduce a heavy overhead when a new picture has to be displayed in place of the previous one. A fourth option is to use a display in which the beam is not constrained to a horizontal path but can move in any arbitrary direction across the screen. These all-points-addressable displays offer advantages in the case of line drawings and vector representation of images.

The television display, though inexpensive, cannot accommodate the 80-character column widths used in business word processing with enough resolution to be easily read by the human eye. Also, in many cases, the availability of colored output offers distinct advantages over a monochrome display (usually white/black, green/black, or orange/black) of equivalent resolution. Currently, medium-resolution color RGB (red, green, blue) monitors in the range of $500–$700 suffice for most application programs in the business environment.

Another display technology compatible with personal computers is the *flat screen display technology* primarily used in portable personal computers. In this case, the display is either built in or is configured with the personal computer unit by the manufacturer. Although the flat panel displays and other new products are beginning to appear in volume, the CRT display remains the primary display technology. The CRT market is growing at 25 percent per year and prices are decreasing at 5–10 percent per year.

A part of the computer's own memory or a separate dedicated memory is used to store the information about the pixels on the screen. Such a "display memory" or "frame buffer" can be built with two access paths—the first path is used by the computer to write, and the second path is used for reading by the refresh circuits. Drawing of a new line requires the computer to alter the contents of the memory locations corresponding to the pixels whose states have to be altered. When a *light pen* is used to draw on the screen, the position of the pen is continuously monitored by the computer and, depending on changes in the position of the pen, the computer makes appropriate changes in the display memory. A *mouse* is a similar device, except that its movement on a horizontal plane is monitored and translated into lines on the vertical screen. The mouse represents a simple cursor positioning device that couples the screen cursor to a mechanical or optical rolling device on the table top. *Tablets* are also available for absolute positioning of inputs from a stylus on a grated surface. *Touch screens* using infrared, LED, or grid technology and offering medium resolution are becoming available on many contemporary personal computers. However, the basic principle of operation of all these devices is very similar. The computer detects the movement and makes appropriate changes in the display memory.

In many environments it is essential to have a hard copy, that is, a copy that can be read by human eyes and that will last for several years. A hard copy output is generated using one of four alternative device technologies. At the low end, *thermal printers* provide inexpensive and relatively quiet hard copy output. Disadvantages include the requirement for special paper and the fading of the thermal image over time. *Impact dot matrix printers*, though a little more expensive, produce near-letter quality text, alphanumerics, 100-dots-per-inch graphics, and, in some cases, limited color output. Units in this category tend to be the most reliable and cost effective for business applications. *Letter quality printers*, based on a Daisy Wheel or Spin Writer technology, offer better print quality and also limited graphics capability. At the top end, *laser printers* are available for high-quality text and graphics output. Laser printers have the ability to produce typeset quality text output as well as near-photographic quality graphics. It is only a matter of time before such units become common table-top personal computer output devices. Just as the plain paper copiers have now become personal (e.g., Canon PC10/PC20), so, too, will the laser printer become the common desk-top hard copy output device.

Both in the case of a display and of hard copy, the output must be "read" by the user. Such "visual" perception of computer-generated outputs has continued to be the predominant mode of computer communication with human beings. Computers that could communicate through the medium of "speech," as conceived in *2001: A Space Odyssey*, offer great advantages in terms of ease of use and in enhancing the quality and power of the man–machine symbiosis. Speech can be used to input information to the computer in the form of spoken, rather than keyboard, commands and data. This process, called *voice recognition*, holds special merit for motivating senior executives to use computers and also for handicapped users and in "hands-free" work situations. The complementary process of *speech synthesis* involves synthesizing or replaying of speech through a combination of voice patterns stored in the computer. Toys like the Texas Instruments Speak 'N Spell and many video games embody the latter capability in a rather primitive manner. Also, the spectrum of spoken words is very limited. It is only within the past two years that speech has been used as a viable communications methodology for generalized applications in conjunction with personal computers.

Speech consists of a sequence of discrete sound segments, called phonemes, linked in time. Each phoneme possesses distinguishable acoustic characteristics. A spoken word consists of several syllables, each comprised of several phonemes, with the characteristics of a given phoneme having been modified as a function of its immediate phonetic environment. The latter effect, called coarticulation, causes the same phoneme to have vastly different acoustic characteristics in different words making it difficult to decompose the word into its constituent phonemes. Further, since the coarticulation effect can occur across word boundaries, too, continuous speech is more difficult to recognize than isolated words. The process is further complicated by the fact that pronunciation varies enormously from person to person and even for a single speaker. A summary of the inherent processing requirements for different types of speech is presented in Table 4 [8].

Because of the enormous computational overhead, the corresponding high costs and low demand, few custom integrated circuits have been developed for speech-related applications. The advent of the Texas Instruments TMS 320 microprocessor [9] used in the TI Professional Computer and in personal computers of other makes has played a major role in equipping personal computers with the capabilities of recognizing isolated words as inputs and of generating outputs in the form of synthesized speech. In view of their lower requirements for computing speed and memory, speaker-dependent systems are more common. In such systems the user first defines the vocabulary of the enrollment phase. Next, the user speaks each word several times to enable the computer to store alternative pronunciations. The system is now ready for use. The system "hears" words spoken by the user and compares them with words in its stored vocabulary database. If a match occurs, the reference word is identified; if not, the

Table 4 Speech-Recognition System Milestones [8]

Recognition Capability	Isolated words, SD[1]	Continuous Speech, SI[2]	Isolated Words, SD	Isolated Words, SI	Continuous Speech, SI
Syntax	Limited	Limited	Unlimited	Unlimited	Unlimited
Vocabulary, words	200	1000	5000	20 000	20 000
Processing speed required mega-instructions per second	1 to 10	100	300	1000	100 000
Technology required	Acoustic pattern matching used to identify individual phonemes Dynamic programming to solve problem of variations in duration of words (Both achieved by Nippon Electric commercial machines)	Beam-search strategy to narrow selection of words Better algorithms to determine word boundaries (Both achieved by Harpy)	Probabilistic approach to determine words on basis of preceding words, for use in supplementing phonetics Faster searches using selectors keyed to individual sounds (Achieved by IBM experimental system, but not in real time)	Language constraints—such as the fact that "vn" never begins English words—to narrow choices Relating acoustic signals to phonemes in form of quantitative rules	natural-language understanding Knowledge base to use context of speech to assist in recognition Learning from errors

[1]SD means speaker-dependent.
[2]SI means speaker-independent.

user makes a fresh attempt or inputs information into the computer using a more traditional mechanism. The size of the mass storage and its retrieval rate determines the maximum size of the vocabulary. The TI system is capable of recognizing vocabularies of up to 50 words each, with spoken words replacing up to 40 manual keystrokes. Also, it allows for recognition of connected words without compelling the user to pause between words.

Speech synthesis, the process of reconstructing speech from stored digital data, is implemented using one of two approaches. Synthesis by rule, also called "constructive synthesis," constructs sounds from text based on linguistic rules. Variations (allophones) of phonemes are prestored in the computer memory. The size of this stored information and the overall size of the set of linguistic rules are used to define the quality of the sound produced. Comparatively less memory and better sound quality can be generated using the alternative approach of *synthesis by analysis*. In this case, the user must first speak the word, and the corresponding information is digitized and stored. At the time of synthesis, the system uses these digitized patterns to generate a speech output that closely resembles the voice of the original speaker. Unlike synthesis by rule where an unlimited number of words could be synthesized, synthesis by analysis allows generation of only those words which are previously known to the system. Data compression techniques are employed to store more words in available memory without appreciable loss of quality. The most common one is the linear predictive coding (LPC) method. The TI system models the human voice with only 2400 bits/s. This enables storage of 16 min of speech on a 320K-byte diskette and 8 h of speech on a 10M-byte Winchester disk. The latter figure is much higher than the unoptimized method of speech storage shown previously in Fig. 1.

Besides communicating with human beings, there is a heavy increase in the level of information exchange between personal computers and between personal computers and host computers (mainframes/minicomputers). Already, personal computers are used in the business environment as intelligent terminals to retrieve files from host computers to be manipulated locally on the personal computer. True networking personal computers operating on a user-transparent basis will become available in the coming years. Currently, many different protocols have been proposed for integration of local personal computer networks. Two protocols that currently dominate the consideration are Carrier Sense Multiple Access (CMSA/CD) and

Tokenpassing. Efficient communication, especially between dissimilar systems, is critically dependent on the protocols and standards for interconnection.

III. SOFTWARE

Between the stage of input of a command or data by the user and the actual execution by the microprocessor, several layers of software come into operation. Undoubtedly the most important, the *operating system,* is used to optimize utilization of resources and to minimize user effort. In addition, there are programming languages and their development tools and user application packages. We consider the operating system first.

Operating System

An operating system is a software program, usually provided by the vendor, that is used for some or all of the following functions:

a) processor management
b) memory management
c) peripheral management
d) file management
e) task scheduling and process management
f) user-oriented facilities such as command-line interpretation
g) miscellaneous functions to support networking, utilities, and high-level languages.

Unlike mainframe computers where the emphasis of the operating system is towards optimizing the usage of the CPU (deemed to be the "costliest" resource in the system) and to support multiple users, operating systems for personal computers are geared more towards supporting single users only and high CPU utilization is no longer the primary objective.

The history of operating systems for microcomputers commences a decade back (1974) when MAA (Microcomputer Applications Associates, later to become Digital Research) developed a small operating system called CP/M (Control Program for Microcomputers). This program enabled applications to be written and compiled on an Intel 8080-based microcomputer. Because of its significant head start, CP/M has become one of the *de facto* standards with most vendors in the United States and Japan which support it on their 8- and 16-bit microprocessors. Another *de facto* standard is the MS-DOS operating system developed by Microsoft—this operating system was introduced in August 1981 in conjunction with the IBM Personal Computer and as such is also called PC-DOS. Its future as a viable standard has been guaranteed by the large base of personal computers of IBM make and the array of plug-compatible hardware from other manufacturers.

A third *de facto* standard is the UNIX operating system. "The name UNIX is a weak pun on Multics" [10]. After Bell Laboratories withdrew from the Multics project at MIT, Kenneth Thompson, an employee of Bell Laboratories, began to implement his ideas about a small but powerful operating system on a discarded PDP-7 computer in 1969 [11]. Originally implemented in assembly language, this operating system was re-implemented in the early 1970s in 'C' programming language on different models of PDP and in the late 1970s on many computers of other makes. The availability of UNIX on personal computers enables these computers to use software originally developed for execution on minicomputers. UNIX offers advantages in multitasking and multiuser environments and hierarchical file systems. Also, it supports linkage and integration of information in a LAN environment.

One of the unique features of UNIX is its "Shell," which allows users to process several system commands with minimal effort through the execution of user-developed Shell files.

Nesting of these files further enhances applicability. The Shell provides a common syntactical format for all system commands and utilities and enables support of several specialized capabilities: *pipes/filters* for passing information between processes; *metacharacter* processing for increasing system flexibility through the use of special characters; and *background process generation* for execution of jobs in the background while the user continues to perform other processes without apparent interruption. UNIX uses a hierarchical file system with three distinct categories of files: *ordinary files* are files created by users and contain user-designated information; *directories* provide mapping between the names of files and the files themselves; and *I/O oriented files* are used within the UNIX structure to denote system devices such as terminals, disk drives, and printers. One drawback of UNIX is its terse command structure. For example, CP means COPY, and RM (for remove) is used to delete files from a directory. But this minor esthetic deficiency can be easily circumvented, and UNIX, overall, is indeed a powerful operating system for multiuser environments.

CP/M on the other hand uses ordinary disk files which can be accessed on either a sequential or random basis. CP/M consists of three main subsystems: *BIOS* (basic input–output system) which handles input–output operations and is heavily hardware dependent; *BDOS* (basic disk operating system) which handles all file transactions and is machine independent; and *CCP* (console command processor) which handles operations relating to the user console. Since CP/M is intended for single-user operation, there are no commands to assign priorities to programs or to enable transfer of information between processes. On the other hand, CP/M offers a dynamic debugging tool (DDT) to facilitate debugging of errors.

The structure and facilities of MS-DOS are quite similar to those of CP/M. Both are intended solely for single-user operation, and as such perform the minimum set of functions usually associated with an operating system. In view of the growing popularity of networks of personal computers and the use of multiple processors within the same personal computer, it is inevitable that UNIX is becoming increasingly important because of its inherent orientation towards multitasking and its acceptance by major manufacturers of microprocessors.

There are two parallel trends in developing the UNIX operating system. Several companies including Microsoft have adapted the code, developed by Bell Laboratories, for several microprocessors. Other companies have opted to rewrite the entire code based on the UNIX design. Meanwhile, Digital Research has expanded their CP/M operating system to support multiuser and multitasking environments. This expanded system is called MP/M.

Even when the same operating system is supported on different computer systems, hardware and architectural differences make it essential to modify application programs to execute under the same operating system on different computers. To mitigate such problems in the migration of software, the UCSD p-system [12], originally developed at the University of California at San Diego, facilitates software portability through use of intermediate code, called p-code, into which all the high-level languages are compiled. Interpreters are available for many processors for translating p-code into the respective native code of the processor. Using this strategy, the same source program can be executed on different systems. The penalty is in terms of reduced execution speed of interpreted code. As microprocessors offer increased speeds and as programming costs continue to escalate, more users will accept the penalty of reduced execution speeds and opt for solutions using such techniques of intermediate code to achieve software portability. The concept of p-systems has been enlarged to establish a network protocol for computers of different makes. Each mode of a network in such a system is assigned a different function.

Application-Oriented Software

Application packages fall into two categories: *specialized packages* oriented towards a specific task or operation, such as payroll or inventory, and *generic tools* used to develop customized models or personalized solutions to problems. Packages in this latter category of "fourth-generation languages" permit the user to develop a structure for his or her data and to perform specific operations on the data. These fourth-generation language tools are extremely powerful and flexible for solving *ad hoc* problems.

Conversion of mainframe and minicomputer software to a personal computer environment represents an interesting challenge. The limited capabilities of the personal computer do not, in general, allow for a mainframe software package to be transported in its entirety to a personal computer. Also, it is not always desirable to move the entire mainframe package as in the case of centralized databases. Frequently, the personal computer will perform all of the terminal emulation, screen handling, and query preprocessing and postprocessing functions. The mainframe retains responsibility for database access, security, and query response. Thus tasks formerly hosted on the mainframe alone can now be split between the personal computer and the host computer to provide more efficient and quicker user response. Such partial migration of software is becoming increasingly prevalent.

Principal *program development languages* in use today are BASIC, Pascal, C, Fortran, and assembly language. Although BASIC is a convenient and easy language in which to prototype algorithms, it lacks structure, self-documentation, and flexible program linkage conventions to make it an efficient application development tool for any but the simplest of programs. Pascal facilitates structured programming and documentation. The key tradeoff between Pascal and C is the strong versus weak typing of data provided by each, respectively. The former is preferred for applications programming while the latter has strengths for systems programming. Pascal and C are not as easy to learn as BASIC. Fortran is a carry-over from minicomputers and mainframes. Assembly language offers high performance, compact code, and intimate control of the hardware. It is used in cases where real-time requirements, input–output device control, and graphics manipulations require programming at the machine level. In many cases, a high-level language is used to develop the general structure and key algorithms, and Assembly language is used to provide specific performance enhancements and device control not achievable in the high-level language. As the costs for software program development become astronomical in terms of programmer time, documentation, maintenance, and field support, off-the-shelf packages are becoming increasingly preferable over in-house software development.

With more than half a million copies having been sold so far, VisiCalc represents the most popular personal computer applications program. Developed by Daniel Bricklin and Robert Frankston in 1979, this "instantly calculating electronic worksheet" uses computer memory and a CRT terminal to store and display a table of 63 columns and 255 rows. Each position of the matrix on the screen corresponds to a record in memory. Each record in memory holds either data, a label, or a formula. The corresponding position on the screen is used to display the label, data, or the result of the calculation using the formula. For example, if the record D8 (D refers to column number and 8 to row number) contains the label "CASH," then at position D8 on the screen the word CASH will be displayed. The same is true for data. The power and flexibility of VisiCalc becomes clearer when we consider what happens with a formula stored in memory. For example, if record A5 contains the formula +A1 + A3, the results of adding the contents of records A1 and A3 will be displayed. If the data in A1 or A3 are changed at any time, the answer displayed at A5 will change automatically. The contents of records A1 and A3 need not be data; they can also refer to another location via a formula. This enables formulation of a particular problem using records as variables. At any given time, 20 rows and up to nine columns are displayed facilitating comprehension of relationships among entries.

Initially, personal computers were used primarily for calculations and for numerical work. The last three years have witnessed the growing popularity of word processors and text-manipulation applications such as checking spellings using extensive dictionaries resident on floppy disks. Only now is it becoming feasible to efficiently undertake storage and retrieval of graphical and pictorial information. In coming years, software will become available to perform integrated sets of operations involving diverse types of information—numbers, text, and

Table 5 Personal Computer Applications

Past	Present	Future
Calculator-Type Functions	Simple Data Retrieval	Integrated Information Retrieval
Hobbyist	Basic Accounting and Spreadsheet	Decision Support Systems, e.g., medical diagnostics, legal information
Games	Elementary Graphics	Artificial Intelligence, Distributed Databases

pictures. Just as the evolution of integrated databases drastically altered the manner in which information was maintained on mainframe computers, the integrated manipulation of dissimilar information structures will revolutionize the role of personal computers and widen the scope of application areas as shown in Table 5.

The evolution of sophisticated graphical and pictorial representation techniques in the limited memory space of personal computers is made possible using several innovative ideas. Logo, a graphics-oriented language designed for school children arose from the Lisp programming language devised at MIT. By building up primitive structures using a cursor—a "turtle" in Logo nomenclature—and integrating them, Logo attempts to introduce thrills, rather than frustrations, in generating complex drawings using personal computers. At the other end, the idea of visual "icons" originally implemented on the Xerox Alto [1] has now been introduced in the realm of personal computers on systems such as the Apple Lisa. The implementation strategy used in VCN ExecuVision reflects an example of an endeavor to implement sophisticated presentation graphics capabilities on inexpensive computers, and to use contemporary data compression techniques to store hundreds of images on a single floppy disk.

The spurt in the number of software products is compelling software developers towards common data structures to enable transfer of information between different programs. The VisiOn Operating Environment is one such example of a unified system that integrates applications programs and presents a common and consistent user interface. Just as portability and standardization of operating systems are now receiving attention, application programs are also undergoing a slow, but distinct, trend towards rationalization and maturity!

IV. ARCHITECTURES

Contemporary personal computers are marked by significant diversity in terms of their architectures and level of performance. Even in the case of the same manufacturer, architectures may differ radically from system to system as in the case of Apple Lisa versus Apple II.

To a large extent, the architecture of the personal computer is dependent on the microprocessor used to handle principal activities. The choice of a particular 16-bit [4] or 32-bit [5] microprocessor as the CPU of the personal computer determines the maximum size of memory, the manner of interconnecting input–output devices, and the "optimal" program development environment for the system. As we will see in subsequent chapters, several personal computer vendors including IBM (Chapter 8), DEC, and Wang (Chapter 6) have opted to use microprocessors belonging to the Intel iAPX 86 family, and it is hardly surprising that these personal computers possess similar architectures. The Motorola 68000 finds use in the HP-200 and the Apple Lisa (Chapter 14) systems.

However, even in cases where the same or a similar chip has been used in several systems, the end products are not necessarily identical. The compatibility aspect between members of the IBM Personal Computer family is examined in Chapter 8. In general, differences in architecture are due to several reasons including personal preferences of different designers, the availability of newer coprocessors and higher density memory chips, and the perceived user needs. There is now a growing trend towards using several dissimilar microprocessor chips within the same system in order to allow different operating systems to run, or to handle different functions. In such cases, efficient mechanisms are designed to handle communications between the multiple microprocessors.

The use of dual-ported memories represents another area of innovation. Since the screen must be refreshed at regular intervals, the memory must be read at a constant rate. In parallel, the computer is also writing to and reading from the memory. Dual-ported memories allow both these functions to occur in parallel, without compromising either the throughput of the computer or the refresh rate of the display. The PC 100 (Chapter 17) manufactured by NEC performs these functions in parallel without using expensive components.

Because of their orientation towards ease of use rather than on raw computing speeds, manufacturers have published little information about standardized applications level throughputs of their respective systems. Macro-level comparisons between the DG and IBM personal computers have been indicated in Chapter 7. Similar comparisons between the DEC Rainbow and the IBM personal computers found in [13], [14] show that these two systems have performance in the same ballpark range. Figures 2 and 3, provided by Apple, show the relative

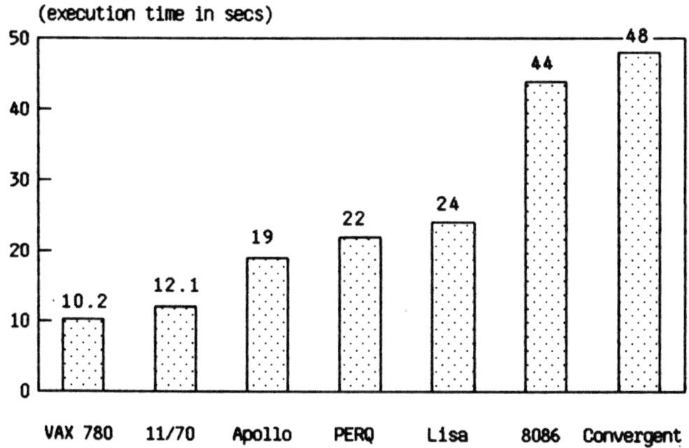

Fig. 2.   Performance evaluation using Pascal "PUZZLE" program.

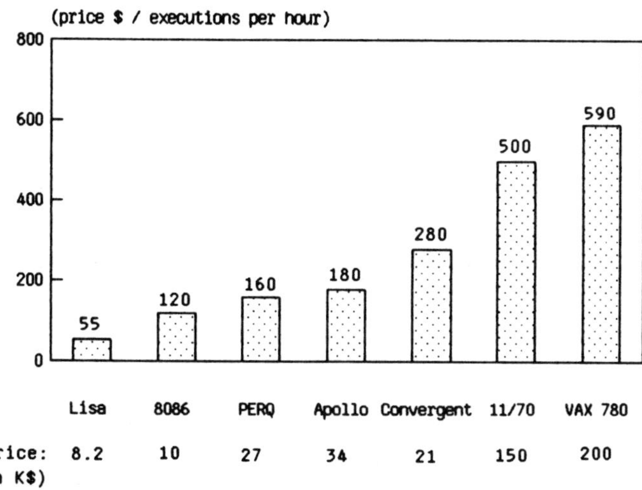

Fig. 3.   Price/performance ratio for "PUZZLE" program.

performance and the price–performance ratio of the Apple Lisa in comparison to minicomputers and other computers not falling within the category of personal computers.

Independent evaluation of several different personal computers is still scarce. The spectrum of options on each system, both in terms of hardware and software, restricts the usefulness of such results. As such, some comparisons simply summarize the specifications in terms of features. One such comparison of portable computers [15] shows the spectrum of functionality available on personal computers. Similar comparisons of desktop computers appear frequently in trade journals. The fast rate of introduction of new personal computer products represents a rapid evolution of traditional mini/micro architectures towards new, innovative system organizations to best utilize the new technologies and best support the end user. By offering performance traditionally available on much larger systems, personal computers are gradually eroding the popularity of minicomputers and even mainframes!

V. Markets

The application of personal computer technology varies substantially between the four areas of usage: home, business, science, and education. Users in any given area have specific needs and expectations as shown in Table 6. Accordingly, manufacturers of personal computer systems as well as software vendors have targeted specific offerings to each of these markets. The major functional requirements of each of these four categories are defined next.

Requirements of the Home Market

a) Low Cost: The home market is very price-sensitive to both hardware configuration costs as well as add-on software expenses. Because it is a consumer market, personal computer technology must be packaged, marketed, and distributed in the same fashion as mass product consumer goods. Price resistance occurs at several levels. For the hardware system these levels are around $100, $500, and $1000. The upper limit on home budgets for a basic computer system

Table 6 Four Primary Markets for Personal Computers

Characteristic	Home	Business	Science	Education
Complete System Price ($)	⩽ 1000	⩽ 5000	⩽ 10 000	⩽ 1000
Overall Need for Storage				
a) Avg. System Primary	64K	256K	256K–512K	64K
b) Avg. System Secondary	100–500K	0.5–1M	5–10M	500K
Computation Intensive	Low	Moderate	Heavy	Low
Hard Copy Output	Dot matrix printer	Dot matrix letter quality	Full graphics	Dot matrix
User Interface	For noncomputer use of graphics, color	Noncomputer user	Computer user	Use of graphics color
Applications Software Price	⩽ $100	$100–700	$1000–2000	⩽ $200
Principal Applications	Games, household tasks, word processing	Spreadsheets, word processing graphing database communications	Similar to business applications; Specialized to each task	CAI, CBT, Classroom instruction

is around $1000. Similarly, in software, the home market centers between $25–$50 for entertainment packages and between $50–$200 for home financial applications.

b) Expandability: The ability to expand the original system by the addition of peripherals, more memory, or communications, and the availability of a growth path to upwards compatible, more powerful computer systems are factors that influence the decision to purchase a computer system.

c) Educational Software: Aside from entertainment, personal computers are used for training and education. This includes learning of BASIC, elementary mathematics, reading, and other school skills and the use of educational programs at the secondary school level.

d) Games: Home computers support entertainment and game software. This application requires the generation of colors and sounds in the system unit.

e) Integration with Other Home Systems: Facilities must exist for the computer to be hooked up to the home entertainment system that currently includes the television set and in the future will include stereos, large-screen TVs, telephone, and data network services such as Videotext.

Requirements of the Business Market

a) Storage: Business applications require sufficient on-line and secondary storage to accommodate moderate to extensive databases. On the average, current-generation business personal computers use 128K bytes of RAM, with secondary storage around 1M byte for floppy technology and 10M bytes for hard disk Winchester technology.

b) Hard Copy Output: The need to produce reports, memos, and graphs in a form suitable for presentation to other parties requires capabilities for both letter quality text as well as high-resolution graphics output. These two requirements necessitate separate types of printer technology driving up the price of business computer systems.

c) Large Software Base: The average business person has neither the expertise nor the resources to develop software in-house. Consequently, such users invest heavily in off-the-shelf software applications programs. Hardware that supports a variety of editors, word processing programs, spreadsheets, graphics, and database programs is naturally preferred.

d) Support: The impact of a system "going down" is much more serious in a business environment than in the home. Thus business users require sufficient support from either the vendor, the distribution channel, or an in-house information center to achieve reasonable "up-time" characteristics.

Requirements of the Science Market

a) Specialized Systems: Scientific users often have a need for special hardware devices and specific software within a narrow application area. For example, the use of a personal computer in a research chemistry laboratory would require interfaces to various noncomputer equipment (e.g., gas chromatographs, multichannel analyzers, spectrometers), and specialized software to integrate the auxiliary systems with the personal computer. If no off-the-shelf software exists, then the scientific user seeks good programming and debugging tools in order to develop software in-house.

b) High Computation Requirements: Since most applications are computation-intensive, the personal computer must provide fast numeric calculations as well as efficient block data moves, possibly through the addition of a coprocessor dedicated to arithmetic and floating-point operations.

c) Programming Environment: Because scientific users often do their own program development, the programming environment must be rich and flexible including tools such as full screen editors, symbolic debuggers, and extensive cross-reference capabilities, and efficient run-time packages.

Requirements of the Education Market

a) Ease of Use: In order to retain the motivation and the attention of students, personal computer systems must present a friendly interface and challenging, easy-to-use software.

b) Cost: Educational institutions are in a period of shrinking budgets and thus are unable to afford high-end systems.

c) Educational Software Base: The personal computer must support self-paced computer-aided instruction (CAI) programs and a large educational software base.

d) Environmental Factors: The classroom environment requires sharing of most personal computer resources in order to reduce the cost per student to an acceptable level. This sharing is enforced by scheduling, by local area networking, or by hardware multiplexing. Another requirement is the need for portability as the personal computer is often used by different groups for different topics at different times within the same institution. Finally, units must be rugged to survive in an educational environment.

The overall trends in the four principal markets in terms of price per system, number of systems, and total dollar volumes are summarized in Tables 7, 8, and 9, respectively.

Table 7 Historical and Predicted Average Price for Personal Computers in the U.S. for Different Applications

Year	Business	Home/ Hobby	Science	Education	Overall Average
1981	$3599	$1997	$3199	$2800	$3099
1982	$2630	$1240	$2355	$1987	$2186
1983	$2502	$1071	$2432	$1325	$2047
1984	$2238	$ 787	$2642	$ 935	$1807
1985	$2182	$ 778	$2696	$ 712	$1752

Table 8 Estimated Number of Units Sold/Projected to Be Sold: By Market Segments: U.S. Only (in Thousands)

	1980	1981	1982	1983	1984	1985
Business	285	385	750	1040	1500	2100
Home	135	175	375	510	750	1075
Science	60	105	200	250	300	400
Education	20	35	60	100	150	225
Total (numbers)	500	700	1385	1900	2700	3800
Total Value: (millions of dollars)	(1140)	(2169)	(3028)	(3889)	(4880)	(6658)

VI. Conclusion

The personal computer is a product of the information revolution. It usually requires a substantial amount of time to disseminate any product of a revolution among the population at large. The benefits of the industrial revolution accrued many decades after the original inventions. In the case of computers, this dissemination process has occurred over a very condensed time frame.

The domain of individually tailored computing power has evolved dramatically over the past decade, and the impact of this evolution continues to escalate. The shift in focus from

Table 9 Total U.S. Market (in Millions of Dollars)

Year	Business	Home/ Hobby	Science	Education	Total
1977	26.5	25.2	8.2	3.1	63
1978	140.25	82.5	38.5	13.75	275
1979	385	175	105	35	700
1980	681.7	228	173.3	57	1140
1981	1385.6	349.5	335.9	98	2169
1982	1972.7	465.1	471	119.2	3028
1983	2602.2	546.3	608	132.5	3889
1984	3356.8	590.2	792.7	140.3	4880
1985	4582.6	836.8	1078.5	160.1	6658

computing power to ease of use has led to concentrated efforts in evolving user-oriented mechanisms such as function-keys, menu-driven interfaces, speech input and output methodologies, and fourth-generation languages. The selective combination of these newer techniques has resulted in a wide variety of personal computers to suit the needs and the economics of different individuals. As in the case of other consumer items, such as cars, a prospective user appreciates the utility of acquiring an asset. However, the process of selecting and configuring a personal computer is becoming increasingly complex as we will see in the final chapter of this book.

Most people involved in scientific, engineering, or business endeavors combine activities that fall under several categories. A typical user will employ the personal computer to prepare and disseminate office memos, professional papers, and data records, to support decision making, and also to learn new skills of both an educational and entertainment nature. The flexibility of a personal computer to carry out such a multitude of functions is what makes it so convenient and desirable to most of us. From the quiet beginning of the personal computer, one could have hardly visualized that within a single decade this technology would be available in a product form to several million people around the world and will become available to many millions more in the very near future. In this chapter some notions about the second decade were presented. No doubt things will look very different by the turn of the century, but hopefully we will view the personal computer with as much excitement, promise, and enthusiasm as we foresee today!

REFERENCES

[1] C. P. Thacker et al., "Alto: A personal computer," in D. P. Siewiorek et al., Computer Structures: Principles and Examples.   New York: McGraw-Hill, 1982.

[2] S. Bereiter, "The personal computer invades higher education," IEEE Spectrum, vol. 20, no. 6, pp. 59–61, June 1983.

[3] H. Mintzberg, The Nature of Managerial Work.   Englewood Cliffs, NJ: Prentice Hall, 1980.

[4] H. D. Toong and A. Gupta, "An architectural comparison of contemporary 16-bit microprocessors," IEEE Micro, vol. 1, no. 2, pp. 26–37, May 1981.

[5] A. Gupta and H. D. Toong, "An architectural comparison of 32-bit microprocessors," IEEE Micro, vol. 3, no. 1, pp. 9–22, Feb. 1983.

[6] G. E. Moore, "Progress in digital integrated electronics," in Proc. Int. Electron Devices Meet., pp. 11–13, Dec. 1975.

[7] High Technology, May 1982.

[8] R. Reddy and V. Zue, "Recognizing continuous speech remains an elusive goal," IEEE Spectrum, vol. 20, no. 11, pp. 84–87, Nov. 1983.

[9] K. McDonough et al., "Microcomputer with 32-bit arithmetic does high-precision number crunching," Electronics, pp. 105–110, Feb. 24, 1982.

[10] B. W. Kernighan and S. P. Morgan, "The UNIX operating system: A model for software design," *Science*, vol. 215, no. 4534, pp. 779–783, Feb. 12, 1982.
[11] E. I. Organick, *The MULTICS System.* Cambridge, MA: MIT Press, 1972.
[12] C. A. Irvine, "UCSD system makes programs portable," *Electron. Des.*, pp. 113–118, Aug. 1982.
[13] A. M. Seybold, "The new top contender," *Digit. Rev.*, pp. 23–27, Oct. 1983.
[14] J. Cohler, "Benchmark: Rainbow versus IBM PC," *Digit. Rev.*, pp. 28–40, Nov. 1983.
[15] D. H. Ahl, "Choosing a notebook computer," *Creative Comput.*, pp. 18–32, Jan. 1984.

3
The Design and Development of a Family of Personal Computers for Engineers and Scientists

GERALD E. NELSON AND WILLIAM R. HEWLETT

Back in 1968 Hewlett-Packard was the pioneer in introducing a sophisticated scientific calculator with transcendental functions implemented in firmware. The original design led to three generations of personal computers with more memory, higher performance, and greater versatility. In this chapter the authors present an insight into the design and development of personal computers geared towards the professional needs of scientists and engineers. The range in performance of Hewlett-Packard scientific computers is examined. The current product, the Hewlett-Packard Series 200, is described in detail.

The Editors

I. INTRODUCTION

In 1968, Hewlett-Packard introduced its first personal computer for engineers and scientists, the HP 9100A [1]. It was called a "computing calculator," weighed 18 kg (40 lbs), and sold for less than $5000. Programs and data were entered either through the 63-key keyboard or by means of wallet-sized magnetic cards capable of holding up to two complete read/write memory images. These "rectangular floppy disks" could be read or written by the 9100A and were used to distribute a wide variety of application programs for business, chemistry, electronics, fluid mechanics, life sciences, mathematics, physics, statistics, structures, surveying, and thermodynamics.

Data in the 9100A were represented as decimal floating-point numbers with two-digit exponents and twelve digits of mantissa precision. Results were displayed on a 5-in electrostatic CRT in three lines (numeric only). Firmware was provided for a full complement of arithmetic, logarithmic, exponential, trigonometric, hyperbolic, coordinate, memory, and programming functions. Typical add/subtract operations completed in 2 ms. Multiply required 22 ms, square-root 30 ms, and trigonometric functions 330 ms. Conditional and unconditional branching using flags and/or arithmetic comparisons were provided, along with program halt, pause, and single-step.

Internal memory in the 9100A was organized into a 368-word by 6-bit read/write coincident current core memory for programs and data; a 64-word by 29-bit, 800 ns, threaded core ROM for control sequences; and a 512-word by 64-bit program ROM for microcode. The latter memory utilized a 16-layer printed circuit board with inductive coupling to sense lines from reference

---

G. E. Nelson is with the Hewlett-Packard Company, Fort Collins Systems Division, Fort Collins, CO 80525, USA.

W. R. Hewlett is with the Hewlett-Packard Company, Palo Alto, CA 94304, USA.

and address lines. This unusual technology achieved a density of 1000 bits per square inch using no integrated circuit chips!

The 9100A was well received and regarded as a significant technical achievement. It was followed within a year by the 9100B which doubled the read/write memory size and provided a true subroutine capability with nesting to five levels. Also introduced in 1969 were a 25- by 38-cm (10- by 15-in) plotter and a 180 line/min strip printer for hard copy output, a card reader which read pencil marks on standard size tab cards, and a large screen CRT display.

Our intent for the 9100 products was very clear in our minds. We were a team of scientists and engineers who wanted to build personal computers for other scientists and engineers. In retrospect, it is interesting to consider to what degree the 9100A should be considered the first mass-produced personal computer. A technology assessment of personal computers was conducted for the National Science Foundation by a research team at the University of Southern California, Los Angeles. The report, issued in September of 1980 [2], acknowledges that it is difficult exactly to define "personal computer," but gives definitions containing the following criteria:

- small, stand-alone
- general purpose
- advanced microelectronics technology (microprocessor)
- operated by a single individual, interactively
- no requisite computer training
- affordable by an individual or small group.

The report concludes: "the distinction of being the first mass-produced personal computer (PC) probably belongs to the ALTAIR 8800 marketed in late 1974 by the small Albuquerque-based firm, MITS, Inc." (The Altair 8800 was based on the Intel 8080 microprocessor which was first delivered in 1973.) The HP 9100 machines substantially satisfied the above criteria. Microprocessors, of course, were not used in the HP 9100 since they did not then exist. Those who would argue that the 9100 was too specialized to be considered the first personal computer would almost certainly agree that the distinction is merited by one of the subsequent 9800 Series computers that provided full algebraic language capability and still predated 1974.

The principal members of the second generation of Hewlett-Packard personal computers were the 9810A, the 9820A, and the 9830A [3]. They featured plug-in memory modules to increase read/write memory size, plug-in ROM modules to add application functions, and customized keyboards. A growing set of input and output peripherals was provided. These included card and paper tape readers, typewriter and line printers, cassette and fixed-plus-removable hard disk storage devices, digitizers, plotters, TTL I/O interfaces, and the HP-IB (IEEE-488) interface bus.

The 9810A was introduced in 1971. It included a built-in strip printer and offered larger memory, faster performance, lower price, and increased versatility relative to the 9100A. Like its predecessor, it was programmed by keystrokes. The 9820A was introduced in January of 1972. This was the first of the 9800 Series to offer programming in an algebraic language, HPL. The 9830A was introduced the following year and provided an interactive, user-friendly BASIC language system. Extensions made it possible for the user to write programs which exercised full control over the set of input and output peripherals. This computer family shared a common hardware processor architecture implemented with TTL SSI and MSI components. The 9830A and a later version of the 9820A, the 9821A, also included an integrated cassette for personal mass storage.

The evolution of the 9800 Series personal computers continued to a third generation of products in the mid-1970s. These were the first Hewlett-Packard personal computers to be based upon a proprietary 16-bit NMOS microprocessor called the "BPC" [4]. The 9825A was introduced in 1976, the 9845A in 1977, the 9835A in 1978, and the 9845B in 1979. These machines offered very significant gains in performance and capability. The 9825A provided HPL and the 9835A and 9845A/B provided enhanced BASIC. The 9845A/B also offered 560 by 455 color raster graphics.

The fourth generation of HP personal computers is the subject of Section III of this chapter. Its definition and the underlying hardware and software design decisions are discussed there.

II. Design Objectives

As stated in Section I, the 9100 and 9800 Series personal computers were designed with the needs of engineers and scientists uppermost in mind. This part of the chapter describes basic requirements and design objectives, emphasizing those elements which are of particular importance to these users.

Any family of personal computers must satisfy the criteria listed in Section I. The computers must be low in cost, easily used by an individual, and provide, in a compact desktop or benchtop configuration, a complete set of computing resources. No prior training in computer operation or programming technology should be required, and the system should operate in a friendly, interactive manner which enhances the user's productivity. In addition to these basic requirements, there are some specialized objectives which also must be met in order to satisfy the technical computing needs of engineers and scientists.

A. Interfacing to the Physical World

A personal computer used for technical applications requires a complete set of peripheral input and output devices, particularly mass storage, printers, displays, and terminal connections to a host computer. In addition, it often needs to connect to instrumentation, experimental apparatus, or high capability graphic input or output devices. This necessitates a wide variety of interface adapter cards and sufficient backplane slots to hold them. This may result in computers of larger size, with extender boxes, and perhaps larger power supplies.

B. Real-Time Data Acquisition

In addition to normal low-speed asynchronous I/O and high-speed file I/O, technical applications frequently require the ability to capture short, high-speed bursts of data, or to issue high-speed command sequences for instrumentation control. The computer hardware and software must be able to respond very rapidly to interrupts caused by external events. This may require operating systems which permit application programs to control input and output devices directly, without the help (and resulting overhead) of manufacturer-supplied I/O access methods and drivers.

C. Computational Power

In the authors' experience, there are few applications which would not benefit from additional computational power. This is particularly true of personal computers employed for technical applications. Adequate response to real-time needs of instrumentation and experimental apparatus depends upon the performance of the processor. Scientific computation involves dealing with floating-point numbers over a range of ten to the hundredth power or more, with precisions of 12 or more digits. The IEEE floating-point standard and specialized hardware for high-speed floating-point and array calculations are indicators of the central character of this requirement. Thirty-two bit data paths and specialized hardware to accelerate arithmetic, trigonometric, transcendental, and statistics calculations are increasingly desirable.

D. Memory Size

Nearly all computers share the need to access large amounts of information on a random basis. Newer programming technologies which trade space and machine cycles for human productivity, as well as nontraditional categories of data such as voice and picture, will continue to require larger and larger main memories. Technical applications which must acquire large amounts of data at high speeds will require large memories to buffer those data. Personal computers used for technical applications must provide the power and card slots for enough memory cards, or must be able to connect to extender boxes without undue loss of performance.

E. Ease of Program Development

Off-the-shelf application and subroutine packages are of significant benefit to all types of personal computer users. It is frequently necessary in technical applications, however, to produce one-time programs or to modify existing applications. These considerations imply that personal computers used for technical applications must provide powerful, easy-to-use program development and debugging systems. They also imply that standard programming languages should be used to facilitate sharing of software and to assure ready portability of off-the-shelf application packages.

F. Software Flexibility

For some time, engineering curricula have included heavy doses of computer experience. Increasingly, engineers and scientists are exposed to state-of-the-art hardware and software systems. To be attractive to such individuals, a personal computer must provide a variety of languages, libraries of subroutines, and a full repertoire of tools and utilities. Means must be provided to permit the user both to trade performance for programming productivity and, in critical timing situations, to optimize object code for maximum performance. Languages and tools must be provided to meet both of these needs.

G. Graphics Capabilities

The graphics human interface needs of technical users span a wide range of capability. Some needs are satisfied by simple two-dimensional graphing of mathematical functions. Other needs require the capability to draw schematics or block diagrams (such as the figures in this chapter). And at the high end, the designers of complex mechanical parts or integrated circuit chips need very high speed, high resolution, large screen color displays on their personal computer workstations. This wide range, coupled with the high cost of the graphic display hardware, leads to the necessity for a range of product configurations having different prices and features.

H. Environmental Requirements

Personal computers for technical applications are often used in industrial factories, in laboratories where sensitive electronic measurements are being made, and in the field. Their hardware designs must be rugged enough to provide dependable operation in such adverse environments. Ambient conditions of 50° and 90-percent humidity must be tolerated. Permissible electromagnetic interference levels are significantly lower than those for home or office. Greater resistance to shock and vibration is important for applications in vehicles, aircraft, or ships. Another frequent requirement is for immunity to power line transients and interruptions that could cause the loss of expensive data.

III. Design Implementation

This section of the chapter describes how the above needs and objectives were addressed by the design implementation of a technical computer family, the Hewlett-Packard Series 200. The discussion will proceed by functional subsystems within the design rather than by topical areas of design objectives as in the previous section.

A. Product Design Configurations

It is virtually impossible to meet the personal computer needs of every engineer and scientist with a single product configuration. Over the past three years, five different models have been developed in the Series 200 family to meet a range of those needs. The photo in Fig. 1 shows the Series 200 family, and the chart of Fig. 2 lists some of the distinguishing hardware features. Here are the primary needs and user design centers for each model:

- **Model 226:** This was the first model in the series to be introduced. It was designed primarily as a controller for laboratory or factory floor instrumentation systems. The package is rack-mountable or stackable with instrumentation. The display size and mass

Fig. 1. Series 200 family portrait.

	Model 216	Model 9920	Model 226	Model 236	Model 236C
CRT Display: Size: (mm diag) Text Capability: Graphics Raster:	229 (9 in.) 25 Lines of 80 Chars. 400x300 pixels	External Monitor 25 Lines of 80 Chars. 400x300 pixels	178 (7 in.) 25 Lines of 50 Chars. 400x300 pixels	 25 Lines of 80 Chars. 512x390 pixels	 25 Lines of 80 Chars. 512x390 4 bits/pixel Color
Built-in Mass Storage:	(None)	(None)	One 264Kb flexible disc drive	Two 264Kb flexible disc drives	Two 264Kb flexible disc drives
Maximum Memory: (Without Expander)	768Kb	3.25 Mb	2Mb	2Mb	2Mb
Maximum External I/O Cards (Without Expander)	2	16	8	8	8
Size: Ht x Wd x Dp (mm)	282x315x488	191x426x377	184x432x654	452x432x654	452x432x705
Weight: (kg)	11.3 (25 lb)	17.2 (38 lb)	24.6 (54 lb)	44.3 (98 lb)	49.9(110 lb)

Fig. 2. Series 200 family hardware distinctions.

storage capability was chosen to minimize the physical height and to meet the more limited needs of this type of use.

- **Model 236:**   This product was developed for the user who interacts with the computer as a major part of his or her activity. It provides a large display screen, dual minifloppy drives, capacity for up to 2M bytes of memory, and higher resolution graphics.
- **Model 236C:**   This is the most expensive version, providing color display capabilities for those computer-aided design and scientific graphics applications that need color to enhance their human interface.
- **Model 216:**   This is the lowest costing, most limited capability version. It was designed to be small in size in order to fit on the desk without consuming all the available space on it. The design center user is the engineer, scientist, or technical manager who needs ready access to a personal computer but does not use it as his or her major job activity. It has the same computing performance as the larger and more expensive models, but is more limited in display features, memory, and I/O space, and has no built-in mass storage.
- **Model 9920:**   This is a rack-mountable box computer, designed to be configured into test systems, larger design workstations, or any other situation that requires a different collection of peripheral resources than is provided by the integrated desktop members of the family. It provides the largest number (16) of backplane slots for memory and I/O adapters.

B. Processor Architecture

The need for processor speed and memory capacity in a technical personal computer is limited only by the cost of providing it. The rapid progress of silicon technology has allowed the processor speed and memory system size of a constant cost personal computer to double every few years. The historic progression of technical personal computers has therefore tended to show a slow increase in price, related to the rate of wage inflation, with an exploding growth in capability.

Development of the Series 200 began in 1977. An important early goal was to provide the next generation of capability from its predecessor family, the 9825, 9835, and 9845. The first of these machines, the 9825, was introduced in 1976. The first Series 200 computer, the Model 226, was introduced in 1981. The goal for processor speed was set at twice that of the BPC microprocessor in the 9825 and memory capacity was targeted to be at least four times larger. Memory addressing range of the processor was a key consideration. The natural 16-bit CPU limit of 64K bytes was circumvented in the earlier family by hardware-assisted paging [5], but this created increased cost and software complications.

The choice of IC technology for the Series 200 processor was dictated by HP's internal technology situation relative to the IC industry in the late 1970s. In 1976, when the BPC was new, the internal NMOS-II process was ahead of the commercially available ones. Today in 1984, the NMOS-III process used in the 9000/500 series of 32-bit computers, is again ahead [6]. But in 1979, when the Series 200 processor choice was made, NMOS-II was obsolescent and NMOS-III was not yet ready. After extensive evaluation of the commercially available 16-bit microprocessors, the Motorola 68000 was chosen. It alone met the objectives of performance together with the timing of volume availability. Some of the key attributes of this chip that made it the best choice were [7]:

- 32-bit internal architecture for performance coupled with 16-bit external bussing for low cost
- 16 megabyte linear address space
- memory-mapped I/O
- a powerful instruction set with 14 addressing modes and 5 main data types
- a register architecture with 17 32-bit registers in addition to the 32-bit program counter and 16-bit status register

- an 8-MHz clock, allowing a memory cycle time of 625 ns and an average instruction time of about 2 μs.

The processor and memory system architecture of the Series 200 has undergone one minor and one major revision since the initial product introduction in mid-1981. The first version used the 8-MHz 68000 chip, a system bus that was a buffered version of the processor connections, and 16K-bit memory chips. The minor revision, introduced in early 1982, replaced the 16K memory chips with 64K parts, allowing a four times improvement in capacity per memory board. The major revision, introduced in late 1983, added cache and memory management hardware to the processor board, along with capability to use the 68012 CPU chip.

The block diagram of the initial Series 200 hardware is shown in Fig. 3. The CPU board provides the 68000 microprocessor, buffers, and control circuits, 16K bytes of ROM for the system boot loader and self-test code, and 64K bytes of RAM. The system backplane address and data busses are buffered forms of the processor busses. Except for a few special-purpose additions, the same is true for the control lines. Various products within the Series 200 family provide different internal peripheral capabilities. Differing numbers of external card cage slots can be used for I/O adapter cards as well as memory.

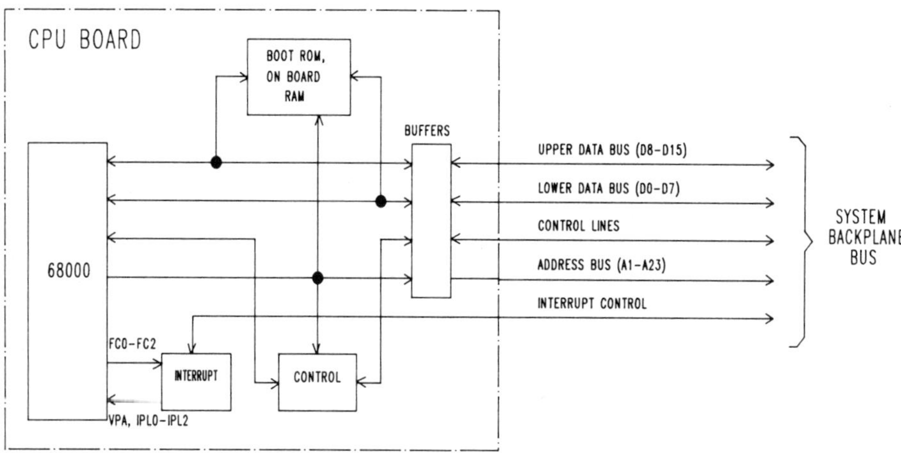

Fig. 3. Series 200 processor block diagram.

The processor and backplane signals are shown in more detail in Fig. 4. The processor status bits indicate the state and cycle type currently being executed. The 6800 peripheral control signals are included to allow for backward compatibility when interfacing to Motorola 6800 family peripheral devices. The system control inputs are used to initialize or halt the processor and to indicate to the processor that a bus error has occurred. The asynchronous bus control lines supply the necessary handshake to coordinate the timing of data transfer. The bus arbitration lines determine which device in the system will be the bus master. Finally, the interrupt control inputs indicate to the processor the priority level of the interrupting device.

The system memory map is shown in Fig. 5. The lowest 4M bytes are assigned to system ROM, including the boot ROM. Since ROMs (read-only memories) are constant in their response time, unlike RAMs (random-access memories) that have refresh cycles to contend with, the CPU board treats this part of the address space synchronously. The processor handshake signal DTACK is sent by the CPU board, creating a five clock-cycle access. The next 4M bytes are assigned to the internal and external I/O devices. This address space is mapped as shown in Fig. 6. The next 1M byte is reserved for internal testing and monitoring, leaving the top 7M bytes available for RAM.

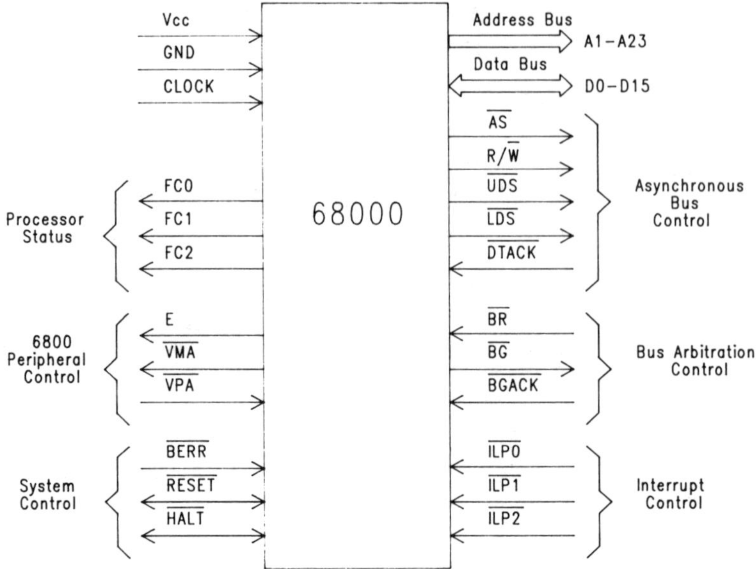

Fig. 4. 68000 processor signals.

At the initial introduction of the Series 200, 16K-bit RAMs were used, and the initial memory board was 64K bytes. Then in 1982, the newer 64K-bit chips allowed the introduction of a 256K-byte board. The memory boards can run either a regular asynchronous access cycle of seven clock periods or a special higher speed synchronous one requiring only five. Except during refresh of the dynamic RAM chips, the synchronous cycle is used. Since late in 1982, a memory expander box has allowed configuration of systems having the maximum possible physical memory.

Late in 1983, the systems software capability of the Series 200 was augmented considerably by the introduction of a multitasking operating system, HP-UX (to be discussed later.) This required some radical changes in the hardware architecture. A new CPU board was designed with a block diagram as shown in Fig. 7. The design objectives for the new board were to provide new functionality for HP-UX, take advantage of the new faster versions of the 68000 processor family, provide hardware support for virtual memory, and retain backward compatibility with the existing software systems, I/O cards, and memory cards. The HP-UX functionality objective was met by providing a memory management unit, or MMU, that allows hardware relocation of processes under operating system control. The MMU separates the physical address bus of the system backplane from the logical address bus of the microprocessor, and allows mapping of any 1K-byte page of logical memory to any other in physical memory. It also performs bounds checking to prevent processes from accessing memory outside of their assigned range. Support for faster processors is provided by a 16K-byte cache memory. This subsystem allows increasing the processor clock and decreasing the in-cache memory cycle time without changing the main memory cycle time or any nontiming-dependent software. The only software control needed is to turn the cache on or off. The memory system performance as a function of processor clock, MMU state, and cache hit/miss is shown in Fig. 8. The initial shipments of this board have used a 12.5-MHz 68000 processor. Extensive use of this version has shown a cache hit ratio of over 80 percent, and a subsequent performance increase of over 50 percent. When it becomes available in quantity from Motorola, the 14.3-MHz 68012 processor will plug into the same board, allowing even faster performance, together with the capability to address up to 256M bytes of memory.

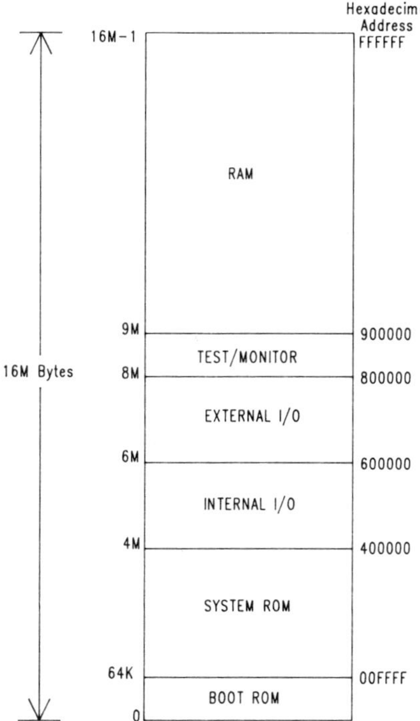

Fig. 5. System memory map.

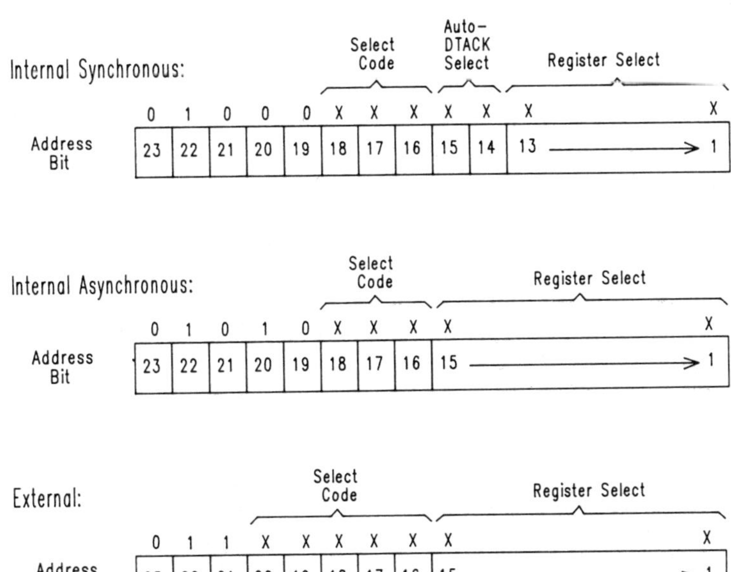

Fig. 6. I/O address bit assignments.

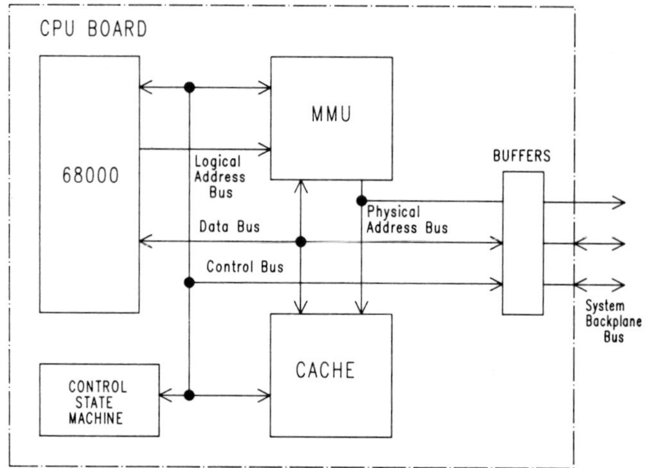

Fig. 7. New CPU with cache and memory management.

		12.5 MHZ CLOCK		14.3 MHZ CLOCK	
		CLOCK STATES	TIME ns	CLOCK STATES	TIME ns
MMU ON	CACHE HIT	4.5	360	4.5	315
	CACHE MISS	8.5	680	9.5	665
MMU OFF	CACHE HIT	4.0	320	4.0	280
	CACHE MISS	8.0	640	9.0	630

Fig. 8. New memory system performance.

C. Interfacing and Networking Hardware

To meet the technical personal computer users' needs for a wide variety of interfacing capabilities, an extensive set of interface adapter cards has been designed and introduced over the past three years. These are as follows:

- a two-channel DMA (direct memory access) controller (98620A) to allow faster data transfers from other I/O cards directly to and from memory at up to 1.2 million transfers per second
- a 16-bit general-purpose parallel I/O card (98622A)
- a BCD (binary-coded decimal) input card (98623A) providing 43 input lines for parallel acceptance of 8 BCD digits, exponent, mantissa sign, and exponent sign
- two different cards for IEEE-488 (HP-IB) devices; a low-cost instrumentation version (98624A) and a high-performance disk mass storage version (98625A)
- two different cards for serial interfacing (RS-232-C or CCITT V.28/V.24); a simple asynchronous version (98626A) and an intelligent, buffered version (98628A)
- a color video output card (98627A), providing display memory and red/green/blue video outputs to drive an external color monitor
- a shared resource management interface (98629A) to permit connection of multiple technical personal computers to a central file system and set of shared peripherals
- a programmable data communications interface (98691A) that can be tailored to meet a wide variety of special serial interfacing needs
- a bubble memory card (98259A) providing 128K bytes of nonvolatile, fast-response, environmentally rugged mass storage

- an EPROM (electrically programmed read-only memory) card that allows up to 256K bytes of program to be permanently stored, together with a programmer card that programs the EPROM chips directly in the Series 200 computer without requiring a separate piece of programming equipment
- a breadboard card (98630A) for experienced hardware designers to use in creating their own special I/O adapter for any purpose not covered by the above products

D. Software Architecture

As described in Section II of this chapter, the wide variety of needs of technical personal computers require a wide variety of software tools to meet them. At the present time, there have been four radically different software systems designed for the Series 200 by Hewlett-Packard, and several more have been contributed by other companies. These range from friendly interpreters to meet the need for rapid program development by non-computer professionals, to powerful compiler and assembler tools for extracting maximum performance from the hardware, to a general-purpose, multiuser, and multitask operating system with emphasis on software compatibility and portability.

1) Boot ROM: In order to facilitate the existence of multiple operating systems on the Series 200, and to be able to load them into the computer's memory when the power is turned on, a surprisingly large amount of code (48K bytes) is contained in a ROM on the processor board. This code is executed when the power is turned on or when the user chooses to go from one system to another. It tests the internal peripherals and memory and then searches all attached mass storage devices, networks, and internal ROM cards for operating systems. If there is more than one available, it waits for the user to select one from the keyboard. To permit unattended startup, if the user makes no response within a short time, the first system found will be loaded and control transferred to it. The boot ROM code is large because of the many mass storage drivers it must provide to accommodate ROM, floppy disk, hard disk, and network access.

2) HPL: To provide a software-compatible growth path for more than 30 000 users of the predecessor 9825A computer, an interpreter system was provided that supports exactly the same language, HPL. This language was first provided on the 9820A Programmable Calculator in 1972 [8], and was designed for scientists and engineers to use in rapidly solving computation and instrument control problems. Its virtue and its weakness are simplicity. Variables are limited to single-letter names. Few structured programming constructs are available. Most keywords are three-letter mnemonics, helping in rapid typing of the program but making the code harder to read.

Conventional wisdom says that high-level, compatible languages are a necessity for software transportability. The development of Series 200 HPL was done by a small, dedicated team of engineers in a short time by direct translation of BPC Assembly code to 68000 Assembly code! Having a strict constraint on the definition and a direct comparison yardstick for testing (the 9825A) was much more important in making the design task straightforward than was the system implementation language.

In order to provide not only compatible language syntax but also compatible execution semantics, the same representation for numbers was used in the Series 200 HPL system as in the 9825A. This is a 12-digit BCD floating-point format. The BPC processor in the 9825A provided hardware arithmetic routines to assist in manipulating this format that the 68000 lacks. Fortunately, the fundamental processor power together with some clever algorithm design yielded equivalent or higher performance. The verification of perfect mathematical compatibility was done by connecting a 9825A computer to a Series 200 computer back-to-back and running millions of operands through all the arithmetic routines and comparing the results [9].

3) BASIC: The primary software system designed for the noncomputer-professional users of the Series 200 was the BASIC Language System. Most BASIC implementations provide a small, simple, low-performance language that is adequate for simple tasks but is severely limited in its functionality. This system provides a very rich and powerful language in an integrated environment emphasizing ease of use. Some of the language features that go beyond the usual BASIC implementations are

- Program structure:
  long variable names (15 character)
  subprograms with completely isolated contexts
  multiple, labeled COMmon blocks
  IF..THEN..ELSE..ENDIF
  WHILE..END WHILE
  REPEAT..UNTIL
  LOOP..EXIT IF..END LOOP.
- Instrumentation I/O:
  ASSIGN @(name) TO (physical device or file)
  ENTER, OUTPUT USING (image format)
  nine HP-IB (IEEE-488) control statements.
- Graphics:
  WINDOW, SHOW, CLIP, VIEWPORT
  MOVE, DRAW, PLOT, IMOVE, IDRAW, IPLOT
  GRID, AXES, GLOAD, GSTORE, LABEL.

The ease of use environment provides:

- full-screen, syntaxing editor that detects and locates syntax errors as soon as the line is typed
- very fast EDIT..RUN cycle due to an interpreter rather than a compiler-based system
- powerful debugging (e.g., direct interrogation of variables)
- direct keyboard execution of virtually all language statements.

The primary challenge in the design of this system was to provide the fastest possible execution speed while preserving the ease of use and user code size advantages of an interpreter [10]. The performance goal, continued from the hardware goal described earlier, was at least twice that of the 9825A. Because BASIC is a much more complex language than HPL, the attainment of this goal was particularly difficult. HPL can use a fixed-length symbol table but BASIC's longer names require a variable-length one. Subprograms in BASIC are independent contexts, adding the context-switching overhead to the calling time. An additional slowdown came from the choice of implementing most of the BASIC system in Modcal, an internal enhanced version of Pascal with systems programming features, some of which were derived from Modula [11].

Several factors contributed successfully to meeting the performance goals. The large, linear address space allowed assuming the existence of sufficient memory for program execution without requiring any overlay techniques—see the memory map of Fig. 9. As much work as possible is done when the program lines are entered and during a pre-run phase, to insure efficient interpretation of the internal representation of the user's program. Arithmetic speed was enhanced by using binary numeric representations, both two's-complement 16-bit integer and IEEE standard 64-bit floating point. Probably the most important factor was the extensive rewriting of 20 percent of the Modcal code in assembly language after the initial system was working, yielding a fivefold speed improvement.

4) Pascal Workstation: The Pascal Workstation System was introduced for the Series 200 in February of 1982 [10]. Most of the commercially available application programs for this computer family have been developed using this set of tools. It supports a modern, well-structured, and widely accepted programming language with the computing performance of compiled code and minimum operating system size and overhead. The primary drawbacks with respect to some other operating systems are lack of support for other language compilers and lack of multitask or multiuser capability. It was designed to meet the need for a complete

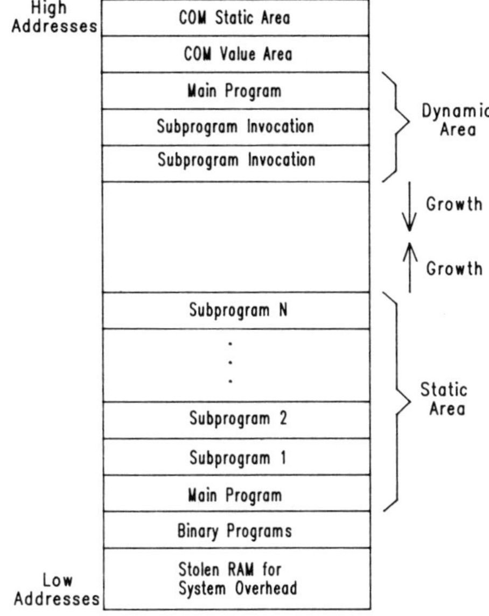

Fig. 9. BASIC system user memory map.

system development toolbox for professional programmers. In fact, the prototype of this system was the internal Modcal Workstation used in developing BASIC. Unlike the HPL and BASIC integrated language systems, the Pascal Workstation is a general-purpose operating system environment with a small memory-resident kernel. It contains a linking loader, file system, and a set of subsystems that are loaded from mass storage when needed. The most important components are

Command Interpreter
Editor
File Manager
Pascal Compiler
Assembler
Debugger
Librarian

The Command Interpreter provides a simple, efficient human interface that is patterned after the portable Pascal development system developed at the University of California, San Diego. This interface provides a menu of single-key commands at the top of the computer's screen such as

Command: Cmplr Edit File Init Libr Run Xcut Ver?

This provides a very effective program development sequence. Typing "E" invokes the Editor. The program source code is then produced. Upon leaving the Editor, the source code is placed in a work file. Typing "R" invokes the Compiler which compiles the source text and creates an object work file. If the compilation was successful, the object code is immediately loaded and executed. If not, the Editor is called with the source reloaded and the edit cursor placed at the point of error.

The Editor is an in-memory, screen-oriented text processor. It has complete search/replace capability, block move, and aids for either document preparation such as automatic margining and word wrap or program entry such as automatic column indenting. The File Manager can create and examine directories, copy, purge, or rename files. It accommodates a wide variety of file formats and directory access methods corresponding to the wide variety of mass storage devices supported by the Series 200.

The Pascal Compiler supports three dialects of Pascal invoked via separate compiler directives: HP Standard Pascal—a superset of the ISO standard, UCSD Pascal (a trademark of the Regents of the University of California), and a set of extensions chosen from the internal Modcal language—allowing separate compilation of modules and giving complete access to hardware features. The compile speed exceeds 4000 lines of source code per minute. This speed of compilation, together with the ability to compile individual modules, is a major enhancer of productivity in code development using this system. Compilation is a one-pass process which translates programs into an internal tree representation from which ready-to-run relocatable object code is generated. The Assembler is a two-pass design, accepting mnemonics in the syntax defined by Motorola [12], and producing object code in the same form as the compiler. Either absolute or relocatable assembly is possible at up to 4000 lines per minute.

The Debugger allows single stepping of the program and interrogation of memory or processor registers. The Librarian provides three library management capabilities: linking, constructing libraries, and disassembling code files. A library in this system is simply a file containing programs or modules of code. The output of the Compiler and Assembler is a library. The Librarian can be used to create complete, stand-alone systems that can be loaded by the boot ROM. The system also includes a standard library of about 150 procedures to perform device I/O and interactive graphics.

5) HP-UX: In December of 1983, the largest and most complete operating system to date for the Series 200 was introduced, the HP-UX. This system is a compatible implementation of the popular System III UNIX Operating System now available from a wide variety of manufacturers. (UNIX is a trademark of AT&T Bell Laboratories, Inc.) HP has made a strong, corporate-wide commitment to the use of HP-UX on many of its new computer products [13]. The primary objective is to eliminate unique software attributes that make transportation of user programs from one computer to another difficult. UNIX is gaining wide acceptance as an industry standard for 16- and 32-bit minicomputers and technical personal computers. Its popularity is partially due to the ease with which it has been implemented on a wide variety of processors and architectures. The main contributions of UNIX (and therefore HP-UX) are

- Multiple user and multiple concurrent task capability.
- Multiple language compilers: C, Fortran, Pascal that generate compatible object code, allowing creation of procedure libraries that can be called from all languages.
- Run-time redirection of I/O, together with the ability to pass data from one concurrent task to another ("filters and pipes").
- A set of tools to support high-productivity software development by teams working on complex projects.
- "On line" documentation—reference manuals stored in the computer's mass storage and instantly accessible.
- Electronic mail and phone line network connections.
- An extremely rich set of system commands and intrinsics.

There are, however, some important disadvantages to the use of UNIX, particularly from the viewpoint of the user of a technical personal computer; these include:

- An expensive hard disk mass storage device is required to contain the large amount of system code and provide "swap" space for processes. Also, more RAM is needed due to the larger operating system kernel.
- The execution performance of instrumentation I/O and real-time data acquisition and control is slower and less predictable.
- The human interface is cryptic and dangerous for the novice user.
- The file system is incompatible with the other Series 200 systems, making it difficult to switch readily between HP-UX and another operating system on the same computer.

The development strategy for HP-UX on the Series 200 has followed the usual course of a UNIX port, beginning with the UNIX Release 3.0 licensed from AT & T and a C language compiler for the 68000 developed at MIT. A major engineering effort has been made to go beyond this base, however. A very large number of quality improvements were made. The HP Standard Pascal compiler was moved to this system. A device-independent graphics library, that has become a corporate standard, was provided. Drivers for many additional peripherals were written. Popular additions from Berkeley UNIX such as the "vi" Screen Editor have been made. In the future, a large amount of engineering work will be done to ameliorate the disadvantages of the initial HP-UX system described above.

IV. FUTURE TRENDS

The personal computer industry is undergoing explosive evolution, and the technical computer portion of that industry is no exception. While it would be inappropriate to disclose here specific product plans of any manufacturer, there are several obvious trends in capability that will occur in the near future.

A. Memory Capacity

Every four years, the IC industry has provided a fourfold increase in the bits per chip for dynamic RAM. The next step to 256K-bit parts will cause the minimum memory size for a 16-bit computer to reach 512K bytes. In the Series 200, a memory card can be designed to hold 1M byte, compared to the current 256K. As the memory capacity increases, however, detection and correction of soft errors is becoming imperative.

B. Floating-Point Computation

Another area that will soon benefit from silicon technology is the addition of VLSI hardware to support faster floating-point arithmetic in personal computer price level products. Chips have recently become available [14] that can provide a tenfold increase in the number of floating-point operations per second relative to software algorithms.

C. Graphics Display

Cathode-ray tube and silicon VLSI technologies are combining rapidly to increase the capability of displays that are appropriate to the technical personal computer price level. Within a few years, resolutions of greater than 1000-by-1000 pixels, 8 bits per pixel, color displays with hardware-enhanced graphics and window-management performance, and arbitrary-font bit-mapped text will be common.

D. Networking

The trend is very strong throughout the industry toward groups of personal technical workstations connected together with a local area network replacing the older multiuser minicomputer systems. This is obvious when one considers the impact that VLSI microprocessors have had on reducing the portion of the computer's cost that is attributable to the central processing unit. Sharing the CPU is no longer a sensible thing to do, although sharing of information among several users' personal computers is very important.

E. Quality and Reliability

Intuition would lead one to suspect that the rapid increase in functional capability and complexity of personal computers at a constant price level would lead to a decrease in reliability with time. Exactly the opposite has been true, however. These increases have come largely through more complex components rather than increased component counts. In addition, some of the increased complexity has been and will continue to be used to provide better reliability and faster repair through self-test hardware and redundancy. Hewlett-Packard has a goal to provide a tenfold increase in the reliability of a given price range set of computers in this decade [15]. The Series 200 is ahead of schedule in meeting this goal.

F. Applications Software

The most rapidly changing and improving aspect of the use of personal technical computers in the next few years will be the applications solutions that are available. The development tools described above have not yet had their full impact on the productivity with which these application programs can be written and transported. The availability of more memory is very significant in allowing more capable programs to be executed. The standardization of operating systems and languages will allow more time and effort to be devoted to developing new and improved applications software instead of rewriting the old packages for a new machine. The technologies that are emerging from artificial intelligence research such as the LISP language and its derivatives, expert systems, and natural language human interfacing can now be implemented on a personal technical computer such as the Series 200.

As an example of the suitability of a personal technical computer for LISP technology, Hewlett-Packard and the Massachusetts Institute of Technology are participating in a joint project to provide a set of personal computer workstations for MIT's introductory computer programming course, 6.001 [16]. This course, which is required of all electrical engineering and computer science undergraduates at MIT, is based on an advanced dialect of LISP called "Scheme." In the past, a large computer with multiple terminals was used.

The hardware set used in this project consists of four groups, each group with 12 Series 200/36 computers. Each group is connected together in a network with a Shared Resource Manager providing a multiuser file system on a shared 66M-byte disk. Each Model 36 computer is equipped with a memory expander and a total of 4M bytes of RAM. The ability to have such large memory per computer is a key factor in establishing the suitability of the hardware for this situation. LISP applications have a tendency to consume a large amount of memory because of a combination of automatic storage management by the system and the large set of services made available to the user. This greatly increases the productivity with which programmers can create and build upon their code.

The software consists of two major pieces, a multiwindow, multiworkspace Editor written in LISP by HP, and the Scheme language system transported from MIT's earlier large computer implementation. The human interface, which is very similar to MIT's EMACS Editor, is used by the students to prepare programs which are sent to the Scheme system for execution. (Both systems are resident in memory in the local computer simultaneously.) The Pascal Workstation operating system provides the underlying file system and driver support.

While not a commercially supported product, the MIT system does represent the future potential of a network of personal technical computers to meet some very sophisticated computing needs. While any given personal computer workstation presents less computing power than a more expensive mainframe, the freedom from sharing the memory and CPU provides much more capability per user. The additional obvious benefit is the increased reliability of the entire system because of the autonomy of each user's hardware and software.

V. Conclusion

This chapter has concentrated on only one of Hewlett-Packard's families of personal computers. It was necessary to do this to limit the size and scope of the topic. By way of conclusion, let us compare and contrast all three of HP's personal computer families, the Series 80, the Series 100, and the Series 200.

Characteristic	Series 80 (86B)	Series 100 (HP 150)	Series 200 (Model 216)
Processor	HP (8-bit)	Intel 8088 (16/8-bit)	Motorola 68000 (32/16-bit)
Memory: Standard/Maximum	128K/640K	256K/640K	128K/768K (w/o expander)
External Interfaces	IEEE-488 Built in Four Ext Slots Eight Cards Avail.	IEEE-488, Dual RS232 Built in Two Ext Slots	IEEE-488, RS232 Built in Two Ext Slots
Operating Systems	(Part of BASIC in ROM) CP/M UCSD P-system	MS-DOS 2.0	(Part of BASIC) Pascal WS
Languages	BASIC (built-in) Assembler UCSD Pascal FORTRAN-77	BASIC	BASIC HP Pascal UCSD Pascal Assembler
Unique Features	Electronic Disc Built-in ROM Language System	Touch Screen Built-in Terminal Optional Built-in Printer	16-bit Processor High Performance I/O
Relative Price and Performance	Lowest	Intermediate	Highest

Fig. 10. HP personal computer family comparisons.

The company has been organized for many years into a collection of geographically separated, semi-autonomous divisions. Each of these personal computer families arose by natural evolution from the product lines of three separate divisions and bears the stamp of the user needs and market concentrations of those divisions. The Series 80 was developed in Corvallis, Oregon, and is the upper end of what began as HP's hand-held calculator line. Its concentration is therefore on personal tools for professionals—business as well as scientific. The Series 100 was developed in Sunnyvale, California, as an outgrowth of HP's computer terminal line. It is the company's "mainstream" personal computer line concentrating on personal office applications and includes built-in terminal capability for connection to host mainframes. The Series 200 was developed in Fort Collins, Colorado, and its ancestry was described in Section I of this chapter. Its concentration is on workstations for engineers and scientists.

The chart of Fig. 10 summarizes some of the salient features and distinctions of the latest and most closely related computers from each family. The strength of HP's strategy in personal computers is the breadth of available models. The corresponding difficulty with it is the lack of leverage of development resources that enables any given product to be provided with the range of capabilities—particularly, applications software solutions that would be desirable. The key strategic challenge for Hewlett-Packard personal computers in the next few years is to increase this leverage while retaining the ability to innovate in meeting the needs of the users.

References

[1] T. E. Osborne, "Hardware design of the model 9100A calculator," *Hewlett-Packard J.*, pp. 10–13, Sept. 1968.

[2] "Technical Assessment of Personal Computers," vols. I, II, Univ. of So. California, Los Angeles, U.S. Dept. of Commerce NTIS, Sept. 1980.

[3] R. M. Spangler, "A new series of programmable calculators," *Hewlett-Packard J.*, pp. 2–4, Dec. 1972.

[4] W. D. Eads and D. S. Maitland, "High-performance NMOS LSI processor," *Hewlett-Packard J.*, pp. 15–18, June 1976.

[5] D. R. Ujvarosy and D. T. Shaffer, "Processor enhancements expand memory," *Hewlett-Packard J.*, pp. 13–15, May 1979.

[6] J. M. Mikkelson *et al.*, "An NMOS VLSI process for fabrication of a 32b CPU chip," in *ISSCC Digest Tech. Papers*, pp. 106–107, 1981.

[7] D. Stewart *et al.*, "Hardware design for an integrated instrumentation computer system," *Hewlett-Packard J.*, pp. 7–17, May 1982.

[8] R. L. James and J. Yockey, "Interactive Model 20 speaks algebraic language," *Hewlett-Packard J.*, pp. 8–13, Dec. 1972.

[9] A. Goris, "BCD arithmetic on the 68000," *Hewlett-Packard J.*, p. 29, May 1982.

[10] K. Y. Kwinn, R. M. Hallissy, and R. E. Ison, "The 9826A/9836A Language Systems," *Hewlett-Packard J.*, pp. 24–32, May 1982.

[11] N. Wirth, "Modula: A programming language for modular multiprogramming," *Software—Practice and Experience*, pp. 3–35, Jan. 1977.

[12] Motorola Inc., *MC68000 16-Bit Microprocessor User's Manual.* Englewood Cliffs, NJ: Prentice-Hall, 1982, Appendix B, pp. 79–182.

[13] F. Clegg, "Hewlett-Packard's entry into the UNIX community," *UNIX Rev.*, pp. 26–30, June/July 1983.

[14] R. D. Grappel, "Floating-point-processing unit improves 16-bit-μP performance," *EDN*, pp. 181–188 Sept. 15, 1983.

[15] J. A. Young, "One company's quest for improved quality," *Wall Street J.*, p. 12, July 25, 1983.

[16] H. Abelson, R. Fano, and G. Sussman, "Course Notes: 6.001 Structure and Interpretation of Computer Programs," Mass. Inst. Technol., Dept. Elec. Eng. and Comput. Sci., Spring Semester 1982.

4

Ease-of-Use Features in the Texas Instruments Professional Computer

J. FRED BUCY, WALLACE W. ANDERSON, MICHAEL L. McMAHAN, RICHARD T. TARRANT, AND HARRY R. TENNANT

Even though computer technology has evolved at such a spectacular pace, the reluctance towards using computers has still not entirely disappeared. The newer generation of computers has been specifically tailored towards supporting ease-of-use features. The Texas Instruments Professional Computer offers two innovative features: a natural-language query system for accessing databases and a peripheral speech processor for verbal input/output. The two features make it much easier for new users to interact with personal computers. The TI Professional Computer which implements both speech processing and NaturalLink capabilities is described.

The Editors

I. INTRODUCTION

In January 1983, Texas Instruments introduced the first member in its family of personal microcomputers, the TI Professional Computer (TIPC), designed primarily to serve the productivity needs of professionals and small businesses. Design of the TIPC was based on extensive research into the needs of professionals and their difficulties with existing systems. This research convinced us that

1) The TIPC must support industry-standard software and hardware.
2) The TIPC must achieve a step-function increase in ease of use.

The TIPC supports the most popular operating systems, including MS-DOS, and many of the most popular applications software packages including Lotus 1-2-3 and WordStar. Programming languages available include BASIC, Cobol, Pascal, and Fortran.

Ease of use is one of the major challenges confronting the microcomputer industry today [1]. The rate of growth of computer skills by nonexpert users will be largely governed by ease-of-use improvements. The focus of this chapter is on significant ease-of-use features in the TIPC, particularly two advanced input/output interface options, NaturalLink and the Speech Command system.

II. TIPC DESIGN

The TIPC (see Fig. 1) is a second-generation desktop modular computer, consisting of a low-profile keyboard, high-resolution CRT display, and an easily expandable systems unit. The physical design of the TIPC reflects attention to ergonomics, the science of making machines operable with greater user proficiency and satisfaction and less fatigue. Both the keyboard and CRT display provide substantial improvement ergonomically over most second-generation desktop computers.

The authors are with Texas Instruments Inc., Dallas, TX 75265, USA.

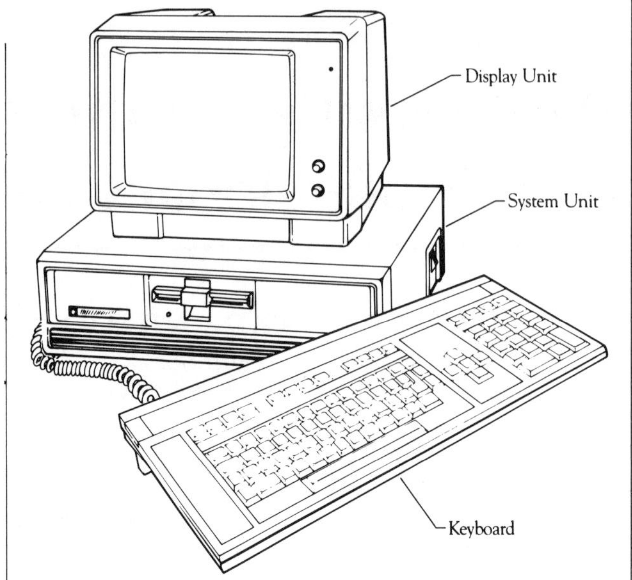

Fig. 1. Texas Instruments Professional Computer.

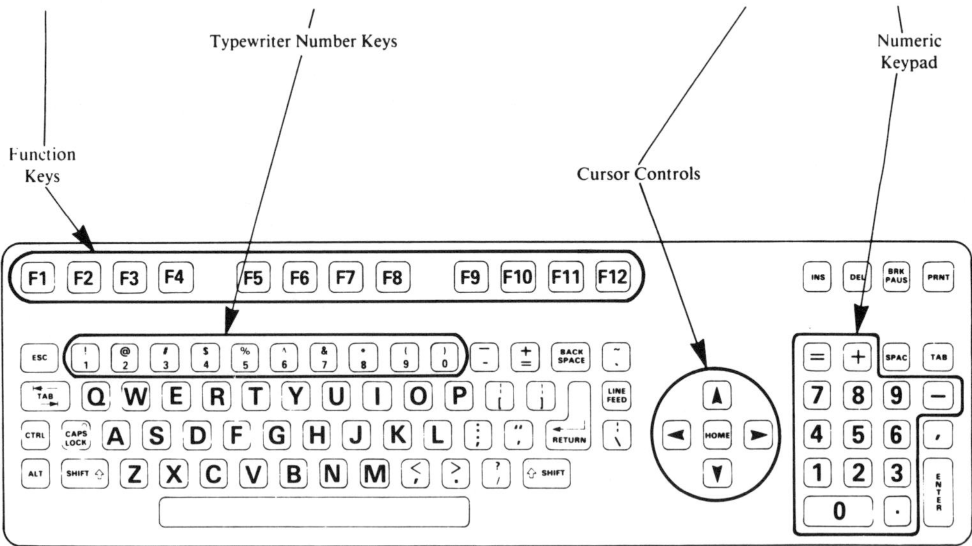

Fig. 2. TIPC keyboard.

The design of the keyboard (Fig. 2) is based on an examination of user performance and preferences [2]. The slope of the low-profile keyboard is continuously adjustable between 5° and 15°, even on the user's lap. Silent operation on the Hall-effect keyswitches has been supplemented with tactile feedback provided by a small silicone dome beneath each keycap. The 97 autorepeating keys are separated into several logical groups: alphanumeric area, cross pattern cursor-control pad, numeric keypad with math functions, programmable and dedicated function keys. The dedicated function keys (Insert, Delete, Break/Pause, and Print) are located in the upper right corner where they are unlikely to be pressed accidentally. The American version of the keyboard follows the standard QWERTY arrangement for the alphanumeric keys, with oversize shift keys and L-shaped return key located exactly as in the IBM Selectric typewriter. The Caps Lock keycap contains a red light-emitting diode (LED) to indicate status.

High-resolution display capability, which reduces eye strain and user errors, is provided for both the standard 12-in monochrome and optional 13-in color CRT displays. Because both the monochrome and color displays use the same format (25 lines of 80 columns; 720 by 300 pixels with the graphics controller option), application programs can operate on either display without modification. The color display has been compared favorably with CAD displays by computer industry magazines [3].

III. SYSTEM ARCHITECTURE

The TIPC system unit contains a 16-bit 8088 microprocessor, 64K bytes of dynamic RAM, support logic, a single 320K floppy disk drive with controller (a second internal floppy or 10M-byte Winchester is optional), a parallel printer port, and a power supply. Memory can be expanded up to 768K bytes. In addition to the memory expansion slot, there are five option slots that can be used for interconnecting a second 10M-byte Winchester, two external drives, and other peripherals. Available option cards include the Winchester controller, a synchronous/asynchronous communications board, internal modem boards (300-Bd Bell-type 103 or 300/1200-Bd Bell-type 212A), graphics memory option (piggybacked to the CRT controller to occupy only one slot), Ethernet LAN, and the Speech Command board.

As illustrated in the TIPC system block diagram (Fig. 3), the 5-MHz 8088 can be augmented with the optional 8087 numeric coprocessor for enhanced arithmetic calculations. The memory and system data buses are separated to improve drive and timing margins. This also allows memory expansion without use of option slots. The CPU bus controller converts CPU status information into memory and I/O control signals which, along with the address and data buffer/latches, allow the CPU to operate in its "maximum" mode.

The interrupt controller provides eight vectored interrupts for use by the system in addition to the dedicated nonmaskable interrupt (used for system parity error and CRT control). The triple timer IC provides two system interval timers plus a programmable speaker oscillator. The oscillator output is transmitted to the speaker amplifier where a second signal can be mixed. This second signal is usually a speech signal. The combination of amplifier and speaker provides a high-quality audio voice signal when used with the Speech Command option board. Of the 1M-byte system memory space, the upper 256K bytes are reserved for the CRT graphics memory (three 32K-byte banks), system/option ROM (48K bytes), and peripherals. It is in this latter space that the Speech Command subsystem resides with 32K bytes of 8088/TMS320 dual-ported RAM.

The Speech Command option board contains the TMS320 signal processor along with 8K bytes of program RAM and 32K bytes of data RAM (accessed through the TMS320 I/O ports). Since the 32K-byte RAM is dual-ported to the 8088 memory space, rapid data transfer occurs between the two processors. Also, the TMS320 program RAM can be uploaded with appropriate algorithms from the 8088 mass storage devices via the common 32K RAM. A boot ROM on the Speech Command board allows the TMS320 to upload its program RAM, then the ROM switches itself out of the program space, and TMS320 execution commences at a designated RAM location. This TMS320 program flexibility allows the Speech Command board to be used for a variety of speech applications and lends itself to general coprocessor applications. Location of the 32K-byte RAM in 8088 memory space is DIP-switch selectable to allow for multiple Speech Command boards, if desired. External I/O channels on the Speech Command board provide for microphone/speaker, headset, and telephone dial-up voice interfacing. A Codec provides A-to-D and D-to-A conversion of the voice signal at an 8-kHz sample rate (64K bits/s). Telephone pulse or tone dialing and touchtone decoding is available on the board to aid application programs.

The TIPC's system architecture supports the use of the 32-bit TMS320 processor for speech recognition and other applications. Two significant ease-of-use innovations available for the TIPC are described in detail in the following sections.

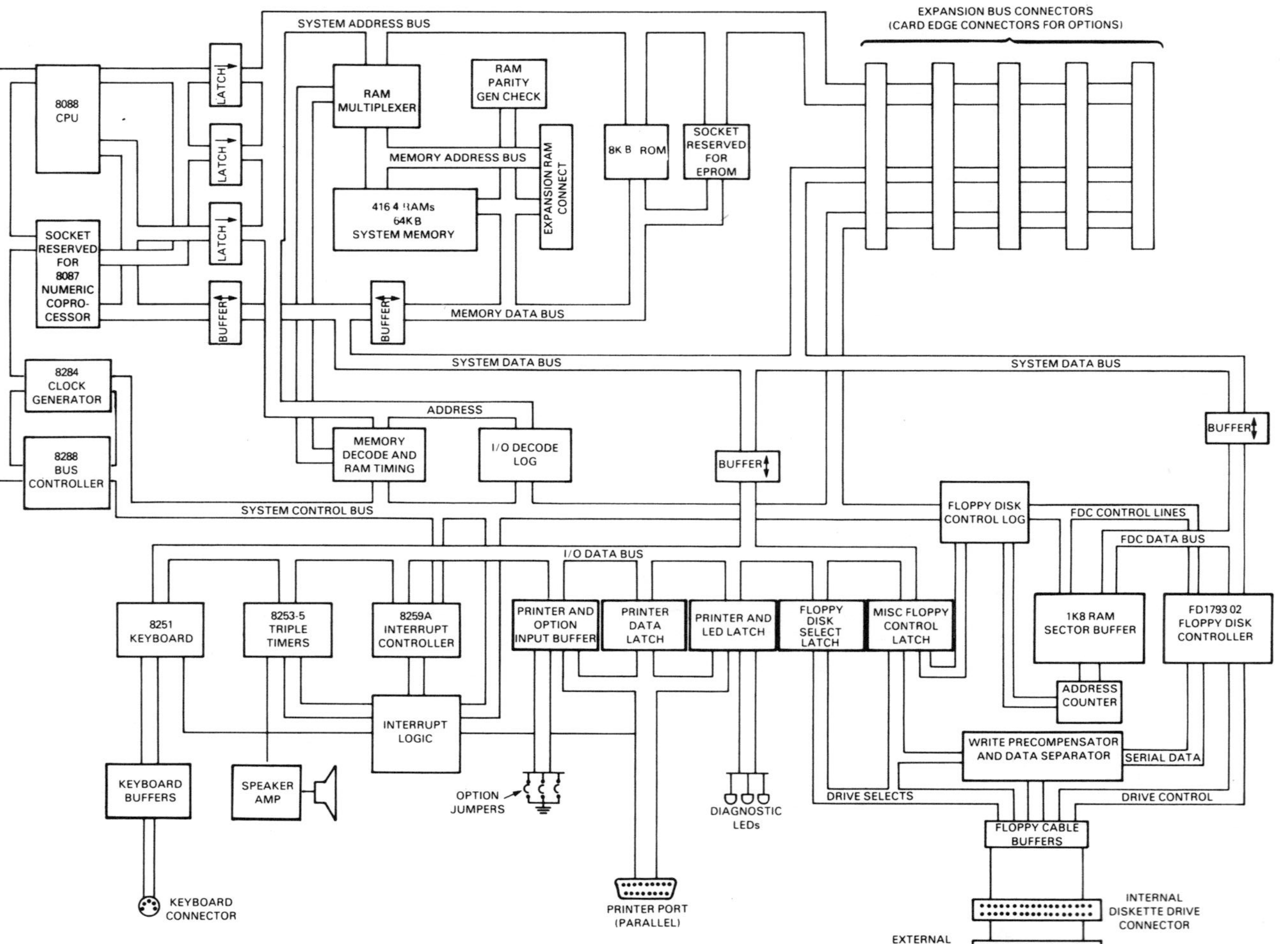

Fig. 3. TIPC system unit board.

IV. NaturalLink

NaturalLink is a software package that facilitates access to databases such as Dow Jones News/Retrieval by allowing users to ask questions about the data in English (or other natural languages such as French, Japanese, etc.). NaturalLink translates the question into a database query-language query, which is sent to the database system. The database system then retrieves the desired data, which are sent back to NaturalLink for display.

Natural language interfaces such as NaturalLink are an outgrowth of artificial intelligence research [4]. However, conventional natural language systems suffer from several problems: they require a user to type and to formulate questions in a way that the system can understand; they cause high failure rates among users; and users often do not use features of the system because they are unaware of them or do not trust them.

NaturalLink solves these problems through a new approach to natural language understanding: grammar-driven menu-based natural language understanding [5]–[7]. NaturalLink provides the user with windows from which words or phrases are selected to form complete sentences for database queries. The contents (or "menu") of each successive window are based upon the selection made in the preceding window. As the user chooses items from the menu, they are inserted into a window on the lower half of the screen so that the user can see the sentence being constructed. Individual function keys allow the user to backtrack a phrase at a time, or to erase the entire question and start over. Phrases can be selected through cursor control keys, a mouse, or other pointing device, or even through the Speech Command interface. The menus are scrollable, in case they happen to contain more elements than can be displayed in the available screen space. They can also be dynamically searched. When a substring of a phrase is typed, the cursor jumps to the first element in the menu that matches. For general operation, however, the user need not know how to type or how to spell. Also, the contents of the database—the range of potential questions he may ask—are revealed to the user by the menu contents.

Because items are selected by cursor, typing effort is greatly reduced. Because each query can be constructed only in a specific manner, invalid queries are eliminated. User failure rate drops to zero. And because the extent of its coverage is apparent, the system encourages experimentation and use of the full range of its capabilities.

A. NaturalLink in Action

Fig. 4 shows a NaturalLink interface to a jobshop database including tables of data on jobcards, operations, orders, pieces, and workers. The user builds a question in the empty window near the bottom of the display from words and phrases selected from the active menus above. As selections are made, the selected phrase appears in the query window, different menus will become active, and the contents of the active menus change to reflect the current context of the question. In Fig. 4 the user has moved the cursor to select "Find all."

Fig. 5 shows that "Find all" has been copied to the query window and the NOUNS menu has become active. The user points to "workers" with the cursor and selects it. Fig. 6 shows that the question now reads "Find all workers," the QUALIFIERS menu has become active and the user is pointing to the phrase "whose wage rate is." The user continues in this way (Figs. 7–9), selecting phrases from active menus until the query is complete.

Fig. 9 shows a complete question, "Find all workers whose wage rate is > 7.55." NaturalLink's database query translation of the question can then be sent to the database. Appearance of the EXECUTABLE option on the bottom line of the display indicates that this question is understood as a complete sentence, and so can be translated into a database query and sent to the database. The option to execute will appear only for complete sentences. Notice that the CONNECTORS menu is active in Fig. 9. The user has constructed a complete sentence, but has the option to further qualify it as necessary. In fact, questions can be made arbitrarily complex, restricted only by the flexibility of the database query language to which the questions are translated. Examples of other questions are shown below.

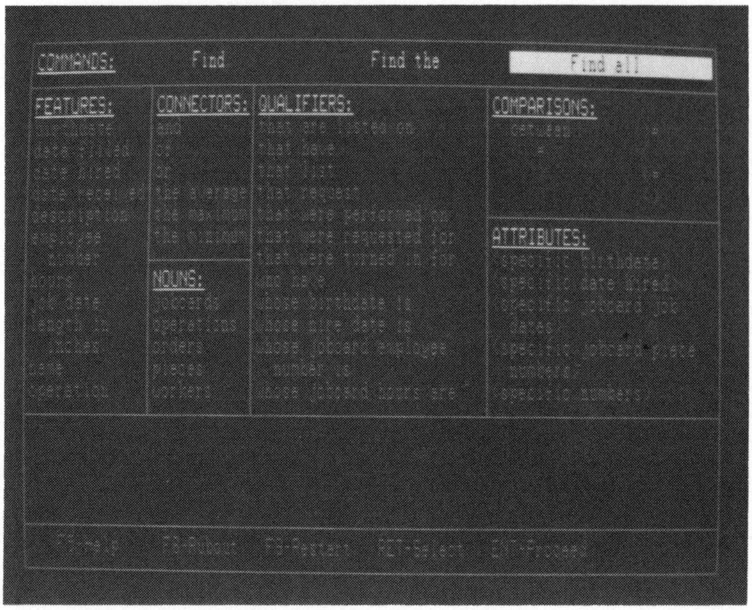

Fig. 4. Building a database query with NaturalLink.

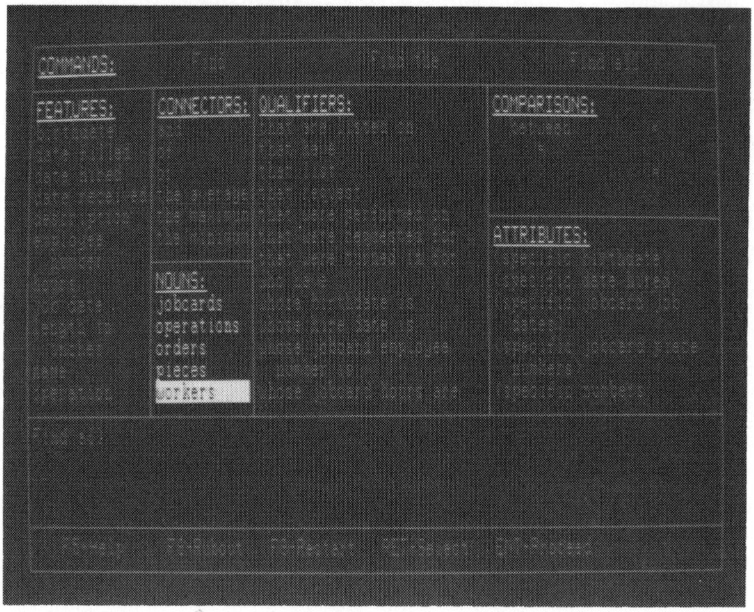

Fig. 5. Building a database query with NaturalLink.

From the jobcard interface:

Find all workers whose wage rate is > 7.55 and who have jobcards whose jobcard pieces done is between the average pieces done of jobcards and 89.

Find the name and wage rate of workers who have jobcards whose jobcard pieces done is > the average pieces done of jobcards.

Find the total quantity of orders that request pieces whose piece name is bushing.

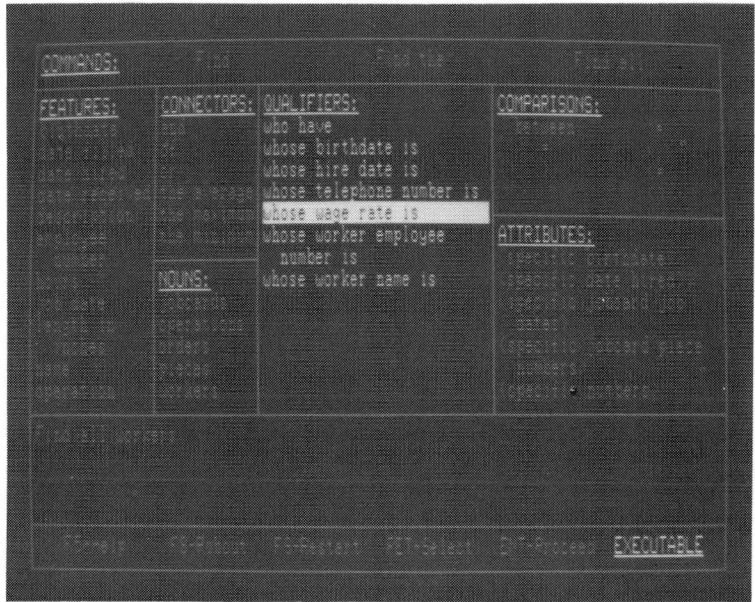

Fig. 6. Building a database query with NaturalLink.

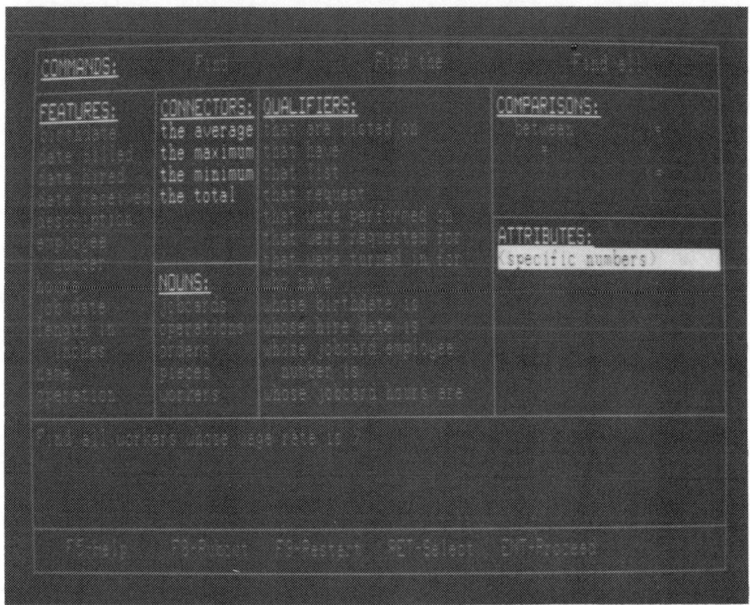

Fig. 7. Building a database query with NaturalLink.

From the Dow Jones interface:

What is the current quote for Sears Roebuck on the New York exchange?

What were the stock prices for Sears Roebuck for the last 12 days?

We find that menu-based natural language interfaces such as NaturalLink are readily accepted and quite usable, even by persons with no computer experience at all. Uninitiated users can

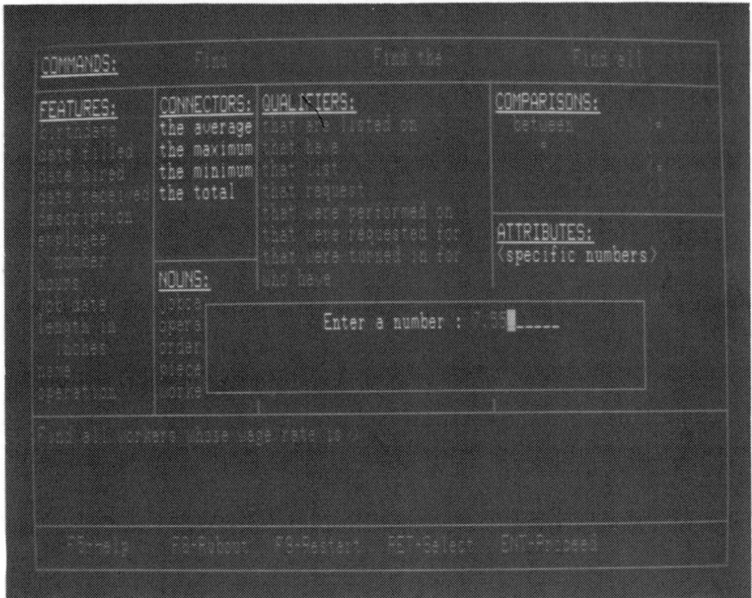

Fig. 8. Building a database query with NaturalLink.

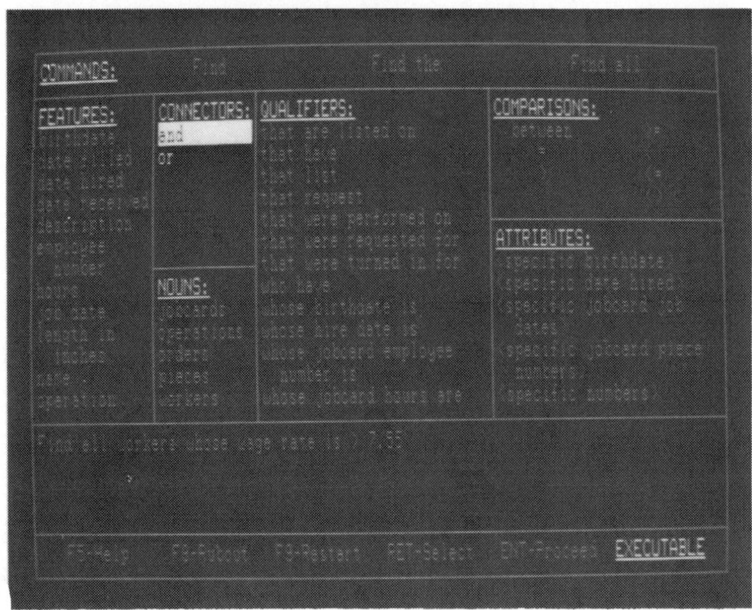

Fig. 9. Building a database query with NaturalLink.

perform complex database queries like those above with NaturalLink after an introduction of only a few minutes to learn how to position the cursor. In the case of Dow Jones News/Retrieval, users can access 22 databases, including current news, current stock market reports, company reports, and financial data on more than 3100 companies. In tests of the ease of NaturalLink in this application, novice users began using it successfully within 30 min, without a manual. NaturalLink also allows for cost-saving efficiency through preparation of inquiries off-line, before transmitting them in a batch.

B. Mixed-Mode Interaction

NaturalLink allows the use of modes other than cursor selection in setting certain query parameters, such as ATTRIBUTES. The ATTRIBUTES menu defines specific database values: weights, dates, colors, locations, and so on. When one of these items is selected, such as "specific numbers" (Fig. 7), a pop-up window appears (Fig. 8). Specific database values are entered through these specialized windows, which may include range checking, triggers, and other features.

ATTRIBUTES windows have been generated in a variety of forms. The form shown in Fig. 8 is the simplest: a type-in window. ATTRIBUTES windows also have been implemented as menus, calculator keypads, and even a map. The map window was implemented for a system where the user is interested in finding airports in specific areas of the country. When the user wants to indicate the desired area of the country, a map of the United States pops up and the user draws a box on the map with the cursor. The map then disappears and the latitude and longitude coordinates of the box are inserted textually into the query. The user can, of course, further qualify the question.

After asking a question, one frequently wishes to follow up with a similar question. NaturalLink supports this feature by allowing limited editing on the question. The user can select specific database elements mentioned in the question and change them. When an element is changed, the same ATTRIBUTES window previously presented to the user for this value is presented again. The user specifies a new value, the window then disappears, and the new value is inserted into the question.

C. NaturalLink Versus Conventional Natural Language Systems

The menu-based approach represents a radical departure from the way natural language interfaces have been viewed. Conventional natural language interfaces [8]–[36] are oriented around the user typing a question into the computer system, which then attempts to understand what the question means in terms of a database query. Frequently, the user enters words and constructions that a conventional natural language system is unable to translate. Users may also ask for information that is beyond the scope of the database and is therefore untranslatable. (In fact, these two problems generally cannot be distinguished by conventional natural language systems.) Attempts to build conventional natural language systems have yielded disappointing results [37].

In contrast, menu-based natural language interfaces successfully translate all of the queries that users generate. This is because the user can select a phrase only if it makes sense given the current context of the question. NaturalLink does this by activating only appropriate menus for each choice and restricting the elements in the active menus to only the sensible ones. For example, in Fig. 5, the user selects "workers" to make the fragment "Find all workers," to be followed by a QUALIFIER. Notice that the inactive QUALIFIERS menu in Fig. 5 includes some qualifiers that do not make sense in the context of "Find all workers" (for example, "that were performed on," a qualifier which modifies operations). But when the QUALIFIERS menu becomes active (Fig. 6), only those qualifiers that make sense in the context of "Find all workers" are presented as choices. A phrase such as "that were performed on," which cannot be translated into a meaningful query, is not available for selection. In this way, NaturalLink allows the user to express anything it can translate, but prevents questions it cannot translate. The user has the same expressive power through menu-based natural language interfaces as through conventional natural language interfaces, but without the frustration of not being understood.

D. NaturalLink Versus Query-By-Example

Grammar-driven menu-based natural language interfaces can be compared with other forms of database interface. Query-by-example (QBE) [38]–[43] is another novel screen-oriented interface technique. In this case, the user indicates how the resultant table should look, and the system then queries the database to fill the table template with data. The user can indicate, through a language of conventions, what columns of the table should be constants, what conditions must hold on the members of columns, and what columns should be joined over for queries involving more than one table.

In some ways, QBE and menu-based natural language understanding are similar. Both are display-based interfaces, both have been applied to database access, both can be readily interfaced to new databases. In other respects, the two are different. In a menu-based natural language environment, the user constructs questions in a natural language, whereas in QBE the user must learn the two-dimensional interaction language before using the system. (It is interesting to note that when QBE is described, example questions are first shown in English versions, then the QBE queries for expressing the questions are illustrated. Our approach does not require the translation—the user deals directly with the English form.) Also, QBE requires the user to deal with the structure of the database fairly directly. When constructing a join, for example, the user must know that the tables are constructed in such a way that a join would be required. In NaturalLink, joins are performed implicitly without the user having to be aware of the structure of the database. For example, the question "Find the total quantity of orders that request pieces whose piece name is bushing" involves a join of the orders and pieces tables over pieces. NaturalLink users construct such questions without any notion of the structure of the database, much less what a join is.

In assessing the usefulness of NaturalLink, two questions arise. First, can users successfully master an interface in which there is only one correct way to state their query? In our studies we find that they can, in spite of occasionally stilted phrasing. Users do not really care how many possible ways a question can be asked; they just want the answer. Secondly, is menu size a problem? Menus must not become too big or the user will be swamped with choices and will be unable to find the right one. For most interfaces we have generated, menu size has not been a problem, since choices earlier in a sentence tend to restrict later choices to a manageable few. NaturalLink menus are scrollable, of course. But eventually, menu size does limit the sort of interfaces for which NaturalLink can be used.

In sum, the significance of NaturalLink is that its enhanced ease-of-use facility allows database access by a much broader class of users, without any prior training in database languages or techniques, for an expanding range of applications.

V.   Speech Command System

The Speech Command system is a TIPC peripheral option that enhances both ease-of-use and user communications capabilities through voice I/O. This system allows users to enter data verbally (see Fig. 10) and to give spoken, rather than keystroke, commands to the TIPC. (This process is called *voice recognition*.) One spoken word can replace up to 40 manual keystrokes, so users no longer have to remember complex sequences of key commands. This feature is especially convenient in "hands-free" work situations and for handicapped users. Speech Command also can digitally record, store, and replay speech (processes called *speech analysis* and *synthesis*). This capability allows the TIPC to serve as a dictation machine and as a versatile telephone management device. Other features include setting up a daily calendar and providing "tickler" prompting of appointments.

Speech Command is a turnkey package consisting of both hardware and applications software. Hardware consists of a speech processor board—actually two boards, arranged piggyback so that they occupy only one option slot in the TIPC. The speech processor board is controlled by a TMS320 microcomputer [44], which executes all speech-related functions. The 8088 host CPU handles only the high-level interface with the user.

The TMS320 microcomputer is one of the fastest devices available for dedicated, real-time digital signal processing, capable of executing commands at rates up to 5 million instructions

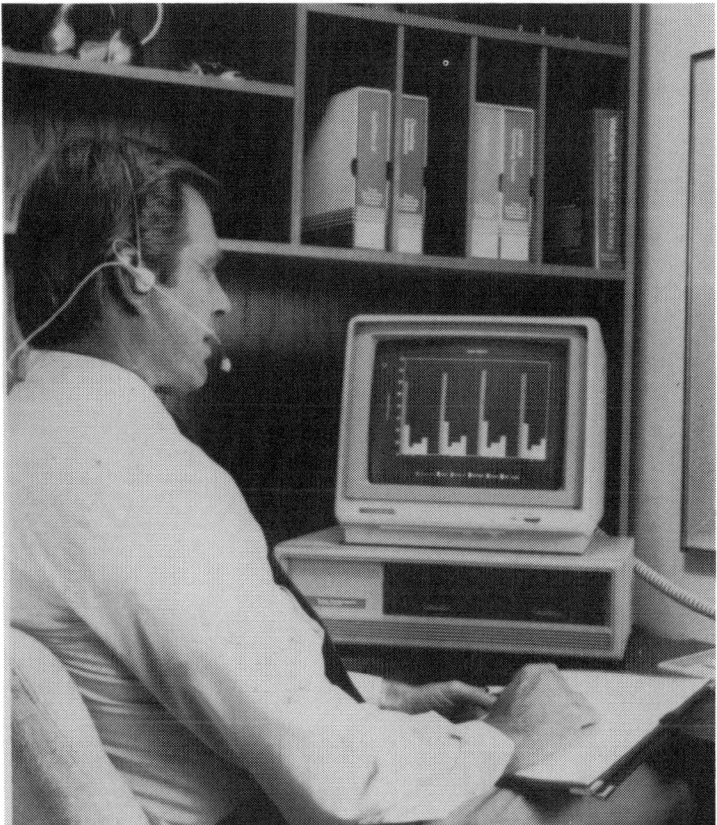

Fig. 10. Verbal input with Speech Command.

per second. However, its capabilities extend well beyond speech processing to include applications such as optical character recognition, spectrum analysis, and high-speed modem functions.

Development of a single-chip, monolithic signal processor such as the TMS320 was crucial to wide commercial introduction of a speech I/O system such as Speech Command for use on a personal computer. Historically, signal processing tasks have demanded mainframes and large minicomputers with powerful array processors for computation. Signal processing algorithms have huge computational requirements, especially the "multiply-accumulate" operations for filtering (a minimum of 200 000 multiply-accumulates per second for speech). These requirements were beyond the range of most personal computers.

The TMS320 provides the required computational power. Equally important, its programmability makes it multifunctional. Until recently, semiconductor technology allowed the solution of only isolated speech problems. Custom integrated circuits could be developed for these isolated problems, but commercial demand for most single-solution chips was too limited for cost-effective production. Recognizing that the future of commercial speech applications lies not in single-function solutions, but rather in flexible combinations of speech analysis, synthesis, recognition, and other operations, we opted for a programmable speech module, not a hard-wired system.

Since it is the TMS320 that gives the Speech Command board its essential computational power, multifunctionality, and cost-effectiveness, it is appropriate first to describe its unique architecture.

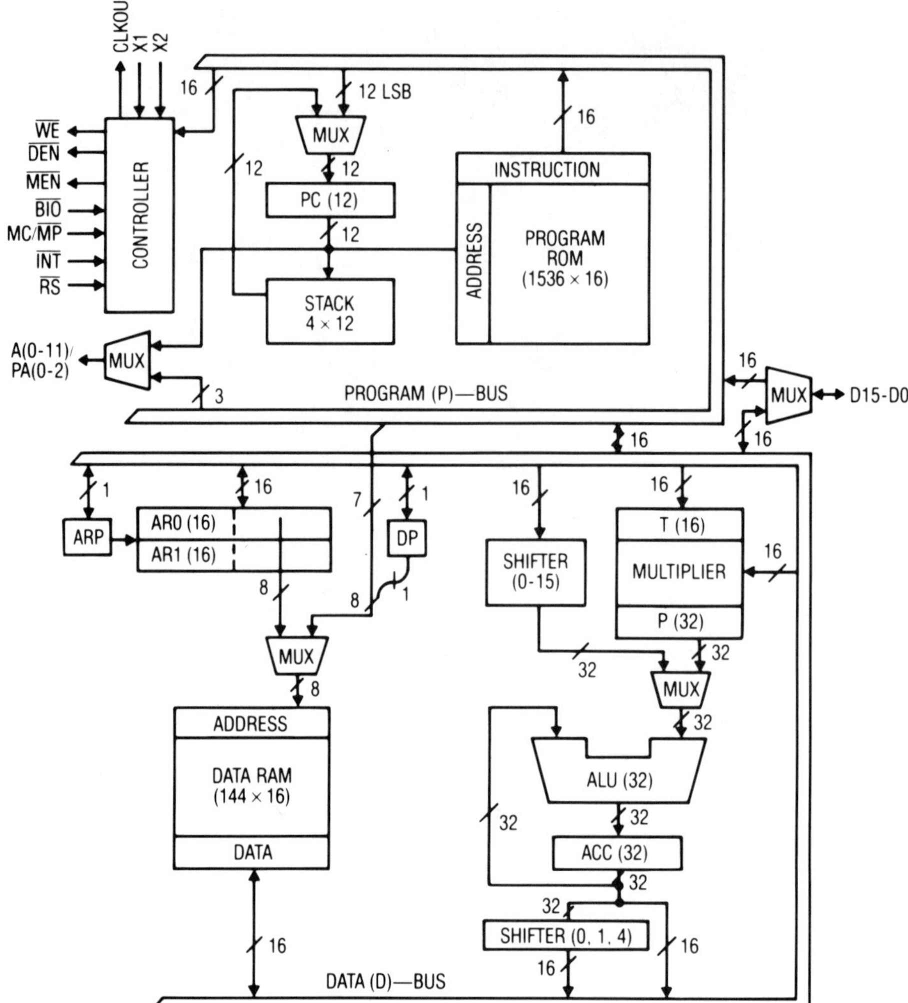

Fig. 11. TMS320.

A. TMS320 Architecture

TMS320 design is based on a modified Harvard architecture (Fig. 11) incorporating separate program and data memory spaces. This configuration permits fetching information from both program and data memory in parallel, overlapping the execution and data memory access of one instruction with the fetch cycle of the next instruction. By using the two separate program and data memory buses and pipelining the instructions, an instruction cycle time of 200 ns is achieved. The traditional Harvard architecture is modified by a special feature that allows crossovers between program and data memories, permitting data values to modify program branches, and permitting data access to constants stored in program memory.

The architecture provides a mixture of 16- and 32-bit data paths. All inputs and outputs use 16-bit words, and both the program and memory data buses are 16 bits wide. The multiplier provides a 16- by 16-bit multiply with a 32-bit result. The bus from the multiplier to the 32-bit accumulator is 32 bits wide, and instructions are provided for move, add, or subtract operations of the product with the accumulator. Additional instructions allow pipelining of the next multiplier load with accumulation, so that a series of multiply-accumulate operations can be executed at a 400-ns rate. In addition, there is a 32-bit barrel shifter available to adjust the resolution of the 32-bit arithmetic. The 16-bit data memory values may be left-shifted by up to 15 bits before operations with the accumulator, and the most significant word of the accumulator may be left-shifted by 0, 1, or 4 bits as it is stored.

The program memory for the TMS320 may reside in either or both of two locations: 1536 words of internal mask programmed ROM, or up to 4096 words of external memory. The capability to use external program memory (not available on other signal processing chips) makes possible the flexibility of Speech Command. The external memory used is RAM, which may be downloaded from the TIPC. Thus one software module provides recognition and synthesis capabilities for recognition applications with prompting by prerecorded messages, and another module provides similar capabilities for dictation and telephone management applications. Additional speech functions may be developed and used with the same hardware, and software improvements may be made by distributing new TIPC diskettes.

The data memory on the TMS320 consists of 144 words of 16 bits each. For Speech Command, this was augmented with external data RAM of 16K words. The external RAM is accessed through I/O instructions, using an address pointer that may be used with either autoincrementing or autodecrementing as well as the regular nonchanging mode. Access to this memory requires a 400-ns instruction cycle. It is used mainly to store the speech recognition templates downloaded from the TIPC, as well as to buffer input and output digital speech samples.

Table 1 summarizes the architectural features of the TMS320 in comparison with similar digital signal processing devices on the market today. Table 2 contrasts performance benchmarks of the TMS320 with those of NEC's μPD7720 chip.

Table 1 Digital Signal Processor Architectural Features

Feature	TI TMS320	NEC μPD7720	AMI S2811	Intel 2920
Data word size (bits)	16	16	16	25
Coefficient size (bits)	16	13	16	(1)
Accumulator width (bits)	32	16	16	28
Saturation arithmetic	hardware	software	hardware	hardware
Boolean logic operations	yes	yes	no	yes
Multiplier implementation	hardware	hardware	hardware	software
Multiplier precision (in × in = out)	16 × 16 = 32	16 × 16 = 32	12 × 12 = 16	12 × 25 = 28
Multiplication time (ns) (worst case)	200	250	300	4800
Parallel I/O (bits)	16	8	8	4 in/8 out
Instruction word (bits)	16	23	17	24
Instruction cycle (ns)	200	250	300	400
Subroutine levels	> 50	4	1	none
Interaction (loop) counter	yes	no	yes	no
Conditional jumps	yes	yes	yes	no
Full-speed external memory expansion	yes	no	no	no
Instruction ROM (bits)	1536 × 16	512 × 23	256 × 17	192 × 24
Coefficient ROM (bits)		512 × 13	120 × 16	n/a
Data RAM (bits)	144 × 16	128 × 16	128 × 16	40 × 25
Z-1 function	yes	yes	yes	no
Look-up tables	yes	yes	yes	no

B. Speech Analysis and Synthesis

The purpose of speech analysis is to compress speech into a compact digital form which can be stored or transmitted, yet retains the information necessary to be expanded back into its

Table 2 Digital Signal Processor Performance Benchmarks

	TI TMS320	μPD* 7720	UNITS
Biquad filter element	2.0	2.25	uS
Sine or cosine	4.8	5.25	uS
u/A law to linear conversion	0.8	0.5	uS
32-point complex FFT	0.254	0.7	mS
64-point complex FFT	0.580	1.6	mS
Normalized Total	1.0	2.7	

*Source: NEC Electronics Digital Signal Processor Data Sheet, 1982 Microcomputer Division Catalog.

original form with only a minimal loss of quality. With Speech Command, this capability can be used for telephone answering, voice messaging (especially once Local Area Networks become common), voice annotation of text messages, and prerecorded prompting of informational messages. For telephone answering, local speech analysis provides the advantages of random access to messages, selective deletion of messages, and archival of important messages through copying to a backup diskette.

Note that Speech Command synthesizes or "replays" speech from stored data derived from voice input. This method should not be confused with synthesis by rule, sometimes called "constructive synthesis," which constructs sounds from text, using linguistic rules, rather than from stored voice data. In that method, variations (allophones) of standardized segments of sound (phonemes) provide the basis for all outputs, implicitly requiring that all known speech parts be stored in the computer memory, together with the rules for constructing speech. Though unlimited as to the number of words that can be synthesized, synthesis by rule produces a distinctly unnatural voice quality.

The method of speech analysis used in Speech Command is linear predictive coding (LPC) [45]. Using this method, speech is represented as an excitation sequence filtered by the vocal tract, as shown in Fig. 12 [46]. The excitation is either a pseudorandom excitation, representing the turbulent air flow through a constriction for unvoiced sounds such as "s," or a periodic pulse train, representing the vibrations of the vocal cords for voiced sounds such as "a." The vocal tract response to this excitation is represented by ten LPC coefficients. The total speech signal is represented by the ten LPC coefficients, a pitch value to specify either an unvoiced condition or the voiced pitch period, and an energy value that represents the amplitude or loudness of the speech.

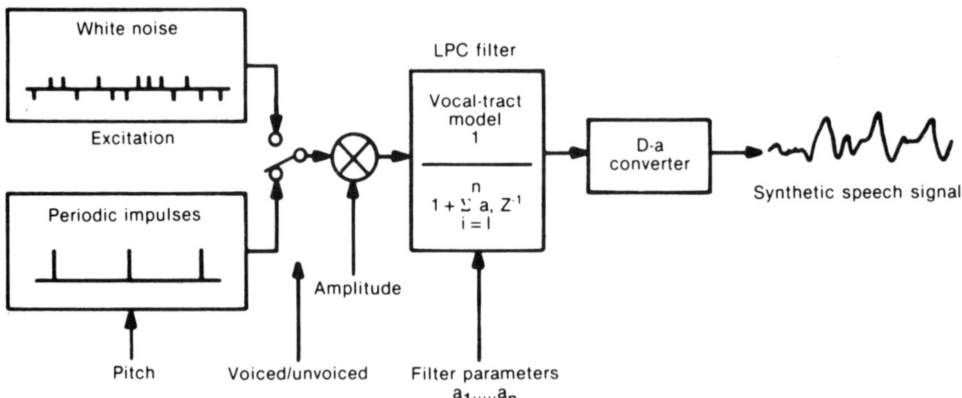

Fig. 12. LPC vocal tract model.

With Speech Command, incoming speech from either a microphone or an attached telephone may be analyzed and stored for later playback. There are two subprocesses involved in the analysis of speech, as shown in Fig. 13. In the spectral analysis subprocess, incoming samples are preemphasized to boost the high-frequency portion of the speech by flattening the spectrum. They are then multiplied by a 30-ms Hamming window, and an autocorrelation analysis is done. The autocorrelation computes 11 coefficients, according to the formula

$$R(i) = \sum_{n=0}^{N-1-i} x(n)x(n+i).$$

The LeRoux, Geugen algorithm [47] iteratively calculates the ten LPC reflection coefficients from the 11 autocorrelation coefficients.

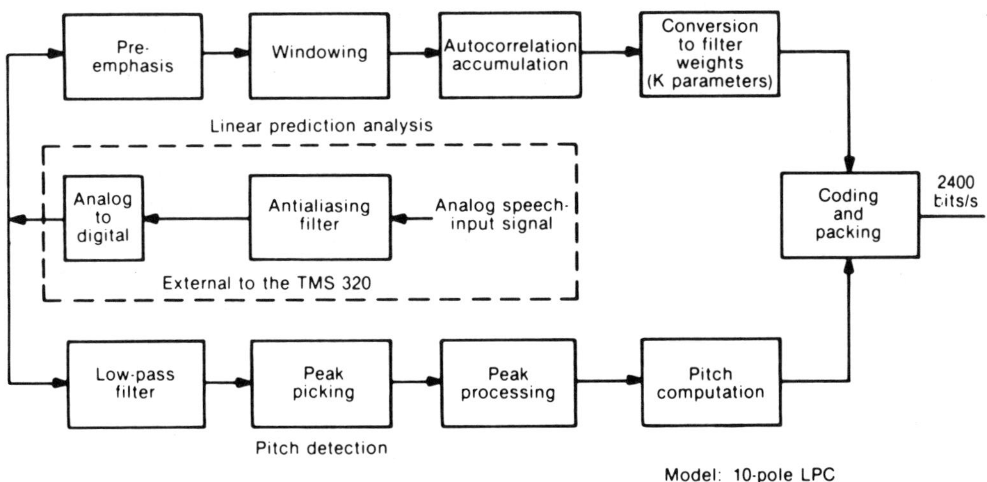

Fig. 13. LPC analysis algorithm flow.

In the other subprocess, the Gold–Rabiner [48] pitch tracker is used to make the voicing decision and to determine the pitch period for voiced speech. The input samples are first low-pass filtered to reduce the higher harmonics of the pitch frequency. Then the samples are examined by six different pitch trackers looking for different combinations of peaks and valleys. Finally, the six pitch trackers vote to determine a single pitch period. If no candidate wins, the frame is declared unvoiced.

The 12 parameters are coded to a total of 48 bits for each frame, representing 20 ms of speech. Thus the total bit rate is the product of 50 frames per second times the 48 bits per frame, giving 2400 bits/s of speech data. Using this method, Speech Command can analyze and record more than 16 min of speech on a 320K-byte floppy diskette. Data storage requirements are also reduced by silence suppression, which compresses pauses and dead spaces. In order to synthesize speech from the 2400-bits/s data stream, the 12 parameters are decoded from the 48 bits/frame. The excitation signal is generated using the pitch and energy information. Finally, the ten LPC coefficients are used to model the vocal tract filter response to the excitation. The speech that is synthesized is slightly degraded from the original, but it is understandable and vocal characteristics of the original speaker are recognizable.

Other methods of speech analysis and synthesis are available that give somewhat better quality than the 2400-bits/s pitch-excited LPC used by Speech Command, but they do so at the penalty of much higher bit rates (up to 32K bits/s). For local speech analysis and synthesis on a microcomputer, the current analysis method provides the best compromise between speech quality and storage requirements.

C. Speech Recognition

Speech recognition systems vary greatly in utility and memory requirements, according to whether they recognize isolated or connected words, and whether they recognize words by a single speaker ("speaker-dependent") or by all speakers ("speaker-independent"). At present, speaker-independent systems are characterized by limited accuracy, vocabularies, and functions, and large computer resource requirements. Speaker-dependent systems, such as Speech Command, are more accurate and versatile, with larger vocabularies and reduced computational requirements.

Speech Command is capable of recognizing vocabularies of up to 50 words each. Additional vocabularies may be stored on disk or may be resident in the system memory. A real-time switching mechanism can provide quick access to these additional vocabularies. In addition, Speech Command is capable of connected-word recognition, as opposed to isolated-word systems that require users to pause between words. This allows a more natural style of input.

Four basic steps are involved in the recognition of speech: feature extraction, pattern similarity measurement, time registration, and decision strategy. An additional task that is required prior to speaker-dependent recognition is referred to as enrollment. This is the process by which speaker-dependent reference patterns are formed to be used during the recognition process. Current speech recognition systems use a variety of techniques to perform these basic steps. Each approach has its own performance and cost mix. The system used in Speech Command is unique in that it provides robust performance in a connected word environment with a relatively low-cost implementation.

The basic speech recognition strategy is to "scan" the incoming speech data continuously, perform dynamic programming, compute a similarity measure or "distance" between the utterance spoken and the stored reference patterns, and decide if the similarity measure is sufficiently small to declare that the utterance is recognized. The flow diagram for this system (see Fig. 14) shows the major algorithm steps: autocorrelation, matched residual energy distance computation, dynamic programming time alignment, event detection, and high-level postprocessing. Parameters for measuring the similarity between input utterances and stored templates are computed by the autocorrelation and residual energy algorithms. Dynamic programming time registration is used to determine the minimum distance between the word spoken and each stored reference pattern. Word-recognition candidates are hypothesized by locating valley points in the minimum dynamic programming distance taken across all candidates. The recognition candidates are passed to high-level decision logic, which applies a threshold comparison test and next-closest error threshold test to determine if the utterance is to be declared.

1) Feature Extraction: A variety of signal processing techniques exist for representing a speech signal in terms of time-varying parameters that are useful for speech recognition.

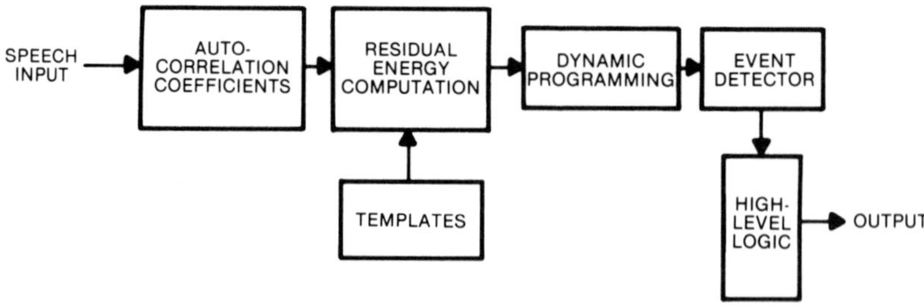

Fig. 14. Speech recognition algorithm flow.

Examples of these signal processing transformations are the direct spectral measurement (mediated either by a bank of bandpass filters or by a discrete Fourier transform), the cepstrum, and a set of suitable parameters of an LPC model [49]. Selection of the parameters depends to a considerable degree on implementation considerations. However, it is generally agreed that the LPC modeling techniques have performance comparable to or better than other techniques for speaker-dependent recognition tasks [50]–[52]. Furthermore, an LPC-based recognition algorithm is attractive because of its compatibility with LPC-based speech analysis and synthesis techniques. For these reasons and for optimum implementation with a digital signal processor chip, Speech Command utilizes a recognition algorithm that is LPC-based.

2) Similarity Measure: After feature extraction, the next basic recognition step is the computation of a similarity measure between a stored reference and the time-normalized parameters extracted from the utterance. The basic similarity measuring technique used in this system is patterned after that of Itakura [53]. In the Itakura approach, recognition is achieved by performing a frame-by-frame comparison of speech data, using a normalized prediction residual. The LPC prediction residual energy is measured by passing the input speech signal (for the frame in question) through an all-zero inverse filter that represents the reference data (see Fig. 15). If the reference data match the input data, then the spectral notches in the inverse filter will match the spectral peaks in the input signal and a low-energy residual output will result. This residual energy is normalized by the residual energy that results when the inverse filter is optimally matched to the input data. The resulting normalized residual error is thus stabilized to be greater than 1. It typically takes on values of less than 1.2 in speaker-dependent word recognition environments.

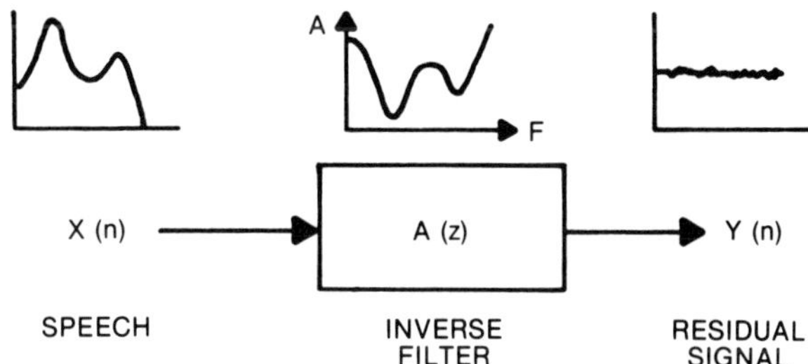

Fig. 15. Distance measure concept.

The prediction residual is computed easily as the inner product of the autocorrelation function of the input with the autocorrelation function of the impulse response of the inverse filter. Normalization by the residual of the input signal is not so simple. In essence, the autocorrelation matrix must be inverted and the traditional method of choice is Levinson's algorithm [54]. LeRoux and Guegen [47] improve on this algorithm by limiting intermediate computations to a magnitude of less than 1. It is this variation of Levinson's algorithm that has been implemented.

3) Dynamic Programming: The measurement of similarity between the incoming speech and stored vocabulary representations requires compensation for changes in the length and timing of the input utterance. Thus it is desirable to time-warp the feature vectors obtained from the incoming data in some optimal sense prior to the comparison with stored feature vectors. The approach utilized in this system is a unique modification of the typical dynamic programming algorithm.

In principle, the dynamic programming procedure is similar to that used by Itakura. Several modifications have been made to the basic Itakura approach, however. The Itakura approach assumes that the reference data are comprised of feature vector measurements obtained from frames of the speech signal that have the same length as the frames utilized during the recognition analysis procedure. The frame period of the input analysis is usually 10 to 20 ms in order to capture dynamic speech events.

The basic difference between the Itakura approach and the approach used here is that reference data are represented only at every other input frame. This approach has three advantages. First, it halves the amount of reference data that must be stored. Second, it halves the number of dynamic programming computations that must be performed. Third, it simplifies the dynamic programming computation by eliminating the memory element required in the basic Itakura technique. Fig. 16 provides a graphic comparison of the basic and modified dynamic programming techniques.

There are two other significant modifications to the Itakura time registration technique as implemented in this recognition system. First and most significant, endpoints are unconstrained. That is, there is no requirement that the dynamic optimization routine be constrained to start

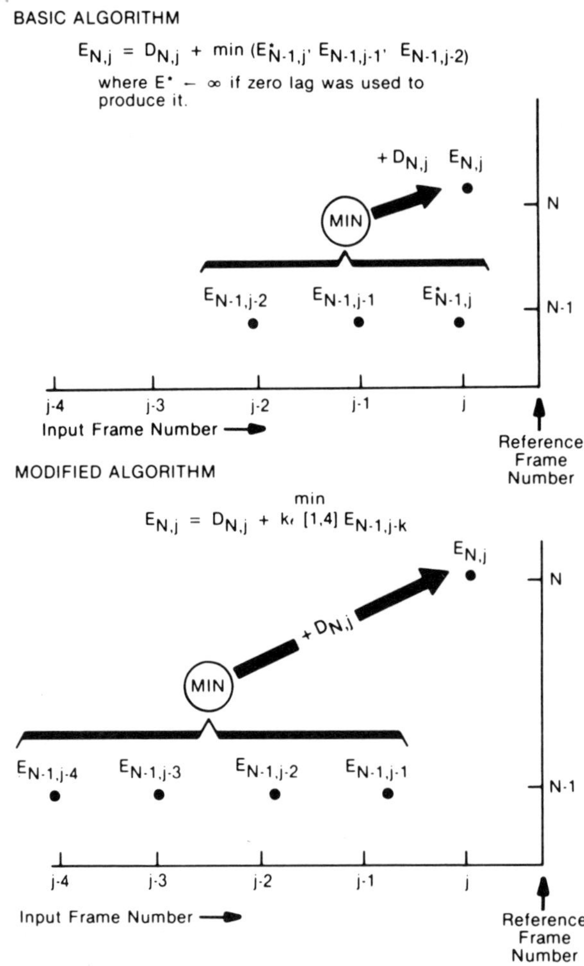

Fig. 16. Basic and modified dynamic programming algorithms.

and end on specific input speech frames. This is a very significant simplification because it separates the high-level word-finding logic from the dynamic programming/recognition processing. Second, penalty errors are added when nonlinear warping occurs. Although a time-warping factor of two still may be achieved, the algorithm prefers utterances with durations equal to the template duration.

Although processing time is substantially increased by not specifying the starting and ending input speech frames, there are two further reasons for having unconstrained endpoints. First, the system reliability is substantially improved by eliminating the requirement for endpoint determination. Accuracy requirements of 98-percent recognition or better would require the reliability of endpoint determination to be at least 98 percent. This is unrealistic, assuming that endpoint determination is based upon information that is not word specific. Second, the system is able to perform recognition of vocabulary words embedded in connected speech. By using the unconstrained endpoint dynamic programming algorithm, this system is able to perform recognition of vocabulary words that are not separated discretely in time. This is a distinct advantage over most other word recognition systems, which require the user to pause between each utterance.

4) Decision Strategy: For each frame of input data, a sequence of scanning errors (similarity measures) are computed assuming that the current input frame corresponds to the last reference frame of each reference pattern. The best and next-best errors are stored along with the corresponding word indices. Before a word in the vocabulary can be hypothesized, a valley point in the scanning error minimum must be declared. The valley-finding process is a key element in simplifying the decision strategy. A valley-finding capability specially designed to satisfy word recognition applications is used. A local valley is defined as the minimum value in a subsequence of errors that begins and ends with values greater than or equal to this valley multiplied by a minimum peak-to-valley ratio. A word is recognized when the following five conditions are met:

a) A valley has been declared.
b) The dynamic programming scanning error is less than some threshold.
c) The next-best error is greater than the error of the best word plus a constant.
d) The prior hypothesis occurred at least TDELT time units ago where TDELT is a constant that is related to the number of reference frames in the templates under consideration.
e) The maximum energy during the utterance has exceeded a minimum threshold.

All accumulated hypotheses are output when "silence" has occurred for a specified amount of time (typically 300 ms). A frame is considered silent when the frame energy is less than a specified fraction (typically 0.1) of the maximum energy in the utterance.

5) Enrollment: The purpose of enrollment is to create for each vocabulary word a set of feature vectors which are utilized in the similarity measurement process during recognition. The enrollment strategy is to provide energy-based definition of start/stop times for an initial reference pattern for each vocabulary word, and then to update these reference patterns through a predefined set of word sequences that admits connected multiple word utterances.

In the initial enrollment mode, one pass is made through the vocabulary and initial reference patterns are formed based upon energy endpoints of each utterance. The actual start and stop times include some padding (typically one frame) to allow conservative, and therefore more reliable, energy endpoint detection. For every reference frame, the speech autocorrelation coefficients are stored. These sets of coefficients determine the inverse filters.

The reference patterns are represented in terms of the autocorrelation function of the inverse filter coefficients. Reference frames that have weak energy levels are weighted less than those with energies above a specified percentage of the maximum energy of a given reference template. This energy weighting is necessary to maintain high performance under noisy operating conditions.

After the initial templates are formed, additional passes through the vocabulary are collected from the user and are used to update the initial templates. The averaging algorithm uses the time registration information obtained from dynamic programming to determine which input coefficients are to be averaged with those stored as reference. For each prompt, the input utterance is compared with the reference data stored for that word. If the utterance is recognized (i.e., the scanning error is less than a threshold), then the template is updated by averaging the appropriate input speech autocorrelation coefficients with those stored as reference. If the utterance is not recognized (i.e., a poor match occurs), then the utterance is reprompted. The above process may be repeated as many times as is desired. More weight in the averaging process is assigned to those templates which have been updated multiple times. For example, during the Nth update the reference template is assigned a weight of $N/(N + 1)$, while the input data are assigned a weight of $1/(N + 1)$. This achieves equal weighting of all input tokens.

Experiments indicate that a significant improvement in performance is achieved by successive updating of each reference template. Substitution error rate decreases substantially as the number of training tokens increases. For example, when five training tokens are used to update the initial template, the corresponding substitution error rate decreases by a factor of three over that measured with one training pass. Improved connected speech recognition performance is achieved by prompting for connected speech and updating the isolated templates as described above.

D. Applications

Included in the Speech Command applications package is a feature called the Transparent Keyboard, which makes it possible to apply voice I/O to any existing TIPC MS-DOS software program. To support the development of recognition vocabularies, the Speech Command software supports vocabulary definition, enrollment, update, and testing. For most effective use of Speech Command, the user's TIPC should have 256K bytes of memory.

Another part of the applications package provides telephone management facility. Fifteen separate directories of ten numbers each can be stored, along with their descriptions, then accessed for speed dialing of individual numbers or of the entire directory. When dialing, the computer can automatically re-dial the number on "busy" or "no answer," and deliver a previously stored message. Functioning as an answering machine, the Speech Command telephone package also can answer incoming calls, deliver a stored voice message, record incoming messages, and interpret touch tone coded commands and respond to them.

A third capability of the applications package offers the equivalent of a computer-based dictation machine that utilizes real-time speech analysis to store verbal inputs in the computer memory. Dictation is stored with file name and description, so the TIPC can sort through a collection of dictated messages and select the one desired. On selection, the dictation can be played back at normal speed, or faster or slower than normal, without changing voice pitch. Computer function keys also can be used to control loudness, as well as to scan rapidly forward and backward in the file material. A "tickler file" also is a part of the Speech Command applications package. This feature allows the computer user to set up agendas and appointment schedules in the computer file for ready reference.

A Speech Command Development Kit includes the programming tools necessary for TIPC users, third-party developers, OEMs, and TI resellers to easily design unique applications using speech technology. The development kit will allow speech technology to be applied to hundreds of applications, thereby enhancing their ease of use.

The Speech Command Development Kit includes routines that provide an application program with convenient access to the capabilities of the Speech Command system. The development kit includes a programmer's guide, the processing algorithms in object code form, device service routines for the Speech Command hardware, and a library of runtime routines for the high-level programming languages MS-BASIC, MS-Pascal, and Lattice-C. Applications written in any of these languages, or in 8088 assembly language, can link the runtime routines with the program in order to use the capabilities of the Speech Command system.

In the future, microprocessor speech capabilities will be applied to a broad range of uses. Voiceprint verification for data security, already an active field, will be extended to other security needs—theoretically, to any lock-and-key situation. Subtle discriminations can be used; for example, voice-recognition ignition locks on automobiles, by recognizing user impairment, could prevent driving while intoxicated. The extent of future applications is potentially limitless, ranging from voice mail to dictation typewriters to foreign language translation machines.

Speech Command represents a significant step in this evolution. In applying voice I/O to the desktop computer—integrated with existing software and practical routines such as telephone management—Speech Command brings speech technology to a new class of users.

VI. SUMMARY

Design criteria for the TIPC assigned highest priority to ergonomic and ease-of-use features. Human factors research contributed greatly to the design process, particularly for the keyboard. Both keyboard and CRT display have been favorably reviewed in the press.

Ease of use is one of the major challenges facing the microcomputer industry today. The growth of computer skills, especially among executives and professionals, will be largely governed by ease-of-use improvements. Such improvements promise to expand greatly both the user base and the range of potential applications. NaturalLink and Speech Command represent significant ease-of-use advances in I/O interface. Although the underlying methodologies had been known for some time, they had not been implemented, prior to their introduction on the TIPC, in a desktop personal computer affordable to a wide range of users.

By simplifying interactive database queries, NaturalLink increases user confidence, decreases training time, and eliminates user failure entirely. Speech Command adds a third, parallel dimension to microcomputer I/O, complementing visual and keyboard communications. By replacing manual keystrokes with verbal input, Speech Command not only enhances ease of use, but also helps adapt computers to hands-free work situations and handicapped users. Speech Command allows the TIPC to serve as a dictation machine and telephone management device as well. Future speech applications range from voiceprint data security and voice mail to text-to-speech conversion and foreign language translation.

Although speech is but one of a number of innovative I/O techniques on the market or under development, it is the most desirable in terms of efficiency and ease of use. It is also one of the most difficult techniques to implement. Speech Command clearly demonstrates the feasibility of such a system and its benefits to nonexpert users. Both Speech Command and NaturalLink are ease-of-use advances certain to be extended in future microcomputer developments.

REFERENCES

[1] A. Gupta and H-M. D. Toong, Eds., *Advanced Microprocessors.* New York: IEEE PRESS, 1983, IEEE reprint book.

[2] R. W. Monty *et al.*, "Keyboard design: An investigation of user preference and performance," in *Proc. Human Factors Soc. 27th Ann. Meet.* (Norfolk, VA, Oct. 1983).

[3] M. Haas, "The Texas Instruments Professional Computer," *BYTE*, pp. 286–324, Dec. 1983.

[4] P. H. Winston, *Artificial Intelligence.* Reading, MA: Addison-Wesley, 1977.

[5] H. R. Tennant *et al.*, "Menu-based natural language understanding," in *Proc. 21st Ann. Meet. Assoc. Comput. Linguistics* (MIT, June 15–17, 1983).

[6] C. W. Thompson *et al.*, "Building usable menu-based natural language interfaces to databases," in *Proc. 9th Int. Conf. on Very Large Databases* (Florence, Italy, 1983).

[7] H. R. Tennant *et al.*, "Usable natural language interfaces through menu-based natural language understanding," in *Proc. Conf. on Human Factors in Computing Systems* (Boston, MA, 1983).

[8] J. S. Brown *et al.*, "SOPHIE/A sophisticated instructional environment for teaching electronic trouble-shooting," Rep. 2790, A1 Rep. 12, Bolt, Beranek and Newman, Cambridge, MA, 1974.

[9] R. R. Burton, "Semantic grammar: An engineering technique for constructing natural language understanding systems," Rep. 3453, ICAI Rep. 3, Bolt, Beranek and Newman, Cambridge, MA, 1976.

[10] E. F. Codd, "Seven steps to rendezvous with the casual user," in *Data Base Management*, J. W. Klimbie and K. L. Koffema, Eds.   New York: North-Holland, 1974.

[11] E. F. Codd *et al.*, "Rendezvous version 1: An experimental English language query formulation system for casual users," Rep. RJ2144(29407), IBM Res. Lab., San Jose, CA, 1978.

[12] F. Damerau, "Advantages of a transformational grammar for question answering," in *Proc. Int. Joint Conf. on Artificial Intelligence.*   Cambridge MA: MIT Press, 1977.

[13] ______, "The derivation of answers from logical forms in a question answering system," Res. Rep. RC 6859.

[14] T. Finin, B. Goodman, and H. Tennant, "Jets: Achieving completeness through coverage and closure," in *Proc. Int. Conf. on Artificial Intelligence*, 1979.

[15] J. M. Ginsparg, "Natural language processing in an automatic programming domain," Ph.D. dissertation, Stanford Univ., Stanford, CA, Memo AIM-316, Computer Sci. Dep. Rep. STAN-CS-78-671, June 1978.

[16] L. R. Harris, "Experience with ROBOT in 12 commercial natural language data base query applications," in *Proc. Int. Conf. on Artificial Intelligence*, 1979.

[17] ______, "User oriented data base query with the robot natural language query system," *Int. J. Man–Machine Studies*, vol. 9, pp. 697–713, 1977.

[18] G. G. Hendrix, "Human engineering for applied natural language processing," in *Proc. Int. Joint Conf. on Artificial Intelligence.*   Cambridge, MA: MIT Press, 1977.

[19] ______, "LIFER: A natural language interface facility," SRI Tech. Note 135, Dec. 1976.

[20] G. G. Hendrix, E. D. Sacerdoti, D. Sagalowicz, and J. Slocum, "Developing a natural language interface to complex data," in *ACM Trans. Database Syst.*, 1978.

[21] A. K. Joshi, S. J. Kaplan, and R. M. Lee, "Approximate responses from a data base query system: An application of inferencing in natural language," in *Proc. Int. Joint Conf. on Artificial Intelligence.*   Cambridge, MA: MIT Press, 1977.

[22] S. J. Kaplan "Cooperative responses from a portable natural language data base query system," Ph.D. dissertation, Univ. of Pennsylvania, July 1979.

[23] ______, "Indirect responses to loaded questions," in *Proc. Second Workshop on Theoretical Issues in Natural Language Processing.*   Urbana, IL: Univ. of Illinois, 1978.

[24] ______, "On the difference between natural language and high level query languages," in *Proc. ACM 78.*   Washington, DC: ACM, 1978.

[25] S. J. Kaplan and A. K. Joshi, "Cooperative responses: An application of discourse inference to database query systems," in *Proc. Second Annu. Conf. of the Canadian Society for Computational Studies of Intelligence*, Toronto, Ont., 1978.

[26] J. Krausse, "Preliminary results of a user study with the 'user speciality languages' system and consequences for the architecture of natural language interfaces," IBM Heidelberg Scientific Center, Tech. Rep. TR 79.04.003, May 1979.

[27] H. Lehman, "Interpretation of natural language in an information system," *IBM J. Res. Develop.*, vol. 22, no. 5, Sept. 1978.

[28] E. D. Sacerdoti, "Language access to distributed data with error recovery," in *Proc. Int. Joint Conf. Artificial Intelligence.*   Cambridge, MA: MIT Press, 1977.

[29] F. B. Thompson and B. H. Thompson, "Practical natural language processing: The REL system as prototype," in *Advances in Computers*, Vol. 13, M. Yovits and M. Rubinoff, Eds.   New York: Academic Press, 1975.

[30] D. L. Waltz, "Natural language access to a large data base," in *Advance Papers of the 4th Int. Joint Conf. on Artificial Intelligence.*   Cambridge, MA: MIT Press, 1975.

[31] ______, "An English language question answering system for a large relational database," *Commun. ACM*, vol. 21, no. 7, July 1978.

[32] D. L. Waltz and B. A. Goodman, "Writing a natural language data base system," in *Proc. Int. Joint Conf. on Artificial Intelligence.*   Cambridge, MA: MIT Press, 1977.

[33] T. Winograd, *Understanding Natural Language.*   New York: Academic Press, 1972.

[34] W. A. Woods, "A personal view of natural language understanding," in *SIGART Newsletter*, no. 61, Feb. 1977.

[35] ______, "Progress in natural language understanding—An application to lunar geology," in *Proc. Nat. Computer Conf.*   Montvale, NJ: AFIPS Press, 1973.

[36] W. A. Woods, R. M. Kaplan, and B. Nash-Webber, "The lunar sciences natural language information system: Final report," Rep. 2378, Bolt Beranek and Newman, Cambridge MA, 1972.

[37] H. R. Tennant, "Evaluation of natural language processors," PhD. dissertation, Dep. Comput. Sci., Univ. of Illinois, 1980.

[38] M. M. Zloof, "Query-by-example: A data base language," *IBM Syst. J.*, vol. 16, no. 4, pp. 324–343, 1977.

[39] ______, "Query-by-Example," in *AFIPS Conf. Proc.*, pp. 431–438, 1975.

[40] ______, "Query-by-Example: The invocation and definition of tables and forms," in *Proc. Int. Conf. on Very Large Data Bases* (Sept. 1975), pp. 1–24.

[41] ______, "Query-by-Example: Operations on the transitive closure," IBM Res. Rep. RC 5526, IBM Thomas J. Watson Res. Cen., Yorktown Heights, NY, 1975.

[42] ______, "Security and integrity within the query-by-example data base management language," IBM Res. Rep. RC 6982, IBM Thomas J. Watson Res. Cen., Yorktown Heights, NY, 1978.

[43] J. C. Thomas and J. D. Gould, "A psychological study of query-by-example," in *AFIPS Conf. Proc.*, pp. 439–445, 1975.

[44] K. McDonough *et al.*, "Microcomputer with 32-bit arithmetic does high-precision number crunching," *Electronics* pp. 105–110, Feb. 24, 1982.

[45] J. Makhoul, "Linear prediction: A tutorial review," *Proc. IEEE*, vol. 63, pp. 561–580, Apr. 1975.

[46] B. Secrest *et al.*, "Speech analysis and synthesis become practical on uC chip," *Electron. Des.*, pp. 129–136, May 27, 1982.

[47] J. LeRoux and G. Guegen, "A fixed point computation of partial correlation coefficients," *IEEE Trans. Acoust., Speech, Signal Process.*, vol. ASSP-25, pp. 257–259, June, 1977.

[48] B. Gold and L. R. Rabiner, "Parallel processing techniques for estimating pitch periods of speech in the time domain," *J. Acoust. Soc. Amer.*, pp. 442–448, Aug. 1969.

[49] J. D. Markel and A. H. Gray, Jr., *Linear Prediction of Speech.* New York: Springer-Verlag, 1976.

[50] ITT RADC Rep. TR-80-75.

[51] Dantrich *et al.*, "On the effects of varying filter bank parameters on isolated word recognition," *IEEE Trans. Acoust., Speech, Signal Process.*, vol. ASSP-31, pp. 793–807, Aug. 1983.

[52] G. Doddington and G. Schalk, "Speech recognition: Turning theory to practice," *IEEE Spectrum*, vol. 18, pp. 26–32, Sept. 1981.

[53] F. Itakura, "Minimum prediction residual principle applied to speech recognition," *IEEE Trans. Acoust., Speech, Signal Process.*, vol. ASSP-23, pp. 67–72, 1975.

[54] N. Levinson, "The Wiener RMS (root mean square) error criterion in filter design and prediction," *J. Math. Phys.*, vol. 25, pp. 261–278, 1947.

5
Digital's Personal Computers

KENNETH H. OLSEN, BARRY JAMES FOLSOM, RONALD J. HAM, AND
JOHN D. CLARKE

Digital Equipment Corporation has been the leading force behind the minicomputer revolution. Although not the originator of personal computers, DEC has designed three different series of personal computers. The hardware architecture of each series is oriented towards specific operating and performance goals. At the same time, the design effort was geared towards adopting common ergonomic standards. This chapter presents an overview of the three families of personal computers and the need for using multiple processors in some personal computers to attain both desired performance and compatibility. Issues relating to job assignment between peer processors are also discussed.

The Editors

I. INTRODUCTION

The Whirlwind computer at MIT in the very early 1950s was, in a sense, the first personal computer. An engineer could sit in front of a cathode-ray tube with a keyboard and do interactive computing. He had a light pen, a joystick, an audio output, and a 16-bit computer. Each bit slice was 2 ft wide and 11 ft high, and the computer took 2500 ft^2 of floor space. So it was not small, but it was truly an interactive computer.

Digital Equipment Corporation was founded 26 years ago to introduce the Whirlwind idea of fast, simple computers to do interactive computing. The result was the minicomputer, with timesharing, communication, and networking, plus the ability to expand to any size and to interact with any piece of equipment. With minicomputers, interactive computing spread rapidly and became the most accepted way to use computers.

After minicomputers became quite well defined in their architecture and in their communications techniques, they were replaced in some applications by machines that had limited expansion possibilities. By leaving out many of the features not needed by an individual user, these computers were optimized for use by one person and became what we now call the personal computer.

Personal computers have replaced minicomputers in applications that are best done on a single-user machine. In many other applications, personal computers have encouraged many new users who can also be satisfied with a minicomputer having multiuser capability and expansion. The techniques developed for the minicomputer made possible the personal computer, and the popularity of the personal computer is making the minicomputer even more important. Together they offer unlimited opportunities to do the exciting things we still have to expect from computers.

In 1982, we introduced three distinctly different personal computers [33]—the Professional series, the Rainbow series, and the DECmate II. The varied, rapidly growing and changing business markets for personal computers clearly demanded ranges of performance, pricing, and

---

The authors are with Digital Equipment Corporation, Maynard, MA 01754, USA.

software resources that we felt could not be effectively provided in a single series of similar models, much less in a single machine.

The Professional 300 series, which currently consists of the 350 and 325 models, are personal minicomputers based on the 16-bit PDP-11 architecture. They are designed to operate as multifunction stand-alone computing systems or as part of distributed information systems. The numerous operating systems available to run on the Professional series currently include two that are PDP-11-oriented—one of them the Professional Operating System (P/OS)—and three that are UNIX-oriented. Software tools are provided for local and host-based development of application programs.

The Rainbow series, which currently consists of the 100 and 100 + models, is designed to execute the many third-party 8- and 16-bit application programs based on the MS-DOS, CP/M-80, CP/M-86, Concurrent CP/M, and UCSD p-System operating systems.

The DECmate II personal computer, which is based on the 12-bit PDP-8 architecture, is designed specifically to perform the two main computing functions in automated offices, word processing, and business accounting. Its operating systems are WPS-8 for word processing and CP/M-80 and COS-310 for business applications.

II.   PROFESSIONAL PERSONAL COMPUTERS

Hardware Architecture

The hardware architecture of the Professional 350 (Fig. 1) reflects its physical modularity [6], [11]–[13]. The basic functional components are linked logically to the internal section of the bus and located physically on the system board. These are the CPU, floating-point instruction unit,

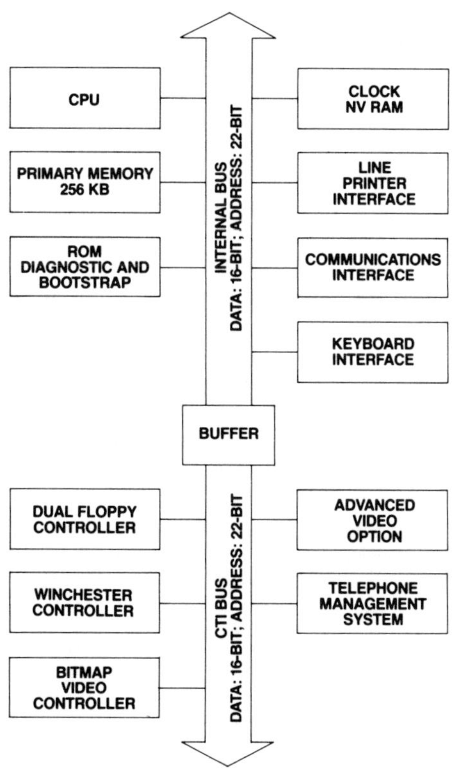

Fig. 1.   Modular system architecture of the Professional 350 personal computer.

main memory on two daughter boards, ROM for diagnostics and bootstrap software, clock, nonvolatile RAM, as well as interface logic for the keyboard, line printer, and asynchronous/synchronous communications.

Mass storage, video controller, and option modules are linked to the CTI (computing terminal interconnect) bus. Modules include the extended bit-map option for interfacing a 13-in color monitor, a real-time IEEE 488 option, and the TMS (telephone management system) module for interfacing external voice and data communications facilities.

Selecting the CPU

At the time of original design of the Professional series, two PDP-11 CPUs were available: the T-11 [3], [4] and the F-11 [1]. The single-chip T-11 and three-chip F-11 CPUs both offer approximately the same performance as Digital's PDP-11/34 mid-range minicomputer. The T-11 CPU was the lower cost approach and required less board space. However, the F-11 CPU was selected because of its memory management unit (MMU). The MMU, which consists of a single DIP (dual in-line package), provides 36 memory management registers (4 for status and 32 for relocation; 16 for users and 16 for the operating system) and memory logic that can directly address 4M bytes of main memory, whereas the T-11 can only address 64K bytes. As of the time of writing, 512K bytes of main memory is more than adequate to handle the present basic and optional functions of the system. Even though it may be difficult today to visualize a need for 4M bytes of main memory in a personal computer, the history of the computer industry has shown that as more memory has become available, developers have found applications for it.

A natural evolution of hardware architecture in the PDP-11 family would be a Professional model based on Digital's J-11 supermicroprocessor [9]. The J-11 is a VLSI implementation of the PDP-11/70 in two CMOS chips mounted on a 60-pin, eight-layer ceramic package. A J-11-based personal computer would offer the full functionality of the PDP-11/70 minicomputer at about twice the performance of the F-11 in the Professional series.

Bus Structure

The Professional's CTI bus uses a new bus structure that facilitates installation of option modules in any slot. This bus provides 22 bits of addressing and so allows access to 4M bytes of main memory. A licensing agreement for the CTI bus enables third parties to design, manufacture, and market options that plug into the bus option slots. The CTI bus is a multiplexed address and data bus that combines 16-bit data signals with the 22-bit address signals on 22 signal lines. It is designed for a maximum of eight option slots (only six of them are currently built into the option backplane). The limited number of option slots permits controlling the electrical characteristics of the bus lines so that there is reduced capacitive loading caused by bus drivers and receivers, less capacitance in circuit connections, and reduced transmission line effects. The lower capacitive loading permits using lower cost octal three-state transceivers. Eight three-state transceivers occupy the same board space as four of the more expensive open-collector devices, resulting in a low-cost connection to the bus. Control of data and address transmission on the three-state bus to avoid contention between two drivers simultaneously sending signals on the data/address line (DAL) is accomplished by the circuit shown schematically in Fig. 2(a). Here, a master device is reading data from a slave device. The MDEN (master device enable) and SDEN (slave device enable) bus signals allow the master to control the bus drivers and receivers during the bus cycle so that information flows in the appropriate direction. In Fig. 2(b), the timing strobes for the read bus cycle are such that MDEN is on during the address portion and SDEN is on during the data portion, so that the slave can return the data at the specified address. Power supply noise spikes and the possibility of data loss associated with noise are thus avoided at the cost of only two additional control signals.

There is DMA (direct memory access) arbitration circuitry on the system module. Any module on the option section of the bus can attain bus mastership for transferring data to any portion of the 4M bytes in the primary memory space. There are three priority levels for bus arbitration:

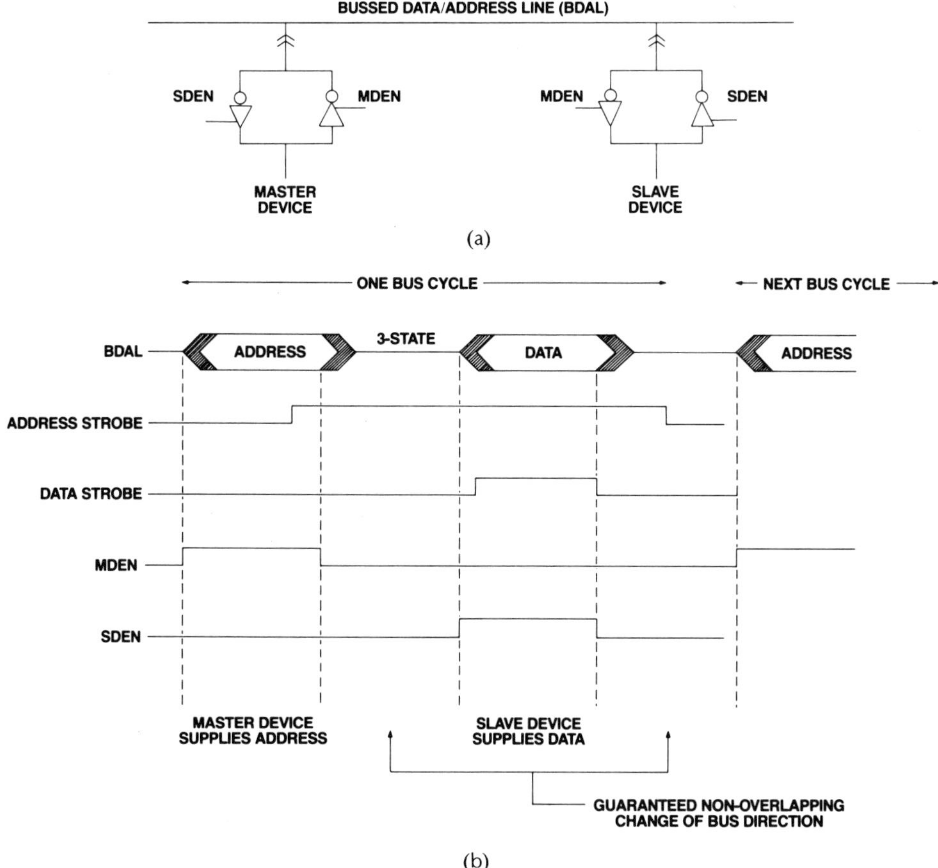

Fig. 2. (a) Circuit for avoiding contention between signals from two drivers on the DAL (data/address line). (b) Timing strobes for the read bus cycle.

level two cannot be preempted by any other level, level one can be preempted only by level two, and level zero can be preempted by either level one or two. If a request is made by a higher priority device, the device currently having bus mastership will relinquish it. Unlike the PDP-11 and LSI-11 buses, however, the device on the CTI bus having the highest current priority retains mastership until the data transfer has been fully completed. Individual applications can be optimized by assigning different priority levels to option modules.

Option Module Flexibility

Packaging flexibility is provided by requiring that the physical position of option modules in the backplane have no effect on the functionality or performance of the system. This is accomplished by avoiding the use of daisy chain signals, which would require that there be no empty slots between modules, and by having interrupt and DMA priority independent of backplane position. This also permits modules to be arranged in the backplane for cabling convenience without potential interference with system operation. Given the confined physical package of a personal computer, cabling convenience is very important.

Flexibility is also provided in the size of the module. The module height is fixed at 5.2 in, so that it may fit in the card cage; however, the width of the card may vary from 4 in to a maximum of 12 in. This allows a cost savings for those simpler options that do not require the maximum printed-circuit size.

Addressing modules is accomplished by assigning fixed addresses to the bus slots themselves and having a module assume the address of the slot in which it is installed. In the memory map in Fig. 3, the registers of the option devices are located in the uppermost 4K-byte segment of addressable memory, which is defined as the I/O page. A 128-byte segment of the I/O page is reserved for each of the eight physical slots. This 128-byte allotment is more than adequate for the majority of modules. Since there can be no more than eight modules, the I/O page cannot be overloaded, and, since fixed addresses are not assigned to options, there are always enough I/O page addresses.

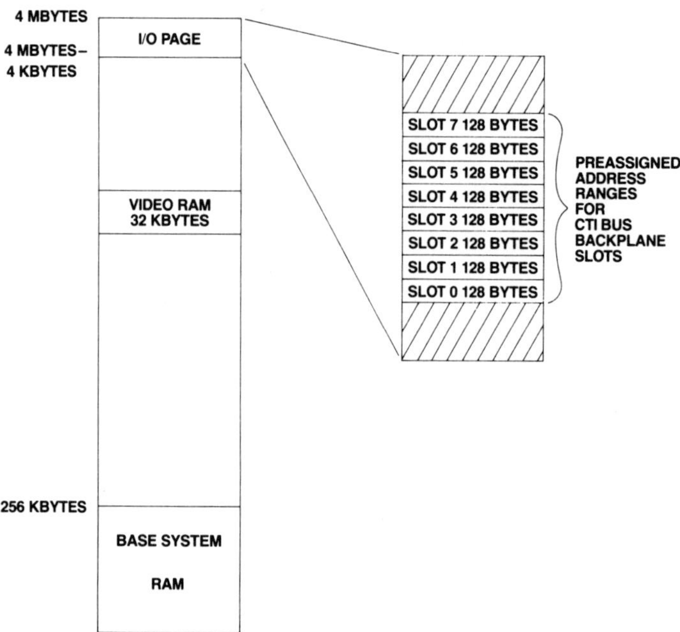

Fig. 3. I/O page of the Professional 350's memory map.

When a decoder on the system board receives DAL signals in the address portion of the cycle, it sends eight slot select signals, one for each slot, down the bus. If the bus address falls into the range for a particular option slot, that slot select signal is asserted. This central decoder hardware is equivalent to one set of decoding hardware if the decoding had been done on the module. The module need examine only its slot select signal and the least significant seven address bits to determine which, if any, of its potential 128 bytes is being accessed.

An "option present" feature of the bus provides a unique signal from each module to the system board on power-up. When the ZIF connector has locked a module into its slot, the option present signal is grounded, and a signal from the module appears as a bit in a designated I/O page memory location. The diagnostics firmware on system board ROM checks the bit positions on that register for the location options. This feature provides a reliable means of determining which slots are occupied.

The system provides complete system verification each time it is powered up. Diagnostics firmware initiated at power-up must verify first the functions on the system board and then those on each of the option modules. The system cannot anticipate what modules are currently in the card cage or what options will be available in the future. Each module therefore carries its own diagnostics in ROM. After the diagnostics firmware on the system board's ROM has been executed, the CPU transfers an image of the diagnostics ROM on each module to the main RAM and executes it. If any faults are detected in the option modules, an appropriate message is displayed on the terminal. Failures are isolated to an assembly that the user is capable of replacing, which permits the user to service the system personally. Service engineers also find the system easier to maintain.

Bit-Map Video Controller

A bit-map architecture was chosen for the Professional video controller (Fig. 4) because of the inherent flexibility of a bit-map display. The bit-map controller driving a raster scan display offers excellent flexibility due to the ability to access and directly control the state of every pixel displayed on the CRT. This flexibility allows both alphanumeric characters and graphics to be displayed using the same video controller.

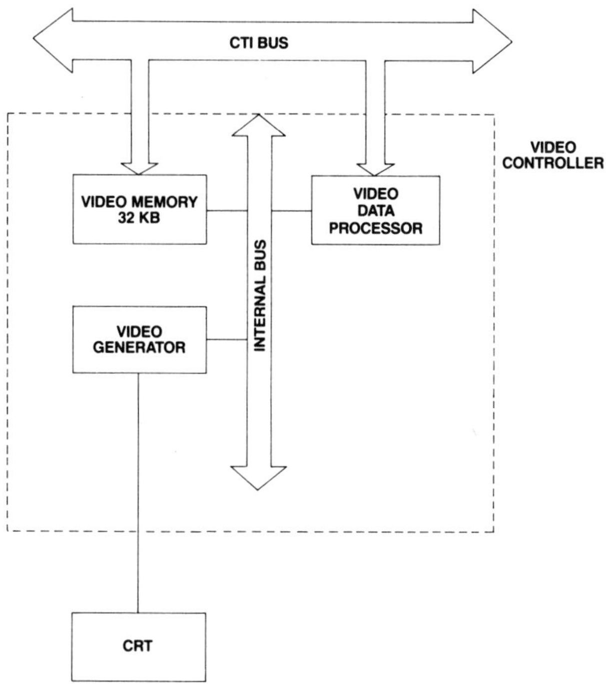

Fig. 4. Block diagram of the bit-map video controller.

The Professional's bit-map display memory can be controlled directly by the F-11 processor executing a video control program resident in system memory. The bit-map memory is directly accessible as 32K bytes of the primary memory space, thus allowing the pixel representations in bit-map memory to be manipulated directly by the PDP-11 instructions. However, this approach involves intensive data manipulation to set and clear the appropriate bits in the correct words. A video data processor, which consists of arithmetic and state machine logic implemented in gate arrays, has been included as a part of the Professional video control hardware to make the task of displaying a character on the screen easier. This video data processor transfers a string of pixels to the video RAM. This string consist of the pattern length (1 to 16 bits), the coordinate of the pixel at which the operation will begin, the number of times the operation is to be performed, and the type of operation to be performed. Possible operations include: move pattern to screen, move complement of pattern to screen, OR pattern to screen contents, AND pattern with screen contents, XOR pattern with screen contents. The video data processor speeds the processing of moving characters to the screen by relieving the F-11 software of the need to deal with character cells being nonaligned with video memory byte boundaries.

The block diagram of Fig. 4 shows that there are two paths into the video memory. The direct path allows the system processor to access the memory directly. This path can be used to quickly save and restore images which have been previously constructed. Images could be stored in system RAM or on a mass storage unit. The second path into the video memory is through the video data processor, which helps in constructing images.

Terminal Control Program

The bit-map controller is utilized by the terminal control program to provide both alphanumeric and graphic capabilities. The alphanumeric capability is the same as provided by Digital's VT102 video terminal. It displays characters in one of two screen formats, 80 characters by 24 lines or 132 characters by 24 lines. The characters in the 80-character width are formed within a 12 (width) by 10 (height) cell, while the characters in the 132-character width are formed within a 7 by 10 cell. Each character may be assigned four attributes in any combination: blink, bold, reverse, and underline. Double width and double height/double width characters are also possible. The character set consists of 204 characters, including line drawing characters and special Western European characters. Commands are provided for inserting or deleting characters and lines of text.

The graphics screen is 960 pixels wide by 240 pixels high. Software supports the generation of circles, curves, and vectors. Graphics-associated text may be displayed in various sizes and angles and in normal characters or italics. In addition to the standard character set, the user may add three more character sets. Several modes of writing to the screen are supported: replace, overlay, complement, erase, and negate.

The extended bit-map option provides enhanced color display capability in the 13-in color monitor. Eight of 256 possible colors may be displayed at one time, and colors may be changed instantaneously by manipulation of the hardware color map.

Natural Images and Color

The 1024 by 256 pixels on the screen—1 bit per pixel—provide the highest black/white resolution with one level intensity (the screen is either dark or light). By folding the memory plane once horizontally through software manipulation of control registers on the I/O page of memory, the resolution can be changed to 512 by 256. In that case, each pixel is represented by 2 bits of data and can therefore be displayed at four intensity levels. If the memory plane is folded once more, the result is a resolution of 256 by 256 (four bit positions per pixel). There can be 16 levels of intensity, which produces nearly the continuous tone appearance of a black/white photograph.

The extended bit-map option module consists of two bit-map video memories identical to the monochrome video memory and provides 1 bit per pixel for each of the colors: red, blue, and green. By folding the memory plane of each of the three colors, it is possible to produce natural images in full color—16 levels of intensity in each of the colors. In concept, the three bit-map video memories can be used to produce images with 12 bits per pixel, corresponding to 4096 different color tones at a resolution of 256 by 256.

Placing all the bit-map video controller hardware on one option module proved to be a difficult layout task. The video controller functions described here would have required a total of 175 discrete MSI/LSI chips. The chip population was reduced to only 75 chips by designing three gate-array chips based on gate-array blanks developed for the VAX-11/750 computer. One gate-array chip is used in the video generator and two in the video data processor.

Telephone Management System (TMS)

Telephone management functions are provided in the Professional by two hardware elements (Fig. 5): the controller module, which is mounted inside the card cage, and the telephone

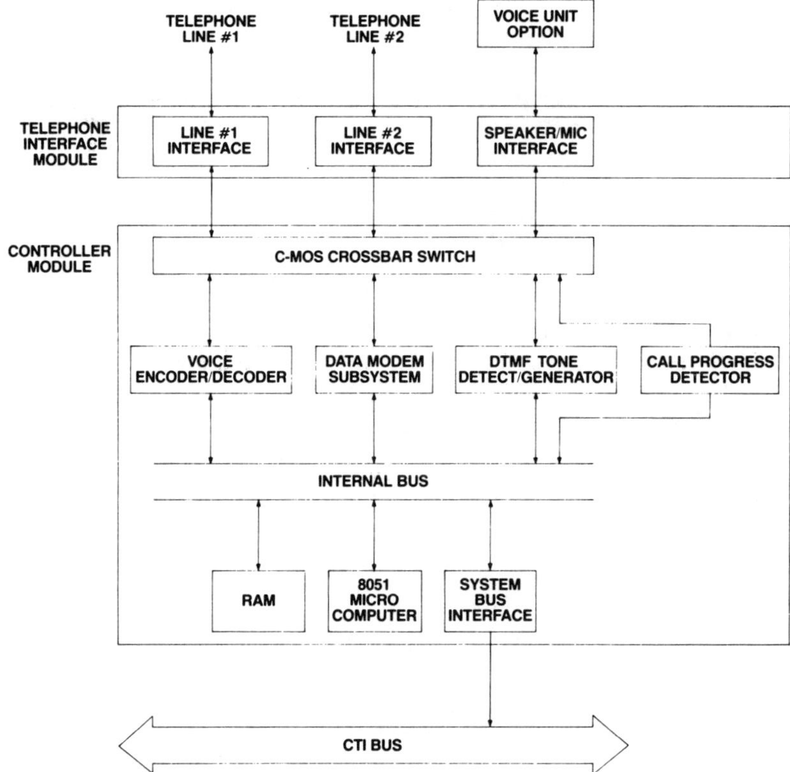

Fig. 5. Schematic diagram of the Professional 350's TMS option.

interface module, which is mounted on the outside of the card cage just behind the I/O connector panel at the back of the system board module.

The hardware elements on the internal bus of the TMS controller module include an 8051 single-chip microcomputer, RAM, a Bell 212A 1200-Bd modem, a 103J 300-Bd modem, a DTMF tone detector/generator, a voice encoder/decoder, and call progress detector. Through a CMOS crossbar switch, any of these internal elements may be connected to external lines through the telephone interface module. This module includes two telephone lines (one may be used for data and the other for voice). The optional voice unit contains an integral microphone for voice encoding and storage, a loudspeaker for playback, and a multifunction keypad with 9 function keys and a 12-key numeric array for dialing. The voice unit functions as a speaker phone for communication over public telephone networks. Accessory jacks allow use of a headphone, an external microphone, and a remote footswitch.

System, Development, and Application Software

The two PDP-11-based operating systems for the Professional personal computers are P/OS and RT-11. P/OS [14], which was derived from RSX-11M-Plus [15], retains the multitasking, memory management, and record management [16] functions characteristic of PDP-11 software architecture. However, the multiuser utility software of RSX-11M-Plus has been deleted as it is not required in a personal computer environment. (The RSX-11M-Plus real-time system and RT-11 single-user system have been standard on PDP-11 computers for many years.) Also, three operating systems based on UNIX [10] are supported: ULTRIX (a Digital-developed version of UNIX), VENIX, and IDRIS. Other current operating systems—all of them implemented to encourage conversion of industry-standard applications to the Professional computers—are UCSD p-System and CP/M-80 [17].

Application software can be developed remotely on a computer running the RSX-11M, RSX-11M-Plus, or VAX/VMS operating systems or locally on a Professional running P/OS. High-level languages are Fortran-77 [19], BASIC [23], PL/I, Cobol-81 [20], Pascal [21], [22], and "C." The Professional developer's toolkit includes PDP-11 utility tools such as editors, FMS (forms management system), DCL command language, and the DATATRIEVE query language and report writer. A library of application management tools permits the program developer to integrate the P/OS menu system, HELP services, and functions keys into the application software. Third-party application programs developed with these tools to date include: NPL Information Management [24], TK!Solver-86, Core Graphics [28], SINGRAPH [26], Maps/PRO [27], and Supercomm-20 Communications [25]. These are all minicomputer-class applications running on the Professional computer with a Winchester disk drive and capable of sharing files with host computers such as the VAX-11/780 superminicomputer.

Communications

Capabilities for communications, distributed data processing, and resource sharing are becoming increasingly important as users seek integration of individually oriented computing with the spectrum of group and remote computing services available to them. Current communications capabilities of the Professional series [18] include: file transfer between Professionals, PDP-11 minis, and VAX superminis; emulation of Digital's VT102 and VT125 series terminals and IBM 3270 terminals; and compatibility with the NAPLPS (North American Presentation Level Protocol System) standard for monochrome and color graphics communications. High-speed communications via DECnet remote networks and Ethernet local-area networks is supported. Ethernet capability is provided by means of a single CTI bus option card, which contains 128K bytes of RAM for Ethernet buffers and DECnet communications software.

Low-cost communication is available via the Digital microprocessor-based mini-exchange, a low-cost circuit-switching device that can be used with all three personal computers. Any combination of these computers can communicate at 9600 Bd through the device's eight RS232C serial lines. A printer connected to one of the ports can be shared by computers on other ports.

III. Rainbow Personal Computers

8 and 16 Bits

The personal computer industry is currently in a state of transition in word length from 8 to 16 bits. Software packages written for 16-bit computers offer more functions and faster response than equivalent applications on 8-bit machines at insignificant additional cost. Because 8-bit personal computers have been applied in the office since the mid-1970s, there are many established 8-bit application packages. A number of 16-bit programs have recently become commercially available and soon they will overtake 8-bit application programs.

The Rainbow 100 and 100 + computers [36], [37] are able to process both 8- and 16-bit application software because they contain two microprocessors, the 8-bit Zilog Z80A and the 16-bit Intel 8088. Both Rainbow models have the same dual-processor architecture and run on either of two operating systems: a) an enhanced version of Microsoft's MS-DOS or b) CP/M-86/80, a hybrid of Digital Research's CP/M-80 and CP/M-86. The Rainbow 100 +, which was introduced in the fall of 1983, provides significant extensions in memory, mass storage, and graphics capabilities.

Dual Hardware Architecture

The dual computer architecture in Fig. 6 represents the Rainbow 100 + but applies as well to the Rainbow 100 [8]. As summarized below, the main differences are in the amount of RAM and

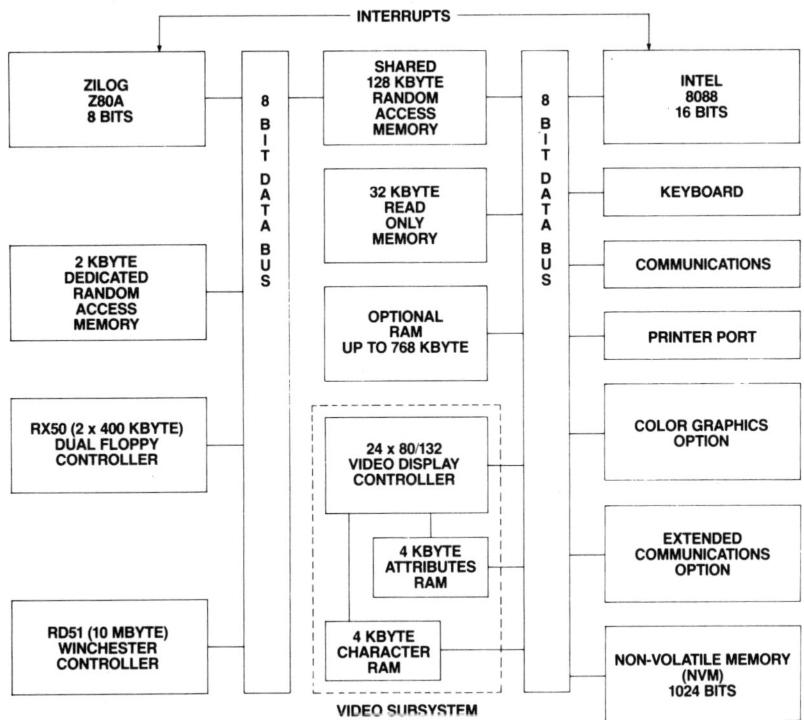

Fig. 6. Dual computer architecture of the Rainbow personal computers (RAM and ROM given for the Rainbow 100 +).

ROM and the fact that the 10M-byte Winchester disk drive is standard and housed in the system unit of the Rainbow 100 + . The optional add-on Winchester subsystem for the Rainbow 100 includes an upgraded power supply, drive, and controller.

The two CPUs each have their own 8-bit bus, share a main memory of 128K bytes of RAM (64K bytes for the Rainbow 100), and synchronize communications with each other by means of interrupts. When either CPU is running an application program, it exchanges data directly with devices on its own 8-bit bus and indirectly with devices on the other 8-bit bus via a buffer "mailbox" in shared memory. Each CPU also functions as an intelligent controller for the devices on its own 8-bit bus. In doing so, it off-loads I/O tasks from the other CPU and thereby helps to improve program execution time and system response.

Shared main memory provides a fast method of transferring data from CPU to CPU. Memory accesses are managed by a finite-state machine in the RAM arbitration logic. The RAM arbiter is notified that either a CPU or DMA device (e.g., the extended communications option) wishes to read data into shared memory or write data out of it. The arbiter either permits addressing memory and establishes the proper timing or locks out the requested data transfer until ongoing activity in memory has been completed. Design of the RAM arbiter was difficult to implement because of the different clocks and execution times of the Z80A and 8088 CPUs.

On the Z80A Side

The basic and optional peripheral devices are assigned to the two Rainbow CPUs so as to optimize overall performance. In the floppy-based Rainbow 100 computer, integral mass storage consists of either one or two 800K-byte dual floppy diskette units and is located on the Z80A bus. Therefore, the Z80A CPU alone has access to the floppy diskette controller and is responsible for controlling floppy data transfers. (This is done through programmed I/O so as to avoid the extra cost and board space of a DMA controller chip.)

Data transfers to and from floppy diskettes are in general extremely slow; one character is handled every 32 μs so that transmitting the nearly 3200 characters in a 132 by 24 screen, for example, takes more than 0.1 s. With the Z80A assuming the burden of these transfers, the 8088 has only to request "reads" or "writes" to specific locations on the diskette drive units. The Z80A CPU's floppy access service was optimized by eliminating unnecessary transfer times. For this reason, the Z80A has been assigned 2K bytes of dedicated RAM (unaccessible to the 8088) for storing its interrupt vectors and any other software that affects floppy access timing. If the Z80A's interrupt vectors were maintained in shared memory, the Z80A might have to execute wait states becuase it was locked out by the RAM arbiter. Interrupt latency is thus minimized because the Z80A accesses its dedicated RAM without wait states.

There is a minimal chance of a floppy disk data transfer being interrupted. If the 8088 is currently processing an application, it has made the data transfer request and it is itself handling the peripheral devices on its bus. And there are no peripherals on the Z80A bus to originate an interrupt. Since the Z80A can only address a total of 64K bytes of memory, it can access only 62K bytes of shared RAM in addition to its 2K bytes of dedicated RAM. The remaining 2K bytes of shared RAM are used for dedicated location of the 8088's interrupt vectors. In this way, the possibility of a collision between Z80A and 8088 interrupt vectors is eliminated.

On the 8088 Side

Data transfer time on the 8088 has been minimized to provide high-speed execution of 16-bit CP/M programs. The 8088 exchanges data with all the peripherals on its side of shared memory via its 8-bit bus. Since the control of floppy disks has been delegated to the Z80A, the Rainbow's 8088 CPU is capable of executing 16-bit programs faster than equivalent 8088-only personal computers. On the Z80A side, in part because of the peripheral I/O tasks performed by the 8088 and in spite of its floppy diskette control responsibility, the Rainbow has been found to execute 8-bit application programs at least as fast as Z80A-only machines.

The Rainbow's 8088 processor makes use of several different types of memory (sizes of memory and mass storage apply to Rainbow 100):

- 64K bytes of dynamic main memory (62K bytes shared with the Z80A CPU).
- 24K bytes of ROM (read only memory): contains bootstrap, diagnostics, and VT102 emulation firmware code for both the 8088 and Z80A CPUs. Digital's VT102 video display terminal is emulated in two modes: console and terminal. In console mode, the Rainbow emulates a VT102 running programs locally as a stand-alone machine. In terminal mode, it appears as a VT102 terminal to a host computer connected to the communications port.
- Optional unshared dynamic memory: additional 8088 RAM of 64K bytes or 192K bytes on an option module (daughter board).
- Video Control RAM: separate 4K-byte RAMs for character and attributes code are used by the 8088 CPU to control characters on the video display.
- 1024 bits of nonvolatile memory (NVM) storage: stores setup parameters that establish characteristics of keyboard, video display, and communications interfaces. In VT102 terminal mode, it is therefore unnecessary to boot the computer after power-up.

The video subsystem provides, in addition to 24 line by 80 or 132 column displays, such VT102 characteristics as smooth scrolling, full screen and split screen, double-height and double-width lines, reverse video, and bold, blinking, and underlined characters. The video display processor accesses the 4K-byte blocks of character and attribute RAM for small periods of time (with the 8088 CPU in a wait state) in order to index an ASCII character code into a character generator and apply attributes information to modify the video data.

There are serial line interfaces to the keyboard, communications port, and printer. The keyboard interface is an RS423 full-duplex connection running asynchronously at 4800 bits per second. Communication with other computers is through an RS232C asynchronous/byte synchronous interface. The general-purpose printer port provides an RS232C interface to a variety of Digital printers.

The color graphics option (on a daughter board) provides the required bit-map memory array and additional video controller logic for use with the monochrome CRT monitor or optional color monitor. A high-level command language is used to draw figures from simple vectors to complex open and closed curves. There are two resolution modes for graphics, 800 by 240 picture elements with two planes and 320 by 240 picture elements with four planes. Four colors are available in the high-resolution mode, and up to 16 colors in the low-resolution mode (from a choice of 4096 for the Rainbow 100 + and 1028 for the Rainbow 100).

The extended communications option for the Rainbow 100 provides a DMA high-speed serial line for a local-area network or custom OEM interfaces and a second communications port with bit and byte synchronous capability.

Sharing Tasks in Floppy-Based System

Typically, one of the two 400K-byte diskettes in a dual floppy drive contains both the operating system occupying about 80K bytes of space and an assortment of 8- and 16-bit programs in the remaining space. After power-up, bootstrap, and diagnostics, code on the 8088's ROM prepares the floppy-based Rainbow 100 for processing an application. As shown in the schematic memory map in Fig. 7, the CP/M-86/80 operating system is loaded into its proper location in the 64K-byte primary memory. The software modules in the CP/M-86/80 fall into two groups, the CP/M-86/80 kernel and the CP/M-80 interface layer. The CP/M-86/80 kernel has essentially the same characteristics and functions as the CP/M-86 16-bit operating system for the 8088 CPU. The CP/M-80 interface layer appears to an 8-bit CP/M-80 application program to be a BIOS (basic input/output system) as defined by Digital Research for the CP/M-80 operating system.

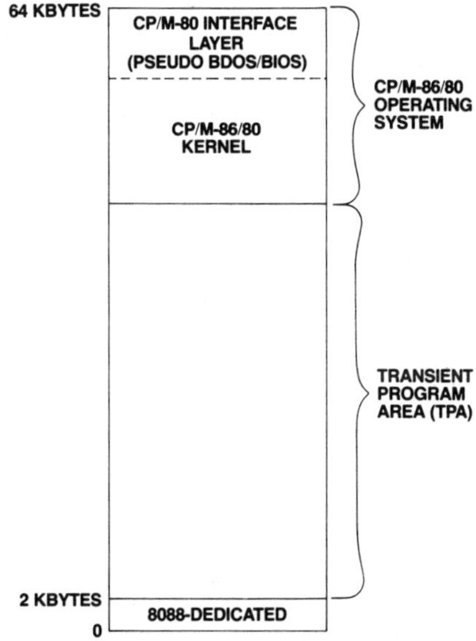

Fig. 7. Schematic memory map of the 64K-byte shared RAM in the Rainbow 100.

When the user keys in a file name for the selected application program, CP/M-86/80 searches for that file name on the floppy diskettes. The operating system is able to "soft-sense" whether it is a Z80A or an 8088 program by the three-character file extensions suffixed to the file names: a file name.COM indicates a CP/M-80 file and a file name.CMD indicates a CP/M-86 file. Such file extensions are customarily used for file organization purposes.

The selected application program is loaded into TPA (transient program array) space in shared memory. If it is an 8088 program, it communicates with the CP/M-86/80 kernel in the usual way. If it is an Z80A program, it instead makes operating system calls to the CP/M-80 interface layer (or pseudo-BIOS). This interface layer stores the call parameters in shared RAM and turns over control to a Z80A service routine in CP/M-86/80. By means of a cross-CPU transfer between the 8088 and Z80A, the Z80A executes the instruction and the results are passed back to the pseudo-BIOS, which returns control to the application program. The program again calls the pseudo-BIOS, and the process is repeated for the next instruction.

The Z80A executes CP/M-80 programs and the 8088 executes CP/M-86 programs, but the two processors do not have equal responsibility or authority. CP/M-86/80 actually runs on the 8088, and so the 8088 performs all operating system functions. Even when the Z80A is executing a program, the 8088 is doing such tasks as handling keyboard code, servicing communications, and processing video screen refresh. The 8088 is always the master and the Z80A the slave, even when the Z80A is logically the master in executing a CP/M-80 program. If a CP/M-80 program is running, the 8088 must tell the Z80A to execute its own instructions. If the Z80A wants to communicate with a peripheral device or requires a service from CP/M-86/80, it makes a system call to the 8088. When an 8088 program is running, the Z80A is inactive but ready (looping) as it waits for an 8088 request for floppy diskette data transfer, which would involve the following sequence:

- 8088 transfers data to a buffer in shared RAM.
- 8088 interrupts Z80A with signals that describe what is to be done and where the data are located in shared RAM.
- Z80A accesses data in shared RAM and transfers them to the indicated disk location.
- Z80A reports to the 8088 that the transfer has been completed.

When the Z80A is executing a program and wants access to the floppy drives, it must still send a request to the 8088, just as if it had to transfer data to or receive data from a peripheral on the 8088's bus.

Diagnostics

The diagnostics software tests all functional units in the basic hardware configuration: Z80A and 8088 CPUs, shared RAM, video subsystem, floppy controller, and arbitration logic. The tests determine and report the nature of the error and identify the field-replaceable unit at fault. The diagnostics process is either automatic (and transparent to the user) or is initiated step-by-step with commands in plain English that the non-computer-oriented person can comfortably handle.

There are three different modes of diagnostics operation:

- *Cold-Start:* performed automatically on power-up. Takes 7 to 10 s, a time which is noticeable but not long enough to be disturbing to the user.
- *Reset:* the computer has been booted, the program execution has started but has later failed in some way. The user presses the SET-UP and control keys on the keyboard to initiate reset diagnostics, which takes about 5 s. This process is less exhaustive than the cold-start diagnostics because shared ROM is assumed to be running properly.
- *Self Test:* this procedure involves inserting a diagnostics diskette into the dual floppy drive and selecting types of tests on several diagnostics menus. Typically, the user has tried reset diagnostics several times without success and now wants to determine whether the malfunction is in the application program or hardware. Checks basic system elements such as floppy diskettes and serial lines more thoroughly and adds tests on optional RAM and video controller, among others.

When the user boots the diagnostics diskette, the main diagnostics menu appears on the monitor screen. The user may decide to run a floppy test for drives A and B, which takes from 3 to 5 min, separately or as the first step in the extended test sequence, which takes from 30 to 45 min altogether. The floppy test checks a number of aspects of the drive: internal registers in floppy controller, timing of head stepping motor, track 0 switch, rotational speed of disk, operation of data separator in floppy controller, disk read and write, and capability for detecting header and CRC data errors.

The extended test sequence checks the floppies, shared RAM, and communications interfaces automatically. RAM tests include:

- *Addressing:* determines that select logic for RAM chips is working properly.
- *Gallop:* validates timing by loading RAM with all 0s and all 1s alternately and checking outputs.
- *Code Execution:* checks capability of processor in handling instructions and data transfers in tight loops by switching data rapidly between adjacent addresses.
- *Refresh:* checks refresh logic by loading data and determining if still present after 3 s (refresh rate is once every 2 ms).
- *Alpha Contamination:* determines whether alpha particles are destroying data in RAM storage.

"Time to complete" on the extended test screen displays how much time remains for each test segment that lasts for over 1-1/2 min.

The communications port tests determine whether there is a malfunction and whether it is in the on-board interface or in an external unit, such as a modem in a communications line or the printer itself. The communications tests are more thorough in self-test procedure than in the cold-start tests. In cold start, for example, the serial lines are tested only under the most common conditions: a data stream with 1 stop bit, no parity, and 7-bit code at 9600 bits per second. In the self-test procedure, the serial lines are checked at a number of baud rates from 50 to 9600 and in several synchronous and asynchronous message formats: 1, 1-1/2, and 2 stop bits; no parity and parity bit; 7- and 8-bit code.

If all individual tests have been run and a malfunction still exists, the user may select a system test. In this procedure, the computer is subjected to worst case conditions with all devices on the two buses requesting access to the two CPUs at the same time. If individual tests have found all units acceptable, the malfunction is likely to be in the interaction between two units and the solution may be to replace the system board.

Loopback Testing

Conventional computer diagnosis routines identify a malfunction as originating somewhere in a peripheral subsystem but cannot go further to identify the specific source; for example, a floppy diskette subsystem would be pinpointed but not whether the problem is in the disk drive, floppy controller, or floppy data separator. Such a distinction is provided in the Rainbow computers.

An internal loopback arrangement, shown schematically for a floppy diskette subsystem in Fig. 8, provides a fast, convenient method of testing for malfunctions. By inserting a loopback multiplexer at the system connection to the floppy diskette drive, a datastream is transmitted under keyboard control from the 8088 CPU to the floppy data separator that emulates the datastream from the diskette drive itself. Failure in this transmission will eliminate the floppy diskette drive as the source of the problem. An error message on the CRT monitor indicates whether the malfunction is on the floppy daughter board, which contains the floppy data separator and floppy controller, or on the system board.

The loopback procedure for checking the video subsystem is similar except that the loopback multiplexer is placed between the video display controller and CRT monitor. A data stream from the 8088 CPU is transferred into the video controller and then looped back to the printer port, converted from serial to parallel form, and read out on the printer.

The loopback arrangement supports testing in cold start, reset, and self-test diagnosis. The user can handle a significantly greater proportion of malfunctions by replacing units rather than by calling on field service staff.

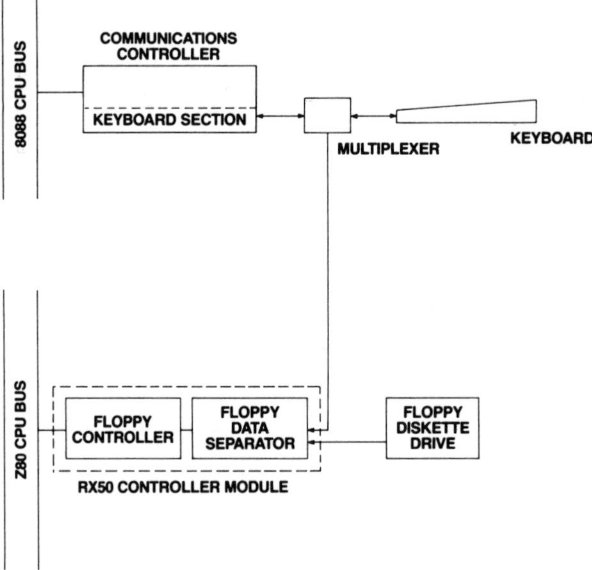

Fig. 8. The Rainbow computers' internal loopback arrangement.

Extended Memory and Graphics

Extending RAM space in the Rainbow 100 + consisted of increasing standard main memory from 64K to 128K bytes and, with more optional RAM, maximum main memory from 256 to 896K bytes. The larger standard memory is adequate for the recently enhanced versions of the MS-DOS and CP/M-86/80 operating systems. The additional standard main memory involved adding eight 64K × 1 chips; the three banks of optional RAM can each contain either 64K × 1 or 256K × 1 RAM chips. The ROM in the Rainbow 100 + was increased from 24K bytes in the Rainbow 100K to 32K bytes (and can be further increased to 64K bytes with high-density ROMs). ROM hardware was reduced from three 8K chips to two 16K chips, which, with the lower cost of ROM devices, involved a negligible increase in cost. The board area previously occupied by the third 8K ROM chip helped in clearing space for the additional RAM.

The increased ROM permitted booting the operating system from the integral Winchester disk rather than from a floppy, a process that is four to five times faster. With the help of only a small amount of extra ROM code, the Rainbow 100 + automatically adjusts to any additional RAM that the user inserts to support application software requiring more memory. In contrast, the Rainbow 100 requires the user to enter any changes in RAM as part of setup; in other personal computers, the user may have to remove the cover of the system unit and adjust switches.

The additional ROM has also permitted improving the international language capability of the Rainbow 100 +. The Rainbow 100 operates in conjunction with 15 different ROM sets, one for each of the 15 Digital personal computer keyboards representing 10 languages (and dialects of several). The Rainbow 100 + instead uses only five three-language ROM sets for all 15 keyboards. One ROM set (English, French, and German) accounts for more than 70 percent of worldwide markets. If the desired keyboard language is not included in the current ROM set, English is the default language for setup screens, opening menu, and diagnostic messages. In all cases, ROM handles translation in both directions between the 8-bit ASCII code used in the Rainbow and the particular 7-bit NRC (National Replacement Character) code corresponding to the keyboard.

Designing an integral Winchester drive into the system unit of the Rainbow 100 required minimizing the space and power consumed by the disk controller. The switching power supply was increased from 120 to 140 W in the same size package by using as the main rectifier for +5 V dc a new Schottky diode (Motorola MUR 3010PT in a T0218 package) having a thermal resistance of only 1.5°C/W. The disk controller uses Western Digital's new 1010 chip [29] with a minimum of interface and support hardware. Use of LSI technology rather than bit-slice and microcode techniques has substantially reduced the controller's chip count and power require- ments. In addition, improvement in the Winchester drive design reduced the turn-on current surge from 4.5 to 3.5 A.

A major reduction in the cost of high-resolution color CRTs permitted providing both monochrome and color graphics on the same monitor on the Rainbow 100 + without signifcant cost penalty. In addition to eliminating the need for two monitors, both monochrome and color graphics are created at a resolution of 800 pixels across. In addition, monochrome graphics has been extended from 4 to 16 shades of gray.

Extended System Software

The MS/DOS and CP/M-86/80 operating systems and their respective sets of unique files reside on the integral Winchester disk drive. The disk space is partitioned so that each operating system recognizes a fixed portion of the disk as its file structure (any other operating system can also coexist on the hard disk as long as it is assigned a unique partition). As part of disk installation with the Winchester's utility diskette, users may partition the 10M bytes of storage in several ways: 5 and 5, 8 and 2, 10 and 0, or four partitions of 2.5M bytes each. Database transfers to and from diskettes are supported by utility software that permits each operating system to both read and write the other system's file structure. That is, MS-DOS can read a CP/M-86/80 diskette file and CP/M-86/80 can write an MS-DOS file, and vice-versa.

Both the MS-DOS and CP/M-86/80 operating systems as supplied by their developers were modified by Digital to take advantage of Rainbow's specific architectural characteristics. For example, the terminal emulation and file-transfer functions of these operating systems were hardware-oriented and so device-dependent. In addition, neither operating system included means for handling communications interrupts or for matching specific operating parameters such as baud rate and parity. By providing device-independent software interfaces for these functions, current Rainbow application programs become directly transportable to future Rainbow models. Two other software extensions support improved video and keyboard perfor- mance with both operating systems. A device-independent fast video out function provides a method for updating screen data a line or block at a time, rather than a character at a time. A 16-bit keyboard interface was added as well to simplify writing application code and speed up program execution. With a level 2 (8-bit) interface, striking a function key generates several characters (as many as five in the Rainbow), which must be read in sequence by application code. With a level 1 (16-bit) interface in the Rainbow, the keyboard generates only one 16-bit quantity, 8 bits of flags and an 8-bit keycode. Computers running CP/M-80 or CP/M-86 customarily replace defective areas of the disk medium at the block level, which on a Winchester disk consists of 4K or 8K bytes. The Rainbow's replacement scheme is instead based on 512-byte sectors, which makes more efficient use of the disk space reserved for replacement.

The memory disk concept has been applied to make use of available RAM space under both MS-DOS and CP/M-86/80 operation. For example, if a Rainbow 100 + has been equipped with maximum RAM of 896K bytes and only 256K bytes are needed for a program, the free space is partitioned as a disk drive with its own name and sized in any multiple of 64K-byte increments. Typically, the memory disk is used for temporary files; without rotational latency or seek time, they are accessed at processor speed. The memory disk is set up at boot time under MS-DOS and at any time under CP/M-86/80 without rebooting.

The incremental backup function on Rainbow personal computers saves time and floppy diskettes by avoiding copying unchanged files. (Note that it takes 22 floppies each of 400K bytes to back up a full Winchester disk.) The user can specify particular Winchester files and/or categories of files for floppy backup, and the remaining files on the disk will not be copied. Similarly, floppy-based backup files can be selectively restored to the hard disk.

IV. DECmate II Personal Computer

DECmate II (Fig. 9) [30]–[32], [34], [35] is built around the 6120 custom CMOS processor chip originally developed for the DECmate I desktop-class computer [2]. The 6120 chip, which employs a 12-bit word length, implements an advanced version of the PDP-8 minicomputer architecture (PDP-8 +), executes an extended PDP-8/A instruction set, and is organized to address two 32K-word memory domains, user memory and control memory.

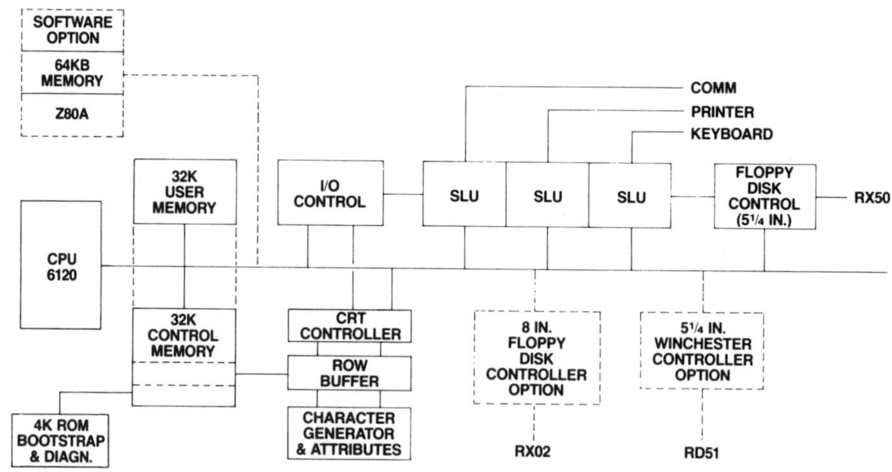

Fig. 9. Schematic system diagram of the DECmate II personal computer.

The user memory contains user programs; the control memory, which is transparent to the user, emulates the terminal functions of the machine. A 32K-word control memory provides the user with 16K words of control memory more than DECmate I, which improves execution of such applications as word processing. When a user sends a character to the screen of a video terminal, for example, an interrupt signal is sent to control memory. Code in control memory, which has a higher interrupt priority than user memory, performs all terminal input–output (I/O) operations on the character and places it in the display buffer.

Functions not available on the DECmate I were incorporated in DECmate II because of the availability of multiple display memory pages. With appropriate software, operations such as horizontal scrolling, windowing, rapid recall of HELP menus, and other advanced video operations can be performed. This superior display performance is achieved by using a portion of the control memory as a display buffer. In DECmate I, a separate 2K-word screen buffer was updated periodically but rather slowly; characters were written to the screen at a speed of about 9600 Bd, which is, maximum for many terminals. In contrast, the DECmate II display controller can perform DMA operations to the control memory at a speed of 50 to 70K Bd, a five- to seven-fold improvement. It takes almost 2 s to perform a full screen update on a DECmate I, and only about 0.1 s to do so on a DECmate II.

Two Floppy Sizes

Transition from the DECmate I 8-in diskette to the DECmate II 5-1/4-in diskette has been provided. In addition, related PDP-8-based word processing systems may also employ 8-in floppies as document diskettes. The new smaller diskette is formatted with 80 tracks and 10 sectors per track, in contrast with 77 tracks and 26 sectors per track on the 8-in floppy; it has a capacity of 204K words (408K bytes), in contrast with 256K words for the larger diskette. The controller for the new floppy diskette drive is incorporated into the basic processor board rather than implemented on separate boards as on the DECmate I. The controller has its own microprocessor and its own ROM and RAM dedicated to handling the floppy. A simple modification of the floppy disk handler permitted DECmate II software to handle the smaller floppy drive.

The disk subsystem for the 5 1/4-in drive utilizes its dedicated microprocessor to run diagnostics on start-up. This is useful in two ways: first, it decreases the burden on the 6120 processor during start-up procedures and, second, it runs a thorough series of tests and makes determinations such as whether a discovered fault lies in the drive or not.

Z80A for CP/M

DECmate II's optional auxiliary processor unit (APU), shown schematically in Fig. 10, is provided in the form of a daughter circuit card with a Z80A microprocessor and 64K bytes of associated memory that plugs into a predefined slot connecting to the internal bus. The APU permits DECmate II, like the other series of personal computers, to run on the CP/M-80 operating system.

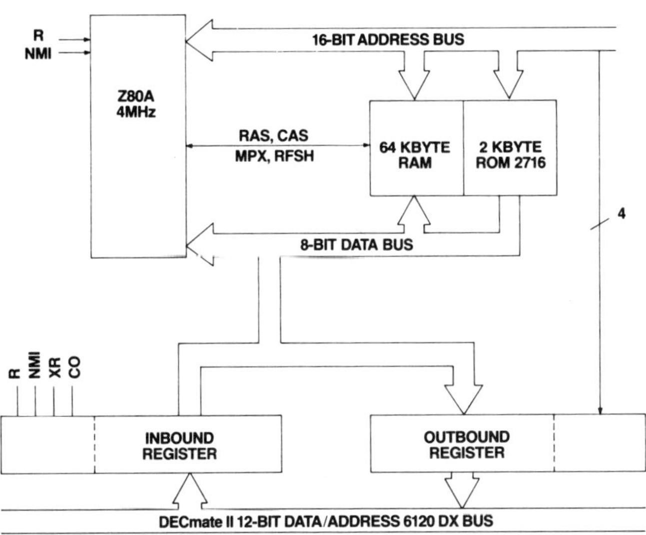

Fig. 10. Block diagram of DECmate II's Z80A-based auxiliary processor unit.

The Z80A and 6120 communicate through inbound and outbound 12-bit-wide registers linked to the DECmate II data bus. The inbound register is split into an 8-bit register for data and a 4-bit register for status, reset, and nonmaskable interrupt signals. Incoming data are either a command from the 6120 or a BIOS-requested byte for the Z80A. The outbound register lines are a combination of the Z80A 8-bit data bus and 4 address bits. Data are placed on the byte portion of the register, and commands on the nibble portion. This arrangement permits the Z80A to request an I/O process and transfer output data in one instruction cycle.

Fifteen of the 17 CP/M BIOS calls require physical input/output. Nine of these are represented in the 4-bit nibble, which leaves room in the nibble for diagnostics requests and commands from the Z80A to the 6120. The six remaining BIOS calls, along with other commands to the 6120, are placed in the data byte for secondary decoding.

At power-up, the DECmate II runs self-test diagnostics, checking CPU, memory, video logic, and floppy controllers. If the user boots a diskette with word processing or business applications running under WPS-8 or COS-310, the Z80A is not initiated. If a CP/M disk has been booted, the computer loads DECmate BIOS support code, which in turn activates a Z80A reset. The Z80A first runs diagnostics from ROM to assure proper operation and tests the Z80/DECmate II interface. At the same time, the DECmate II loads the Z80A BIOS, basic disk operating system (BDOS), and console command program (CCP) into its main memory. When the self-test is completed, the Z80A upline-loads BIOS, BDOS, and CCP into its RAM at memory transfer speeds. The CP/M remains in DECmate II memory, so warm start occurs without reloading from disk again. From then on, the Z80A becomes the CP/M master, with the 6120 slave functioning as an intelligent input/output controller, resulting in excellent CP/M performance.

The disk controller tests and identifies disks by format and content. Z80A diskettes can be mounted in the same drive used for 6120 diskettes. Application programs for DECmate II are stored in the same format as for other Digital personal computers running CP/M operating systems; thus, 48-tpi (tracks per inch) RX180 diskettes can be read and copied onto the 96-tpi diskettes used with the Professional and Rainbow series. Another daughter-board slot was added to allow use of an optional internal 5 1/4-in 10M-byte Winchester disk drive. This disk allows all four DECmate II operating systems—WPS-8, CP/M-80, COS-310, and OS/78—to coreside. A third daughter-board slot permits adding a four-plane color graphics option. This provides DECmate II users with VT125 terminal emulation.

Another component implemented on the mother board is the communications controller. This controller uses a single line and provides a full-duplex serial port for either asynchronous or synchronous operations. In synchronous operations, the user may select either bit- or byte-oriented protocols. Full modem control is provided.

V. BASIC CONFIGURATIONS

While each of the three personal computers has unique performance characteristics, their basic configurations are physically and visually similar and include two common, interchangeable modules [5], [7]. Each personal computer consists of three modules: the system unit (containing the CPU and mass storage, among other things), the keyboard, and the monochrome or color CRT (cathode-ray tube) monitor. The keyboard and CRT monitor are identical for all five current personal computer models. The multifunction system unit for the Rainbow series and DECmate II is narrower and lighter in weight than the Professional system unit. The same packaging concepts were applied for all smaller system units; they are the same size, look very much alike, but have many electronic and structural differences inside.

System Units

The larger system unit for the Professional series is 23 1/4 in wide by 14 5/8 in deep by 6 1/2 in high and weighs just under 35 lb. The user removes the cover of the system unit by actuating the two latches holding it in place at the ends. Fig. 11 shows the modules, subassemblies, and printed circuit option modules that occupy the system unit of the Professional 350. The mounting methods for all modules are designed to simplify assembly and disassembly and minimize the possibility of errors in doing so. The power supply, for instance, is aligned on the chassis by means of four post-to-hole tapered connectors, and the module is freed for removal by actuating two push–pull slides at the left end of the chassis.

The Winchester disk drive (either 5 or 10M bytes) and dual 5 1/4-in floppy diskette drive (2 by 400K bytes) are identical in size, 3 3/8 in high by 5 3/4 in wide by 9 in deep. Either type of mass storage unit, therefore, fits into the central mass storage position in the system unit; system software running on the Professional automatically determines which of the two types of mass storage is in position.

The Professional 350 system board is released by means of a lever which is accessed through the chassis between the mass storage unit positions. The board automatically slides out the back of the system unit about 1/2 in so that it can be easily grasped and removed. Each memory unit is released by depressing the release lever in the front of the chassis. Option modules are located in a six-slot card cage. Users slide the modules in and out of a backplane within the card cage on custom-designed ZIF (zero insertion force) connectors.

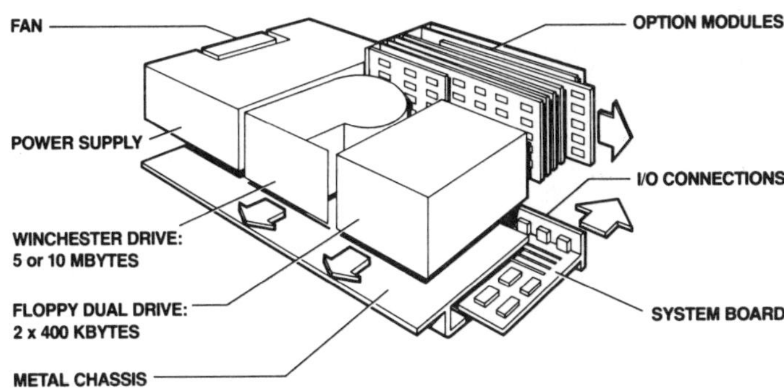

Fig. 11. System unit of the Professional 350 personal computer.

The power supply, which is contained in a 8 1/2-in wide by 4 1/8-in high by 13-in deep aluminum housing, was custom-designed to provide the 208 W of power required for the Professional 350 configuration. All hardware is located inside the enclosure (no exposed wiring), including an integral circuit breaker button. A power on/off switch projects through an opening in the front of the system box cover. The power supply meets U.S. and European standard specifications.

RFI (radio frequency interference) protection requires that most high-speed logic devices be surrounded with metal. Rather than making the cover of the system unit out of metal (it would have been heavier gauge and more expensive to fabricate), each module containing logic devices is separately enclosed in metal. To comply with FCC requirements, it is necessary that there be positive grounding contact between logic enclosures at no greater than 4-in intervals. Flat springs spaced along the card cage and I/O connector panel press against the aluminum surface of the chassis. Grounding contacts at the rear of the mass storage units are spring-loaded against the chassis. An aluminum shield around five sides of the floppy disk drive blocks RFI, and a band of magnetic shielding limits EMI (electromagnetic interference) interaction between the floppy disk and monitor when the computer is operated with the monitor on top of the system unit.

The Professional 350's system board module consists of the 10.4-in by 16-in system board, card cage, and I/O connector panel. The system board (Fig. 12) includes most of the basic elements of the system: among other things, the central processor; interface hardware for the keyboard, line printer, and asynchronous/synchronous communications; battery pack for nonvolatile on-board memory; and a backplane with six slots for option modules. The first 256K bytes of main memory are located on two 3.2-in by 5.2-in daughter boards mounted on the system board through box connectors. Each daughter board has an array of 16 64K-bit RAM chips. Another 256K bytes of main memory are provided on a backplane option module.

Fig. 12. System board and other major components of the Professional 350 personal computer.

There were several advantages in locating all nonoptional functions on one large system board—the Professional 350's board is the largest that can be economically fabricated and assembled and is very nearly the largest that can fit in the system box. The assembly, handling, and test costs of a single large board are lower than for a group of smaller boards of uniform size, even though actual IC (integrated circuit) cost is the same. Faster data transfers and savings in hardware and space may be achieved in the primary memory controller, printer interface, and other nonoptional on-board functions by linking them directly to the internal bus. A 4 1/2-in-diameter propeller fan mounted in the chassis subassembly delivers a minimum of 30 ft^3/min of cooling air over the memory units, power supply, and card cage on top of the chassis and over the chips on the system board below.

The multifunction system unit (shown in Fig. 13 without its cover) is a modification of the Professional system unit based on the needs of the Rainbow 100 and DECmate II computers. The latter two computers were to be smaller, lighter, and lower in cost than the Professional series. The lower functionality and smaller power supply (137 W) could be accommodated on a 10.4-in by 14-in system board (2 in narrower than the Professional 350's system board). The multifunction system unit is 4 in narrower and 7 lbs lighter than the Professional system unit. Daughter-board modules for the fewer options in the multifunction unit are mounted directly on the system board like the RAM modules in the Professional, thus eliminating the card cage entirely. The size and functions of the option modules were left up to the Rainbow 100 and DECmate II designers, as long as total power remained within 137 W. The reduced power requirement permits a more compact power supply, which is placed in the former location of the card cage. The cooling fan and power switch enclosure is mounted on the end of the chassis subassembly. An opening in the top of the chassis at the back corner accommodates a dc power cable connection and a link to the floppy controller module on the system board.

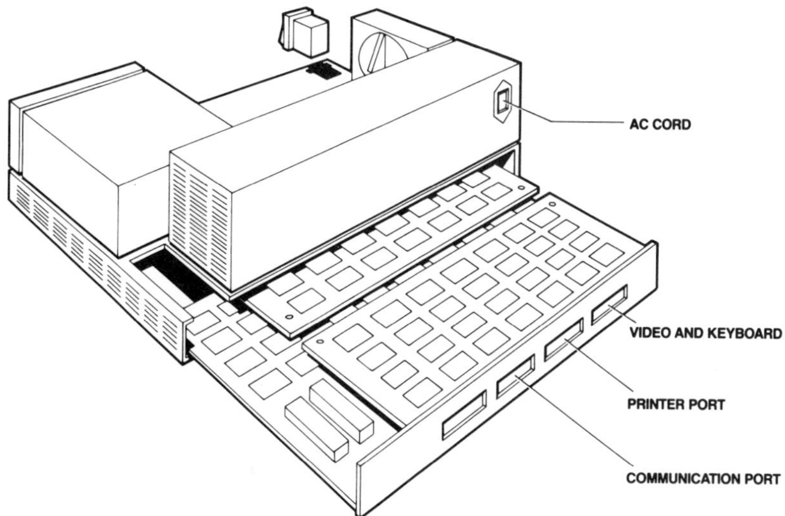

Fig. 13. Multifunction system box of the Rainbow and DECmate II computers.

Monitors

The wedge-shaped monochrome monitor (with OCLI filter) in Fig. 14 weighs 15 lbs and is 13 3/4 in wide by 11 1/2 in high by 12 1/4 in deep, very slightly larger than the CRT itself (the 12-in screen displays 24 lines by 80 or 132 columns). The color monitor has a 13-in screen but is otherwise similarly packaged. The CRT is furnished without the customary ears on the tube band because it can then be secured to the screen bezel in less space. Space is saved as well by designing the internal CRT chassis with wire forms. The viewing angle for the user can be tilted between $+5°$ above horizontal to $-25°$ with an adjustment on one side of the monitor chassis. The monitor is held steady on a thin rubber pad underneath the screen and yet can be easily swivelled to change the horizontal viewing angle. The monitor also includes a built-in handle to facilitate carrying.

The wedge-shaped control logic board, which is attached to the wire form monitor chassis with four clips, includes both control logic and the I/O panel, which is exposed through an

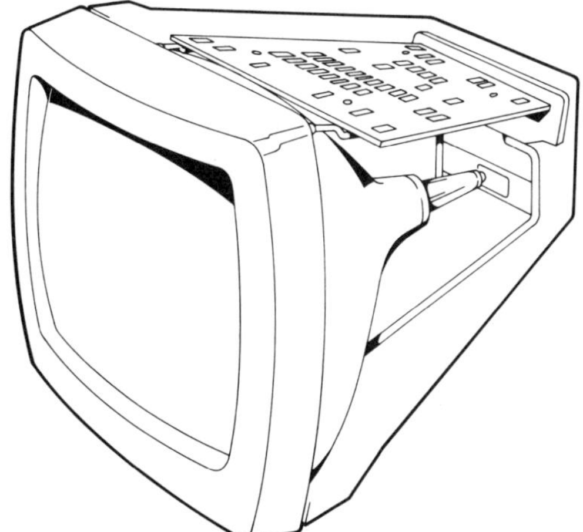

Fig. 14. Common monochrome CRT monitor of Digital's personal computers.

opening in the plastic enclosure. The I/O panel includes thumbwheels for brightness and contrast controls and receptacles for cable connectors to the system box and keyboard. One screw located just below the I/O panel secures the entire enclosure to the monitor chassis. The monitor package can accommodate either a standard commercial CRT or an OCLI-filtered CRT, which is a bonded-in 1/4-wavelength glass filter. The OCLI-filtered CRT is comparatively expensive, particularly for computers designed for price-competitive markets. High glare protection was considered vital, however, for office installation where ceiling fluorescent lighting, windows, and other glare sources are often uncontrolled.

Keyboard

The 8051-microprocessor-driven keyboard (Fig. 15), which is 21 in wide and 6 3/4 in deep, has an array of 103 keys in separate sections for standard typewriter characters (text and command entry), numerical keypad (data entry), and inverted-T cursor controls. The most demanding packaging constraint is the European ergonomics specification that the homerow (A, S, D, etc.) of the typewriter character section be no more than 30 mm above the surface the keyboard is resting on.

Fig. 15. Common keyboard of Digital's personal computers.

The single row of 16 undesignated keys at the top of the keyboard provides for specific functions in different types of applications. Function key identification strips, which are mounted just above the function keys, are kept in a covered compartment at the top edge of the keyboard. From a receptacle on the bottom of the plastic keyboard base, a 6-ft-long coil-type cord goes to the monitor's I/O panel. The cord can be pressed into a groove on the bottom of the base so that it extends out from either the left or right edge of the keyboard, whichever is more convenient for the user. The 2-in by 9-in printed circuit board containing the encoding microprocessor is mounted with the keyboard click speaker between the base enclosure and the keyboard frame assembly.

Much of the cost of electromechanical keyboards is due to a large printed circuit board on which are mounted individual switch mechanisms for each key. A membrane switch design was used instead for the keyboard to save space and reduce cost. A special key design integrates the plunger, keycap, and keycap retainer in one plastic molding.

VI. Conclusion

Table 1 summarizes the major system characteristics of the three Digital families of personal computers as of the time of writing. Many of these characteristics represent upgrades and additions since the design of the original computers—particularly in operating systems, main memory, and mass storage.

The vitality of the markets for personal computers and the intensely competitive nature of the industry present both challenge and opportunity to Digital and other personal computer manufacturers. Whatever the changes in the marketplace—and experience has shown that no

Table 1 Summary of Major System Characteristics of the Three Digital Families of Personal Computers

CHARACTERISTIC	PROFESSIONAL SERIES		RAINBOW SERIES		DECmate II
	350	325	100	100+	
MAIN MEMORY STANDARD–KBYTES MAXIMUM–KBYTES	 512 1280	 512 768	 64 256	 128 896	 96 160
MASS STORAGE 2 X 400-KBYTE DUAL DISKETTE	 •	 •	 •	 •	 •
10-MBYTE WINCHESTER INTEGRAL	 •		 •	 •	 •
CPU(S)	FII (PDP–11/23)		Z80A/8088 DUAL MICROPROCESSORS		6120 (PDP-8+) MICRO– PROCESSOR AND Z80A (OPTIONAL)
OPERATING SYSTEM(S)	P/OS RSX-11M-PLUS RT-11 ULTRIX, VENIX, IDRIX(UNIX) UCSD p-SYSTEM CP/M-00		MS-DOS CPM-86/80 CONCURRENT CP/M UCSD p-SYSTEM		WPS-8 COS-310 CP/M-80 OS-78
OPTION SLOTS	3	1	3		3
SYSTEM UNIT SIZE SMALL (19¼"x14⅝"x6½")			•	•	•
LARGE (23¼"x14⅝"x6½")	•	•			
VIDEO 12-IN. MONO MONITOR 13-IN. COLOR MONITOR GRAPHICS	 • • •		 • • •		 • • •
I/O PORTS PRINTER (SERIAL RS232C)* COMMUNICATIONS (ASYNCH/SYNC TO 9600 B)	 • •		 • •		 • •

*LA50 PERSONAL PRINTER, LETTERPRINTER 100, OR LQP02 LETTER QUALITY PRINTER

one can predict what they will be—innovative design concepts and advancing technologies will lead to a constant flow of new personal computers.

REFERENCES

[1] D. Dickhut, B. Hashizume, and W. N. Johnson, "LSI trio calls the tunes in microcomputer's CPU," *Electronics*, vol. 53, pp. 130–135, July 17, 1980.

[2] C. P. Gerstle and D. A. White, "Custom microprocessor powers office work station," *Electronics*, vol. 54, pp. 116–119, Oct. 6, 1981.

[3] R. Ochester, "Low-cost 16-bit microprocessor has performance of midrange minicomputer," *Electronics*, vol. 54, pp. 129–133, Nov. 3, 1981.

[4] B. A. Maskas, "Single-board controller extends PDP-11 family's reach," *Electronics*, vol. 55, pp. 133–137, Mar. 10. 1982.

[5] C. N. Abernathy, E. M. Comstock, and C. W. Fontaine, "Make personal computers more effective by applying ergonomics," *Comput. Technol. Rev.*, vol. II, pp. 101–105, Spring–Summer, 1982.

[6] P. C. Kotschenreuther and W. A. H. Engelse, "Personal computer packs a minicomputer punch," *Electronics*, vol. 55, pp. 99–104, July 18, 1982.

[7] R. Gonzales, "Personal computers—A packaging challenge," *Electron. Packag. Production*, vol. 22, pp. 63–76, Aug. 1982.

[8] B. J. Folsom, R. McNamara, and M. Sheffield, "Paired processors boost micro's performance," *Comput. Des.*, vol. 21, pp. 101–106, Nov. 1982.

[9] P. I. Rubinfeld, "Two-chip supermicroprocessor outperforms PDP-11 minicomputers," *Electronics*, vol. 55, pp. 131–136, Dec. 15, 1982.

[10] K. Thompson, "The UNIX Operating System," *Bell Syst. Tech. J.*, vol. 57, no. 6, pt. 2, p. 1931, July–Aug. 1978.

[11] *PRO TK Users Guide* (AA-N617B-TK), Digital Equipment Corp., Maynard, MA, Oct. 3, 1983.

[12] *PRO Users Guide for Hard Disk Systems* (AA-N603A-TH), Digital Equipment Corp., Maynard, MA, Feb. 28, 1983.

[13] *PRO Users Guide for Diskette Systems* (AA-U708A-TH), Digital Equipment Corp., Maynard, MA, Aug. 29, 1983.

[14] *PRO TK P/OS System Reference Manual* (AA-N620A-TK), Digital Equipment Corp., Maynard, MA, Feb. 2, 1983.

[15] *RSX-11M/M + Executive Reference Manual* (AA-L675A-TC), Digital Equipment Corp., Maynard, MA, Mar. 29, 1982.

[16] *RMS-11 Users Guide* (AA-L669A-TC), Digital Equipment Corp., Maynard, MA, July 5, 1983.

[17] *PRO-CP/M-80 Users Guide* (AA-V449A-TH), Digital Equipment Corp., Maynard, MA, Oct. 3, 1983.

[18] *PRO/Communications Manual* (AA-N602B-TH), Digital Equipment Corp., Maynard, MA, Aug. 29, 1983.

[19] *PRO TK FORTRAN-77 Installation Guide/Documentation Supplement* (AA-R387A-TK), Digital Equipment Corp., Maynard, MA, Oct. 30, 1983.

[20] *PRO TK COBOL-81 Installation Guide/Documentation Supplement* (AA-R758A-TK), Digital Equipment Corp., Maynard, MA, July 5, 1983.

[21] *PRO TK Pascal Users Guide* (AA-U046A-TK), Digital Equipment Corp., Maynard, MA, Aug. 29, 1983.

[22] *PRO TK Pascal Language Reference Manual* (AA-U047A-TK), Digital Equipment Corp., Maynard, MA, Aug. 29, 1983.

[23] *PRO/BASIC Language Manual* (AA-N601B-TH), Digital Equipment Corp., Maynard, MA, Oct. 3, 1983.

[24] *NPL Information Management Users Guide* (AA-W849A-TH), Digital Equipment Corp., Maynard, MA, Oct. 3, 1983.

[25] *Supercomm-20 Handbook* (AA-W924A-TH), Digital Equipment Corp., Maynard, MA, Aug. 29, 1983.

[26] *SINGRAPH Product Overview* (AA-W861A-TH), Digital Equipment Corp., Maynard, MA, Aug. 29, 1983.

[27] *Maps/PRO Graphics Users Guide* (AA-X577A-TH), Digital Equipment Corp., Maynard, MA, Oct. 30, 1983.

[28] *PRO TK Core Graphics Library Manual* (AA-619A-TK), Digital Equipment Corp., Maynard, MA, Feb. 28, 1983.

[29] J. V. Jaworski, "Flexible controller mates with popular Winchester drive," *Electron. Des.*, vol. 31, no. 9, pp. 175–182, Apr. 28, 1983.

[30] *DECmate II* (EB-24827-18), Digital Equipment Corp., Maynard, MA, 1983.

[31] L. H. Eisenberg, "Gold key unlocks barriers between personal computing and office automation," *PERSONAL and PROFESSIONAL*, pp. 40–44, June 1983.

[32] M. J. Forbes, *Word Processing Procedures for Today's Office* (EY-00019-DP). Bedford, MA: Digital Press, 1983.

[33] *Guide to personal computing*, 2nd ed. (EB-24501-18), Digital Equipment Corp., Maynard, MA, 1983.

[34] *DECmate II Programmers Reference Manual* (EK-DECM2-RM-001), Digital Equipment Corp., Maynard, MA, May 1983.

[35] *DECmate Word Processing Technical Notebook* (AA-J356B-TK), Digital Equipment Corp., Maynard, MA, Apr. 1983.

[36] A. M. Seybold, "The new top contender," *Digital Rev.*, pp. 23–27, Oct., 1983.

[37] J. Cohler, "Benchmark: Rainbow vs. IBM PC," *Digital Rev.*, pp. 28–40, Oct. 1983.

6

The Wang Professional Image Computer: A New Dimension to Personal and Office Computing

FREDERICK A. WANG, AHMED H. M. EL-SHERBINI, STAN FRY, MIKE SMUTEK, AND NANCY WEBB

Wang Laboratories has been at the leading edge of office automation technology. The Wang Professional Image Computer (PIC) offers image processing technology for the office environment. This computer can capture, create, display, alter, store, retrieve, and transmit images in real time. Using the system, it is feasible to process numeric, textual, and pictorial information. In this chapter the architecture and the technical features of this personal computer are described.

The Editors

I. INTRODUCTION

Office automation is based on the development and application of six technologies [1]:

1) Data Processing
2) Word Processing
3) Image Processing
4) Audio Processing
5) Networking
6) Human Factors

In spite of all the office automation products available today, the user's needs for image processing capabilities and advanced systems integration have not yet been met [2]–[6]. The storage of and access to written information which comes into an organization from the "outside world" is still a manual process, even if the organization has office automation equipments. Companies that produce documents that require input from many different sources need to have the ability to create, modify, and transmit documents with images quickly and efficiently.

Traditionally, computer manipulation of images was a task that only large machines could accomplish [7], [8] because of the following reasons:

1) Dealing with digitized images means manipulating huge amounts of data (several million bits per image) which was beyond the capabilities of small machines.
2) Real-time performance required in many applications (such as the office) was not possible due to the limited speeds of the available microcomputers.

The authors are with Wang Laboratories Inc., Lowell, MA 01851, USA.

Fig. 1. A PIC photograph.

3) The memory capacity required far exceeded that available on the small machines.
4) Permanent storage of such large amounts of data was very expensive.

Now, the Wang Professional Image Computer (PIC), shown in Fig. 1 offers image processing technology at the desktop level.

Based on the Wang Professional Computer (PC), the PIC includes a desktop, cameralike scanner to digitize images from a sheet of paper, a high-resolution monitor capable of displaying the image, and a desktop thermal printer capable of printing the image. The PIC image processing software permits users to scan, digitize, create, display, alter, store, retrieve, and transmit images. These images can be merged with text. The PIC can handle image information that includes pictures, handwritten notes, margin notations on correspondence, drawings, as well as text. With PIC, the ability to process images, words, and data, and to communicate and transmit that information locally or remotely within Wang's entire family of compatible office products is now available in a single workstation.

The PIC is an integration of the six technologies on one system. With its imaging capabilities, the PIC is more than a personal computer, more than an image storage and retrieval device, more than a facsimile machine, and more than a management workstation. It is a synergistic computer with all the fundamental features adding up to make it a superior office automation tool.

The next section gives a brief description of the Wang PC on which the PIC is based. Section III presents an overview of the PIC, Sections IV, V, and VI give a detailed description of the PIC hardware and software components, the architecture, and the applications.

II. Wang PC

The Wang PC [9] is a key element in our overall office automation strategy. Its main characteristics are summarized in Table 1. The Wang PC uses an Intel 16-bit 8086 microprocessor running at up to 8 MHz; an optional 8-MHz 8087 co-processor can be installed for high-performance numeric data processing. The 8086 and its 8087 co-processor communicate

Table 1 Wang Professional Computer Summary

	Standard	Optional
Processor	8086 16-bit microprocessor	8087 numeric data processor
Memory	128K-byte RAM	128K bytes, 256K bytes, or 512K bytes for a total of up to 640K bytes
Storage	320K-byte diskette drive	2nd 320K-byte diskette drive or 5M-byte fixed Winchester drive
Communications	RS-232C adapter	Asynchronous Communications: TTY 2236DW terminal emulation Synchronous Communications: 2780/3780/WPC protocol Emulation of the following terminals: VS 2246S VS 2256C OIS 5536-4 ALLIANCE 5536-4
Operating system	Microsoft DOS	CP/M 80 emulator
Languages	Microsoft BASIC-86 interpreter	Microsoft BASIC compiler Microsoft COBOL Microsoft FORTRAN Microsoft Pascal
Applications		Wang PC-Word Processing PC Database PC Multiplan Third-party general business applications
Printer	Parallel printer connector	20 CPS Daisy 80 CPS Matrix Third-party parallel printers Third-party serial printers
Monitor		Wang Monochrome Display with Character or Character and Graphics capabilities, or a customer-supplied NTSC B & W or color television, or B & W or RGB color monitor

with each other via a local interprocessor bus. Both processors communicate with memory and I/O components via the system bus by means of address latches, data transceivers, and a bus controller chip. The processor block diagram is shown in Fig. 2.

The system board memory includes 128K bytes of dynamic RAM that can store system programs, application programs, or data. The 64-kbit RAM chips that are used have 200-ns access time and 350-ns cycle time, achieving high memory array density at reasonable cost. An optional extended memory board augments the 128K bytes of standard system memory with 128, 256, or 512K bytes of extended dynamic RAM with parity check. The four-channel DMA Controller (direct memory access) allocates one channel for dynamic RAM refresh, leaving three channels available for general use. It transfers only byte data, not word data. The maximum DMA transfer rate is 300K bytes/s. The controller is programmed for rotating priority to give

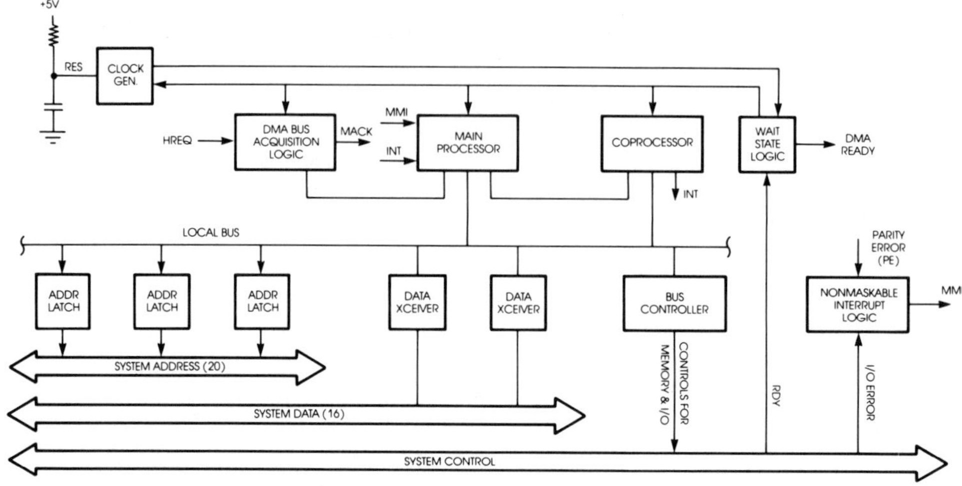

Fig. 2. Wang PC processor block diagram.

every channel equal access to the system bus. The system bus provides 16 bidirectional data lines, 20 address lines, and miscellaneous control signals. The 8086 is normally the bus master; it relinquishes the bus and grants it to the DMA controller or the 8087 when either device requests a bus cycle. A programmable interrupt controller provides eight levels of maskable priority interrupts.

The PC comes with a separate and detachable, ergonomically designed keyboard. The keyboard contains a dedicated microprocessor that accepts commands from the 8086 while retrieving both keyboard status data and keystroke data. The PC's operating system is the Microsoft Disk Operating System (MSDOS), which is a 16-bit industry standard operating system. As enhanced by Wang, this operating system has a user interface designed to be used by the professional. The system is interactive and menu driven.

The system has an Extended Programmable Communication Interface (EPCI) which is programmed by the 8086 to support RS-232C asynchronous serial data communications in full or half-duplex mode. It also has a parallel peripheral interface chip (PPI) which implements the Parallel I/O interface. The floppy disk controller (FDC) operates one or two 5.25-in double-sided, double-density, floppy disk drives recorded at 48 tracks/in (320K bytes). The diskette drive is enclosed in the lightweight, compact enclosure.

Table 2 PIC System Required and Optional Hardware and Software

	Required	Optional
Hardware	• PC chassis—8-slot *OR* 5-slot • 512K-byte Memory Expansion Card • 10M-byte Winchester Disk and Controller Card • Text/Image/Graphics Card • Wang Image Monitor • PC Keyboard	• Scanner/Printer Card • Image Scanner • Wang Thermal Printer • LIS-12 Laser Imaging System • Local Communications Option • Local Interconnect Option • Remote Communications Option
Software:	• Image Processing • Image Composition	• Integrated Word Processing • Integrated Notebook • Integrated Database • Image Forms-Fill

III. OVERVIEW OF THE PIC

The PIC is a highly integrated office product designed to capture, manage, and communicate various forms of information, including image, text, data, and voice. With its extensive communications and networking capabilities, the PIC is also a multifunction workstation which can be linked to other Wang systems, including the VS, OIS, and Alliance. The PIC's design is based upon the Wang PC. The imaging capabilities enable several operations: scan, display, alter, integrate with structured and unstructured information, store, retrieve, and communicate. These capabilities are enabled by compatible plug-in controller cards and add-on imaging components and imaging software. Required and optional system components are summarized in Table 2. Fig. 3 shows the data flow in the PIC, while Fig. 4 shows the PIC system cards and connections.

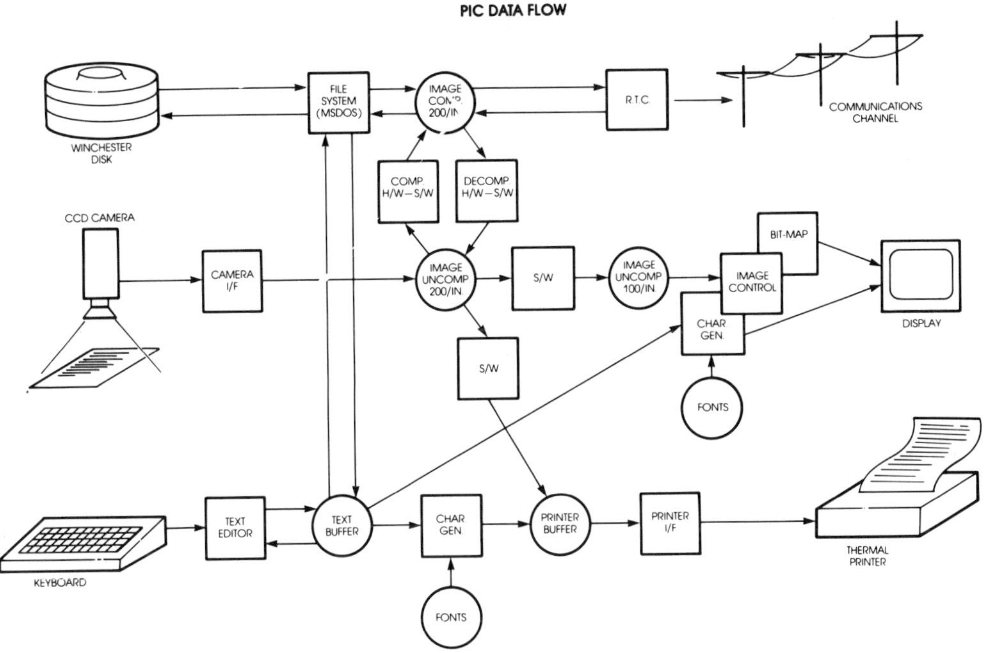

Fig. 3. PIC data flow diagram.

IV. PIC HARDWARE

The major hardware components that upgrade the Wang PC into a PIC are the image scanner, the thermal or laser printer, the camera/printer interface card, the high-resolution monitor, and the CRT controller.

The Image Scanner

The PIC image scanner, pictured in Fig. 5, is a desktop scanning device used to input images into the PIC. It consists of a flat base upon which the material to be scanned is placed face up. An adjustable upright column mounted to the base supports the scanning assembly above the document and lets the user zoom in or out. A reticule projected down through the lens of

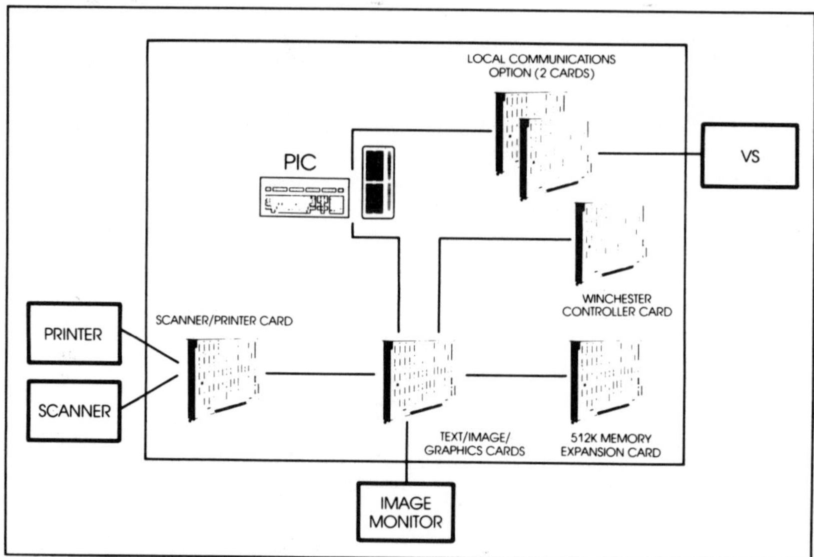

Fig. 4. PIC system diagram.

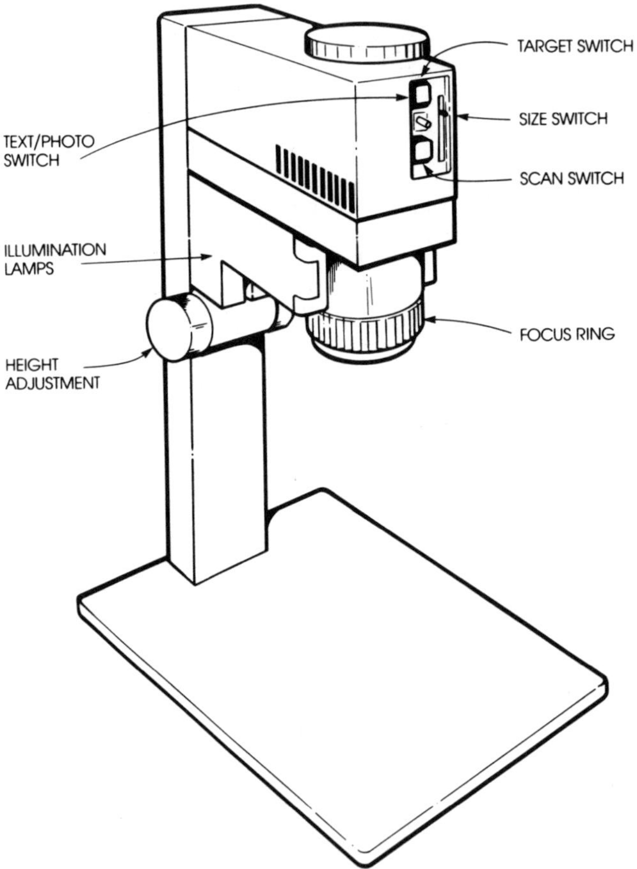

Fig. 5. PIC image scanner.

the scanning assembly and onto the document provides a visible frame for positioning the document and targets for adjusting the focus. Lamps for illumination are provided in fold-out arms mounted to the scanning assembly.

The face-up scanning arrangement is an important part of the camera design. It gives the user the ability to easily scan thick material, such as books or magazines, and sections of oversize material, such as engineering drawings or blueprints. It makes it easy for a user to target in on a specific area, and to point to or write on the document while it is in scanning position.

The scanner supports two modes of operation: a text mode and a photo mode. In the text mode, the camera is set to scan any document that contains text or typing, and in the photo mode the camera will output a dithered or "half-tone like" images which are useful for media containing photographs [10]–[12]. The scanner uses a custom designed fixed aperture lens. The lens focuses the input document onto a linear CCD array which is 1728 X 1 pixels in size. The array, which moves smoothly across the image plane while scanning, is mounted on a movable carriage driven by a lead screw. A complete scan cycle takes approximately 12 s: 2 s to move the reticule out of the way, 4 s active scan time, and 6 s to return to the rest position. The scanner digitizes at a resolution of 200 dots per inch, providing resolution equivalent to group-3 facsimile system.

The electronics in the scanner consists of a microprocessor, an analog-to-digital converter, and a high-speed signal processor. The microprocessor performs control functions of communicating with the host interface, monitoring and responding to the controls on the operators panel, turning the lamps on and off, operating the motor which drives the lead screw, performing power-on diagnostics, and providing input to the signal processor. The signal processor thresholds the digital video signal to produce the binary image data. It is programmed to dynamically adjust its threshold to compensate for variations in document contrast and lighting [13].

The data out of the signal processor are sent serially to the interface board within the PIC chassis. There the data are deserialized and transferred via direct memory access (DMA) into the main memory of the CPU. The data are clocked at 1.25 MHz during the active part of each scan line with a dead time of about 430 μs between scan lines. A large FIFO register buffers the data to accommodate the worst case latency of the DMA channel. During the active portion of the scan, the data transfer rate of the present camera averages about 120 000 bytes/s. Once begun, the scan cycle proceeds without interruption so the CPU is required to accept the entire 475 200 bytes of image data within just 4 s. A block diagram of the scanner electronics is shown in Fig. 6.

CRT Monitor and Controller

The PIC uses an interlaced monochrome display with an active display area of 800 X 600 pixels which can show both characters and bit-mapped image. The 12-in screen has an active area of approximately 8 by 6 in, producing equal pixel density of 100 pixels/inch in each direction and eliminating anamorphic distortion. Furthermore, at normal size, the displayed data have been decimated to a nominal density of 100 pixels/inch so that an image as viewed on the screen is close to its true size.

The display is used in both negative and positive contrast modes. Images (and images combined with text) are usually displayed as black on a white background, a feature that avoids giving the impression that the displayed image is a "negative" or a "blueprint." Furthermore, because large areas are often illuminated as a result, a white color (rather than green phosphor) was preferred because it is more pleasing to look at. Text-only screens such as menus are usually displayed as white characters on a black background, a presentation common for most CRT displays.

The CRT controller is self-contained and includes bit-map, text, and font memory on a single 8 X 12-in printed circuit board which fits in a standard "option" slot in the chassis. The

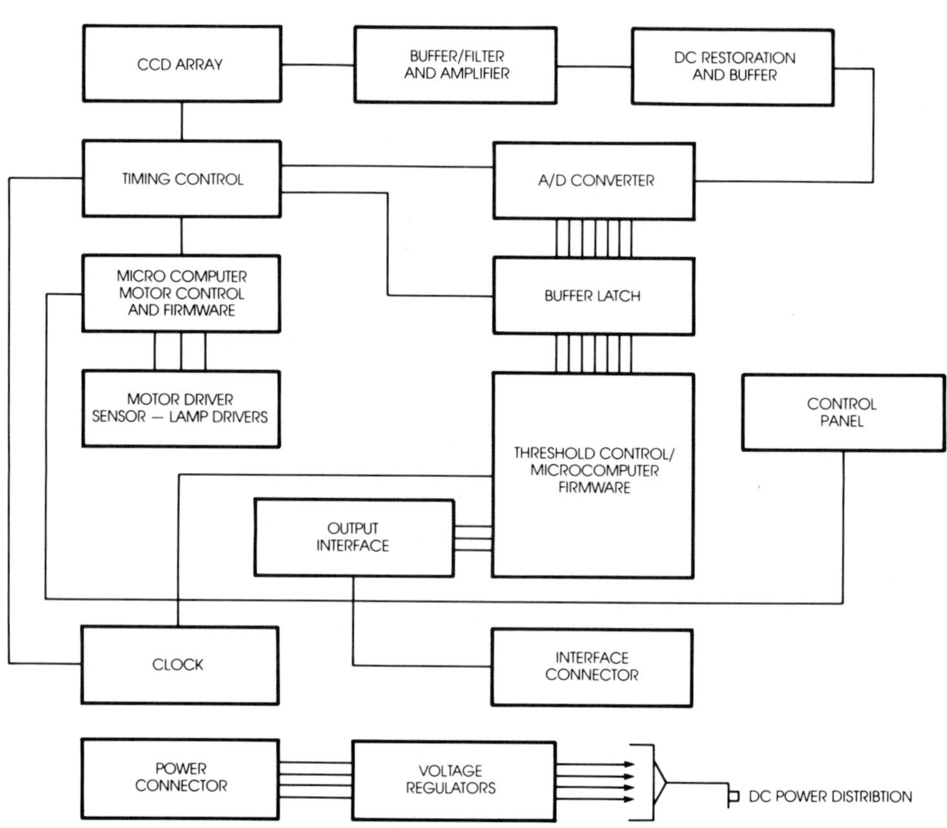

Fig. 6. Block diagram of scanner electronics.

implementation uses two graphic controllers (GCs), one for text and the other for image and graphics. All of the memory on the controller board is accessed through the GCs which arbitrate memory accesses and perform memory refreshes. None of the memory appears in the PC memory address space. Bulk data transfers can be performed in either direction by DMA through the graphic controllers and the DMA facilities of the CPU.

The number of pixels of data which must be delivered to the screen in a given time is proportional to the refresh rate, i.e., the vertical frame rate of the display. In general, supporting a higher frame rate requires faster memory devices or a wider data path. To help keep the memory bandwidth and device costs down, the display employs interlace at a vertical rate of 40 Hz. The interlace technique works well as long as the display's spatial frequencies are band limited in the vertical direction. Fortunately, for most actual images this is true and the resultant display is flicker-free.

The controller provides two separate display planes, one for characters and one for bit-maps. The two planes are operated by separate GC controller devices which are synchronized but otherwise operate independently. The two GC devices must be synchronized by the software initially at power up and whenever the basic timing parameters of the GCs are changed. The GC controlling the character display is designated as master and the bit-map GC as the slave. During synchronization, the slave monitors the timing signals of the master and "locks-on" within a few frame times after which both GCs are "started." Once started, the GC's synchronization process is over and both free run independently. Obviously, the timing parameters for the two must be equivalent or they will immediately get out of synchronization. Also, both are driven by clock signals derived from the same crystal-controlled oscillator to prevent any long-term drift in their timing. The video signals from the two planes are combined for display by a loadable look-up table arrangement which provides considerable flexibility.

Printers

For hardcopy printouts, the PIC supports two high-quality printers: the Wang thermal printer and the laser imaging system model LIS-12.

The Wang thermal printer, which connects to the scanner/printer card, can print both image and text. This compact (4.4-in height, 11.4-in depth, 16.5-in width, and 12-lb weight), high-resolution peripheral prints at 200 dots/in.

The LIS-12 laser imaging system provides high-quality outputs for PIC generated images, text, and documents integrating image and text. The LIS-12 prints at speeds of up to 12 pages/min at a print resolution of 300 dots/in. LIS-12 consists of a laser xerographic printing system and a text/image/graphics processing unit containing all the printer electronics. The printer supports numerous paper sizes up to 11 × 14 in and 26 different character sets including Boston, Courier, Geneva, Gothic, and Prestige elite [14].

V. PIC SOFTWARE

The PIC offers six major software functions which provide the generic tools required to create custom applications. One of the key areas of the PIC is the ability to maintain structured and unstructured information in a database. Integrating images with the tools of a database permits the user to perform functions not available on existing personal computers or host computers. Coupling the powerful query capabilities of the database products with the PIC attached to the hosts systems permits the user to store and retrieve large volumes of information. Images have been integrated with three database products on the PIC. Another key area of the PIC is the composition of images and the integration of images with word processing. The PIC functions are described in the following subsections.

Image Processing

The image processing core software allows the user to create, review, print, delete, send, and receive documents containing image pages. Once an image document has been created, the user can capture (scan and digitize) images, manipulate image content, and store images on disk. When an image page is displayed, the user can perform operations such as view half of an image, view an image in the positive (white background) or in the negative (dark background), scroll through an image horizontally and vertically, and lighten or darken an image. The aspect of an image can be changed from portrait (vertical) to landscape (horizontal), that is, rotating the image 90° [15], [16]. Furthermore, a portion of the image can be viewed at the size that it was originally scanned, and can be enlarged or reduced by a factor of 2 [17]–[20]. The user can also insert image pages into any location of the document, replace, delete, or print image pages (either on the thermal or the laster printer), and enter search words to aid in the recall of particular documents for reviewing or printing.

In terms of actual file structure, each image file contains one "image document." There may be several separate images ("pages") in a file, each identified by a unique image ID. This image ID is the method by which the various keywords and data blocks which make up an image are logically combined into a "page." Throughout this chapter, the terms "document" and "page" will refer to image files and individual images. There are four types of information stored in PIC image files:

1) An index block which allows for reconstruction of an Integrated Index entry.
2) A Page Table which maps images into "pages" in an image "document."
3) A header block for each image which describes parameters specific to that image.
4) The actual image data. Image data are stored in 2K blocks and referenced by CBAM (compressed B-tree access method) pointers [21], [22].

Table 3 Compression Ratios of the Two Coding Schemes

	Picture Resolution—100 dots/in	Picture Resolution—200 dots/in
1-D Modified Huffman Code	5.025	8.794
2-D READ Code ($k = 4$)	9.05	12.955

Every image is compressed (coded) before transmission or storage on the disk. Compression reduces storage requirements and allows for faster transmission [23]–[26]. The compression scheme that we use is the one-dimensional modified Huffman run length code [27]. This coding scheme is the CCITT (the International Telephone and Telegraph Consultative Committee) Recommendation T.4 for group-3 facsimile machines [28], which makes Wang PIC compatible with most of the existing facsimile machines. Huffman code is a compact uniquely decodable code and is implemented in an efficient table look-up fashion. Several compression schemes were considered (e.g., two-dimensional READ code [29]) but the one-dimensional Huffman was chosen for ease of implementation, reduced memory and processing time requirements, and compatibility reasons [28]–[31]. Table 3 shows the average compression ratios of the two coding schemes for different picture resolutions. On the average, 100 compressed images can be stored on the 10M-byte disk.

Image Composition

Full-page images often include areas which are not needed by the application into which the images are integrated. In addition, it is desirable to be able to create new images and new visual effects by combining sections from a number of images. This created a need for a method to define areas of images, and to associate these areas in a manner which would be easy for an application to access.

The PIC uses a composite structure of descriptions defining image cropping parameters, relative positioning of image sections, display formatting information, etc. This general structure allows for combining many different types of media, although currently it is implemented only for images. The full-page image is cropped by reference, leaving the original data intact. By accessing images only by reference, many composites can share the same image data without the storage overhead of multiple copies of the same data. This also provides the ability to return to the original data and recrop if the desired effect was not achieved by the initial definition. Changes to a "master" image can be made without necessarily having to respecify all composites which reference it. Storage requirements can be reduced further by physically cropping portions of the image which the user decides will never be needed, or by scanning shorter sections of an image.

The Composite Editor is part of the Image Processing Editor. Using the standard PC keyboard, rectangles may be defined and positioned into a composite. A group of image descriptions is given a unique name which can be accessed by applications. Using the Composite Editor, "libraries" of composites are created which may be accessed globally throughout the system. Simply stated, the image composition package allows the user to perform composition of image information in a manner similar to "cut-and-paste" operations performed with paper.

Integrated Word Processing

The first application into which images were integrated was the PC Word Processing (WP) package. Since the PC/WP was a released product with a defined document structure already in use in the field, images had to be integrated in a way which did not change the existing document structure. Documents created by PIC/WP had to be editable on PCs without the imaging option.

This led to the implementation of the composite token and the complex information descriptor (CID) file. Each WP document has associated with it a file which contains descriptions of images in that document (composites). The composites are referenced by token characters in the document text stream. Each token has an associated ID number which refers to an entry in the CID file. The token is a flag to the Word Processing Editor to escape to software which can interpret the external data. Since the specifics of the composite are generally unknown to word processing, this allows the flexibility to add other media, such as graphics, without a major impact on WP. The composite token occupies the space of a standard text character, thus the document structure is not affected. To a WP editor which does not include image processing capabilities, it is an unrecognizable character which can be displayed although not interpreted. This also facilitates manipulation of the composite within the document. To the user, the token is simply another character which can be accessed via normal WP functions (copy, move, search, etc.).

There are two methods of inserting a composite into a document. In either case, a composite token is placed into the document, and an ID is allocated in the CID file. The composite is taken from a global library of composites, or created interactively as a composite private to the document. In the first method, a composite library is specified, and a composite name selected from within that library. A copy of the composite is placed in the CID file. In the second method, the Image Processing/Composite Editor is invoked from within Word Processing. This makes available the full range of image processing functions. A composite built using this method may be assembled from existing and/or newly scanned images. It may be inserted in a global library, or defined solely for the use of the current document. In the latter case, the composite is placed directly in the CID file. In either case, the image sections defined by the composite are displayed at the specified position in the document. The two-plane display of the PIC provides flexibility for formatting text with images. The text may be formatted around the images, or may be entered over them. Even with the flexibility of text formatting, it may be necessary to make minor adjustments to the positioning of image sections within a composite. A "mini-editor" can be accessed during word processing without the overhead of invoking the entire image processing editor. Using the mini-editor, individual image sections may be selected and moved horizontally or vertically within the composite, while viewing the text into which the image has been placed. The repositioning is performed on the CID copies of the composite, therefore neither library composites nor image data are affected.

An example of output generated using the PIC image and text integrating capability is shown in Fig. 7.

Integrated Notebook

Integrated Notebook permits the user to define textual information (notes) and attach images and image documents to each note. The notes can be retrieved through free format text retrieval based on word or set of words in the note. Fig. 8 shows an example of attaching images in the Integrated Notebook.

This package allows the user to organize mixed information (notes/images) in a form which conceptually resembles "paper" file folder (notebook entries with images attached). Information can be created, reviewed, printed, and/or deleted. The information may be purely textually entered notes or may contain both the note and related image information. When a user creates or edits a note, the user may attach an image document (which can contain multiple image pages) by signaling to the system that image information is to be associated with the currently selected note. The image document can also be accessed by any of the other image software packages. When a user has selected (through positioning and/or searching) a note, a single keystroke will bring the associated image to the screen and the Integrated Notebook package enters normal image processing.

With the Integrated Notebook, categories can be established to aid in the organization of both text and image information; information search, at the note level, is fully word indexed

WANG LABORATORIES, INC.
One Industrial Avenue, Lowell, Massachusetts 01851

The Wang Professional Image Computer

At the heart of the Professional Image Computer is the Wang
Professional Computer. Since it uses standard PC components, the PIC
can run all of the usual PC applications including Wang's renowned
word processing, the Multiplan spreadsheet package, and business
graphics.

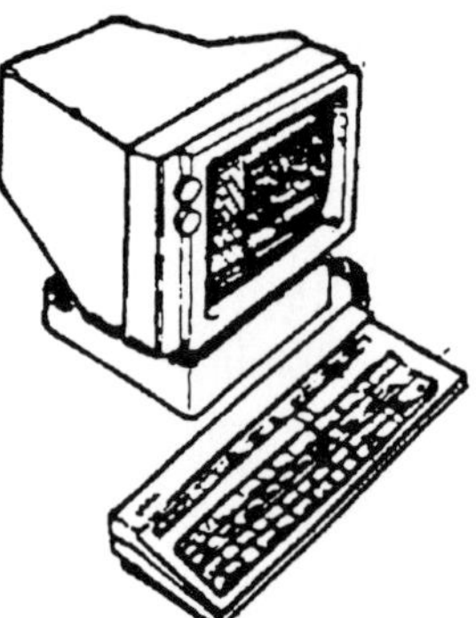

It can be used as a stand-alone personal
system, as a node in a network of PICs,
or as a workstation attached to an OIS or
VS system. The Image Capable Workstation
includes a high resolution display of 800
by 600 dots for clear, crisp images. It
has a full page bit-map which can contain
a full 8.5" x 11" image and a separate
plane of text memory which holds over
4000 characters. This allows images and
text to be combined. This display is an
option on the standard PC but is required
for imaging capabilities.

For output the Professional Image Computer
includes a quality dot-matrix thermal printer.
The printer complements the image scanner and
permits images, text, and graphics to be output
quickly, quietly, and cleanly. Together with the
small size and low cost, these features will make
the printer an irresistable component at every
workstation.

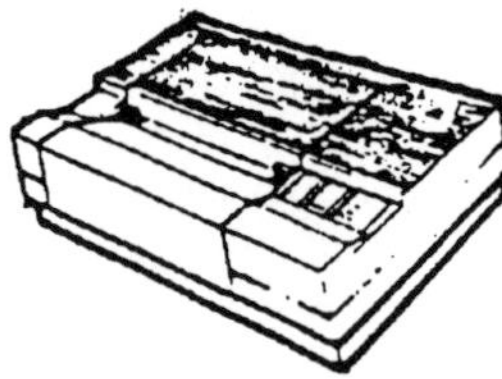

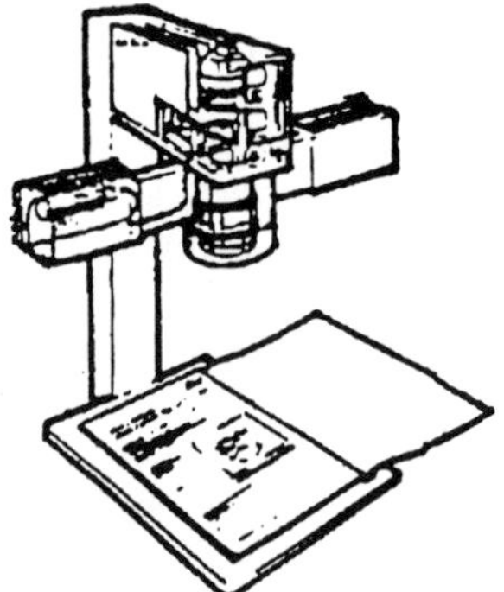

The Wang Image Scanner is the most
unique component of the system.
Advanced image scanning techniques let
it scan full pages with amazing clarity
and definition. Yet, true to the Wang
tradition, the operation of the scanner
is easy and uncomplicated. Best of all,
the scanner is priced so that it is
reasonable to include one with every
workstation.

Fig. 7.   Example of a page produced by using the PIC image and text integrating capability.

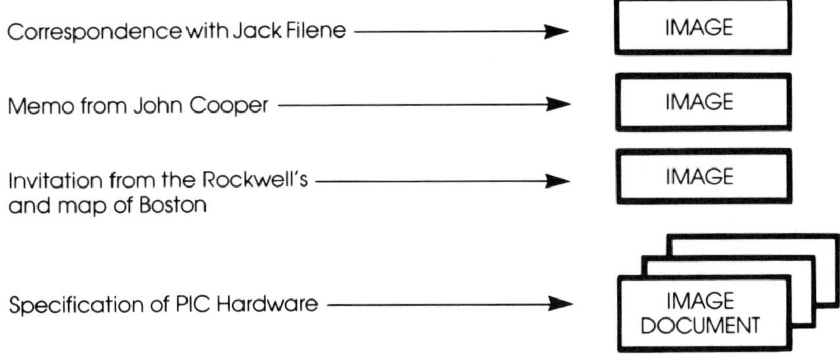

Any word or words in the text could be entered to retrieve the note and image(s).

Fig. 8.   Example of attaching images in the Integrated Notebook.

allowing the user to search and recall notes fitting the entered criteria. Operation of the notebook, down to the note level, is identical to that of PC Notebook [32]. The new image feature of notebook allows the user to "attach" specific notes to specific image documents.

Integrated Database

Integrated Database is a relational database which permits the user to define structured data and text and to relate images with each data record. Fig. 9 shows examples of data records in the Integrated Database. Queries may span many record types, and can be based on any of the information within the record, including the identification of the images in the data record. Information search within the database for image fields or text fields is word-indexed allowing

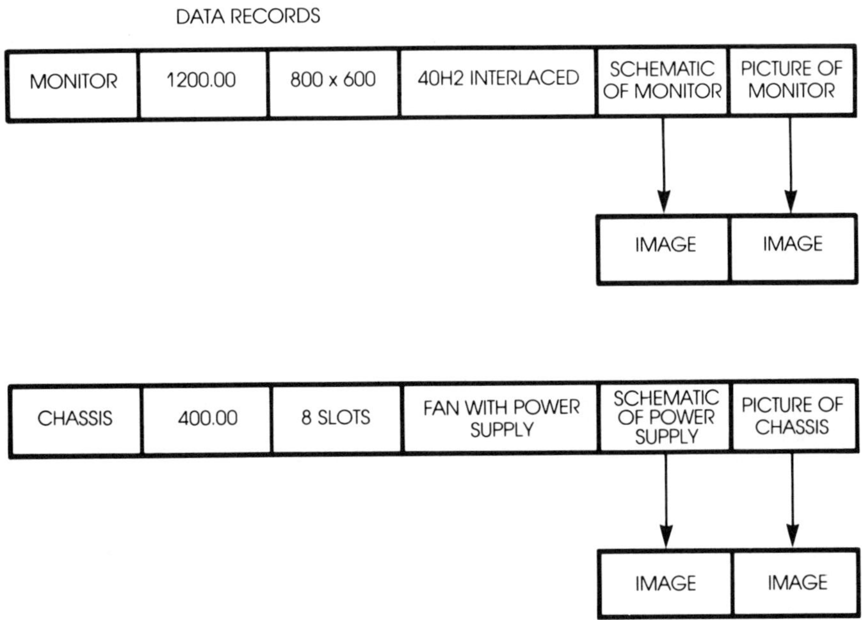

Fig. 9.   Examples of data records in the Integrated Database.

the user to enter categories of information to aid in the search and recall of the images and the associated data records.

When Integrated Database is selected, the same PC database selections are available to the user from the database main menu. Operations of database, down to the record and field levels, are identical to those of PC database [32], [33]. The new image feature of database allows the user to "attach" specific fields to specific image document.

If a field is to point to an image document, it is created normally (up to a maximum field length of 50 characters) and designated as an image field. All words entered in the field are automatically word indexed and are used as a descriptive narrative of what the image document contains. The user presses the GOTO key to automatically create the image document which holds the image information. The particular field is then associated with the specific image document until the field is deleted. The image document can also be accessed by any of the other image software packages. When a user has selected (through positioning/search functions) a field, a single keystroke will bring the associated image to the screen. Fields which allow images to be attached are identified to the user through a change in the database menu options at the bottom of the screen.

Image Forms-Fill Processing

Forms-Fill provides the capability of using a relational database which is defined and manipulated through a form. The form can be a standard paper form which has been captured in the system. Fields may be defined in free format anywhere on the form.

This package allows the user to define forms, databases, records, and fields which contain both image and data information. The significant advantages of this approach are

- An image form can be used as the background for form/field definition, data entry and edit, query and response, sort, and print.
- The image form can be aligned to allow the precise positioning of fields.
- In addition to the standard field definitions (alpha, numeric, and date), a new field definition option for image information has been provided. This allows the user to go from data information to image information based on conventional data processing techniques.
- Both the image form and specific data records can be merged within word processing documents.

Five field types are supported within Forms-Fill processing: Alpha, Numeric, Date, Auto Dial, and Image Reference.

Any character or set of characters may be used as prompts and entered during format definition. The literal corresponds exactly to the typical prompting portion of normal data processing during screen definition. That is, "Enter Customer Name" would be a literal/prompt.

During form definition, the user can optionally designate an image form to be the form background information. With normal image processing, the real form can be placed under the scanner and the digitized image scanned into the system. If the user desires, the scanned form can be modified for alignment with actual field placement. The alignment would normally be used for forms where the typed entry falls slightly above or below the space designated on the form. A single copy of the background form is stored and used with each data record of the file for viewing, editing, etc. This reduces the system's storage requirements.

An "image field" is the descriptor of the image document and serves as the link to attach images to specific records in the database. The entered information for an image field "links" the current data record to image documents. Because of the flexibility that this field adds to traditional applications, an example is provided below on how this field (combined with image processing (scan and store) and traditional data processing) may be employed.

Most organizations maintain personnel databases which contain such pieces of information as individuals' names, addresses, phone numbers, positions, and salary levels. Other information associated with an individual's profile such as resumes, reviews, letters of appreciation, is filed separately on paper. With the PIC, both the data and the paper information related to individuals can be maintained in the same information database. Traditional data fields about the individual can be established on the form (name, address, etc.). Paper information attachments can also be added to the data record through image fields which have scanned documents associated with them. A record could consist of not only the data information, but image information such as a current resume, all reviews, correspondence to personnel about this person, etc. From this base of information, very detailed forms could be created that would allow for more accurate information to be maintained on employees. Once a form definition of this type has been established, individual personnel information is entered.

At any time, any individual's record can be recalled based on traditional search criteria (name, social security, employee number) as long as that information has been entered into the database. Once the record is recalled, the user can review the data portions and/or position to any image field and direct the system to go to the image document which corresponds to that field. For example, the user may wish to review the individual's letters of appreciation. The system will then enter image processing mode directly and display the image document which contains those letters. When the user is finished reviewing the information, the system is directed back to the individual's form.

All fields are automatically identified as "indexable" fields. Therefore, all data entered into the system can be searched. Information can be recalled and processed through the query function. Lists which satisfy the query request can be built, sorted, and output. While a user is executing the integrated word processing package, information within the image/forms database can be recalled, and both the image form as well as the record information can be added to (or inserted to) the integrated word processing document. When the system is directed to print information from the information database, both the form background (if used during the form definition) and the data record are output.

VI. Image Communications

One of the most important uses of image processing is the communication of image information to other systems, which is an active area of research and development [34]–[38]. A properly configured Wang PIC system equipped with the image processing software, can scan, transmit, and exchange images. It provides the following three communication options [39]:

1) local communication option
2) local interconnect option
3) remote communications option.

The communications protocol for the transfer of images requires synchronous modems, switched or leased lines, and a minimum transmission speed of 4800 bits/s.

Two applications have been created with the use of communications of images: these are TELE-SEND and TELE-MAIL.

The TELE-SEND application is used when a system user is having a phone conversation and wants to transfer (paper) information which is to be discussed in the conversation. The TELE-SEND application can be invoked and the paper can be scanned and transmitted to the receiving party. When the transmission is complete the voice conversation can continue on the same phone line.

The TELE-MAIL application permits the user to transmit images, image documents, word processing documents, or databases to a specified user. When the destination is identified, the system will deliver the specified information to the user's mailbox either through the telephone network or through local network connections.

VII. CONCLUSION

In developing the PIC, we have created an architecture that allows applications to be integrated efficiently, to fit the office business needs, in a low-cost workstation. As price/performance continues to improve, image processing will become an integral part of the office information processing environment. Among the future trends in office automation, the following topics are advancing rapidly and will reshape the future office workstations:

- Development of high-performance specialized processors
- Further integration of images with office business needs
- Integration of optical character recognition (OCR) capabilities with image processing, for efficient mixed document processing
- Development of high-capacity/low-cost storage devices
- Automatic speech recognition and synthesis, and further integration of images, speech, and text
- Powerful networking capabilities for office equipment.

The speech subsystems for the PIC will be released in the future. This combination of sophisticated image and speech processing capabilities will add a new dimension to the power of personal computers for office automation applications.

REFERENCES

[1] F. Wang, "Office automation," *Mini-Micro Syst.*, pp. 198–207, Dec. 1982.

[2] R. A. Myers, "Trends in office automation technology," *IEEE Commun. Mag.*, pp. 10–16, Sept. 1982.

[3] A. Gupta, "Emerging trends in office technology," in *Office Information Systems*. Amsterdam, The Netherlands: North-Holland, 1982, pp. 599–626.

[4] K. J. King and F. J. Maryanski, "Information management trends in office automation," *Proc. IEEE*, vol. 71, no. 4, pp. 519–528, Apr. 1983.

[5] B. R. Gaines, "From word processing to image processing in office systems," in *Proc. Int. Electrical Electronics Conf.* (Toronto, Ont., Canada, Sept. 1983), pp. 622–625.

[6] N. Naffah, "Editorial," in *Office Information Systems*. Amsterdam, The Netherlands: North-Holland, 1982.

[7] *Proc. IEEE* (Special Issue on Image Processing), vol. 69, May 1981.

[8] E. Hall, *Computer Image Processing and Recognition*. New York: Academic Press, 1979.

[9] *The Wang Professional Image Computer Guide*, Wang Labs., Lowell, MA, Dec. 1982.

[10] B. E. Bayer, "An optimum method for two-level rendition of continuous tone pictures," in *Proc. IEEE Int. Conf. on Communications*, pp. 11–15, 1973.

[11] D. Anastassiou and K. S. Pennington, "Digital halftoning of images," *IBM J. Res. Develop.*, vol. 26, pp. 687–697, Nov. 1982.

[12] J. F. Jarvis, C. N. Judice, and W. H. Ninke, "A survey of techniques for the display of continuous tone pictures on bilevel displays," *Comp. Graph. Image Process.*, vol. 5, pp. 13–40, 1976.

[13] A. Moyer, "Adaptive threshold for low cost fax," Internal Rep., Wang Labs., Lowell, MA, Mar. 1983.

[14] P. Archibald, *Fonts Manual, Version 2*, IBM Thomas Watson Res. Cent., Yorktown Heights, NY, Sept. 1977.

[15] M. Smutek, "Rotation by 90 degrees in the Wang PIC," Internal Rep., Wang Labs., Lowell, MA, Mar. 1983.

[16] R. W. Floyd, "Permuting information in idealized two-level storage," in *Proc. Symp. on Complexity of Computer Computations*. New York: Plenum Press, 1972, pp. 105–110.

[17] I. E. Abdou and K. Y. Wong, "Analysis of linear interpolation schemes for bi level image applications," *IBM J. Res. Develop.*, vol. 26, no. 6, Nov. 1982.

[18] A. Moyer, "Interpolation algorithm for Fax output and display," Internal Rep., Wang Labs., Lowell, MA, Apr. 1983.

[19] A. El-Sherbini, "Linear interpolation for the PIC," Internal Rep., Wang Labs., Lowell, MA, May 1983.

[20] ______, "Display of dithered images on the PIC monitor," Internal Rep., Wang Labs., Lowell, MA, Dec. 1983.

[21] D. Comer, "The ubiquitous B-tree," *ACM Comput. Surv.*, vol. 11, no. 2, June 1979.

[22] A. Waisman and R. Wenig, "Compressed B-tree access method for 8086," Internal Rep., Wang Labs., Lowell, MA, May 1983.

[23] A. N. Netravali and J. O. Limb, "Picture coding: A review," *Proc. IEEE*, vol. 68, no. 3, pp. 366–406, Mar. 1980.

[24] D. Ting and B. Prasada, "Digital processing techniques for encoding of graphics," *Proc. IEEE*, vol. 68, no. 7, July 1980.

[25] A. N. Netravali, F. W. Mounts, and J. D. Beyer, "Techniques for coding dithered two-level pictures," *Bell. Syst. Tech. J.*, pp. 809–819, May–June 1977.

[26] A. El-Sherbini, "An efficient coding scheme for dithered images," Internal Rep., Wang Labs., Lowell, MA, Nov. 1983.

[27] D. A. Huffman, "A method for the construction of minimum redundancy codes," *Proc. IRE*, vol. 40, pp. 1098–1101, Sept. 1972.

[28] R. Hunter and A. H. Robinson, "International digital facsimile coding standards," *Proc. IEEE*, vol. 68, no. 7, pp. 854–867, July 1980.

[29] "Proposal for draft recommendation of two-dimensional coding scheme" (a proposal by the Japanese Government), CCITT SGXIV Doc. No. 24, Aug. 1978.

[30] A. Moyer, "Evaluation of Fax run-length compression techniques," Internal Rep., Wang Labs., Lowell, MA, Feb. 1983.

[31] H. G. Musmann and D. Preuss, "Comparison of redundancy reducing codes for facsmile transmission of documents," *IEEE Trans. Commun.*, vol. COM-25, no. 11, Nov. 1977.

[32] The Professional Computer NCC Announcement, *FOCUS*, May 16, 1982.

[33] *The Wang Professional Computer Database Reference Guide*, Wang Labs., Lowell, MA, Jan. 1984.

[34] H. Teramura *et al.*, "Experimental facsimile communication system on packet switched data networks," *IEEE Trans. Commun.*, vol. COM-29, no. 12, pp. 1942–1951, Dec. 1981.

[35] O. Johnsen and A. N. Netravali, "Progressive transmission of two-tone images," *IEEE Trans. Commun.*, vol. COM-29, no. 17, pp. 1934–1941, Dec. 1981.

[36] W. Horak, "Interchanging mixed text image documents in the office environment," *Comput. Graph.*, vol. 7, no. 1, pp. 13–29, 1983.

[37] H. Tominaga and R. Itoh, "Mix mode image processing for document transmission," in *Proc. Globecom '83* (San Diego, CA, Nov.–Dec. 1983), pp. 179–183.

[38] T. Kawasaki *et al.*, "A 4800 bps full-duplex communication system for combined voice and facsimile data," in *Proc. Globecom '83* (San Diego, CA, Nov.–Dec. 1983), pp. 1261–1267.

[39] A. El-Sherbini and M. Smutek, "The Wang professional image computer: An overview," in *Proc. Micro-Delcon '84* (Delaware, Mar. 1984).

7
Data General Desktop Generation Model 10: Architecture and Implementation

ROBERT C. MILLER, DONALD A. WADE, AND CHRISTINE WALLIS

The implementation of any new product is always influenced by corporate and marketing goals. In order to benefit from the latest technology, new systems must be developed in relatively short periods of time. These factors played a key role in finalizing the design and the implementation strategy of the Data General Desktop Generation Model 10 personal computer. This chapter focuses on the salient characteristics of this computer. In particular, it focuses on the strategy of using two dissimilar processors to enable support of a broad software base as well as to facilitate future growth.

The Editors

I. INTRODUCTION

In the last three years, the nature of computing has changed dramatically. Few will argue that the product which most exemplifies the direction and magnitude of the change is the IBM Personal Computer. If only by the sheer number of systems shipped since its introduction, the IBM PC has become a *de facto* standard for desktop computing [1]. But the volume of shipments is not the sole issue. Currently, most innovative software offerings are being made in the area of personal, desktop products. Hardware vendors are challenged by this large body of horizontal and vertical software to develop systems which can take advantage of it [2]. The combination of the IBM PC and broad spectrum of user-tailorable spreadsheet programs has gone far beyond the functionality offered initially by the combination of the Apple II and Visicalc.

The low end of the computer market is also characterized by its rapid rate of change. While the lifetime of a processor at the high end of the computer market can be as long as 10 years (3–5 years typically), that of a processor at the low end is as short as 18 months. This is not a situation that encourages long study phases, followed by pilot programs, field tests, and many other stages. A new product must be brought to market quickly.

Another key characteristic of the personal/desktop market is its extreme price sensitivity [3]. Market segments can be defined within $2000 to $4000 bands. By contrast, other areas of the computer industry (e.g., mainframes and scientific systems) are more sensitive to features and performance. Individual computer buyers are increasingly aware that the real cost of owning a system only begins with the purchase price. Cost of ownership must be measured over the life of a product. Maintenance and repair costs can dwarf the original expenditure [4]. For a product to have a cost of ownership which is acceptably low, the user must be able to diagnose and fix a system failure with little or no external help.

Data General has made a large investment in operating systems, hardware diagnostics, communications software, language compilers, and database software. Additionally, DG OEM

The authors are with Data General Corporation, Westboro, MA 01580, USA.

120

Table 1 Desktop Generation Model 10 Market Requirements

Requirement	Office Automation	Small Business	Technical OEM
Access to third-party software	X	X	X
Cost-effective single user	X	X	
Concurrent communications	X		X
Small size	X		X
High-performance multiuser	X	X	
Run in hostile environments		X	X
CEO engine	X		
Physically attractive	X		
Office electrical power	X		
Floating-point capability			X
Configurability			X
Bit-mapped graphics			X

customers have made substantial investments in applications software and in Data General compatible hardware. Many companies have run into difficulties in attempting to field a new architecture which orphans their existing account base, requiring users to spend significant amounts of money to take advantage of the new "Hot Box." Our approach has been to design personal computers that are compatible with and offer the full potential of existing DG minicomputer software. We identified three broad market areas: small business, technical OEM, and office automation. The requirements for these markets are shown in Table 1.

A. Small Business System

The requirement to make third-party software available to new customers was the overwhelming consideration in this area. One objective was to add additional terminals to a low-price single-terminal system to give a cluster or "branch office" system. Clustering permits pooling of local resources and sharing of peripherals (disks, printers, etc.). Since a small business system may be used almost anywhere (an office, a back room, a warehouse, etc.), the system must be reliable, simple to operate, and survive in semi-hostile physical environments.

B. Product and System OEM

OEMs in technical areas such as engineering and CAD/CAM require a scientifically oriented workstation with fast floating-point and robust graphics capabilities. Technical OEMs have the highest need for configurability. Many add their own controllers and peripherals to the hardware supplied. They resist paying for hardware capabilities or packaging they do not use.

C. Office Automation and Decision Support

In this area we needed a workstation which could function as an engine for our CEO (comprehensive electronic office) office automation package [5]. The workstation had to offer full-fledged concurrent communications facilities to support CEO's capability of routing and sharing data of various types (messages, files, records, etc.) [6]. To provide an integrated application environment, the software would need to accept common word processor document formats and output from popular third-party applications programs. The office environment also dictated a packaging scheme which would use office electrical power, run quietly, take up little space, and be harmonious with office decor.

We wanted to design products that could be implemented quickly. Our intention was to ship systems within 12–14 months of the inception of this project.

II. Design Alternatives

Many alternative designs, running the gamut from purely hardware to purely software, could achieve the corporate and marketing goals described above. The following three were examined in greater detail.

A. Rehost DG System Software on an Industry Standard Micro

This solution met the objective of supporting industry standard hardware and third-party operating systems such as MS-DOS and CP/M-86, facilitating the availability of the applications that run under those operating systems. The processor design effort was considered to be minimal.

This approach had serious disadvantages, however. We would have to build up a complete line of peripheral controllers for a non-DG bus architecture. The magnitude of the software effort would have been overwhelming. Recoding Data General operating systems which had been written primarily in assembly language to run on another incompatible processor would be a nontrivial task. Much of our communications and data management software is also written in assembly language. While the time to develop hardware would have been short, software development would have taken substantially longer. Also, the software problem could not have been solved without compromising the company's commitment to a compatible product line.

B. Rehost Third-Party Operating Systems and Applications on a DG Processor

This approach is roughly the opposite of the previous one. (DEC's Professional Series is an example [7].) Here, most existing DG proprietary and OEM software would come for free and the engineering solution could be derived primarily from past DG processor implementations. The major problem would lie in convincing software vendors to adapt their application programs and distribution channels to stock this software for different architectures. Most third-party software companies are small and interested in adding new functionality to their products to leverage their limited resources, not in rehosting existing functionality on another machine. Clearly, this approach takes the in-house software problem and gives it to someone else with fewer resources (and possibly less incentive) to solve it. While the proprietary pieces of the product can be developed quickly, the goal of availability of third-party software is rarely met.

C. Two Processors in the Same Box

In general, software performs best when it runs on the system for which it was originally coded. Though many microsoftware vendors are recoding their applications in high-level languages to increase their portability, most applications have been optimized to the hardware characteristics (at least the instruction set) of the processor on which they originally ran.

The third approach—the one we eventually pursued—is based on an architecture which offers maximum operational efficiency. It is efficient because it runs DG system software concurrently with third-party PC/DOS, MS-DOS, and CPM-86 applications on the CPU for which they were designed. A microECLIPSE processor coupled to an 8086 minimizes both the hardware and software efforts, and permits the smooth integration of third-party software at the low end of the existing DG product line while offering excellent performance characteristics. The total system cost of this dual-processor implementation is only slightly higher (less than 5 percent) than a single-processor equivalent. Before details of this design approach are discussed, it is relevant to present the specifications of the microECLIPSE.

III. MicroECLIPSE Microprocessor

The Model 10 is built around a proprietary chip set produced at our Sunnyvale semiconductor facility. The microECLIPSE chip set is implemented using an NMOS silicon-gate process with 3.5-μm channels, 10.2-μm metal pitch, and 650-Å gate-oxide thickness. It consists of a CPU chip, one to three External Microcontroller Chips (CROMs), and a System Input/Output (SIO) chip. These are interconnected by a 16-bit parallel system bus.

The microECLIPSE chip set employs a two-level microarchitecture. The CPU chip executes the kernel of the 16-bit ECLIPSE instruction set and accepts external microcode from the CROM's via a dedicated 8-bit bus. The SIO chip controls programmed I/O and Data Channel transfers and implements both ECLIPSE and microNOVA I/O busses. The SIO chip also contains a power monitor, a programmable interval timer, a real-time clock, and an asynchronous communications port. A soft-console monitor interface section provides break-key detection and scratchpad RAM.

The two-level microarchitecture of the chip set substantially reduces the size of the CPU chip's control store without significantly degrading response times. The first level, or vertical, microinstructions are 18 bits wide. Six bits are used to select one of sixty-four 35-bit second level, or horizontal, microinstructions. Two 4-bit fields, supplied by the vertical, can be substituted for two fields in the selected horizontal. The remaining 4 bits control the sequencing of vertical microinstructions. Substituting vertical fields into horizontal fields multiplies the power of each horizontal microinstruction. The result is an orthogonal horizontal microinstruction set which provides a general yet bit-efficient set of control primitives.

The performance of the CPU chip is enhanced by supporting concurrent operations within a single microcycle. This involves the macroinstruction prefetch unit, the four-bus internal data path, and self-modifying temporary registers. First, the macroinstruction Instruction Register (IR) pipeline is filled by autonomous fetch control logic whenever the system bus is idle. A separate pipeline Program Counter is maintained in parallel to establish a correlation between prefetched instructions and their addresses. This permits calculation of return addresses and program counter relative addresses. Second, two precharged busses transmit operands from the Register File to the ALU. A third bus is used for writing data into the Register File; this bus can be driven with either the ALU result or with external data during system bus read operations. A fourth bus is used to provide addresses to the pad transceivers directly from the Register File. Third, each of four temporary registers in the Register File can perform a specific transformation independently of the ALU. These four functions are increment, decrement, shift left, and shift right. By coordinating a combination of these "in-place" functions with the ALU operation, many instruction executions are optimized. For instance, only one microcycle is required every multiply or divide iteration step. Additionally, incrementing or decrementing the stack pointer during context saves and restores allows each register push/pop to occur in only one microcycle [8].

With the addition of external translation RAMs on the Model 10, a physical address space of up to 2M bytes is supported by the memory management and protection logic included in the chip set. This logic provides protection against unauthorized execution of I/O instructions, allows specific logical memory segments to be either write or validity protected, and limits the number of levels of indirection permitted in one memory reference.

Each CROM monitors the system bus to maintain a duplicate of the CPU's macroinstruction pipeline, allowing the CPU and multiple CROMs to simultaneously decode macroinstructions. When a CROM recognizes a resident macroinstruction, it provides the vertical microinstructions necessary for the execution of that macroinstruction and overrides normal sequencing (internal microcode) of the microECLIPSE processor. Only one unused microcycle follows the decode. The CROM then supplies one vertical microinstruction each microcycle by time-multiplexing 8 pins. This feature (originally intended to provide extensions to the internally supported ECLIPSE instruction set) was used in the Model 10 to minimize system cost while maintaining total compatibility with existing software. For example, certain I/O instructions to TTI/TTO (historically the system console device), memory management and I/O maps, diskettes and line printers are trapped. A combination of firmware and hardware masks the differences and presents the standard device interface to the system software.

The CPU can execute the entire 16-bit ECLIPSE instruction set including floating-point and character extensions. Execution of 16-bit register-to-register operations requires a single 500-ns microcycle, and memory-to-register moves require only 2 microcycles.

IV. PRODUCT IMPLEMENTATION: SYSTEM PROCESSING UNIT

A block diagram of the Model 10 is shown in Fig. 1. The System Processing Unit (SPU), outlined by the dashed square, consists of the following elements:

- Two 16-bit central processing units (CPUs): the Data General microECLIPSE CPU integrated circuit with one to three external microcode controller chips (CROMs) and an Intel 8086 microprocessor IC, referred to as the attached processor, or ATP.
- A multidevice section based on a microECLIPSE system I/O (SIO) IC, containing a full duplex asynchronous communications interface (called the printer port), a real-time clock, a programmable interval timer, the interface to the microNOVA I/O bus, a powerfail monitor, and an SPU status register.
- Bus arbitration as well as DMA and I/O control logic.
- 16K bytes of read-only memory that contains a self-test program, a virtual console program, and instruction emulation code (this ROM is supplemented by an additional 6K bytes of reserved RAM).
- Two memory allocation and protection units (contained in one physical memory array)—one for each CPU, along with selection logic to route the addresses to the memory.
- 128K or 256K bytes of dynamic random-access memory and associated parity checking logic.
- A diskette interface that supports one or two minidiskette drives and provides direct memory access (DMA) for diskette data transfers.
- Bit-mapped video and keyboard support logic, including a firmware graphics/alphanumerics video generator for the standard monochrome monitor of the system console.
- Decoding logic for memory-mapped I/O control and system timing signal generators.

The 8086 processor shares its main memory with the microECLIPSE CPU. Only one processor can access memory at a time, so the processors run serially. The operational cycles of the two processors are synchronized so that their memory accesses occur during the same relative timing phase: a memory access for either processor requires 500 ns. Each processor has its own memory allocation and protection (MAP) unit.

The microECLIPSE MAP translates 15-bit logical addresses into 20-bit physical addresses and the 8086 MAP translates 19-bit logical addressees into 20-bit physical addresses. The mapping operation translates 2K-byte logical blocks (called pages) into 2K-byte physical blocks. The blocks are not required to be mapped contiguously, and microECLIPSE and 8086 blocks can be interspersed. Since mapping and all I/O devices are under the control of the microECLIPSE processor, the 8086 program must make requests to the microECLIPSE if it requires a change of the MAP or access to an I/O device. Ownership of the MAP and I/O devices by the microECLIPSE protects the DG environment from contamination by 8086 program errors.

If any interrupt occurs while the 8086 processor is running, and if microECLIPSE processor interrupts are enabled, the 8086 is paused, and control passes immediately to the microECLIPSE CPU. After the microECLIPSE handles the interrupt, it normally restarts the 8086 processor.

Communication between the microECLIPSE and the 8086 processor is conducted using a Data General standard I/O interface. This interface supports processor calls from the 8086 to the microECLIPSE, vectored 8086 interrupts, and shared memory mailboxes. Software, which will be discussed in Section VI, determines the location and format of the mailboxes.

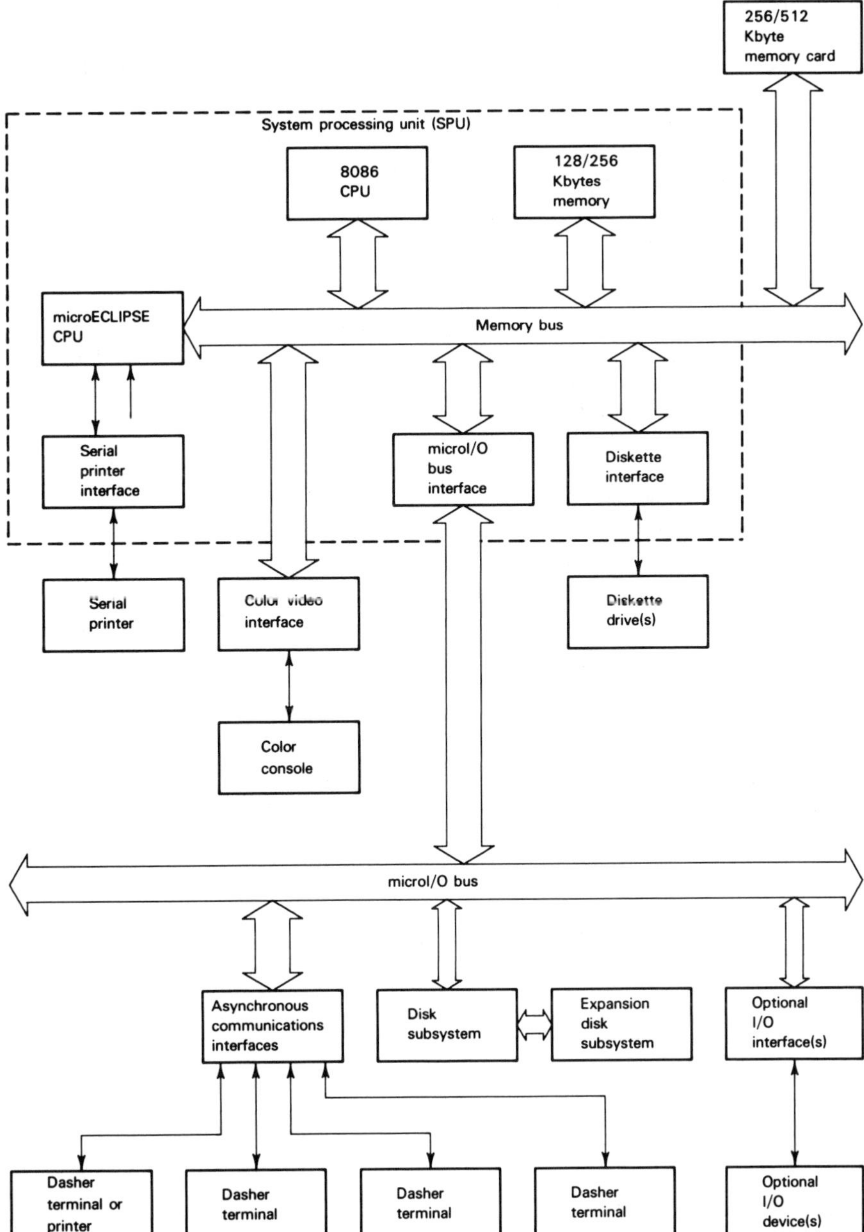

Fig. 1. Desktop Generation Model 10 system block diagram.

The microECLIPSE uses the ATP Status Register and ATP Interrupt Register, Busy and Done flags to pass control to the 8086, to specify the first address to be used by the 8086 processor, to determine its status, and to reset it. The 8086 returns control to the microECLIPSE by executing an OUT instruction. The Busy flag, when set to 1, indicates to the microECLIPSE processor that the 8086 processor has been paused and that its interrupts are enabled. Once the Busy flag is reset by the microECLIPSE, the 8086 processor either continues execution at the previous PC address or responds to an 8086 interrupt request using the ATP interrupt vector (discussed later).

The Done flag, when set to 1, initiates an interrupt request to the microECLIPSE CPU (unless interrupts are disabled, or the Interrupt Request bit in the ATP status register is set to 1). The ATP Status Register is loaded using a Set ATP Status instruction (DOA). If bit 15 is set to 0, the ATP issues an interrupt request to the microECLIPSE processor when the ATP Done flag is 1 (due to OUT instruction or validity fault). If bit 15 is 1, the ATP will not issue any interrupt requests. A microECLIPSE program reads the register by issuing a Read ATP Status instruction (DIA). This returns the values of the Done and Busy flags, and information on whether control is being returned to the microECLIPSE because of a validity trap (logically equivalent to the 8086 running out of memory) or an OUT instruction. It also returns the previously set interrupt request status. The microECLIPSE program uses a Load ATP Interrupt Vector instruction (DOB) to load an 8-bit vector into the ATP Interrupt Address Register. The 8086 uses this value to determine the address at which to begin execution when it resumes operation. Four additional programmed I/O instructions, two addressed to the ATP interface, and three addressed to the microECLIPSE CPU allow the CPU to

- alter program flow determined by the state of the Done flag (IOSKP);
- issue a Start or Clear flag command without a programmed input/output transfer (NIO);
- identify an interrupting source (INTA);
- initialize the interface (IORST).

Emulation of a DGC standard alphanumeric console (device codes 10 and 11) is provided by trapping I/O to the console in an external microcode controller chip and dispatching to the terminal emulator program that resides in reserved main memory. This program generates characters on the master console's bit-mapped display of 640 by 240 pixels. On power up, the keyboard has only rudimentary alphanumeric capabilities. These capabilities may be supplemented by loading additional code into reserved main memory.

V. Product Implementation: Bit-Mapped Color Graphics

The interface for the system console color monitor consists of eight major functional blocks:

1) the drive circuitry for the color monitor,
2) the color selection palette,
3) the CRT controller circuitry,
4) the alphanumeric character memory,
5) downloadable character generation,
6) the graphics memory,
7) the status and timing circuitry,
8) the interface circuitry to the Model 10 processor.

All of these elements are under the control of the console emulator and command interpreter programs of the Model 10. The interface between the controller and the processor is a DG memory bus interface.

The color monitor is a noninterlaced display which uses a bit-mapped screen of 640 by 240 pixels. As a color monitor, the display uses three separate guns (red, green, and blue) to illuminate its screen. Each gun is driven by a 4-bit digital-to-analog converter which gives 16 intensity levels for that color. Thus 4096 different colors are available for use on the display. However, since supporting all colors at all times for each pixel would have required large amounts of memory, the controller supports one active subset of the 4096 colors at a time. The active colors are specified by a selected color palette. The set of color palettes consists of a 1024 by 12-bit high-speed memory array. The 12 bits of the array output drive the three D/A converters for the color guns (4 bits for each color). The 1024 locations of the color palette array are divided into four subsets of 256 palette addresses. Only one of these four subsets is active at any one time as determined by the status and control register. Eight bits are used for addressing these palette locations. Arbitration logic determines the source of the addresses for the color palette. When operating with both graphics and characters, the arbitration logic gives priority to character blocks, character fonts, character background, or graphics. This encoding is done in the character attribute field along with transparent character color specification.

The CRT controller circuitry is initialized by the emulator program to operate with an 8 by 10 dot matrix to form characters. In addition, the program initializes the screen into 80 characters per line, 24 lines per screen. The CRT controller always acts as if it were painting the screen and forming characters. It assumes it will address 80 characters in a line and step through the 10 horizontal scans needed to paint the entire line. The CRT controller then adds 80 to its base count and repeats the process for the next 10 horizontal scans of the screen. This process continues until all 24 lines of characters have been painted. For each address, the CRT controller sends out, auxiliary circuitry generates the 8 horizontal dots for the character being displayed. The CRT controller operates in this manner independent of whether the system is working in graphic or alphanumeric mode. To simplify memory organization and management, alphanumeric characters and graphic data reside in independent memories.

Because of the dimensions of the screen, 2K words of memory are adequate to store the raw characters to be displayed and their attributes. Attribute information for each character is stored in the low-order byte and the character itself is stored in the high-order byte of a given word. Characters are stored by rows, with the first line of the display occupying the first 80 words of memory, etc. A second attribute byte (Attribute byte 2) for each character allows selection of additional features for displaying characters. These features include the underscoring of individual characters, reversing the character font color with the background screen color (reverse video), selecting an alternate character color from the color palette, and implementing the character dimming operation. Only 4 of the 8 bits of Attribute byte 2 are currently used.

Each time the CRT controller circuitry sends out an address and a scan line number, hardware generates information for 8 pixels on the screen using a 32-bit-wide memory for graphics information. Since there are 19 200 pixels, a 20K × 32-bit memory has been used. This memory is divided into two banks, each 16 bits wide, in order to make it usable by the 16-bit microECLIPSE processor. Bank 0 contains the information for the first 4 pixels expected by the CRT controller while Bank 1 contains the information for the fifth through eighth pixels. Set up in this manner, 80 consecutive memory locations (each 32 bits wide) contain the graphics data needed for one horizontal sweep of the display screen. However, the next 9 horizontal sweeps will also generate those same 80 addresses because the CRT generator is expecting 10 horizontal sweeps to paint the screen, just as it would if it were displaying characters. To keep the memory addressing simple, we set up 10 areas in memory, each area occupying two map slots of the CPU's physical address space. Using the scan line number to select the appropriate memory area, we have an addressing scheme which satisfies the CRT controller's expectations.

Two principal registers reside in the status and timing circuitry—the status and control register and the pixel region register. Each of these registers appears as a memory location to the system. Eleven of the 16 bits of the status and control register are used in the controller. These bits perform the following functions: enable/disable the display, enable/disable graphics, enable/disable characters, enable/disable graphics blinking, enable/disable character blinking, enable/disable character cursor blinking, respond or not to user space, select one of the four color palettes, and indicate the horizontal and vertical sync periods for the display. The pixel region register is used solely in conjunction with the graphics memory. One bit selects the bank (0 or 1) for loading and reading the memory by the CPU. Four bits specify the scan line address used for loading and reading the 10 memory areas by the CPU. This technique allows the entire 20K-double words of screen memory to be mapped into one page of processor memory.

VI.   PRODUCT IMPLEMENTATION: SOFTWARE

The 8086 attached processor (ATP) "environment" runs as directed by the host (microECLIPSE) processor in a manner that isolates the Data General operating system's characteristics from the ATP application program. This layered architecture is depicted in Fig. 2. Running in the

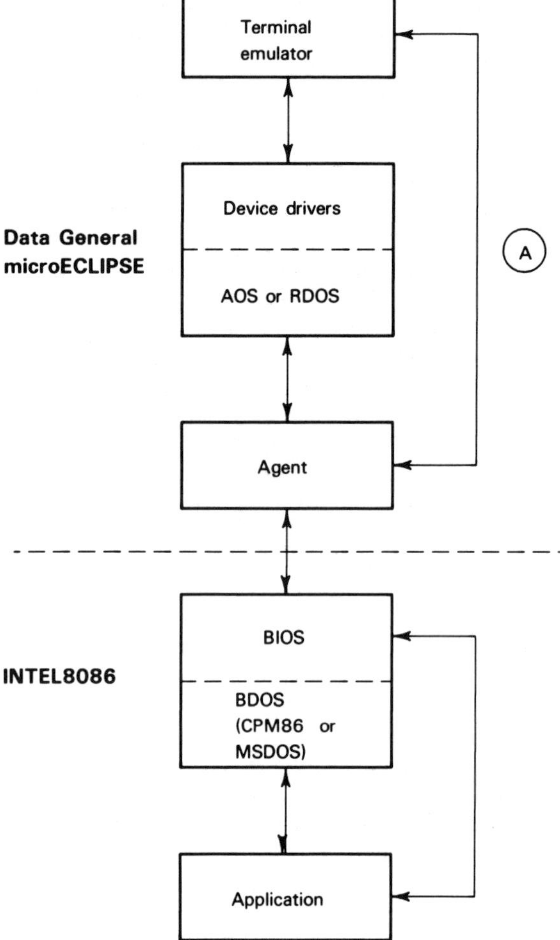

Fig. 2. Desktop Generation Model 10 layered software architecture.

microECLIPSE are the terminal emulator, the host operating system (either AOS or RDOS), and
the ATP Agent. Running in the 8086 are the operating system (either CP/M-86 or MS-DOS),
consisting of BIOS (Basic I/O System) and BDOS (Basic Disk Operating System), and user
application program. When power is applied to the system, self-tests are performed and the
host operating system begins running. Software configurations are offered in which entry into
either CP/M-86 or MS-DOS is automatic. Alternatively, the user may elect to run either
CP/M-86 or MS-DOS as an application program under a DG operating system. In this case,
entry into either CP/M-86 or MS-DOS is at the discretion of the user.

A. MicroECLIPSE Software

At system start-up, the terminal emulator program is automatically loaded by the operating
system into the reserved main memory. This emulator controls the console keyboard and the
monitor. It supplements the ROM resident terminal emulator by providing full alphanumeric
(for English and several foreign character sets) and graphics support.

Either of two Data General host operating systems can be used. RDOS is small (runs in 128K
bytes of memory with a single diskette) and easily configured to run memory-resident which
makes it suitable for real-time applications [9]. It provides support for two user processes. When

the 8086 is in use, it is controlled by the RDOS "background process." The "foreground process" can run other DG or user-written application programs. AOS is a more sophisticated operating system that provides a multiprocess environment for timesharing applications [10]. It runs in a minimum of 0.5M byte of memory and requires a hard disk.

Both RDOS and AOS provide the same facilities for controlling the ATP environment, so for brevity we will refer only to AOS. To initiate an ATP operating system, the user types in its name. This causes AOS to load into memory a program called the "Agent," which then loads the ATP operating system into the 8086. The Agent process controls the ATP and remains in memory while the ATP operating system is running. It is multitasked to provide support for simultaneous system-level functions (for example, concurrent use of master console and secondary communications line) by an 8086 application program.

B. Attached Processor Software

The ATP operating systems (CP/M-86 and MS-DOS) use the same software "hierarchy." The BDOS and BIOS layers actually comprise the operating system itself. When a program makes a system call to the BDOS, functions which are relatively independent of machine architecture are performed. A command such as "read a file from disk" or "send a character to the printer" causes the BDOS to translate the request into a smaller set of primitives which are handled by the BIOS layer. BIOS handles hardware-dependent requests from BDOS as well as directly from an 8086 application program. In the Desktop implementation, the BIOS builds a request packet for a function such as "read disk sector X from disk drive 0 into memory location Y" and places it in shared memory for the Agent.

C. Interprocessor Communications

An application running in the 8086 makes a system call to either the BDOS or BIOS layer of the ATP operating system. The BIOS makes a resource request of the microECLIPSE by placing a packet of information in shared memory where it will be found by the Agent and sets the Done flag. The Agent process is activated by AOS, converts the ATP BIOS request into an AOS system request, and pends. In some cases, the 8086 processor remains stopped until the request is satisfied (for example, in the case of a disk read). In other cases, the Agent initiates another task within its own address space and proceeds to reactivate the 8086 immediately.

Under AOS, processes are scheduled using an algorithm which tend to favor the Agent over other processes in the system. Once the request is completed, the Agent is restarted as the active process by the DG operating system. The Agent fills the status (or the result of the system call) in the shared memory and acknowledges the request by resetting the Busy flag. Processor arbitration logic pends the microECLIPSE and execution continues in the 8086 at the location following the completed request.

D. Disk Support

The Desktop computer supports 360K-byte diskettes and 15M-byte Winchester disks. In order to run either ATP operating system, both of which have unique file systems, the concept of a "virtual disk" was implemented. A virtual disk is a randomly organized file within the DG operating system's file system that has an internal structure consistent with the requirements of an ATP operating system [11]. Thus when an ATP operating system is manipulating files, it is normally operating within a virtual disk, which is a fixed length file on a physical DG disk. ATP logical disks may exist on either physical diskettes or hard disks.

Due to size constraints, a diskette may have only one virtual disk, but a hard disk may have many virtual disks. On a 15M-byte hard disk, a user will typically set up a number of DG format directories, each of which may contain a number of virtual disks. The ATP operating systems are configured to allow the user simultaneous access to a maximum of two physical and two logical drives.

E. Fast Screen Calls

Existing mechanisms in both RDOS and AOS permit a user program to gain direct access to peripherals [12]. These mechanisms are used most frequently by applications in real-time environments. In the Model 10 system, the Agent signals AOS that it wishes to do direct I/O to the master console. Entry points in the terminal emulator implement a variety of functions including character, line, and block move commands. When the application executes an EHYP instruction, it jumps directly into the emulator code at one of these entry points. This path bypasses the device-independent Read and Write system calls, as shown by line *A* in Fig. 2. This direct screen access is particularly useful in applications like spreadsheets which need to move blocks of text on the screen quickly.

Overall, a high degree of compatibility with the IBM PC implementation of MS-DOS has been achieved through this approach. We have found that existing applications which use BDOS calls run unchanged on the Desktop Generation Model 10. Applications which go directly to the BIOS level or which rely on the ability to directly modify memory locations in the BIOS may require recoding. Diskette and file formats are fully compatible.

VII. Product Implementation: Packaging

Experience on an earlier product, the MPT100, showed that a totally enclosed desktop package including monitor, keyboard, CPU, and peripherals is workable in very few environments. Everyone wants to add just one more card or peripheral than can be supported—and each addition is different every time. Moreover, if one assumes that a user will be troubleshooting down to the box level, then the smallest possible replaceable unit in this style of system is the whole system.

Another approach, the "pieces and parts packaging style" used in early systems such as the Apple II, leaves the user's desk covered with a collection of little boxes of various sizes containing CPU, diskette drives, and other peripherals. While a malfunctioning part is more easily separated from the system for repair, this form of integration is not as reliable as others. Moreover, the system is aesthetically unattractive.

A third packaging technique, that of the IBM PC and XT among others, uses a horizontally mounted system board, slots for additional memory and peripheral controllers, and 1 or 2 diskette/Winchester disk modules. This rectangular box is typically placed under the system monitor on a user's desk. However, disassembling two systems (IBM PC and DEC Rainbow) indicated that this approach would still not offer the extendability required in some configurations. Certain XT configurations in which multiple horizontal boxes must be stacked vertically constitute a regression to the Apple scheme. Because of the inadequacies of the existing techniques, a new packaging design was adopted.

The Model 10 system consists of between three and six modules connected horizontally to form a single desk- or shelf-top unit. In an in-house survey, the industrial design group discovered that while desk space is almost always at a premium, virtually everyone has a bookcase or shelf on which a unit would be placed if it were the right size and shape. Even in situations where floor space is scarce, shelf space is available. Fig. 3 illustrates our modular design. There are six module types: the power-supply module (always the rightmost unit in a system), the CPU logic module (immediately to the left of the power supply module), the (optional) logic expansion module, the (optional) disk module, the diskette module, and the (optional) tape module. Each module is 4.8 inches by 12.8 inches by 10.7 inches in size. It consists of a metal cage with a base plate and removable plastic front, rear, and top panels. End modules have a removable plastic side panel. Adjacent cages mechanically interlock with one another easily and require no tools to connect and disconnect. The logic expansion and disk modules each contain two intermodule connectors, one at each end. The CPU logic and diskette module back panels each contain one intermodule connector, located on the left end of the CPU logic module back panel and the right end of the diskette module back panel.

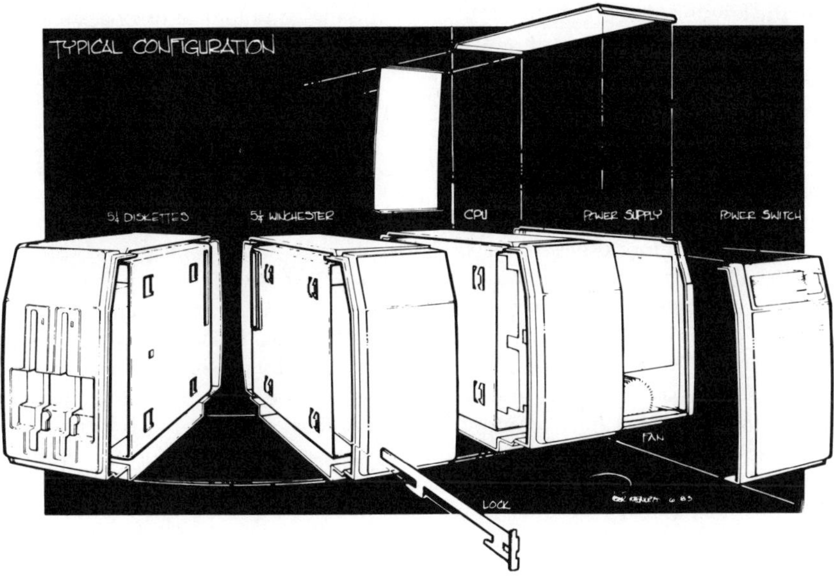

Fig. 3. Desktop Generation Model 10 packaging.

Logic modules (CPU and expansion) each accept up to five DG standard 7-by-9 inch boards. Since the SPU cards take up two slots and include diskette, printer port, and console control, the base Model 10 configuration has three empty slots. This is adequate for most configurations, and the addition of an expansion module permits another five I/O boards to be added [13]. Because the packaging scheme implements a standard DG bus (microNOVA bus), virtually all of the preexisting 7-by-9 inch boards, including multiplexors, IEEE 488 bus controllers, and parallel interface boards can be used. Also, the packaging scheme enables the Model 10 to meet class "B" FCC compliance with approximately 15-percent margin in the base level configuration. The vertical arrangement of the printed circuit boards allows air to circulate freely, resulting in efficient cooling [14]. Thus the Model 10 in any allowable system configuration is environmentally qualified to 38°C.

VIII. Final Product

The Desktop Generation program began in the summer of 1982 and the first system was shipped approximately 16 months later. This short development cycle was due to the use of the microECLIPSE, the existing 7-by-9 inch form factor, and the microNOVA bus structure.

Half a million lines of diagnostic code were available from previous generations of ECLIPSEs and peripheral controllers. Language compilers, utilities, communications software required little or no modification. These are luxuries that one does not have when debugging a processor, peripherals, and diagnostics simultaneously. Only drivers for new peripherals, such as the Winchester disk, had to be written for the operating systems. The high level of integration in the SPU boards and the ability to emulate selected functionality in software resulted in low cost.

Operating systems, in general, are quite long lived—RDOS has been shipping for over 10 years. To minimize the number of versions of an operating system that must be maintained, software-visible divergence between implementations (for example, to support a new processor instruction set) must be avoided. Running the Agent as a standard system application process permitted the product to be implemented without extensive operating system modification. In the case of AOS (the more complex of the two DG operating systems), less than 400 lines of code were written or modified, excluding new peripheral support. This is less than 0.03 percent of the operating system total. XODIAC [15], a networking communications package, runs intact on the Model 10. A small amount of new code (less than 1 percent of the total) was written to permit the package to use the system asynchronous multiplexor driver. This allows the Model 10 to function as a node in a XODIAC network over an ordinary phone line as well as support multiuser configurations. Synchronous lines are also supported.

The Desktop Model 10 fulfills all the marketing requirements described in Table 1. Further, the comprehensive electronic office software package (CEO) is supported at various levels. In the simplest configuration, the system functions as a self-contained "branch office" system supporting from one to four user terminals. The addition of a communications protocol permits the system to function within a corporate SNA or X.25 network and supplies file transfer, remote database access, and other facilities. In the distributed configuration, the Desktop Model 10 functions as a CEO terminal connected to a host DG processor, but allows compute- and screen-intensive operations such as word processing to be performed locally on the Model 10 in a fashion transparent to the user. File storage can be local or remote, permitting file archiving on the host and local control of private files when desired. Since support for distributed resources is a CEO generation option, the same product runs on both host and Desktop insuring compatible user interface, data, and text files.

IX. System Performance

We evaluated system performance in several different application environments. All tests were run as follows: the IBM PC and XT were used for comparison. The Model 10 configuration included two diskette drives, one 15M-byte Winchester disk drive, and 768K bytes of memory. The XT configuration included one diskette drive, 10M-byte Winchester disk drive, and 512K bytes of memory. All programs ran under MS-DOS rev. 2.0.

The first series of tests consisted of six programs which measured system performance in three general areas—CPU, disk, and screen I/O. A C compiler and binder written by Microsoft (Bellevue, WA) [16] were used. The C compiler was used to test heavy disk switching, CPU, and memory access. The binder was used to test sequential disk usage followed by heavy usage of the CPU. The compiler and binder were used to prepare a program (the SIEVE of ERATOSTHENES) [17] for execution. The SIEVE program was executed to test heavy CPU access. A string and character output program written in C was used to force full screen output and heavy scrolling of the screen. Finally, a pure disk read and write program written in C was used to perform disk I/O. The results are summarized in Table 2.

Table 2 Desktop Generation Model 10 Overall Performance

Test	Diskette		Winchester	
	IBM-PC	Model 10	IBM-XT	Model 10
SIEVE compile	31	66	11	20
SIEVE bind	40	43	8	11
SIEVE execution	110	65	116	56
Video execution	40	25	37	22
Disk read	17	18	9	6
Disk write	23	27	12	18

The use of two operating systems can degrade performance if the system is not designed carefully. For example, if a single character is written to the master console screen from an application program running under an ATP operating system in the 8086, it must traverse the entire software hierarchy of both operating systems. This specific problem was successfully handled by the fast screen calls which support output to the screen at an effective rate of over 19.2 kBd. To verify that screen I/O performance was acceptably fast, we ran a second set of tests using Microsoft's Multiplan [18] Electronic Worksheet. On both machines, all Multiplan

Table 3 Desktop Generation Model 10 Multiplan Performance

Test Description	Model 10 Avg. Time	IBM-XT Avg. Time
Bringing up Multiplan (entering name, displaying Multiplan logo, blank worksheet)	6	4
TRANSFER LOADing previously built worksheet:	3	3
COPY DOWN (20 calls, labels, no RECALC)	1	2
COPY FROM (1 formula cell to create new 20 × 20 worksheet, no RECALC)	5	9
COPY FROM (1 formula cell from 50 × 50 worksheet to new 20 × 20 area, no RECALC)	28	68
DELETE (50 rows, no RECALC)	15	20
INSERT (50 columns, no RECALC)	4	4
SORT 50 × 50 worksheet by Col. 1	7	15
Recalculate in 50 × 50 worksheet, with 50 × 48 section containing formulas, changing one figure at R2C2 ("what if analysis")	23	49
Scrolling page (3 × right, full screens)	6	7

commands ran from main memory, giving neither system an advantage. Each command was executed three times and the average times were rounded to the nearest second. The results of these tests are shown in Table 3.

Overall, the results summarized in Tables 2 and 3 show that the DG Model 10 is slightly slower than the IBM PC or XT for diskette intensive applications, and is roughly twice as fast for compute- and screen-intensive applications.

X. Conclusion

Coupling multiple processors in a single product is a powerful implementation technique. This approach gives the user access to applications software available under multiple operating systems without requiring the purchase of multiple complete systems, effectively minimizing the total system price. For a vendor, a dual-processor product maximizes the amount of available software while minimizing the time and effort required to implement and maintain that software. It can obviate the need to turn an existing software product inside out in order to make it run in an environment which could not have been forseen when the program was originally written. Companies that find a way to permit access to new generations of software and smoothly integrate those products with existing software and hardware will succeed in the long run.

Since the introduction of the Desktop Generation, IBM has announced a similar architecture in the XT/370 [19], linking their mainframe software with PC software [20]. Clearly, our situation —having a large body of software both internally in proprietary code and externally through its installed base—is not unique. Multiple processor architectures will prove increasingly attractive to the large number of vendors in this situation, and to large numbers of users who want low-cost access to a wide range of software.

References

[1] P. Issacson and E. Juliussen, *Personal Computer Industry Views*, Future Computing, Inc., pp. 2–7, Mar. 28, 1983.

[2] Dataquest, *Small Computer Industry Service*, vol. II, pp. 6.1–26, June 12, 1981.

[3] International Data Corp., *Microprocessor Markets and Trends*, pp. 41–45, Sept. 1982.

[4] Yankee Group, "Communications and Information Systems," *Pulse*, vol. 1, pp. 31–33, 137–152, 1983.

[5] Data General Corp., "A preview of CEO, Comprehensive Electronic Office," Rep. 069-032, pp. 15–41, Nov. 1981.

[6] International Resource Development, "DG tackles the electronic office," *Electron. Mail Message Syst.*, vol. 5, no. 23, pp. 6–9, Dec. 12, 1981.

[7] Datapro Research Corp., "DEC Professional 300 Series," *Directory of Small Computers*, Doc. No. SC30-384-301, Dec. 1982.

[8] R. Rubinstein *et al.*, "Compatibility and speed: Goals of a small machine," *Comput. Des.*, vol. 21, no. 8, pp. 69–76, Aug. 1982.

[9] Data General Corp., "Introduction to the Real-Time Disc Operating System (RDOS)," Rep. 069-000002, p. 18, June 1982.

[10] Datapro Research Corp., "Data General desktop generation," *Directory of Small Computers*, Doc. No. SC30-304-201, Dec. 1983.

[11] Data General Corp., "Using AOS on the Desktop Generation System," Rep. 069-000058, pp. 15-7–15-20, Oct. 1983.

[12] Data General Corp., *Advanced Operating System (AOS) Programmer's Manual*, Doc. No. 093-000120, pp. 8-7–8-8, May 1982.

[13] Data General Corp., "Desktop Generation Model 10 and 10SP Computer Systems Technical Reference," Rep. 014-000760, pp. 8-2–8-13, Oct. 1983.

[14] E. Humm, "Novel cooling scheme resolves packaging dilemma," *Electron. Packag. Prod.*, vol. 26, no. 9, pp. 118–119, Oct. 1983.

[15] Data General Corp., "Xodiac network management system guide for managers and operators," Rep. 093-000260-01, pp. 1-1–1-6, Oct. 1981.

[16] Microsoft, "C Compiler for 8086 and 8088 Microprocessors and the MS-DOS Operating System," Doc. No. 8415-104-00, 1983.

[17] J. and G. Gilbreath, "Eratosthenes revisited: One more through the sieve," *Byte Mag.*, vol. 8, no. 1, p. 283, Jan. 1983.

[18] Microsoft, "Multiplan Electronic Worksheet for MS-DOS," Doc. No. 8901-105-00, 1983.

[19] Management Information Corporation, "PC XT/370 architecture," *Small Business Comput. News*, vol. X, no. 11, pp. 20–31, Nov. 1983.

[20] C. Daney, "The XT/370, a technical overview," *PC Mag.*, vol. 3, no. 1, pp. 151–154, Jan. 24, 1984.

8
The IBM PCjr

PHILIP D. ESTRIDGE, DAVID J. BRADLEY, AND DAVID A. KUMMER

After the spectacular success of the IBM Personal Computer, IBM decided to launch a lower priced personal computer. In implementing this new system, designers frequently had to choose between retaining compatibility with the IBM Personal Computer and the need to make the changes necessary to allow for a lower cost system. This chapter describes the IBM PCjr and the design aspects relating to the compatibility issue.

The Editors

I. INTRODUCTION

In mid-July 1980 IBM formed a task force to develop a small, personal-use computer designed for individuals in business, at home, and in the classroom. A year later, on August 12, 1981, the company introduced the IBM Personal Computer. Since then, the IBM Personal Computer has enjoyed a level of acceptance that has surprised almost everyone: demand for the systems has far exceeded most observers' expectations; and an entire industry has grown up around the IBM PC, ranging from a dozen magazines dedicated to IBM PC-related material to hundreds of companies developing and producing thousands of applications and hardware peripherals designed for IBM Personal Computers.

While being described by many observers as a standard for the personal computer industry, the PC has also become the foundation for a family of systems subsequently introduced by IBM. The first extension of the product line was the IBM Personal Computer XT. Introduced in March, 1983, the XT built upon the flexibility of the IBM Personal Computer offering a range of standard features and design characteristics that make it especially suitable for handling large amounts of information. In October 1983, IBM introduced the IBM Personal Computer XT/370 and IBM 3270 Personal Computer, again offering more memory capacity, specialized functions, and flexibility. And, in November 1983, IBM introduced the IBM PCjr, which is easy to use yet flexible and powerful enough for many sophisticated computer applications.

A key consideration in the design of each IBM Personal Computer system is compatibility—enabling different members of the IBM Personal Computer family to use many of the application programs developed for other models. Ensuring compatibility throughout the product line is challenging in light of the many factors that must be considered: the level of the purchasers' experience with personal computers; the range of applications which may be run on the system; the initial as well as potential future configuration of the computer and peripherals; and even the price of the system.

IBM has met these challenges in the design of the PCjr. The most affordable computer ever offered by IBM, it is designed for people with little or no computing experience. Yet, it also offers much of the function found in the IBM Personal Computer and the IBM Personal Computer XT as well as the flexibility to grow along with the user's needs.

The authors are with the Entry Systems Division, IBM Corporation, Boca Raton, FL 33432, USA.

The first part of this chapter describes the hardware architecture of the PCjr, its characteristics and features [2], [3], [12]. The second part focuses on compatibility issues.

II. THE PCJR

System Description

The base PCjr consists of the system unit, a power transformer, the cordless keyboard for the IBM PCjr, and a display unit. Fig. 1 shows a typical PCjr configuration. The display unit can be either an IBM Color Display or any other television frequency display, such as a direct drive monitor, a composite video monitor or, with an optional RF modulator, a home television set. A diskette drive, a modem, and additional storage can be added in the system unit. Additional options can be attached to the system's I/O channel.

Fig. 1. PCjr system photograph.

Hardware Architecture

A block diagram of the PCjr system is shown in Fig. 2. At this level of abstraction, the PCjr appears very similar to the IBM Personal Computer. There are, however, significant differences between them. The system unit of the PCjr houses most of the electronics including the power supply, system board, and optional diskette drive. The power supply has two stages. The first stage is an external desktop transformer that produces a low-voltage ac output. The second stage is inside the system unit, and it converts the low-voltage ac output into the three dc output levels used by the system.

The system board of the PCjr contains the central processor and its support circuitry, the display and memory subsystem, and several I/O functions and connectors. The system board develops the I/O channel for internal connections and busses the signals to the right-hand side of the system unit. An external connector allows I/O features to be installed by horizontally "stacking" them with the system unit. Each I/O device passes the bus signals through the unit, allowing more units to attach. Each device connects to the bus signals that it requires for operation.

The PCjr uses the Intel 8088 microprocessor, the same processor used in the other members of the IBM Personal Computer family [1], [5], [6], [9], [10]. The 8088 is the 8-bit data bus version of the 8086 processor. The 8088 has a 1M-byte address space and does 16-bit arithmetic internally. Choosing the 8088 allowed us to build a system with an 8-bit data bus, with the corresponding savings in connection costs. The 8088 runs at 4.77 MHz, which is the oscillator frequency of 14.318 MHz divided by three. We chose this oscillator frequency since it is four times the color burst frequency of 3.579 MHz necessary to display color on composite monitors and television sets. The 8088 runs in the minimum mode. This precludes using an 8087 math coprocessor, but it saves the cost of an additional bus controller.

The PCjr has nine prioritized levels of interrupt, eight of which come from the 8259A Programmable Interrupt Controller. Five of the eight are connected to system board devices—the timer, serial port, modem port, diskette port, and display vertical retrace. The remaining three go to the system I/O channel so that external features may use them. The ninth interrupt is the Non-Maskable Interrupt (NMI) of the 8088. The NMI signals the 8088 that the cordless keyboard is transmitting a character to the system. The 8088 must deserialize the characters sent from the keyboard. This operation is explained in the section on the cordless keyboard.

Video and RAM

Unlike the IBM Personal Computer, the color graphics circuitry of the PCjr is on the system board and is an integral part of every system. The video system generates a television frequency signal that can drive the IBM Color Display or any similar monitor. The PCjr cannot drive the IBM Monochrome Display because of the difference in horizontal frequencies.

We designed the color graphics system of the PCjr to be as compatible with the IBM Color Graphics Adapter (CGA) as possible. The PCjr supports all the operating modes of the CGA, including two general modes of operation—the text mode and the graphics mode. Fig. 3 shows the text and graphics modes supported by PCjr. As this figure shows, the PCjr has several new modes beyond those offered by the CGA. The figure also shows the modes that require high memory bandwidth and, consequently, need the 64K memory and display expansion.

The system board of the PCjr has 64K bytes of RAM which is shared between the processor and the video logic. This was done to reduce the cost, since the system needs only one set of memory modules. The system board also has a connector for an additional 64K bytes of memory, allowing up to 128K bytes of memory within the system unit. The display and processor also share this additional storage. When both banks of memory are installed, the PCjr can operate in the higher bandwidth display modes.

The video logic has two major components: the 6845 CRT controller and the Video Gate Array (VGA). The video logic also contains a character generator ROM, a composite video generator, and memory controls. The 6845 provides the basic raster and display information, such as display memory address, horizontal and vertical retrace signals, cursor timing, row scan information for the character generator, and light pen logic. The character generator contains the dot patterns for characters in the text mode. The composite video logic converts the direct-drive video signals (intensity, red, green, blue, horizontal, and vertical sync) into a single composite video signal used by composite monitors and television sets.

The Video Gate Array controls the memory and arbitrates the memory sharing between the processor and the display [11]. The VGA also takes the information from memory or the character generator, formats the data depending on the mode, assigns color to the data, and shifts the color out to the CRT. Fig. 4 shows how the VGA cycles the RAM. Every 1.1 μs, three memory cycles occur. Two of these cycles are for the display; the remaining one is available for

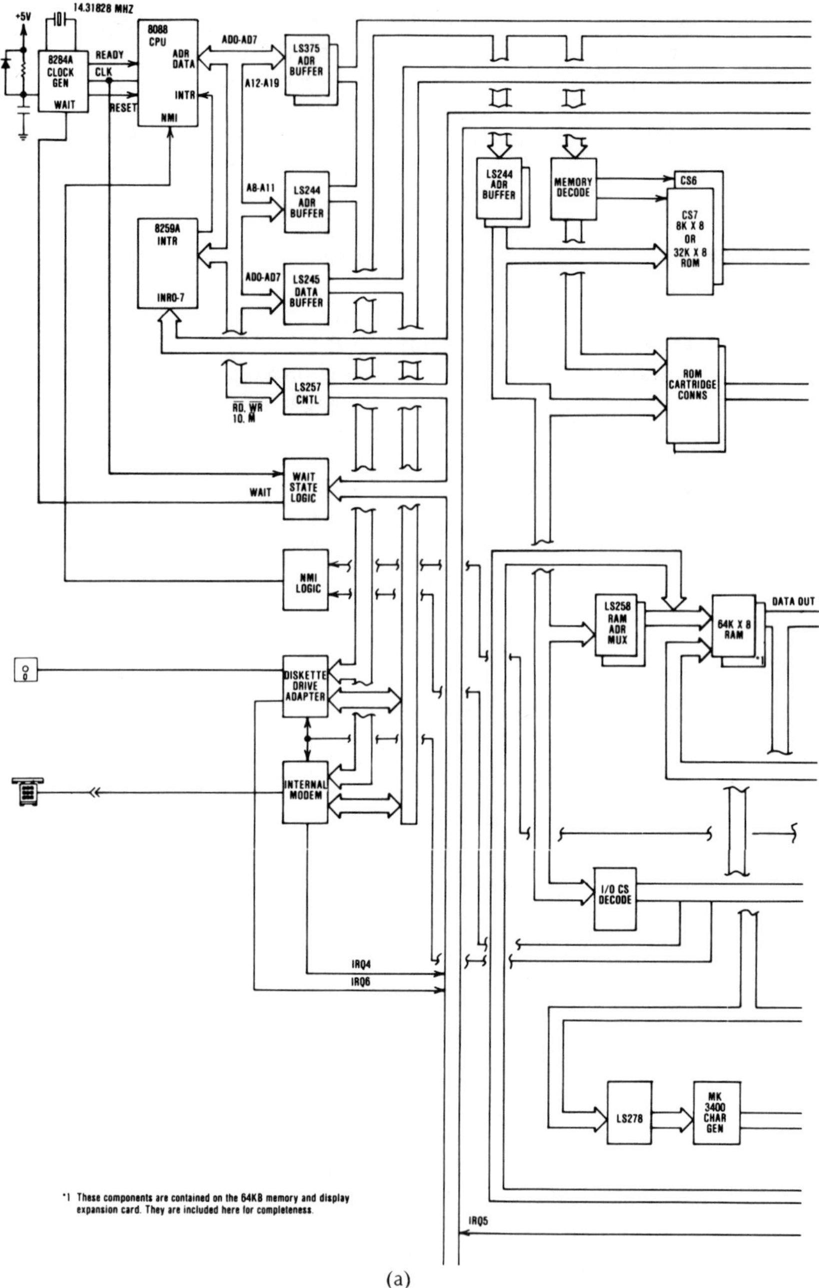

Fig. 2. (a) PCjr system block diagram.

the processor. The processor uses its memory cycle only if it needs it; otherwise, that cycle is unused. The processor must wait until the next available processor cycle when trying to address the RAM. This places wait states into the processor RAM read and write cycles, slowing down program execution from RAM. This strategy also allows the program to use as much of main storage for the display buffer as it requires. The 40-column text mode requires only 2K bytes, while the 320-by-200 16-color mode requires 32K bytes.

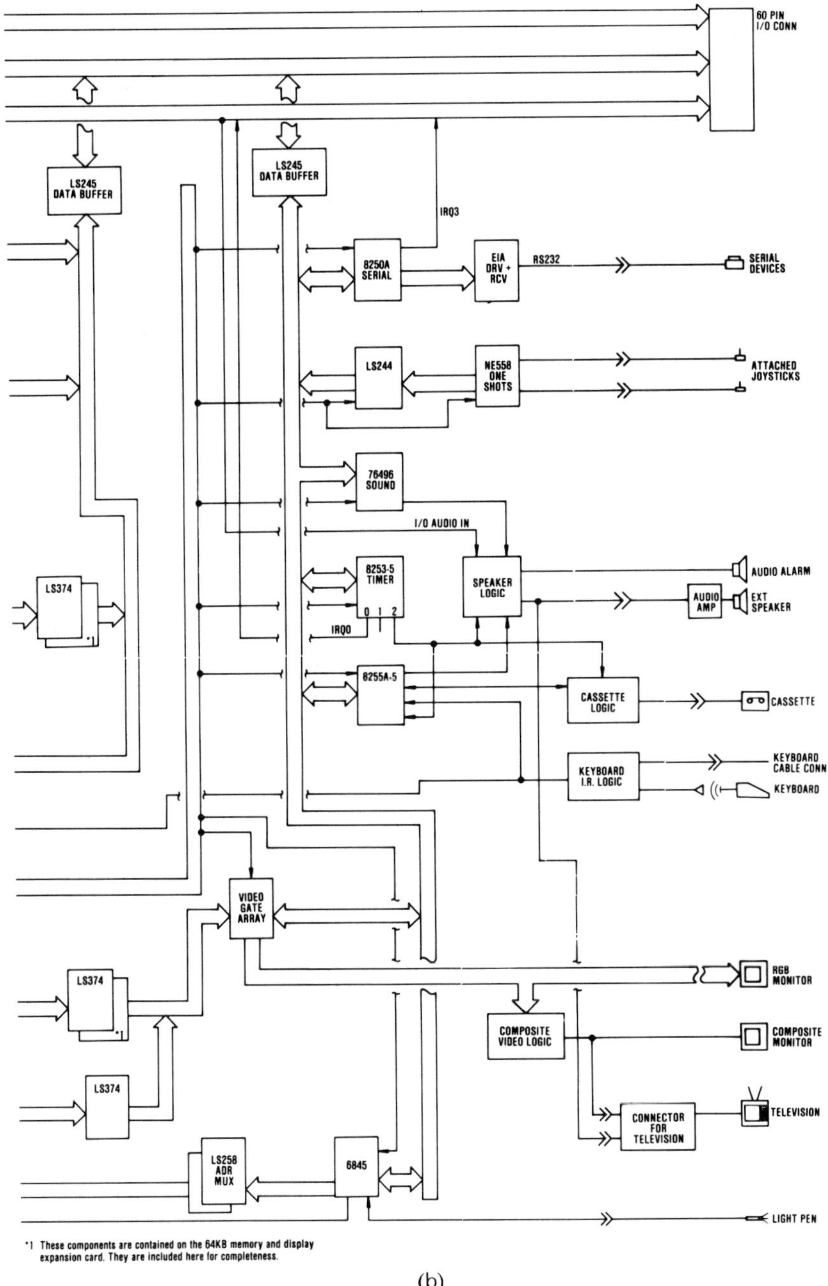

(b)

Fig. 2. *Continued*

In the text modes, either 40-column by 25 lines or 80-column by 25 lines, the display system specifies each character position with 2 bytes of storage. The even byte of each pair contains the ASCII representation of the character. The odd byte is the attribute byte, which tells the system how to display the character. This byte specifies the foreground color, the background color, and whether the character will be blinking. The attribute byte allows the programmer to choose colors on a character-by-character basis.

Mode	Number of Colors	Compatible With Color/Graphics Adapter	Requires 64KB Memory and Display Expansion Option	Buffer Size
40-column alpha	16	Yes	No	2KB
160 x 200	16	No	No	16KB
320 x 200	4	Yes	No	16KB
640 x 200	2	Yes	No	16KB
80-column alpha	16	Yes	Yes	4KB
320 x 200	16	No	Yes	32KB
640 x 200	4	No	Yes	32KB

Fig. 3.   PCjr display modes.

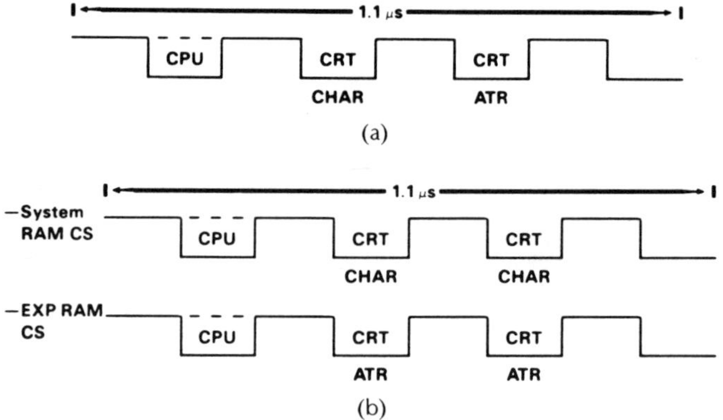

Fig. 4.   Memory sharing—processor and display.

In the 40-column text mode, a low-bandwidth mode, the display system fetches a character byte and an attribute byte every 1.1 μs. Low-bandwidth graphics modes likewise fetch two display bytes during the 1.1-μs interval. However, the high-bandwidth 80-column text mode requires a character and an attribute every 550 ns. The system accomplishes this by using the base 64K-byte memory and the 64K-byte memory and display expansion card. When the expansion card is in the system, the base memory occupies the even addresses while the expansion memory is at the odd addresses. During each display memory cycle, the display system fetches, in parallel, a character from the base memory and an attribute from the expansion memory. Therefore, two characters and two attributes go to the display in 1.1 μs, which meets the bandwidth requirements of the 80-column text mode. High-bandwidth graphics modes work in a similar manner.

The VGA contains a 16-word by 4-bit palette. This register array takes the encoded color information from the display and converts it to the desired display color. This color look-up table lets an application change rapidly from one color to another, without rewriting all of the color information in the display buffer. The change is accomplished by changing the colors assigned to the memory data by the palette. The VGA converts the RGB information into the appropriate 3.58-MHz phase. This is then used by the video logic when generating composite video. This logic also converts the color information into different shades of gray for a pleasing appearance on a black-and-white monitor or television set.

ROM and Cartridges

The 64K bytes of ROM on the system board is comprised of two 32K × 8 ROM modules. This ROM is located at the high end of the address space. The ROM contains the Power-On Self-Test, the Basic Input/Output System, Cassette Basic, Customer Diagnostics, and a user tutorial/game called Keyboard Adventure.

The PCjr also has two ROM cartridge slots which can contain up to another 128K bytes of ROM. Both cartridge slots are wired exactly the same and contain address, data, and 6 chip select lines. The system decodes the chip select lines at 32K-byte boundaries in the address space. Two different cartridges can be inserted, providing they use different chip selects. Two of the chip selects are the same as the base ROM. These, along with two inputs on the cartridge slots, called Base ROM in Cartridge 1 and 2, allow a cartridge to overlay the ROM on the system board. This lets the cartridge gain complete control of the machine at power-on or reset time. The cartridge slots also have a reset tab which resets the machine whenever the user installs or removes a cartridge. This *L*-shaped connector ensures that the system will respond correctly to the change in a cartridge. This reset connection is just one of 36 connections on the cartridge connector. Besides the reset tab, the remaining connections on the cartridge provide power and ground, the 8-bit data bus, a 15-bit address bus (to address within the 32K-byte chip select), 6 chip selects in the range D0000H through FFFFFH, and the 2 base ROM in cartridge signals. This interface design for the cartridge minimizes its cost since it needs to include only one or more 32K-byte ROM modules. No chip select logic is necessary.

Sound

The PCjr has four sound sources: the 8253 timer, the TI SN76496 Complex Sound Generator, the cassette input, and the I/O channel. The system can choose any of these sound sources to send to the audio output jack and the RF modulator connector. This allows an external device, like a television set or an audio amplifier system, to play the sound. The PCjr also has a small audio alarm on the system board which only the 8253 timer can drive. This portion of the sound system is compatible with the sound on the IBM Personal Computer. It generates a sound that is always a square wave with constant amplitude. Fig. 5 summarizes the sound subsystem. All of the components in this block diagram are found on the system board of the PCjr. The external channel signal comes from the I/O channel connector, while the outputs are presented at rear panel connections.

There are three sound channels and one noise channel on the SN76496 Complex Sound Generator. Each sound channel can be programmed for a frequency and one of sixteen amplitude levels. Also, the noise channel can be programmed for either random noise or periodic noise at one of sixteen amplitude levels. The output of the SN76496 is always a sine wave for the three sound channels.

A program can send either the cassette input or an I/O channel line to the audio output through the multiplexer. This allows a program to pass sound from the cassette or an external

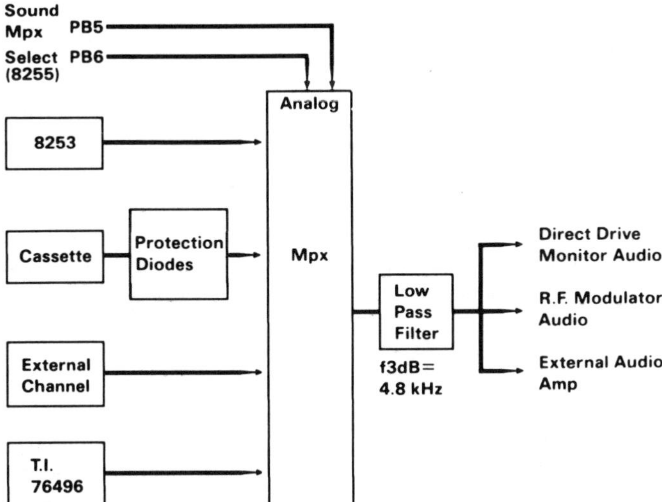

Fig. 5. Sound subsystem block diagram.

I/O feature to the amplifier/speaker combination attached to the system. A program developer is thereby given the ability to intermix computer-generated music and sound with an external, prerecorded audio source. This is advantageous for training programs that use human voice and computer music as intermixed portions of the program. Similarly, the I/O channel connection allows an external feature, such as voice synthesizer, to use the same audio output as the rest of the system. The audio multiplexer has a variable gain or attenuation for each input channel and produces a normalized output independent of the channel selected. When switching between channels, it maintains a consistent output level.

System Board I/O

The system board of the PCjr has a serial I/O port which is RS232C compatible, but it does not use the standard 25-pin D-Shell connector. A special cable is needed to connect the port to standard asynchronous communication devices. The serial port uses the National 8250 Asynchronous Communications Element (ACE). This port is connected in exactly the same way as the alternate Asynchronous Communications Adapter is connected on the IBM Personal Computer, providing program compatibility. The clock rate, however, is different from that on the PC adapter card, so a different divisor value is required in the communication setup routine. If a program uses BIOS for asynchronous initialization, the BIOS support adapter handles the difference with no change in the calling interface.

The joystick interface on the system board is compatible with the IBM PC Game Adapter. It has four switch inputs and four resistive inputs. The circuit converts the resistance input into a variable time-delay output with an *RC* time circuit. The program can convert the time delay into a digital value by timing the pulse length.

The PCjr provides cassette support with a minimum of hardware, relying extensively on software for correct operation. An output bit controls a relay for turning the cassette motor on and off. The cassette program writes data to the cassette by varying the output frequency of one of the timer channels, using different frequencies for ones and zeros. The cassette input is a simple signal conditioning circuit that presents its output to a digital input. The cassette program reads data by examining the signal transitions on the input port and timing them. This technique gives the IBM PCjr the ability to store programs and data on inexpensive cassette tape, without significantly adding to the product cost.

I/O Channel

The I/O channel for PCjr is an extension of the 8088 microprocessor bus. The I/O channel contains 20 address lines, an 8-bit bidirectional data bus, control signals, a clock, three interrupt request lines, and power distribution. Alternate bus masters can be added to the I/O channel with the hold request and hold acknowledge signals. This allows DMA or alternate processors to be added to the system.

The channel has some other unique features. The audio input line for external sound synthesizers was described previously. The channel has a ready line for attaching slow memory or peripherals. It also has a card select line for the feature adapters. Feature cards use this line to signal their activation. This signaling simplifies bus expansion design. The expansion logic can easily determine the location of a selected memory or I/O device and drive the data bus accordingly.

Cordless Keyboard

The PCjr cordless keyboard transmits data to the system unit using infrared (IR) light. The keyboard has no wire connection to the system unit and is battery powered. An optional cable can be installed to power the keyboard and eliminate the need for batteries. The cable also disables the IR transmission allowing multiple PCjrs to operate in the same room.

The CMOS logic used in the PCjr keyboard allows long battery life. An 80C48 microprocessor provides the intelligence for this remote unit. The keyboard consumes negligible current, in the range of 50–70 μA, when no keys are depressed. Depressing a key powers up the 80C48. The processor then scans the keyboard for the correct key and transmits the scan code for that key over the IR link. The 80C48 then powers down until the next key is depressed. During the power up time, the keyboard consumes about 10 mA for the electronics. The IR diodes use considerable power, consuming about 450 mA when activated. To minimize battery drain and provide a detectable carrier frequency, the diodes are pulsed at 40 kHz with a 50-percent duty cycle. Each pulse lasts for 62.5 μs, with one pulse per bit. The bi-phase encoding places the pulse at the beginning of the data cell for a "1" and in the middle of the cell for a "0."

The PCjr keyboard uses a rubber-dome, carbon-contact technology which results in a full-travel, low-profile keyboard. Although the keys differ in size from normal typewriter keys, the center-to-center spacing is identical to that on a typewriter keyboard. Likewise, the key travel of about 4 mm from the rest position to the activated position is standard.

The PCjr keyboard offers excellent touch characteristics at a low cost. The keys have no symbol designations and are identified by a plastic overlay. Since all the keyboard encoding is done in system software, it is easy to redefine the keyboard by changing the keyboard decoding routine and using a different overlay.

Infrared Link

An IR receiver in the system unit of the PCjr receives IR light from the keyboard and converts it into a digital data stream. The keyboard sends data with a 40-kHz modulated IR signal using a biphase data transmission. The keyboard transmits a start bit, 8 data bits, and a stop bit followed by 11 additional stop bits. The start bit activates the NMI on the system board. The 8088 NMI routine then deserializes the data stream with the help of the 8253 timer. This BIOS software also provides some signal processing and error detection. The effective data rate of the IR link is 2200 Bd.

The PCjr uses 11 stop bits to give the processor some time between keystrokes to honor other interrupts. Timer interrupts occur regularly, and serial communication may be in progress. The system can receive serial data at up to 1200 Bd while simultaneously handling keystrokes.

Diskette

The optional diskette adapter card plugs into a dedicated connector on the system board of the PCjr. The diskette drive adapter uses the NEC μPD765 diskette controller to manage the drive and the serial data stream. PCjr does not have a direct memory access controller, so the diskette device control program must transfer the data with processor instructions. The timing constraints on the data transfer are so close that PCjr cannot accept any keystrokes during the diskette data transfer interval. Any keystroke attempted during that time sets a latch. After the data transfer, the BIOS control program will sound the alarm, alerting the user to the lost keystroke. The ROM BIOS device handler takes care of all these actions. Asynchronous communications operating as a background task also must handle this timing restriction. During a diskette transfer, the interrupt handler for communications may not gain control within the required time, resulting in data overrun. The communications program must ensure that no data are transmitted to it during a diskette operation.

The diskette drive is a slim-line, double-sided drive with 40 tracks on each side. This gives 360K bytes of formatted data using nine sectors of 512 bytes each per track. The diskette drive has a media cooling fan which insures reliable operation within the temperature range specified for the system unit.

The IBM PCjr was optimized as a single-diskette drive system. The power supply and the enclosure do not have the capacity to handle a second diskette drive or a fixed disk. Likewise, the diskette adapter card does not have drive select logic or the drivers and receivers necessary for connecting a second diskette drive; yet, the system I/O channel, described earlier, is fully capable of supporting almost any device. That device, however, must provide its own power and cabinet.

Internal Modem

The optional modem adapter card plugs into a dedicated modem connector on the system board. The modem is a Bell 103 compatible 300-Bd modem with auto-answer and auto-dial capability. Communication to the modem is through an 8250 ACE. The I/O bus connection of this adapter is compatible with the primary Asynchronous Communications Adapter of the IBM Personal Computer. Any program using the COM1: port of the Personal Computer will use the modem of the PCjr. The modem connects directly to the telephone line with a modular phone jack.

DOS 2.1

The IBM Personal Computer Disk Operating System (DOS) 2.1 is an enhanced release of DOS 2.0 and has the same functions and storage requirements as DOS 2.0. DOS 2.1 supports the IBM Personal Computer, the IBM Personal Computer XT, and the IBM PCjr, and becomes the DOS for the IBM Personal Computer family.

All DOS commands and functions are supported in the 64K-byte entry configuration of the IBM PCjr. DOS 2.1 also automatically redirects the printer operations to the serial port, allowing the IBM Compact Printer to be used when no parallel printer is attached. DOS 2.1 also has some modifications to handle the specific diskette drive characteristics of the PCjr. The most significant change is the addition of cartridge support. During the initialization of DOS, it scans for a cartridge. A specific cartridge architecture, documented in the IBM PCjr Technical Reference manual, allows for a DOS command file to be located in the cartridge, rather than requiring it to be loaded into RAM. DOS remembers these cartridge file names and transfers control to the cartridge when that file name is presented as a command. An example of this is the BASIC cartridge. DOS transfers control to the BASIC cartridge in response to the BASICA command, rather than searching the diskette for that file.

III. COMPATIBILITY

Although compatibility with the IBM Personal Computer was the key design requirement for the IBM PCjr, the requirement was not absolute. As with any design, an engineering decision was made when compatibility conflicted with the goal of lower costs or higher functionality. Most often the decision was made in favor of compatibility. Had every decision been made in favor of compatibility, the IBM PCjr would have looked the same and cost the same as an IBM Personal Computer. Clearly, some compatibility had to be sacrificed to build a new system.

The success of the IBM Personal Computer has largely been attributed to the amount of software that runs on it. With so large a body of available programs, it would have been inappropriate to design a new computer that could not take advantage of those programs. Consequently, the engineering decision was not one of total compatibility but rather, "which programs will run and which will not?"

Processing Speed

One incompatibility of the PCjr and the IBM Personal Computers is the processing speed of the 8088. All three systems use the same processor clock, 4.77 MHz. The difference in processing speed is due to the difference in display adapters. In the Personal Computer, the display memory is self-contained on the display adapter. This dual-ported memory serves the video controller most of the time, but it can be read and written by the processor. The processor encounters delays only when accessing the display memory storage area. In the PCjr, the system memory contains the display refresh buffer. As explained earlier, the CPU gets only one of every three possible memory cycles. A program that fetches instructions and data from this RAM area will run slower than a comparable PC program. This is because of the wait states that the PCjr inserts during processor memory cycles to synchronize the memory accesses to the available memory cycles. This degradation is limited to RAM accesses. Any fetches from ROM are unhindered, resulting in a performance loss that depends on the frequency of RAM access.

Although this performance difference is minimal, there are some programs that fail because of the timing differences. Any program that requires identical instruction timing executes differently on the PCjr than on the PC. To help programmers design and code programs that need external timing without resorting to instruction timing, the 8253 timer/counter on the PCjr is identical to that of the PC. The I/O control functions are also identical, as is the input frequency to the timer. Thus an external time base is available, if necessary.

BIOS

The design of the IBM Personal Computer attempts to insulate the programmer from the hardware specifics of the machine through a system program called Basic Input/Output System. These routines, contained in the ROM, provide a set of device drivers that interact directly with the machine's hardware. The intent was to have all programs use BIOS for any hardware interaction. The BIOS routines have served their purpose admirably, but not completely. As programmers strove for the ultimate in performance or special effects, they found they could gain some advantage by bypassing the BIOS routines and programming directly to the hardware. Also, the original BIOS design did not anticipate every programming requirement for the hardware. There are some functions for which no BIOS routine is available.

The PCjr has a BIOS program that provides for all of the functions found in the PC; however, that is not enough. Portions of the machine's hardware must duplicate the functions of the IBM PC exactly. The system must appear identical to the IBM Personal Computer in several key areas to ensure that the majority of programs continue to execute correctly. The following sections show some of the areas where hardware compatibility was required.

Component Selection

The processor, interrupt controller, and timer of the PCjr are identical to those of the IBM Personal Computer. The processor was an obvious choice, giving both an identical instruction set and a low cost. We used the same interrupt controller and timer primarily for compatibility reasons. The 8259 interrupt controller prioritizes and controls eight individual interrupts. The PC has no BIOS function for the manipulation of the interrupt controller. Some programs require direct interaction with the interrupt controller to set or clear the interrupt mask and to signal the end of an interrupt.

Similarly, the three-channel 8253 timer/counter provides a portion of the sound capability of the PC. There is no BIOS function in the PC for the timer/counter, and programs requiring sounds had to directly control the timer. This was changed in the BIOS for PCjr, which contains a sound interface to control not only the timer but also the sound generator. Future systems will probably not require the same measure of hardware compatibility, since the BIOS function can mask the hardware differences. For the design of PCjr, however, the timer control had to match the PC design exactly.

Direct Memory Access

The Personal Computer has a four-channel DMA controller as part of the system board. This controller does the dynamic memory refresh and provides I/O functions. For PCjr, we felt it would be economical to remove the DMA controller from the system, for several reasons. First, PCjr's video activity keeps the system memory refreshed. The display subsystem constantly reads the system memory for video information. By connecting the system memory appropriately, all of it remains refreshed. Second, the BIOS routines are the primary user of the DMA controller. The only component in the base Personal Computer system that uses DMA is the diskette adapter. Most application programs use diskette BIOS to read or write the diskette, rather than dealing directly with the hardware. The diskette BIOS for PCjr has been written to provide the same functions as the PC diskette BIOS, but without the use of DMA. This is a good example of how BIOS was used to mask an underlying hardware change.

The removal of the DMA controller does compromise total compatibility. Some programs directly control the diskette hardware, and consequently, the DMA. These programs do their own diskette BIOS, primarily for copy protection of diskettes. Diskette copy protection falls more into the area of art than science. Most copy protection schemes rely on special diskette characteristics, and some require identical processor timing. In all probability, it seemed that attempting to save diskette copy protection schemes would have resulted in a significantly more expensive system. The lack of DMA also affects programs that do not deal directly with it. The background asynchronous communications problem described earlier occurs because there is no DMA to handle the diskette data flow. Sometimes compatibility requirements cannot be determined simply by looking at the software that uses a particular feature.

Finally, the other adapter cards that require DMA capability (fixed disk and SDLC adapters) are not available in the form factor for the PCjr. This means that the cards need to be redesigned before they can be used on PCjr. At that time, they can be changed to include DMA capability directly, since the I/O bus of the PCjr allows for other system masters, such as a DMA controller, on the external bus. Overall, a considerable cost savings was achieved by removing the DMA controller from the system.

Display Compatibility

The display area imposed the greatest compatibility requirements on the design of PCjr. Although the IBM PC has a BIOS routine that handles nearly all display operations, many programs work directly with the hardware primarily to accelerate the performance of their applications. In particular, changing large sections of the display (other than by scrolling) can take a long time if a program uses the BIOS functions of single character read and write. This is due to the overhead associated with setting up the parameters and issuing the software interrupt for each character. Since the display adapters for the PC are memory mapped, a program can store the graphic information directly into the display buffer without BIOS intervention. The performance improvement is significant.

For these reasons, we felt that the video section had to emulate the IBM Personal Computer exactly in one area—the character map for text modes and the bit map for graphic modes. Consequently, the display memory map of the PCjr exactly duplicates the memory map of the IBM Color/Graphics display adapter in those modes which they have in common. In the text mode, the character code appears at the even-byte address, with the attribute for that character at the odd-byte location. In the graphics modes that are common to the PC and PCjr, the pixel map is identical. This includes the even- and odd-field addressing used by the Personal Computer in the graphics modes. We also used the same video controller chip, the 6845, for compatibility. Even though it is not advisable, some programs directly manipulate the controller registers to manage the cursor position or screen effects. By including a 6845 as part of the display design in the PCjr, a number of programs can run successfully, instead of requiring a change to their display handling.

Display Paging

As mentioned previously, many programs directly address the display refresh buffer. On the PC, these display buffers are located high in the address space. Specifically, the display buffer for the Color/Graphics display adapter is at B8000H. PCjr uses system memory for display refresh. This system memory occupies the lowest section of the memory space. Thus a program that writes directly to the Color/Graphics Adapter (CGA) will not store data in the display refresh buffer of the PCjr. This was changed by designing a memory address redirection system. To simulate the CGA, the system redirects any processor reference to the address range B8000H through BBFFFH into the system memory area. A page register determines the section of system RAM that the processor reads or writes are redirected to. Fig. 6 shows this method. Using this scheme, a program written to execute directly on the hardware of the CGA will write its data into the correct location for the display hardware of the PCjr.

This method also uses a second page resister. The display subsystem fetches its data in the system memory from the area identified by this page register. Normally, both registers point to the same area of system memory, which is usually the last 16K bytes of system RAM. The Power-On Self-Test establishes this area as the default region. For special effects, such as a quick switch of the displayed image, the processor can write into one area while the display shows a different region. Changing the display page register immediately changes the displayed region to the one pointed at. The processor can then begin changing a different region of memory for later use as the displayed image. This paging scheme is invaluable for doing real-time animation on the display.

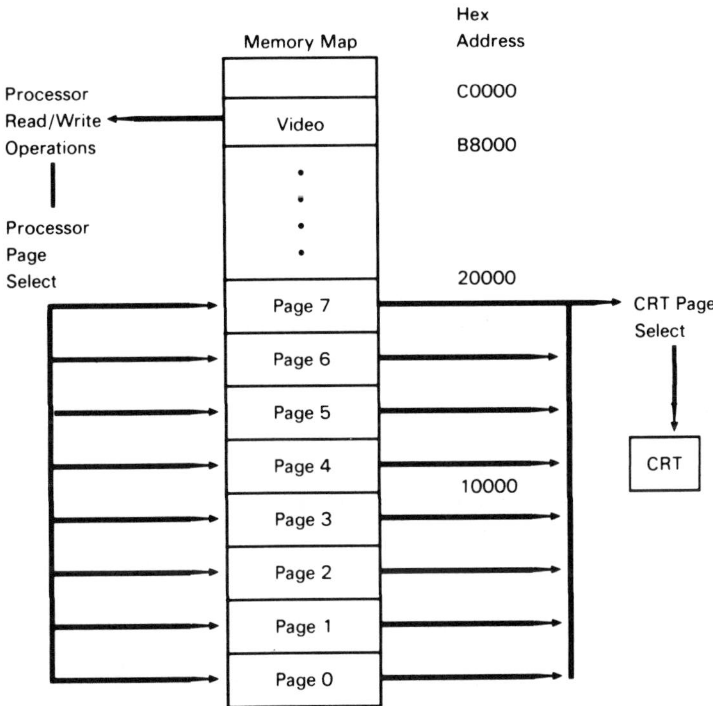

Fig. 6. Display memory paging.

Keyboard

Since the PCjr cordless keyboard has 62 keys, as compared to the 83-key Personal Computer keyboard, the operater must use a new function key (see Fig. 7) in combination with the other keys to produce all of the 83 keystrokes available on the PC keyboard. However, the keyboard functions still must be program compatible. Many programs read the keystrokes directly from the hardware keyboard input buffer on the PC, rather than using the BIOS functions available for the keystrokes. To remain compatible with such programs, each keystroke from the cordless

IBM Personal Computers 83-key Keyboard Function	IBM PC*jr* Cordless Keyboard Mapping
F1-F10	Function key + 1-0 (F1-F10)
Ctrl Break	Function key + B (Break)
Ctrl PrtSc (Echo Print)	Function key + E (Echo)
Shift PrtSc (Print Screen)	Function key + P (PrtSc)
Ctrl NumLock (Pause)	Function key + Q (Pause)
Scroll Lock	Function key + S (ScLock)
Numeric keypad region:	
Num Lock (Number keypad 1 through 10 becomes key scan codes.)	Alt + Function key + N (1 through 0 becomes numeric-key scan-codes)
PgUp key	Function key + cursor left (PgUp)
PgDn key	Function key + cursor right (PgDn)
Home key	Function key + cursor up (Home)
End key	Function key + cursor down (End)
Numeric keypad – sign	Function key plus the – sign
Numeric keypad + sign	Function key + = sign
\ key	Alt + /
' key	Alt + '
! key	Alt + [
~ key	Alt +]
* with PrtSc	Alt + .
Numeric keypad .	Shift + Del
All 256 extended codes: Alt + numeric value from numeric keypad	NumLock then Alt + numeric value (1 through 0)

Fig. 7. Keystroke mapping.

keyboard goes through several distinct software operations. First, the serial communication link with the keyboard creates a Non-Maskable Interrupt. The NMI handling routine converts the serial data from the keyboard into the scan code that corresponds to the key struck or released on the cordless keyboard.

Since this scan code is not identical to the scan codes produced by the 83-key PC keyboard, a second software routine now comes into play. The NMI routine invokes the scan code mapping routine through software interrupt 48H. This routine converts the 62 scan codes of the cordless keyboard to the 83 scan codes of the PC keyboard. This is the routine that tracks the current state of the function key and converts the multiple keystrokes of PCjr into a single PC equivalent keystroke. The output of this routine is a scan code identical to one created by the PC keyboard. The interrupt 48H routine places the PC compatible scan code into a special hardware register, at port 60H. The PC uses this port as the hardware register for the keyboard scan code. The PCjr emulates this port for program compatibility.

The final section of the software mapping is a program similar to the keyboard interrupt handler in the PC. When the mapping routine places a scan code into the port 60H register, it invokes a software interrupt 9. This is the hardware interrupt that the PC uses to signal a keystroke. Any program that replaces this interrupt to directly follow the keystrokes will gain control at this point.

The three layers of software give a great deal of flexibility as well as compatibility. The serial decoding routine is driven from the hardware interrupt. When it has recovered the scan code, it invokes software interrupt 48H for conversion into a PC scan code. Any program written specifically for PCjr that needs to intercept keystrokes can do so at this point. Finally, the hardware port 60H and the PC compatible conversion routine at interrupt 9 bring compatibility to programs written for the PC family. This combination of actions allows the lower cost 62-key keyboard to emulate all of the functions of the 83-key PC keyboard, in a fashion that is transparent to an application program.

IV. Summary

The IBM PCjr is a low-cost member of the IBM Personal Computer family. Although lower in price than the IBM Personal Computer, it offers equivalent and, in some cases, advanced functions. Most importantly, the IBM PCjr is a compatible member of the family. IBM has invested both hardware and software in the system design to ensure the greatest degree of compatibility within the system constraints.

References

[1]   *The 8086 Family User's Manual.* Intel Corp., 1980.
[2]   *Technical Reference Manual for the IBM Personal Computer.* IBM, Inc., Boca Raton, FL, 1983.
[3]   *Technical Reference Manual for the IBM PCjr.* IBM, Inc., Boca Raton, FL, 1983.
[4]   D. Bradley, *Assembly Language Programming for the IBM Personal Computer.* Englewood Cliffs, NJ: Prentice-Hall, 1984.
[5]   M. DePrycker, "A performance comparison of three contemporary 16-bit microprocessors," *IEEE Micro,* vol. 3, no. 2, pp. 26–37, Apr. 1983.
[6]   S. Fehr and A. C. Hartmann, "VLSI architecture for software structure: The Intel 8086," *IEEE Micro,* vol. 1, no. 2, pp. 57–69, May 1981.
[7]   F. Guterl, "Personal computers," *IEEE Spectrum,* vol. 20, no. 1, pp. 36–37, Jan. 1983.
[8]   C. Montague, D. Howse, B. Mikkelsen, D. Rein, and D. Mathews, "Technical aspects of IBM PC compatibility," *BYTE,* vol. 8, no. 11, pp. 247–254, Nov. 1983.
[9]   R. N. Noyce and M. E. Hoff, "A history of microprocessor development at Intel," *IEEE Micro,* vol. 1, no. 1, pp. 8–21, Feb. 1981.
[10] S. P. Morse, B. W. Ravenel, S. Mazor, and W. B. Pohlman, "Intel microprocessors—8008 to 8086," *Computer,* vol. 13, no. 10, pp. 42–60, Oct. 1980.
[11] R. Walker, R. Derickson, and K. Lobo, "CMOS logic arrays: A design direction," submitted to *Comput. Des.*
[12] G. Williams, "Inside the IBM PC," *BYTE,* vol. 8, no. 11, pp. 76–78, Nov. 1983.

9
The Anatomy of a Portable Computer

JOHN V. ROACH, STEVEN W. LEININGER, AND WILLIAM T. WALTERS

Although personal computers carry computing power to the masses, most of these computers cannot be readily moved around. Although the definition varies, portable computers are usually small enough to fit in a briefcase. In such computers both physical space and power consumption are at a premium. In this chapter one strategy is identified to make optimal use of these scarce resources. This chapter concludes with a prediction of the functionality of future portable computers.

The Editors

I. Introduction

The Radio Shack TRS-80 Model 100 Portable Computer represents a major innovation in the field of portable personal computers. Its true portable nature combined with its memory-based programs and data that are immediately available to the user at power-on have introduced a new era in the utility and simplicity of microcomputers. The computer, pictured in Fig. 1, is a battery-operated, fully self-contained computer system. It features a liquid-crystal display with eight 40-character lines, full-size typewriter-style keyboard, five ready-to-run application programs, and a built-in modem with an auto-dialer all enclosed in a compact (2 in × 11 7/8 in × 8 1/2 in) package that weighs less than 4 lb.

The computer has been designed for the business person who needs to be able to perform several different computing and communications tasks at the office desk, at a customer's office, in meetings, and while traveling. The TRS-80 Model 100 is the result of a team effort by Tandy Corporation of Fort Worth, TX, Microsoft Corporation of Bellevue, WA, and Kyocera of Tokyo, Japan.

To be truly portable, the computer must be able to operate with an internal power source. CMOS (complementary metal–oxide–semiconductor) integrated circuits, noted for their low power consumption, have been improving in speed and functionality in an evolutionary process [1]. While CMOS logic gates have been available for some time, it was not until the development of low-power CMOS memories, microprocessors, and peripheral LSIs (large scale integrated circuits) that one could design a complete system based on this power-saving technology. Similarly, large liquid-crystal displays (LCDs) have previously been available only as samples. Several Japanese manufacturers (such as Hitachi [2], Epson [3], and Optrex [4]) have finally perfected their manufacturing techniques, and low power consumption displays of eight rows or more are becoming affordable. Such large character and graphic displays remove some of the barriers to effective software design for a portable product.

The authors are with Tandy Corporation, Fort Worth, TX 76102, USA.

150

Fig. 1. The Radio Shack TRS-80 Model 100 Portable Computer main menu shows its five ROM-based application programs on the 8-line, 40-character liquid-crystal display.

II. THE MODEL 100

The initial product description for the TRS-80 Model 100 was motivated by several considerations. First, to be truly portable, the computer would have to be small enough to fit in a briefcase. Second, the computer would have to be able to run off of batteries. (Incidentally, several Radio Shack "pocket computers," which are a hybrid between a computer and a calculator, meet these two criteria.) Third, it was decided to support a full-sized typewriter format keyboard, and a display capable of handling a reasonable amount of text. Fourth, the computer should support useful and easy-to-operate software. Fifth, since an increasing amount of emphasis is being placed on communications from computer-to-computer and terminal-to-information service in the business environment, the ability to support different telecommunications standards was deemed necessary. Sixth, since we do not yet live in a "paperless society," a built-in printer interface would be necessary. Finally, some means of external data storage, such as cassette tape or floppy disk, should be available.

These general directions were refined to the following list of features:

1) Battery operation on AA batteries, for 20 h.
2) 240 × 64 dot graphics display, capable of displaying 8 rows of 40 characters.
3) Selectric-style keyboard with 16 function keys.
4) BASIC, word processing, address book, terminal, and scheduling software built into the system.
5) Parallel printer interface, conforming to Centronics standard.
6) Interface to external audio cassette, for program and data loading and storage.
7) Internal clock/calendar circuit to perpetually monitor time.
8) Auto dial, answer/originate Bell 103 compatible modem with direct line interface.

III. SOFTWARE

The Radio Shack Model 100 primary software consists of five programs permanently stored in memory. These programs are described below [5].

A. BASIC Interpreter

BASIC, despite some of its purported shortcomings, has become the standard programming language for nearly all personal computers. The Model 100's BASIC interpreter is similar to the Microsoft BASIC used in most of the personal computers on the market. The processing speed of the BASIC interpreter is comparable to that of the Radio Shack TRS-80 Model III personal computer and the Apple II computer [6]. In addition to the normal functions, commands, and statements usually supported by BASIC, there are additional graphics statements and functions which take advantage of the bit mapped liquid-crystal display. For example, the statement LINE X1,Y1 — X2,Y2 draws a straight line between two points.

Perhaps the most significant extension to previous versions of BASIC is the enhanced file handling capability on the Model 100 computer. By using BASIC's OPEN file command, program and data files can be assigned to any of 6 devices. RAM (in memory storage) and CAS (cassette tape storage) files constitute actual stored files which can be written and read under program control. COM (RS-232C communications line) and MDM (telephone line modem) files are transmission files, where the device being communicated with will send and/or receive the file data. LCD and LPT (line printer) files facilitate program directed output to the liquid-crystal display screen and the parallel printer port, respectively.

B. Text Processing

TEXT, the built-in text processing program, is a simplified "cut and paste" text editor which can be used for word processing and for other applications that require creation and manipulation of text. TEXT can be used to create document files for use in the other application programs in the Model 100 computer. The cut and paste technique allows the user to select a block of text and move it to the "paste buffer," an area in memory which remembers the last block of text CUT or COPYed. To paste the cut block of text back into the document (or another document, for that matter), the location for the insert is found using the cursor positioning keys, and the PASTE key is pressed. The entire block of text from the paste buffer is then inserted into the document at the point selected. In addition to the cut and paste functions, TEXT supports control code editing functions which provide additional control over cursor movement, file operations, and cut and paste editing.

C. Schedule Organizer

The SCHEDL program keeps track of and locates dates and times for appointments or events. Because it uses a text-oriented file, additional items such as expenses and action items can be recorded. The user first creates the NOTE.DO text file with information such as meeting date, time, and subject using different characters to differentiate between schedule entries and expenses. For example, the following file NOTE.DO could be set up:

```
#10/25  9:00 Status meeting regarding Project X
#10/27  3:00 Plant visit by board of directors
$10/26 Glass cleaner—Joes Hdwr 2.50
*Get passport information from post office
$10/25 Lunch for Project X staff McD 23.75
*Order new drafting table
#11/2 11:30 Lunch with Mike
```

In this example, "#" was chosen to represent a scheduled event, "$" for an expense item, and " *" tags an item for the "to do list." Upon entering SCHEDL, we can then type "Find *" to display our to-do list:

*Get passport information from post office
*Order new drafting table

Because SCHEDL is a text scanning program, it allows for free-form formatting of data records. This allows the user to tailor the file format to fit individual needs.

D. Address Organizer

The program ADDRSS lets the user retrieve information from a file named ADRS.DO created previously using the TEXT program. The records in the ADRS.DO file typically contain name, phone number, address, and additional information as desired. For example, we may want to set up a file of business contacts by name, phone number, occupation, and city. Further, there may be some data in each record for simplifying operations in the telecommunications program (discussed later). In this example, the initials of each business contact are used as a keyword to that record. The file consists of entries like

Peter Jones :1-817-555-1700: PJ, Insurance, Fort Worth
Sam Smith :555-2673: SS, TV Repair, Dallas
Ed Brown :1-408-555-2600: EB, TV Games, San Jose

Now, if we needed to find out who our insurance agent was, we could press the "Find" function key and type INS. The entries would be searched, and those which had the string "INS" in any part of their record would be displayed. In our case, the "Peter Jones" record would be listed in its entirety. Because all records are searched, we could print a list of all contacts somehow involved with television by using the "Lfnd" function key followed by the text "TV." The Lfnd function causes all matched records (Smith and Brown records in this case) to be output to the parallel printer port.

E. Telecommunications

The TELCOM program performs several functions related to the exchange of information between the Model 100 computer and outside data sources, phone dialing, and serial I/O setup. The phone dialing feature uses the same ADRS.DO file which was created for the ADDRSS program. Each line in the file could contain the name of the person to call, that person's phone number, and maybe a list of keywords to facilitate lookup. The function keys can be used to FIND a given string in the file. For example, to locate the entry with Peter Jones in it, the user would press the FIND function key (or type FIND) and then type Jones (his last name), PJ (his initials), or maybe INS (for insurance, his occupation in our example). The program would respond by displaying all records that match the request. In this case, it would find the first record. To place the phone call (assuming the computer is already connected to the phone line), the user would simply press the CALL function key. The Model 100 would print "Calling Peter Jones" and the phone number digit by digit as it pulse-dials it. Of course, typing "Find TV" would result in two entries being found. The user can either dial the current entry shown by pressing "Call" or look at the next entry by pressing the "More" key. In addition, TELCOM also provides terminal functions for use with dial-up databases such as Compuserve and the Source. The Bell 103 compatible modem allows the user easy access to such resources with either direct phone line connect, or if on the road, acoustic coupler connected to the handset of a standard telephone.

F. The File Manager

The File Manager is a ROM-based operating system which maintains the directory, allocates RAM, and provides the main menu functions. While not an applications program like the five programs reviewed so far, the file manager is perhaps the most innovative portion of the internal software. The Model 100 computer's operating environment is unique in several respects. First, the RAM is continuously battery backed-up, so data are not lost in a power-down condition. The software does not require any form of mass storage other than that which is provided as RAM in the system. All programs are entered through the main menu. Because all of the data and program files must coexist in the same 8K to 32K bytes of RAM, the file manager must insure integrity of all data and programs while allowing maximum functionality of the currently running program. The file manager maintains a directory of program names, their memory location pointers, and information regarding what type the program is (ASCII text, compressed BASIC, or machine language) [7]. Within the RAM memory space, BASIC program files are stored at the lowest addresses available. Text files are directly above the BASIC programs, with machine language immediately above the text files. The memory at the very top of RAM is reserved for pointers, LCD screen buffer, the telecommunications buffer, and the directory. The space between the last machine language file and the memory reserved at the top is called the working storage area. It is used as the variable storage area when executing BASIC programs or as the text buffer area when inputting a file.

IV. HARDWARE

As Fig. 2 illustrates, the block diagram for the TRS-80 Model 100 is elegant in its simplicity [8]. Since components which consume low power often cost the most, and both low power and low cost were desired, the final product is the result of efficient hardware design, in which

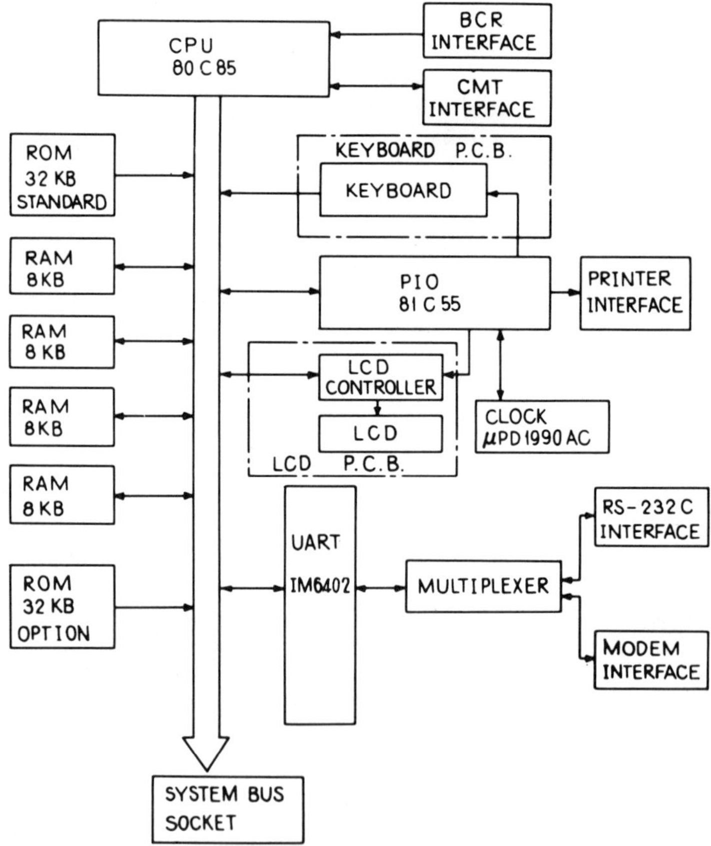

Fig. 2. The block diagram of the Model 100 computer.

readily available CMOS logic and LSI are connected together with the fewest number of parts. The computer consists of a central processing unit, memory, and LSI integrated circuits for input, output, and special functions. The bar code reader circuitry and the cassette tape interface electronics connect directly to the CPU chip. The IM6402 Universal Asynchronous Receiver/Transmitter provides the serial interface to the RS-232C circuitry and to the modem electronics. The 81C55 Parallel Input/Output (PIO) integrated circuit, which has 3 parallel digital ports and a 14-bit programmable counter/timer, provides interface and timing signals to the keyboard array, the parallel printer interface, the clock/calendar chip, and the liquid-crystal display electronics. To minimize hardware, many system features, such as keyboard scanning and decoding, bar code reader timing, and cassette tape reading and writing have been implemented in software.

All of the circuitry for the Model 100 Portable Computer is contained on three printed circuit boards (Fig. 3). The largest board contains practically all of the electronics, with the exception of the LCD control logic, which is mounted on the rear of the liquid-crystal display. The keyboard printed circuit board holds the 56-key typewriter array, the 8 programmable function keys, the 4 command keys, and the 4 cursor control keys.

Fig. 3.   The three printed circuit boards of the Model 100 computer include the main logic board on the left, the LCD driver board on the upper right, and the keyboard printed circuit board on the lower right.

A. Central Processing Unit

The central processing unit is an OKI 80C85, the CMOS equivalent of the Intel 8085 microprocessor. The 80C85, in addition to having a low power consumption, has the same instruction set as the Intel 8080 [9], which helped reduce the software development time for the Model 100. The ROM-resident BASIC in the Model 100 computer was licensed from Microsoft Corporation, and is an expanded version of the BASIC written by Microsoft in 1975. The multiplexed data and address bus is demultiplexed on the printed circuit board as required by the system memory.

The 8085 includes a serial I/O port which is supported by two instructions not available in the older 8080 [10]. This feature is used to simplify the hardware design of the cassette tape interface, as will be described later.

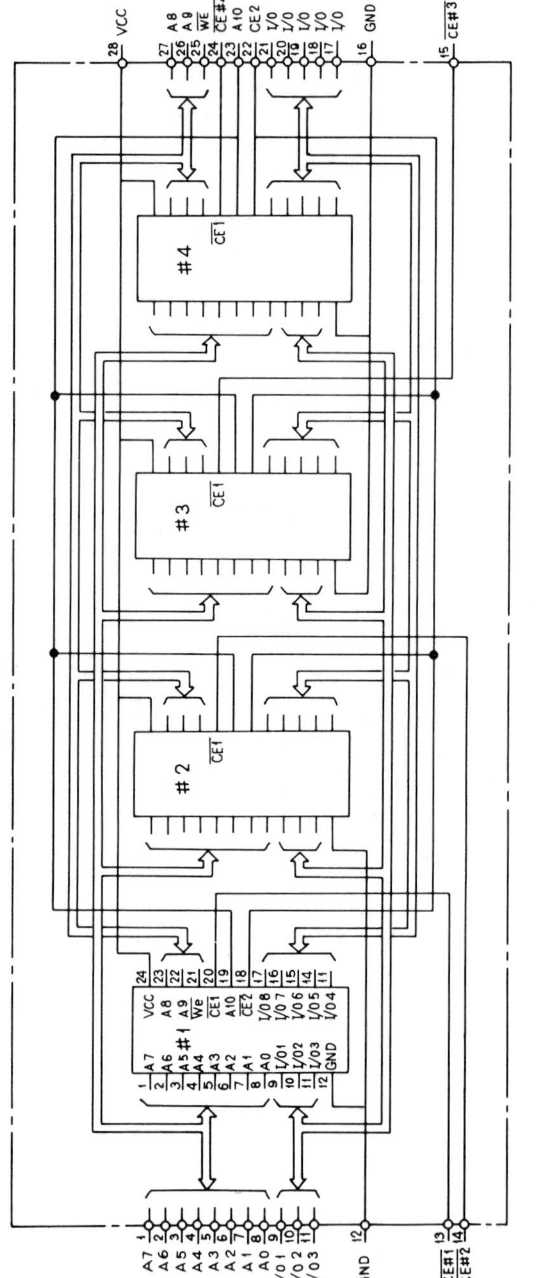

Fig. 4. The 8K × 8 CMOS static RAMs in the computer are in reality four 2K × 8 RAMs connected together on a ceramic hybrid substrate.

B. Memory

The TRS-80 Model 100 has a 32K (32K = 32768) byte read only memory that contains the five application programs, the peripheral and I/O control routines, and the bit patterns for the alphanumeric and graphic character sets. A single chip was preferred over multiple chips of lower storage density based on printed circuit board requirements. Also a CMOS ROM was selected instead of an NMOS ROM because of the lower power consumption of the CMOS chip. The Model 100 also contains 8K bytes of random access memory used for saving user data when the computer is turned off. While some 8K byte RAMs are available, their cost is much greater than the cost of four 2K byte CMOS RAMs. To conserve valuable printed circuit board area, a hybrid 8K CMOS RAM was developed. This hybrid consists of four 2K byte CMOS static RAMs mounted on a ceramic chip carrier and connected as shown in Fig. 4. The Model 100 can be expanded from 8K bytes of RAM to 32K bytes by adding three additional 8K RAM modules onto the main printed circuit board.

The address decoding and related logic circuitry necessary to interconnect the various system components is implemented with 7400 series pinout compatible CMOS chips. This address decoding circuitry, in addition to providing the chip select for the 32K byte ROM and the one to four RAM modules, allows the computer to turn off the main ROM and turn on an optional ROM which can be plugged into the ROM expansion socket on the bottom of the computer. This expansion ROM can be used for ROM-based software such as the Multiplan spreadsheet program and other programs designed for special applications. The ability to choose either the standard ROM or the optional expansion ROM is called bank selection. On the Model 100 computer, this is implemented with a selection bit from a latch addressed as an output port and a CMOS digital decoder IC. The memory map for the computer is shown in Fig. 5.

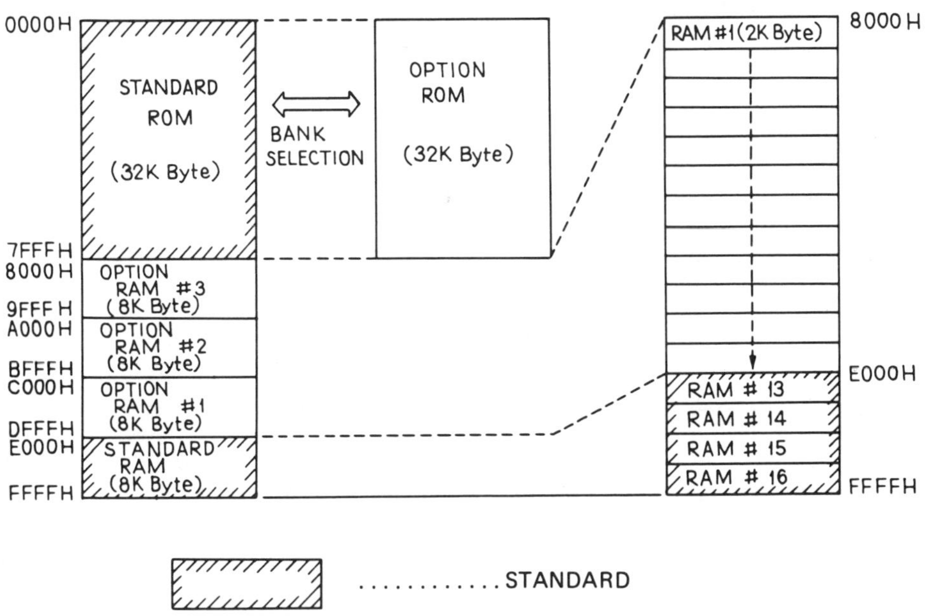

Fig. 5.   The memory map of the TRS-80 Model 100.

C. Keyboard

The Model 100 Portable Computer has a mechanical contact keyboard which is "scanned" and decoded by the 80C85 microprocessor. Unlike the keyboards used in the Apple II computer, the IBM Personal Computer, or the Radio Shack TRS-80 Model 12, there is no

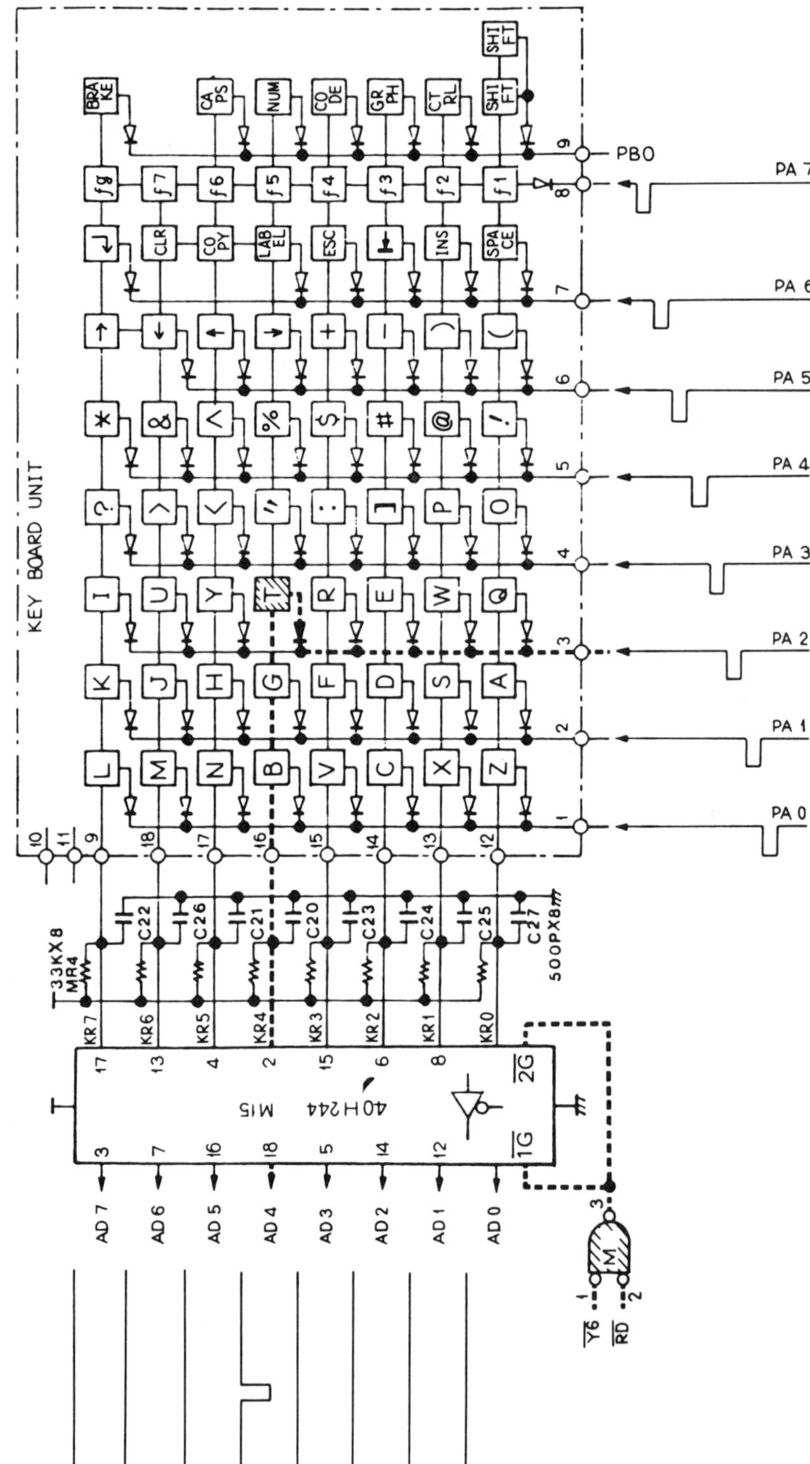

Fig. 6. The keyboard array is scanned and decoded under software control. The row data out of the buffer IC represents the data read when column PA2 is scanned and the "T" key has been depressed.

microprocessor dedicated to detecting key depressions and calculating the output code. Instead, the 80C85 microprocessor performs a matrix switch routine to determine which key has been depressed, and, through a look-up table, outputs the corresponding value [11]. The keyboard is a full travel mechanical contact keyboard with diode isolation. The microprocessor "scans" the keyboard by outputing a byte to the 81C55 parallel interface circuit, looking for a depressed key, and translating the key position information into an ASCII character through table look-up. The example in Fig. 6 shows the output signal of the 40H244 buffer IC corresponding to bit PA2 from the 81C55 parallel port being set low while the "T" key is depressed. Data bit AD4 is read as a logical "0," indicating that a key has been pressed in row 4 of the keyboard. The keyboard look-up routine then generates an index into the ASCII look-up table by multiplying the column number (in this case 2) by eight and adding the keyboard row number (in this case 4). The ASCII representation for "T" is then found by reading the value of the ROM memory location 20 bytes from the beginning of the look-up table.

D. Cassette Interface

The cassette interface is similar to those used on several of the home computers on the market. A digital bit output is filtered to make its frequency content compatible with a standard audio cassette recorder. The output of the cassette recorder is converted back into a digital pulse train by a simple comparator circuit. In the Model 100, the SID (serial input data) and SOD (serial output data) I/O pins on the 80C85 are used for the data into and out of the system, respectively, instead of the usual external latch and buffer normally required. This is an example of an area where logic requirements have been minimized to keep the system costs low. The input and output timing is done in machine language counting loops as with most other personal computer cassette interfaces.

E. Liquid-Crystal Display

The LCD used in the Model 100 is a TN (twisted nematic) type liquid crystal. The liquid crystal operates as an "electric shutter" that controls the passage of light. The liquid crystal is sandwiched between the front and rear polarizers, which are at right angles to each other. If no voltage is applied to the liquid crystal, the light entering the front polarizer is twisted 90° allowing it to pass through the rear polarizer and reflect off of the reflector and thus appear bright (see Fig. 7(a)). When voltage is applied to the liquid crystal, the polarized light from the front filter is passed through to the rear polarizer at right angles. Since the light cannot pass through the rear filter, no light is reflected showing up as a black dot or pixel (picture element) on the screen (Fig. 7(b)). To cut down on the number of wires necessary to address all 15 360 pixels (240 dots/line × 64 lines) on the Model 100's LCD, the display is decomposed into 2 sections each of 32 lines and 240 columns. The display is driven in a multiplex mode with 2 rows at a time. This circuit uses 10 shift registers with 50 parallel outputs each. Custom-designed integrated circuits for performing those functions are mounted on the back of the display interface printed circuit board. The signals for driving one of 32 rows at a time emanate from 2 additional ICs. One of the row driver ICs is the master timing generator for the LCD panel, providing clock and synchronization signals to the other row driver and the ten 50-bit-wide shift registers.

Everything on the liquid-crystal display is handled in a byte graphics mode. The CPU writes the bit patterns to the column driver/shift register ICs, and the synchronous logic automatically multiplexes the data to the liquid-crystal display. The bit patterns are 8 bits wide and are oriented vertically, so that only six 8-bit bytes need to be written into the control logic to define a character.

F. Telecommunications Interface

The Model 100 supports several modes of communications, including RS-232C serial and Bell 103 compatible modem. The heart of the communications circuitry is the IM6402 CMOS UART

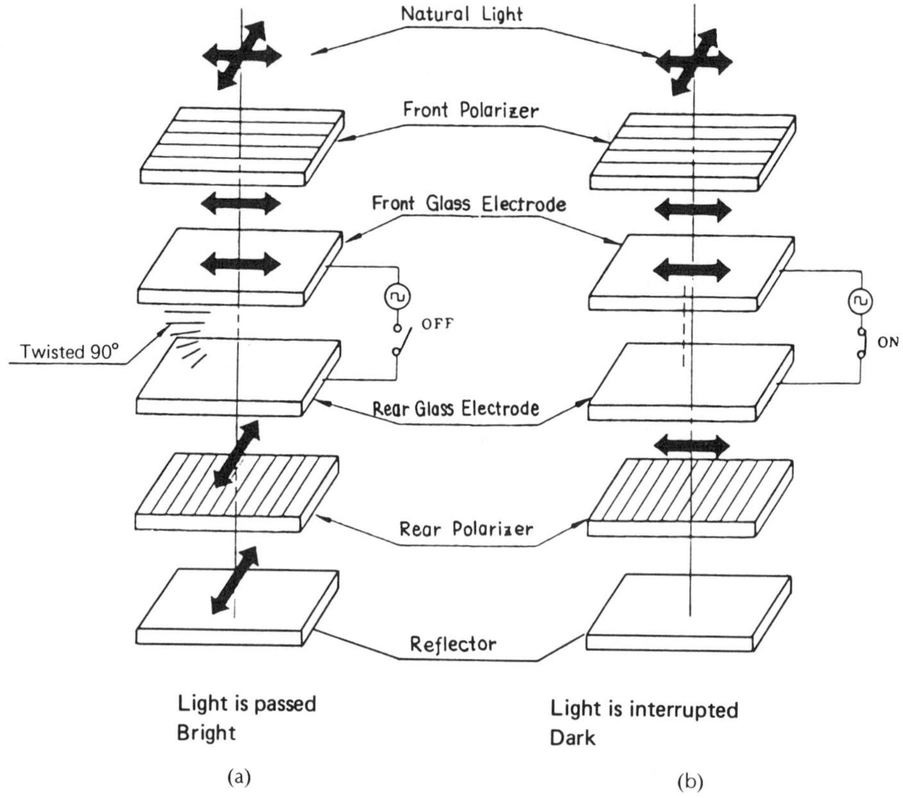

Fig. 7. The liquid-crystal controls the angle of the incident light on the rear polarizer, permitting transmition to the reflector only if no power is applied. (a) Voltage is not applied. (b) Voltage is applied.

(Universal Asynchronous Receiver/Transmitter) and the timer portion of the 81C55. The IM6402 (Fig. 8) is one of the first CMOS digital communications integrated circuits to be available at low cost. The UART is split into two sections, the transmitter and the receiver. The transmitter consists of a buffer register followed by a parallel-to-serial converter. The transmitter timing logic shifts the data bits out of the transmitter shift register at a data rate determined by the transmitter clock input (TRC). In the Model 100 computer, the clock input to both the transmit and receive portions of the UART comes from the 14-bit counter in the 81C55, which is loaded with an appropriate divisor to produce a clock signal sixteen times the desired baud rate, as required by the IM6402. The receiver logic samples the incoming serial data signal and clocks the bits into the serial-to-parallel receiver register. When the entire data byte has been reassembled in the receiver register, the byte is transferred to the receiver buffer register, so that the shift register is ready for the next incoming data. Status signals from the UART indicate conditions such as Transmitter Buffer Register Empty (TBRE), Data Ready (DR), and various receive error conditions.

Because the IM6402 is a single-channel UART, digital logic is used to switch between the modem circuitry and the RS-232C drivers and receivers. This multiplexing logic is under software control to provide "switchless operation." The modem is a Motorola MC14412 Modulation/Demodulation LSI [12], and is supported by analog transmit and receive filters. The modem chip (Fig. 9) is capable of producing and decoding standard FSK (Frequency Shift Keying) signals that are compatible with Bell 103 modems. When in the "originate" mode, the

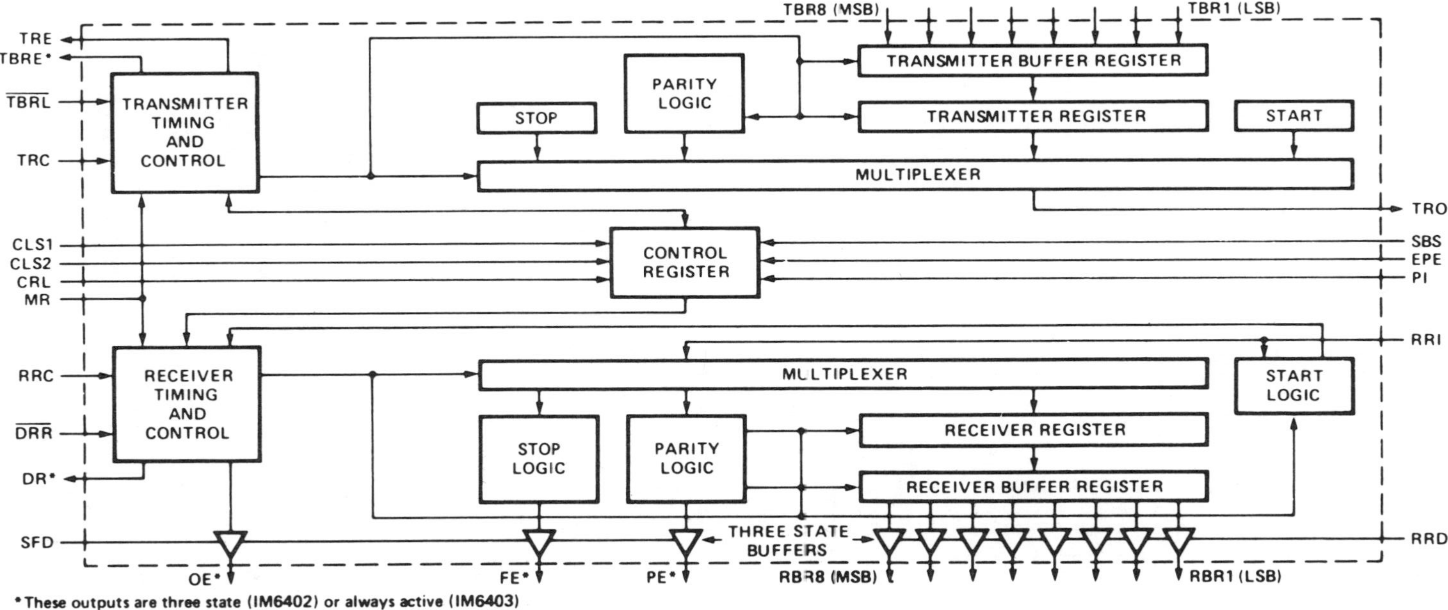

*These outputs are three state (IM6402) or always active (IM6403)

Fig. 8. The internal block diagram of the IM6402 UART shows the data transmit and receive registers.

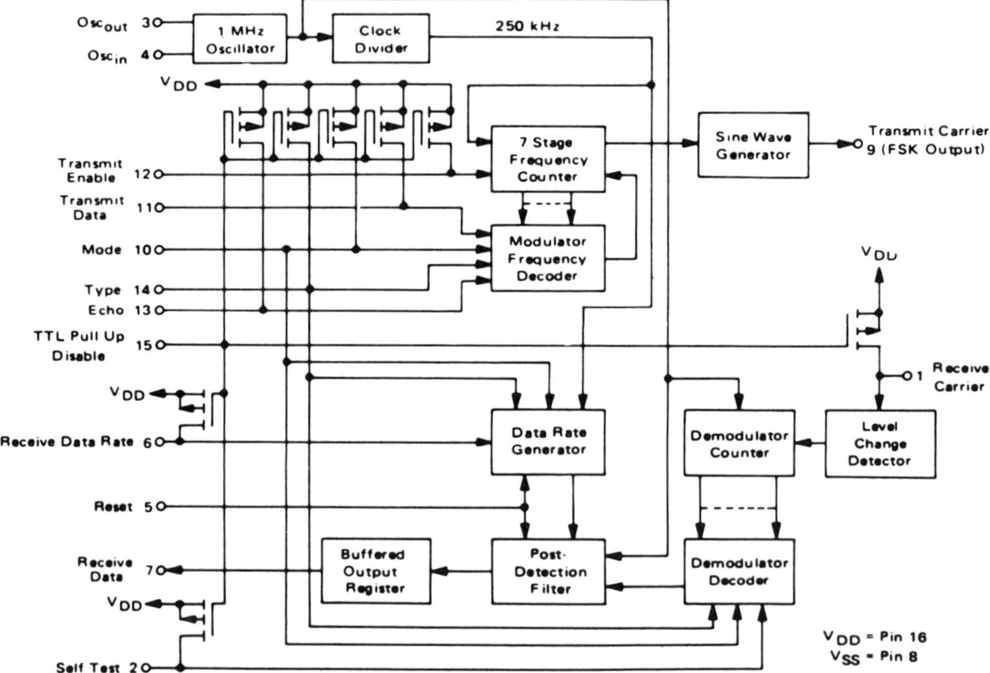

Fig. 9. The MC14412 modem integrated circuit generates and decodes standard 300-Bd FSK communications signals.

modem transmits a logical "1" bit as a 1270-Hz tone and a logical "0" bit as a 1070-Hz tone. The receiver, or demodulator portion of the MC14412 decodes incoming tones with a frequency of 2225 Hz as a logical "1" and those of 2025 Hz as a logical "0." When the "answer" mode is selected, the transmit and receive frequencies are reversed.

The modulator portion of the MC14412 consists of a 7-bit counter, an input clock of 250 kHz, a modulator frequency decoder, and a sine wave generator. The sine wave frequency is determined by the mode (answer or originate) and the state of the serial data stream from the UART. These two data signals adjust the period of the seven-stage frequency counter which drives the sine wave generator at sixteen times the desired output frequency. The sine wave generator outputs a 16-segment sine wave approximation which is filtered to produce a relatively pure FSK signal.

The demodulator portion of the MC14412 takes the digital pulse train input from the communications line filters and limiter circuitry and determines the incoming frequency by counting the number of cycles from the 1-MHz reference clock in the modem chip. The demodulation decoder then outputs a logical data bit stream, which is the recovered NRZ signal to be sent to the UART receiver. A digital low-pass filter, the postdetection filter, reduces the amount of digital glitch noise to an acceptable level for accurate data recovery.

The modem can be connected to the phone line directly using the phone line interface circuitry built into the Model 100, or it can be acoustically coupled to a standard phone handset using the optional acoustic coupler cups. The telephone line interface also contains a relay connected across the phone lines, to serve as a pulse dialer under software control. This relay, when activated by the TELCOM software in the Model 100, pulse-dials the selected number at either 10 or 20 pulses per second as selected by the user.

In the RS-232C configuration, the UART can support communications speeds ranging from 75 to 19200 Bd. The RS-232C interface is primarily used for connecting to other computers, higher speed modems, or to non-Tandy printers.

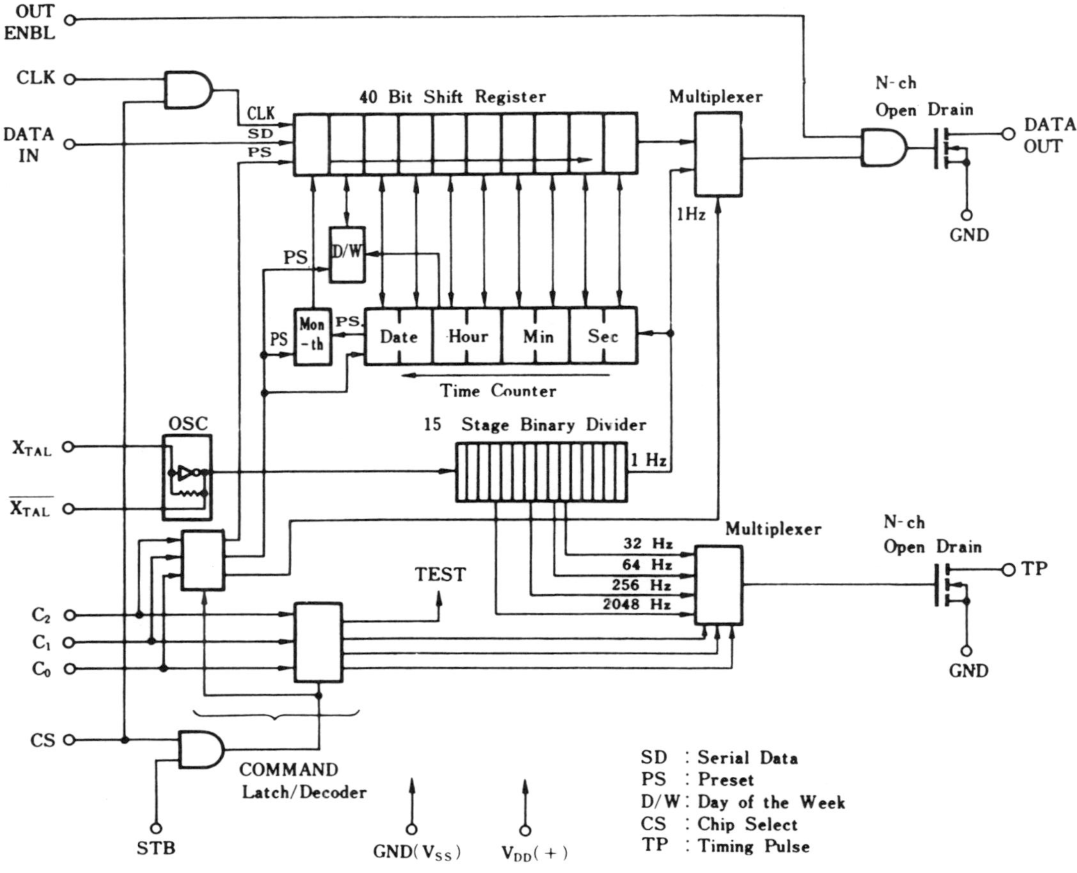

Fig. 10. The CMOS clock calendar chip internal architecture, showing the 1-Hz signal generator, the time counter, and the 40-bit shift register used for reading and writing the time counter.

G. Parallel Printer Interface

The Centronics-type parallel printer interface has been adopted by Radio Shack for all computers primarily intended for business use. The output port transmits in parallel the 8-bit ASCII representation of the character to be printed. These 8 bits of data are the latched 8 bits from the 81C55 PIO. The only other signal from the computer is the strobe signal, which latches the data into the printer. Two signals coming back from the printer are BUSY and its inverse. These two signals are used by the printer to indicate that the printer is performing some function, such as carriage return, which does not allow any further characters to be accepted. The inverse signal may be used to halt the printing operation in the event of a "Paper Out" condition.

H. Perpetual Clock/Calendar

The internal clock/calendar chip, a μPD1990 from NEC, allows the Model 100 computer to always have the current time and date available for use in the applications and programming language. This IC, shown in Fig. 10, generates an internal 1-Hz signal by dividing the 32.768-kHz crystal oscillator output signal by 32768. This signal is used to increment the seconds counter, which overflows at 60 seconds to increment the minutes counter, and likewise through the hours, days, and months counters.

The μPD1990 is written to and read from using a clocked serial interface (see Fig. 11). The time and date are initialized by clocking in the binary-coded decimal data corresponding to each or the respective counters. The clocking operation is accomplished by raising and lowering the CLK signal while applying the serialized data to the DATA IN pin on the IC. Both these digital signals are generated by 81C55 PIO under software control. In a similar manner, the data are read back by setting the output enable signal high, clocking the data out of the clock/calendar chip, and reconstructing the binary-coded decimal representations of the time and date in the CPU under software control. The clock, like the CMOS RAM, is always powered, even when the Model 100 is turned off. Thus there is no need to reset the time and date whenever the computer is turned on.

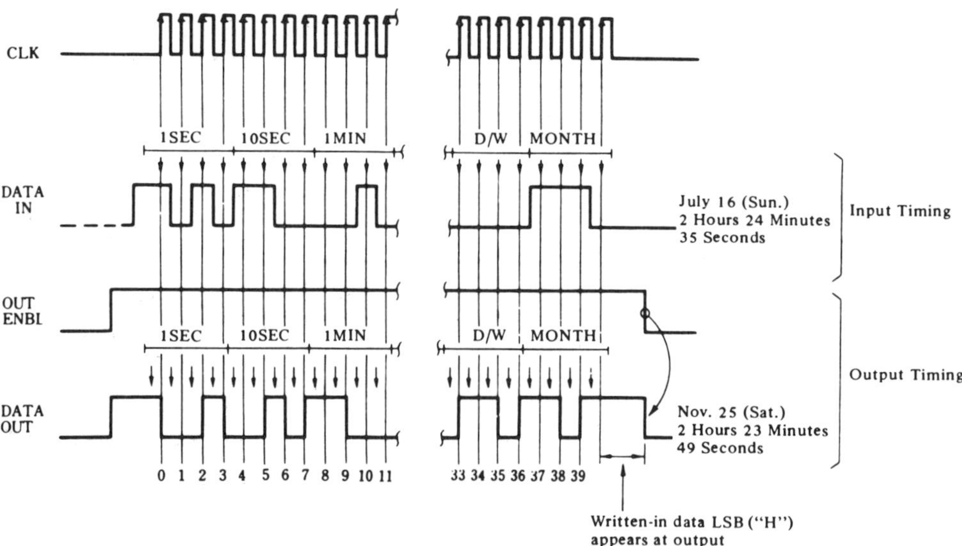

Fig. 11. The input and output data for the clock/calendar chip are transferred according to this timing diagram.

I. Barcode Reader

The barcode reader interface is an input which can be monitored under software control, and decoded to read UPC, 3 of 9, or most other standard barcodes. The input is set up to generate an interrupt which causes the microprocessor to vector to a jump table which directs the CPU to the appropriate decoding algorithm. Because of the number of different kinds of barcode wands and types of barcodes, the timing software for reading, converting, and interpreting the scanned codes must be first loaded into the computer.

J. Sound Output

A software-controlled bit is used to produce sound on the Model 100. A bit from the 81C55 can be toggled on and off at a software-determined rate to drive the piezo-speaker output. Additionally, one of the timer outputs of the 81C55 can be used to generate a tone directly.

K. Power Supply

The power supply for the TRS-80 Model 100 consists of a switching power supply which supplies positive and negative 5 V of direct current from the 4 AA cells in the computer or from the external ac adapter. The oscillator in the switching power supply can be turned off by toggling a output bit on the 81C55. When the oscillation stops, the power supply goes into a power-down mode. To restart the converter, the power switch must be turned off and then back on again.

There are two conditions when the computer will automatically turn itself off. The first condition is a low battery condition, which is sensed with a voltage comparator. When the battery voltage drops to about 3.7 V, a signal is generated which initiates a TRAP interrupt to the 80C85. The TRAP interrupt is a nonmaskable restart interrupt which causes the microprocessor to jump to memory location 0024H [13]. The Model 100 computer has a routine there which prepares for a graceful system power down by resetting the necessary program pointers and toggling the oscillator control bit to shut down the power supply. The second condition which turns off the computer is a lack of program operation for about 10 min. The control bit is toggled automatically so that the power supply will not drain the batteries when the computer is inadvertently left on. The waiting period until power off is adjustable using the BASIC command POWER *n*, where *n* is the number of tenths of minutes of no activity. The POWER CONT command is used to disable the automatic power down feature.

L. Performance

Since the Radio Shack Model 100 portable computer was announced in the spring of 1983, a number of other briefcase-size computers have been introduced. In a study comparing 14 of the so-called "note-book computers" [14], the Model 100 running a speed and accuracy benchmark was shown to be slower, but more accurate than two thirds of its competition. The slowness can be attributed to the use of double precision numbers in the Radio Shack computer as compared with the single precision numbers which most of the competition defaults to. It was our feeling that the numeric accuracy was, in general, more important to our customers than the speed.

V. Conclusion

The Radio Shack TRS-80 Model 100 Portable Computer combines easy to use software with an efficient hardware architecture to bring a high level of programming power to the micro-computer user. As advances in hardware and software technology take place, the portable computer will evolve into a more powerful, easier to use tool.

The number of characters on the LCD display will soon equal those of a CRT terminal. Memories will have increased capacity with reduced power consumption. VLSI modem technology will crack the 1200-Bd barrier with cost effective, high-speed implementations. Integrated software environments featuring "windowing" and shared data will evolve. Even the low power supply will improve with advances in battery technology [15].

New portable computers will evolve from existing portables and popular desktop personal computers, so that the new product can take advantage of an existing applications software base. And when these new computers reach the market, at least part of their roots will be in first-generation products, such as the TRS-80 model 100.

REFERENCES

[1] D. L. Wollensen, "CMOS LSI—The computer component process of the 80's," *Computer*, vol. 13, no. 2, pp. 59–67, Feb. 1980.
[2] *Hitachi Dot Matrix Liquid Crystal Display*, Hitachi, Ltd., Nov. 1982.
[3] *Large Capacity LCD Graphics Modules*, Epson America, Inc., July 15, 1983.
[4] *Graphic Liquid Crystal Display Module*, Optrex Corporation, Oct. 1983.
[5] *TRS-80 Model 100 Owner's Manual*, Tandy Corp., 1983.
[6] R. Malloy, "Little big computer, the TRS-80 Model 100 portable computer," *Byte*, vol. 8, no. 5, pp. 14–34, May 1983.
[7] B. Walters, "Delving into the darkest reaches of the Model 100's memory," *Portable 100*, vol. 1, no. 5, pp. 16–19, Jan. 1984.
[8] *TRS-80 Model 100 Portable Computer Service Manual*, Tandy Corp., 1983.
[9] R. N. Noyce and M. E. Hoff, Jr., "A History of microprocessor development at Intel," *IEEE Micro*, vol. 1, no. 1, pp. 8–21, Feb. 1981.
[10] S. P. Morse *et al.*, "Intel microprocessors—8008 to 8086," *Computer*, vol. 13, no. 10, pp. 42–60, Oct. 1980.
[11] *M6800 Microprocessor Applications Manual*, Motorola Inc., 1975, pp. 5-1 to 5-11.
[12] *CMOS Integrated Circuits*, Motorola Inc., 1978, pp. 7-244 to 7-228.
[13] *Microprocessor and Peripheral Handbook*, Intel Corp., 1983, pp. 2-10 to 2-25.
[14] D. H. Ahl, "Choosing a notebook computer," *Creative Comput.*, vol. 10, no. 1, pp. 18–32, Jan. 1984.
[15] B. Margolin, "Batteries—A key ingredient for portability," *Electron. Prod.*, vol. 25, no. 13, pp. 75–77, Mar. 18, 1983.

10
Microprocessors—The First Twelve Years

AMAR GUPTA AND HOO-MIN D. TOONG

During the first twelve years of their existence, microprocessors have evolved at a dramatic pace in terms of numbers, technology, power, functionality, and applications. This chapter begins with a technical explanation of key microprocessor specifications. Four generations of microprocessors are considered in detail, along with case studies of popular chip families. Special-purpose processors, software issues, and performance evaluation techniques are other areas of discussion. Overall industry trends are presented.

I. INTRODUCTION

Looking at the wide array of sophisticated microprocessors available today to support virtually all conceivable applications, it is difficult to believe that microprocessors have been in existence for just over a decade. The term "microprocessor" was first used in 1972. However, the era of microprocessors commenced in 1971 with the introduction of the Intel 4004, a "microprogrammable computer on a chip" composed of an "integrated CPU complete with a four-bit parallel adder, 16 four-bit registers, an accumulator and a push-down stack on a chip" [1]. The 4-bit 4004 CPU contained 2300 transistors and could execute 45 different instructions. Successive generations of microprocessors, using 8-bit, 16-bit, and 32-bit chips, commenced in 1972, 1974, and 1981, respectively. During their twelve years of existence, the number of devices per chip has increased by a factor of 200, the clock frequency by a factor of 50, and the overall throughput of the microprocessor has increased by two to three orders of magnitude. By all standards, the pace of the microelectronic revolution is unparalleled—it even outstrips the pace of advancement of the computer. The time elapsed between the original invention and the adoption of 32-bit word size is just one decade in the case of microprocessors, almost half the time lag as in the case of computers. "After only a single decade, in fact, microprocessor design has evolved from a situation in which it lagged far behind conventional computer design to a place where it is beginning to take the lead" [2]. This is both in terms of computing power and architectural sophistication.

A *microprocessor* is the central arithmetic and logic unit of a computer scaled down so that it fits on a single silicon chip (sometimes several chips) holding tens of thousands of transistors, resistors, and similar circuit elements [3]. Early microprocessors performed basic functions only. Additional chips were required to generate timing signals, to provide primary memory for program and data storage, and to interface with peripheral units. During their first years of existence, microprocessors were used almost exclusively as *microcontrollers* on a dedicated basis in process control applications. They offered a limited instruction set and needed to be programmed directly in machine language. Over the years, the evolution of superior system architectures, the availability of improved higher level languages, and the increase in power and

The authors are with the Sloan School of Management, Massachusetts Institute of Technology, Cambridge, MA 02139, USA.

flexibility has greatly broadened the domain of microprocessor usage [73], [74]. Microprocessors have been the direct cause of the computer game explosion and the personal computer revolution [64].

Early microprocessors were fabricated using p-channel MOS technology. In 1974 RCA introduced the 1802, the first microprocessor fabricated in CMOS technology. Over the years microprocessors have been fabricated in almost all available semiconductor technologies. The Intel 8080 used n-channel enhancement-mode MOS, the Intel 8085 used n-channel depletion-mode MOS [18], the Fairchild 9440 used bipolar technology, and the Fairchild 16-bit processor uses $I^2 L$ technology [17]. In view of the large number of transistors, most manufacturers prefer using MOS technology in preference to bipolar transistor technology. Currently, the most popular MOS technology is n-channel MOS (NMOS) by virtue of its high packing density and fast switching speeds. To emphasize the high-performance aspect, Intel prefers to call it HMOS. The Intel 8086, introduced in 1978, contained 29 000 transistors implanted in an area of 48 400 mil^2; the Intel 80286, introduced in 1982, has three times the circuit density with 130 000 devices in an area of 70 225 mil^2 [14]. Such design innovations will enable NMOS to remain popular at least until the mid-1980s [77], [78]. A leading competitor is complementary MOS (CMOS) technology [76], [80] which provides faster speed and lower power consumption than circuits implemented with traditional PMOS and NMOS technology; the disadvantage of CMOS lies in its lower packing density. Classical CMOS logic designs have an equal number of n- and p-channel devices. Newer CMOS designs use a higher number of n-channel devices than p-channel devices in order to implement higher circuit densities. High-density CMOS microprocessor circuits have been implemented among others by Bell Laboratories [4], by Rockwell International [5], and by Hewlett-Packard [15]. In coming years, CMOS will become the most popular technology for fabricating microprocessors because of the advantages offered by CMOS in terms of faster speed, lower power consumption, and higher noise immunity [6], [75], [76].

The most significant single criterion for evaluating and selecting microprocessors is the word size of the microprocessor which reflects the basic unit of work. A larger word size implies higher processing power and greater addressing capabilities. In the early years of microprocessor evolution, the size of register, the width of internal instruction paths and data paths, and the width of external instruction paths and data paths were almost always identical. This is rarely true now. Larger external paths require the chip package to have a large number of pins, which increases the total packaging and production costs. Thus chips nowadays tend to have larger internal paths than external paths. For example, the Motorola 68000 and the National NS 16032 have 32-bit internal paths and 16-bit external paths. A true 32-bit microprocessor has all paths and all internal units designed to communicate or process 32 bits in parallel; some of these paths may, in fact, be wider than 32 bits. For example, a 32-bit by 32-bit multiply yields a 64-bit result, and some 32-bit microprocessors are designed to store intermediate results with higher accuracy. If one assumes that a generation ends with the introduction of the pioneer chip of the next generation, then the 4-, 8-, and 16-bit microprocessor eras lasted for 1, 2, and 7 years, respectively. Now 32-bit chips are beginning to dominate the market. Also, smaller word-width microprocessors are used for a whole range of control applications, where there is no requirement for either the higher power or the greater addressing capabilities of costlier microprocessors with larger word width.

Microprogramming capabilities are now becoming a standard feature. Unlike early microprocessors which used "hard-wired architectures," a microprogrammed processor, though inherently slower, offers greater flexibility in terms of easier incorporation of changes or additions to the instruction set. To minimize the size of the control store area, a two-level control structure is frequently employed. First, the machine instructions are converted into sequences of microinstructions in the microcontrol store. These microinstructions serve as pointers to nanoinstructions in the nanostore. The nanocontrol store contains an arbitrarily ordered set of unduplicated machine-state control words, which control the execution unit. In the case of the Motorola MC68000, the two-level structure requires 22.5 kbits of control store, 50 percent less than the control store requirements for a single-level implementation. However, the two-level structure increases total access time. Even though microprogrammed architectures are now standard, very few chips can be microprogrammed by the user. The NCR Corporation four-chip 32000 series 32-bit microprocessor [7] offers external microprogramming capability; with this chip set, a Texas Instruments 9900 16-bit microprocessor operating system and instruction set can be emulated using 12K bytes of external store and an optimized Cobol virtual-language machine can be emulated with 25K bytes. With such microprogramming capabilities, one can emulate popular minicomputer and mainframe computer instruction sets at a small fraction of the cost involved in buying an entire computer system.

In 1975, Moore [16] had predicted that by the end of the decade the increase in complexity of VLSI chips would approximately double every two years rather than every year as in the preceding decade. In terms of chip complexity, microprocessors have been at the leading edge of technology. An excellent example is the Hewlett-Packard 32-bit microprocessor chip, the heart of an HP-9000 computer system, with 450 000 transistors on a single chip [8], [72]. One advantage of the increased transistor density is the ability to implement instruction repertoires that are much larger and much more powerful than the ones they offered previously, enabling more compact programs [88]. Frequently, the same chip uses instructions of varying sizes depending on instruction type, size of data, and addressing mode used; this variable size increases architectural complexity but reduces code size. Also, individual instructions are becoming increasingly powerful. On several systems a single instruction can control the transfer of an entire block of data from the memory, or manipulate several registers simultaneously. Such single instructions can replace several instructions of earlier systems. The contemporary instructions have close resemblance with instructions of higher level languages [19], facilitating compilation of such programs by performing in hardware an increasing number of functions traditionally done in software. As instruction size and complexity have increased, the complexity of the chip has increased and so has the design effort [110] from under a man-year to over 100 man-years of engineering time. Patterson [9], [89] has implemented reduced instruction set architectures to enable better utilization of the potential of evolving technology. In coming years, commercial microprocessors are unlikely to offer larger instruction repertoires—instead the focus will be on increasing the power of individual instructions and on supporting instruction sets with an established base. The T-11 chip [11] emulates the PDP 11 instruction set and offers an execution speed comparable to that of the PDP 11/34. The IBM System 370 instruction set has also been implemented on a single chip [12] though additional chips are still needed for supporting general-purpose registers and control storage. Other vendors, too, are expected to adopt instruction sets that have an established user base.

Over the years, the addressing capability of microprocessors has increased very significantly. The number of auxiliary addressing modes (like indirect, indexed, autodecrementing) has also increased. Most vendors offer specialized memory management chips, like the Motorola 68451 [81] and the National Semiconductors NS16082, to facilitate access to larger memory sizes and to assure adequate memory protection. However, the Intel iAPX 286, unlike its predecessor, the 8086, incorporates the memory protection function on the microprocessor chip itself [13]. Almost all new chips support virtual memory, giving an overall address space of the order of gigabytes. This virtual memory enables execution of very large programs and assists in simultaneous support of multiple users; virtual storage techniques make use of disk storage to augment main memory (RAMs and ROMs) for program storage and execution. Cache memories, on the other hand, are very fast memory units of relatively small size; information needed by the processor is prestaged from the main memory (or possibly from the disk) to the cache memory to enable faster processor execution. The increase in throughput is determined by the "hit ratio"—the fraction of times the processor finds the desired information in the cache.

Microprocessors differ significantly in their ability to store and manipulate different types of data. Although data in the form of bytes and words are generally supported on contemporary microprocessors, data in other forms, like bits, binary-coded-decimal (BCD) words, floating-point numbers, and character strings are not always directly supported. For example, data, in bit form, generally used in control applications, are not supported on the Intel 8086. BCD digits are not supported on the Intel iAPX 432. Floating-point numbers are not supported on the Bellmac-32A, and character strings, used in text processing applications, are not directly supported on the Motorola MC68000. The availability of support for a greater variety of data types makes the microprocessor suitable for a larger range of applications. Unfortunately, supporting multiple data types involves increased design complexity and an increased number of devices. In some cases, additional data types can be supported by using auxiliary processor chips. For example, the Intel 8087, the Motorola 68881, and the NS16081 floating-point chips can be used with the 16-bit microprocessors of the respective manufacturers. The proposed IEEE standard P754 on floating-point arithmetic is one data format that all chips attempt to support, either directly or through use of coprocessors.

The microprocessor revolution represents a trend towards implementing all the components of a computer on a small number of chips [63], [82]. Any computer system, irrespective of size power, and capabilities, combines three classes of subsystems—CPUs (for arithmetic, logic, and control functions), memories (READ/WRITE (RAM) and/or READ ONLY (ROM)), and input/output interfaces for peripheral control. Early microprocessors performed the basic CPU functions only. As better technology became available to enable integration of larger numbers of devices on the same chip, it became feasible to implement an increasing number of auxiliary functions on the microprocessor chip itself, resulting in increased popularity of computers built with very few chips. A *microcomputer* [86] combines a microprocessor with memory and input/output capabilities on one or several chips. *Single-chip microcomputers* [83] constitute an important subset of microprocessors in which all functions, including memory, are implemented on the same chip. In view of the chip area devoted to auxiliary functions, there is always a time lag between the introduction of a microprocessor chip of a given word size and the introduction of a microcomputer chip of an equivalent word size. For example, the first 8-bit single-chip microcomputer, the Intel 8048, was introduced in 1976, four years after the introduction of the first 8-bit microprocessor, the Intel 8008 [1].

There are several characteristics that distinguish single-chip microcomputers from conventional architectures. Because of the large volumes in which single-chip microcomputers are purchased, real estate per chip must be minimized. For instance, a 25-percent savings on a $2 microcomputer can result in savings of $500 000 for a million units. This optimization requires careful consideration of architectural trade-offs, memory design factors, instruction sizes, memory addressing techniques, and other design constraints with respect to area, performance, and run-time parameters [65]. Soon a typical commercial chip will contain about a million transistors offering a tremendous potential for implementing many sophisticated features in hardware. The processor section of the chip could include on-chip memory hierarchy, multiple homogeneous caches for enhanced execution parallelism, support for complex data structures and high-level languages, a flexible instruction set, and communication hardware [63]. More than four-fifths of the transistors on the chip are expected to be allocated for memeory functions. Although, architecturally, this computer-on-a-chip will compare favorably with modern computers, in terms of throughput, implementation of processing power comparable to the CRAY-1 on a single chip is not likely to happen until the end of the 1980s.

At the other extreme of the spectrum, there are applications that require higher computing power or better accuracy than that provided by single-chip microprocessors. For such applications, *bit-sliced organization* [66] enables linking several identical modular chips in parallel to achieve higher accuracy. Also, since these chips are implemented in either bipolar or emitter-coupled logic (ECL) technology, bit-sliced chips offer higher throughput than MOS chips. Thus by using multiple 4-bit chips of this kind, one can easily integrate systems offering an effective word size of 8, 12, 16 bits, or even more. The 2900 series of 4-bit chips manufactured by MOS Technology and Advanced Micro Devices has been very popular. Note, however, that although the Intel iAPX 432 uses a three-chip set, it does *not* represent an example of bit-sliced architectures, as the three chips are neither capable of operating individually, nor are they identical to each other. With the advent of wider word size, general-purpose microprocessors, the primary merit of using bit-sliced microprocessors for higher accuracy has gradually eroded over the years. Designers of these chips claim that they can continue to boost speed by 30 percent every two years by using ECL internal circuitry and advanced device processing techniques. It is useful, however, to note an example of a phenomenon that occurs in the semiconductor industry—in 1972, just a year after the commencement of the microprocessor era, American Micro-Systems Inc. announced the AMI 7200, the first 8-bit processor slice, or "byte-slice"; such slices became a commercial reality only with the introduction of the Fairchild F100200 in 1979 [66]. The need for caution in depending on chips using the leading edge of technology cannot be overemphasized.

II. 4-Bit Microprocessors

Although the Intel 4004 and the Rockwell PPS-4 were introduced earlier, the TMS-1000 series introduced in 1974 has made Texas Instruments the leading manufacturer of 4-bit processors used by millions in games, toys, calculators, and other low-end controller applications. The low price of less than $1 per chip is made possible by two major factors—first, the PMOS technology has become a mature technology and, second, the widespread usage of such chips has reduced production costs through economies of scale. Equivalent microprocessors implemented in CMOS (for low-power applications, for example, CMOS TMS 1000) or bipolar technology (for higher performance) cost more. The 4-bit CMOS microprocessors are used in conjunction with liquid-crystal displays (LCDs) for a wide array of hand-held products. Low-cost microprocessors continue to have a tremendous potential use in industrial (testing, process control, instrumentation, manufacturing), commercial, and consumer applications (see [20]). Like the basic TTL NAND gate, it is unlikely that the basic 4-bit processor will ever disappear.

The wide spectrum of additional capabilities implemented on 4-bit processor chips includes the following:

a) significant on-chip ROM and RAM;
b) versatile instruction set;
c) flexible I/O protocols;
d) on-chip A/D converter as on TMS2100;
e) multiple CPUs on same chip (e.g., the National Semiconductor COP2440 contains two identical CPUs along with ROM, RAM, system timing, and internal logic);
f) ability to drive displays directly—NEC (LCD) [79], Hitachi (LCD), ITT (LCD), and TI (Vacuum Fluorescent).

This trend of supporting additional functions on the same chip sustains interest in 4-bit microprocessor chips.

III. 8-Bit Microprocessors

Although the second generation commenced with the introduction of the Intel 8008 in 1971, the domain of 8-bit microprocessors witnessed several significant improvements in hardware and system concepts with the introduction of the Intel 8080 and the Motorola 6800 in mid 1974. The Intel 8080 commenced the trend of using NMOS technology, of executing decimal and BCD arithmetic, and of the 16-bit address bus. Unlike other microprocessors that required multiple power supplies, the Motorola 6800 was the first 5-V single-power-supply microprocessor. Also, instead of relying on TTL chips for interfacing, peripheral processors became available for supporting interface functions such as CRT and floppy disk control.

In sharp contrast to early 8-bit microprocessors with a structure supporting uniform 8-bit data paths, current 8-bit microprocessors frequently have 16-bit or even 32-bit internal data paths. The Intel 8088, the Texas Instruments 9980, and the Motorola 6809 all offer 8-bit external buses, but process data internally as 16-bit words. The NS16008 uses an 8-bit external bus and a 32-bit internal architecture. Such a structure enables retaining compatibility at the bus level with earlier 8-bit microprocessors, while enabling users access to new software. The newer 8-bit microprocessor chips are versions of popular 16-bit or 32-bit architectures intended for low-cost applications.

Since the introduction of the first 8-bit, single-chip microcomputer, the Intel 8048 in 1976 [1], several families of 8-bit microcomputers have become available. In most cases (Motorola and Rockwell, for example), these microcomputers are enhancements of the respective 8-bit microprocessor family. However, the Zilog Z8 is architecturally dissimilar to the Zilog Z80.

Depending on the intended application scenario, system designers demand microcomputers with one or more of the following characteristics:

a) high speed
b) low power consumption
c) large sized ROM
d) large sized RAM
e) microprogramming
f) easy interfacing of I/O
g) low cost.

Since there is no global optimal solution, vendors now offer whole families of chips, each family with a particular architecture; different members of the same family offer different combinations of ROM, RAM, and auxiliary functional capabilities. Examples include Intel [21], Motorola [22], Rockwell [23], Zilog [24], and Texas Instruments [25].

IV. 16-BIT MICROPROCESSORS

The era of 16-bit microprocessors began in 1974 with the introduction of the PACE chip by National Semiconductor. The Texas Instruments TMS 9900 was introduced two years later. Subsequently, the Intel 8086 became commercially available in 1978, the Zilog Z8000 in 1979, and the Motorola MC68000 in 1980. Several higher performance versions of the original chips are now available [84]. It is difficult to analyze in depth the characteristics of all 16-bit microprocessors that have been developed, or even the subset of chips [96], [97] that is currently available. We concentrate on the trends exemplified by the more popular chips.

The characteristics of leading 16-bit microprocessors are summarized in Table 1 [26]–[29]. The first five columns show the trend over the years of increasing functional capabilities, the addressing range, the diverse types of data supported, and clock speeds. The Intel 80286 is a higher capability version of the Intel 8086 [94] and displays the problems inherent in using new technology while retaining compatibility with an earlier chip. Upward compatibility often prohibits any major changes in chip architecture; this, in turn, restricts implementation or support of newer functions and data types. The five-fold increase in the number of transistors is used to increase performance six-fold, and to perform memory management and protection functions on the chip itself. Similarly, the Motorola MC68010, introduced in 1982, retains the basic architecture of the original MC68000, but provides additional support for virtual memory [121]. This similarity of architectures enables many different 16-bit microprocessor chips to be studied through evaluation and comparison of a few families of chips.

The basic structure of the Texas Instruments 9900 is shown in Fig. 1. It is a very simple design with no instruction prefetch or pipelining. The processor contains three registers—the program counter, the status register, and the workspace pointer; in addition, 16 general-purpose "workspace" registers are set up in memory. By altering the content of the workspace pointer, a new set of workspace registers is obtained. This simple "context switching" mechanism enables handling of interrupt and subroutine calls without need for saving or stacking the contents of the old set of workspace registers. All memory is accessed directly, a 16-bit word at a time; thus the maximum memory size is 64K bytes. However, the 9900 has byte instructions to perform operations on either of the two bytes fetched from memory. The microprocessor, memory, and I/O devices are interconnected by a local bus. The communications register unit (CRU) handles I/O interface using special instructions to address external devices via the CRU lines and

Table 1 Specifications of 16-Bit Microprocessors not Including Functions Provided by Coprocessors or Auxiliary Chips

	TI 9900	Intel 8086	Zilog-Z8000	Motorola 68000	NS 16032	Intel 80286
Year of Commercial Introduction	1976	1978	1979	1980	1982	1982
No. of Basic Instructions	69	95	110	61	82	121
No. of General-Purpose Registers	16	14	16	16	8	14
Pin Count	40	40	48/40	64	48	68
Direct Address Range (Bytes)	64K	1M	48M*	16M/64M	16M	16M
Number of Addressing Modes	8	24	6	14	9	
System Structures						
Uniform Addressability	X	X	X	√	√	X
Module Map and Modules	X	X	X	X	√	X
Virtual	X	X	X	X	√	√
Primitive Data Types						
Bits	√	X	√	√	√	X
Integer Byte or Word	√	√	√	√	√	√
Integer Double-Word	X	X	√	√	√	X
Logical Byte or Word	√	√	√	√	√	√
Logical Double-Word	X	X	X	√	√	X
Character Strings (Byte, Word)	√	√	√	X	√	√
Character Strings (Double-Word)	X	X	X	X	√	X
BCD Byte	X	√	√	√	√	√
BCD Word	X	X	X	X	√	X
BCD Double-Word	X	X	X	X	√	X
Floating-Point	X	X	X	X	X	X
Data Structures						
Stacks	√	√	√	√	√	√
Arrays	√	X	X	X	√	X
Packed Arrays	√	X	X	X	√	X
Records	√	√	√	√	√	√
Packed Records	X	X	X	X	√	X
Strings	X	√	√	X	√	√
Primitive Control Operations						
Condition Code Primitives	√	X	√	√	√	X
Jump	√	√	√	√	√	√
Conditional Branch	√	√	√	√	√	√
Simple Iterative Loop Control	√	√	√	√	√	√
Subroutine Call	√	√	√	√	√	√
Multiway Branch	X	X	X	X	√	X
Control Structure						
External Procedure Call	X	X	X	X	√	√
Semaphores	X	√	√	√	√	√
Traps	√	√	√	√	√	√
Interrupts	√	√	√	√	√	√
Supervisor Call	√	X	√	√	√	√
Compatibility with other microprocessors	X	X	X	X	X	√

*6 segments of 8M each.

address bus. The CRU mechanism can address up to 4 kbits each of input and output. All CRU data transfers to and from I/O devices are handled serially. There are eight addressing modes in all. In 1981, Texas Instruments introduced the 9995, with 256 bytes of internal RAM, higher I/O workspaces, and an instruction trap (MID instruction interrupt) to enable simulation of new instructions and to trap on illegal opcodes. The new 99000 family [30], [85] offers single instruction prefetch, an internal oscillator and clock generator, long-word arithmetic, test-and-set primitives, and support for multiprocessor and DMA configurations

The basic structure of the Intel 8086 is shown in Fig. 2. The CPU consists of two separate processing units, the execution unit (EU) and the bus interface unit connected by a 16-bit ALU

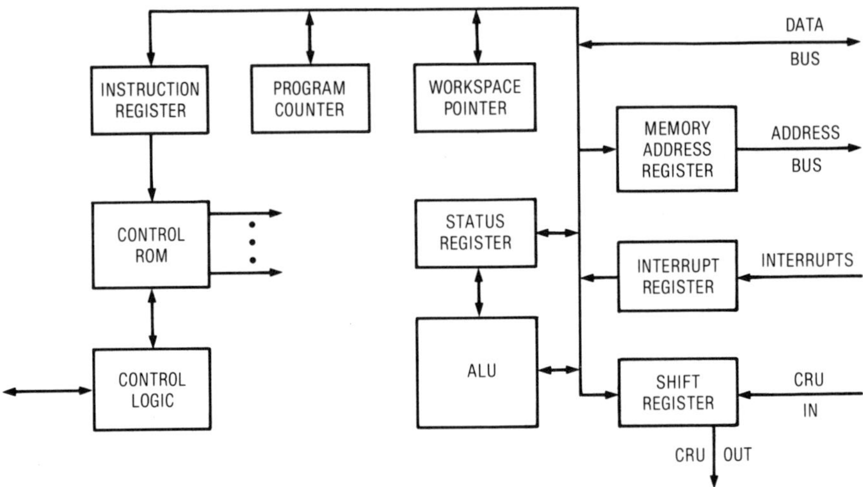

Fig. 1. Basic structure of the 9900.

data bus and an 8-bit Q bus. The EU obtains instructions from the instruction prefetch queue, IQ, maintained by the BIU, and executes instructions using the 16-bit ALU. The EU accesses memory and peripherals through requests to the BIU, which is the second processing unit, performing all bus operations for the EU on a demand basis; the BIU is also responsible for prefetching instructions. The 6-byte instruction prefetch queue feeds instructions to the EU in 8-bit segments. A substantial number of the 95 basic instructions are only a byte long. In the few 16-bit instructions, only the first byte is used for operation codes; the second byte specifies data displacement. Instructions longer than 2 bytes use the remaining bytes for specifying data. The 8086 instruction set is an expanded version of the 8080 instruction set. However, base segment registers have been added to enable programmers to do process swaps with relative ease, and to increase memory addressing capabilities. The 1M byte of real addressing space is treated as a group of segments, each segment 64K bytes in size. Four segments are addressable at one time, providing up to 64K bytes of code, 64K bytes for stack, and 128K bytes for data. Multiple concurrent stacks are not feasible. The Intel 8086 execution unit contains four 16-bit pointer and index registers and four 16-bit data registers addressable on an individual byte basis. These eight registers are used implicitly by the instruction set, providing compact encoding at the cost of reduced flexibility. The BIU contains additional registers for addressing purposes. The 8086 utilizes two types of multimaster buses, the local bus and the system bus. Microprocessors are always connected to a local bus, and memory and I/O usually reside on a system bus. These two buses are linked by interface components. The system bus is functionally and electrically compatible with the Intel Multibus. The Intel 8086 has a 64K-byte separate I/O space. A memory-mapped I/O capability that can respond like a memory device is available for linking I/O devices. Any memory reference instruction can be used to access an I/O device, providing additional programming flexibility. High-speed I/O operations can be carried out with traditional DMA controllers. Intel also offers the 8089 IOP, an independent processor with two DMA channels and an instruction set tailored for I/O operations. Overall, the 8086 instruction set provides automatic repetition of many instructions, decimal operations, error traps, and a large I/O space through indirect addressing. Designed to be used as a coprocessor, the Intel 8087 Numeric Data Processor [101] supports 32-, 64-, and 80-bit data structures and floating-point arithmetic. The Intel 80186 introduced in 1982 offers twice the performance of the standard Intel 8086, and offers twelve additional instructions. The new instructions facilitate string operations, subroutine operations, context switching, and detection of out-of-range

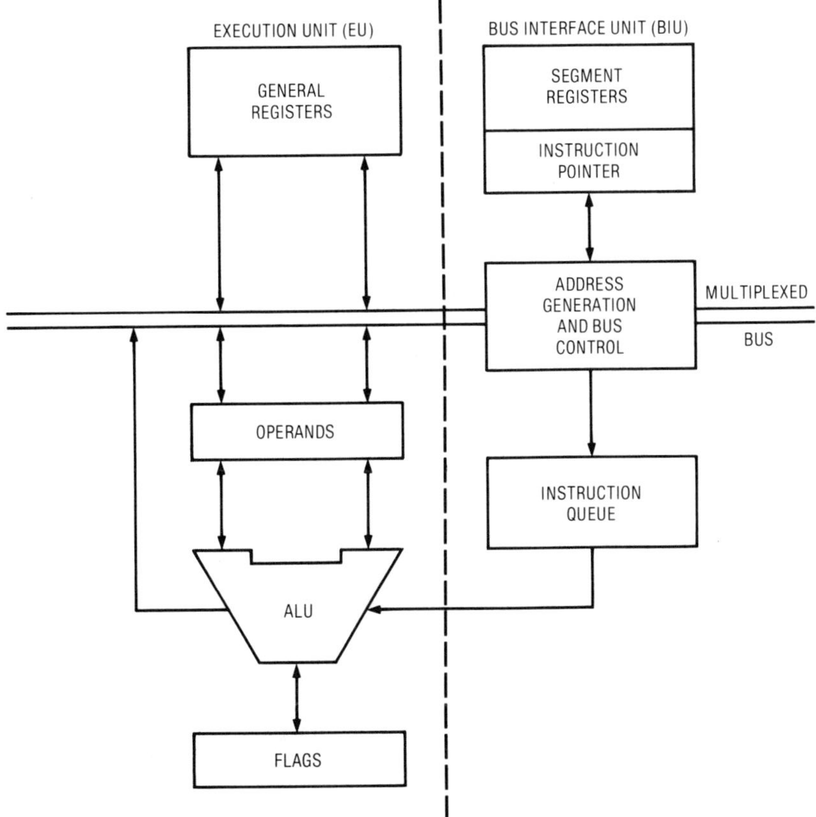

Fig. 2. Basic structure of the Intel 8086.

values. The Intel 80286, also introduced in 1982, offers still higher performance (up to six times that of the 8086), virtual memory, on-chip memory management, a four-level memory protection hierarchy, and is directed towards the multiuser environment [31], [32]; the 80286 uses a superset of the 80186 instruction set with sixteen additional instructions.

The basic structure of the Zilog Z8000, architecturally different from the Z80, is shown in Fig. 3. The internal 16-bit data bus is used for internal addressing and data communication. The instructions are fetched through the Z-bus interface and executed by the instruction execute control unit. Throughput is enhanced through "limited" pipelining, which allows prefetching of the next single-word instruction (or the first word of the next multiword instruction) from the memory into the instruction buffer. This occurs only during the execution of the current instruction, provided the current instruction does not require the bus to complete the execution cycle. Unlike the 8086, the Z8000 does not use implied registers. All sixteen 16-bit general-purpose registers can be used as accumulators and all but one can be used as index pointers or memory pointers. The one exception is an escape mechanism for address changes. The general register architecture avoids bottlenecks inherent in dedicated or implied registers. Memory addresses are always expressed in bytes. The 8M bytes of directly addressable memory is split up as 128 segments, each of 64 kbytes. To increase the address range beyond the nominal limits, code, data, and stack spaces in the CPU's system and normal modes can be physically separated using the Z8010 memory management unit (6 × 8M bytes = 48M bytes). Unlike the 8086, the Z8000 permits multiple concurrent stacks; stacks can be located anywhere in memory and are addressed via stack pointer registers. Any register, barring one, can serve as a stack pointer by means of PUSH and POP. Call return, interrupts, and traps use implied stack. The system stack can be accessed only in system mode, whereas the normal stack can be accessed in both modes. The Z-bus interconnects Z8000 family components [33] in a master/slave fashion. The CPU obeys the Z-bus protocol directly at the chip level, and no extra circuitry is needed to generate bus signals. Multiplexing of addresses and data minimizes pin count; multiplexing does not affect read times, but degrades write times. Almost in all cases, reads outnumber writes three or four to one, and as such, multiplexing does not result in any significant performance loss. Demulitplexing is performed when necessary within the individual modules. The daisy chain serial priority philosophy resolves interrupts/traps, bus requests, and requests for shared resources. In the system mode, two different I/O instructions transfer data between the CPU and peripherals, and special I/O instructions transfer data to and from external support chips. Processor status information enables separation of address spaces. The I/O addressing scheme is identical to the basic memory addressing scheme. For DMA operations, two signals—bus request and bus acknowledge—are available. Inhibited from controlling the bus during DMA operations, the CPU must wait for the bus to be given up by the DMA controller. The instruction set facilitates multiprogramming through a context switching facility. Other instruction highlights include signed 32-bit multiply and divide, decimal operations, multiple load, vector-based instructions, and the test-and-set instruction for multiprocessor applications, as well as support for floating-point operations [87]. Addressing schemes include indexing, with or without displacement, and multiple increment indexing.

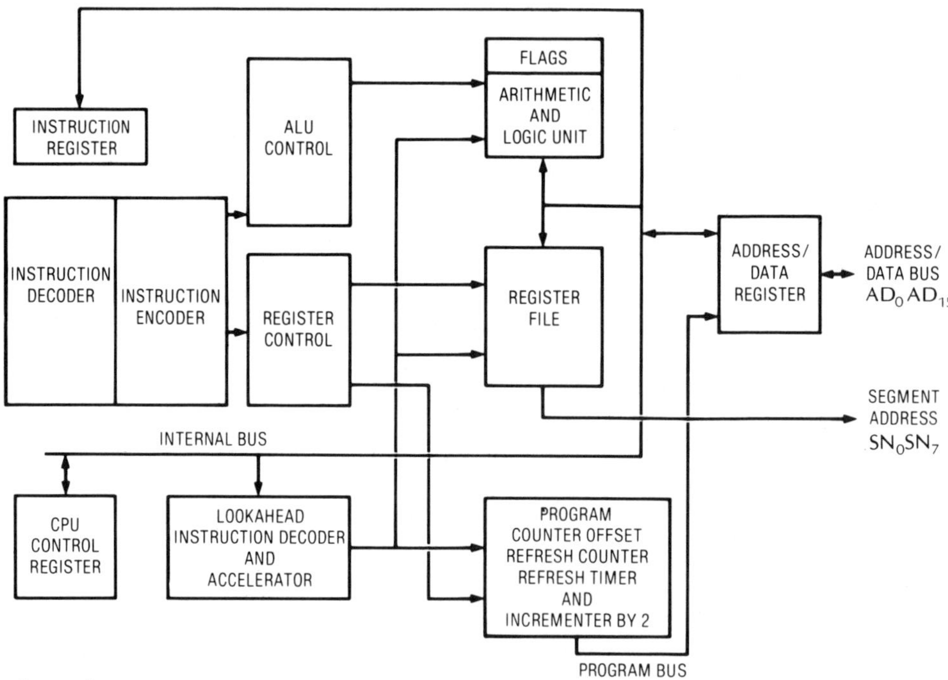

Fig. 3. Basic structure of the Z8000.

The Motorola MC68000 (see Fig. 4) is architecturally [34] quite different from the TI 9900, the Intel 8086, and the Zilog Z8000 chips. The microcode-based CPU is centered around a microprogram-controlled execution unit. Most internal data structures are 32 bits wide. To minimize the control store area size, a two-level structure comprised of a microstore and a nanostore is used which, however, increases total access time. An attempt has been made to overcome this by means of a pipelined architecture, in which the instruction fetch, instruction decode, and instruction execute cycles are fully overlapped across every macroinstruction boundary. In branch conditions, the prefetch is associated with the most likely branch condition. The MC68000 execution unit is a dual-bus structure that performs both address and data processing. There are eight 32-bit data registers, seven 32-bit address registers, and two implied 32-bit stack pointers. The data registers can be addressed as byte, word, or double-word registers. The address registers are used for 32-bit base addressing, 32-bit software stack operations, and word and long-word address operations. The implied stack pointers are used for 32-bit base addressing and for word and long-word operations. The MC68000 views memory as a linear space of up to 16M bytes with no internal segmentation. Although words are normally addressed, single bytes can be read or written using upper and lower data byte strobes. Instructions and multibyte data are always aligned on even byte boundaries. The memory management unit, MC68451, supports management and protection of 32 variable-sized segments, ranging from 256 bytes to 16M bytes in increments of 256 bytes. Multiple concurrent user stacks and queues can be created and maintained by employing the address register indirectly with post-increment and predecrement addressing modes. The MC68000 possesses no separate I/O space. All I/O is memory mapped and all I/O protection must occur at memory protection level. Three signals—bus request, bus grant, and bus grant acknowledge—allow master devices to get control of the bus for DMA operations. The 68000 family is supported by two different master/slave-based multimaster buses for interconnection of components—the local bus and the global bus. The local bus connects microprocessor, memory, and I/O devices to form individual microcomputer modules, and the global bus interfaces to various local buses through bus arbitration modules. Versabus [95] is an extended version of the local bus. Overall, the MC68000 has a regular instruction set and provides multiuser support. It emphasizes space-efficient code through "quick" instructions and short jumps on loops. The MC68000 offers the advantage of excellent debug tools like single-step execution, traps on illegal instructions, and debug mode. Context switching facilitates multiprogramming, and the test-and-set instruction aids in multiprocessor and database applications. Other advantages include complex push and pop capabilities, the 32-bit internal structure, and instructions for multiple load and signed multiply and divide. Real-time control applications are aided by multilevel interrupt and seven auto-vector interrupt capabilities. The MC68010 [35], introduced in 1982, offers virtual memory facilities, and superior operating system support through relocatable exception vectors and additional system control registers. The MC68020 [35] offers full 32-bit capability. The MC6881 [35] floating-point coprocessor can only be used in conjunction with the MC68020.

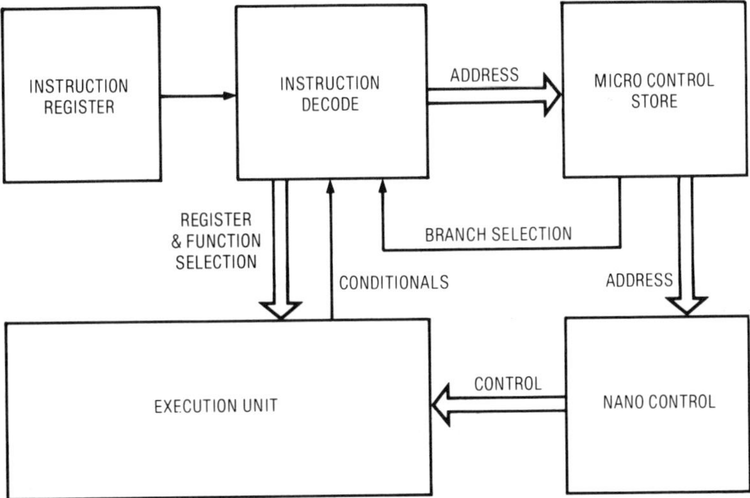

Fig. 4. Basic structure of the MC68000.

The National NS16032 (see Fig. 5), sometimes classified as a 32-bit microprocessor [36], [90], contains several similarities to the MC68000 architecture. It, too, uses 32-bit data paths and 32-bit address arithmetic to access memory without the overhead of segmentation registers; externally, it uses a multiplexed address and data bus with 24 bits of external address of 16 bits of external data. The NS16032 also uses a two-level microcode that enables sharing of microcode routines by all instructions and avoids time-consuming subroutine calls and space-consuming repeated microcode flows. The instruction queue, in the case of the NS16032, consists of a double-ended 8-byte first-in first-out, with 16-bit input and output buses. As microinstruction n is executed, microinstruction $n + 1$ is decoded, and microinstruction $n + 2$ is selected by the microcode ROM address decoder. There are eight general-purpose registers, all 32 bits wide, and eight dedicated registers of smaller size. The NS16032 provides a 16-byte uniform address space and nine types of address modes. The length of the address mode offset constants are encoded in the upper 2 bits of the offset so that small offsets (-64 to 63) require only 1 byte in the instruction stream, and larger offsets take 2 or 4 bytes. Instructions are of variable length. Common zero-operand instructions, such as a branch instruction, have a 1-byte opcode. The one-operand and two-operand instructions use a 2-byte basic instruction. All instructions can use all applicable addressing modes—this is termed an orthogonal instruction set and reflects the general industry trend. Instructions are aligned on byte boundaries, for code compactness. The NS16032 offers instructions to operate on packed decimal quantities, on arrays, and on blocks. The ability to operate on variable-length character strings makes the processor suited for text processing applications. The NS16081, which is the floating-point coprocessor of the NS16032, provides 32-bit and 64-bit floating-point capabilities, and the memory management unit, the NS16082, provides demand paged virtual memory facilities. Virtual address to real address translation is accomplished through two levels of page tables and offset specifications. Each page, 512 bytes in size, is assigned a protection code, and this provides an access control mechanism. The memory management unit has eight registers and provides a flow-tracing facility for both sequential and nonsequential instructions. The NS16032 has a hardware backup mechanism that saves contents of the processor status register, the stack pointer, and the program counter, and automatically restores them to their original values in case of an instruction retry. In view of the architectural orientation for support of virtual memory, the NS16032 is quite similar to the Motorola MC68010. The 32-bit version, the NS32032, uses the same architecture but provides 32-bit external data paths like the Motorola MC68020.

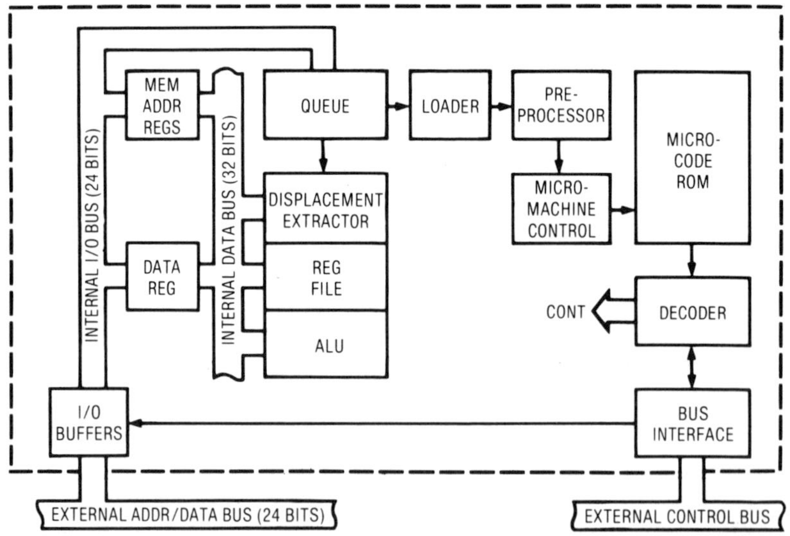

Fig. 5. NS16032 CPU block diagram.

The 16-bit microprocessors considered so far are second-sourced by several companies outside the United States. A significant portion of the NS16032 design work was done by the National Semiconductors subsidiary in Israel. Some other design efforts deserve mention here. Philips Data Systems in Europe has implemented the SP 16C/10 microprocessor in NMOS; this chip also offers virtual memory and support for coprocessors and multiple processors [37]. Fujitsu of Japan has implemented in CMOS a 16-bit processor with on-chip error detection, virtual memory support, and four hierarchical levels of operation to efficiently handle multi-processing [38]. Within the United States, single chips have become available that replace entire CPUs of popular minicomputers like the PDP 11 [39] and the Data General Eclipse [40].

In this world of increasing variety of 16-bit microprocessor chips, the task of selecting a particular chip is a difficult one. Apart from hardware and architectural details which we have discussed so far, it becomes essential to evaluate system performance at multiple levels [41] as follows:

a) Instruction Level: At this level one compares timings on an instruction-by-instruction basis. This level is especially relevant when the chip is not physically available such as is the case of newly announced or newly released processors.

b) Routine Level: Sample user tasks coded in assembly language are often represented as competitive analyses between processors by manufacturers. The application programs frequently reflect advantages unique to the "winning" microprocessor.

c) Support Task Level: The sophistication of operating systems support is evaluated. An example of a support task would be a multilevel queue management used by the process scheduling algorithm of the operating system.

d) System Functions Level: Specific operating system and user tasks are encoded, e.g., memory management algorithms for segmentation.

e) User Job Level: This benchmark spawns many processes, thereby exercising the operating system and all lower level benchmarks.

16-bit microprocessors have been compared and evaluated by Heering [42], by Grappel and Hemenway [43], [44], by Rajulu and Rajaraman [117], by Toong and Gupta [26], [41], and by Prycher [120]. Table 2, based on information from [26], [27], [36], compares performance at the

Table 2 Execution Speeds (in Microseconds) of 16-Bit Microprocessors [26], [27], [36] (Note that different chips use different clock frequencies)

Operation	Data Type	Chips and Clock Frequency					
		TI 9900 at 3 MHz	Intel 8086 at 5 MHz	Zilog Z8000 at 5 MHz	Motorola MC68000 at 8 MHz	National NS16032 at 10 MHz	TI 99110 at 6 MHz
Register-to-	Byte/Word	4.60	0.40	0.75	0.50	0.30	0.50
Register Move	Double-Word	9.80	0.80	1.25	0.50	0.30	1.00
Memory-to-	Byte/Word	7.30	3.40	3.50	1.50	1.00	0.83/0.67
Register Move	Double-Word	14.60	6.80	4.25	2.00	1.50	1.33
Memory-to-	Byte/Word	9.90	7.00	7.00	2.50	1.70	1.00/0.83
Memory Move	Double-Word	19.80	14.00	8.50	3.75	2.50	1.67
Add Memory	Byte/Word	7.32	3.60	3.75	1.50	1.20	0.83
to Register	Double-Word	21.30	7.20	5.25	2.25	1.60	2.00
Compare Memory	Byte/Word	9.90	7.00	7.25	3.00	1.70	1.00
to Memory	Double-Word	19.80	14.00	9.50	4.00	2.50	2.00
Multiply	Byte	21.90	13.00	20.25	N/A	3.50	4.17
Memory to	Word	21.90	23.00	16.00	8.75	5.10	4.17
Memory	Double-Word	180.64	115.20	85.75	43.00	8.30	26.38
Conditional	Branch Taken	3.60	1.60	1.50	1.25	1.60	0.50
Branch	Branch Not Taken	2.90	0.80	1.50	1.00	0.80	0.50
Modify Index							
Branch if Zero	Branch Taken	7.60	2.20	2.75	1.25	1.30	1.00
Branch to							
Subroutine		7.90	3.80	3.75	2.25	2.00	1.00

Table 3 Comparison of Performance of 16-Bit Microprocessors (n, in the case of the hash algorithm, denotes the number of searches before an open slot is found)

Level	Example Used	Performance Intel 8086	Z8000	MC68000
Routine	(a) Booth's Multiplication Algorithm	1.00	1.41	1.26
	(b) Polynomial Evaluation	1.00	1.80	1.97
Support Task	(a) Stack Exerciser	1.00	8.42	3.49
	(b) Hash Algorithm	$144 + 48*n$	$188 + 66*n$	$141 + 54*n$

instruction level. Comparison at higher levels of the evaluation hierarchy are summarized in Table 3 [41] based on the same clock frequency. As seen from this table, the performance is heavily dependent on the choice of algorithm. Comparison at higher levels is even more application dependent. Thus all general comparisons must be used with extreme caution.

V. 32-BIT MICROPROCESSORS

Microprocessors with 32-bit internal paths and 16-bit external paths have been in existence since 1980. However, the era of true 32-bit microprocessors begins in 1981 with the commercial introduction of the Intel iAPX 432. IBM's implementation of the IBM 370 on a single chip in 1980 [45] is generally overlooked because of the lack of commercial production of the device.

As mentioned in the previous section, the Motorola 68020 and the National 32032 are very similar to their respective 16-bit processors; as such, they are not analyzed here. We discuss general trends by considering three different 32-bit microprocessors chosen on the basis of their architectural innovativeness and the availability of good documentation [46]. These are the Bellmac-32A microprocessor (also called the Western Electric 32000 microprocessor) from Bell Laboratories [47], [48], the "no name" 32-bit CPU chip from Hewlett-Packard [49], [50], and the Intel iAPX 432 [51]-[53]. Even though the former two are designed for internal use, they are harbingers of similar products in the public domain.

General Characteristics

The general characteristics of the three microprocessors are summarized in Table 4.

The Bellmac-32A single-chip CPU has been fabricated in twin-tub CMOS technology that dissipates less than 1 W of power and uses new "domino circuits" that operate at twice the speed of previous CMOS circuits and enable a single clock pulse to activate many circuits simultaneously. A single 40-MHz clock is used to generate two 10-MHz phase-shifted clock signals. The Bellmac-32A chip has been designed to provide support for the programming language C. Single instructions can move blocks of data from memory to memory, or push and pop a group of registers with respect to the stack. Sophisticated hardware facilities include a barrel shift circuit that shifts 0 to 31 bits in a single cycle. The operating system can be included in the address space of every process, and includes a hardware interface for a process-oriented operating system and a set of exception-handling mechanisms. The exception structure provides four levels of execution privilege. It is intended for real-time control applications. Neither floating-point nor decimal arithmetic are supported. An auxiliary processor to perform such operations is at the investigation stage [48]. At present, "extension" instructions are provided to perform these functions. There is little compatibility with any existing microprocessor. The development of the Bellmac-32A chip was accomplished in a relatively short time using extensive computer-aided design techniques [91]. A mask generation program permits "technology updatability" enabling old mask sets to be updated to new rule(s) easily; the simulation files are generated automatically to benefit from the evolving technology that permits thinner

Table 4 General Characteristics of 32-Bit Microprocessors [46]

	Bellmac-32A	HP 32-Bit CPU	Intel iAPX 432
Year of Commercial Introduction	1982*	1982*	1981
Technology	2.5-μm Domino CMOS	1.5/1.0-μm NMOS	HMOS
No. of Transistors	146 000	450 000	219 000 on 3 Chips
Size of Chip	160 000 Mil^2	48 400 Mil^2	100 000 Mil^2 Each
Power Dissipation	0.7 Watt at 8 MHz	4 Watts	2.5 Watts/Chip
Pin Count	63 Active 84 Total	83	64 per Chip
Basic Clock Frequency	10 MHz	18 MHz	8 MHz
Direct Address Range (Bytes)	2^{32}	2^{29} Real; 2^{41} Virtual	2^{24} Real; 2^{40} Virtual
No. of General-Purpose Registers	16 User-Visible	28 (Not All General-Purpose)	No Registers Visible to User
No. of Basic Instructions	169	230	221
No. of Addressing Modes	18	10	5

*Currently for internal use only.

linewidths. On the chip itself, access is available to most registers for test and debug purposes via special internal access features. Unlike the Hewlett-Packard chip (discussed next), there is no facility for automatic self-test during the power-up sequence.

The HP 32-bit CPU chip has the highest circuit density—450 000 transistors implemented on a single chip using a 1-μm pitch n-channel MOS double-layer-metal technology. This microprocessor uses two nonoverlapping clocks each of 18-MHz frequency (generated from an external 36-MHz clock), and is microcoded using 9K (38-bit) words of ROM control store addressed via a set of 14-bit registers in the sequence stack. The microinstructions are decoded by PLA. Most microinstructions execute in a one clock cycle of 55 ns. Pipelining of memory operations permits initiation of 32-bit memory read every two states (110 ns) even though the access time is longer. The self-test routine, executed by the CPU during the power-up sequence, automatically tests operations internal to the chip. This HP chip offers several sophisticated hardware and software features. The hardware implemented N-bit barrel shifter can shift a 32-bit quantity right or left 0 to 31 places in a single clock cycle. The load instruction includes automatic bounds checking and takes only 550 ns. The arithmetic and logical instructions can manipulate 32- and 64-bit IEEE standard floating-point operands. Text editing capabilities are inherent in the move and string instructions that manipulate byte arrays and string-type data. All communication to and from the chip involves use of the memory-processor bus. This 32-bit-wide multiplexed address/data bus permits pipelined data transfers at 36M bytes/s transfer rate. Facilities to communicate with the memory and with peripheral devices are provided by the memory controller chip and the I/O processor chip, respectively.

In many respects, the Intel iAPX 432 is very different from our previous examples. First, just as the Burroughs 5000 introduced a trend two decades ago of architectures especially designed to support high-level languages, the Intel iAPX 432 is designed to be programmed entirely in a high-level language, and the system architecture is consciously oriented toward supporting Ada, the programming language sponsored by the Department of Defense. Secondly, whereas the other 32-bit processors are single-chip CPUs, the Intel iAPX 432 is designed as a three-chip set [100]. These three chips are connected to each other though a processor-memory interconnection bus, which is different from the traditional Intel Multibus. The General Data Processor System, usually referred to as GDP, consists of two chips—the iAPX 43201 [53], [98], with 110 000 transistors, which is responsible for instruction decoding, and the iAPX 43202 [51], [93] with 49 000 transistors, which performs actual instruction execution. The iAPX 43203 I/O interface processor [52], [92] containing 60 000 transistors, maps I/O bus addresses into the main memory address space, and also provides attached I/O processors with a set of interprocess communication primitives. Two other chips, the 43204 Memory Control Unit (MCU) and the 43205 Bus Interface Unit (BIU), are used in larger configurations with multiple memories, processors, and buses. The Intel iAPX 432 is architectually very different from its predecessors, namely, the 8080, 8085, and 8086; this difference, although providing technological enhancements, newer functions, and higher overall throughput, greatly limits the programming compatibility which exists among the earlier Intel products. On the Intel iAPX 432, the total physical address size is limited to 2^{24} bytes. The upper limit on the logical address space is 2^{40} bytes. However, at any instant, the logical addressing environment of a program is restricted to 2^{32} bytes. The instructions are of variable length ranging from 6 to 344 bits in size; each instruction's operator can have 0, 1, 2, or 3 operands. The general processor flexibility is accompanied by adequate built-in security mechanisms that restrict access to program and data on a "need-to-know" basis. Other highlights include hardware-implemented concurrent programming functions, self-dispatching processors with hardware-implemented process scheduling, Ada high-level language support, and the capability to perform specialized functions, for example, floating-point operations and string operations, without the need to attach auxiliary, specialized chips.

Technology

All the chips reflect a conscious attempt toward the integration of an enormously large number of transistors. Even with a significantly smaller chip size, Hewlett-Packard has packaged the largest number (450 000) on a single chip, almost twice what Intel has packaged on three chips put together. In order to achieve this intense packaging density, Hewlett-Packard uses an electron beam to generate masks that provide 1.5-μm-wide lines and 1.0-μm spaces with ± 0.25-μm tolerances. The large number of devices and the low width of the lines contribute to the higher power dissipation (4 W). The packaging technology used by Hewlett-Packard consists of a copper core, on which the CPU and auxiliary chips are directly mounted and four layers of interconnect, separated by low-capacitance Teflon dielectrics. The Intel iAPX 432 is also implemented in NMOS (Intel prefers to call it n-channel silicon-gate HMOS technology). However, as compared to Hewlett-Packard, the transistor density is much lower, permitting implementation of wider 3.5-μm structures.

Because of the CMOS implementation, the Bellmac-32A chip is the least power-consuming microprocessor. The twin-tub CMOS process (Fig. 6) gives high switching speed in both n- and p-channel devices, because each tub is separately implanted for optimum doping. The process takes advantage of reduced geometries for denser design and the n^+ substrate layer avoids the thyristorlike latchup characteristic usually found in CMOS circuits. The optimization of per-

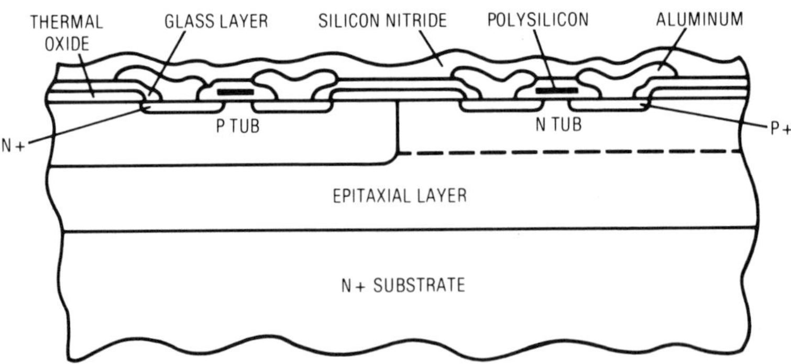

Fig. 6. The Bellmac-32A implemented in domino CMOS [54].

centages of n- and p-channel components has enabled implementation of high circuit densities while retaining the CMOS advantages of fast speeds and low power consumption.

Basic Principles of Operation

The structure of the Bellmac-32A microprocessor is shown in Fig. 7. It consists of two distinct functional units—a fetch unit which controls interactions with the external memory and an execution unit which controls the manipulation and processing of data. Both units, as well as the bus, have full 32-bit capability. The instruction stream is byte oriented. The first byte specifies the addressing mode and the register, and the subsequent bytes specify additional data. All byte and halfword operands are sign or zeros extended to 32 bits when they are fetched. Instructions are monadic, dyadic, or triadic depending on the number of operators being 1, 2, or 3, respectively. Instructions fetched from the memory are stored in the instruction queue, and translated into a series of microinstructions using a PLA. The arithmetic address unit performs all address calculations. The arithmetic logic unit in the execute block performs the actual execution of microinstructions. The emphasis on support for a process-oriented operating system generates a need to store all instructions, data, and register values associated with a process at times of switching from one process to another; the Bellmac-32A microprocessor performs these functions in hardware.

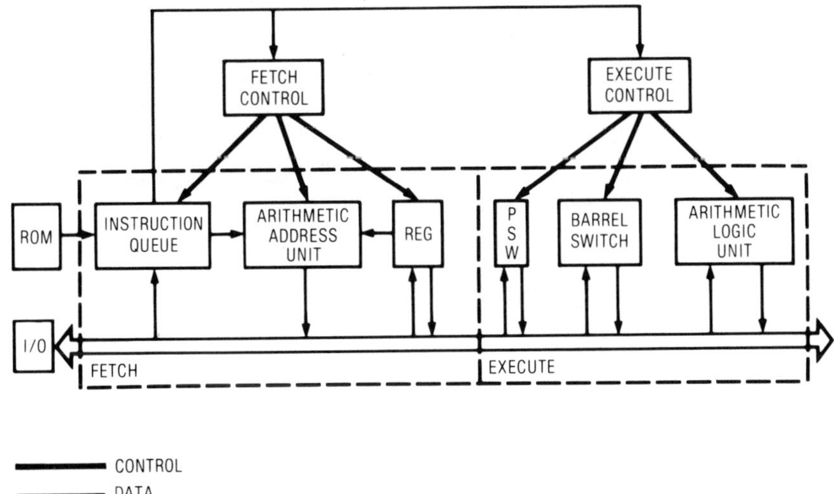

Fig. 7. Bellmac-32A CPU architecture.

The Hewlett-Packard 32-bit chip, shown in Fig. 8, uses a microcode control store ROM of 9216 words, each of 38 bits. Microinstructions accessed from the ROM are decoded by the PLA and drive control lines which determine the operations of the 32-bit register stack and the ALU. The flow of instructions to the PLA is controlled by the sequencing machine which contains a microprogram counter, a set of incrementers, three registers for microcode subroutine return addresses, and a machine instruction opcode decoder. The opcode decoder generates the starting address in control store for the microcode routine that implements each machine instruction. The test condition multiplex facilitates conditional jumps and skips in the microcode. The ALU contains an n-bit shifter, a 32-bit logical selector, and a 32-bit full look-ahead adder, which also performs integer multiplication and division using special hardware.

The operation of the iAPX 432 involves communication between the iAPX 43201 instruction fetch and decode unit and the iAPX 43202 instruction execution unit via a microinstruction bus. The iAPX 43203 I/O interface unit is connected through the processor-memory interconnect bus as shown in Fig. 9. The characteristics of these chips are summarized in Table 5. Data can be

Fig. 8. The Hewlett-Packard 32-bit microprocessor.

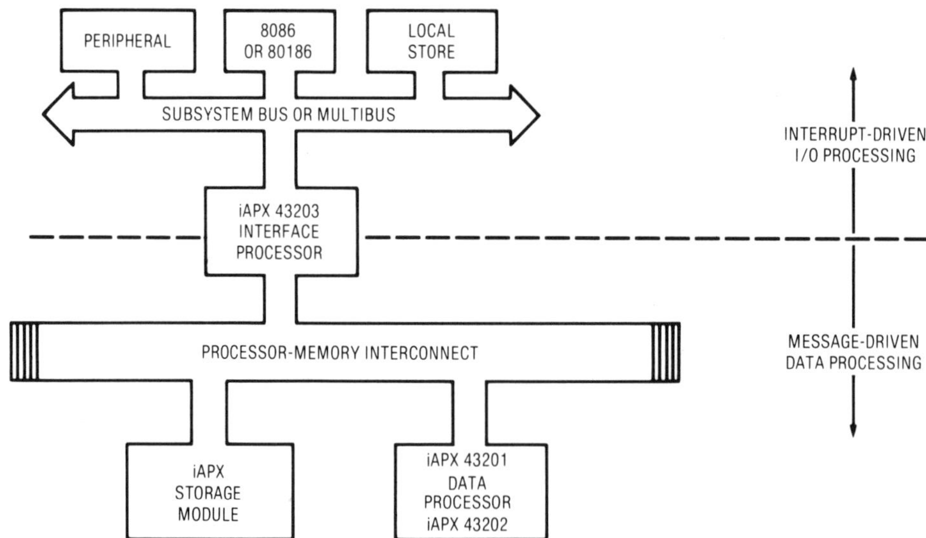

Fig. 9. Intel's iAPX 432 three-chip 32-bit microprocessor.

Table 5 Characteristics of the General Data Processor

Characteristic	iAPX 43201		iAPX 43202		iAPX 43203	
Die Size (in Microns)	318 × 323		366 × 313		358 × 326	
Total Device Placements	110 000		49 000		60 000	
Function of Unit	Instruction fetch and decode		Instruction execution		I/O Interface	
Functional Subunits	Instruction decoder	Microinstruction Sequencer (MIS)	Data Manipulation Unit (DMU)	Reference Generation Unit (RGU)	Data Acquisition Unit (DAU)	Microexecution Unit (MEU)
Function of Subunit	Decode variable-length, bit-aligned instructions	Sequences vertically encoded micro-instructions and inputs them to the MEU	Contains operand and units to implement the macro-instruction set efficiently	Contains registers and functional units for logical-to-physical address translation and access rights verification	Performs prefetch and post-write buffering of data and generates main system memory accesses	Performs system access environment manipulation, interprocessor communication, and address map set-up

manipulated in the form of 8-bit characters, 16/32-bit ordinals, 16/32-bit integers, 32/64/80-bit floating-point variables, bit strings, arrays, records, and as "objects" which are data structures containing information in an organized manner. These objects can be referenced as a single entity, and their internal organization is hidden and protected from all other procedures by hardware mechanisms. Each object has defined for it a set of operations (procedures or instructions) that are permitted to manipulate it directly. Examples of hardware-defined objects are as follows:

a) processor objects: represent the physical processors;
b) process objects: represent the individual computing tasks;
c) context objects: represent the activation of a program unit;
d) dispatching port/ objects: provide a stream of work for a set of processors;
e) communications port objects: supports interprocess communication and synchronization.

The iAPX 432 instruction set supports objects through messages (SEND, WAIT), context (CALL, RETURN), storage pools (ALLOCATE, TYPE), and processes (SCHEDULE, DISPATCH). Objects permit each program module (e.g., an Ada package) to operate as an individualized "virtual machine" for more reliable operation, since errors in the module are confined to its virtual machine. They also provide simpler compilation, since each virtual machine has its own address space.

Register Organization

The Bellmac-32A microprocessor contains a special program counter register and fifteen other registers (32 bits wide) that can be referenced in any addressing mode. Of these fifteen registers, three are used to support operating system functions (as interrupt stack pointer, process control block pointer, processor status word) and can be written when the processor is in kernel execution level. Another three registers are used as a stack pointer, a frame pointer, and an argument pointer by certain instructions.

At the heart of the Hewlett-Packard chip, there is a register stack containing 28 identical general-purpose registers (not all accessible by software), each 32 bits wide and an ALU with four operand/result registers. The register stack uses two databases and contains auxiliary logic such as top of stack registers and instruction registers. In any register, each of the 32-bit cells can receive data from or dump data to either of the two data buses, as determined by the PLA outputs.

On account of its multichip organization, the register structure of the iAPX 432 cannot be compared with the others on an equitable basis. The microinstruction execution unit performs several functions traditionally associated with registers. Its functional subunit, the reference generation unit (RGU) contains a 43-bit by 20-entry register array to support logical-to-physical address translation and access rights verification. The other functional unit, the data manipulation unit (DMU), contains its own set of operand registers, implemented as double-ended queues, to optimize arithmetic calculations on variable length operands with a fixed length (16-bit) bus. Intel claims that the compiler complexity is reduced by keepings registers "behind the scenes" rather than as visible features of the architecture [99].

Instruction Set

The 32-bit processors offer powerful instruction sets and support a wide spectrum of distinct data structures. These capabilities are summarized in Table 6.

The Bellmac-32A offers 169 instructions, more than twice the number on the NS16032. It supports bytes, halfwords, words, and bit fields. Strings are supported by special block instructions, and the string format conforms to the C language. This design objective is manifest in the implementation of the instruction repertoire. The result of unary operations Negate and Complement (implemented as a move instruction) can either replace the existing datum or be placed in a new location. The dyadic form stores the result in the second operand and the triadic form places the result in the third operand, with the first two unaltered: these dyadic and triadic forms of instructions are available for all operators. High-level procedure linkage operations assist in manipulating the stack frame, saving registers, and in transferring control between procedures. Also, explicit instructions (Call Process and Return to Process) are provided for switching processes by the operating system. On the negative side, the Bellmac-32A does not support floating-point or decimal arithmetic.

The Hewlett-Packard 32-bit chip offers a still larger repertoire of 230 instructions and 32- and 64-bit floating-point arithmetic capability. The Load and Store instructions can transfer double words in addition to the bits, bytes, halfwords, and words. Move and String instructions manipulate both unstructured byte arrays and structured string data. Hardware support includes four top of stack registers to handle push and pop operations and to provide "data valid" indication. The large number of transistors enables hardware implementation of features that have traditionally been done by software. For example, there is support for run-time bounds checking of addresses performed on all memory accesses.

The iPAX 432 processor supports integer data in the form of features that have traditionally been done by software. For example, there is support for run-time bounds checking of addresses performed on all memory accesses. The iAPX 432 processor supports integer data in the form of halfwords and words, and floating-point data in the form of words, double words, and as 80-bit quantities. The usual 80-bit-wide quantities, called temporary reals, are used to store intermediate results to improve accuracy of final results. Instructions are bit-variable in length and are not constrained to coincide with byte or word boundaries. The total number of instructions is 230 and the longest is 344 bits long. By allowing both stack arithmetic and memory-to-memory arithmetic, the iAPX 432 has the potential of providing denser code and faster speeds at evaluating expressions. An instruction contains four fields. The first two fields, the class field and the format field, specify how many operands are in the instruction and how they are to be accessed. The third field, the reference field, contains the logical addresses of up to three operands. The last field specifies the operator itself. The processor reads an instruction segment in units of 32 bits. The instructions are decoded by the 43201 decoding chip, and the resulting stream of microinstructions are executed by the 43202 execution chip.

Memory Organization

The Bellmac-32A chip offers several addressing modes: literal, byte/halfword/word immediate, register, register deferred, short offset (for frame and argument pointers), absolute, absolute deferred, byte/halfword/word displacement deferred, and expanded operand type.

Table 6 Characteristics of Different Microprocessors (Without the use of Coprocessors or Auxiliary Chips

	Bellmac-32A	HP-32	Intel iAPX 432
System Structures			
Uniform Addressability	√	√	√
Module Map and Modules	X	X	√
Virtual	√	√	√
Primitive Data Types			
Bits	√	√	√
Integer Byte or Halfword	√	√	√
Integer Word	√	√	√
Logical Byte or Halfword	√	√	√
Logical Word	√	√	√
Character Strings (Variable)	√	√	√
BCD Byte or Halfword	X	X	X
BCD Word	X	√	X
32-Bit Floating Point	X	√	√
64-Bit Floating Point	X	√	√
80-Bit Floating Point	X	X	√
Data Structures			
Stacks	√	√	√
Arrays	√	√	√
Packed Arrays	X	X	X
Records	X	X	√
Packed Records	X	X	X
Strings	√	√	√
Primitive Control Operations			
Condition Code Primitives	√	√	√
Jump	√	√	√
Conditional Branch	√	√	√
Iterative Loop Control	X	√	√
Subroutine Call	√	√	√
Multiway Branch	√	√	√
Orthogonal Instruction Set	√	√	√
Control Structure			
External Procedure Call	√	√	√
Semaphores	√	√	√
Traps	√	√	√
Interrupts	√	√	√
Supervisor Call	√	√	√
Objects	X	X	√
Hierarchical Operating System	√	X	√
Others			
User Microcode	X	X	X
Debug Mode	√	√	X
Compatibility with Other Microprocessors	X	X	X
Self-Test During Power-Up	X	√	X

The Bellmac-32A chip includes hardware interface for a process-oriented operating system and a set of exception-handling mechanisms; this operating system can be included in the address space of every process, enabling each process to execute independently.

The Hewlett-Packard 32-bit processor views the memory space for each program as an active code segment (one of 4096 code segments), a stack segment, a global data segment, and a set of 4096 external data segments. Segment pointers, maintained in 32-bit on-chip registers, include base and limit register for the code, stack, and global data segments, the current instruction address in the code segment, the address of the most recent stack marker in the stack segment, and the address of the top of stack in memory. External data segments are

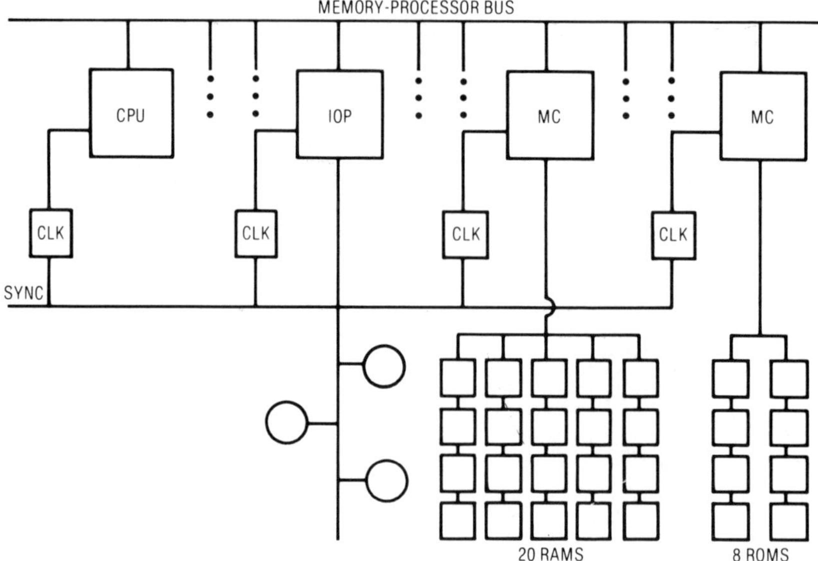

Fig. 10. Hewlett-Packard 32-bit system configuration.

accessed via a set of memory resident tables. A memory controller chip is used to control 256K bytes of RAM (20 chips each of 128K) or 512K bytes of ROM (8 chips each of 640K), as shown in Fig. 10. The memory-processor bus has a transfer rate of 36M bytes/s, and the overlapped access method permits high throughout. The memory controller maps logical to physical addresses in 16K-byte blocks, and permits byte, halfword, word, and semaphore operations.

The iAPX 432 uses a segmented memory scheme with up to 2^{24} segments, each segment 2^{16} bytes long yielding a total virtual space of 2^{40} bytes. A two-step mapping process separates the relocation mechanism from the access control mechanism. Segments are of two types: access and data. The latest release of 432 microcode allows segments to contain both access and data. Access quantities are protected by means of an addressing fence in each segment. Values below the fence are access, while those above the fence are data. The location of the fence is determined by the object represented. The iAPX 432 provides four addressing modes: the base and index direct is used to access scalers; the base indirect, index direct is used to access records; the base direct, index indirect is used to access static arrays; the base and index indirect is used to access dynamic arrays. The emphasis is on addressing objects through use of access descriptors in the form of directory index and segment index. This object-oriented architecture facilitates implementation of high-level languages like Ada [102], [103], Pascal, and PL/I.

Performance Estimates

The timing estimates for several elementary operations summarized in Table 7 must be interpreted with caution. Actual throughput is a function of the exact instruction sequence, displacements, data lengths, clock frequency, and other factors. Also, since the figures have been provided by the respective manufacturers, it is appropriate to assume the figures to reflect optimal performance estimates. The NS16032, though not a true 32-bit microprocessor, has been included for comparison purposes. Notice that the comparison is being made at dissimilar clock frequencies, and that in the Intel case several chips are involved, and the timing includes some operating overhead.

Hansen *et al.* [55] have used four programs (string search, sieve, puzzle, and Ackermann's function) to evaluate iAPX 432 performance in comparison to 16-bit microprocessors and VAX 11/780. Using a VAX 11/780 operating in a VMS Pascal environment as the base, the relative code size is summarized in Table 8. These figures indicate that in spite of bit-variable length

Table 7   Timing Estimates in Microseconds Unless Otherwise Specified [46]

Operation	NS 16032	Bellmac-32A	HP	Intel 432
General: Clock Speed	10 MHz	10 MHz	19 MHz	8 MHz
Move: Memory to Register	1.5	0.95	0.56	0.75
Add: 32-Bit Integer	1.6	0.4	0.055 (hardware time) 0.275 (instruction time)	0.5
Add: Floating Point	9.3 with NS 16081	Not supported in hardware	6.0 (for 64-bit) 4.7 (for 32-bit)	19.125 (for 80-bit)
Multiply: 32-Bit Integer	8.3	1.8 to 9.5 depending on operands	1.8 (hardware time) 2.9 (instruction time)	6.375
Multiply: Floating Point	7.1 (for 64-bit) with NS 16081	Not supported in hardware	10.4 (for 64-bit) 5.1 (for 32-bit)	27.875 (for 80-bit)
Divide: 32-Bit Integer	9.2	Dependent on operands	9.4 (64-bit/ 32-bit) 5.2 (32-bit/ 32-bit)	10.625
Divide: Floating Point	10.8 with NS 16081	Not supported in hardware	16.0 (for 64-bit) 6.5 (for 32-bit)	48.25 (for 80-bit)

Table 8   Relative Code Size (Numbers smaller than 1.0 indicate more compact code than on VAX)

Machine	Language	Word Size	Ratio to VMS Pascal (< 1 = > Smaller)				
			Search	Sieve	Puzzle	Acker	Avg ± SD
VAX-11/780	C	32	0.60	0.38	0.77	0.45	0.5 ± 0.2
	Pascal (UNIX)	32	0.95	1.24	1.49	0.72	1.1 ± 0.3
	C	32	0.79	0.55	1.01	0.50	0.7 ± 0.2
68000	Pascal	16	0.72	0.29	0.60	0.36	0.5 ± 0.2
	Pascal	32	0.74	0.31	0.64	0.38	0.5 ± 0.2
8086	Pascal	16	0.94	0.85	0.79	0.91	0.9 ± 0.1
432 (Rel. 3)	Ada	16	0.76	0.44	0.84	0.42	0.6 ± 0.2

instructions, the code size was larger on the iAPX 432 as compared to the 68000, probably because of the inability of the former to refer to a local variable or constant using fewer than 16 bits of address. The execution timings are summarized in Tables 9 and 10 [56]. In all these performance evaluation exercises, the iAPX 432 is tested as a high-level language uniprocessor for integer and character programs; thus potential benefits of transparent multiprocessing, data security, and increased programmer productivity are not reflected [55]. Also, the timings for the Hewlett-Packard and National chips must be taken with caution as they have not been verified by any independent organization.

Overall, the performance of the newer microprocessors approaches the performance of mainframes. The Intel 432 at 8-MHz clock frequency takes 6.375 μs for a 32-bit integer multiply and 27.875 μs for an 80-bit floating-point multiply. The equivalent figures for the IBM 370/148 are 16.0 and 38.5 μs, respectively. In terms of basic computational power, the iAPX 432 is superior to an IBM 370/148, and the Bellmac-32A and the Hewlett-Packard processors are expected to be superior compared to an IBM 370/158. However, whereas the IBM 370 family is supported by extensive software in terms of compilers and application programs, it would take some time for similar facilities to be available on 32-bit microprocessors. A typical end user has to decide among several options: wait for the desired application software to become commercially available; develop the software in house; or use an earlier generation microprocessor that provides the software needed.

Table 9 Execution Times

Machine	Language	Word Size	Time (Milliseconds)			
			Search	Sieve	Puzzle	Acker
VAX-11/780	C	32	1.4	250	9400	4600
	Pascal (UNIX)	32	1.6	220	11 900	7800
	Pascal (VMS)	32	1.4	259	11 530	9850
68000 (8 MHz)	C	32	4.7	740	37 100	7800
	Pascal	16	5.3	810	32 470	11 480
	Pascal	32	5.8	960	32 520	12 320
68000 (16 MHz)	Pascal	16	1.3	196	9180	2750
	Pascal	32	1.5	246	9200	3080
8086 (5 MHz)	Pascal	16	7.3	764	44 000	11 100
432/Rel. 3 (8 MHz)	Ada	16	4.4	978	45 700	47 800
80286 (8 MHz)	Pascal	16	1.4	168	9138	2218
80286 (10 MHz)	Pascal	16	1.1	135	7311	1774
HP 32-Bit CPU* (18 MHz)	Pascal	32	NA	NA	7450	2590
NS 16032** (7 MHz)	Pascal	32	NA	NA	24 000	9900

*Indicates experimental prototype.
**Indicates vendor provided information.

Table 10 Performance at 8 MHz

Wait States	Machine	Language	Time (Milliseconds)			
			Search	Sieve	Puzzle	Acker
4	68000	Pascal	5.3	810	32 470	11 480
	432 (Rel. 3)	Ada	4.4	978	45 700	47 800
	8086	Pascal	4.6	448	27 500	6938
0	68000	Pascal	2.6	392	18 360	5500
	80286	Pascal	1.4	168	9138	2218

VI. SYSTEM ISSUES

Concurrent with the development of basic processors, manufacturers have developed sophisticated chips for auxiliary functions-memory management, control of DMA operations, control of peripherals, bus management and arbitration, control of communications, and control of input and output functions. However, a particular chip of this kind is designed to support only a particular family of microprocessor chips of a particular vendor. Exhaustive lists of chips are published annually in several trade magazines. Usually there is a time lag between the introduction of the processor chip itself and the introduction of support chips. This results in extra effort in implementing systems based on recently introduced microprocessors.

In order to take over applications previously handled by minicomputers and mainframes, users demand that microprocessor based systems offer high throughput, ease of use, and friendliness of the system [104]. To optimize utilization of resources and to minimize user effort, an *operating system* is used. It is used for some or all the following functions:

a) processor management,
b) memory management,
c) peripheral management,
d) file management,
e) task scheduling and process management,
f) user-oriented facilities like command-line interpreter,
g) miscellaneous features to support networking, utilities, and high-level languages.

In order to fully comprehend the emerging trends in microcomputer software, it is relevant to know a little about the history of the popular operating system.

The earliest uses of microprocessors were in embedded control applications. Programs were written on mainframe computers, cross-assembled for the micro, and loaded as object code into the micro's memory for execution. To aid the writing of such control programs, Intel, in 1972, hired MAA (Microcomputer Applications Associates, later to become Digital Research) to design and implement a systems programming language. This language, called PL/M (Programming Language for Microcomputers) used ideas from PL/I, Algol, and XPL, the command-writing language. PL/M became quite popular and is still used.

Along with PL/M, MAA proposed a small operating system, called CP/M (Control Program for Microcomputers), to enable applications to be written and compiled on the Intel 8080-based microcomputer. As Intel was reluctant, MAA developed the product independently in 1974. CP/M subsequently became the most popular operating system for microcomputers; now there are 200 000 installations using a wide spectrum of hardware configurations. It has become a *de facto* standard with most vendors in both the United States and abroad supporting it on their 8-bit and 16-bit microprocessors [105]–[107]. CP/M dominates the single-user environment.

UNIX, developed during the 1970s at Bell Laboratories, is the premier example of an operating system optimized for program development by professional programmers in a multiuser interactive environment. The popularity of UNIX can be judged by the vast number of look-alike operating systems, such as Coherent and Xenix on the 8086; Zeus, Onix and Xenix on the Z-8000; Uniflex, Idris, Coherent, and Xenix on the 68000; Cromix, UNIX, and Idris on the Z-80; and Idris, Xenix, and Coherent on LSI-11 and PDP-11 systems.

According to Kenneth Thompson, the principal architect of the UNIX operating system, "the UNIX kernel consists of about 10 000 lines of C code and about 1000 lines of assembly code. The assembly code can be further broken down into 200 lines included for the sake of efficiency (they could have been written in C) and 800 lines to perform hardware functions not possible in C. The assembly code represents 5 to 10 percent of what has been lumped into the broad expression *the UNIX operating system*. The kernel is the only UNIX code that cannot be substituted by the user to his own liking" [57]. Some companies like Microsoft have adapted this hardware-dependent code for several microprocessors. Other like Mark Williams Company have chosen to rewrite the entire code based on the UNIX design.

Inspired by UNIX, Digital Research, the originator of CP/M, has developed the MP/M operating system. Similar to UNIX, MP/M is a multiuser, multitasking operating system. But unlike UNIX, MP/M has a real-time kernel that can be either interrupt-driven or dependent upon device polling. Also, MP/M uses multilevel directories rather than the tree structure provided by UNIX. In the UNIX environment, a fast disk file is used as a buffer to communicate between two processes. Such "pipes" are opened and closed as standard files, but are limited to character I/O only. MP/M permits variably sized messages to be written to and to be read from an unlimited number of processes, through buffers maintained in the memory. Each such "queue" has a name and is treated like other disk files. Further, queues can be optimized for message sizes. UNIX, on the other hand, offers a large array of excellent system development tools, and the ability to link utilities through a single command. The advent of personal computers has resulted in a growing popularity of the MS-DOS operating system developed by Microsoft. This operating system is supported on many leading computers of U.S. and Japanese make.

Unfortunately in all these cases, even though the same operating system is supported on several computer systems, the differences in hardware make it essential to modify application programs to execute under the same operating system on different systems. New techniques are evolving that enable such differences to be transparent to end users. For example, the UCSD p-system [116], originally developed by the University of California at San Diego, permits maximum level of software portability through use of intermediate code, called p-code, into which all the high-level languages are compiled. When a new processor is introduced, the p-system is implemented simply by writing an interpreter that translates p-code into the new processor's native code. The penalty is in terms of reduced execution speed of interpreted code. The advantage is in terms of ability to execute the same program under different environments like 8086, Z8000, 68000, TI 9900, and others. As microprocessors offer increased speeds, and as programming costs continue to escalate, it is likely that more users will accept the penalty of reduced execution speeds, and opt for using such techniques of intermediate code to aid conversion of programs to achieve software compatibility.

In the domain of large computer systems, Fortran and Cobol became industry standards by virtue of their availability on a large number of systems. This does not, however, imply that all vendors offered identical languages. The traditional problem of incompatible higher level languages has been carried over to the microprocessor area. Although BASIC is supported on almost all systems, the different vendors offer significantly different versions, depending on word size, memory addressing, and other factors. Frequently, multiple versions of BASIC are available for the same machine (for example, on the IBM Personal Computer alone there are three versions of BASIC available). The current trend in new operating systems is to support Pascal and Ada. These two languages are likely to be major forces in coming years. The increasing use of higher level languages will mitigate the problems of soaring software development costs [69]. The operating systems themselves are also written entirely in higher level languages, e.g., the iMAX for iAPX 432 is written in Ada [118].

Unlike the early years of microprocessors when stand-alone applications dominated the scene, the need to transmit and receive data and programs is an important characteristic of current generation systems [108], [109]. Communication between microprocessor-based systems can be analyzed at different levels. The International Organization for Standardization has developed a Reference Model of Open Systems Interconnection (ISO-OSI) comprised of seven layers as follows [58], [59]:

1) the physical layer,
2) the data link layer,
3) the network layer,
4) the transport layer,
5) the session layer,
6) the presentation layer,
7) the application layer.

The *physical layer* deals with transmission of raw bit stream, and the electrical protocols. For example, RS 232 is a physical link protocol that specifies the required voltages, number of wires, and transmission speeds over a serial communication link. The *data link layer* deals with issues of converting unreliable transmission links into reliable ones by using techniques like checksums to validate information received over the line. Although virtually every leading vendor is proposing a somewhat different protocol, two protocols (carrier sense multiple access (CMSA/CD) and Tokenpassing) currently dominate the consideration for standards embodied in the IEEE 802 specification. The *network layer* deals with conventions that govern the transmission of data messages over the communication highway, for example, X.25. The *transport layer* is used to shield the customer's portion of the network from the carrier's portion; thus a change in carrier should be transparent to the computers at the two ends of the link. The *session layer* deals with setting up, managing, and splitting down process-to-process connection. The *presentation layer* deals with transformations (like data compression) on the data to be transmitted. The *application layer* is at the discretion of the users and refers to the ability of appliction programs involved in communication to freely exchange data and programs. Although the goal is to enable efficient communication at the application level, this goal involves efficient communication at the other levels as well. Efficient communication, especially between dissimilar systems, is critically dependent on the protocols and standards for interconnection. Interconnection standards [113], like other standards, are usually based on the design adopted by a large vendor. For example, the IEEE 802 [114] is based on the Hewlett-Packard design, and the IEEE P796 is based on the Intel Multibus [115]. With multiple standards, conversion of information from one standard to another involves an unproductive overhead.

Note that multiple communication standards are inevitable especially because interconnection of computing resources can be at several distinct levels. At the basic hardware level, *backplane busses* such as Multibus, S-100, and VME are used to communicate (over very small distances, usually of less than 1 m) data and information between processors, processor and memory, and between processors and fast peripheral units. At the next level, *I/O busses* such as the IEEE 488 bus standard are used to communicate between the processor and I/O units. Then, local area networks (LANs) are used to provide data communication capabilities in buildings and over a few square kilometers of area. In this chapter, we only consider the role of backplane busses used in multiprocessor configurations.

VII. Multiprocessor Capabilities

To increase computational bandwidth and/or system resilience, integration of several microprocessors in a single system frequently becomes necessary. The overall throughput and efficiency of such systems is directly dependent on the hardware and software interconnection mechanisms supported by the basic microprocessor chips. Many different interconnection systems have evolved over the years. The single timeshared bus offers distinct advantages as an interconnection mechanism for multimicroprocessor systems. Under such a scheme, different modules can share the bus resource equally on a time-multiplexed or demand-multiplexed basis. We concentrate on the Intel multiprocessing strategy to illustrate these interconnection characteristics.

A typical iAPX 432-based multiprocessor configuration is shown in Fig. 11. Different iAPX 432 processor pairs (43201, 43202) are connected to a single processor–memory interconnect bus which Intel refers to as a Packetbus. It operates on a split-transaction basis. For example, if a processor needed to access some data from memory, it would send a message to the appropriate storage module. The actual transfer of the message on the bus will occur when the arbitration mechanism grants the bus to the particular CPU. When the request for the data is received by the storage module, it accesses the data, but during this period of data access, the bus is freed up for use by others. And, finally, when the storage module is ready with the data, it requests the bus, gets them, and sends the "reply" to the CPU. By freeing up the bus during the period of memory access, which is significantly longer than the bus service time, more processors can communicate on the same bus in a given span. On the iAPX 432, variable length (1 to 10 bytes) of data messages are used for request/reply packet, and a 32-bit word can be transferred in 250 ns. The split-transaction protocol used by Intel offers maximum benefits in

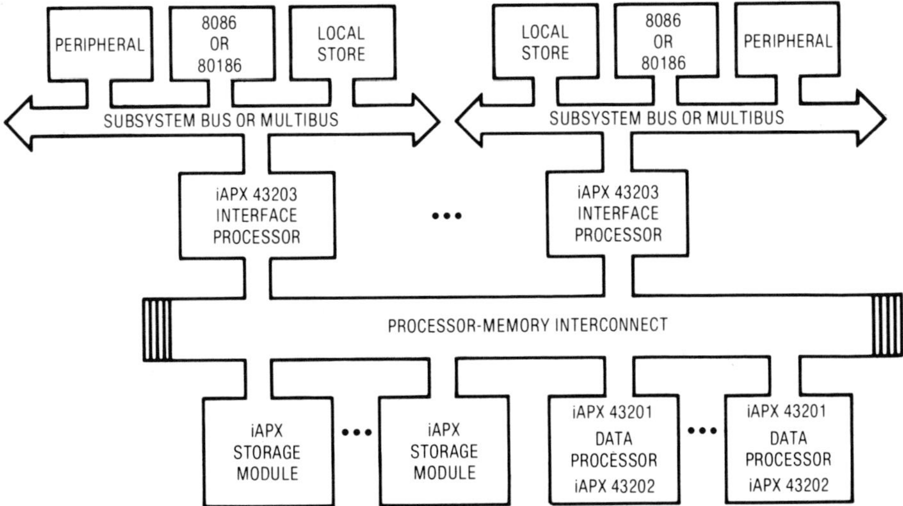

Fig. 11. A typical multiple iAPX 432 based system.

the "homogeneous" multiprocessing case with identical processors being used to permit any processor to handle a given task. "Heterogeneous" multiprocessing, for I/O or special-purpose applications, involves use of different types of microprocessors. Unfortunately, no 16-bit microprocessor can be interconnected directly to the Packetbus. One option to interconnect an Intel 8086 is through a Multibus and an iAPX 43203 interface processor as shown in Fig. 11. Although the iAPX 43203 can undertake additional responsibilities, besides the interconnect function, the overhead of code conversion and differences in protocol between the Multibus and the Packet makes such heterogeneous multiprocessor configurations less efficient than homogeneous multiprocessor configurations. The iAPX 43204 and iAPX 43205 support multiple busses to reduce contention problems. However, multiple busses introduce time delays and impose higher overhead than a single bus configuration.

Hewlett-Packard also uses a demand multiplexed bus [60] with a single CPU using 30 percent of the total bus bandwidth for typical instruction mixes. In general, as the number of processors increases, there are more bus users leading to increased bus contention. Also, there is additional overhead in terms of control and coordination of multiple resources. The latter overhead is difficult to estimate, and most studies simply neglect to take it into account. Fig. 12 reflects Intel's estimates of effective number of processors versus actual number of processors using a single bus. Since a dual-processor configuration is indicated as having twice the processing power of a single one, the exclusion of software overhead is evident. Notice that the curve flattens off quickly, and irrespective of the number of physical processors used, it is possible to get an aggregate performance exceeding four times the power of a single one using a single memory bus. Hewlett-Packard [60] claims that with four processors the overall performance with multitasking ranges from 2.9 to 3.7 times the uniprocessor performance, depending on the instruction mix. According to an anonymous reviewer, systems using eight iAPX 432 processors have been designed. With proper interface circuitry and bus protocols, one can integrate up to 25 processors on a single bus with positive incremental increases on overall system throughput [61], and facilitate enhanced concurrent operation of all system resources [62]. Also, the minimal cost of processing elements enables duplication of system resources, and peer or self-testing of these resources. Thus using multimicroprocessors and efficient bus operation techniques, several recent computer systems offer both high throughput and significant fault tolerance at much lower prices than before. In view of these advantages, these systems are becoming increasingly popular for transaction processing applications.

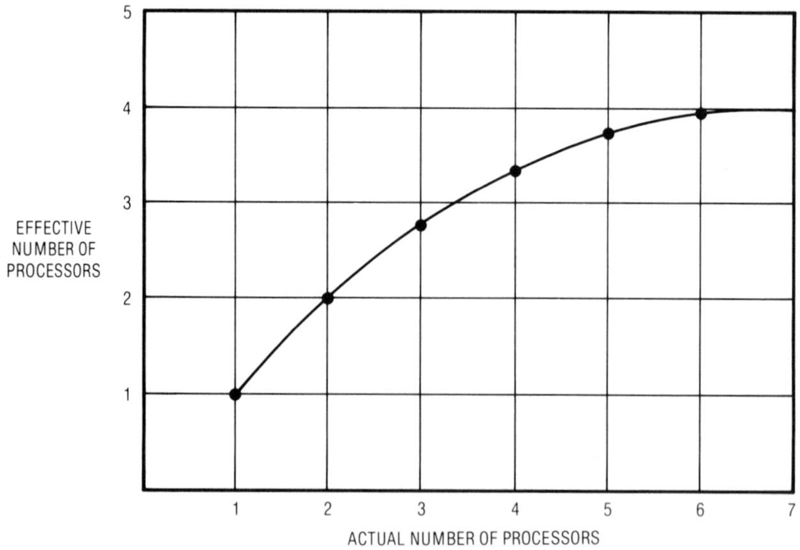

Fig. 12. Intel estimated iAPX 432 bus efficiency for a single memory bus multiprocessor system.

VIII. SPECIAL-PURPOSE PROCESSORS

During their first decade of existence, the focus was on general-purpose microprocessors and microcomputers. In 1981, Intel announced the 2920 analog processor with an on-chip D/A converter, which could also be used for A/D conversion using the successive-approximation algorithm. The precision of conversion is 9 bits, but internal arithmetic is done with 25 bits. An on-chip PROM can hold a 192-instruction program, which is executed in sequence with no program jumps. Since an instruction takes 400 ns, the program execution time is 76.8 μm or less, corresponding to a sampling rate of 13 kHz. This enables the processor to sample and process analog waveforms with a bandwidth of 6.5 kHz which is quite adequate for high-quality speech applications.

In 1982, Texas Instruments announced the TMS320 single-chip microcomputer for digital signal-processing applications [68]. Unlike conventional von Neumann architecture, the Harvard architecture of the TMS320 uses a dual-bus design for parallel fetching of code and data to support high-speed complex arithmetic. This chip has been optimized for speed, rather than for size or power consumption. As such, significant parallelism has been implemented using a large number of devices. A fully parallel 2's complement 16-by-16 multiplier is incorporated enabling multiplication in just one cycle of 200 ns, plus another 200 ns to latch the result. It does not, however, have an on-chip A/D or D/A converter. Intended applications include digital filtering, signal handling, data compression, and fast Fourier transforms. Microprocessors for signal-processing applications have also been developed by AMI (S28211 family) and by NEC (μPD 7720). The AMI 29500 signal processor uses the 2900 type bit-slice architecture to implement a sum-of-products number crunching capability for array processing applications. It has been designed to perform a 1024-point complex fast Fourier transform in 2 ms (400 ns per butterfly).

The trend in the special-purpose processor domain is towards systolic data architectures to increase computational throughput without increased memory bandwidth. Unlike traditional architectures, where data are moved one at a time through a processing element, a systolic architecture relies on an array of processing cells. Data are pumped through the array, undergoing changes at each cell, before returning to memory, similar to the manner in which blood circulates from and to the heart. Since speech- and video-processing techniques rely heavily on fast Fourier transforms, which can be implemented as an array of definite processing operation, systolic data architectures offer great potential for use in newer processor chips specifically geared towards speech and video applications. An excellent summary of research on alternative design methodologies for special-purpose processors can be found in [70].

IX. CONCLUSION

The ability to implement increasing numbers of devices on the same chip has enabled microprocessors to offer increased functional capabilities at diminishing costs over the years. The enhanced capabilities are in the areas of processing power, peripheral support, and in terms of software. These trends are likely to continue. The domain of microprocessors constitutes a dynamic world, and we can always expect newer and more powerful chips.

X. GLOSSARY

Accumulator A register that is used to store results of arithmetic and logical operations.

Arbitration The process of selecting who will use a resource next in the light of requests from several entities (typically processors).

Arrays Refers to a set of data that is organized in a matrix format.

Barrel shift circuit A circuit that enables all data stored in a particular register to be shifted left or right by an arbitrary number of bits—such circuits are used in implementing fast multiplication techniques.

BCD Binary-coded decimal, a technique to store each decimal digit as a combination of four binary bits.

Bit-sliced organization Refers to use of multiple, but identical, microprocessors, each with "small" word sizes to generate a processor with larger effective word size.

Cache memory Very fast, but limited capacity, memory used for prestaging operands and data needed by the processor. By reducing effective memory response time, the overall computer system throughput is enhanced.

CMOS Complementary metal–oxide–semiconductor technology uses both n- and p-channel devices. This combination yields faster devices and lower power consumption than either N- or PMOS alone.

Concurrent user stacks In earlier systems, none or only one user-defined stack was supported. New chips allow multiple stacks to be used concurrently. This development allows users greater flexibility.

Context switching Refers to the processor ceasing execution of one program, and initiating execution of another program in a multiprogrammed environment. A context switch incurs the overhead of saving the status of the discontinued program and of loading the status, or context, of the new program to be run.

DMA Direct memory access enables direct transfer of information between memory and peripherals without information passing through the processor.

ECL Emitter-coupled logic used for implementing systems with very fast speeds. This technology suffers higher power consumption and lower device densities than MOS techniques.

Hardware-implemented process scheduling Scheduler algorithm hardwired or in firmware.

Interface processor A processor used to convert codes and protocols to allow interfacing of two entities, such as communications lines, computers, terminals, etc.

Microprocessor The semiconductor central processing unit manufactured usually as a single physical device.

MOS Metal–oxide–semiconductor, refers to a device that is the result of processing a semiconductor material in various stages with deposited metals such as aluminum and oxide layers to form basic switching and electrical circuit elements.

Multilevel memory protection hierarchy Refers to the ability to distinguish between several levels of requests for memory operations and to enable enhanced degrees of memory protection.

Multiple homogeneous caches Refers to the ability to support several cache memories of identical characteristics.

Multiplexing of address and data Refers to the use of the same physical pins or bus wires to carry both address information and actual data on a time-multiplexed basis.

NMOS n-channel MOS; in such devices electric current is constituted by a flow of negative charges.

On-chip memory hierarchy Storage of different types of memory organizations on the same (processor) chip.

Orthogonal instruction set An instruction set that allows all (relevant) addressing methods to be used with all instructions.

Packed arrays Arrays that are compressed to contain all information in the original array in the minimum storage space.

Packed records Records that are compressed to contain all information in the minimum storage space.

Pipelining The mechanism of fetching next sequential program operand or data while the present instruction is being executed.

PLA Programmed logic array, a structured matrix of chip interconnections accomplished by mask programming. Often used to implement instruction decode and control logic.

PMOS p-channel MOS; in such devices electric current is constituted by a flow of positive charges.

Self-dispatching processors Processors, in a multiprocessor environment, that are seeking tasks on a continuous basis; as soon as a new task enters the system, an idle self-dispatching processor will immediately direct itself to start executing the task.

Stack A last-in first-out (LIFO) buffer used for storing data and interrupts. Also referred to as a FILO (first-in last-out).

Trap A special condition during program execution which, if encountered, will cause special action or exception processing to occur.

Vector-based instructions Powerful instructions that enable many sequential operations to be carried out atomically. A vector instruction may take an interrupt, store the machine state, branch to the appropriate device or handle stacks and allocate a stack frame in a few microseconds. This process would take several sequential subroutines if it were executed using traditional operating systems.

Virtual machines Multiple copies of the system's complete hardware-software interface are efficiently replicated through a combination of hardware and software.

References

[1] R. N. Noyce and M. E. Hoff, Jr., "A history of microprocessor development at Intel," *IEEE Micro*, vol. 1, no. 1, pp. 8–21, Feb. 1981.

[2] D. Moralee, "Microprocessor architectures: Ten years of development," *Electronics and Power*, pp. 216–221, March 1981.

[3] H. D. Toong, "Microprocessors," *Sci. Amer.*, pp. 146–161, Sept. 1977.

[4] R. H. Krambeck, C. M. Lee, and H. F. S. Law, "High-speed compact circuit with CMOS," *IEEE J. Solid-State Circuits*, vol. SC-16, pp. 614–618, June 1982.

[5] D. W. Best *et al.*, "An advanced-architecture CMOS/SOS microprocessor," *IEEE Micro*, vol. 2, no. 3, pp. 10–26, Aug. 1982.

[6] D. L. Wollesen, "CMOS LSI—The computer component process of the 80's," *Computer*, pp. 59–67, Feb. 1980.

[7] W. R. Iversen, "32-bit chip set will offer huge microprogram store," *Electronics*, pp. 47–48, Sept. 8, 1982.

[8] J. W. Beyers *et al.*, "A 32-bit VLSI CPU chip," *IEEE J. Solid-State Circuits*, vol. SC-16, no. 5, pp. 537–542, Oct. 1981.

[9] D. A. Patterson and C. H. Sequin, "A VLSI RISC," *Computer*, vol. 15, no. 9, pp. 8–21, Sept. 1982.

[10] G. Radin, "The 801 minicomputer," in *Proc. Symp. Architectural Support for Programming Languages and Operating Systems*, Mar. 1–3, 1982, pp. 39–47.

[11] R. Ochester, "Low-cost 16-bit microprocessor has performance of midrange minicomputer," *Electronics*, pp. 129–133, Nov. 3, 1981.

[12] C. Davis *et al.*, "Gate array embodies System/370 processor," *Electronics*, pp. 140–143, Oct. 9, 1980.

[13] P. Heller *et al.*, "Memory protection moves onto 16-bit microprocessor chip," *Electronics*, pp. 133–137, Feb. 24, 1982.

[14] S. M. S. Liu *et al.*, "HMOS III technology," *IEEE J. Solid-State Circuits*, vol. SC-17, no. 5, pp. 810–815, Oct. 1982.

[15] F. A. Ware *et al.*, "64-bit monolithic floating point processors," *IEEE J. Solid-State Circuits*, vol. SC-17, no. 5, pp. 898–907, Oct. 1982.

[16] G. E. Moore, "Progress in digital integrated electronics," in *Proc. Int. Electron Devices Meet.*, pp. 11–13, Dec. 1975.

[17] H. Hingarh *et al.*, "A 16-bit microprocessor for realtime applications," in *Proc. Int. Solid-State Circuits Conf.*, Feb. 23–25, 1983.

[18] S. P. Morse *et al.*, "Intel microprocessors—8008 to 8086," *Computer*, pp. 42–60, Oct. 1980.

[19] J. Rattner and W. W. Lattin, "Ada determines architecture of 32-bit microprocessor," *Electronics*, pp. 119–126, Feb. 24, 1981.

[20] P. M. Russo, "VLSI impact on microprocessor evolution, usage and system design," *IEEE Trans. Electron Devices*, vol. ED-27, no. 8, pp. 1332–1341, Aug. 1980.

[21] ——, "Intel 8048 and 8051 family of chips," *EDN*, pp. 126–133, Oct. 27, 1982.

[22] E. Peatrowsky, "EPROM MCU's reduce hardware liability," in *Proc. MIDCON 1981*, session 21, paper 2, pp. 1–3, Nov. 1981.

[23] D. E. Smith, "New high performance one chip microcomputer," *Electron. Eng.*, pp. 56–65, Feb. 1982.

[24] P. R. Brown, "Advanced hardware features of the Z8 microcomputer family," in *Proc. MIDCON 1981*, session 21, paper 5, pp. 1–10, Nov. 1981.

[25] M. Patrick and J. Millar, "An innovative microcomputer for the 1980's," in *Proc. MIDCON 1981*, session 21, paper 4, pp. 1–13, Nov. 1981.

[26] H-M. D. Toong and A. Gupta, "An architectural comparison of contemporary 16-bit microprocessors," *IEEE Micro*, vol. 1, no. 2, pp. 26–37, May 1981.

[27] R. V. Orlando and T. L. Anderson, "An overview of the 9900 microprocessor family," *IEEE Micro*, vol. 1, no. 3, pp. 38–44, Aug. 1981.

[28] ——, *Introduction to the iAPX 286.* Intel Corp., Feb. 1982.

[29] S. Bal *et al.*, "The NS16000 family—Advances in architecture and hardware," *Computer*, pp. 58–67, June 1982.

[30] D. Laffitte, "New-generation 16-bit microprocessors—Fast and function-oriented," *Electron. Des.*, vol. 29, no. 4, pp. 111–117, Feb. 19, 1981.

[31] R. J. Markowitz, "iAPX 286: Virtual memory and distributed computing," in *Proc. WESCON 1981*, session 9, paper 2, pp. 1–7.

[32] G. Louie *et al.*, "A 16-bit microprocessor with on-chip memory protection," in *Proc. ISSCC 83*, session II, Feb. 1983.

[33] R. Mateosian, "Benefits of Z8000 family planning," in *Proc. WESCON 1981*, session 1, paper 5, pp. 1–7.

[34] J. W. Browne, Jr., "MC68000—Break away from the past," in *Proc. WESCON 1981*, session 1, paper 4, pp. 1–8.

[35] ——, *68010, 68020 Product Preview.* Motorola Semiconductors, 1982.

[36] A. Kaminker *et al.*, "A 32-bit microprocessor with virtual memory support," *IEEE J. Solid-State Circuits*, vol. SC-16, no. 5, pp. 548–557, Oct. 1981.

[37] J. Beekmans *et al.*, "Chip set bestows virtual memory on 16-bit minis," *Electronics*, pp. 134–138, June 2, 1981.

[38] N. Inui *et al.*, "16-bit C-MOS processor packs in hardware for business computers, *Electronics*, pp. 182–186, June 16, 1981.

[39] R. Ochester, "Low-cost 16-bit microprocessor has performance of midrange computer," *Electronics*, pp. 129–133, Nov. 3, 1981.

[40] R. Rubinstein *et al.*, "Compatibility about μECLIPSE and speed: Goals of a small machine," *Comput. Des.*, pp. 69–76, Aug. 1982.

[41] H. D. Toong and A. Gupta, "Evaluation kernels for microprocessor performance analyses," *Perform. Eval.*, vol. 2, no. 1, pp. 1–8, May 1982.

[42] J. Heering, "The Intel 8086, the Zilog Z8000 and the Motorola MC68000 microprocessors," *EUROMICRO J.*, vol. 6, pp. 135–143, 1980.

[43] R. Grappel and J. Hemenway, "Evaluating the 16-bit chips," *Mini-Micro. Syst.*, pp. 152–162, Dec. 1980.

[44] ——, "A tale of four μPs: Benchmarks quantify performance," *EDN*, pp. 179–185, Apr. 1, 1981.

[45] C. Davis *et al.*, "Gate array embodies system 1370 processor," *Electronics*, Oct. 9, 1980.

[46] A. Gupta and H. D. Toong, "An architectual comparison of 32-bit microprocessors," *IEEE Micro.*, vol. 3, no. 1, pp. 9–22, Feb. 1983.

[47] B. T. Murphy *et al.*, "A CMOS 32b single chip microprocessor," in *Proc. IEEE Solid-State Circuits Conf.*, pp. 230–231, Feb. 1981.

[48] A. D. Berenbaum *et al.*, "The operating system and language support features of the Bellmac-32 microprocessor," in *Proc. Symp. Architectural Support for Programming Languages and Operating Systems*, pp. 30–38, Mar. 1982.

[49] J. W. Beyers *et al.*, "A 32-bit VLSI CPU chip," *IEEE J. Solid-State Circuits*, vol. SC-16, pp. 537–542, Oct. 1981.

[50] J. M. Mikkelson *et al.*, "An NMOS VLSI process for fabrication of a 32-bit CPU chip," *IEEE J. Solid-State Circuits*, vol. SC-16, pp. 542–547, Oct. 1981.

[51] D. L. Budde *et al.*, "The execution unit for the VLSI 432 general data processor," *IEEE J. Solid-State Circuits*, vol. SC-16, pp. 514–521, Oct. 1981.

[52] J. A. Bayliss *et al.*, "The interface processor for the Intel 432 32-bit computer," *IEEE J. Solid-State Circuits*, vol. SC-16, pp. 522–530, Oct. 1981.

[53] J. A. Bayliss *et al.*, "The instruction decoding unit for the VLSI 432 general data processor," *IEEE J. Solid-State Circuits*, vol. SC-16, pp. 531–537, Oct. 1981.

[54] A. F. Shackil, "Microprocessors," *IEEE Spectrum*, pp. 32–33, Jan. 1982.

[55] P. M. Hansen *et al.*, "A performance evaluation of the Intel iAPX 432," *Comput. Architecture News*, vol. 10, no. 4, pp. 17–26, June 1982.

[56] D. A. Patterson, "A performance evaluation of the Intel 80286," *Comput. Architecture News*, vol. 10, no. 5, pp. 16–18, Sept. 1982.

[57] K. Thompson, *Bell Syst. Tech. J.*, vol. 57, no. 6, pt. 2, p. 1931, July–Aug. 1978.

[58] H. Zimmermann, "OSI reference model—The ISO model of architecture for open systems interconnection," *IEEE Trans. Commun.*, vol. COM-28, pp. 425–432, Apr. 1980.

[59] A. S. Tanenbaum, "Network protocols," *ACM Computing Surveys*, vol. 13, no. 4, pp. 454–489, Dec. 1981.

[60] D. Seccombe, Hewlett-Packard, Nov. 8, 1982, personal communication.

[61] H-M. D. Toong, S. O. Strommen, and E. R. Goodrich II, "A general multi-microprocessor interconnection mechanism for non-numeric processing," in *Proc. the 5th Workshop on Computer Architecture for Non-Numeric Processing*, pp. 115–123, 1980.

[62] A. Gupta and H-M. D. Toong, "Increased concurrency in m-n multiprocessor systems," in *Proc. 3rd Int. Conf. on Distributed Computing Systems* (Miami/Ft. Lauderdale, FL, Oct. 18–22, 1982), pp. 146–151.

[63] D. A. Patterson and C. Sequin, "Design considerations for single-chip computers of the future," *IEEE J. Solid-State Circuits*, vol. SC-15, pp. 44–52, 1980.

[64] H-M. D. Toong and A. Gupta, "Personal computers," *Sci. Amer.*, pp. 88–99, Dec. 1982.

[65] H. Cragon, "The elements of single-chip microcomputer architecture," *Computer*, pp. 27–41, Oct. 1980.

[66] J. P. Hayes, "A survey of bit-sliced computer design," *J. Digital Syst.*, vol. V, no. 3, pp. 203–250, 1981.

[67] K. Thompson, "the UNIX operating system," *Bell Syst. Tech. J.*, vol. 57, no. 6, pt. 2, p. 1931, July–Aug. 1978.

[68] K. McDonough *et al.*, "Microcomputer with 32-bit arithmetic does high-precision number crunching," *Electronics*, pp. 105–110, Feb. 24, 1982.

[69] R. Bernhard, "More hardware means less software," *IEEE Spectrum*, pp. 30–37, Dec. 1981.

[70] P. C. Treleaven, "VLSI processor architectures," *Computer*, vol. 15, no. 6, pp. 33–45, June 1982.

[71] A. Gupta and H-M. D. Toong, *Advanced Microprocessors*. New York: IEEE Press, 1983, IEEE reprint book.

[72] J. W. Beyers *et al.*, "A 32-bit VLSI CPU chip," in *Dig. Tech. Papers, 1981 IEEE Int. Solid-State Circuits Conf.*, pp. 104, 105.

[73] ——, "Microprocessors," *Electron. Eng.*, pp. 60–85, Sept. 1981.

[74] H. M. J. M. Dortmans, "Application of microprocessors," *J. Phys. E. Sci. Instrum.*, vol. 14, pp. 777–782, 1981.

[75] D. G. Fairbairn, "VLSI technology," *Computer*, pp. 87–96, Jan. 1982.

[76] C. M. Lee and C. G. Lin-Hendel, "Current status and future projection of CMOS technology," in *Proc. COMPCON, Fall* (Sept. 20–23, 1982), pp. 716–719.

[77] D. J. McGreivy and K. A Pickar, *VLSI Technologies Through the 80's and Beyond*. New York: IEEE Computer Soc. Reprint Book, 1982.

[78] R. Rice, *VLSI Support Technologies—A Tutorial*. New York: IEEE Computer Soc. Reprint Book, 1982.

[79] T. Knowlton, "μPD7500 family of 4-bit microcomputers—Big jobs with small programs," in *Proc. MIDCON 1981*, session 24, paper 5, pp. 1–5.

[80] R. M. Cushman, "CMOS microprocessor and microcomputer ICs," *EDN*, pp. 88–100, Sept. 29, 1982.

[81] J. F. Stockton, "A virtual breakthrough for micros," *Comput. Des.*, pp. 153–162, Aug. 1982.

[82] H. W. Lawson, Jr., "New directions for micro and system architectures in the 1980s," *Proc. Nat. Computer Conf.*, 1981, pp. 57–62.

[83] ——, "Single-chip microcomputers: Performance and features," *Electron Des.*, pp. 130–139, Oct. 14, 1982.

[84] D. Bursky, "16-bit families swell with greater integration," *Electron. Des.*, pp. 103–112, Oct. 14, 1982.

[85] W. D. Hopkins, "Speed/cost tradeoffs of using the TMS 99110 microprocessor," in *Proc. ELECTRO 1982*, session 18, paper 3, pp. 1–7.

[86] W. D. Huston, "Microcomputers—Heritages and the future," *IEEE Trans. Consum. Electron.*, vol. CE-26, pp. 129–141, Feb. 1980.

[87] D. Stevenson, "Floating-point processing with Zilog's Z-8000 CPU," in *Proc. ELECTRO 1982*, session 18, paper 4, pp. 1–2.

[88] J. T. Twardy, "Fourth generation architecture allows performance of larger jobs with smaller programs," in *Proc. ELECTRO 1982*, session 25, paper 4, pp. 1–8.

[89] D. A. Patterson and R. S. Piepho, "Assessing RISCs in high-level language support," *IEEE Micro*, pp. 9–19, Nov. 1982.

[90] L. Kohn, "A 32b microprocessor with virtual memory support," in *Proc. IEEE Solid-State Circuits Conf.*, pp. 232–233, Feb. 1981.

[91] H-F. S. Law, "Layout technology for high performance VLSI," in *Proc. COMPCON, Fall* (Sept. 20–23, 1982), pp. 40–43.

[92] J. A. Bayliss *et al.*, "The interface processor for the 32-bit computer," in *Dig. Tech. Papers, 1981 IEEE Int. Solid-State Circuits Conf.*, pp. 116–117, 263.

[93] D. L. Budde *et al.*, "The 32-bit computer execution unit," in *Dig. Tech. Papers, 1981 IEEE Int. Solid-State Circuits Conf.*, pp. 112–113, 261.

[94] J. Klovstad, G. M. Catlin, and T. Zingale, "16-bit μP crams peripheral support on chip," *Electron. Des.*, pp. 191–196, June 10, 1982.

[95] J. Black and J. Kister, "VERSA bus: A powerful structure for multiprocessing applications," in *Proc. MIDCON 1981*, session 25, paper 6, pp. 1–6.

[96] W. Twaddell, "EDN's ninth annual μP/μC chip directory," *EDN*, pp. 98–204, Oct. 27, 1982.

[97] ——, "General-purpose microprocessors: Performance and features," *Electron. Des.*, pp. 118–139, Oct. 14, 1982.

[98] W. S. Richardson *et al.*, "The 32 bit computer instruction decoding unit," in *Dig. Tech. Papers, 1981 IEEE Int. Solid-State Circuits Conf.*, pp. 114–115, 262.

[99] ——, *Intel 432 System Summary: Manager's Perspective*, Intel Corp., Manual Number 171867-001, 1981, p. 29.

[100] W. W. Lattin *et al.*, "A 32-bit VLSI micromainframe computer system," in *Dig. Tech. Papers, 1981 IEEE Int. Solid-State Circuits Conf.*, pp. 110–111.

[101] T. Zingale, "Broadening the scope of microcomputer numeric applications with the 8087 numeric processor extension," in *Proc. ELECTRO 1982*, session 18, paper 1, pp. 1–7.

[102] S. Ziegler *et al.*, "Ada for the Intel 432 microcomputer," *Computer*, pp. 47–56, June 1981.

[103] F. J. Pollack *et al.*, "Supporting Ada memory management in the iAPX-432," in *Proc. Symp. on Architectural Support for Programming Languages and Operating Systems*, Mar. 1982.

[104] M. Schindler, "Operating systems help micros act like minis," *Electron. Des.*, pp. SS41–SS45, Mar. 18, 1982.

[105] ——, "The latest in microcomputer operating systems," *Electron. Des.*, pp. SS46–SS64, Mar. 18, 1982.

[106] G. Kotelly, "EDN's third annual μC operating systems directory," *EDN*, pp. 80–157, Sept. 15, 1982.

[107] R. C. Johnson, "Operating systems hold a full house of features for 16-bit microprocessors," *Electronics*, pp. 113–120, Mar. 24, 1982.

[108] H. A. Freeman and K. J. Thurber, Eds., *Microcomputer Networks—A Tutorial*. New York: IEEE Computer Soc., 1981.

[109] P. L. Borrill, "Microprocessor bus structures and standards," *IEEE Micro*, vol. 1, no. 1, pp. 84–95, Feb. 1981.

[110] E. H. Frank and R. F. Sproull, "Testing and debugging custom integrated circuits," *ACM Comput. Surv.*, vol. 13, no. 4, pp. 425–451, Dec. 1981.

[111] S. P. Joshi, "Ethernet controller chip interfaces with variety of 16-bit processors," *Electron. Des.*, pp. 193–200, Oct. 14, 1982.

[112] R. Gilbert, "The general-purpose interface bus," *IEEE Micro*, vol. 2, no. 1, pp. 41–51, Feb. 1982.

[113] M. Graube, "Local area nets: A pair of standards," *IEEE Spectrum*, pp. 60–64, June 1982.

[114] T. J. Harrison, "IEEE project 802: Local area network standard," in *Proc. ELECTRO 1982*, session 17, paper 1, pp. 1–11.

[115] R. Dilbeck and J. Barthmailer, "The multibus/IEEE P796 bus standard and microcomputer system architecture for the 80's," in *Proc. MIDCON 1981*, session 25, paper 2, pp. 1–8.

[116] C. A. Irvine, "UCSD system makes programs portable," *Electron. Des.*, pp. 113–118, Aug. 1982.

[117] R. G. Rajulu and V. Rajaraman, "Execution-time analysis of process control algorithms on microprocessors," *IEEE Trans. Ind. Electron.*, vol. IE-29, no. 4, pp. 312–319, Nov. 1982.

[118] K. C. Kahn *et al.*, "iMAX: A multiprocessor operating system for an object-based computer," in *Proc. 8th Symp. on Operating Systems Principles* (ACM, Dec. 1981), pp. 127–136.

[119] C. B. Peterson *et al.*, "Two chips endow 32-bit processor with fault-tolerant architecture," *Electronics*, pp. 159–164, Apr. 7, 1983.

[120] M. De Prycher, "A performance comparison of three contemporary 16-bit microprocessors," *IEEE Micro*, vol. 3, no. 2, pp. 26–37, Apr. 1983.

[121] D. MacGregor and D. S. Mothersole, "Virtual memory and the MC68010," *IEEE Micro*, vol. 3, no. 3, pp. 24–39, June 1983.

11
A Processor Family for Personal Computers

ROBERT E. CHILDS, JR., JOHN CRAWFORD, DAVID L. HOUSE, AND ROBERT N. NOYCE,

The evolution of personal computers is intimately linked to advances in microprocessor technology. The Intel 80286 microprocessor offers sophisticated multitasking and memory management capabilities. This new microprocessor offers object code compatibility with the 8086/8088 CPU chip used in a number of popular personal computers. This chapter discusses the highlights of the 80286 microprocessor, its four-stage pipelined architecture and its other powerful capabilities that will radically impact the design of personal computers of tomorrow.

The Editors

I. INTRODUCTION

With the overwhelming amount of information now available electronically, a growing class of new users has turned to computer technology in hope of easily transforming data into a form meaningful for each user's own environment. These individuals are generally not computer professionals, but view information-handling technology as merely another office tool. As such, these users are typically relatively intolerant of poor performance, such as delayed or slow execution of tasks.

Because of the need to serve these users, the personal computer industry is faced with the unique problem of providing a very high degree of functional capability in a high-performance operating environment—all accessed through an easily understood user interface at very low cost. As described in this chapter, advanced very large-scale integrated (VLSI) circuits like those in the iAPX 86 family of processors meet this need through direct hardware support of key software structures. Furthermore, the availability of high-performance hardware support from low-cost VLSI circuits continues to encourage the development of the personal computer from one that found use only among computer-hardware hobbyists to one easy enough to use by individuals from more diverse backgrounds. Thus just as the 8086 improved on the 8080 by providing hardware support for the high-level language environment, a new microprocessor like the 80286 builds on the 8086 and offers direct hardware support for the multiwindow (multitasking) operating environments beginning to appear in personal computers.

From its inception in 1975 [1], the personal computer industry has moved from a low-volume market (0.1 million units) to one expected to surpass 50 million units by 1987 [2]. The first hobbyist machines based on Intel's 8080 microprocessor have stepped aside to machines like IBM's personal computer based on Intel's 8088 (Chapter 8), serving the business sector. In fact, the business community's need to deal with information on a corporate-wide basis is further motivating the widespread interconnection of personal computers and attachment to

---

The authors are with Intel Corporation, Santa Clara, CA 95051, USA.

mainframes, such as in the IBM PC XT/370, which provides virtual-service connections to IBM mainframes running VM/CMS [3]. Connected to other machines through a local-area network, low-cost personal workstations enjoy most of the benefits of large mainframes in sharing data, while still maintaining high performance during peak usage.

For this information to be usable to the average office worker, it has to be presented in a familiar environment, such as the office metaphor. Although historically users have adapted to the needs of the machine's operating environment, the situation is now the converse: from the user's point of view, the machine must now create an efficient electronic emulation of the physical environment. For the computer industry, this metaphor extends to more subtle notions like information protection through partitioned access control. Thus not only must personal data be guarded from intrusions within a company, but also company-proprietary information must be protected from unauthorized access across worldwide computer networks. In replacing physical media like paper and file cabinets with electronic counterparts, the computer industry must meet the challenge to provide an alternative that is at least as easy to use and as secure as the original environment.

Furthermore, the industry must deliver all this capability in a high-performance environment. The need for high-performance hardware support for multitasking stems directly from the need for easy to use, yet sophisticated user interfaces to integrated operating environments. Earlier trials into advanced user environments, like the Xerox Star [4], have demonstrated the advantages of graphic-oriented integrated operating environments. New users can rapidly perform useful tasks with minimal training thanks to the system's mouse-driven and menu-directed multiple-window interface. This interface presents a working environment using a desktop metaphor familiar to users. For example, Star users manipulate a variety of features (icons) that represent objects found in the typical business office, such as file drawers and mailboxes, thereby creating an electronic analog of the natural business environment.

Apart from this initial effort, the software industry now must concentrate on providing multiwindow environments that are easy to use and also preserve compatibility with the existing software base. But from the user's standpoint, not only must new integrated operating environments like MS-Window [5] and VisiOn [6] account for software compatibility, but they must also respond rapidly. Consequently, because the underlying model is a multitasking operating system, the long-term success of these important new systems rests heavily on their high performance and on the availability of high-performance multitasking support in hardware.

To meet these needs, Intel's 80286 microprocessor [7]–[14] (Fig. 1) provides direct hardware support for multitasking [15], memory management [16], and protection [17]. This processor is another member of the iAPX 86 family, which includes the 8086/8088 CPU and the newer 80186/80188 chip. The latter part integrates a direct memory-access controller, timer, interrupt controller, bus controller, and clock generator with a CPU in a single VLSI device [18], [19].

The Intel 80286 central-processing unit provides direct hardware support for this model of task-oriented software. In particular, the 80286 explicitly boosts multitasking performance through several data structures recognized directly by the CPU hardware. In dealing directly in hardware with the same software structures used to implement multitasking systems, the iAPX 286 bridges what has been called the semantic gap [20] between operating system structures and the hardware architecture. Thus the 80286 will contribute to greater software reliability, higher system performance, and reduced operating system size as well as offer a standardized model for operating system support of multitasking.

Often overlooked, standards are the unifying factors that permit software to be ported, data to be exchanged, and hardware to be upgraded without a major software impact. With the rapidly expanding software base even now available for personal computers, the importance of ensuring a compatible operating environment for the next generation of personal computers assumes major importance in the computer industry. The 80286 is able to directly execute software originally developed for the 8086/8088. In turn, though, the 80286 provides a hardware baseline for the next generation of multitasking (multiwindow) operating environments utilizing virtual memory.

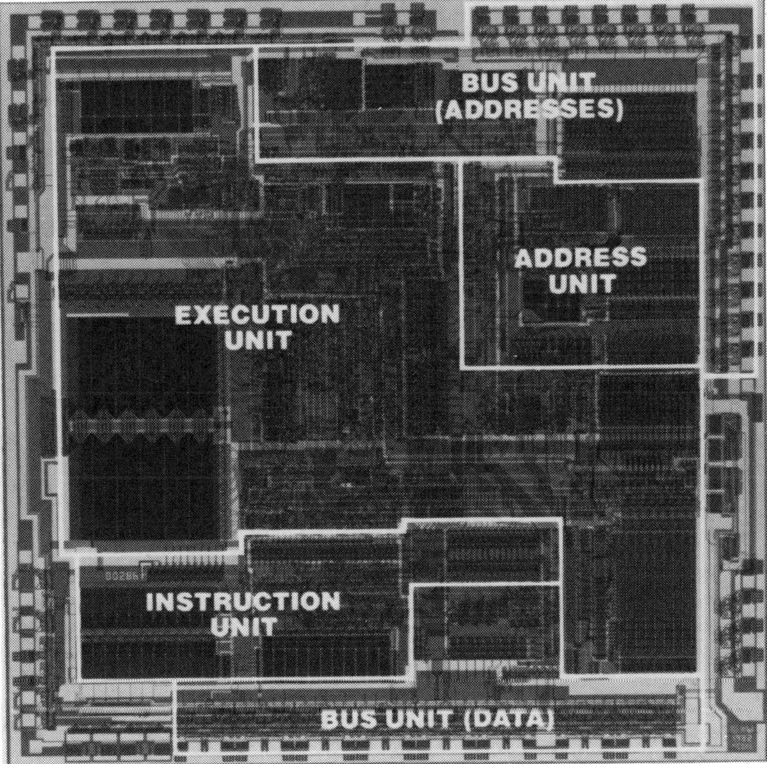

Fig. 1. Photograph of 80286.

This chapter delves deeply into the 80286 architecture. The next section describes details of the software structures supported by the 80286, and is therefore of concern primarily to someone writing an operating system, rather than to a user or someone writing an application program. Section IV describes how these features are implemented in hardware. Finally, Section V reveals future directions for the iAPX 86 family, in particular, the future 80386 CPU.

II. SOFTWARE STRUCTURES

A. Instruction Set

With the evolution of the iAPX 86 family has come a progression of the instruction set from the basic instruction set of the 8086/8088. With the 80186, the instruction set expanded to encompass further features for high-level languages like procedure entry and exit, parameter validation for index computations, and block I/O. Now with the memory management, protection, and multitasking features of the 80286, the instruction set has broadened significantly [21]. Yet within this extensive instruction repetoire, the programmer finds a simple schema of four disjoint instruction types.

Comprised of the usual instructions for traditional operations like arithmetic operations or conditional branches, one subset of the processor's instructions provides a conventional instruction set. Instructions in this subset, such as MOV (move), ADD, and PUSH, access arbitrary registers and memory in the conventional and fully symmetric manner.

Although similar from the point of view of the programmer, a second class of instructions, attuned to compiler heuristics, is specialized for compactness and is deliberately asymmetric in order to support highly frequently used forms. These instructions are register specific, such as the MOV and ADD instructions that are specific for the AX register, and have a 1-byte form.

A third subset applies to specific business application areas served by personal computers, such as text processing. Instructions in this subset include those such as the move-string instruction MOVS, the XLAT (translate) instruction for character-set translation, and the ASCII to BCD conversion instruction. Thus this subset extends the fundamental binary arithmetic- and logical-based instruction set of conventional CPUs with instructions intended to directly support business applications.

However, in the last subset, programmers find an unconventional category of instructions— those that change the environment. All the instructions dealt with thus far have been embedded within an implicit framework of an addressing environment, which is explicitly described by a special set of registers, called segment registers, and their contents. Indeed, compilers emit code for this implied execution environment. Changing of the execution environment is supported by instructions such as the long call (inter-segment CALL) and load long pointer instructions (such as LDS).

Separating these instructions from the rest of the instruction set particularly eases the complexity of linkage, relocation, and restarting instructions due to virtual memory "not-present" traps. Direct support for virtual memory is a natural extension and is easily implemented. The absence of a required segment in real memory can be noted and a hardware trap can be executed without the need to restore any data structures or register contents. For example, the processor can trap on a data segment "not-present" exception, swap in the required data, and restart without any difficulty.

B. Coprocessor Extensions

Besides these categories of instructions within the iAPX 86 family, however, the basic set of instructions available to a programmer is expanded through the use of special-purpose companion processors, like the numerics processor extension. Capable of sharing a local bus with the processor chip, the 80287 numeric processor extension provides full hardware support for floating-point functions traditionally performed in software and integrates them with the CPU instruction set at the systems level. The 80287 permits numerical operations in a variety of formats including 32-, 64-, and 80-bit floating point, 16-, 32-, and 64-bit integer, and 18-digit BCD [22]. In keeping with its conformance to the specifications of IEEE Standard 754, the 80287 also reports various exception conditions, such as zero divide, underflow, and overflow among others.

Besides floating-point operations, another arena sufficiently well-defined to be able to receive hardware support is communications. Conforming to IEEE 802, the 82586 local communications controller and 82501 Ethernet serial interface can offload low-level communications tasks from the host CPU. This pair implements the Physical and Data-Link Levels of the International Standards Organization's Open Systems Interconnection Reference Model [23].

Coprocessors such as these for floating-point operations and for communications increase overall system performance by offloading functions previously performed by the CPU in software. To the present personal computer user, this can be of critical importance. However, to the user of succeeding generations of hardware and software, coprocessors provide a further function. By implementing well-defined software interfaces in hardware, coprocessors help safeguard the compatibility of an existing software base through successive generations of hardware.

C. Segmentation

A multitasking environment is characterized by many processes that serve specific applications or systems functions. In any machine, a process consists of a number of segments. The 80286 supports this model through its use of segments as the fundamental unit of organization of code and data. Expanding the segmented view of organization found in Intel's 8086/8088, the 80286 further provides the memory management and protection features possible with segmented organization.

In the iAPX 86 family of processors, including the 80286, memory is organized into distinct segment types. A group of four segments form the execution environment at any instant in time. The execution environment is explicitly defined by the contents of four segment registers: the code segment (CS), data segment (DS), stack segment (SS), and extra segment (ES) registers.

All members of the iAPX 86 family use a 32-bit value as an address pointer—a 16-bit segment number and a 16-bit offset (Fig. 2). Processors that deal with real addresses (8086, 8088, 80186, 80188) utilize the segment number as a real memory base address to form a 2^{20}-byte physical memory address. The iAPX 286 recognizes this organization of memory in its Real Address mode. Existing 8086/8088 code (which is implicitly based on real-address segments) can be executed on the 80286 directly in Real Address mode.

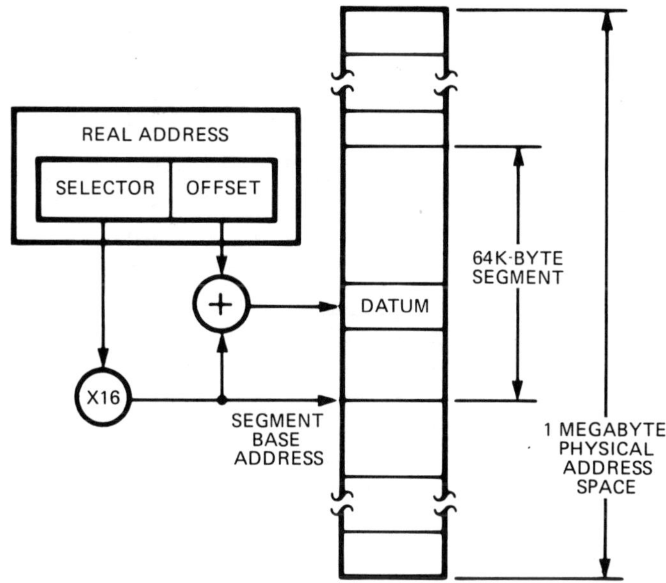

Fig. 2.   Real address mode segment selector interpretation.

Notes: 1)   The selector identifies a segment in physical memory.
2)   A selector specifies the segment's base address (modulo 16) within the 1M-byte address space.
3)   The selector is the 16 most significant bits of a segment's physical address.
4)   The values of selectors determine the amount by which they overlap in real memory.
5)   Segments may overlap by increments of 16 bytes. Overlap ranges from complete to none.

D. Memory Mapping

Besides providing a more efficient use of existing physical memory, memory management also simplifies software development because of the resulting position independence of code and lack of constraints in using address space in programs for either code or data. Furthermore, as an economic necessity, memory management provides a cost-effective alternative to massive amounts of semiconductor memory—which continues to maintain a significant disadvantage in cost per bit over disk storage.

However, the 80286 considerably extends the view of memory organization with its Protected Virtual Address mechanism. Here, much as in the Burroughs B 5000 [24] or Multics Honeywell 645 [25], the 16-bit segment portion of the pointer becomes a selector, or index, into a table of descriptors that define the virtual-to-physical address translation (Fig. 3). After the linkage process converts a segment name to a segment selector, software designed originally for real addresses can execute in Protected Address mode, where it can additionally exploit the chip's protection and multitasking mechanisms. Although the programmer only specifies a selector into the descriptor table, the processor uses the information in the descriptors in its virtual-to-physical address translation process. These descriptors contain the physical base address of a 1-byte to 64K-byte segment. Each task can address up to 2^{14} (16 384) of these segments for a total address space of 2^{30} bytes of virtual memory (mapped into the CPU's 16M-byte physical address space).

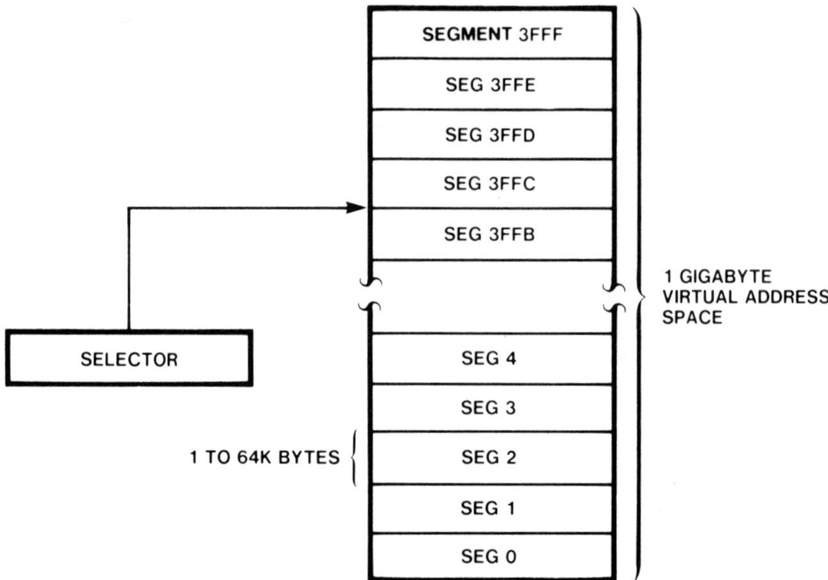

Fig. 3. Protected mode segment selector interpretation.

Notes: 1) A selector uniquely identifies (names) one of 16K possible segments in the task's virtual address space.
2) The selector value does not specify the segment's location in physical memory.
3) The selector does not imply any overlap with other segments (this depends on the base address of the segment as specified via the memory management and protection information).

E. Descriptors

In the iAPX 286, descriptors fall into two classes—segment descriptors for code and data and special-purpose descriptors for system and control mechanisms (Fig. 4). Code and data descriptors contain a 24-bit physical base address of a segment as well as a 16-bit field, the limit field, which contains the maximum size (largest offset) of the segment. Thus a segment can be located on any byte boundary and the segment size can range in value between 1 and 65 536 bytes. Consequently, programmers can exploit on-chip memory protection in the 80286 while remaining free to deal with software modules of arbitrary size. Additional control bits indicate descriptor type, protection level, and presence of the information in real memory. The processor sets another control bit in data and code segment descriptors whenever the descriptor is accessed to assist a swap handler that supports virtual memory in maintaining a usage profile.

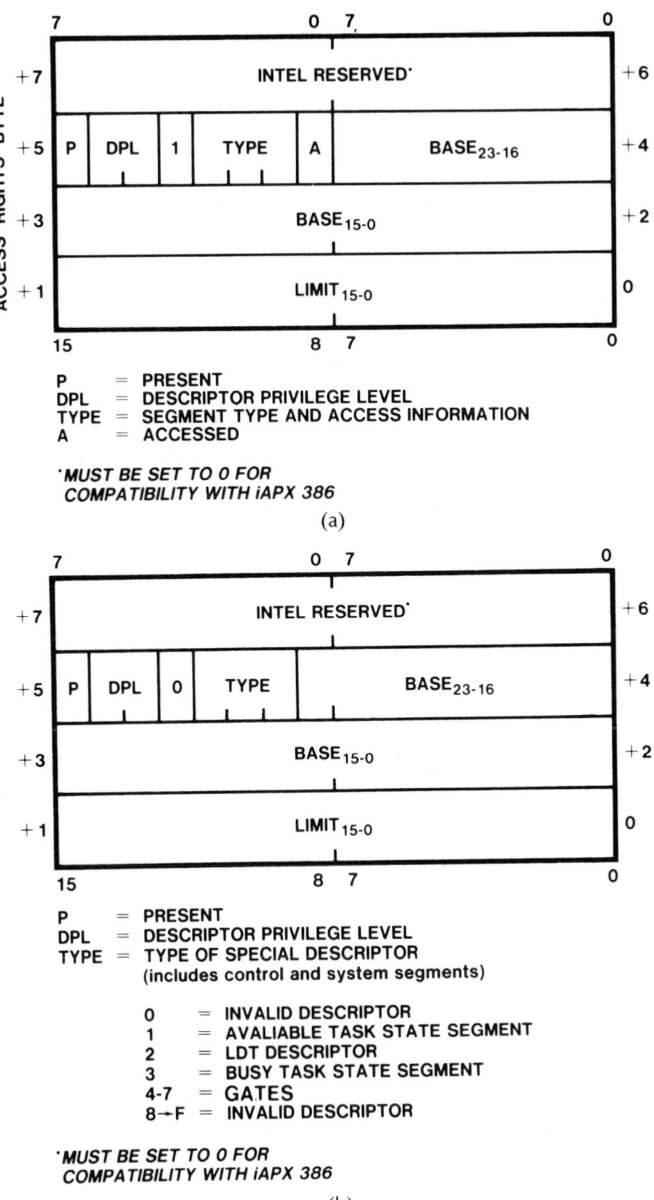

Fig. 4. Descriptors. (a) Segment descriptor. (b) System control and special system segment descriptors.

F. Virtual Address Space Partitions

The 80286 divides its 2^{30}-byte virtual address space into two equal partitions—global and local virtual memory—which are mapped by two separate descriptor tables. Thus each task in a multitasking environment possesses one-half gigabyte of private virtual address space mapped by the local descriptor table (LDT) and shares a one-half gigabyte global virtual address space mapped by the global descriptor table (GDT) with other tasks, subject to the protection provisions discussed below. Consequently, in a multitasking environment, multiple descriptor tables exist—one for each particular task and a unique table for global descriptors.

Because of the implied execution environment, the 80286 accesses these descriptor tables only when an operation requires code or data external to the current environment. In this case, although the programmer need only specify the remote linkage name, the instruction specifies a 16-bit selector and 16-bit offset. The processor proceeds to use the selector as an index from the base of the local (or global) descriptor table in order to acquire the descriptor that provides the physical base address, limit, and attributes of the desired segment (Fig. 5). If the needed segment does not reside in physical memory, a not-present (missing-segment) exception will cause a trap to the appropriate system handler.

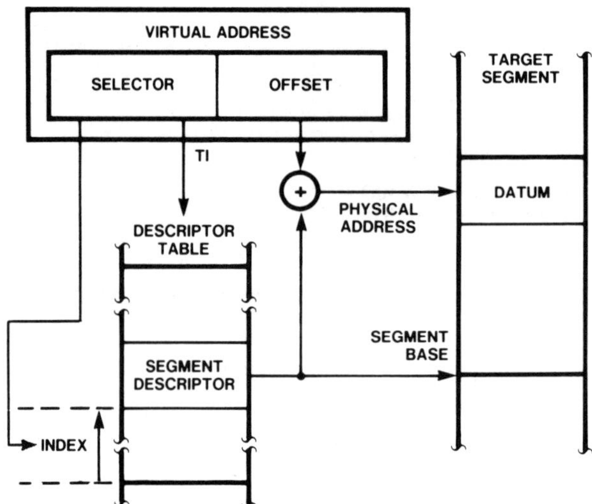

Fig. 5. Virtual-to-physical address translation.

The 80286 keeps track of the base address of each of these descriptor tables—themselves special-purpose segments called system segments—through a set of separate registers—the global descriptor table (GDT) register and the local descriptor table (LDT) register. The GDT is the root of the table structure, and so cannot be within the segment structure, but is specified by a physical base and physical limit.

The 80286 accommodates multitasking environments specifically by means of a system segment, called an LDT segment, for each task. The LDT segment provides the task's LDT base and size. The processor automatically loads the LDT register and the fields containing the base and limit in the LDT descriptor into on-chip registers during a task-switch operation (Fig. 6).

Thus the hidden fields of the segment and descriptor registers serve as a memory-management cache in the 80286. When a program accesses any segment, it uses the cached descriptor values to determine base address, size, and access rights of the segment.

G. Memory Management

Allocating memory can occur statically—through the Intel System Builder [26]—or dynamically through a system loader and memory manager, which is a system module for dynamic allocation of physical memory [27]. In the segmented memory model of the iAPX 286, free space (unused segments) would be linked into lists and filled as needed using an appropriate algorithm [28]. In accessing a free area of memory, the memory manager would dynamically create descriptors to address the various boundary tags and free-space linkage pointers.

An operating system that supports virtual memory would further include a system manager responsible for swapping segments between memory and secondary storage. The 80286 directly

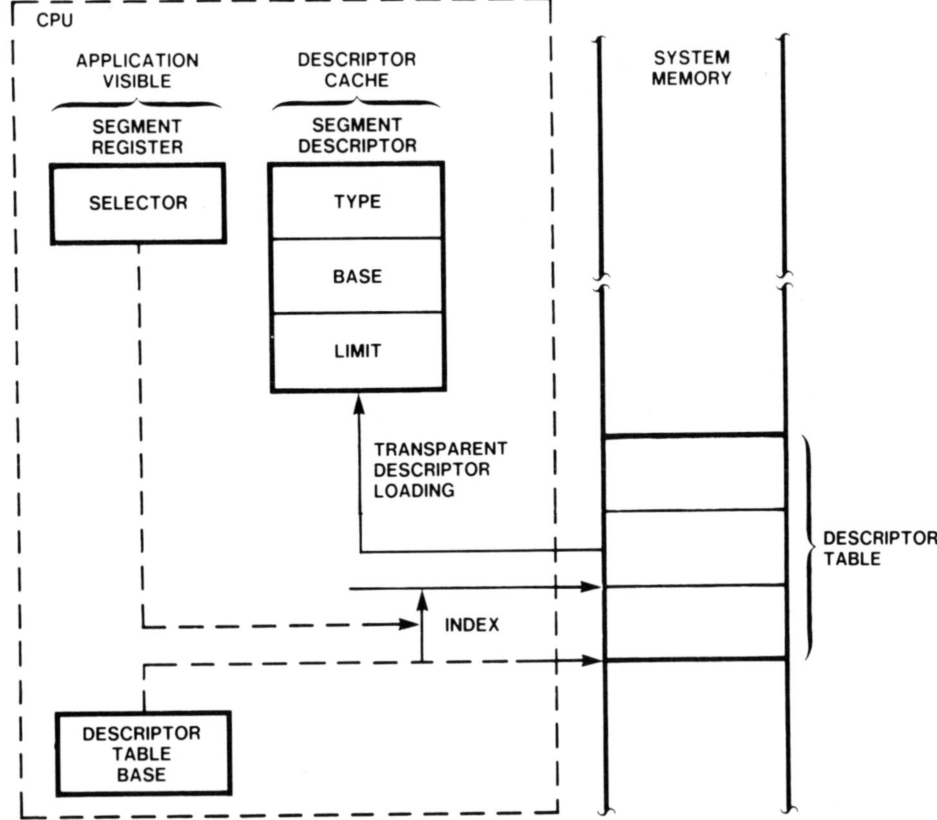

Fig. 6. Descriptor loading.

supports fundamental mechanisms for swapping algorithms [29] through the accessed bit and present bit in segment descriptors. Thus a handler would check the present bit in the descriptor to determine if the corresponding segment needs to be swapped in. The handler would check the accessed bit to determine which segment could be swapped out according to a least recently used algorithm, for example.

H. Multitasking

Task switching with memory management in traditional multitasking systems has been a complex sequence of operations that typically proceeds as follows:

1) Save the current task state.
2) Test for the presence of the new task in the MMU.
3) Set up for a (partial) reload of the MMU.
4) Scan the list of running tasks for the LRU entry.
5) Free the least recently used entry in the MMU.
6) Load free entries with new translation information.
7) Restore the context of the new task.

Because of the need to resort to complex system software in the traditional task-switch mechanism, task-switch times have frequently exceeded a millisecond in such systems. With the task-oriented software architecture of the new multiwindow systems for personal computers, personal computer systems can be expected to undergo continual task switches. In order to provide the responsive and high-performance functions demanded by the user in these environments, the iAPX 286 expends some of its silicon budget on direct hardware support for task switching. As a result, the processor can completely change from executing one task to executing another in a single hardware operation consuming only approximately 21 μs.

Once again maintaining a consistent segmentation model, from the point of view of the programmer, the key structure in a task-switch operation is yet another instance of a particular system segment, called a task state segment (TSS). To initiate a task switch, the programmer deals only with a selector into a descriptor table containing a system descriptor called the TSS descriptor. Then, based on the current TSS, the 80286 hardware saves the current task state, and then uses the new TSS descriptor to access and load the required TSS (Fig. 7).

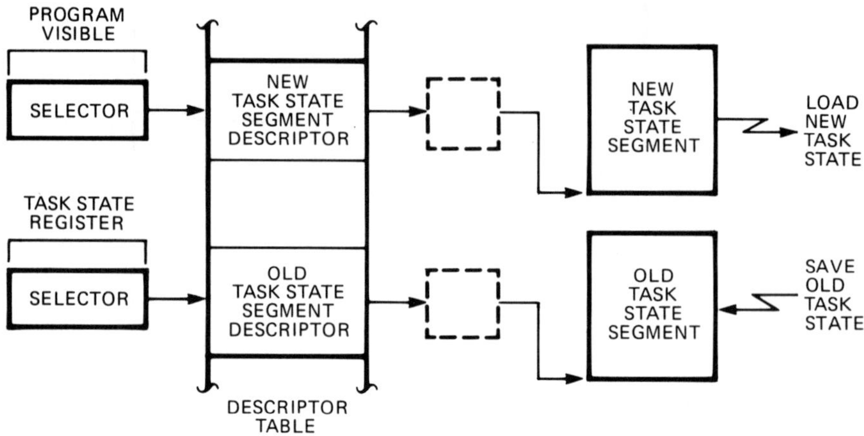

Fig. 7. Task switch.

In its 44 bytes, the TSS holds the LDT selector for the task, copies of the contents of the general registers and segment registers, pointers for the privileged stacks, and a back-link pointer to the previous task (Fig. 8). In a multitasking operating system, other control information would be included with these specific hardware-recognized 44 bytes to make up a conventional process control block.

The back-link pointer deserves special attention. It is essential for support of interrupt tasks in the case where the current task is interrupted under hardware control by another task.

Rather than using a set of special instructions for task switching, the scheduler code to perform a task switch in the iAPX 286 is a simple JUMP to a global segment, which in this case is a TSS. Of course, no code is required for interrupt-initiated task switches. (To allow coroutine implementation, application software can also initiate task switches through a simple CALL instruction.)

I. Multiprocessing

To complement its hardware support for multitasking, the hardware supports multiple processor configurations with certain instructions that permit mutual exclusion [30] when multiple 80286 processors share critical resources. An explicit lock can be added to any instruction to prevent other potential bus masters from assuming control of the bus until the instruction has completed. In addition, lock signals implicitly occur during interrupt–acknowledge sequences, descriptor-table accesses, and during the XCHG (exchange) instruction. The XCHG instruction, which exchanges the contents of one of the CPU registers with memory, is the key function needed to implement semaphores.

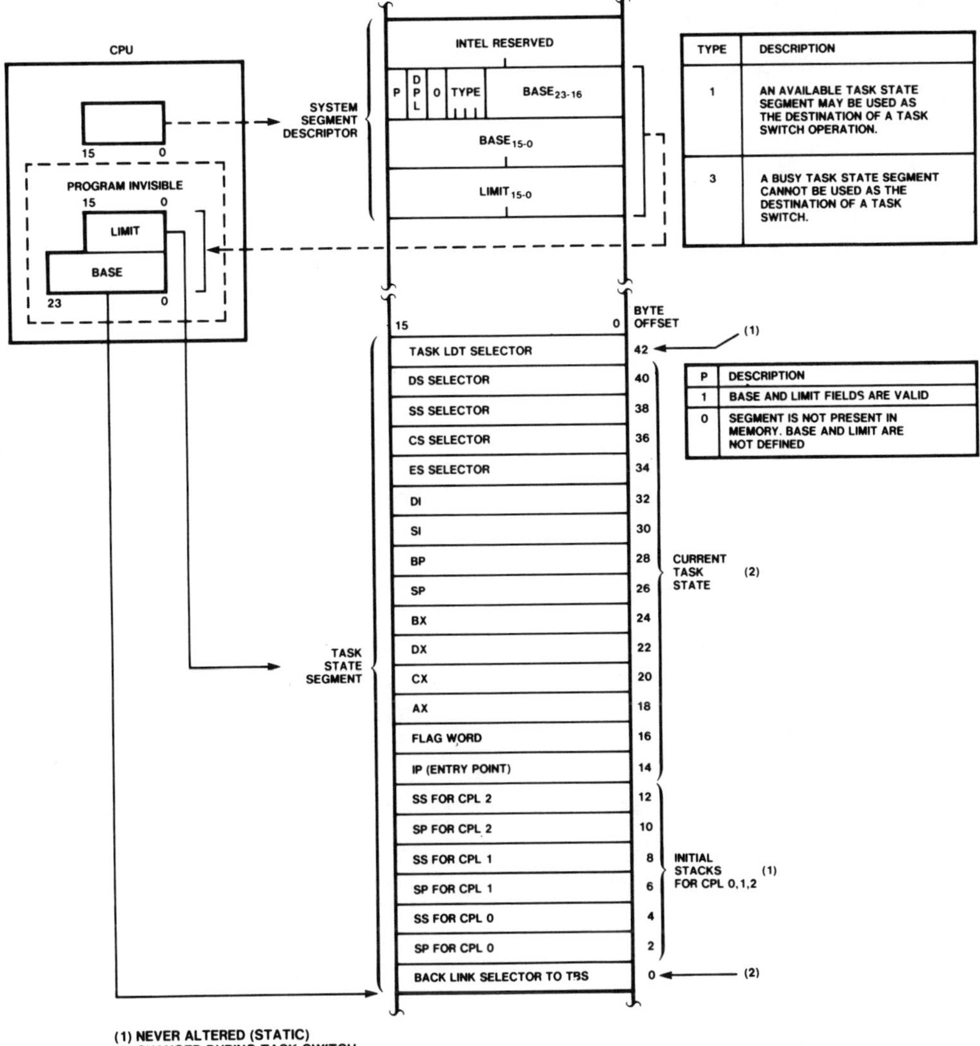

Fig. 8. Task state segment and TSS registers.

J. Protection

A multitasking system must be sufficiently robust to withstand the inadvertent incursions into system software often experienced in program development. In addition, with the expected growth in communications between personal computers, a multitasking system must be able to survive more determined attempts to violate system security policies. Just as the office environment now provides various graduations of physical security ranging from locked desks to locked or guarded buildings, microprocessor-based systems must be capable of employing a variety of safeguards to protect code and data at multiple levels of security.

Protection exists at various levels in the 80286 processor chip to directly support a variety of protection mechanisms [30]–[33]. The separate virtual address partition available to each task ensures that a task accesses segments only within its certain bounds. Segments private to another task cannot even be addressed. Even within its own partition, however, a task may not deviate from the strict segment typing enforced by the protection model. In addition, iAPX 286 hardware applies specific privilege-rights checks to every memory access at the segment level. Thus a security policy may adopt whatever granularity is deemed appropriate, rather than be constrained to fixed-sized pages.

K. Multiple Privilege Levels

Traditionally, central-processing units have provided a simple pair of protection levels—supervisor and user—based on the traditional types of software existing in a system: system and application. In the 80286, four levels of protection (numbered 0 through 3) allow a further refinement of systems and applications privileges. Most trusted code and data are placed at the highest privilege level (PL0), while least trusted information, such as user application code and data, would remain at the least trusted level (PL3).

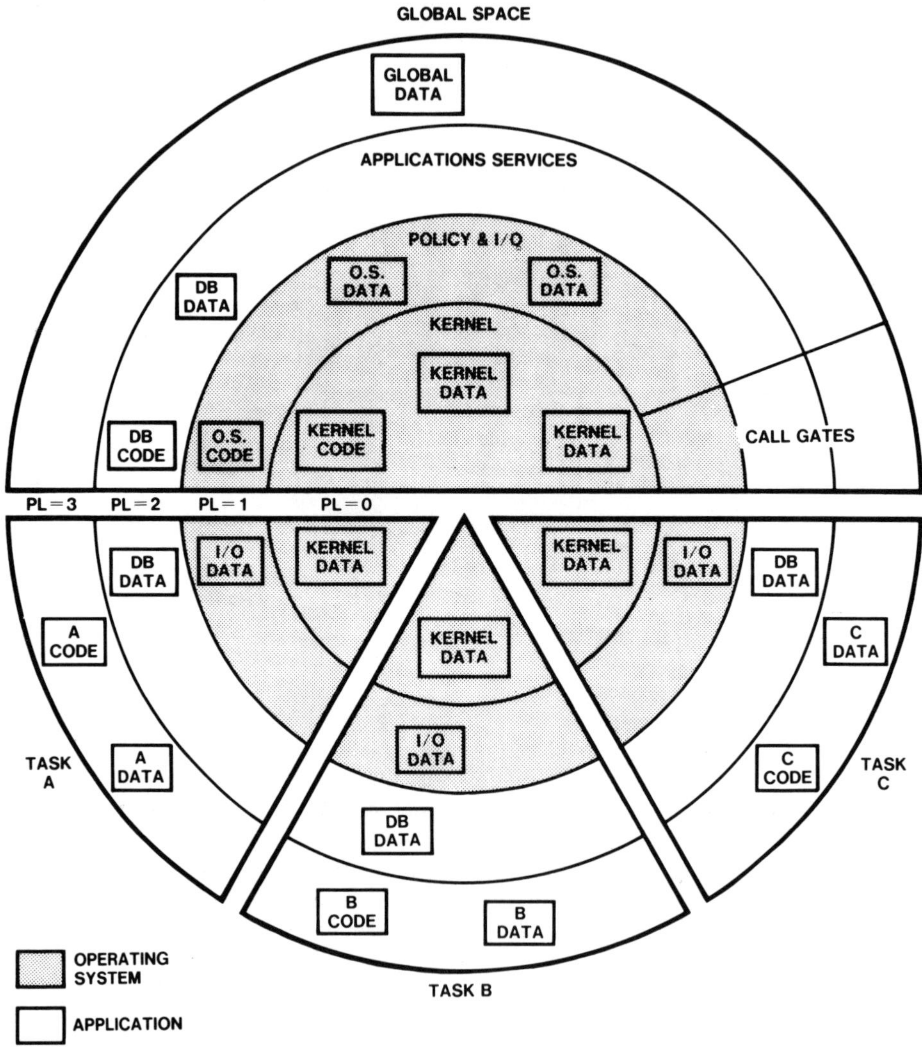

Fig. 9. A four-level protection structure.

Various operating system services and extensions would typically be assigned to intermediate levels (Fig. 9). Thus, for example, the kernel—the code and data needed to implement the most basic mechanisms of an operating system—could be placed in PL0. PL1 could contain system utilities and access-protection and policy-enforcement procedures. (For example, code and data to carry out a system's security policies, such as access table checks, might be placed in PL1 in a secure operating system.) Abstract OS services or customizing extensions to the operating system could be placed in PL2. Finally, applications could be relegated to PL3.

In the protection scheme implemented in the 80286 chip, access rights are unidirectional. Tasks that are executing at a more privileged level (possessing a lower numerical value) may directly access data only at the same or less privileged (numerically greater) levels. On the other hand, tasks may directly access only those code segments (through jumps or calls) that are at the same privilege level.

Hardware enforces this protection by comparing the 2-bit wide descriptor privilege level (DPL) field in a descriptor with the current privilege level (CPL) maintained within the processor during execution. The CPL associated with the current task is maintained in the least significant two bits in the code segment register. When the 80286 accesses a descriptor for a data segment, it must find that DPL is numerically greater than or equal to the CPL, or a general-protection trap will occur. Similarly, the DPL for a code segment must be numerically equal to the CPL. Unlike the DPL, which is statically defined by the system programmer, task privilege level (CPL) is a dynamic quantity, which takes on the value of the DPL of the code segment it is in the process of executing.

L. System Calls

In Multics [25], access to higher levels occurs only through well-defined gates, where access privileges can be verified before a less-privileged task is allowed to execute more-privileged code. The 80286 directly supports this concept through its implementation of a special access protocol mediated by similar structures. Specifically, the processor identifies four different types of special control descriptors—called the call, task, interrupt, and trap gates (Fig. 10)—that reside in the descriptor tables.

Gates redirect control to a destination address that cannot be directly accessed by the caller. For most application-level software, gates form the only vehicle for calls (control transfers) to code at more-privileged levels. Thus a call instruction originating from a less-trusted level is able to reach code segments at more-trusted privilege levels indirectly through a call gate. As demonstrated in Fig. 11, applications (or application servers) located in less-trusted privilege levels would access system utilities (typically located in PL1) through a call gate located at PL3. Locating the call gate at progressively more-trusted levels would prohibit access from corresponding less-trusted levels in the protection model.

When a less-privileged task uses a call gate to access a subroutine located at a more-privileged level, from both the application and system programmers' points of view, the subroutine call proceeds just as a call from the same privilege level. That is, the caller uses the stack to pass parameters to the target subroutine. However, the protection model of the 80286 requires a separate stack at each privilege level.

The 80286 solves this apparent contradiction by copying the subroutine parameters from the stack of the caller's privilege level to another separate stack at the target privilege level. (The TSS contains the pointers to stack segments for privilege levels 2, 1, and 0.) A count field in the call gate descriptor specifies the number of words to copy from the originating stack. Once the target subroutine has terminated, it is free to return results or pointers through one of the registers or by reference to the caller's data area in the normal manner. As a result, operating system calls in the 80286 are much cleaner than the traditional technique of passing through a library trap handler or single supervisor-call operation. A conventional supervisor-trap handler passes control to an operating system routine that must copy parameters onto the system stack before calling the actual service function. The straightforward use of call instructions for

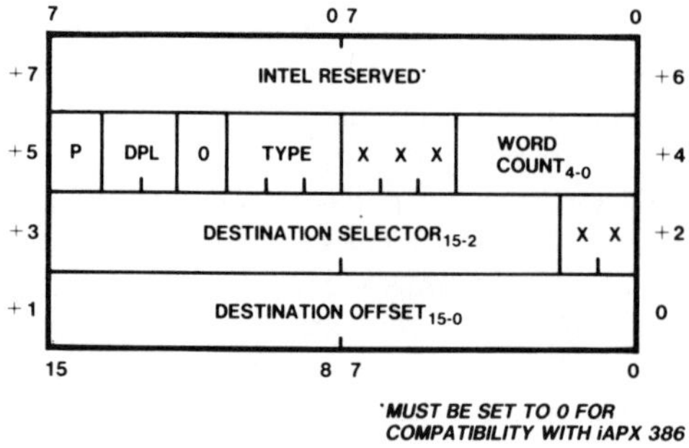

Gate Descriptor Fields

Name	Value	Description
TYPE	4 5 6 7	—Call Gate —Task Gate —Interrupt Gate —Trap Gate
P	0 1	—Descriptor Contents are not valid —Descriptor Contents are valid
DPL	0-3	Descriptor Privilege Level
WORD COUNT	0-31	Number of words to copy from callers stack to called procedures stack. Only used with call gate.
DESTINATION SELECTOR	16-bit selector	Selector to the target code segment (Call, Interrupt or Trap Gate) Selector to the target task state segment (Task Gate)
DESTINATION OFFSET	16-bit offset	Entry point within the target code segment

Fig. 10. Gate descriptor format.

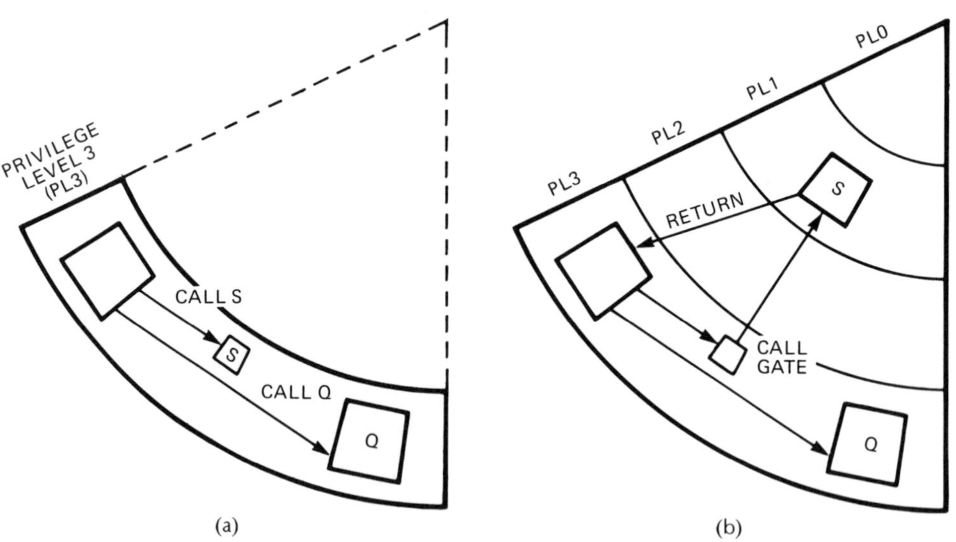

(a)   (b)

Fig. 11. Gated interlevel call and return. (a) Application view. (b) System view.

operating system services in the 80286 results in an overhead of only approximately 12 μs for a 5-word parameter OS call, much less than the 80–200 μs common in other systems that utilize supervisor traps, or calls.

The other three types of gates—trap, interrupt, and task—function similarly to transfer control upon the occurrence of a processor trap or external interrupt. Trap and interrupt gates that appear only in a separate system global descriptor table—the interrupt descriptor table—differ from each other only in that the trap gates do not disable the 80286's maskable hardware interrupts, unlike interrupt gates. Task gates are used for invoking system tasks, such as hardware-driven I/O tasks.

The 80286 provides one other mechanism for tasks executing at a less trusted level to access code and data at a more trusted level. In order to permit execution of global code segments that might be contained in more privileged levels, a special control bit, the conforming bit, in an executable segment descriptor indicates that the current privilege level should be set to the calling task's privilege level, rather than the DPL of the called descriptor as is normally the case. These segments, called conforming segments, are especially useful for permitting global access to library routines, such as numeric or graphics packages.

III. Secure Systems

Although the increasing expansion of personal computer networks into wider facets of business, government, and personal life promises to heighten information transfer, it also opens the door to infiltration and compromise of confidential information [34]. Particularly worrisome to the user dependent on safeguarding information are government reports that pinpoint computer crime and abuse as the most rapidly growing form of larceny [35].

In this light, the highly flexible memory protection available in hardware with the 80286 gives system designers the ability to implement sophisticated security policies without sacrificing performance. In fact, the 80286 meets the four general criteria to support a kernel-based secure operating system [36]:

1) support for multiple processes,
2) protection of large segmented virtual memory,
3) minimum of three execution domains, and
4) control of access to I/O devices.

The 80286 multitasking support, segmented memory management and protection, four privilege levels, and I/O protection mechanism account for each of these specific points. A secure operating system based on the 80286 has been mentioned for embedded applications [37]. Furthermore, Schell [38] has described a security kernel—targeted for the 80286—that is intended for more general-purpose programming environments.

IV. Hardware Implementation

A simple 80286 system using the 8207 dynamic RAM controller can operate at 8 MHz with zero wait states using 100-ns dynamic RAMs [39] (Fig. 12). Because of the 80286's pipelined architecture, the 8207 controller has time to respond to memory requests with not-ready signals only when necessary, rather than requiring additional wait states, which are additional clock cycles added between memory request and response to allow slower memory to work with a faster CPU. But even in larger systems, the 80286 exhibits performance surpassing that of a VAX 11/780 [40] (Fig. 13 and Tables 1 and 2).

In keeping with the demands of users for rapid task initiation and execution, the iAPX 286 maximizes performance while holding down the requirements for fast (and expensive) memory chips. The chip manages this by incorporating a pipeline of four separate state machines for bus interface, instruction decode, execution, and address decode. High throughput demands a high degree of integration of function on-chip to maintain a steady flow of instructions to the

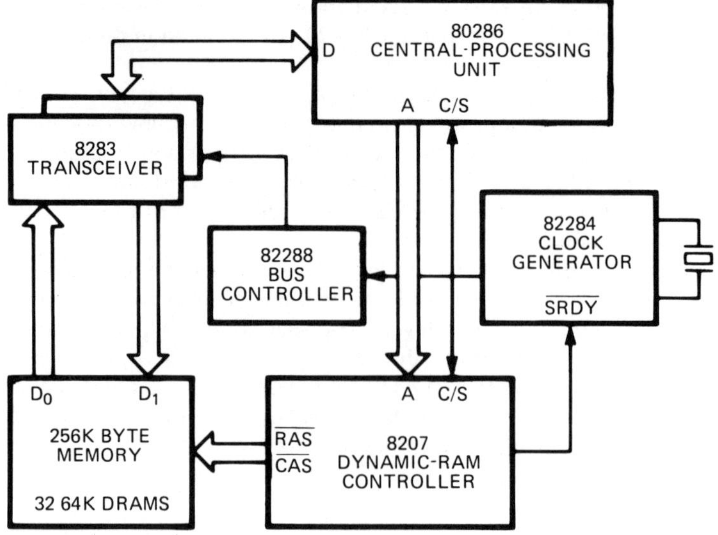

Fig. 12. iAPX286 system configuration.

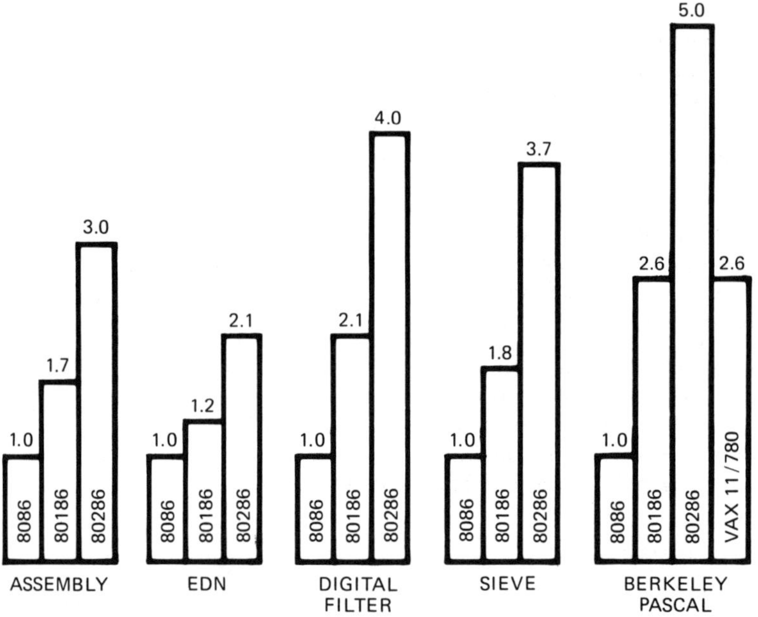

Fig. 13. CPU to CPU benchmark comparisons; 8-MHz, zero wait states.

Table 1 Execution Times (After [40])

Machine	Language	Word Size	Search	Sieve	Puzzle	Acker
				Time (ms)		
	C	32	1.4	250	9400	4 600
VAX-11/780	Pascal (UNIX)	32	1.6	220	11 900	7 800
	Pascal (VMS)	32	1.4	259	11 530	9 850
8086 (5 MHz)	Pascal	16	7.3	764	44 000	11 100
80286 (8 MHz)	Pascal	16	1.4	168	9138	2 218
80286 (10 MHz)	Pascal	16	1.1	135	7311	1 774

Table 2 Performance Relative to VAX-11/780 (After [40])

Machine	Language	Word Size	Ratio to VMS Pascal (> 1 means faster)				
			Search	Sieve	Puzzle	Acker	Avg + SD
	C	32	1.0	1.0	1.2	2.1	1.3 + 0.4
VAX-11/780	Pascal (UNIX)	32	0.9	1.2	1.0	1.3	1.1 + 0.2
	Pascal (VMS)	32	1.0	1.0	1.0	1.0	1.0 + 0.0
8086 (5MHZ)	Pascal	16	0.2	0.3	0.3	0.9	0.4 + 0.3
80286 (8MHz)	Pascal	16	1.0	1.5	1.3	4.4	2.1 + 1.4
80286 (10MHz)	Pascal	16	1.3	1.9	1.6	5.6	2.6 + 1.7

execution unit. The combination of on-chip memory management and a pipelined architecture (Fig. 14) have several benefits at the systems level both in performance and in cost of personal computers. To achieve higher performance, designers could simply scale the processor cycle to higher frequencies. Unfortunately, this approach throws the problem of creating low-cost systems back into the lap of the system designer, who is now forced to employ higher speed (and more costly) memory chips. This problem is particularly exacerbated when memory-management functions require off-chip access. Because of the concomitant increased latency of address translation, designers must opt for yet faster and more expensive memory parts in order to maintain satisfactory system performance.

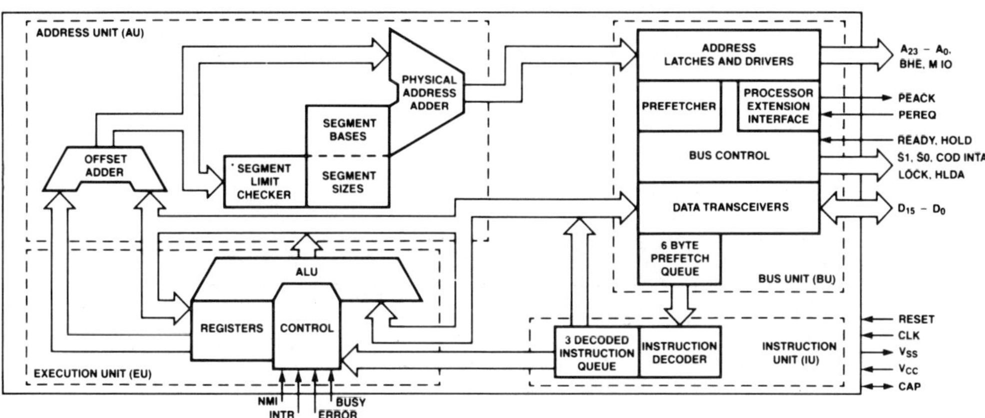

Fig. 14. 80286 internal block diagram.

Furthermore, a design philosophy based on a separate chip for memory-management functions leaves the door open for designers who adopt the strategy of attempting to squeeze the last cycle out of a microprocessor-based system by removing the memory-management function. Though in so doing they eliminate the related overhead in memory-access time, they completely lose the benefits of memory management and protection. In particular, the future widespread use of memory management and protection seems empirically to require holding the costs to less than 5 percent in both performance and memory space. Otherwise, practical designers will consider it acceptable to bypass or eliminate memory management and protection. Thus the 80286 completes effective address calculation, address translation, and access-rights verification in a single clock cycle.

In addition to the low translation latency, the four separate pipelined units cooperate to ensure a continual flow of instructions through the processor. The bus unit fetches instructions and data as needed by the other three units. In addition, it fetches data for the coprocessor extensions. The bus unit continually performs memory access for these units following the priority:

1) HOLD request from an external bus master (highest),
2) processor extension data transfer,
3) address unit, and
4) code prefetch (lowest).

For sequential instructions, the bus unit prefetches instructions when at least 2 bytes of the prefetch queue are empty. However, if the instruction unit loads its queue with an instruction that could potentially cause a branch, it notifies the bus unit to momentarily cease prefetching instructions in order to avoid over-prefetching. Because the 80286 extends its pipelined model to the system memory, external devices may also exploit the advantages of a pipelined system design (Fig. 15). All bus operations occur every 2 clock cycles and complete within 3, resulting in a total bus bandwidth of 8M bytes/s.

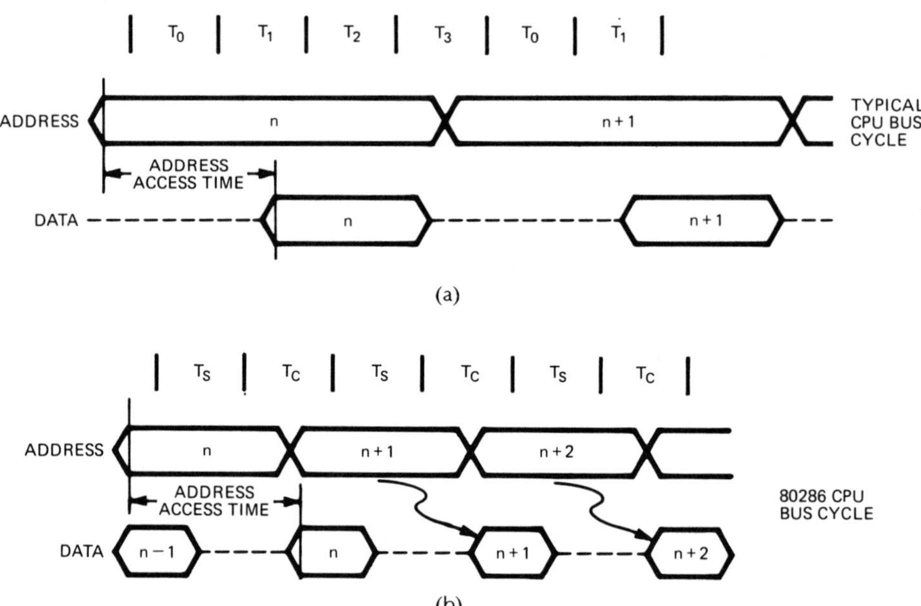

Fig. 15. (a) Typical operations. (b) Pipelined operations.

All four units in the 80286 function autonomously. For example, when on-chip logic arbitrates local bus control among several potential bus masters, only the bus unit is directly affected. When an external device requests the bus, it asserts a line called HOLD. (When the 80286 is ready to release the bus to the requesting device, the 80286 in turn asserts a line called HOLD ACKNOWLEDGE.) Because the four units of the 80286 are autonomous, however, only the bus unit is directly affected when HOLD is asserted by an external device requesting bus control. Instruction execution stops only when the execution unit explicitly requires a bus cycle or after it has exhausted both the instruction queue and the prefetch queue.

The effect of pipelining on performance further explains the fact that performance degradation with wait states is not as severe as might be predicted. A significantly slower memory subsystem that requires one wait state per access results in a 50-percent loss in bandwidth. However, benchmark studies show that overall CPU execution time increases not by the 50 percent that might be expected, but increases only by approximately 25 percent. This results from the fact that in a typical mix of instructions, the average instruction execution is in the range of 2 to 3 clocks. Consequently, the execution unit may continue to operate out of the instruction and prefetch queues even while the bus unit is handling a wait state.

The instruction decode unit extracts instructions from the prefetch queue and creates a 69-bit internally formatted macroinstruction used by the execution unit. The execution unit extracts this fully formatted macroinstruction from the instruction queue. This instruction then initiates the appropriate microsequence in a 1536-word by 35-bit control ROM in the execution unit.

Finally, the address unit performs translations from logical to physical addresses for the other units. A cache in this unit contains the extended 48-bit descriptor information for all of the segments (physical base address, limit, and access-rights information). Address translation and access verification occurs in a single clock cycle. In the first half-cycle, the effective address specified in the instruction is computed by adding together a base register, index, and displacement; during the second, the physical base address is added to this effective address to form the physical memory address. The limit check and access rights check are performed in parallel with the physical base addition operation.

V. Future Directions

In the natural evolution of the iAPX 86 family to the 32-bit 80386 processor, software compatibility with its predecessors is held as a principal objective, even as the 80386 increases the family's address space, performance, and functional capability. In this future product, which will be manufactured in a complementary high-speed metal–oxide–semiconductor process, physical memory will expand to 2^{32} bytes (4096M bytes). Virtual address space will jump to 2^{46} bytes, with 64 terabytes (65 536 billion bytes) available to each task.

The 80386 will incorporate a two-level paging mechanism to manage physical memory—all beneath a segmentation model of logical memory that is logically identical to its predecessors, though parameters like segment physical base address and limit size are larger. In addition, the protection and tasking model of the iAPX 286 will be carried forward to the iAPX 386. As a result of the need for more on-chip function and still greater performance, the processor pipeline will stretch to seven stages. In turn, the microarchitecture will be extended to include 32-bit registers, 32-bit operations, and 32-bit segment offset values.

Still, much of the new microarchitecture is the same as that of the 80286. Four of the seven stages are essentially identical in function to those in the 80286. However, even while squeezing more functions on-chip, the 80386 will include a number of notable differences that help it reach its anticipated performance increase of 2–3 times that of the 80286 while still maintaining compatibility. In the bus unit, a more intelligent prefetcher will support the enhanced performance through the 32-bit bus. Furthermore, an on-chip instruction cache will permit the CPU to execute out of high-speed on-chip memory with a direct reduction in bus bandwidth used for instruction fetch. Subsequent stages in the pipeline will also widen for improved throughput. For example, the instruction unit will expand to over 100 bits, while the register file will double in width, as will the ALU, address unit, and internal busses.

Intel plans to maintain the coprocessor concept of the iAPX 86 family for the 80386's. Consequently, software developed for the 80286 and 80287 will be able to migrate smoothly to 80386-based systems employing a coprocessor and immediately exploit its higher performance.

VI. Conclusion

In order to fulfill users' demands for integrated operating environments with interfaces that are easy to use, the personal computer industry relies on the availability of high-performance microprocessors able to provide direct hardware support for critical functions. Based on an underlying model of a multitasking operating system, multiwindow user interfaces are in particular need of hardware support in order to satisfy users who are typically intolerant of delayed or slowed execution. Intel's 80286 microprocessor provides direct hardware support for multitasking, and further serves the needs of personal computer users with its support for memory management and protection.

However, even as new hardware becomes available, vendors and users alike will seek to ensure the continued viability of the installed software base. Consequently, new microprocessors like the 80286 and future ones like the 80386 will ensure an upward migration path for software—adding new functions on top of a fundamental foundation. In addition, coprocessors in the iAPX 86 family will continue to permit further extension of the processors' instruction set into specific and well-defined areas.

One particular area—communications—has extensive implications that extend back even to the underlying hardware base. As personal computers connect into more extensive networks, system security will assume major importance to users. With the four-tiered protection model of the 80286 and 80386, designers can implement a variety of security models. Furthermore, since this protection is applied at every memory access at the segment level, systems can be designed with security applied to objects of arbitrary granularity.

As personal computers settle more firmly into the office, users will look for a more faithful electronic reproduction of their natural physical environment. Driven by this demand, the evolution of the personal computer will depend heavily on the availability of even higher performance processors like the 80386 for critical system functions like multitasking and protection as well as the management of an ever larger information base.

REFERENCES

[1] H. D. Toong and A. Gupta, "Personal computers," *Sci. Amer.*, vol. 242, Dec. 1982.
[2] *EDP Industry Report*, July, 1983.
[3] M. A. Harris, "IBM moves to lock up office market as it puts 370 on the desk," *Electronics*, p. 47, Nov. 3, 1983.
[4] A. C. Kay, "Microelectronics and the personal computer," *Sci. Amer.*, vol. 237, no. 3, Sept. 1977.
[5] S. McGregor and A. Lewis, "Windowing software gives bit-mapped screen a graphics interface," *Electronics*, Dec. 1, 1983.
[6] W. T. Coleman, III, and S. Warren, "The VisiOn operating environment," *IEEE Quart. Bull. Data Base Eng.*, Sept. 1983.
[7] A. Gupta and H. D. Toong, *Advanced Microprocessors*. New York, NY: IEEE PRESS, 1983.
[8] "Introduction to the iAPX 286," Tech. Rep. 210308, Intel Corp., Santa Clara, CA, 1982.
[9] "iAPX 286 Hardware Reference Manual," Tech. Rep. 210760, Intel Corp., Santa Clara, CA, 1983.
[10] P. Heller, "Advanced system architecture concepts for 16-bit microcomputers," in *Wescon/82 Conf. Rec.* El Segundo, CA: Electron. Conventions, 1982.
[11] R. J. Markowitz, "The architectural evolution path of the 8086 to operating systems environments," in *Weston/80 Conf. Rec.* El Segundo, CA: Electron. Conventions, 1980.
[12] ______, "iAPX 286: Virtual memory and distributed computing," in *Wescon/81 Conf. Rec.* El Segundo, CA: Electron. Conventions, 1981.
[13] ______, "iAPX 286: Virtual memory and distributed computing," in *Midcon/81 Conf. Rec.* El Segundo, CA: Electron. Conventions, 1981.
[14] R. M. Schell, "Multi-user systems from advanced processor chips," *Comput. Des.*, vol 21, no. 11, Nov. 1982.
[15] G. Alexy, "iAPX 286: A microsystem for the new generation of operating system intensive applications," in *Wescon/82 Conf. Rec.* El Segundo, CA: Electron. Conventions, 1982.
[16] G. Alexy, R. Childs, and J. Crawford, "Integrating Memory Management into the CPU," *Electronic Products*, Oct. 25, 1982.
[17] P. Heller, R. Childs, and J. Slager, "Memory protection moves onto 16-bit microprocessor chip," *Electronics*, Feb. 24, 1982.
[18] "iAPX 186 high integration 16-bit microprocessor," Tech. Rep. 210451-003, Intel Corp., Santa Clara, CA, July, 1983.
[19] "iAPX 188 high integration 8-bit microprocessor," Tech. Rep. 210706-002, Intel Corp., Santa Clara, CA, Nov. 1982.
[20] G. J. Myers, *Advances in Computer Architecture*. New York, NY: Wiley, 1978.
[21] "iAPX 286 Programmer's Reference Manual," Tech. Rep. 210498, Intel Corp., Santa Clara, CA, 1983.
[22] "80287 80-bit HMOS numeric processor extension," Tech. Rep. 210920-001, Intel Corp., Santa Clara, CA.
[23] "The complete VLSI LAN solution," Tech. Rep. 210783-001 Intel Corp., Santa Clara, CA, 1982.

[24] D. P. Siewiorek, C. G. Bell, and A. Newell, *Computer Structures: Principles and Examples.* New York, NY: McGraw-Hill, 1982.

[25] E. I. Organick, *The Multics System: An Examination of Its Structure.* Cambridge, MA: MIT Press, 1972.

[26] "iAPX 286 system builder user's guide," Tech. Rep. 121935, Intel Corp., Santa Clara, CA, 1982.

[27] "iAPX 286 operating systems writer's guide," Tech. Rep. 121960, Intel Corp., Santa Clara, CA, 1983.

[28] D. E. Knuth, *Fundamental Algorithms*, Vol. 1. Reading, MA: Addison-Wesley, 1973.

[29] P. J. Denning, "Virtual memory," *Comput. Surv.*, vol. 2, no. 3, Sept. 1970.

[30] P. B. Hansen, *Operating System Principles.* Englewood Cliffs, NJ: Prentice-Hall, 1973.

[31] B. W. Lampson, "Dynamic protection structures," presented at the Fall Joint Computer Conf., 1969.

[32] ______, "Protection," in *Proc. 5th Princeton Symp. on Information Sciences and Systems* (Princeton Univ., Princeton, NJ, Mar. 1971), reprinted in *Operating Syst. Rev.*, vol. 8, no. 1, Jan. 1974.

[33] G. S. Graham and P. J. Denning, "Protection—Principles and practice," presented at the Spring Joint Computer Conf., 1972.

[34] D. E. Denning and P. J. Denning, "Data security," *Comput. Surv.*, vol. 11, no. 3, Sept. 1979.

[35] K. Berney, "Washington takes on computer crime," *Electronics*, p. 102, Nov. 17, 1983.

[36] S. R. Ames, Jr., G. Gasser, and R. R. Schell, "Security kernel design and implementation: An introduction," *Computer*, vol. 16, no. 7, July 1983.

[37] C. E. Landwehr, "The best available technologies for computer security," *Computer*, vol. 16, no. 7, July 1983.

[38] R. R. Schell, "A security kernel for a multiprocessor microcomputer," *Computer*, vol. 16, no. 7, July 1983.

[39] "iAPX 186, 286 benchmark report" Tech. Rep. 210826, Intel Corp., Sanata Clara, CA, 1983.

[40] D. Patterson, "A performance evaluation of the Intel 80286," *Computer Arch. News*, vol. 10, no. 5, Sept. 1982.

12
Structure and Capabilities of Key Personal Computer Operating Systems

MEICHUN HSU AND STUART E. MADNICK

An operating system is a piece of software that is used to optimize use of resources and to minimize user level of effort. It performs functions such as processor allocation management, memory management, peripheral management, file management, user-oriented facilities like command-line interpreter, and miscellaneous features to support networking, utilities, and high-level languages. In the realm of microcomputers, CP/M represents the first popular operating system. The phenomenal success of the IBM Personal Computer has made the MS-DOS operating system equally popular. Meanwhile, the UNIX operating system developed at Bell Laboratories has been adopted for use on personal computers. This chapter provides an overview of these three popular operating systems. The conclusion contains a comparison of the features available on the three operating systems.

The Editors

I. INTRODUCTION

An operating system (OS) is a program that is both a resource manager of and a user/programmer interface to the hardware and software resources of a computer system [1], [2]. Although operating systems have been widely used on large "mainframe" computers for many years, the first microcomputer operating system to gain much visibility was the Intel 8080 microprocessor based CP/M (Control Program for Microprocessors) operating system, developed by Digital Research Inc. It dominated the microcomputer OS market until the phenomenal success of the IBM Personal Computer (PC) brought wider popularity to the MS-DOS (Microsoft-Disk Operating System) developed by Microsoft Inc. (The version of MS-DOS used on the IBM PC is referred to as PC-DOS.) In the meantime, UNIX, a minicomputer operating system developed at Bell Laboratories and widely used in universities and research laboratories throughout the last decade, has also been gaining prominence as an OS for personal computers [3]–[5].

CP/M and MS-DOS were initially designed for single-user, single-tasking environments and therefore support fewer functions than UNIX, which is a multiuser, multitasking operating system. However, the more recent versions of CP/M and MS-DOS (for example, Concurrent

M. Hsu is with the Division of Applied Sciences, Harvard University, Cambridge, MA 02138, USA.

S. E. Madnick is with the Sloan School of Management, Massachusetts Institute of Technology, Cambridge, MA 02139, USA.

CP/M and MS-DOS Version 2.0) have added some of the more advanced functions found in UNIX. This chapter provides an analysis of three key personal computer operating systems: DOS 2.0, Concurrent CP/M, and UNIX System V.

Framework for Analyzing an Operating System

An operating system can be studied along three dimensions: resource management, command language user interface, and system architecture. These aspects provide a useful and comprehensive framework for a comparative analysis, and are briefly elaborated in the following paragraphs.

a) Resource Management

Resource management refers to the manner in which the operating system controls the hardware and software resources of the computer to accomplish users' tasks. The critical hardware resources include i) the main memory, ii) the central processor unit (CPU), iii) the input/output devices, such as the console, printer, and communication lines, and iv) the information (file) storage devices (hard disks and floppy diskettes).

The goal of *memory management* is to control and to minimize the amount of main memory necessary to perform a particular task without compromising performance. In a single-user, single-tasking system only one program is running at a time; therefore the memory management task is relatively straightforward. Under this type of simple environment, it is a challenge to run a program which is logically larger than the size of the physical memory available. "Virtual memory" is a solution used on many large mainframe computers, but it requires more sophisticated memory management hardware than normally exists in most personal computers. Overlay planned by programmers is the other solution. In this case the memory management routines may help by providing primitives for programmers to request allocation and deallocation of memory as needed.

In a multitasking or multiuser system, several programs may be loaded in main memory. By switching the CPU among them, the OS produces the illusion that all programs are being executed at the same time (i.e., multiprogramming). The challenge of memory management lies in making it possible for programs to be loaded and run anywhere in the physical memory, so that wherever there is free space, that space can be utilized. The phenomenon of fragmentation occurs when small chunks of free space are available in memory but each individually is too small to hold a program, and therefore part of the memory is wasted. To alleviate fragmentation, a scheme called segmentation is often used. Segmentation involves dividing a program into several logical pieces that can be loaded into nonadjacent physical memory areas. The need to accommodate programs that are larger than the size of the physical memory still exists in a multiprogrammed environment, and overlay or virtual memory schemes can be used to satisfy this need.

The goal of *processor management* is to make effective use of the processor so that processor idle time is minimized, work is accomplished efficiently, and response time to the user is optimized. Processor management is relevant only when multiprogramming exists. Since the "execution of a program" is often called a "process," processor management is essentially process management. This involves assigning or dispatching the CPU among several concurrent, live processes and coordinating these processes.

I/O device management also aims at increasing utilization and optimizing response time. For example, "spooling" refers to a way of solving the problem of sharing a slow, dedicated device (e.g., a printer) among several processes. Under this scheme, data to be printed for a user are first collected and stored at high speed in a file on a secondary storage device, such as a disk. The user does not have to wait for the actual printing to be done before continuing with his or her next task. At a later time, when the printer is free, the operating system will automatically cause the actual printing to take place.

Information stored within a computer system is an important software resource that an operating system must also manage. The part of the operating system that manages information or files is called the file system. Issues involved in a file system include directory management, record management, file sharing, protection, integrity, and security. Secondary storage management (i.e., the actual assignment of space on the disk for a file) is also a natural part of the file system.

b) Command Language Processor

Managing the above resources involves policies and strategies. These policies often vary from system to system, depending on trade-offs among the policies, complexity of implementation, and the need of the target environment. A well-managed system offers performance advantages over those that are poorly managed. However, resource management, especially management of hardware resources, is an aspect of the operating system which is often not visible to end-users and programmers in well-designed operating systems. This reduces the amount of hardware details that a user must wrestle with, and enables programmers to develop programs that are isolated from and can survive evolution of hardware.

Most modern operating systems accomplish this hardware transparency by using the command language interface and the function call interface of the operating system. In essence, a programmer is expected to use only these interfaces to request services from the operating system rather than to directly "fiddle" with the internals of the operating system. When a new generation of hardware becomes available, the operating system will be modified and extended to take better advantage of the new hardware resources, but the command language and the function call interfaces of the old system will be preserved. If a program depends on knowledge of how the operating system works internally, it runs the risk of facing obsolescence when new hardware or resource management strategies are introduced for that family of systems.

c) System Architecture

An operating system can be understood to be architecturally composed of a resource management kernel, whose interface is the function call, and a command language processor, often built on top of the former, whose interface is the command language. A schematic view of this operating system architecture is shown in Fig. 1. The goal of the design of a command language processor is to offer flexibility and ease of use. This goal inevitably influences, and is constrained by, the algorithms and architecture of the resource management kernel.

In this chapter, we will concentrate on the kernel and the command language components of the three operating systems under discussion. We will ignore other programs that are some-

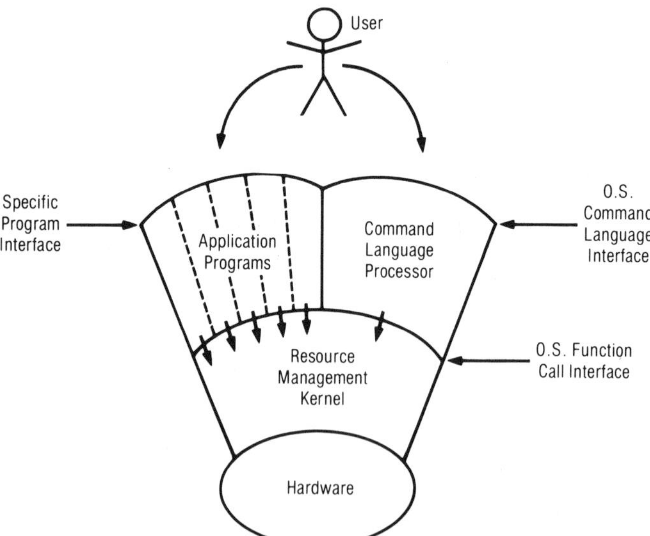

Fig. 1. The role of the operating system: resource management and command language processing.

times bundled into an operating system, such as language processors, text editors, and other utilities, which, strictly speaking, are not part of an operating system.

II. DOS 2.0

DOS 2.0 is a single-user, single-tasking system which contains file system enhancements over its predecessor, DOS 1.1. This section is primarily based on material taken from [6]–[8].

Resource Management

a) Memory Management

Since there is no multiprogramming in DOS, memory management is fairly straightforward. The physical memory is simply divided between resident DOS software and user programs. As there is no virtual memory or segmentation, the entire address space of the user program is loaded into a single, contiguous block of physical memory.

DOS 2.0, however, does provide the facility for a program to grow and shrink dynamically during execution, making it possible for programmers to manage space required by data structures within the program and to conduct planned overlay in order to accommodate programs that are too large to fit in memory all at once. This facility consists of three DOS function calls available to programs to request allocation and deallocation of variable-size memory blocks, and adjustment of the size of an existing block. The first-fit algorithm is used to service memory allocation requests. Because memory blocks can be dynamically added to and subtracted from a program's address space, a program may actually occupy discontiguous blocks

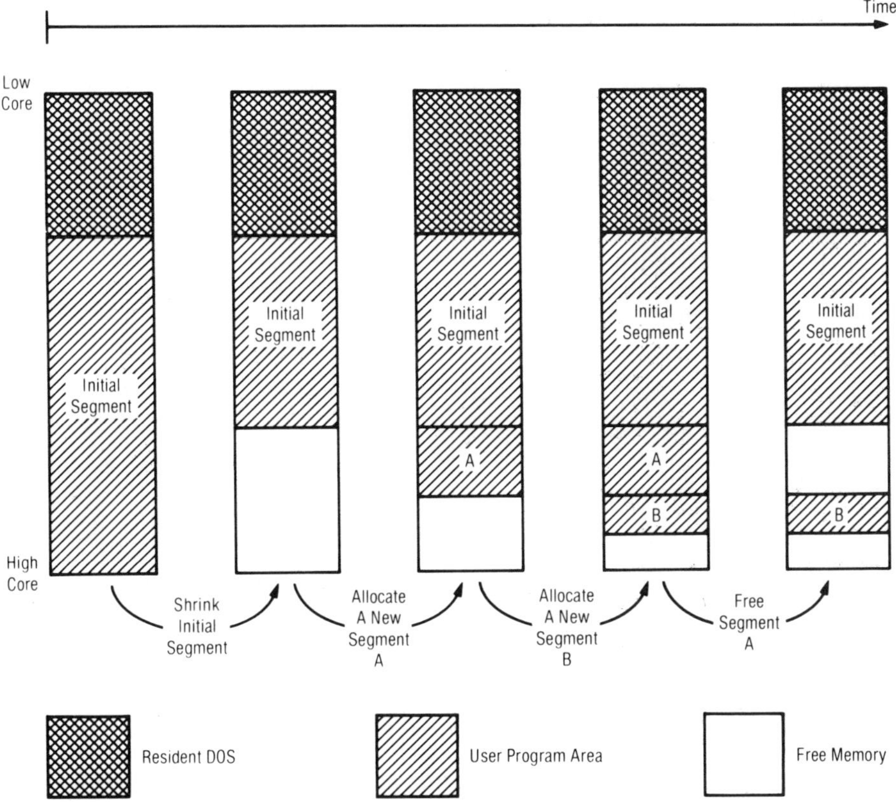

Fig. 2. An example illustrating the dynamics of main memory utilization in DOS.

of memory during execution. An example illustrating the dynamics of memory utilization in DOS is shown in Fig. 2.

b) I/O Buffer Management

DOS provides a buffer management facility which is more than just simple buffering of logical records. The user may select the number of buffers to be used by the operating system. Each buffer can hold one physical record which usually consists of several logical records. When the user program requests to read a logical record from an I/O device, the operating system checks to see if the physical record that contains that logical record is already in one of the system buffers. If so, the logical record can be extracted and provided to the user program without incurring physical I/O. The number of buffers determines the number of physical records that the system is allowed to hold in main memory at a time. DOS uses a least recently used (LRU) method to replace physical records in the buffers and to make room for new records to be read in from the secondary devices. This facility, commonly used by larger computer systems to manage buffer pools, can significantly improve the performance of DOS since most I/O devices for personal computers (e.g., floppy disks) are quite slow. The effectiveness of this scheme depends on the choice of the number of buffers. If the number is too large, it diminishes the physical memory available for the user programs and unproductively increases the CPU time required to search the buffers for the existence of the desired logical record. If the number is too small, it increases the number of I/O operations needed to run the application. It will be seen that this buffer management is very similar (but not identical) to that provided in UNIX.

c) Processor Management

Being a single-user, single-tasking operating system, processor management is quite simple in DOS 2.0. However, one interesting aspect of DOS 2.0 is how the EXEC function call is serviced. In essence, EXEC, when called from within a running program, causes DOS to load another program into available physical memory space. In most cases this newly loaded program is treated like a new process, with its own "program segment prefix" which is similar in nature to process environment control information in some multiprogramming systems. The calling program is sometimes referred to as the "parent process." The parent process then waits until the "child" process finishes before it continues from where it left off when EXEC was issued. The "child" inherits standard input and output devices as well as environment variables from the parent. (The meaning of standard I/O devices will be discussed shortly in another section.) While there is no true multitasking, this arrangement makes it convenient to implement some of the features offered by DOS 2.0's command language processor, notably I/O redirection and command piping. This implementation strategy, as will be seen, closely follows that of UNIX.

d) Device Management

SPOOLING facility: While DOS is a single-tasking system, it does provide a PRINT command which allows a user to print files while running other programs. This facility is normally implemented in a multiprogramming computer system by dedicating the task of printing to a process that can run concurrently with other user processes. In the case of DOS 2.0, this can be accomplished in a more specialized manner by making use of the device interrupt mechanism.

Filelike devices: One interesting architectural feature of DOS 2.0 is its support of filelike devices. The basic idea is that I/O devices are just like special files to a programmer, and that accesses to devices such as consoles, printers, and disks are always routed through the file system. The access function calls are identical, regardless of which device the accesses are eventually directed to, making programs device independent. This notion is illustrated in Fig. 3. The nature of a file is contained in the file control block (FCB) which is established when the file is opened. If a user wishes to direct the output of a program to a printer, all that is needed is to designate in the FCB of the output file that the file is actually a printer device file.

Field installable device drivers: A device driver is a program that interfaces to a specific I/O device. A device driver consists of a strategy module and an interrupt routine. The former takes care of queuing requests for the device, and is always synchronously invoked by the system when a request is received. The latter actually performs necessary I/O operations, and may be invoked synchronously by the system or may be interrupt-driven.

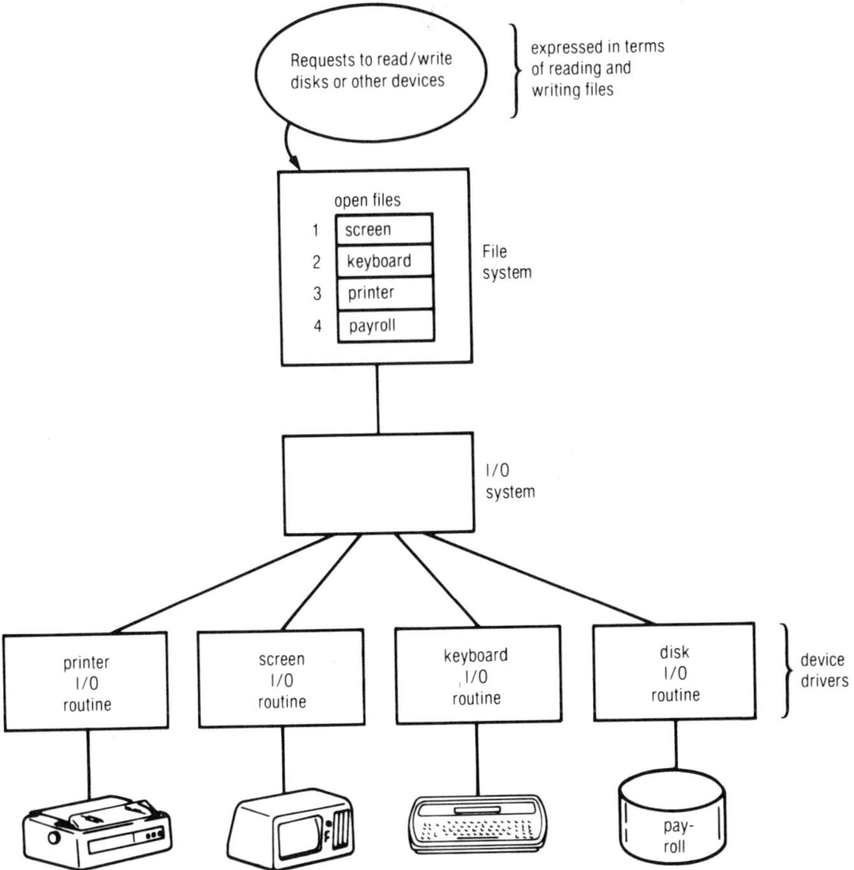

Fig. 3.   The notion of filelike devices.

The concept of field-installable device drivers enables device drivers to be modularly incorporated into DOS without having to modify the internals of the operating system. A new device driver can be installed by a DEVICE command in the CONFIG.SYS file, which the system automatically reads during initialization. The DEVICE command tells the system which file contains the device driver. The initialization routine of DOS will then chain the device driver to other device drivers already in the operating system. This modular design greatly simplifies the task of installing new or optional devices, and enhances portability of these user-written drivers to new releases of the operating system.

e) File Management

File system directory: DOS 2.0 is among the first non-UNIX operating systems for personal computers to provide a tree-structured file directory system. The tree-structured directory is often attributed to the UNIX operating system, and has been widely recognized as an efficient tool for organizing files.

An example of a tree-structured file directory is shown in Fig. 4. Each node in the figure is a file. The root directory is analogous to a file drawer in which information about other files is stored. Some of these files (e.g., dbproj) can be directories, which in turn contain many subfiles. Among these, some (e.g., writeup) may again be file directories. This directory structure provides an interesting way of naming a file. Since a file is a node in the tree, the path from the root of the tree to this node uniquely identifies the node, and therefore in such a system the file-name is also the path-name. Therefore, the file that contains the first chapter of the writeup of dbproj in our example has the path-name dbproj \ writeup \ chap1.

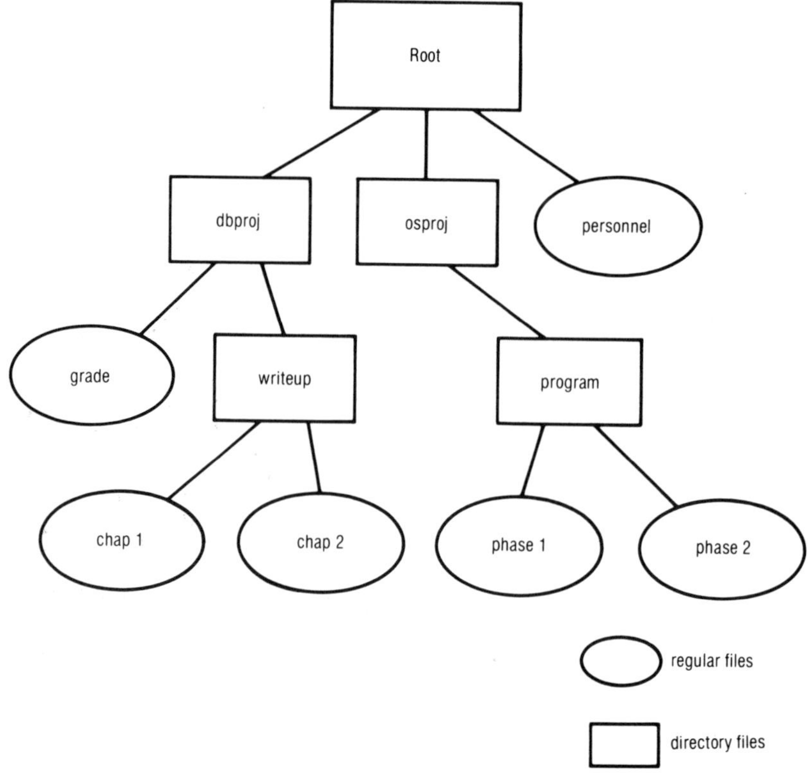

Fig. 4. An example of tree-structured file directory.

In a tree-structured directory file system, a user may be working with a particular directory node in the tree at a time. This node is called the working directory of the user. The path-names issued by a user would be prefixed with the path-name of the working directory by the system. Therefore, when a user uses dbproj as his working directory, the path-name writeup \ chap1 would be interpreted as dbproj \ writeup \ chap1. A user may move around the tree by the *change directory* (CHDIR) command.

The tree-structured directory capability is also important if the personal computer is to be shared among several individuals, though only used by one person at a time. Each individual's files can be gathered together into a separate directory. If each user stays within his or her own file directory, conflicts in the choice of file names and accidental deletion of someone else's files can be eliminated.

Record management: A file is composed of fixed-length logical records. Logical records can be accessed sequentially or randomly by logical record number. Every open file has a "pointer" associated with it which points to a "current" logical record. A program can retrieve (or writing to) the current logical record, or move the pointer to an arbitrary logical record number via a function call. Blocking and buffering is automatically provided by the system (refer to the buffer management section.)

File protection and backup: The DOS file system maintains information about certain attributes of files which enable read-only and archive files to be recognized. The system protects files specified as read-only from being modified. It automatically sets the archive attribute whenever the contents of a writable file are changed. When the file backup command is executed, backup copies of appropriate files are made.

Secondary storage management: DOS uses a dynamic scheme for allocating space for files on the disks. The unit of allocation is a cluster of contiguous sectors on the disk. As a file grows, clusters are dynamically added to the file. The file system keeps track of the free clusters on the disk and the chaining of clusters belonging to the same file via the use of a file allocation table (Fig. 5). Every entry in the table corresponds to a cluster on the disk, and the content of the entry indicates whether the cluster is free. If the cluster is not free, then the entry contains the next cluster number for the file to which this cluster belongs, unless this is the last cluster of a file. In addition, the directory entry of each file contains a pointer to the first cluster of the file. This, combined with the information in the table, forms a complete chain of all the clusters belonging to that file. This scheme is illustrated in Fig. 5. The file allocation table enables efficient management of free space allocation and computation of the cluster number to be accessed for either sequential or random file retrievals. On each secondary device two copies of its file allocation table are stored to guard against hardware or software damage to one of the copies.

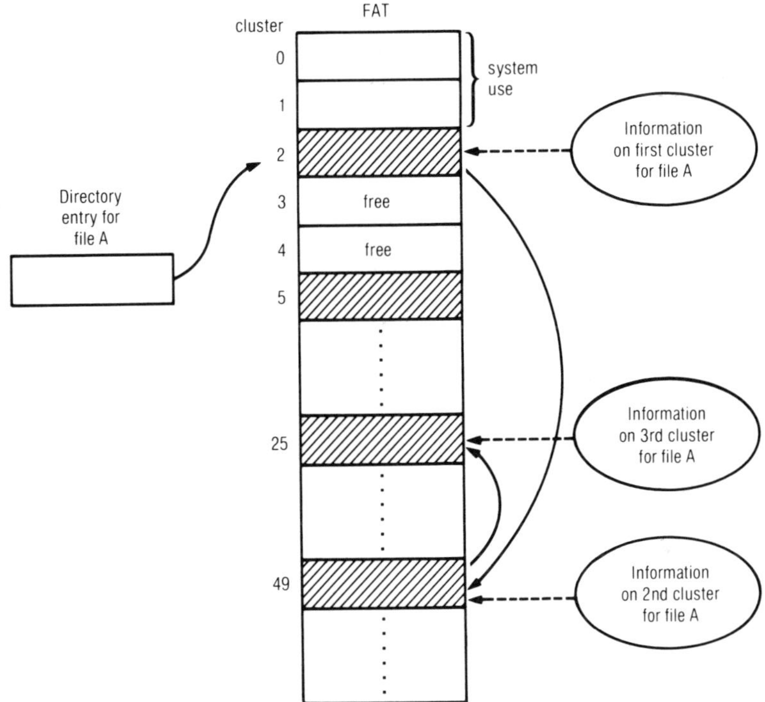

Fig. 5. An illustration of the file allocation table (FAT). The table shows that clusters 3 and 4 are free, and file A is stored on clusters 2, 49, and 25, in that sequence.

The Command Language

Much of the user interface of an operating system is embodied in the command language. In this section we examine the features of the command language processor.

a) Batch Processing

A user can group several DOS commands into a file and submit the file for execution by simply typing the name of the file. This command file has the file type ".BAT" and may contain simple execution flow control primitives such as "if", "for", and "goto". Commands in a command file may also reference arguments passed during invocation.

The batch command processor is used to tailor the syntax of the command processor. Since the command file is invoked by simply entering the name of the file and arguments, a user may group a frequently used sequence of commands into a .BAT file and name the file with something that mnemonically represents what that sequence is supposed to do, and make the system appear as if it now is capable of processing a new command. In addition, a user may specify, via the PATH command, the directories to be searched if the command is not found in the current directory. For sophisticated users, this is a powerful tool for personalizing the command processor.

DOS 2.0 also provides an "autoexec" batch file facility which enables the command file AUTOEXEC.BAT to be executed automatically whenever the user starts up the system.

b) Global Characters for File Names

Both "*", indicating any string, and "?", indicating any character, can be used in the file name(s) referenced in a command line, provided that it is a legal argument to the command. So, for example, if the file directory contains the following files:

file1.bat, file2.bat, myprog.ext, myprog.a

then a reference to file?.bat would be matched with file1.bat and file2.bat, and a reference to myprog.* would be matched with both myprog.ext and myprog.a.

c) I/O Redirection

This is another feature that is often attributed to the UNIX operating system. In essence, every command or program has associated with it a standard input device, which is normally the keyboard, and a standard output device, which is normally the monitor screen or a printer. However, a user can instruct the command language processor to obtain the input from an existing file or to direct the output to another file. For example, the command TREE would normally result in the directory tree being displayed on the console. However, a user may use the special character " > " to redirect the output to a file. For example, the command TREE > MY.CAT would result in the directory listing being saved in a file called MY.CAT and the user can later display MY.CAT to examine the directory listing.

d) Pipes and Filters

This is also a feature familiar to UNIX users. The special character "|" separating two commands is used to indicate to the system that the result of the first command is to be used as input to the second command. In other words, the output from the first command will be "piped" into the second command for further processing. For example, the command line TREE | SORT > MYCAT.SRT would take the result of the TREE command, which is the directory listing, and pipe it through the program SORT, which rearranges the listing in alphabetical order, and then save the sorted directory listing on a file called MYCAT.SRT. Since DOS 2.0 does not support multitasking, piping is accomplished by running the programs one at a time, saving the output of the first program in a file which is later used as input when the second program is started, etc.

A program such as SORT is often used to further process an output file, and is therefore referred to as a "filter." DOS 2.0 provides several filters such as SORT, FIND and MORE. (MORE is a program that displays a file one screenful at a time.) Pipes, I/O redirection and filters make it easy to combine various programs and tools to perform tasks that otherwise would have required extensive reprogramming.

System Architecture

DOS 2.0 is composed of three major program modules: BIO.COM, DOS.COM, and COMMAND.COM. In addition, there is BIOS, residing in read only memory, which handles very low level operating system tasks. This architecture is shown in Fig. 6.

The purpose of BIO.COM and BIOS is to provide low-level I/O handling capabilities. Since BIOS is permanently in memory, it provides the capability to load other parts of the operating system, most notably BIO.COM, from disk into memory. DOS.COM is the heart of the operating system and it implements most of the function calls and interrupt handling routines. The core of the memory management tasks and file management tasks is also included in this module. Finally, there is COMMAND.COM, the command language processor which interacts directly with end users and also with programmers.

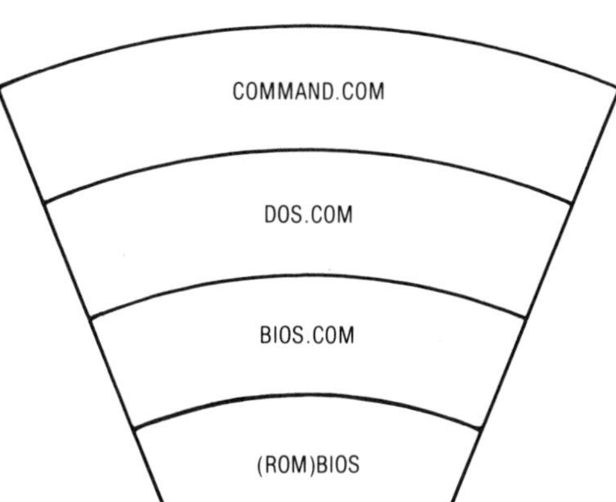

Fig. 6. The structure of DOS 2.0.

Filelike devices, field-installable device drivers, and the nature of the "EXEC" function calls, all discussed previously, are clearly distinctive architectural features of DOS 2.0. They simplify the construction and maintenance of DOS and user programs. In addition, DOS 2.0 has a "replaceable" command language processor, as elaborated in the following paragraphs.

The command language processor, COMMAND.COM, takes care of interpreting user commands and then uses the facilities of DOS.COM to load and execute the programs that carry out these commands. A user may opt to devise his or her own command language processor to replace COMMAND.COM. This can be achieved by using the SHELL command in the CONFIG. SYS file to specify the name of the program file that contains the new command language processor. The effect of the SHELL command is that all future commands would be interpreted by the new program, allowing the system to have a totally different appearance to the user.

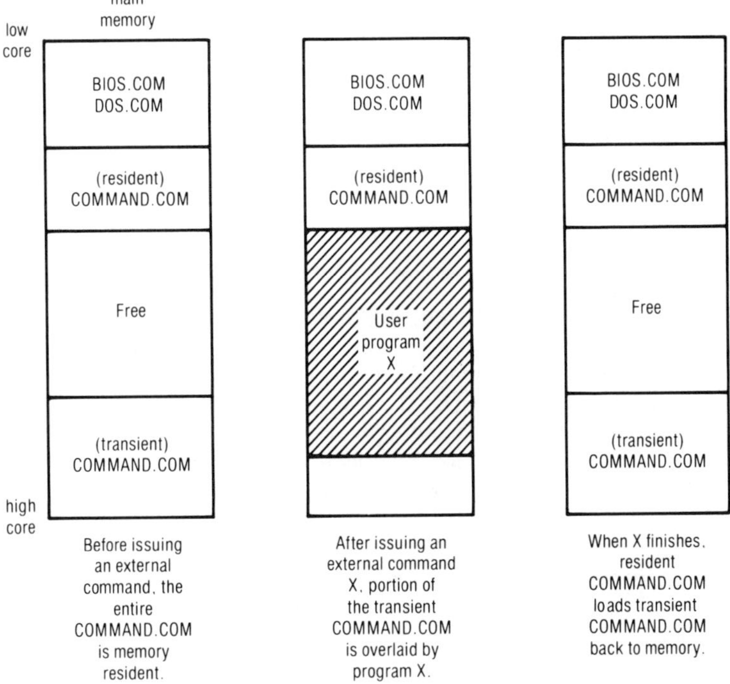

Fig. 7. Effect of dividing COMMAND.COM into a resident portion and a transient portion.

While there are some details to be wrestled with, such as interfacing to COMMAND.COM, and in practice not many users would have the need to write their own command language processor, this modular design makes the system easier to understand and to evolve. In addition, it makes invoking a secondary command language processor from within a user program a relatively straightforward task. This design is quite close to that of UNIX SHELL (to be discussed later), though not identical.

COMMAND.COM is partitioned into a memory resident portion and a transient portion. The former includes a loader which is capable of loading the transient portion of COMMAND.COM. Under this arrangement the transient portion does not have to occupy main memory when a user's program is running. The transient portion includes the routines that implement DOS internal commands, a batch command processor, and an external command loader. (External commands are simply program files that implement those commands.)

When a command that is not a DOS internal command is issued by a user, COMMAND.COM finds the command file on the secondary device and loads it into the main memory (which often causes the transient portion of COMMAND.COM to be overlaid) and transfers control to it. When the latter is finished, control is transferred back to the resident portion of COMMAND.COM which, if needed, loads the transient portion of COMMAND.COM back into main memory. This explains why the DOS system disk, COMMAND.COM in particular, is frequently called for at the end of a command, if it had been physically removed to allow use of other program or data disks. This structure of COMMAND.COM is illustrated in Fig. 7.

III. Concurrent CP/M

Concurrent CP/M is a single-user, multitasking operating system. It allows a user to run up to four processes ("virtual consoles") at the same time. One of the virtual consoles runs in the foreground, interacting with the user through the screen and the keyboard, and the rest run in the background. The background processes may save their output in a file residing on a secondary storage devices. The user may switch from one virtual console to another, achieving the effect of attending to multiple jobs at the same time. To enable a user to view the progress of more than one process, a window manager can be used. It divides the screen into multiple areas, or "windows," each of which can be used to display the output or the status of a particular process.

Multitasking makes resource management an even more challenging task. Multiple processes compete for limited main memory, CPU-time, and shared files. Synchronization and communication among concurrent processes are also needed. This section is based primarily on material from [9]–[10].

Resource Management

   a) Memory Mangement
Concurrent CP/M uses an extended fixed partition scheme for memory management. When a process is created, the entire address space of the process must be loaded. However, in Concurrent CP/M-86, a limited segmentation scheme (without virtual memory) is supported. A process address space is basically composed of a code segment, a data segment, an extra segment, and a stack segment. By making use of the four segment base registers in the processor, these four segments do not have to be loaded into a single contiguous memory area. In fact, CP/M also supports additional "auxiliary" segments, even though the programmer must take care of loading the base registers with the correct base addresses set up by the loader for these segments before addressing them. In sum, a program can be divided into up to eight segments, each being loaded into an independent block of memory. This form of segmentation, albeit limited, alleviates the problem of memory fragmentation and leads to a more efficient use of memory in a multiprogrammed environment than would a strictly contiguous scheme. Fig. 8 illustrates the allocation of memory for a single process. (Note that the term "segment" as used

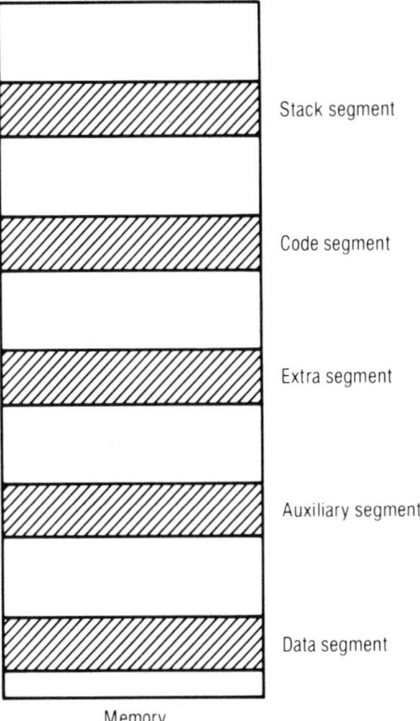

Fig. 8. Segmentation in Concurrent CP/M: the address space of a process is distributed in memory.

here is referred to as "segment group" in Concurrent CP/M-86's terminology, which may consist of multiple "memory segments" each of up to 64K in size.)

Concurrent CP/M also supports dynamic memory allocation during run time. Like DOS 2.0, function calls which service memory allocation and deallocation requests are available. Blocks of memory thus allocated are variable in size, and may be located anywhere in the physical memory address space. As there is no memory protection facility, one process may overwrite memory occupied by another process. In addition, there is no buffer management that corresponds to that offered by DOS 2.0 and UNIX.

b) Processor Management

The task of process management is performed by the real-time, multitasking nucleus of Concurrent CP/M. Its responsibilities include process synchronization and process scheduling.

Process creation and scheduling: Every virtual console is constantly monitored by a terminal message process which reads the user command and loads the program file that implements the command. Like DOS 2.0, a new process is then created to execute the program. The terminal message process therefore becomes the parent process of the command program process. The parent process then waits for the child process to terminate before continuing its terminal monitoring.

A running process may be blocked due to message queue operations, I/O events or voluntary time delays. When a running process is blocked, Concurrent CP/M attempts to find another ready process in the system to dispatch. Concurrent CP/M keeps track of current processes through process descriptors maintained in the system data area. Processes are dispatched based on priority. Processes of the same priority are dispatched using the round-robin algorithm. Timer interrupts are used to enforce time slices on CPU-intensive processes.

Process synchronization: Concurrent CP/M makes use of message queues to provide for process synchronization. Each message queue is named and consists of a fixed number of fixed-length message fields. These queues are created through function calls and are kept in the operating system data area. Messages can be written to (i.e., added) or read from (i.e., removed)

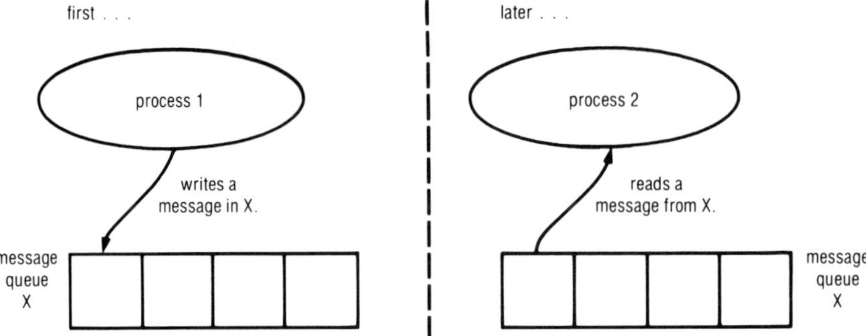

Fig. 9. In Concurrent CP/M, processes communicate through individually named message queues.

the queue in a first-in first-out (FIFO) order. Processes can therefore communicate by operating on a common message queue. Message queues are illustrated in Fig. 9.

These message queues can also be used to guarantee mutual exclusion. The read or write operation on the message queues can be either conditional or unconditional. For example, in writing to a queue *unconditionally*, if the queue is full, the writing process will be suspended until space for a message becomes available in the queue. On the other hand, in writing to a queue *conditionally*, if the queue is full, the calling process is informed of the situation rather than being suspended. It is easy to see that under this scheme, other synchronization techniques can be accomplished. For example, semaphores are just special types of queues and "test-and-set" are conditional operations on special types of queues. It will be seen later that this scheme of process synchronization provides different capabilities than the "message pipe" scheme provided in UNIX.

c) Device Management

A user who wishes to print out a file while working on some other task can simply start the print job in one of the virtual consoles and then work on the other task in another virtual console.

Separation of the file system module from the character device control module is one of the key design differences between CP/M and DOS 2.0. In other words, unlike DOS 2.0 (and UNIX for that matter), CP/M does not follow the philosophy of filelike devices. The access function calls that interface with these two modules are different. A program written for use with one kind of device must be modified for use with another device. This explains why, in CP/M, it is not as easy to achieve the kind of device-independence that DOS 2.0 or UNIX provide. In addition, Concurrent CP/M does not conveniently support the field installable device driver feature.

d) File Management

File directory: Concurrent CP/M implements a limited (two-level) hierarchical directory system. The root of the directory contains up to 16 child directories each of which is labeled by a user number. Each user directory cannot contain any subdirectory. However, file types and some file attributes can be assigned by users to group relevant files together, thereby emulating additional levels of hierarchy, albeit a limited one. Fig. 10 is an illustration of the CP/M file directory.

Files belonging to the directory of one user are generally not visible to the system and therefore cannot be used by another user. One user cannot "link" to another user's file. If one wishes to use another user's program, it must be copied into his or her own directory. Therefore file sharing across user directories is excluded.

Record management and buffering: Like DOS 2.0, CP/M provides both sequential access to logical records in a file and random access by logical record number. It also allows insertion of a new record by its record number. Logical record size is normally 128 bytes, while actual I/O is

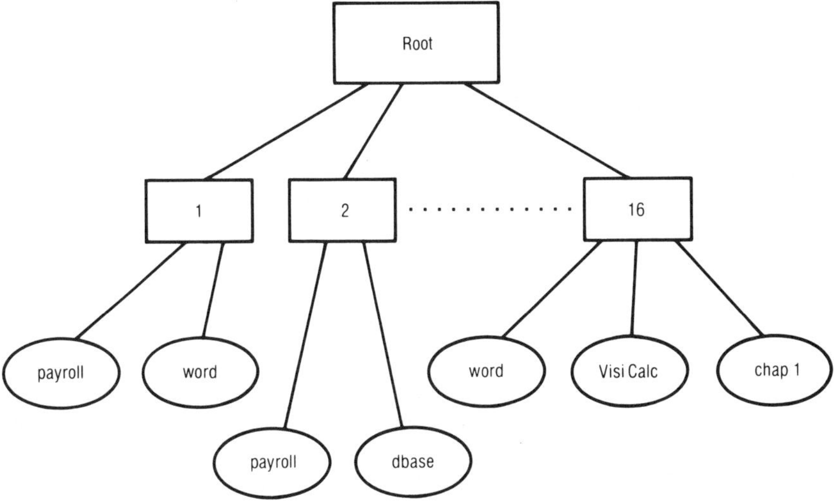

Fig. 10. 2-level hierarchical directory of Concurrent CP/M.

conducted at the physical record level, the size of which is dependent on the secondary storage media. For example, for a device which is less than 64M bytes, the size of the physical record is 1K byte. The system automatically performs blocking and buffering. A flush primitive is provided by the system to force out the content of an I/O buffer.

File protection and integrity: The read-only file attribute is supported. In addition, since the memory-resident file control block associated with every open file in the system is critical to correct operations on the file, a check-sum mechanism is used to verify the correctness of the information to prevent reading or writing a file whose file control block has been accidentally corrupted, possibly by another concurrent process which has failed.

File security: While DOS 2.0 does not dwell on file security, password security is provided for each file in concurrent CP/M. A file can be assigned a password in one of three modes: read, write, or delete. The proper password must be provided before accesses to a file is granted.

Secondary storage management: Like DOS 2.0, a dynamic allocation scheme is used to allocate space on the secondary storage to files. A file is allocated new space only when it is needed. Allocation is done one physical record at a time. If an insertion by record number is performed against a file, only the physical record that contains that logical record needs to be allocated.

CP/M uses a bit map to keep track of the status (free or allocated) of each cluster of sectors on the disk. In addition, the directory entry of each file includes a disk allocation map which maps blocks of logical records to sectors. Disk sectors, once allocated, will not be returned to the free sector pool even if all records in that sector are deleted, until the file itself is deleted. Therefore, for a file that goes through frequent record insertion and deletion, the user must periodically copy the file and then delete the old copy to reclaim such space.

Concurrent access: The issue of concurrent access to files does not arise in a nonmultiprogrammed system such as DOS 2.0. In Concurrent CP/M, extensive file and record locking is supported for coordinating accesses to the same file by concurrent processes. A file can be opened under one of three lock modes: locked, unlocked, and read-only. The locked mode enables exclusive access of a file by a single process. The read-only mode enables simultaneous read-only accesses by multiple processes. The unlocked mode allows simultaneous read- and write access to the same file by concurrent processes. However, such processes must use record-level locking to prevent simultaneous access to the same record.

The Command Language

CP/M supports batch command file processing. Such files have the file type ".SUB" and can be invoked by the SUBMIT command. Like DOS 2.0, simple control flow primitives are provided for a user to write a command procedure, and arguments can be passed when invoking the procedure.

CP/M also supports the global characters "*" and "?" for naming files in certain commands. In sum, the major difference between CP/M's command language and that of DOS 2.0's is the lack of support in CP/M for I/O redirection, pipes, and filters.

System Architecture

Concurrent CP/M is composed of several modules. The real-time monitor (RTM) is responsible for process management. The MEM module keeps track of memory allocation. The hardware-independent portion of the file system is contained in BDOS, while the console and the printer I/O is controlled by the CIO (Character I/O) module and the virtual console screen manager. Finally, the XIOS module directly interfaces with the hardware environment, including conducting physical I/O and responding to interrupts. In addition to these resource kernel modules, the TMP (terminal message processor) and the CLI (command line interpreter) modules constitute the command language processor. A schematic view of Concurrent CP/M is shown in Fig. 11.

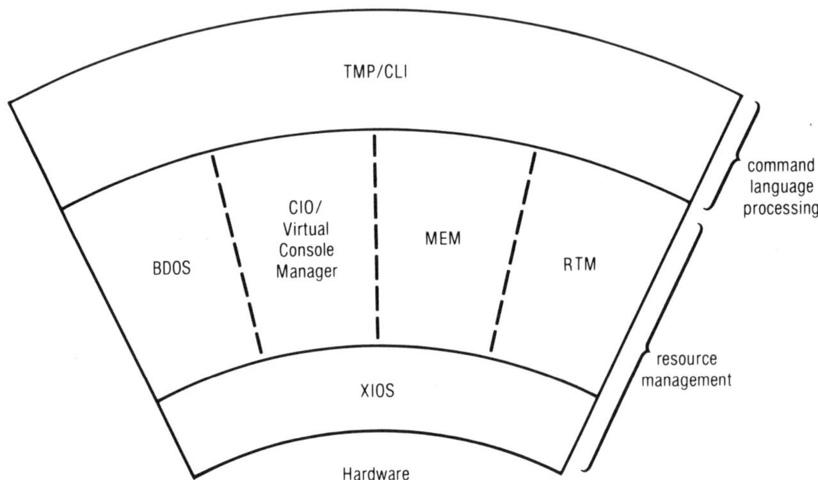

Fig. 11. Structure of Concurrent CP/M.

It was mentioned previously that CP/M's command language does not support I/O redirection and pipes. In fact, the architecture of CP/M is not particularly suitable for supporting such features since they are intimately dependent on key architectural design decisions such as filelike devices and standard I/O devices. Files are accessed by function calls to the BDOS module while character devices (such as consoles) are accessed by calls to the CIO module. This is different from the way DOS 2.0 is implemented. Also, Concurrent CP/M does not provide a convenient way to replace the standard command language processor modules TMP and CLI, the way DOS 2.0 provides with its SHELL command.

In summary, Concurrent CP/M provides a flexible and an easy-to-use multitasking environment, which can be further enhanced by a window manager. The process communication and synchronization capabilities and the extensive concurrent file sharing capabilities are unusual qualities among personal computer operating systems.

IV. UNIX

UNIX was designed by AT & T's Bell Laboratories for use as an in-house time-sharing system on minicomputers around 1970. UNIX has been licensed to outside entities, mostly educational institutions, for more than a decade. Over this period of time, several versions have been released, the more significant ones being (in chronological order) the sixth edition, the seventh edition, and PWB/UNIX (Programmer's Workbench). In addition to Bell Laboratories, other organizations, most notably the University of California at Berkeley, have also produced their own enhancements. Based on the UNIX Seventh Edition, two versions of Berkeley enhancements, known as UNIX BSD 4.1 and BSD 4.2, have become popular at educational institutions.

In late 1981, an update of the Seventh Edition, called UNIX System III, was introduced by AT & T. PC/IX, a single-user multitasking UNIX operating system officially offered by IBM for its PC/XT personal computers, is based on this version. XENIX, an enhanced version of the Seventh Edition, was adopted by IBM for its first multi-user microcomputer system, the PC/AT. In January 1983, the latest version, UNIX System V, was proposed by AT & T as an industry standard. It is used in AT & T's 3B line of microprocessor-based multiuser computer systems and has been licensed to several other computer manufacturers.

This section is based primarily on material from [11]–[16]. We focus on fundamental characteristics of UNIX as well as on significant features of the latest version called the System V [17].

Resource Management

a) Memory Management

The standard version of UNIX uses a variable partition scheme for allocating space to concurrent processes. Like DOS and CP/M, virtual memory is not supported. The entire address space of a process must be loaded before running. However, unlike DOS or Concurrent CP/M, UNIX supports code sharing. Basically, the address space of a process is composed of three logical segments: a code segment, a data segment, and a stack segment. The code segment is write protected once loaded in memory, and can be shared by multiple users or processes if they happen to be running the same program. For example, if several users are editing files at the same time, only one copy of the editor needs to be loaded, achieving a significant saving in memory space. On the other hand, data segments and stack segments are private to each individual processes and are not sharable. The implication of this on process synchronization will be further discussed.

Data segments can be dynamically extended during run time by function calls. Stack segments are automatically extended by the system when needed. Whether or not the entire address space of a process needs to be contiguous in main memory depends on the memory management hardware available. However, in UNIX, there is a strong reason for keeping the address space of a process contiguous in main memory: swapping, which will be discussed shortly. To accomplish this goal of contiguity, whenever a process's address space grows, a new memory area big enough to hold the new, extended address space is found and the entire address space is copied into the new area, freeing up the old area. The first-fit algorithm is used to identify this new area. (Note that neither DOS 2.0 nor Concurrent CP/M would respond to a request to grow an existing segment beyond the free memory available adjacent to that segment.)

I/O buffer management: The UNIX operating system maintains a number of 512-byte buffers, called the buffer pool, in main memory. This arrangement is very similar to that provided by DOS 2.0 as discussed before. When a read or write operation is to be performed, the system searches in the buffer pool first for that block. If it is already in the buffer pool, no physical I/O is incurred for that operation. Otherwise, the system uses a least recently used algorithm to determine a buffer to be emptied, and copies the newly requested block from disk into the buffer, and then carries out the operation in the buffer. Buffer management has other implications that will be further discussed under the file system.

Swapping: Swapping is the mechanism by which the code and data segments of some live processes may be removed from main memory and temporarily saved on the disk. These processes are removed to make room for other processes that would not otherwise fit into the main memory at the same time. Swapping is a fairly effective memory management scheme in a multiuser (time-sharing) environment, in which users often incur long "think time" between issuing commands. While one user is thinking, his or her process is blocked waiting for terminal input that may take a long time to occur. Meanwhile, if there is another process ready for execution but there is not enough room in main memory to hold its address space, the blocked process may be swapped out to free up enough memory for the ready process to run, as shown in Fig. 12. This mechanism increases the number of processes the system can support (i.e., increases the level of multiprogramming,) because the live nonactive processes do not have to occupy memory. However, to make the I/O operation needed for swapping more efficient, it is often desirable to have the process's address space contiguous in memory. This tends to aggravate the memory fragmentation problem. In addition, swapping must be well coordinated with process management, which is discussed next. Furthermore, swapping incurs significant I/O activity that may be lengthy to perform and may interfere with I/O activity needed for the file system.

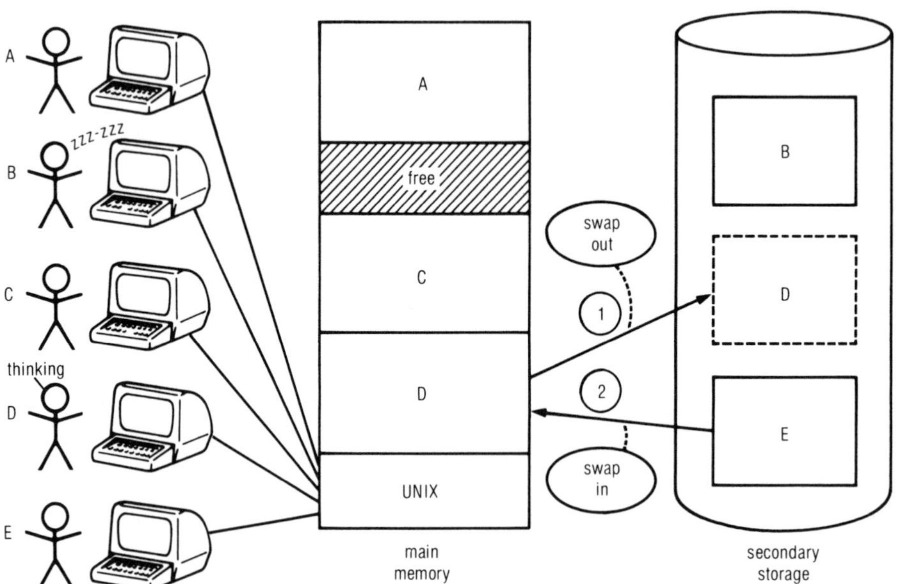

Fig. 12. Swapping: User D is swapped out to make room for User E.

b) Processor Management

Process creation: UNIX processes are created by making a copy of (i.e., forking) the creating process. The FORK function call results in a new process, i.e., the child being born is identical, in terms of code, data, and open files, to the calling process, the parent. The return values of the FORK function call are different for the parent and child and, by testing this return value, the child process may move onto its independent path, performing whatever function it has been created for. This way of creating processes proves to be ingenious when fitted into the rest of the UNIX system.

Process scheduling: UNIX, not unlike Concurrent CP/M, uses a preemptive priority scheduling algorithm to dispatch processes. Priority is assigned in such a way that CPU-intensive processes tend to get lower priority than the I/O-intensive ones, and system processes are always ahead of user processes. In addition, the processes that have been in memory for a long time and those that have been waiting for slow external operations to be completed tend to be the ones selected to be swapped out, while those that have been disk-resident for a long time tend to be the ones to be swapped in. The algorithm contains elements of robustness that deter system thrashing, that is, the situation in which excessive swapping is going on while little useful work is being done.

Process synchronization: UNIX's approach to synchronization is different from that of CP/M. Internally, the UNIX kernel makes use of "event waits" to coordinate processes. When a process is blocked, it waits for some event to occur in order to be awoken. That event can later be signaled by another process. Signaling an event awakes all processes that are waiting for that event. If there is no process waiting at this time, the signal causes no action. This can cause problems if one process signals an event before the other process is ready to wait—the signal is lost. Even though this mechanism is very primitive, it is adequate for the system to perform the task of process switching.

However, in the original design of UNIX [12], a user process could not create an event and communicate with other processes by signaling that event, the way a Concurrent CP/M user can create a message queue and communicate with other processes by reading and writing messages in the queue. The traditional mechanisms for interprocess communication in UNIX are between parent and child processes through the WAIT and SIGNAL function calls and through the pipes. A wait call issued by a parent process puts the parent to sleep until one of its children dies. The primary use of WAIT in UNIX is to implement SHELL. A pipe is treated like a file such that a process can create and open and then have the child-process inherit it as one of its open files. The parent and the child can then communicate through the pipe by reading from and writing to it, and the synchronization of accessing pipes is automatically taken care of by the system.

The pipe is a powerful abstraction and can be used very efficiently for many applications. However, the pipe mechanism has some limitations. For example, suppose several independently created processes need to share a table but only one process may operate on the table at a time. This mutual exclusion requirement cannot be easily achieved in UNIX by way of pipes. Another problem occurs if a parent process is expecting to receive messages from several child processes, each through its own pipe (e.g., each child process is monitoring a different device). The parent process has no way of knowing which pipe currently contains messages. If it attempts to read from an empty pipe, it will be blocked until a message is sent through that pipe, even though there may be messages in the other pipes. These deficiencies in the original UNIX design have troubled some developers in the past [18].

UNIX System V, the version of UNIX released in January 1983 by AT&T, contains many additional powerful interprocess communication features that eliminate the earlier deficiencies. These include conditional read on pipes, message queues similar to CP/Ms, counting semaphores and shared memory data segments; all these can be created by user processes through function calls. This rich ensemble of process synchronization mechanisms greatly facilitates multi-user shared applications.

c) Device Management

UNIX supports spooling by creating a special process, sometimes called a "demon," "phantom," or "friendly spirit," for each dedicated device. All requests for that device are sent to that process to be queued up and eventually serviced. As mentioned earlier under DOS 2.0, UNIX supports the notion of filelike devices which improves device-independence of programs.

d) File Management

File directory: UNIX supports a hierarchical directory system as described in the DOS 2.0 section. In addition, in UNIX, a user in one local directory may link to files in another directory. For example, suppose a user working under the directory/dbproj/writeup issues the following command:

ln /osproj/book osbook

Then the file book in the directory/osproj also becomes a local file called osbook in the directory/dbproj/writeup as shown in Fig. 13. This file becomes shared in these two directo-

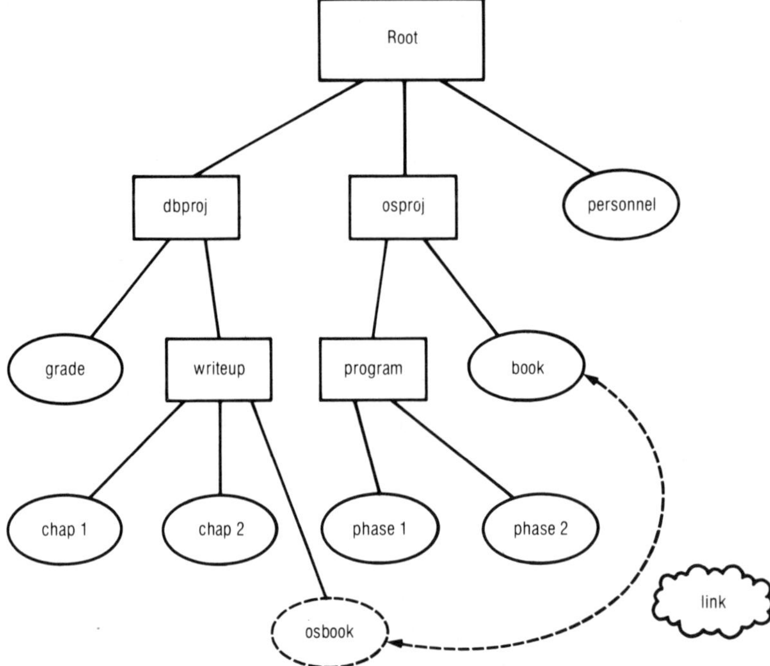

Fig. 13. The notion of "link" in a hierarchical directory system: /dbproj/writeup/osbook and /osproj/book are the same file.

ries. In essence, UNIX implements a hierarchical naming system on top of the files in the system and it allows a file to be accessed via several naming paths. In contrast, in DOS 2.0, either the full path name of a file in another directory must be specified each time, or a copy of the file must be made, in order for the file to become accessible as a local file in another directory. Note, however, for implementation reasons, no link to a directory is allowed in UNIX.

File protection and security: One of three types of accesses can be specified: read, write, and execute. For security, UNIX allows the owner (i.e., the creator) of a file to specify what access rights are to be given to three different user categories: owner, file group, and all others. For example, a user may grant write permission to himself, read permission to a group of users in the same project, and no access rights to any other user. These file protection attributes can be dynamically changed by the owner. Note that this mechanism differs from the password protection mechanism that CP/M provides.

Record management and buffering: Unlike the other two operating systems, UNIX does not provide any explicit record management. Under UNIX, a file is merely an arbitrarily long byte stream. (It is implemented as a series of 512-byte blocks.) Every read and write to the file is directed to a sequence of bytes in the file. These bytes can be accessed sequentially or randomly by an offset into that file. Using this basic byte stream mechanism, almost any desired record management facility (e.g., fixed-length records, variable-length records, indexed records) can be implemented by the user.

Buffering at the block level, as previously discussed in the memory managment section, is provided to reduce the number of physical I/O's and to increase efficiency. A subtle difference between the buffering scheme used in UNIX and that used in DOS 2.0 has bearing on the integrity of the file system. In UNIX, a write request results in the block in the buffer being updated. Except in the case of a flush command the actual writing of that block to the secondary device will take place later when that buffer has to be emptied to make room for another file block [14].

In other words, UNIX adopts the "write-behind" strategy in handling buffered data. Under this strategy, writing to disks does not necessarily occur when the write request is issued.

Therefore if the system crashes (due to, say, a power interruption) the content of the main memory can be suddenly lost, leaving the consistency of the content of the files on the disk questionable. For example, it is possible for a user to make a request to write a file block A, then write a file block B, with the intention that the changes to B are correct as long as the changes to A have been recorded. The intervening buffering scheme, however, may later write out block B to disk while keeping A in main memory. At this point, if the system crashes, the changed B would be preserved on disk while the changed A is not. The integrity of the files involved will be lost. This is the reason why the UNIX file system is sometimes referred to as being "fragile" [19]. In contrast, the buffer system of DOS 2.0 adopts the "write-through" strategy in handling buffered data. It always writes the content of a changed buffer immediately after the user has issued an access which is beyond the boundary of the block contained in that buffer. The performance penalty of not being able to perform delayed writes is the price one pays in DOS 2.0.

Secondary storage management: UNIX also adopts the dynamic disk allocation scheme used in DOS and CP/M. What differs is the exact algorithm by which free space is recorded and how the file map is implemented. In UNIX, free sectors on disks are chained together by storing the chain pointers in the free sectors, while the file map (i.e., the disk addresses of blocks belonging to a file) is kept in the file's directory entry. The directory entry contains enough space for specifying ten disk addresses (i.e., for ten blocks). For larger files additional disk addresses will point instead to blocks in which the disk addresses of the actual file blocks reside. By using up to three levels of indirect addressing, it is possible to map a very large file.

Concurrent accesses: While UNIX is a multiuser system, it has a very limited facility for coordinating concurrent accesses to files as compared to Concurrent CP/M. Files can be opened and accessed by multiple processes at the same time, but no concurrency control such as the locking facility in Concurrent CP/M, is provided. For example, a file containing customers' information may be opened for write by two processes at the same time. While one process changes a customer's address, the other may change the balance. Improper sharing of the same record by two concurrent processes may result in one of the updates being lost without the file system being aware of it. In contrast, Concurrent CP/M directly provides both file- and record-level locking primitives, enabling file sharing to be performed at a fine level of granularity. This problem is often solved in UNIX by dedicating a single process to managing that file and having all concurrent application processes forward their requests to that process through pipes or message queues.

UNIX was not originally designed for applications where large files are concurrently used by multiple processes. It is oriented more towards a typical time-sharing system in which each individual user does his or her own thing, uses his or her own files, and rarely has the need to share information concurrently with other users. This orientation explains the lack of sophisticated file-locking and process synchronization capabilities in early versions of UNIX. Use of the new UNIX System V's interprocess communication features solves many of these problems.

The Command Language Processor—Shell

SHELL, the command language interpreter, is one of the most interesting components of UNIX. Some of the features that were discussed under DOS 2.0's command language processor have their origin in SHELL. These include I/O redirection and piping. In addition, SHELL itself embodies a reasonably powerful language processor, such that a user may write procedures, called shell procedures, or shell scripts, consisting of SHELL commands. A shell procedure can then be submitted to SHELL for execution. This is very similar to the batch command processor feature of DOS and CP/M, but SHELL is much more sophisticated in the kinds of primitives it provides to write these procedures. For example, control flow primitives available include "for," "while," "case," "if/else," and "do."

SHELL also supports wild card characters such as * and ?. This facility in SHELL is called "file name generation," and goes beyond what is available in DOS and CP/M. For example, square brackets [and] together with a hyphen can be used to match a range of characters. Thus a reference CHAP.[1–9] would be matched with all files CHAP.1, CHAP.2,···, CHP.9 in the directory. Characters such as *, ?, [, and] are called meta characters, and are processed by SHELL before invoking the actual command. In essence, every command line is first interpreted by SHELL. The command line consists of a command name and a list of arguments. SHELL examines the list of arguments to identify special characters. For example, if an argument MYCAT* is encountered, SHELL expands it into a list of file names whose first five characters match with MYCAT. After the file name generation is performed, the expanded list of arguments is passed to the program that implements the command. This uniform treatment of meta characters in a command line, independent of the command itself, is an example of modularity.

UNIX provides user multitasking by allowing users to run processes in a background mode through the use of another special character. A command line ended with "&" is understood by SHELL to be a command that will be executed in the background. Thus, for example, a command

ls > listfile &

would cause a listing of the files in the current directory to be generated and to be written to a new file "listfile." However, SHELL immediately returns and displays a prompt on the screen after the "ls" command is started even though the "ls" task is not finished. The user may enter another command and have it executed while the system is performing the "ls" task in the background. In this fashion, a user may spawn many tasks in the background, while attending to something else in the foreground. SHELL provides a command, ps (process status), which enables a user to examine the status of all foreground and background processes. When a background job is done, a user may examine the results of that task.

Shell implementation: The strategy adopted by UNIX to implement SHELL greatly simplifies the task of supporting I/O redirection, piping, and background processing. In essence, a user console is constantly monitored by a SHELL process. When a command is entered, this SHELL process first performs all the meta character substitution and file name generation. It sets up a data structure which contains all the information of the command line, and then creates a new process by forking itself. As mentioned earlier, FORK creates a child process which is identical to the parent process, with the child process inheriting the standard input and output files as well as all other open files from the parent process. The parent SHELL process issues a wait and goes to sleep until the child process terminates. The first thing the child process does is to change its identity (i.e., its image) by an EXEC call using the data structure saved for it by the parent process. As a result, the new process loads the program that implements the command and starts executing the program. When the program is finished, the child process terminates, causing the parent SHELL process to be awoken and to continue its console monitoring.

Under this scheme, I/O redirection is accomplished by having the child process replace its standard input and output file designations before issuing EXEC. Background process is achieved by not making the parent SHELL process go to sleep after forking, but coming back to monitor the console immediately. Batch command processing (i.e., shell procedure processing) is accomplished by having the child process replace its standard input file with the shell procedure file, load the image of another SHELL, and start executing this secondary SHELL. When this secondary SHELL encounters an end of file in the shell procedure, it terminates and causes the parent (i.e., the first level) SHELL process to awaken and to continue. Finally, piping between processes is achieved by replacing the standard output file of the first process and the standard input file of the second process with a common pipe. It is interesting to see that concepts such as filelike devices, standard input and output files, pipes, and command processing by forking processes complement each other so well in producing a flexible and modular system. In contrast, even though DOS 2.0 has followed many of these concepts and implementation ideas very closely, it is not put together as tightly as UNIX is in this particular respect.

The ease of use of the SHELL is not entirely without quibbles [20]. Many have criticized the syntax of its command language for being terse and inconsistent. Others have found its lack of interactive response offensive. Nevertheless the power of its features remains impressive and its influence is likely to last for a long time. Furthermore, its flexibility and modularity make it easy to customize the appearance of SHELL to match the user's preference.

System Architecture

UNIX is composed of a kernel and the command language processor SHELL. Many other programs such as text editors and formatters, the C compiler and debuggers, program development tools, and many utility/filter programs are often provided as part of the UNIX operating system, which makes the system seem very large in comparison with DOS and CP/M. In reality, the kernel of the standard UNIX consists of 10 000 lines of C code and about 1000 lines of assembly language code [14]. As a result of its simplicity, modularity, and extensive use of the C programming language, it has been relatively easy to implement UNIX on a wide variety of processors ranging from microcomputers (e.g., AT & T 3B) to minicomputers (e.g., DEC VAX) to large mainframe computers (e.g., IBM 3033). In this regard, it is sometimes referred to as the first, and probably only, "universal operating system." In comparison, DOS and CP/M do not provide the functions normally expected in mini or mainframe computers nor does their implementation lend them to easy conversion to processors radically different from their original targets, such as the Intel 8080.

The interesting architectural features of UNIX include i) the capability of the system to completely decouple the command language processor—SHELL, ii) filelike devices which enhance device independence, iii) standard input and output devices associated with each process which facilitates ease of I/O redirection and building large systems from small building blocks, iv) program execution by process forking which makes it easy to implement multitasking, v) modular device drivers, i.e., device drivers that can be configured into the system by adding their entry points into a configuration array of the system, and vi) portability, that is, the use of the C high level language for a large portion of the operating system making it easy to convert UNIX to operate on processors of various sizes, designs, and from different manufacturers.

V. Concluding Remarks

A summary of key characteristics of the three operating systems under review is tabulated in Table 1. Although there are many similarities among them, with traces of influences of UNIX on the design of both DOS 2.0 and Concurrent CP/M, the differences provide significant advantages or disadvantages depending upon the user's needs. These differences provide the motivation for other operating systems such as XENIX [21] and PC/IX [22]–[23]. XENIX is a version of UNIX developed by Microsoft Corp. specifically for microcomputers and is offered by IBM for its PC/AT personal computer along with DOS. It is based on the UNIX Seventh Edition with a number of enhancements. PC/IX is a single-user version of UNIX, based on UNIX System III, developed by Interactive Systems Corp. and is offered by IBM for its PC/XT personal computers along with DOS and CP/M.

In order to solve some of the problems in UNIX Seventh Edition regarding process synchronization, file and data sharing, and file integrity, XENIX offers features of shared data segments, improved interprocess communication, and automatic file repair after crash. AT & T solved these problems by developing UNIX System V, as noted earlier. PC/IX, on the other hand, is not concerned with these problems, and the designers have apparently decided that the multiuser capability is not necessary or practical on an IBM PC/XT. Instead they have added capabilities to make the PC/IX coexist with other operating systems, such as DOS, and to transfer files between them.

Operating systems for personal computers are still evolving. The users who are using personal computers in increasingly sophisticated applications will always demand more. Developing and

Table 1 A Comparison of DOS 2.0, Concurrent CP/M, and UNIX

	DOS 2.0	Concurrent CP/M-86	UNIX
General Characteristics	single-user single-tasking	single-user multitasking	multi-user multitasking
Memory Management			
Run-time memory allocation services	Yes	Yes	Yes
Segmentation[1]	No	Yes	Yes
Segment sharing	NA	NA	Code segments only
Buffer pool[2]	Yes, with "store through"	No	Yes, with "store behind"
Swapping[3]	NA	No	Yes
Process Management			
Scheduling	NA	Priority round robin	Priority round robin
Synchronization	NA	Individually named fixed-length message queues with conditional and unconditional operations	Filelike variable-length pipes; in UNIX system 5, counting semaphores, message queues and shared data segments are available
Device Management			
Spooling	Via PRINT for printer output	Via multitasking	Via dedicated "demon" processes
"Filelike devices"	Yes	No	Yes
Field-installable device drivers	Yes	NA	By modifying device driver entry table
File Management			
Hierarchical directory	Yes	Limited (2-level)	Yes, with "link" facility
Record management •logical record	Fixed-length	Fixed-length	No explicit record management; files are byte-addressable byte streams
•access	Sequential or random by record number	Sequential or random by record number	Files are byte-addressable byte streams
•blocking/buffering	Yes	Yes	Yes
Protection/security	"Read-only" protection	"Read-only" protection/ password security	"Read-only" and "execute only" protection; security via authorization

Table 1 (*Continued.*)

	DOS 2.0	Concurrent CP/M-86	UNIX
Secondary storage management	Dynamic allocation	Dynamic allocation	Dynamic allocation
Concurrent accesses to shared files	NA	Yes, with adequate file-level and record-level locking facility	Yes, but without automatic concurrency control
Command Languages			
Control primitives in "batch" procedures	Moderate	Moderate	Very powerful
"Wild card" or "global characters"	"*" and "?" for file-name generation	Yes, similar to DOS 2.0	Yes, but more powerful than DOS 2.0 and CP/M
Standard I/O devices and I/O redirection	Yes	No	Yes
Command piping	Yes[4]	No	Yes
"Replaceable" command language processor	Yes	No	Yes
Number of background tasks	NA	Up to 3; user may switch between them	No theoretical limit

[1]No virtual memory.

[2]Also an issue for device management and file management.

[3]Also an issue for process management.

[4]Simulated by use of temporary files.

extending operating systems to efficiently support networking, windowing software, and sophisticated database applications in cooperation with more powerful hardware will be the next step. The end of this continuing evolution is still not on the horizon. This evolution is still continuing but the increasing convergence of the features of DOS, CP/M, and UNIX make the acceptance of an industry standard operating system possible with significant benefits to both developers and users.

REFERENCES

[1]   S. E. Madnick and J. J. Donovan, *Operating Systems.*   New York: McGraw-Hill, 1974.

[2]   M. Deitel, *An Introduction to Operating Systems.*   Reading, MA: Addison-Wesley, 1984.

[3]   M. A. Husted, "Comparison of CP/M and UNIX operating system," in *Proc. of IEEE COMPCON*, 1983, pp. 177–181.

[4]   R. Dress, "A comparison of Apple DOS and UNIX operating system," in *Proc. of IEEE COMPCON*, 1983, pp. 169–176.

[5]   L. A. Ramsdell, "Analysis and comparison of IBM DOS and UNIX," in *Proc. of IEEE COMPCON*, 1983, pp. 182–191.

[6]   W. G. Wong, "MS-DOS 2.0: An Overview," *Microsystems*, vol. 5, no. 2–4, 1984.

[7]   *DOS 2.0 User's Manual*, IBM Corp., Boca Raton, FL, Jan. 1983.

[8]   *Personal Computer Technical Reference Manual*, IBM Corp., Boca Raton, FL, 1983.

[9]   *Concurrent CP/M User's Manual*, Digital Research Inc., Pacific Grove, CA, 1983.

[10]   *Concurrent CP/M Programmer's Manual*, Digital Research Inc., Pacific Grove, CA, 1983.

[11]   K. Christian, *The UNIX Operating System.*   New York: Wiley, 1983

[12]   D. M. Ritchie and K. L. Thompson, "The UNIX time-sharing system," *Commun. Ass. Comput. Mach.*, vol. 17, no. 7, July 1974.

[13] S. R. Bourne, "An introduction to UNIX shell," *Bell Syst. Tech. J.*, vol. 57, no. 6, July–Aug. 1978, pp. 1971–1990.

[14] K. Thompson, "UNIX implementation," *Bell Syst. Tech. J.*, vol. 57, no. 6, July–Aug. 1978, pp. 1931–1946.

[15] D. M. Ritchie, *The UNIX Programmer's Manual*, Vol. 2, (supplementary document), 7th ed. Murray Hill, NJ: Bell Laboratories, Jan. 1978, Ch. 32.

[16] *UNIX Programmer's Manual Seventh Edition*, Bell Laboratories, Jan. 1979.

[17] *UNIX User's Manual Release 5.0*, Bell Laboratories, June 1982.

[18] M. Stonebraker, "Operating system support for database management," *Commun. Ass. Comput. Mach.*, vol. 24, no. 7, July 1981.

[19] B. Daniels, "The architecture of the Lisa personal computer," in *Insights Into Personal Computers* (This Book). New York: IEEE Press, 1985, Ch. 14.

[20] D. A. Norman, "The trouble with UNIX," *Datamation*, Nov., 1981.

[21] R. G. Greenberg, "The UNIX operating system and the XENIX standard operating system," *Byte*, June 1981.

[22] *PC/IX General Information Manual*, IBM Corp., Boca Raton, FL, 1983.

[23] S. Libes, "PC/IX: A directional signal for IBM systems," *PC Week*, vol. 1, no. 11, Mar. 1984.

13
Graphics—The New Direction in Personal Computer Software

HOO-MIN D. TOONG AND AMAR GUPTA

The "personalization" of computers is made possible by three major factors—advances in microelectronics, the availability of inexpensive software for a spectrum of applications, and the increased user-friendliness of computer systems. This chapter examines the trends in software development and presents estimates of the escalating costs involved in such development. Several studies show that the need is for more sophisticated and effective communication tools rather than for more computing power. Effective communication often pivots around the impact of diverse types of information—numeric, textual, and pictorial. Current endeavors are directed towards refining and integrating several existing technologies to implement software that enables programmers and nonprogrammers alike to readily manipulate images comprised of different types of information. This chapter examines the emerging field of presentation graphics software and presents details of a new product in this nascent field. The conclusion emphasizes the impact of graphic computing in enlarging the spectrum of personal computer applications.

I. INTRODUCTION

In terms of basic computing power, the mainframes of the early 1960s, the minicomputers of the early 1970s, and the personal computers of the 1980s are all in the same performance bracket [1]. However, the popular applications of these systems differ significantly due to several reasons. The diminishing cost of computing and the increasing cost of human resources have resulted in a marked shift in the optimal ratio of computer to human resources (Figs. 1 and 2) [2], [3]. Further, the evolution of superior techniques has vastly improved the human–machine symbiotic relationship and has reduced time delays. Cumbersome machine languages, consisting of strings of zeros and ones, have given way to English-like languages that can be learned and used much more readily. The batch environment characterized by system turnaround times of hours and even days has given way to the interactive mode characterized by virtually instantaneous responses, encouraging users to analyze more issues and in greater detail than before. Unlike earlier when computers were used only for well-structured jobs such as payroll accounting on a periodic basis, personal computers of today are used for *ad hoc* types of analyses on a nonperiodic basis. Computers are used as "decision-support" tools that enable quick analysis of alternative solutions, and answers to "What ... if ...?" type questions without the overhead of extensive programming effort. Rather than constituting a distinct breed, personal computers represent the end result of several decades of "personalization" of computers.

The explosive growth of personal computers has no doubt been catalyzed by the plummeting prices of computer hardware—by 25–40 percent each year. Today's personal computers offer more basic computing power than the largest computer did 25 years ago. But two other reasons are even more important. First is the availability and range of inexpensive software products to

---

The authors are with the Sloan School of Management, Massachusetts Institute of Technology, Cambridge, MA 02139, USA.

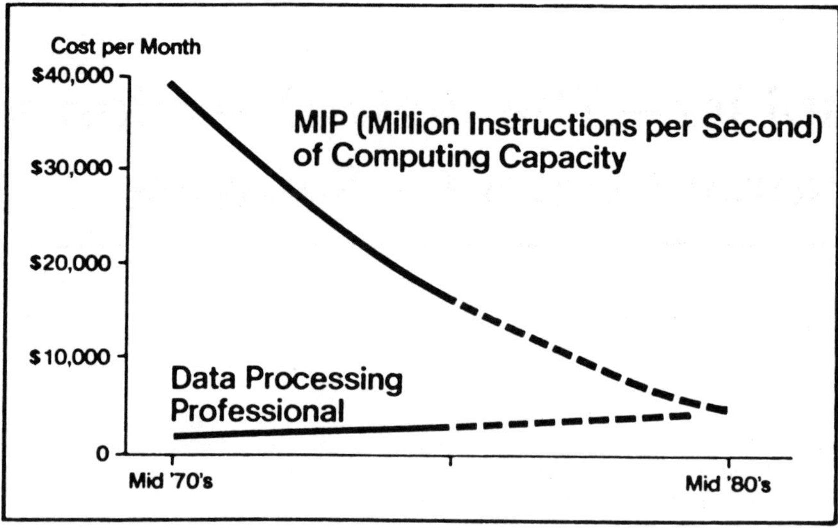

Fig. 1. Relative costs of DP hardware and expertise [2].

suit virtually all individuals and application environments. Second is the increasing "user-friend-liness" of the system. No longer does one need to go through the agony of learning counter-intuitive languages just to be able to indulge in the pleasures of automation. Computers of today can comprehend human beings much more readily. Although advances in microelectronics will continue to play a supporting role, the real impetus for the sustained growth of the personal computer industry will come from innovations in software and in equipping machines to appear more "friendly."

Unlike computer hardware, there is no well-defined scale on which evolution of software can be measured. Frameworks for identifying discrete generations of software evolution have been proposed by several authors. Two such frameworks, summarized in Table 1, highlight the facts

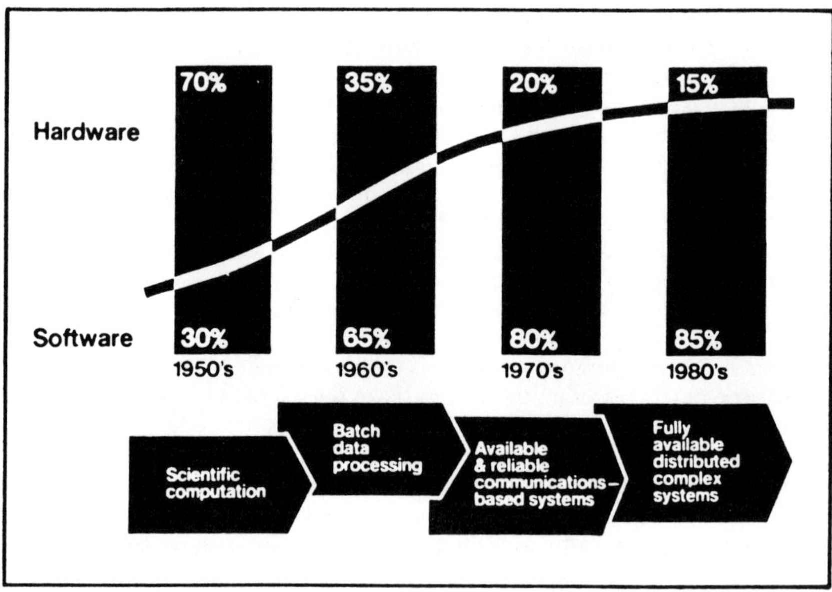

Fig. 2. Hardware/software cost trend [3].

Table 1 Five Generations of Computer Software

	Generation Number				
Characteristic	1	2	3	4	5
A. Withington [4]					
a) Period	1953–1958	1958–1966	1966–1974	1972–1982	1982–
b) New software	None	Compilers, input/output control systems	Multifunction operating systems	Virtual machines	Interactive languages, convenient simulators
c) Facet	Gee-whiz	Paper-pushers	Communicators	Information custodians	Action aids
B. Gupta [5], [6]					
a) Period	1954–1960	1961–1967	1968–1974	1975–1981	1982–
b) Characteristic	Machine languages	Assembly languages	Higher level languages	Management information systems	Decision support syst.; nonprocedure oriented
c) Primary applications	Generating tables	Payroll	Scientific	Business	Diverse

that contemporary software is characterized by emphasis on action and interaction, and that diversity of applications is the norm of the present generation. In this chapter we delineate a current trend in the evolution of software.

II. SOFTWARE

Software resident on a personal computer can be categorized into three hierarchical levels. At the lowest level, directly above the hardware, is the *operating system* which holds responsibility for coordinating system functions such as memory management, task scheduling, user interface, and peripheral control. The next level in the software hierarchy is constituted by *system programs* which include program tools such as editors, assemblers, and compilers. At the highest level are *user application programs*. These are of two generic types: a) programs for particular problems, e.g., a cardiac monitoring program, a diet tracking program; and b) generic tools that facilitate solutions in a wide variety of areas, e.g., spreadsheet programs, database, charting, and graphing programs. The latter category is sometimes termed the fourth generation of programming languages in recognition of the fact that such generic tools offer greater programming functionality and a higher level of portability than third-generation higher level languages such as Fortran and Cobol. A VisiCalc environment, for example, offers users a reasonably friendly environment to execute commands that directly focus on the application problem.

At the dawn of the era of personal computers, a typical application used 3K bytes of memory at a hardware cost of $100 to hold an application program of 1000 lines of assembly language code. Considering productivity in 1975 to be around 10 lines per day of finished, documented, and debugged code and manpower costs of $40 000 including overhead, this program would have taken less than one half of a man-year to complete at a cost of $20 000. By 1980 the software development cost had escalated to nearly half a million dollars if done in assembly language and to $100 000 if done in a higher level language. Such costs now exceed $750 000 for a typical program developed from scratch including runtime libraries and utilities. These industry estimates (Table 2) reflect the underlying fact that software development costs can be prohibitive. In 1980 the development of a reasonably sophisticated spreadsheet package is estimated to have consumed around $500 000 including all coding, testing, documentation, and support necessary to bring the product to market. Because of these high costs, personal computer programs are geared towards activities with a large potential customer base. More-over, smaller organizations with lower overhead structures than large organizations can develop

Table 2 Software Development Costs for a Typical Microprocessor Application (Industry Estimates)

Year	Hardware Cost of Memory	Bytes of Memory	No. Lines of Finished Code[†]	Man Years	Software Development Expenditure
1975	$100	3K	1K	0.5*	$ 20 000
1980	$120	40–45K	13K ASL	6.5**	$450 000
			3K HLL	1.5**	$100 000
1985	$250	500K	20K HLL[††]	~ 7.0***	$875 000

* ~ 10 lines/day; $40K/man year including overhead.
** ~ 10 lines/day; $70K/man year including overhead.
*** ~ 15 lines/day; $125K/man year including overhead; note that this assumes a 50-percent increase in programmer productivity over 1975 and 1980 figures.
[†] Lines refer to debugged, documented, finished lines of code that appear in the final product.
[††] Includes allowance for run-time libraries and utilities.

microcomputer applications for substantially smaller costs than shown in Table 2. Consequently, an entire cottage industry of individual entrepreneurs working out of their homes, or similar low-overhead environments, has provided the lion's share of microcomputer software development activity.

Whereas programs for specialized functions (and smaller customer bases) are typically priced between $500 and $5000, home-oriented software usually is priced under $50. In between these two extremes are the general business packages such as VisiCalc, VisiPlot, and 1-2-3. It is products in this middle range ($100–$500) that hold the potential for revolutionizing the work environment altogether, of making "electronic cottages" [7] a reality, and of further nucleating the widespread use of personal computers.

Interaction with computers is interesting and challenging when a user can do meaningful tasks with it. Otherwise it evokes adverse emotions. "The first of these is a *fear of falling behind*, or a worse manifestation, the *fear of showing it... .* The second observed emotion is a general annoyance with the programming *fraternity* or *priesthood*. The *laity* is made to feel excluded and inferior because they don't know the mystical *incantations* and haven't been *initiated*" [10]. The conscious endeavor towards not intimidating novice users is one of the principal characteristics of newer personal computer software products. Examples include the orientation towards natural languages and the support of speech input and output capabilities that dispense with the need for good typing skills.

One good example of this phenomenon is the predominant use of "menus" in personal computers, while mainframes and minicomputers continue to depend primarily on command languages. Hierarchically organized menus permit users to do complex tasks with efficiency and with no errors since the user is able to select only a "valid" choice. Also, there is no longer any requirement to memorize different options—one needs only to be able to "recognize," rather than recall, an option [11]. While the maximum number of menu options varies from product to product, the number '7' is sometimes chosen as a starting point in systems design based on the hypothesis by Miller [12] that the human being is able to retain 7 ± 2 distinct items for short periods of time. In recent years, the efficacy of alternative menu structures has been studied and published in [13]–[15]. While menu structures differ from program to program, personal computers are standardizing around menu-driven user interfaces. Menu-driven interfaces are already standard in the case of spreadsheet packages which are used for manipulating sets of numbers. Similar techniques are becoming popular for database packages, too.

III. Office Environment

Although promoters of data processing equipment claim that their machines can do almost everything, productivity is certainly not yet rampant in the American office. The increase in

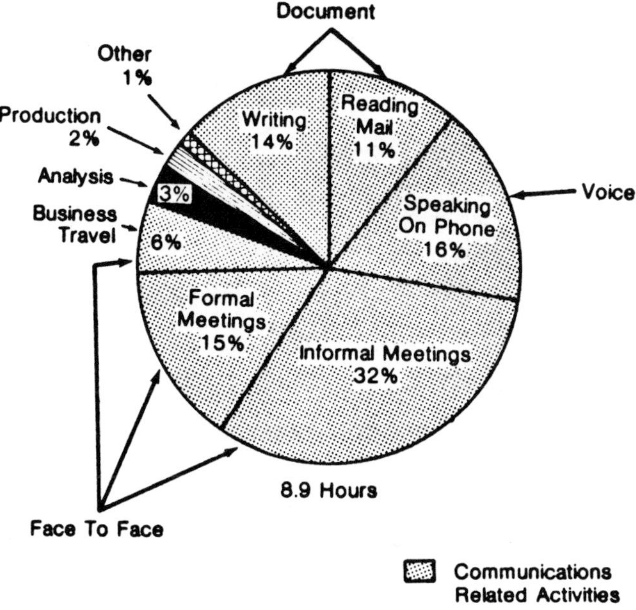

Fig. 3. Display distribution of executive time spent in communications during a typical 8.9-h day [9].

productivity of office workers has been insignificant as compared to the increase in productivity of blue collar workers—and the automated office does little to meet the specific needs of the executive. The ability to process information does not generally aid in the successful communication of information and, consequently, productivity suffers.

Top managers are noted to spend four-fifths of their time attending meetings—delivering or receiving presentations and reports, communicating, and gathering information for successive meetings [8]. Meetings are the most prominent, time-consuming element of an executive's job. The results of an extensive AT & T study (see Figs. 3 and 4 and Table 3) reiterate the fact that since white collar workers spend 80 to 95 percent of their time communicating and managing information, improvement in communication processes has enormous leverage potential on operating expense control, as well as substantial potential for improving the inputs to decisionmaking for managers [9]. Rather than more computing power, executives need more productive and effective communication tools.

One reason why computers have so far failed to serve as effective communication tools is because traditionally computer application software has maintained a strict distinction between different types of information—numeric (figures), text (letters), and images (pictures), making it necessary to use separate application packages for each. Thus word processors could process text but not manipulate numbers, and graphics programs produced colorful video outputs but lacked numeric and text processing capabilities. Although by no means the most complex, the "office" environment involves several types of interrelated information. An annual report, for example, contains accounting numbers, descriptive text, and full color pictures. In the 1970s, computers were used only to generate the numbers. By the early 1980s, computers were used to process and update the text. At present, business personal computers only represent information in numeric form, in text, and in simple charts and graphs. A crucial missing component is the ability to present and manipulate visual, pictorial data. More important is the absent ability to integrate data imagery with textual, numeric, and graphical representations. A new layer of fourth-generation software will bridge the gap from the present position of supporting num-

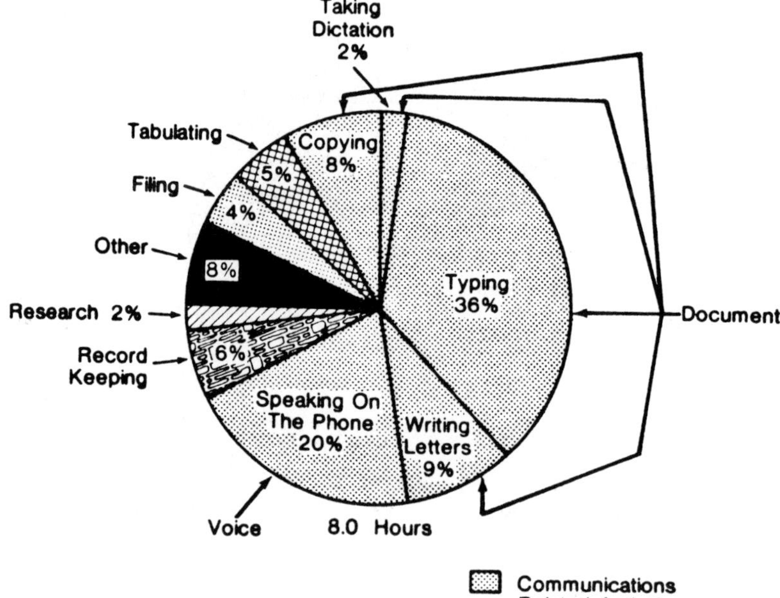

Fig. 4. Display distribution of secretarial time spent in communications during a typical 8.0-h day [9].

Table 3 Distribution of Average Time Spent by All Levels of White Collar Workers in Face-to-Face, Voice, and Document Communications. Remaining Time Also Shown (from [9])

	Executive (percent)	Manager (percent)	Professional (percent)	Secretary (percent)
Face to Face	53	47	23	negl.
Document	25	29	42	55
Voice	16	9	17	20
Total	94	85	82	75
Other	6	15	18	25

bers, text, and transformations on numbers (plotting and charting) to supporting business communications with sophisticated images and color [30].

IV. GRAPHICS

Just as integrated databases replaced the need to duplicate data for use by various application programs, integrated software will eventually permit manipulation of information irrespective of the manner in which it has been stored. In this endeavor towards this final goal, it is first necessary to design more efficient mechanisms of storing and manipulating graphic images. At present, based on the end-application, the use of graphics on personal computers can be classified into four major categories as follows:

a) Home graphics: Packages in this class of software are primarily directed towards entertainment. The emphasis is towards simple animation techniques and the ability to manipulate small objects in real time. A low-resolution output is the general rule. Frequently, the graphics is coupled with an elementary sound output mechanism.

b) Business graphics: This expression connotes the display of business data in the form of line diagrams, bar charts, pie charts, and histograms. VisiPlot and 1-2-3 are examples of software packages that facilitate translation of tables into figures and graphs. With many of these packages, the historical trend can be extrapolated to make forecasts for the future and both past and future datapoints included in the display. The focus in these business graphics packages is on easier comprehension of numbers and trends.

c) Presentation graphics: Packages in this class of software facilitate the creation of pictures for meetings and presentations. Unlike business graphics where the orientation is primarily on the informational content of numeric data, the focus in presentation graphics is towards including numeric, textual, and pictorial information. "Instead of armies of artists manually producing slides, charts and overhead transparencies, much of this work is now being done automatically" [21]. Presentation graphics is one step ahead, and is a superset of traditional business graphics in the evolution of graphic capabilities.

d) Workstation/engineering graphics: By containing more powerful hardware than an average personal computer, a workstation is able to support higher resolution graphics and more extensive computational capabilities. Whereas a two-dimensional representation suffices for business applications, many engineering applications in the CAD and CAM areas need three-dimensional graphics with shading and real-time simulation capability. The diminishing costs of computing power and storage allow such sophisticated graphics capabilities to be incorporated into high-end personal computers. Such software will become widespread before the end of this decade.

We live in a visual world. Color adds depth and effectiveness. Current personal computer technology lacks good color capabilities. Unlike outputs of numeric calculations and word processing where the cosmetic quality of output generated using personal computers can be enhanced using good quality output devices such as laser printers, personal computers are unable to provide good color output because of low screen resolution and the lack of an extensive repertoire of colors commonly found on larger systems. This limitation can be better comprehended by examining the underlying color model for personal computers.

The principal hardware-oriented models are RGB (red, green, blue), CMY (cyan, magenta, yellow), and YIQ (modified RGB broadcast model). These three models are used in color TV monitors, color printing devices, and broadcast TV color systems, respectively. Because these models do not relate directly to our intuitive notions of hue, lightness, and saturation, another set of models known as HSV (hue, saturation, value) and HLS (hue, lightness, saturation) are frequently used.

The most common model is the RGB Cartesian coordinate system. The primary colors (red, green, blue) are additive meaning that individual contributions of each primary color are added together to form the result. The complementary colors (cyan, magenta, and yellow) are subtractive primaries because their effect is to subtract color from white. The RGB color cube shown in Fig. 5 denotes the presence of grey levels along the primary diagonal between black and white.

The Tektronics HLS color model is based on a cylindrical system and represents a geometric representation of the RGB model. Hue, lightness, and saturation represent the three axes in this coordinate system. Hue numbers are measured in degrees around the central axis with blue being arbitrarily assigned a hue angle of zero. The hues are arranged in spectral order with numbers increasing from blue to red to green. Lightness is measured along the vertical axis from 0 which is black to 100 which is white. The saturation axis is radial from the vertical axis and uses numbers that describe the maximum number of saturation for a given lightness level. This model can be represented as a double cone as shown in Fig. 6. All colors at the edge of the cone are assigned a saturation number of 100 although fully saturated colors originate on the lightness plane of 50. This color model—which has been adopted by the ACM Society for Graphics (SIGGRAPH)—is implemented using a raster display system designed such that colors which are combinations of brightness values for each electron gun (RGB) are associated with a look-up table or color map. The number of display colors depends on the number of bit planes/pixel. The bit pattern per pixel is used as an index to the look-up table. For example, if each D-A converter associated with each of three electron guns (RGB) has 4 bits of resolution

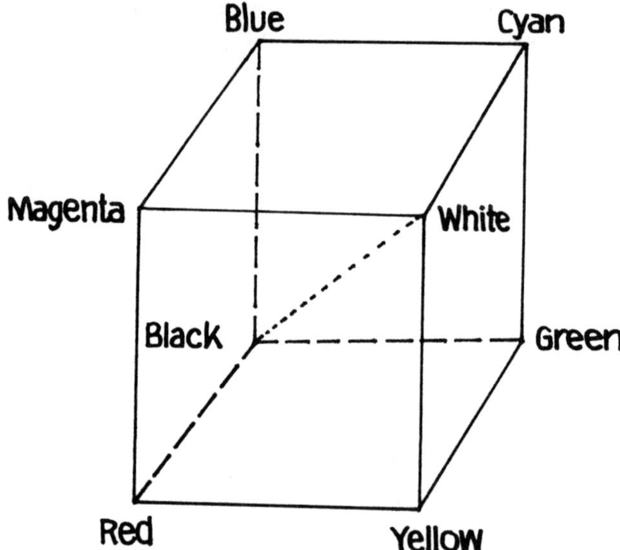

Fig. 5. Red, green, and blue are primaries while cyan, magenta, and yellow are subtractive primitives.

to provide a total of 4096 colors, and if the display system implements 4 bits per pixel (i.e., four display planes), then only 16 colors out of the total of 4096 colors can be displayed at any one time. The design of default color maps for varying dimensions of bit planes is discussed in [22].

As they are based on our concepts of tint, shade, and tone, the HSV and HLS models are more intuitive. However, the implementation of these models requires larger display memory space than normally available in personal computers. Generally, screen resolution is limited by the size of memory and address space. Current personal computers utilize 16K–64K bytes for display, whereas mainframes and professional workstations dedicate between 128K bytes to 4 Mbytes to provide a high-resolution color output.

With the advent of the 256K bit RAM and its 1M bit-chip successor, and the extended computer address spaces of 16M bytes (and even more) available with newer 16/32-bit microprocessors, personal computers will handle up to 4096 colors. This will allow full pictorial representation and the ability for true integration of text, data, and visual graphics. At the present time, however, we must visually accommodate the lower resolution and number of colors. For example, this book is being printed at a resolution of about 300 black dots per inch of white paper. Full color reproduction of images requires similar densities with color dots. However, most personal computers operate with 300–700 dots across the full screen face, which may be up to 8 inches in width, thus yielding a color dot density of only 40–90 dots per inch. To achieve a density of 300 dots per inch and to support 256 colors (out of a total of 4096 colors) on an 8-in × 6-in display surface requires 4M bytes of storage. This is not in the range of current or near-future personal computer systems configurations. Another limiting factor is the computational bandwidth available to provide interaction and manipulation of images on such displays with reasonable response times. For these reasons, personal computers are not commonly used to support three-dimensional graphic manipulations for engineering applications.

Among the various categories of personal computer graphics, the business-oriented environment is rapidly becoming the dominant area [1]. In order to be effective, such graphics packages must contain elements that can enhance the productivity of the business user. Several key elements are described in the following paragraphs.

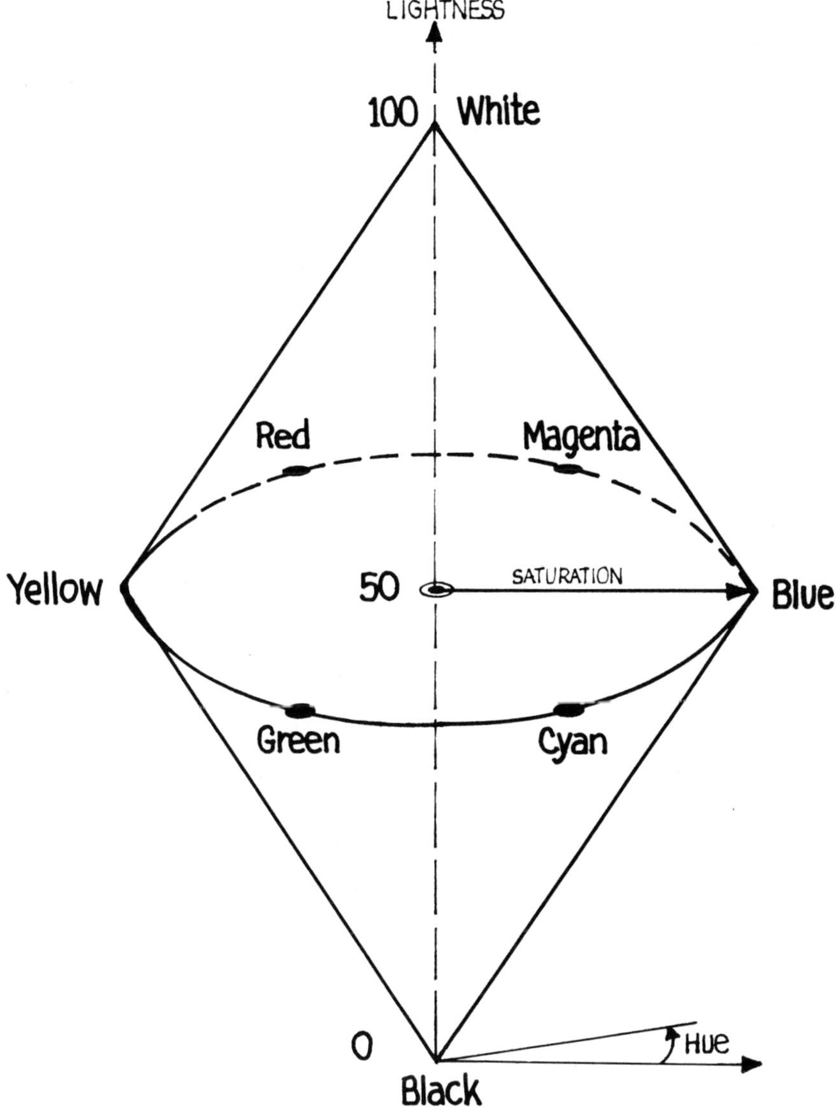

Fig. 6. Double-cone HLS color model.

User-Friendly Interface

Since the beginning of the computer era, users have been forced to struggle with mnemonic and cryptic interfaces that reflect the preferences of hardware designers and programmers. In order to be an effective tool for business use, especially in the graphics area, the application package user interface must be "friendly." This means the interface should not intimidate the user, who is often a first-time computer user. The methodology by which the user directs the operation of the graphics package should reflect an intuitive structure either in commands, menus, or icons. "Help" functions must be backed up by comprehensive and easy-to-read information. Uniformity of the interface across the entire package must be maintained. For example, if certain control or function keys are used to manipulate palette colors in one part of the program, the particular keys must have the same meaning throughout the program. Although the user interfaces should also provide uniformity between families of software products that can run on the same personal computer, the large number of software authors and publishers makes such uniformity very difficult to achieve. The latest generation of windowing software provides a paradigm for providing a uniform user interface at a metalevel. This windowing software provides a single interface for using multiple application packages [30].

Business Graphics

A graphics package for the business user must provide for the automatic plotting of bar, line, and pie charts. Extended functions such as three-dimensional representations, exploded views, and rotation operations are useful but not always essential. Also, the business graphics package must interface to other numeric- and text-oriented packages to capture data for display in a graphics format.

Image Data

A graphics package must provide high-quality images that are capable of being integrated, just as in ordinary life, with text and data. In a business environment it is important to provide pictures of quality comparable to that produced by the corporate art department. The user must be provided with the ability to

- cut and paste arbitrary portions of the image field
- access a large library of prerendered images for incorporation in the presentation information
- manipulate geometric objects whose data structure is in a separate class from pictorial data
- do creative sketching and drawing with a variety of brushes and colors
- store and retrieve integrated presentation material.

Acceptable Output

Business-oriented graphics packages must support a range of output media, both electronic as well as traditional, hard copy. Table 4 illustrates the current personal computer graphic output formats, the normal business-user presentation graphics needs, and the outputs which a graphics software package should provide.

A particular software implementation that fulfills these needs is described in the next section.

Table 4 Business Requirements for Graphics

Most Common PC Graphics Outputs	Business Users Presentation Needs	PC Graphics Software Required Output
Monitor screen	Vu-graphs or foils	Vu-graphs or foils
B & W or color printer/ plotter hardcopy	35-mm slides	35-mm slides
Bit-map data on disk	Projection video	Screen output
	Videotape	Projection video
		Hard copy color

V. Presentation Graphics Software

In the words of an independent software analyst, "What a word processor is to words, VCN ExecuVision is to graphics" [17]. This sentence sums up the essence of this graphics software, released commercially in the fall of 1983 [16], [20]. In designing the product for the personal computer user, VCN ExecuVision has been engineered to enable anyone to design for himself or herself the materials he or she will use in staff meetings, demonstrations, proposals, seminars, and conferences and effectively transforms the personal computer monitor into an artist's canvas. The user can quickly determine and produce the exact look needed to effectively communicate the message.

The program provides a large variety of picture making capabilities. Graphs, charts, and other visual presentations can be drawn, colored, displayed, and modified by the user of the material, not by an in-house or external artist whose time appreciation may be different than the person whose presentation is scheduled for the next morning. A user may choose the style, color, and size of various typefaces for the printed material; one may color-copy, sketch, and manipulate an assortment of forms and elaborate depictions, and create charts and graphs automatically. Electronic cutting and pasting to present numerous images simultaneously and the animation of images using various motion alternatives are other capabilities.

VCN ExecuVision encompasses the following features:

- simple keyboard interface and on-screen explanations of each menu option and function
- easy creation, manipulation, scaling, and movement of objects and images
- automatic pie, bar, and line graphs
- ten different text fonts and typefaces with rescaling and color options
- electronic cut-and-paste capabilities
- complete and continuous color copying for exact copies of any image (either on-screen, through printing capabilities, or when transferred to slides through appropriate hardware)
- multiple built-in animation techniques
- color command to paint areas, objects, images, and texts with 64 color schemes
- availability of art libraries containing professionally rendered images on slides and floppy disks for incorporation into presentations
- electronic tool box for drafting and designing of images
- image manipulation capability to enable the user to catalog, arrange, reorder, and store images with directories for print and on-screen review
- manual and automatic run-time options for time-sequencing
- ten speed variations for animation motion techniques
- compatible for VisiTrend/Plot program.

VCN ExecuVision represents an attempt to develop graphic capabilities that provide a major increase in flexibility and functionality over the graphic software tools hitherto available on personal computers. The primary emphasis is towards enabling graphic information to be generated and to be manipulated with as little effort as generation and manipulation of numbers on traditional computers, and similar operations on textual information using word processors.

The above task has inherent complications. For centuries the four fundamental operations of arithmetic have been widely known, and all other operations can be decomposed into these fundamental operations. Operations with textual information, for example, replace "programme" to "program," can also be easily decomposed into well-defined compare and replace operations. Such well-defined operations are, however, less identifiable in the case of pictorial information. Also, definition of pictures using complicated mathematical structures would defeat the objective of ease-of-use.

In general, a picture consists of several, in fact many, different entities. A forest landscape may contain trees, hills, and water; a city landscape may contain cars, buildings, and people; and a picture of a person such as Albert Einstein will contain a face with very individualized features. In order to generate some basic framework for pictorial representation and manipulation, pictorial structures have been categorized into two sets as follows:

a) *Regular structures:*   These structures have definite shapes and can be defined unambiguously using simple geometric concepts. Rectangles, circles, and triangles are examples of such regular structures. A circle is defined by its center, its radius, and its color. A rectangle is defined by a vertex, its length, its height, and its color, etc. By simple variations in these parameters, it is feasible to *move*, to *copy*, to *scale* (up or down in either one or both dimensions), or to change the color of the structure. An organizational chart, for example, can be generated using several rectangles, connecting lines, and letters. In VCN ExecuVision, such regular structures are termed *objects*.

b) *Irregular structures*: Structures such as trees and peoples' faces fall under this category. In such cases, the first problem is drawing the structure. The second is of manipulation. While graphic operations like *move* and *copy* still make sense, a one-dimensional scaling feature is rather irrelevant in this case.

Primitive graphics software focuses only on a); hence it is used primarily for drawing line charts, pie graphs, and to represent time variations on a set of data. Implementing complex structures on personal computers in a meaningful way represents the real challenge.

A typical user neither has the inclination nor the ability to spend hours after hours drawing a single picture on a personal computer. To mitigate this problem, a two-pronged strategy was adopted. On one side the graphics software has been backed by several libraries of finished pictures with each library containing hundreds of pictures pertaining to a particular profession or discipline. On the other side, a set of programs has been developed that allows pictures to be merged in any way and further enables the user to supplement such pictorial information using the *menu-driven interface*. In order to elaborate on the latter approach, we distinguish between two forms of pictorial representation. A *slide* refers to a picture occupying an entire screen. Such slides can be stored on and retrieved from the disk. Retrieval of a slide erases the previous picture on the display. A *pix* is a subset of a picture. The size and content of a pix is determined by the user by moving and scaling a *pix-rectangle* on the screen and enclosing the desired section of the screen in this rectangle. Like a slide, a pix can also be stored and retrieved. However, unlike a slide, retrieval of a pix from the disk does not cause erasure of the previous information on the screen. This strategy of *pix* allows users to create small pictures one at a time, to modify each picture individually, to store them on a disk, and to compose a larger picture using the pix library—the latter comprised of both user-generated pictures and pictures from the library supplied.

A user can sketch a picture or a pix using the cursor. Altering the size of the cursor leads to the provision of *sketch-brushes* of different thickness. The line is drawn as the user moves the cursor in any direction. Alternatively, the beginning point and the end point can be specified, and a line connecting these two points is drawn by the software. The color of the line can be changed using a function key. The system also provides a flexible electronic "scissors" function which enables cutting of "pieces" of the pictures and their "re-pasting" at different locations on the screen. For example, if a person is promoted, the organizational chart need not be redrawn anew—only the block affected can be cut out, that is, deleted, from its present position and reinserted at a different position. This electronic cut-and-paste function can be used for any object, text, pix, or slide element.

VCN ExecuVision is designed to run on an IBM Personal Computer or any compatible personal computer with 128K bytes of memory, two floppy disk drives, and a color display. The impact of the 64 alternative color schemes, used for providing background and foreground colors, is somewhat lost if a black-and-white display is used. The software supports a variety of hard copy printing styles: reductions, enlargements, horizontals, verticals, and continuous printing. Traditionally, when one runs a color picture through a black-and-white process, such as ordinary photocopying, the resulting picture is a poor representation of the original picture—the different colors are not discernable separately on the copy. Distinction between different colors on a black-and-white printer is provided by printing colors in various shades of grey. This is another example of an area where technology has existed for providing better quality outputs, but rarely have software designers exploited this capability.

Seeing a single slide is one thing, seeing an aggregate of slides is another. VCN ExecuVision supports slide shows in which the transition from one slide to another can be controlled either manually (pressing a key causes display of the next slide) or automatically (by invoking the AUTO-RUN feature). More significant is the support of *animation* techniques which give an illusion of seeing a running movie rather than a slide show. Animation gives the impression of a letter slowly falling down in a letter box or a bird flying across a city horizon. In traditional animation techniques, the sequence of slides is retrieved at frequent intervals of time from storage and displayed on the screen [18]. This method consumes too much storage space and requires very fast disk access times in order to perceive fast transitions on the screen. In VCN ExecuVision, only a single slide is retrieved in its entirety from the disk. Subsequent information relates only to the particular subset of the slide that needs to be moved. This technique allows animation effects to be created using relatively slow speed secondary storage devices.

The IBM Personal Computer supports only two fonts. VCN ExecuVision offers ten different text fonts. Further, the text can be "written" in any color, and the sizes of the characters can be scaled. Both the scale and the color options are selected by using function keys. The availability of diverse font styles, supplemented by the pre-rendered library of borders, enhances the quality of slides (see Fig. 7(a) through (d)). The impact of changing colors is illustrated in Fig. 8(a) through (d).

As in the case of all sophisticated software packages, storage space is always at a premium. In this particular case, the problem is amplified because of the support of several types of fonts and hundreds of images in the library. Each slide contains about a quarter million pixels, and several bits are required to store a single colored pixel. Thus only 20 slides can generally be stored on a single floppy disk. A new data compression algorithm was devised to mitigate this problem. This algorithm reduces storage requirements by a factor ranging typically between two and ten. A hundred slides of average complexity or about 30 complex slides can now be stored on a disk. Both compression and decompression are done on-the-fly and the entire process is transparent to the user.

The full potential of the above set of fairly sophisticated graphical capabilities can be tapped without undergoing lengthy training or memorizing codes and numbers. The entire process is done through a hierarchical menu procedure which displays to the user the options that are available; selecting an option results in the display of alternatives possible under that option, and so on. In spite of these facilities, if a user does perform an illegal operation, for example, attempts to write beyond the boundary of the screen, the erroneous user command is automatically overridden. The user is cautioned that the last command was ineffective and why it was so.

Fig. 9(a) through (f) depicts the sequence of operations involved in the generation of a final picture. The inclusion of text in these pictures allows them to speak for themselves. Aggregates of such pictures comprise an electronic book. Feiner, Nagy, and Van Dam have stated: "Paper documents are inadequate for creating, storing and accessing much of today's information.... They are difficult to keep up-to-date where timeliness is crucial. They provide static, predominantly textual displays where dynamic, pictorial representations of complex information are becoming increasingly important" [19]. While these three authors used a DEC VAX 11/780 to implement their interactive graphic system, VCN ExecuVision uses much cheaper hardware. The samples displayed here are examples of the unprecedented graphics quality generated using inexpensive personal computers. Such capabilities have so far been provided by dedicated graphic systems costing more by an order of magnitude. Rather than introducing any dramatically new technologies, VCN ExecuVision brings sophisticated graphics capabilities to the realm of personal computers thus vastly expanding the horizons of personal computer applications in all four domains—office, home, science, and education.

VI. APPLICATIONS

Personal computers have so far been displacing calculators, typewriters, and word processors. The advent of presentation graphics software equips these computers to replace overhead projectors and slide projectors, too. Besides providing a more efficient mechanism for storing

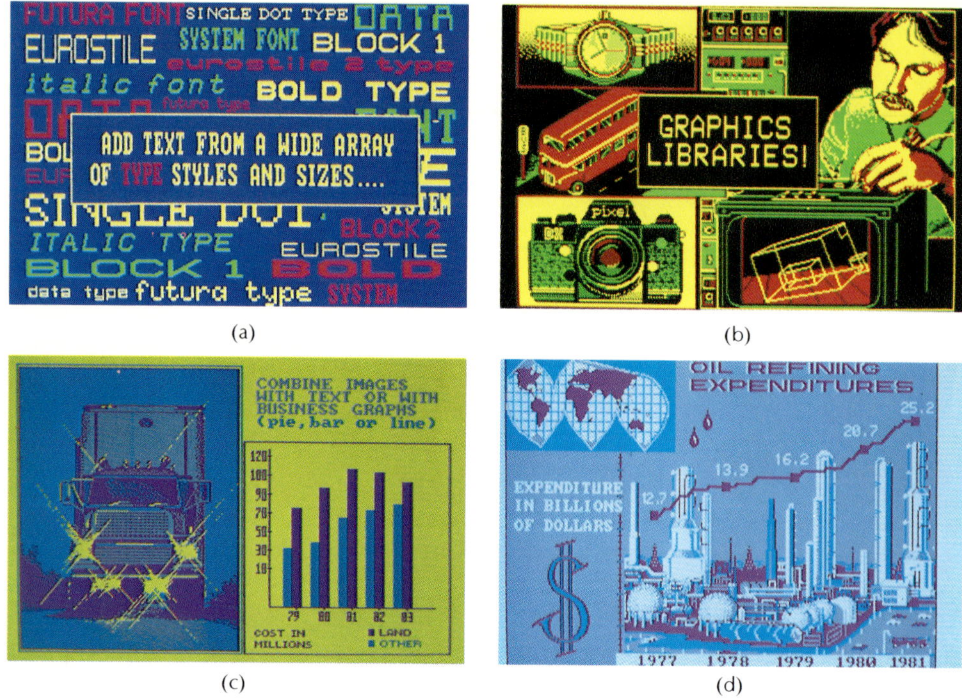

(a)   (b)
(c)   (d)

Fig. 7. (a) and (b) Samples of alternative fonts and pre-rendered images, respectively. Parts (c) and (d) emphasize the greater impact of images which integrate numeric, textual, graphical, and pictorial information in a coherent and logical manner.

(a)   (b)
(c)   (d)

Fig. 8. (a)–(d) Role of colors in presenting alternative impressions of the same picture. The same New York skyline is perceived as (a) winter, (b) spring, (c) summer, and (d) fall. The change is accomplished by simply altering the foreground and background colors.

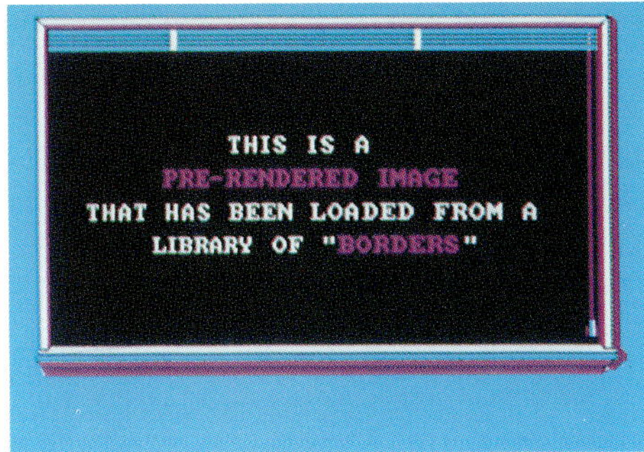

(a)

(b)

(c)

(d)

(e)

(f)

Fig. 9. (a)–(f) Steps involved in generating a final slide. A pre-rendered image is first loaded (a), and augmented using additional images (b). Part (c) highlights the role of "cut-and-paste" to generate copies of images. Part (d) shows the impact of altering colors. Additional images have been incorporated in (e). The final slide, ready for use in a presentation, is shown in (f). Note that the integration of text in the respective figures enhances the value of each figure.

ideas and slides, such software holds tremendous potential for improving the productivity of office workers, sales personnel, and especially top-level executives.

So far, the dominant use of home personal computers has been for recreational purposes. This explains the myriad of game packages that blitz the television advertising time. No wonder children are heavy users of home computers, especially in the first few months of personal computer acquisition. Personal computers are useful aids in doing school assignments and in learning through self-paced courses. An extension of VCN ExecuVision geared towards training applications is expected to be released commercially during this year.

But perhaps the most significant use of graphics capabilities will be in dedicated systems, in professional workstations, and in the area of CAD/CAM. The ability to treat pictorial information in a manner similar to other types of information allows personal computers to serve as the basic building unit in such systems. This trend will be reinforced by the commercial availability of inexpensive optical disks with storage capacities of 100M bytes and more. With each optical disk capable of holding thousands of pictures, users have a virtually infinite selection of pictures to choose from without having to change the disk.

In parallel, technological evolution is facilitating newer low-cost mechanisms to produce color hard copy outputs. Color images are printed in the same way as used for displaying monochrome images. However, in this case, four sets of halftone dots are printed. In addition to the three primary colors, black is printed separately as combinations of the primary colors are unable to generate a deep black color. Different color dots are printed very close to each other, and the human eye spatially integrates the picture to present a continuous colored appearance. As in the case of displays, more colors can be displayed at the expense of resolution. As memory costs diminish, and as color printers become progressively cheaper, color printers will eventually replace the present generation of black-and-white printers just as color photography has virtually replaced black-and-white photography. The availability of good color printed outputs will add a whole new dimension of personal computer applications.

The integration of personal computer technology and efficient graphic methodologies has far-reaching ramifications for the whole computer industry as analyzed in the next section.

VII. Frameworks for Analyzing Trends

So far technologies relating to storage and manipulation of numeric information, textual information, and pictorial information have evolved independent of each other. When a figure, say 5, is stored as a number, it is converted into an equivalent binary floating-point number and stored. The same figure is stored differently when it is stored as part of the text by a word processor. A graphics package stores the figure as a bit-map comprised of dots. The diverse methods for storing the same number makes it impossible to manipulate the information without first converting it from one format to another. As techniques evolve to mitigate these overheads, the demarcation between different categories of computers will become blurred.

At present, computing systems can be categorized into six distinct classes as follows:

- mainframes—32-bit computer systems used for supporting large integrated databases
- minicomputers—16/32-bit architectures which originated for scientific and engineering computing but now used heavily for business computing
- workstations—primarily engineering-oriented single-user systems with software and hardware dedicated to image processing, communications, and local database applications
- word processing—8/16-bit machines primarily based in the office environment for text and document preparation
- personal computers—8/16-bit architectures representing the latest innovations in desktop computing
- calculators—1/16-bit architectures with dedicated functionality for scientific, engineering, and business calculations

A plot of these six categories of computing systems on a cost/performance grid reveals a

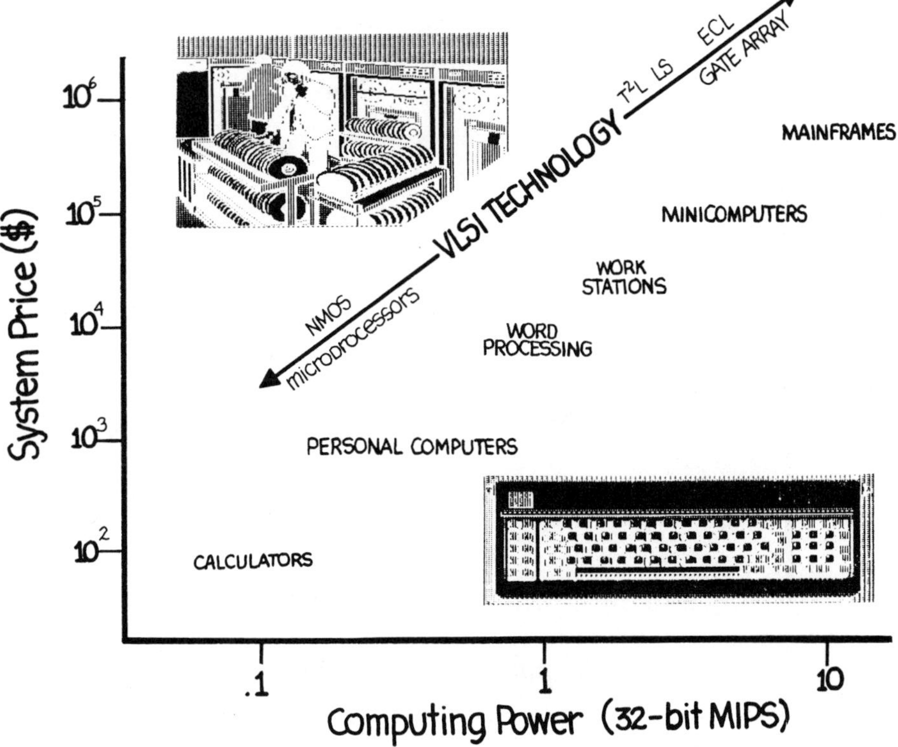

Fig. 10. Six categories of computing systems.

distinctly linear relationship as shown in Fig. 10. Advances in hardware and software are giving rise to overlap between adjacent computing categories in the spectrum. For instance, the 32-bit minicomputers of the VAX 11/780 or MV 10000 class are starting to overlap with the low-end 4300 mainframe computing systems. In another area, professional workstations are starting to encroach upon traditional 16-bit minicomputer markets. The rapid growth of personal computers is posing a threat to the traditional word processing computing systems (for instance, the IBM Display Writer is being converted to personal computer compatibility), and in some cases the 16-bit personal computer architectures are affecting the market for 16-bit minicomputer systems. The shifts along the cost–performance grid, delineated in Fig. 11, also emphasize that newer 16/32-bit personal computers have the functionality and computing power of previous generation workstations and minicomputers.

As at present, computing systems will continue to be distinguished by the applications software made available as well as by the marketing and distribution channels into which each system is directed. For example, when a 16/32-bit personal computer that is capable of performing scientific and engineering computations for real-time process control is marketed to the business community, it will be designated as a desktop productivity tool and offered with spreadsheet, accounting, and word processing programs. Marketing considerations will continue to drive personal computers towards business, education, and stand-alone scientific computing. Over the next five years a significant realignment of the six major categories will occur. Instead of being a separate computing category, word processing will be incorporated as a software application in a personal computer or workstation environment. Minicomputers will exist only as high-end 32-bit systems that compete with the middle- to low-end mainframe market. Workstations and personal computers will evolve into the general category of desktop computing systems. Calculators will become more specialized and narrower in market focus as

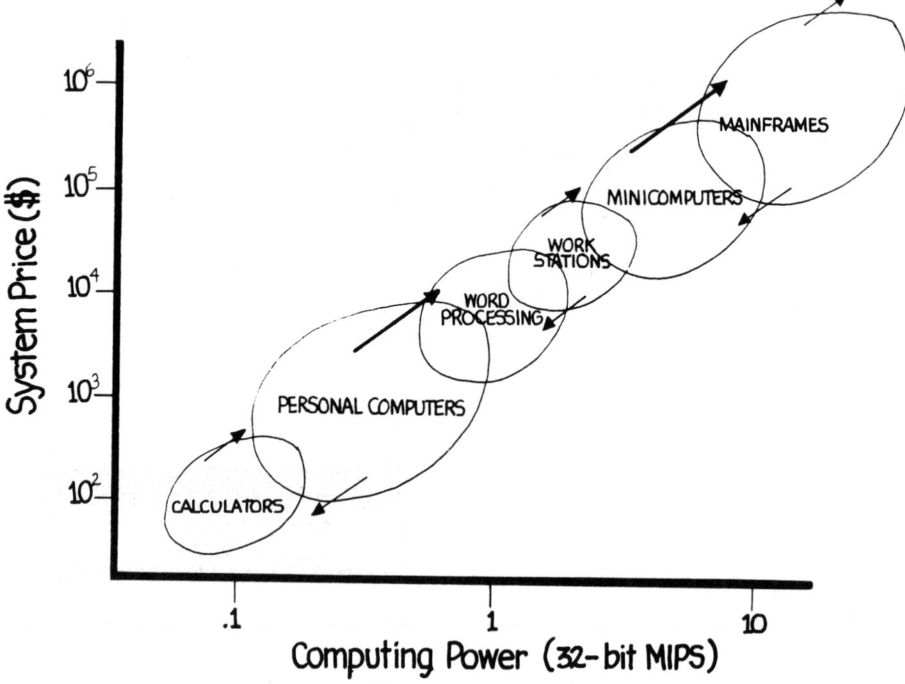

Fig. 11. Overlapping price–pertormance among the major categories of computing. Arrows indicate major shifts in price–performance as systems employ new technologies, achieve economics of scale, and/or expand into new markets.

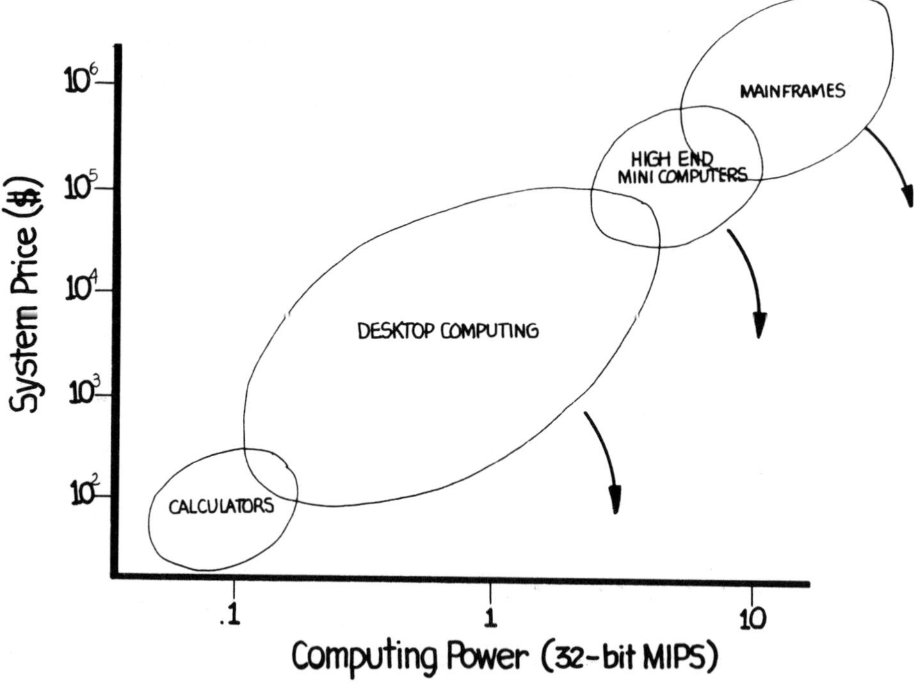

Fig. 12. Continual shift of price–performance axis enables increased computing power at the same price and/or the same computing power at an asymptotically decreasing price. These trends will cause the major computing categories to gradually rotate towards the horizontal axis—more computing power for decreasing amounts of money.

the personal computer becomes cheaper and invades the home. This situation is shown in Fig. 12. At present, the cost and performance of personal computers varies linearly over the spectrum ranging from low-cost home computer systems, through the floppy-based business system, to the $10 000 Winchester-based personal computing system. Technology and market forces will cause the movement of these systems horizontally from left to right as the same computing power is achieved at decreasing costs over time. Since the same set of basic technologies (VLSI, microelectronics, magnetics, electromechanics) is used, the entire spectrum of personal computing systems will shift towards the horizontal axis. Although the linear relationship between cost and computing power will still be preserved, the line relating them (in Figs. 10–12) will rotate clockwise over time, and personal computers will encompass the whole range of functionality presently performed using word processors, minicomputers, and even current generation workstations. Like the contemporary automobile which has replaced several traditional modes of transportation, personal computers are poised to become the dominant category of computers of the 1980s.

References

[1] H. D. Toong and A. Gupta, "Personal computers," *Sci. Amer.*, vol. 247, no. 6, pp. 88–99, Dec. 1982.
[2] L. M. Branscomb, "Bringing computing to people: The broadening challenge," *Computer*, p. 71, July 1982.
[3] ______, "Electronics and computers: An overview," *Science*, vol. 215, no. 4534, p. 759, Feb. 12, 1982.
[4] F. G. Withington, "Five generations of computers," *Harvard Bus. Rev.*, pp. 99–108, July–Aug. 1974.
[5] A. Gupta, "Emerging trends in office technology," in *Office Information Systems*, N. Naffah, Ed. Amsterdam, The Netherlands: North Holland, 1982.
[6] ______, "An overview of contemporary office automation technology," *Behaviour Informat. Technol.* (London, England: Taylor and Francis), vol. 1, no. 3, pp. 217–236, July–Sept. 1982.
[7] A. Toffler, *The Third Wave.* New York: William Morrow, 1980.
[8] H. Mintzberg, *The Nature of Managerial Work.* Englewood Cliffs, NJ: Prentice Hall, 1980.
[9] S. L. Teger, "Factors impacting the evolution of office automation," *Proc. IEEE*, vol. 71, no. 4, pp. 503–511, Apr. 1983.
[10] R. A. Thompson, "Users' perceptions with experimental services and terminals," *IEEE J. Selected Areas Commun.*, vol. SAC-1, no. 2, pp. 337–342, Feb. 1983.
[11] J. D. Grimes, "A knowledge oriented view of user interfaces," in *Proc. Hawaii Int. Conf. Syst. Sci.* (Honolulu, Jan. 1979), pp. 158–163.
[12] G. A. Miller, "The magical number seven, plus or minus two; Some limits in our capacity for processing information," *Psychol. Rev.*, vol. 63, pp. 81–97, Mar. 1956.
[13] H. Dunsmore, "Designing an interactive facility for non-programmers," in *Proc. ACM Nat. Conf.*, pp. 475–483, 1980.
[14] S. K. Card, "User perceptual mechanisms in the search of computer command menus," in *Proc. Human Factors in Computer Systems Conf.* (Gaithersburg, MD, Mar. 1982), pp. 190–196.
[15] R. B. Allen, "Cognitive factors in the use of menus and trees: An experiment," *IEEE J. Selected Areas Commun.*, vol. SAC-1, no. 2, pp. 333–336, Feb. 1983.
[16] V. Puglia, "Pretty pixels," *PC Mag.*, vol. 3, no. 4, pp. 143–146, Mar. 6, 1984.
[17] W. J. Hawkins, "Bits and bytes," *Popular Sci.*, Jan. 1984.
[18] A. C. Kay, "Microelectronics and the personal computer," *Sci. Amer.*, pp. 124–135, Sept. 1977.
[19] S. Feiner, S. Nagy, and A. Van Dam, "An experimental system for creating and presenting interactive graphical documents," *ACM Trans. Graphics*, vol. 1, no. 1, pp. 59–77, Jan. 1982.
[20] *VCN ExecuVision—The Presentation Graphics Program.* Cambridge, MA: Visual Communications Network, and Englewood Cliffs, NJ: Prentice-Hall, 1983.
[21] T. Whitted, "Some recent advances in computer graphics," *Science*, vol. 215, pp. 767–774, Feb. 12, 1982.
[22] D. H. Straayer, "Hoisting the color standard," *Comput. Des.*, pp. 123–130, July 1982.
[23] S. Jessen and K. Pannill, "Device independent color graphics language for micros," *Comput. Des.*, pp. 137–141, July 1982.
[24] M. F. Gordon and S. V. Cope, "Coprocessing to ease the graphics burden," *Comput. Des.*, pp. 147–152, July 1982.
[25] C. L. Denbrook, "Artistry in layers: Generating color transparencies," *Comput. Des.*, pp. 155–163, July 1982.
[26] D. S. Roark, "Toward realtime interactive color graphics," *Comput. Des.*, pp. 167–173, July 1982.
[27] F. E. Langhorst, "Working toward standards in graphics," *Comput. Des.*, pp. 177–182, July 1982.
[28] J. Richardson, "Bit map brings refined graphics to personal work station," *Electronics*, pp. 133–136, Nov. 17, 1982.
[29] M. W. Dickens and L. A. Dorie, "Chips of many colors," *Comput. Des.*, pp. 113–118, July 1982.
[30] F. Guterl, "Personal computers," *IEEE Spectrum*, vol. 21, no. 1, pp. 41–46, Jan. 1984.

14
The Architecture of the Lisa™ Personal Computer

BRUCE DANIELS

Apple Computer Inc. has been the company that made personal computers into consumer items. In keeping up with their reputation of translating ideas from the laboratory to working devices of general interest, Apple Computer Inc. refined known concepts and integrated them into the Lisa computer system. This chapter focuses on software issues and, in particular, on the user interface which allows novice users to quickly grasp the techniques needed to solve problems using this computer.

The Editors

I. Background

In 1979 there was a desire within Apple Computer Inc. to develop a new kind of personal computer product. Personal computers like the Apple II made computing affordable enough to meet the needs of a single person. For just a few thousand dollars, one could purchase a real computer to do word processing, accounting, spreadsheet calculations, and other applications. However, there is a critical limitation with such personal computers, as well as with the older minicomputers and mainframe computers. All these computers are difficult to learn to use. They require the understanding of a whole world of new computer concepts and jargon such as programs, data files, file directories, command languages, etc. Because these computers operate in ways that are not even self-consistent, they present a formidable barrier to their use [19].

It has been observed by the training department of Apple Computer Inc. that it takes about 20 to 30 hours of instruction and practice before a person can learn enough to begin using a traditional computer. This represents a real obstacle to the widespread use of computers to help solve people's problems. Most people are not willing or able to spend the time required to learn to use a traditional computer. Such computers are unfortunately limited to those people who are computer proficient or are willing to become proficient.

The Lisa Charter

The Lisa charter was to build a revolutionary computer that was truly easy to use and thereby to mitigate the limitation of existing computers. A computer which is *revolutionary* may not be compatible with existing products or even with various industry standards and practice. Naturally the Lisa would not be incompatible just for the sake of being different but to be better. Developing a computer which is an order of magnitude easier to use than traditional computers requires major departures.

The author is with Apple Computer Inc., Cupertino, CA 95014, USA.

™Lisa is a Registered Trademark of Apple Computer Inc.

Design Goals

The first design goal for the Lisa was to be intuitive. This implied departing from traditional computer usage which employs textual communication through a formal command language and with an alien vocabulary. Only by building on what the user already knows and working the way the user expects could the Lisa fulfill its charter.

The second goal was that the Lisa be consistent. If a capability works a certain way in one part of the system, then it must work the same way throughout the system. This means that once the user learns to use a standard feature in one place, then he automatically knows how to use it everywhere. More complex capabilities are built on the principles that the user has already learned. Therefore, complex tasks are possible with only a little more effort.

The third goal was an integrated system conforming to the ways in which people actually work. Day-to-day work consists of a variety of diverse activities that are in progress at the same time. People should not be required to terminate one activity before starting another. Instead people should be allowed to easily switch back and forth from one to another. These activities may be related so that information from one activity should be transferable to another with minimum effort.

The fourth goal was to get enough performance to do the job and do it in a way that minimizes its cost and complexity. High system performance is necessary to satisfy the heavy demands of the unique Lisa software, particularly its graphics capabilities. However, high performance is not inexpensive. It increases the complexity, the speed, and therefore the cost of the processor, the hardware bus, memory, etc.

The fifth goal was to provide an open architecture to facilitate the addition of new software, hardware, and peripherals by not only Apple Computer Inc. but also other developers. The Lisa system was announced with a rather extensive selection of hardware and software. However, the Lisa must be expandable to be able to continue to meet all the needs of its diverse community of users.

The sixth goal was reliability. The Lisa must operate day after day in a correct and accurate fashion. When a rare failure occurs, the problem should be quickly detected, isolated, and fixed. After such a failure when the system is restarted, the user's data must be in a state just as they were before the failure.

The Lisa's final goal was to be pleasing and fit naturally into the everyday work environment. It should not consist of units interconnected with a maze of cables or be a massive and noisy cabinet sitting beside the desk.

II. THE LISA HARDWARE

The Lisa hardware [3] consists of a compact, desktop unit that contains the screen, removable power supply, hardware boards, and the floppy disk unit. In addition, a detachable keyboard, mouse, hard disk drives, printers, and other peripherals plug into the main unit as illustrated in Fig. 1. The hardware modules inside the unit are accessed by removing the front and back panels which causes the Lisa to be turned off by the panel safety interlocks. The entire unit can be easily disassembled for service in less than a minute without any tools.

The Lisa hardware consists of four main logic boards: a processor board, an I/O board, and two memory boards. The mother board provides the buses that interconnect these main logic boards. A small video board generates analog signals that actually drive the monitor. Three expansion slots on the mother board accommodate additional logic boards.

The Lisa Processor

Initially, the possibility of using a special Apple Computer Inc. designed processor was investigated. This processor would have provided a special instruction set tailored for the efficient execution of Pascal code. It was to be constructed out of standard 2901 bit-slice microcode circuits. However, designing a new instruction set and its processor for the Lisa

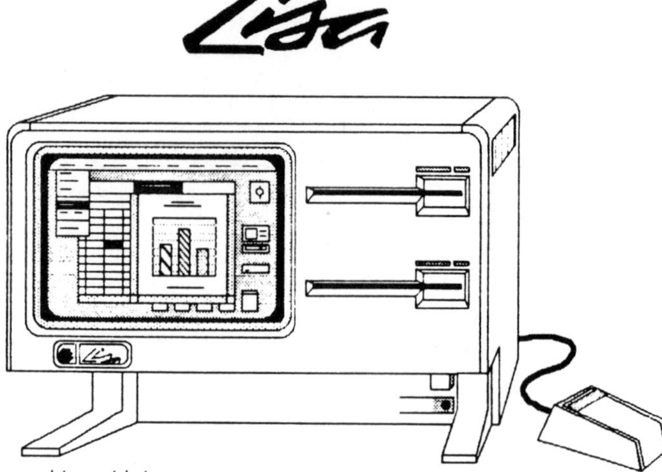

Fig. 1. The Lisa machine with its mouse.

could not be justified on economic or engineering grounds. The cost of a standard, off-the-shelf processor drops significantly with mass manufacturing.

Existing 8-bit processors did not offer the levels of high performance that was necessary. The 16-bit processors offered better performance but suffered from a limited architecture. The Motorola MC68000, which had just become available, was chosen as it had a rich architecture with a 32-bit internal data path, multiple addressing modes, and an addressing range of 16M bytes [18]. The powerful set of instructions and their fast execution offered high performance. The broad repertoire of instructions could compile high-level languages efficiently. In particular, since the majority of the Lisa software was to be written in Pascal, it was important to minimize the code size.

The Memory Management Unit

The MC68000 processor generates 24-bit logical addresses to access data and instructions. Therefore, it provides a logical address space of 16M bytes. In the Lisa this 16M-byte logical address space is divided into 128 segments. Each segment consists of up to 128K bytes in blocks of 512 bytes. The upper 7 bits of a 24-bit logical address is the segment number and the remaining 17 bits is the offset within that segment. The offset consists of 8 upper bits which is the logical block number and 9 bits of the displacement within the block. This can be seen in Fig. 2. To access actual locations in the Lisa hardware, logical addresses are translated into physical addresses by a section of logic on the processor board known as the memory management unit (MMU) [24]. The MMU hardware permits the operating system to control the entire relocation process. The MMU prevents a particular process from accessing areas of memory outside of the portion assigned to it.

The Lisa's RAM memory occupies 2M bytes of physical address space. This would imply that only 16 segments, each of size 128K bytes, could be meaningfully used. However, each segment does not necessarily occupy the full 128K bytes allotted to it in logical address space. Each segment can be mapped into as little as one 512-byte block. Therefore, more than 16 logical segments can map into 2M-byte physical memory. Areas larger than 128K bytes can be accommodated by treating multiple logically contiguous segments as one segment. The translation of a logical address to a physical address by the MMU is performed on a segment-by-segment basis. Associated with each segment in the MMU is its origin which is the 12-bit block number in the physical address space where the corresponding segment begins. The logical block number from bits 9–16 of the logical address is added to the segment's origin value to produce the physical block number to be accessed. The nine displacement bits from the logical

Logical Address (24 bits)

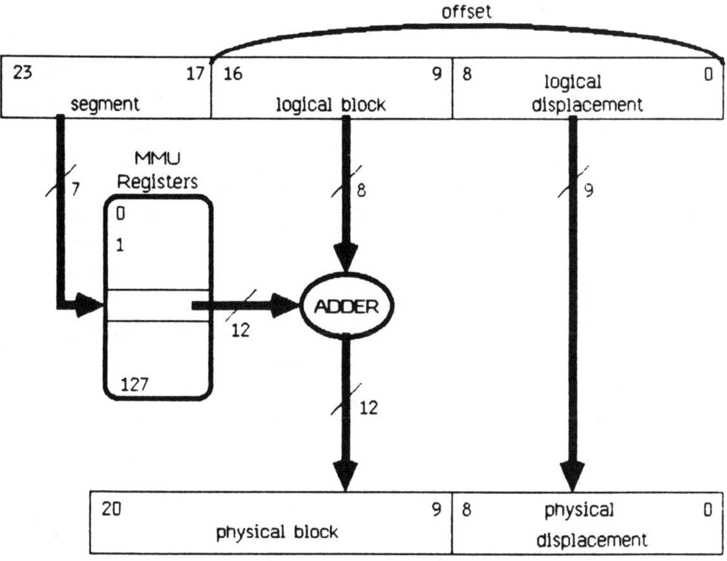

Physical Address (21 bits)

Fig. 2. MMU address transformation.

address translate directly into the physical displacement. This translation process is illustrated in Fig. 2.

The MMU also performs access checks to verify that the requested access is allowed. The MMU checks each access to ensure that it does not exceed the bounds of the specified segment. In addition, an attempt to access a segment which is not mapped or an attempt to write into a read-only segment will generate an access violation. These access violations trap to the operating system for handling.

Within the MMU there are four distinct sets of translation registers, each representing a different mapping from logical addresses into physical addresses. Each set is called a *context*. Only one context is current at any given time. Context 0 is reserved for use by the operating system. Contexts 1, 2, and 3 are used for client processes supported by the operating system. However, more than three processes are possible by using the three MMU contexts as a "cache" of the three most recently used processes. By simply switching contexts, rapid switching among processes and the operating system is accomplished. The Lisa automatically selects context 0 whenever an access is made in Supervisor mode. Thus a TRAP instruction can be used to generate a call from a user process to the operating system. Normally the context is changed while executing in the operating system in Supervisor mode. Execution in the new context begins when user mode is entered.

The Lisa Display

Traditional personal computers employ a text-only display that restricts the output to a limited set of characters at fixed positions on the screen. The Lisa uses a high-resolution bit-mapped display which allows virtually unlimited graphics and the use of multiple sizes and styles of text fonts, including proportionally spaced fonts. Considerable time and effort went into the selection of the dimensions, resolution, composition, and refresh rate of the Lisa's display.

When the refresh rate of the screen is too slow, it produces a maddening flicker of the screen. A high refresh rate demands a higher memory access bandwidth which requires either fast and expensive RAMs or it significantly degrades system performance. On the other hand, a slower refresh rate can be employed if one uses a slow phosphor in the CRT. However, a slow phosphor causes objects removed from the display to slowly fade away on the screen and moving objects to smear. It was found after much experimentation that a responsive yet solid display required a moderately fast phosphor and a noninterlaced refresh rate of 60 Hz [22], [23].

Another important property of a display is its dimensions. When the development of the Lisa began, some research computers, for example see [28], provided a *full page* bit-mapped display that allowed a complete 8 1/2- by 11-in sheet of paper, or up to 66 lines by 102 characters to be shown at once. However, the CRT tube for such a large display is rather expensive. In addition, a full page display places great demands on the memory access bandwidth. For example, a full page display requires a bit map approximately 768 pixels wide by 1024 high, which corresponds to 96K bytes of memory. With a screen refresh rate of 60 Hz, a memory bandwidth of 5.76M bytes per second would be required for just the video alone!

Although a full page display is convenient, the Lisa's half page display provides most of the benefits but at a considerably reduced cost and complexity. A *half page* display still shows the full 8 1/2-in width of a page but only about 5 or 6 inches of the height. Such a smaller display reduces the video bandwidth requirements by half. Another way that the Lisa reduces the video bandwidth is to employ different resolutions for the horizontal and vertical dimensions. The most demanding use of the video resolution is for the display of text. However, the display of sharp and accurate text requires a higher resolution in the horizontal dimension than it does in the vertical dimension. Therefore, on the Lisa display there are 3 pixels in the horizontal dimension for every 2 pixels in the vertical. These different resolutions do complicate, slightly, the design of the Lisa graphics software. For example, the software must remember that a graphical object 150 by 100 appears as a square, however 100 by 100 is a rectangle. Because of its half page size and different resolutions, the bit map for the display (720 pixels wide by 364 pixels high) requires only 32K bytes corresponding to a memory bandwidth of 1.92M bytes per second, which is only one third that of a full page display.

There is one other subtle aspect of the Lisa display that is worth mentioning. Ordinary computers display white characters on a black background. The bit map display hardware for such a computer is implemented with 1 bit per pixel, a black pixel as a Zero and white as a One. To display a character, the computer software sets the appropriate bits to binary One or white. In contrast, the Lisa display shows black characters on a white background to mimic the way text actually appears on a real printed page. Ergonomic studies [23] have shown that when looking back and forth from the screen to a real piece of paper, it is actually easier on the eyes if the screen is the same black on white as the paper. Display of black characters on a white background can be accomplished in software by resetting the appropriate screen bits to binary Zero (black). However, it is much faster and easier with the MC68000 and most other processors to set selected bits to One, using the OR instruction, than it is to reset selected bits to Zero, which requires a NOT-OR-NOT instruction sequence. As a result, the Lisa bit map display can operate faster by representing a black pixel as a One and white as a Zero.

The Lisa does not have a color display. The hardware necessary for really good color is not available. For a low resolution color display, a CRT tube from a standard color television is suitable. However, a color CRT tube suitable for the Lisa must have sufficiently high resolution to display sharp text so that one can do word processing on the machine all day long without getting fatigued. Such a high-resolution color CRT tube and the associated video electronics would add thousands of dollars to the price of the Lisa. In addition, color on the video screen is rather futile unless one can also produce color on the printed page. High-resolution color printers and office copier machines are even more expensive and difficult to obtain. Many of the Lisa applications, such as word processing and spreadsheet calculation, do not have any important use for color. There are certainly some applications, such as graphs and drawings, where color would be convenient. But even with these applications, the Lisa's use of multiple shades, stripes, cross-hatchs, and patterns eliminates the necessity to have color in order to distinguish and emphasize various graphical objects.

The Lisa Hardware Bus

The hardware bus of the Lisa provides access to the physical memory. This physical memory consists of three separate address spaces. The main memory space contains up to 2M bytes of RAM memory for storage of programs and data. Parity checking of this RAM memory is supported to ensure reliable operation. The I/O space provides access to status and control registers of various peripheral devices, both built-in and external. A special I/O space provides access to the bootstrap ROM and special system registers.

Both the MC68000 processor and the video display contend with each other for access to memory. To simplify this contention problem, the Lisa has adopted the same technique used in the Apple-II bus, [2], [31]. Video access to memory alternates regularly with the processor access to memory. This interleaved memory access guarantees the video display the regular, dependable access to memory that it needs for a flicker-free display. To give the video sufficient memory bandwidth, the principal bus timing is an 800-ns cycle consisting of one 400-ns video access to memory followed by one 400-ns processor access. The timing considerations of the Lisa bus lead to a 5-MHz 68000 clock with a clock period of 200 ns. Since either a read or write cycle of the MC68000 processor requires four clock periods, then such a read or write will require 800 ns. This is the same as the Lisa 800-ns bus cycle. While the video access is being performed, the MC68000 is preparing its 24-bit logical address and presenting it to the Lisa's MMU for mapping into a physical memory address. If one of the Lisa's three expansion slots requires direct memory access (DMA), then its request will take priority over and delay the processor's memory access.

The architecture of the Lisa hardware bus allows for a simple and low-cost implementation while still providing some powerful capabilities such as DMA and memory management. This is the primary reason why the Lisa did not adopt some other bus standard such as MultiBus. In addition, the Lisa's hardware boards must be specially designed and shaped anyway to fit into the Lisa's compact cabinet.

III.   THE LISA SOFTWARE

Never before has software been such a large part of the development of a personal computer or been so crucial to its total system architecture. The Lisa Operating System [4] provides virtual memory, multiple processes, and a reliable, device independent file system. The Lisa user interface defines how the software appears and interacts with the user. The software library provides a rich set of primitives for graphics, windows, printing, etc. The Lisa Desktop Manager functions as a system executive in performing filing operations and running application programs. There are seven specific application programs developed by Apple Computer Inc.: LisaCalc—spreadsheet, LisaGraph—business graphs. LisaWrite—word processing, LisaList—personal database, LisaDraw—graphics editing, LisaProject—project management, and LisaTerminal—data communications, see [30] and [11]. The Workshop software development system includes compilers, editors, linkers, etc., and is available for the programming languages: Pascal, BASIC, Cobol, and C. QuickPort and the Toolkit are software packages that aid the software developer in producing software applications for the Lisa. In this exposition of the Lisa software architecture we concentrate on the Operating System, the Lisa user interface, the software library, and Lisa Desktop Manager. The additional software components are not mentioned here, not because they are uninteresting or unimportant, but because they are not central to the exposition of the fundamental Lisa software architecture.

The Lisa Operating System

To support the kind of advanced, integrated software that was planned for the Lisa, a powerful multitasking operating system is required. This requirement eliminated all the popular personal computers operating systems such as CP/M, MS-DOS, the UCSD System, and Apple DOS. Their primary design constraint is that they work in just a small portion of the restricted memory space of existing PCs.

The UNIX operating system [21], [29], seems to be more suitable. It does provide multitasking, good memory management, and a powerful device and file system. However UNIX is a relatively large operating system with several features such as a multiuser timesharing capability, user accounting, and protection which would be wasted in a *personal* computer such as the Lisa. Since the Lisa would be used by people who were not computer experts, the system must be very robust. However, the UNIX file system is fragile and unreliable [10], [14]. If the power is interrupted or a system crash occurs the UNIX file system can easily be damaged. Unless a systems programmer is present to repair the damage, a user can easily lose all his data. In addition, UNIX does not provide the general inter-task communication facility that the Lisa requires. UNIX memory management does not offer sophisticated sharing of code and data between tasks. Finally, UNIX and all other operating systems do not provide the support for graphics, multiple windows, the mouse, integration, etc., which are essential to the Lisa. Such capabilities cannot be built on top of an operating system but must be built in to work correctly and efficiently. An attempt to modify UNIX to overcome all of these deficiencies would have taken longer than designing a new operating system with all of the needed capabilities.

The Lisa Operating System (the Lisa OS) performs four main functions: file management, process management, memory management, and event and exception handling. The file system provides for a uniform naming mechanism for objects (peripheral devices, disk volumes, files, etc.) as in Multics [8] and UNIX [21]. Before a device or disk volume can be accessed, it must be mounted by using the MOUNT system call. Mounting an object logically connects it into the name space of the system. In addition, mounting a disk volume makes the files on the volume accessible. The file system provides device-independent I/O to objects which means that I/O is performed the same way, whether the ultimate destination or source is a disk, a printer, or something else. The file system treats I/O as an uninterpreted stream of bytes. Special device-control functions are available to perform any device specific functions needed, such as setting the baud rate of a serial device.

Some operations apply only to disk objects. New disk files are created, removed, and renamed by changing entries in the disk's catalog. In addition to the data in a disk file, the file itself has certain system attributes, such as its size and creation date. Programs can define their own attributes in a special label associated with each file. System calls are available to access these file attributes. When writing to a disk file, space is allocated as needed. Since this space need not be contiguous, such automatic allocation could result in a severely fragmented file. The resulting performance degradation can be avoided by using system calls to pre-allocate contiguous space for a file. This also ensures that space on the disk will not be exhausted while writing.

To reduce the impact of a system crash, the file system maintains distributed, redundant information about the files on disk storage [17], [20]. Duplicate copies of critical information are stored in different forms and in different places on the media. For example, the information in the central disk catalog about a file is also stored in a special disk block at the head of that file. Also each block on the disk specifies the part of the file to which it belongs. Since all the files and blocks are able to identify and describe themselves, there are several ways to recover lost information. A utility called the scavenger is able to reconstruct damaged catalogs from the redundant information stored about each file.

A Lisa OS process is an instance of an executing program, its stack, and associated data. When the OS is booted, it creates a "shell" process which can then create other processes for the user. Since every process is created by another process, the resultant structure is a tree of processes. Each newly created process has the same standard system capabilities which can then be changed by system calls. A process can suspend, activate, kill, or otherwise control any other process. When a process terminates, all of its descendant processes are also terminated. The CPU is multiplexed among the runnable processes by using a priority based, nonpreemptive scheduling algorithm. This nonpreemptive scheduling policy guarantees correct access to shared resources, such as the bit-mapped display, by interactive processes without the performance penalty of having to explicitly lock and unlock these resources for each access. The memory accesses of an executing process are restricted to its own logical address space. Processes can share their code and data, but each has its own stack. Processes can communicate with other processes by using shared files, shared data segments, and events.

The Lisa OS memory manager provides a segmented virtual memory capability. It is concerned with memory segments and their location in physical memory or on the disk. Memory segments are of two basic types: code segments and data segments. Each process has a data segment that the OS automatically creates for it to use as a stack. This stack segment is automatically enlarged by the OS as more space is needed by the process. Up to sixteen additional data segments can be acquired by the process for uses such as heaps and interprocess communication. These data segments can be either private, accessed only by the creating process, or shared, accessible by any process that opens those segments. The maximum size of a shared data segment is 128K bytes. The OS allows a private data segment to be as large as the physical size of the system (2M bytes) by employing multiple sequential MMU registers.

Code segments allow a program to be constructed as multiple, independently swappable parts. The division of a program into these named code segments is dictated by the programmer through commands to the Compiler and Linker. The MMU allows up to 106 code segments. A given program consists of both intrinsic and regular code segments. Intrinsic code segments, such as the units in the Lisa software library, are shared by all processes. Regular code segments are shared by just those processes executing the same program. The maximum size of a code segment is 128K bytes.

Code segments are automatically swapped into physical memory as they are needed. Since they are write protected, code segments do not have to be swapped out. Although instructions in the MC68000 processor are not generally restartable, we have empirically determined that the four instructions that access code segments, JMP, JSR, RTS, and RTE, are restartable. When one of these four instructions attempts to reference a code segment that is not currently present, it causes a bus error which traps to the OS. The OS memory manager can then load the missing segment and restart the instruction without the client process having to be aware of what has happened. This mechanism allows the Lisa to support full swapping of code without the expense of a second processor to handle swapping. Because the instructions that reference data are not all restartable, the system does not do automatic swapping of data segments. The memory manager must swap in all data segments needed by a process before that process is allowed to execute. However, the OS gives programs the ability to *unbind* data segments that are not needed in the memory while a particular part of the program is executing. Since an executing process requires only its current code segment and its bound data segments to be in physical memory, the total amount of logical memory used by a single process may actually exceed the physical RAM of the Lisa.

When the memory becomes full, the system uses a clock algorithm [7] to determine which segments to swap out or to replace. There is a segment descriptor block (SDB) in the memory manager for each code or data segment currently in use. These SDBs are chained together in a circular list which constitutes the "clock face" of the clock algorithm. The memory manager has a pointer to a current SDB which constitutes the "hands of the clock." A segment will be in one of three states: on disk (not in memory), an *overlay candidate* (in memory but not mapped), or not an overlay candidate (in memory and mapped). If the memory manager needs to swap in a segment and there is insufficient free physical memory available, then the clock hand is advanced to the next SDB and this segment is examined. If the segment is not an overlay candidate, then it is made an overlay candidate and the clock hand is advanced again. If the segment is an overlay candidate then it is swapped out (written to the disk if it is a data segment) and its space is added to the free pool. The clock hand continues to advance around the circular list until enough free space is accumulated to satisfy the current request. Since a code segment which is an overlay candidate is not mapped, any attempt to reference it will generate a bus error just as if it were not in memory. The memory manager handles such a bus error by changing the code segment to not-an-overlay candidate, remapping the segment, and restarting the code reference. A segment is changed to an overlay candidate whenever the clock hand passes by; but, if referenced frequently, is changed back before the hand has gone around again. However, a segment which is used infrequently will remain an overlay candidate and will be swapped out. Therefore, the memory manager uses its bus error mechanism both to handle a reference to a missing code segment and also to determine which segments in memory have not been used recently.

An OS exception is an unexpected condition in the execution of a process (an interrupt). System exceptions are generated by various sorts of errors such as divide by zero, range check out of bounds, illegal instruction, and illegal address. Default exception handlers are supplied that terminate the process. However, a process can supply its own exception handlers if it wants to recover from the error. The exception handler is passed information about the interrupted environment: register contents, condition flags, and program state which it can examine and modify. User exceptions can be declared and exception handlers supplied to process them. A program can then use these new exception handling mechanisms.

An event is a message from one process to another sent through an event channel. The event is a fixed-size data block consisting of a header and some text. The header contains control information, the identity of the sending process, and the type of event. The header is written by the system, not the sender, and is readable by the receiving process. The event text is written by the sender; its meaning is defined by the sending and receiving processes. The name of an event channel is cataloged by the file system and can be accessed by any process. An event channel with no name is used by a process to receive system-generated events pertaining to its descendant processes. A process that expects a message can wait for an event on a channel. If the receiving process is not ready to receive the event, then the event channel queues the event. In addition, an event channel can be made to generate a user exception whenever a message arrives.

The Lisa User Interface

Traditional user interfaces are textual with input coming from characters typed at a keyboard and output being printed text. Many of these user interfaces do not even make use of the random access and editing properties of CRT terminals. Such interfaces work equally well with hardcopy terminals. The command language form of user interface has been in existence since the very start of computing itself. It is based on the same sort of formal syntactic structure as the various programming languages. In fact, some of the programming techniques that are used to parse programming languages can be used to parse command languages. A command language user interface is a very precise, rigid form of interaction and the language itself seems very artificial to a new user. If the correct command is ERA then it does no good to type REMOVE, DELETE, KILL, or even ERASE. The precise order of arguments to a command is critical. Even the details of punctuation may be important, such as a comma, semicolon, slash, or whatever. A menu-based user interface frees the user from remembering the exact names and spelling of commands, [1], [25]. However, because a menu displays a set of choices and then forces the user to pick one, it imposes a rigid structure of its own. Multiple menus are usually required, since the number of choices that can be displayed in a single menu is limited. This produces a hierarchical menu structure with menu choices from the root menu serving to bring up additional submenus. Choices from such submenus may bring up further subsubmenus and so on. To return from the lower level menus back up to the root menu requires some sort of QUIT menu item. To invoke a particular command, the user is required to navigate around this maze of menus to find the proper menu in which the command appears.

The user interface ideas of the Smalltalk system, as developed at Xerox PARC, [13], [32], [27], provide alternatives to the traditional user interfaces, and form the conceptual basis for the Lisa User Interface. Smalltalk is a heavily graphics oriented user interface presenting an image of multiple, overlapping pieces of paper on a grey electronic desktop. Each piece of paper, or window, can be a separate activity which can proceed independently of the others. Smalltalk makes use of the "mouse," [6], [12]. For example, a window is indicated not by typing its name but by simply pointing at it with the mouse. The most important use of the mouse is as a single, uniform method for selecting data objects. Using the mouse to operate a scrolling mechanism brings the desired data into view on the window. One then selects the data by pointing at them, irrespective of whether the data are textual, numeric, graphical, spreadsheet, or of any other kind. If you can see the data then you can select them with the mouse. Another use of the mouse is to invoke commands from menus. Two of the three buttons on the mouse cause menus to "pop-up" on the screen. The mouse is used to select the desired command. These Smalltalk concepts were refined, augmented, and made more efficient and practical to form the user interface of the Lisa (see Figs. 3 and 4).

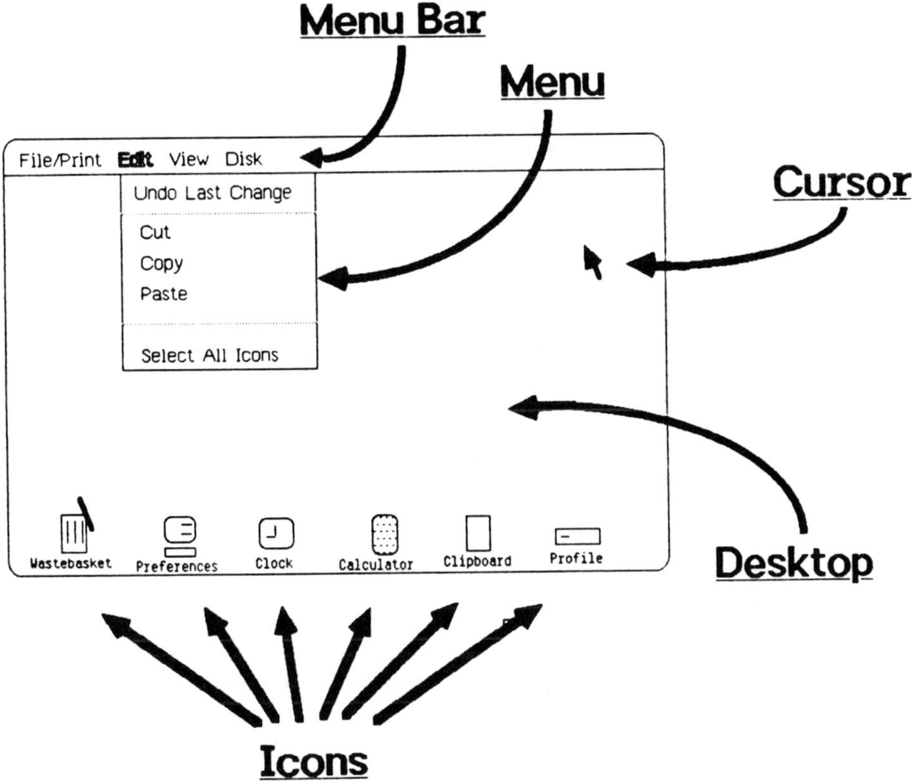

Fig. 3.   The Lisa user interface.

Early user tests demonstrated that a single button mouse was much easier for new users to learn. With a multibutton mouse the user would stop and look at the mouse and try to remember which button did what. With a single button mouse, the Smalltalk concept of using the extra buttons to pop-up menus was not possible. However, these pop-up menus were too limited in number for the sophisticated applications that were desired for the Lisa. The Lisa solution was to place a special menu bar along the top of the screen. This menu bar contains the titles of up to twelve menus that are simultaneously available. Clicking on one of these menu titles causes the corresponding menu to "pull-down" from the menu bar for selection of the desired command. Since each menu can contain twenty or more entries, there are literally hundreds of commands that are available. For the sophisticated user, frequent commands can be invoked directly from the keyboard.

The Lisa user interface employs its mouse and graphics to provide a more intuitive and consistent way for people to interact with a computer. The Lisa display shows graphic images of

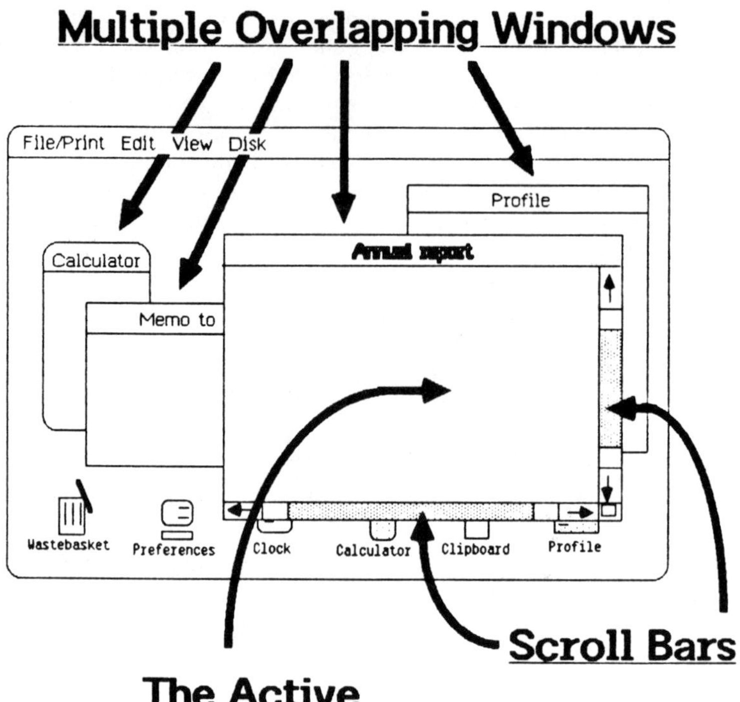

Fig. 4. More of the Lisa interface.

familiar objects on an electronic desktop. The user controls the machine by simply manipulating these images, called *icons*, [26] rather than by typing command sequences. Using the mouse, one selects the desired object by pointing at it, and then chooses the desired command to operate on the selected object. All the conventional "filing" operations are performed by pointing with the mouse. For example, to delete a document one points at the document icon with the mouse and then drags it over on top of the Wastebasket icon. Just as something thrown into a real wastebasket can be retrieved, the last object placed in the Lisa Wastebasket can be retrieved. To create a new document one points at a stationery pad icon and then clicks the mouse button twice to tear off the new document. To copy an existing document one duplicates the document icon, then points at the location where the copy should be placed. A document can be renamed by simply pointing at the icon and typing its new name. Deletion of a document, or file, is accomplished on the Lisa in the same fundamental way as on UNIX and other systems (remove its entry from the catalog and return its disk blocks to the free pool). The difference is that the Lisa provides a more intuitive and visual means to express this and other operations.

An icon can be selected and then opened into a window on the desktop in order to get access to its contents. The icon for a ProFile™ Winchester hard disk drive or floppy diskette can be opened to show, as a window containing icons, what is on the disk. A folder icon, which can be used to group related objects on a disk, can be opened to show its contents. By placing folders inside of folders, which in turn are inside other folders, and so on., the user can arrange information exactly as is possible on a conventional hierarchical file system. A Preferences icon can be opened to allow the user to adjust system parameters such as screen brightness or to configure peripherals or disks. Document icons indicate visually not only that the object is a document, but also the type of document: spreadsheet, business chart, drawing, list, text, etc.

Opening a document icon shows the information so the user can work on it. The user does not have to run programs, called *tools* in the Lisa. Opening a document automatically causes the appropriate application program to be run which then will interpret, display, and allow the user to manipulate its data. Opening a text document "ALPHA" on the Lisa accomplishes the same fundamental operation as a command like "Edit ALPHA" on a conventional system (i.e., run the Edit program on the ALPHA file), but, again, in a more intuitive and visual way that shields the user from unimportant details.

The Lisa Software Library

An integral part of the Lisa system is a vast library of software units (see Fig. 5). These units establish protocols to be followed across all the applications to implement cooperatively a consistent Lisa user interface. The library consists of over half a megabyte of code with 4000 callable routines.

The capabilities for the management of the graphics screen are provided through the close cooperation of various library units, the Lisa OS, and the actual application programs themselves. The **QuickDraw** unit is the Lisa's high-speed bitmap graphics unit. It is significantly more

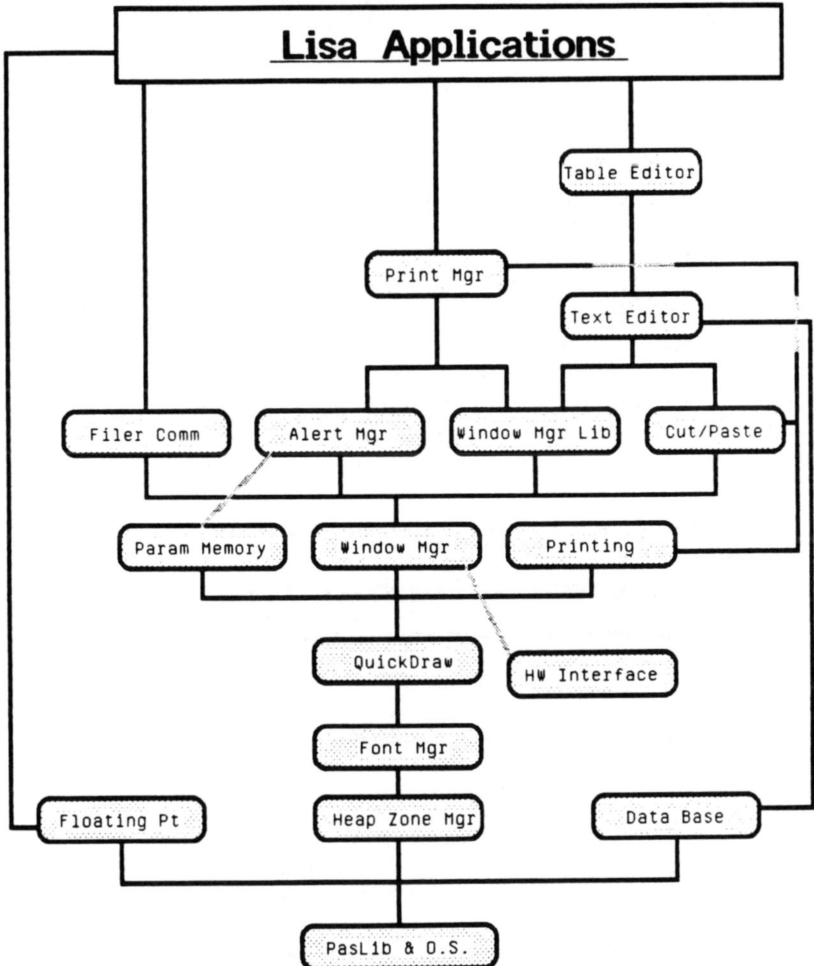

Fig. 5. Structure of the Lisa software library.

powerful than the BITBLT capability of previous bitmap graphics routines [15], [16]. QuickDraw automatically clips all of its output to nonrectangular *regions* to support a multiple, overlapping window environment. QuickDraw, in conjunction with the **Font Manager** unit, draws text to any starting pixel from a variety of fonts which are automatically swapped into memory as needed. It supports proportional widths, multiple drawing modes (OR, XOR, and BIC), and display styles such as bold, italic, underlined, and shadowed. Both fonts and QuickDraw bitmaps can be automatically stretched or shrunk to fit into a destination, giving multiple sizes of these objects. QuickDraw supports the primitive graphical shapes: lines, rectangles, ovals, arcs, and rounded corner rectangles. These shapes can all be drawn with specified pen width, height, and texture pattern and with a variety of drawing modes (OR, XOR, BIC, etc.). The same QuickDraw *region* mechanism that is used for clipping can also be used to define, manipulate, and display new shapes. A QuickDraw *picture* object represents an arbitrary piece of graphics through a compact transcript of the drawing calls. These pictures are used as the universal medium of exchange of graphical information between applications. While providing all these unique, powerful capabilities, QuickDraw is still able to offer high performance such as displaying 4000 characters per second, 800 lines per second, and 160 large solid rectangles per second.

The **Window Manager** unit is responsible for keeping track of the number of open windows, the location of each window on the screen, the size of each window, and which windows are in front of or behind the other windows. The Window Manager knows the process which "owns" the window and is responsible for its actions. For each window that is covered by other windows and therefore partially obscured, the Window Manager calculates the region of the window that is currently visible (see Fig. 6). QuickDraw automatically restricts or clips any output to that window to the portion of the display that is visible. An application process can safely draw into its window at any time without having to know about the windows in front of it. When windows are moved, resized, or otherwise changed, the Window Manager makes sure that the portions of windows that have been uncovered are redisplayed. This is accomplished by the Window Manager keeping a QuickDraw picture for each window which is drawn, but can also be accomplished by asking the application to redisplay the missing content. As a result, the application designer does not need to be aware of where on the screen the window is located or what portion of it is currently visible.

Support for the mouse and the keyboard are provided by two library units in conjunction with the Lisa OS. The **Hardware Interface** unit responds to interrupts from input devices such as the mouse or keyboard. It queues information about these input events so that they are not lost even if the system is busy. Since the keyboard and mouse are shared by all the windows for

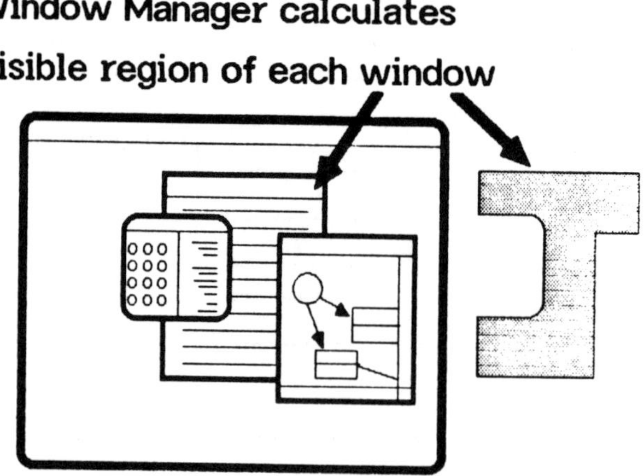

Fig. 6. Visible region of a window.

their input, the Window Manager defines one window as the *active* window with which the user is currently interacting. The Window Manager classifies input events and routes them to the process of the active window for handling. The processes of other windows which request input are blocked until they become active. Additional shared resources such as the menu bar and the alert box for messages are owned by the active window. To switch context and make a different window active, the user simply points at it with the mouse. The Window Manager sends a deactivate event to the process of the currently active window and then an activate event to the process of the new window. The Window Manager keeps the priority of the active window process higher than those of other windows or any background processes so that this interactive process is guaranteed the best performance from the OS.

The guiding philosophy behind the Lisa's advanced printing technology is "What you see on the screen is just what you will get on the printed page." In the past this had been accomplished by restricting output to very high resolution, and very expensive, laser printers. The Lisa **Print Manager** represents the first time that this philosophy has been accomplished with a much cheaper device, such as the less than $700 Apple Dot Matrix Printer, and with even a nonraster device, such as the Apple Daisy Wheel Printer. The Print Manager matches fonts to the specified print device and uses QuickDraw's ability to automatically stretch and shrink objects in order to print to the resolution of its output device. It is capable of printing good quality graphics as well as the usual text on the Daisy Wheel Printer. The Print Manager supports background printing so the user can continue working while printing is in progress. This is accomplished by recording on the disk a QuickDraw picture of each page to be printed.

The **Menu Manager** unit is used to display and select commands from pull-down menus. Another unit allows different portions of a document to be viewed using scrolling. The **Alert Manager** unit displays messages informing the user of errors. There are other software units to enter and edit simple lines of text, to perform floating-point computations, to access database information, and for other specialized applications. Just a few of the one hundred available units have been described. The Lisa software library provides an unusually rich and complete set of capabilities and, therefore, establishes a firm foundation for the applications.

The Lisa Desktop Manager and Applications

The Lisa Desktop Manager serves the same basic functions as the Shell or command interpreter in conventional systems. It provides a mechanism for the user to create and manage documents or files (copy, move, rename, delete, etc.), to run tools or programs, and, in general, to control the system. The desktop image, implemented through the Window Manager, is treated as a special window that is always open to the full width and height of the screen, is always behind any other open windows, and has a grey background pattern rather than the usual white. The Desktop Manager displays the icons that are out on top of the desktop and the icons in any open windows associated with disk, diskette, or folder icons. The Desktop Manager recognizes the user's manipulations of any of these icons and responds interactively with the appropriate visual feedback. The Desktop Manager also performs any filing operations such as file deletion or copying implied by such manipulations, invoking the necessary OS file system calls, and then displaying the resultant visual image. When a user "opens" any document icons, the Desktop Manager first determines the exact type of document which the user desires to open. Associated with each document type is a Lisa tool, or application program. The Desktop Manager then creates an OS process running the desired tool. Next the Desktop Manager calls the Window Manager to establish a window with the same size and position on the screen as the document had when it was last opened. The Desktop Manager sends a DocOpen event to the new process passing both the window to be used and the identity of the document to be opened. When the application process receives the event, it opens the document files and displays the document in its window. Finally, the Desktop Manager makes the new window be the active window so that the user can proceed to manipulate and edit its contents.

The Clipboard is a desktop icon that serves as the medium of information exchange, or integration, in the Lisa. When the user selects some information and performs a cut or copy operation, data are placed on the Clipboard that allows this information to be put into another location with the paste operation. The architecture of the Clipboard supports the transfer of information within a single document, between documents of the same type, and also between documents of different types. In fact, the architecture supports transfer between documents of not only the existing applications but also of future applications. The Clipboard is implemented as a common shared data segment that is accessed by all application processes. Data structures that define the information to be moved are placed into this data segment. No single data structure will suffice for all information transfers. Such a single data structure would tend to lose information even for transfer between documents of the same type. For example, spreadsheet data must include not only the visible cell value but also the formula to compute the value, the column width, the numeric format, etc. The Clipboard data structures are self-describing so that it is possible to distinguish spreadsheet data from any other kind of data. This description allows new kinds of data, for example voice data, to be defined and added in the future. Applications can accept only those kinds of data that they can recognize and handle and can reject unknown kinds of data. However, the Clipboard architecture also allows two application programs, which do not recognize and accept each others data, to transfer information between themselves. To accomplish this, information is placed into the Clipboard in more than one data format. These multiple data formats are arranged in a sequence of increasing generality. The least general format is "application specific data," such as the spreadsheet data that have already been described. If an application does not understand this application specific data, then it can attempt to use a so-called "universal text" form of the same information. This consists of just text characters and formatting commands such as tab and carriage return. For example, a word processor would not be expected to recognize and accept the application specific form of spreadsheet data, but would accept the universal text form which would be cell values represented as text and separated by tabs and carriage returns. The most general form of information is called "universal graphics" and consists of a QuickDraw picture which can be used to generate an image of the information. For example, a word processor could accept this form of information in order to paste a picture of a bar chart, a project schedule, a drawing, or anything else into the middle of a written report.

IV. SUMMARY

The hardware and software of the Lisa establishes a new standard of innovative architecture among personal computers. The contrast with the primitive architectures of the personal computers available even a few years ago is immense. In fact, the hardware and software architecture of the Lisa can be reasonably compared with those of the newer minicomputers. For the first time, a personal computer like the Lisa with the performance, capacity, and architecture offered by a super minicomputer can now be placed on an individual's desk for less than $3500. Software applications which were just not possible or affordable with previous personal computers or time-shared minicomputers have now become possible. By building upon the architecture of the Lisa, these programs are able to more than fulfil the original charter of the Lisa project to build a computer that is ten times easier to learn than traditional computers.

REFERENCES

[1]   R. B. Allen, "Cognitive factors in human interaction with computers," in *Directions in Human/Computer Interaction*, A. Badre and B. Shneiderman, Eds.   Norwood, NJ: Ablex Publishing Corp., 1982, Ch. 1, pp. 1–26.
[2]   Apple Computer Inc., *Apple II Reference Manual*, Cupertino, CA, 1979.
[3]   Apple Computer Inc., *Lisa Hardware Reference Guide*, Cupertino, CA, 1983.

[4] Apple Computer Inc., "Operating system reference manual for the Lisa," in *Lisa Pascal Manual Set*, Cupertino, CA, 1983.

[5] Apple Computer Inc., "QuickDraw reference manual," in *Lisa Pascal Manual Set*, Cupertino, CA, 1983.

[6] S. Card, W. English, and B. Burr, "Evaluation of mouse, rate-controlled isometric joystick, step keys, and text keys for text selection on a CRT," *Ergonomics*, vol. 21, no. 8, pp. 601–613, 1978.

[7] R. Carr and J. Hennessy, "WSCLOCK—A simple and effective algorithm for virtual memory management," in *Proc. 8th Symp. on Operating Systems Principles* (ACM), vol. 15, no. 5, pp. 87–95, Dec. 1981.

[8] F. J. Corbato and V. A. Vyssotsky, "An introduction and overview of the Multics system," in *Proc. AFIPS Fall Joint Computer Conf.*, pp. 667–668, Oct. 1971.

[9] B. Daniels, "Lisa's alternative operating system," *Comput. Des.*, vol. 22, no. 9, pp. 159–166, Aug. 1983.

[10] H. M. Deitel, "Case study: UNIX," in *An Introduction to Operating Systems*.   Reading MA: Addison-Wesley, 1983, Ch. 18, pp. 479–504.

[11] J. L. Ehardt, "Apple's Lisa: A personal office system," *The Seybold Rep. Office Syst.*, vol. 6, no. 2, pp. 1–26, Jan. 24, 1983.

[12] W. English, D. Engelhart, and M. L. Berman, "Display-selection techniques for text manipulation," *IEEE Trans. Human Factors Electron.*, vol. HFE-8, no. 1, pp. 21–31, 1967.

[13] A. Goldberg and D. Robson, *Smalltalk-80 The Language and Its Implementation*.   Reading MA: Addison-Wesley, 1983.

[14] R. B. Greenberg, "The UNIX operating system and the XENIX standard operating environment," *BYTE*, vol. 6, no. 6, pp. 248–264, June 1981.

[15] D. H. Ingalls, "The Smalltalk-76 programming system: Design and implementation," in *Proc. Principles of Programming Languages Symp.*, pp. 9–16, Jan. 1978.

[16] _____, "The Smalltalk graphics kernal," *BYTE*, vol. 6, no. 8, pp. 168–194, Aug. 1981.

[17] B. W. Lampson and R. F. Sproull, "An open operating system for a single user machine," in *Proc. 7th Symp. on Operating Systems Principles*, pp. 98–105, 1979.

[18] Motorola Inc., *MC68000 16-Bit Microprocessor User's Manual*, 3rd ed.   Englewood Cliffs, NJ: Prentice-Hall, 1982.

[19] D. A. Norman, "The trouble with UNIX," *Datamation*, vol. 27, no. 11, pp. 139–153, Nov. 1981.

[20] D. D. Redell *et al.*, "Pilot: An operating system for a personal computer," *Commun. ACM*, vol. 23, no. 2, pp. 81–91, Feb. 1980.

[21] D. M. Ritchie and K. Thompson, "The UNIX time-sharing system," *Bell Syst. Tech. J.*, vol. 57, no. 6, pt. 2, pp. 1905–1930, July–Aug. 1978.

[22] B. E. Rogowitz, "The human visual system: A guide for the display technologist," *Proc. Soc. Inform. Display*, vol. 24, no. 3, pp. 235–252, July 1983.

[23] B. A. Rupp, "Visual display standards: A review of issues," *Proc. Soc. Inform. Display*, vol. 22, no. 1, pp. 63–72, Jan. 1981.

[24] S. Schmitt, "Virtual memory for microcomputers," *BYTE*, vol. 8, no. 4, pp. 210–238, Apr. 1983.

[25] H. Simpson, "A human-factors style guide for program design," *BYTE*, vol. 7, no. 4, pp. 108–132, Apr. 1982.

[26] D. C. Smith, C. Irby, R. Kimball, and E. Harslem, "The Star user interface," in *AFIPS Proc. Nat. Comput. Conf.*, vol. 51, pp. 515–528, 1982.

[27] L. Tesler, "The Smalltalk environment," *BYTE*, vol. 6, no. 8, pp. 90–147, Aug. 1981.

[28] C. P. Thacker, E. M. McCreight, B. W. Lampson, R. F. Sproull, and D. R. Boggs, "Alto: A personal computer," in *Computer Structures: Principles and Examples*, D. Siewiorek, C. G. Bell, and A. Newell, Eds.   New York: McGraw-Hill, 1982.

[29] K. Thompson, "UNIX implementation," *Bell Syst. Tech. J.*, vol. 57, no. 6, pt. 2, pp. 1931–1946, July–Aug. 1978.

[30] G. Williams, "The Lisa computer system," *BYTE*, vol. 8, no. 2, pp. 33–50, Feb. 1983.

[31] S. Wozniak, "System description: The Apple II," *BYTE*, vol. 2, no. 5, May 1977.

[32] Xerox Learning Research Group, "The Smalltalk-80 system," *BYTE*, vol. 6, no. 8, pp. 36–48, Aug. 1981.

15
Design of Personal Computer Software

RICHARD A. ROSS

Microcomputer software can be classified into three major categories: operating systems, utility programs, and application software. The evolution of personal computers has been catalyzed to a great extent by the availability of a wide spectrum of application programs for professional and business environments. In spite of differences inherent in dealing with different types of information, there are still some design aspects which are similar to all packages including spreadsheets, database programs, and word processing software. The common thread linking diverse types of application programs is analyzed in this chapter. In addition, an overview of some of the innovative design features of Lotus 1-2-3 is presented.

The Editors

I. INTRODUCTION

Overview

Modern software for personal microcomputers includes many tools that increase professional productivity, by allowing today's "knowledge worker" a greater facility for data manipulation. For a successful software product, the manipulation of data, whether text, numbers, dates, graphics, or structured charts, must be fast, accurate, and easily performed.

Microcomputer software is classified into three major categories:

- *Operating systems* software allows other programs to utilize hardware capabilities of the machine by interfacing directly with the keyboard, video display, disk drives, and other associated devices.
- *Utility programs*, such as compilers, linkers, and debuggers, help programmers in designing their products.
- *Application software* performs specific functions for general business and home consumer communities.

Within the applications area, there exist several subcategories: specialized products for the scientific and engineering community; educational programs for the scholastic community and entertainment programs for the home; specific software packages intended for either one business function (such as accounting software) or for one industry (such as software for dentists or doctors); and general "business productivity" programs for the office. This latter class is of the greatest interest to us. (See reference [2] for a more comprehensive review of the software industry.)

The author recently formed Metatron, Inc., Berkeley, CA 94708, USA.

There are five major product types of business productivity software:

- *Editors* and *word processors* allow the user to prepare text documents and format them (prepare italicization, centering, paragraph justification, pagination, etc.) for output to a printer.
- *Database* programs allow the user to create a set of structured numeric and text data (structured into *records*), to manipulate and summarize the data, and to search for specific records of interest.
- *Spreadsheet* programs allow the user to set up tabular numeric and text data, and to perform simple arithmetic operations upon the numeric data.
- *Graphics presentation* programs allow the user to manipulate numeric data to produce graphs and charts.
- *Telecommunications* software allows the user to access data from either an external mainframe computer or another microcomputer (attached via modem, for example).

These five types of productivity software account for almost all software revenues in the subcategory of business productivity tools; the first three types (spreadsheet, database, and word processing) account for approximately ninety per cent (by dollar) of productivity software sold in this country. [2]

Four of the top five firms in the microcomputer software sector generated their revenues through sales of productivity software. The dominant firms in this industry (and their respective sales figures for 1983 [6]) are as follows:

1) Micropro International of San Rafael, CA, manufacturers of the *Wordstar* text editor ($60 million);
2) Microsoft of Bellevue, WA, producers of the *Multiplan* spreadsheet, and a host of systems and utilities software ($55 million);
3) Lotus Development Corporation, of Cambridge, MA, creators of the *1-2-3* integrated spreadsheet ($53 million);
4) Digital Research, of Pacific Grove, CA, the only major firm in the industry to generate most of its revenues via sales of systems and utilities software ($45 million);
5) VisiCorp, of San Jose, CA, the publishers of *VisiCalc*, the first major spreadsheet program ($43 million).

Microcomputer software for the professional environment typically operates on machines with 128K to 512K bytes of main memory (1K is 1024 bytes), processor speeds of two to eight million machine cycles per second, and an auxiliary storage device ("floppy disk") of about 160K to 400K bytes of storage. "Hard disks," with up to greater than 24 million bytes of storage, are also increasingly used as auxiliary storage devices for personal computers. Hardware costs for a full microcomputer system exceed several thousand dollars. As the hardware provides no service without adequate software, it is reasonable to assume that the cost of a set of software products should nearly match the total cost of the hardware.

Note that while software products such as those mentioned above are sold for $200 to $800 per program, these products cost between $15 and $50 to manufacture! Software is currently priced according to the presumed value to the purchaser; the price of a software product is relatively independent of its manufacturing cost. The net result is that extraordinary profits can easily be made, on a per-item basis.

As large profits can be made in the software industry by small companies, the venture capital community has become interested in the sector as a potential area for investment. Software commonly takes approximately $1 million, or less, to develop [8]; to market a successful product (such as Lotus 1-2-3) may take upwards of $3 million or more. The venture community has contributed much of the capital for the development and marketing of products such as those discussed above [5].

II. Technical Issues

The fundamental technical issue in the design of microcomputer software is one of *resource allocation*: what is the best use of memory and of the processor to create a fast, flexible program? The program is limited by a small capacity main memory (of which the program itself may typically utilize more than half); the processor is not as fast as the developer would wish (especially in contrast to larger machines with which the developer may have a greater familiarity), and disk accesses for data are extremely slow, in comparison with the execution speed of the processor. The program must interact quickly with the user, but tuning for speed takes up code space, which may be better used by allowing more room for data. The same may be said of adding more features to a product. Furthermore, highly tuned, complex programs are difficult to write and debug, making it more difficult to develop and market the product quickly (and timeliness on the market is important in the determination of a product's success).

The problem of resource allocation has been the fundamental one in software design since the advent of computers; the microcomputer software design environment does not alleviate this challenge, but presents new engineering restrictions. Old mainframe systems were batch-oriented, and were under the control of the data processing department of a large firm, while the modern microcomputer user may be a professional in a small firm with perhaps limited knowledge of (or interest in) computers; he or she demands quick response to keyboard invocations. The old trade-off of response time *versus* full utilization of system resources (necessary in the days when computer systems cost millions of dollars) is no longer of paramount importance: it is not necessary if all cycles of the processor are used, as long as the program appears to respond quickly to the user. The "friendly" program must provide informative error messages, as appropriate, which affect software architectural decisions; the program must use the keyboard and other interactive input media intelligently; it must provide the functionality demanded by the user in as natural a fashion as possible, avoiding arcane command sequences.

Features of Successful Software Products

As an example, Lotus 1-2-3 is an integrated spreadsheet (with graphics and database functionality) for the IBM PC (personal computer), and was the single most successful product in 1983; technical challenges such as the above were faced during its design and implementation. The features of this product epitomize those necessary in all successful software.

The financial success and well-deserved approbation of 1-2-3 offer proof that the product met a real market need. The product provided the fastest spreadsheet available for the IBM PC at the time of its introduction (primarily due to the fact that it was entirely written in the machine's assembler language). Also, graphing of data and simple database functions (the most basic sorting and searching) were integrated into the spreadsheet functions via a consistent, menu-driven interface; this interface, along with a simple tutorial system, allowed the naive user to become proficient in a short period of time. The added functionality, though merely an incremental improvement upon prior spreadsheets, was perceived by the market as adding greatly to the value of the product. Although 1-2-3 was neither a major product innovation (as was VisiCalc), nor the first integrated spreadsheet (a distinction held by the Context MBA), the quality of its implementation and design has allowed it to make a revolutionary impact on the personal computer industry.

To enumerate, the necessary qualities of a successful software product are as follows:

- the program must run very fast;
- it must be easy to use and easy to learn;
- it must provide a consistent user interface, which takes advantage of the intrinsic hardware (for example, 1-2-3 uses a keyboard-driven interface, which takes advantage of the IBM PC's cursor movement keys);

- it must provide broad functionality, and these functions should both share a common interface style and manipulate the same data;
- except in rare and well-documented cases, the program should do what the user expects, without requiring the user to make unnatural choices (that is, the system defaults to the correct mode of operation, as necessary—the "principle of least surprise").

No program is flawless. (In 1-2-3, for example, menus are sometimes obscure, some graphs may look poorly done, a few of the data statistical functions are difficult to use, and there are inconsistencies in feature use.) However, programs with the features noted above demonstrate remarkable integrity; such features as speed, ease of use, consistency and "friendliness" of interface, flexibility, and natural functionality are now requisite for product acceptance by the mass market.

A product's external features are a reflection of the internal architecture, algorithms, and data structures used in its design. The exact set of functions calculated and features supported are independent of much of the internal design *per se*, but the speed at which calculation is accomplished, for example, is crucially dependent upon proper design. The basic data structures and memory management methods allow a product to be fast, and to make full use of system space resources; a proper ("natural order") recalculation method for numeric or textual dependencies speeds processing time, and may eliminate awkward or arbitrary restrictions on the user's data; an intelligent menu processing methodology presents a consistent interface, and allows for functional integration; a tutorial system provides a means for the novice to quickly learn how to use the product. These internal design issues are examined in detail in the following subsection.

Memory Management

The memory manager controls allocation and deallocation of data space from the microcomputer's memory. The space reserved for dynamic data is known as a *heap*. Space in the heap is segmented into *nodes*; a node may be *free* or *used*. Used nodes contain information pertinent to the program; free nodes contain no useful information at all.

In the most common manner of memory allocation, free nodes are connected to one another via a singly linked chain, known as the *free list* (see Fig. 1). Alternatively, the ordered free list may be doubly linked, at a cost of space for the extra pointer, which would reference the previous node of the free list; one saves a little complexity in the code, for the processing need do no "look-ahead," as do some of the algorithms to follow. The savings in code complexity is small compared to the cost in space necessary for the extra link. As another alternative, the free list may also be supported implicitly, using no links at all! As each node (whether free or used) contains a word which indicates its length, free nodes may be easily found by sequentially scanning the heap from one node to the next. As in the singly linked method, free nodes are found in order of their address on the heap.

When data space from the heap is needed by the program to store a text string or a number, for example, memory is allocated from the heap by finding a node of appropriate size on the free list. When a node is deallocated (the data space is no longer required), it is added to the free list. Free nodes are kept on the list in order of their location, from the lowest address to the highest. Nodes are allocated from the free list according to the *first-fit* strategy: if a node of size n is required, the first node found on the free list of this size or larger is allocated. (Other allocation strategies, such as *best-fit*, may also be used [3], [7], [1].) The search starts from the beginning of the free list and proceeds towards its end at high memory. (It may be noted that starting the search in the middle of the free list, and wrapping around at the end, is frequently a more efficient method.)

The following two algorithms indicate the exact method for allocation and deallocation of nodes.

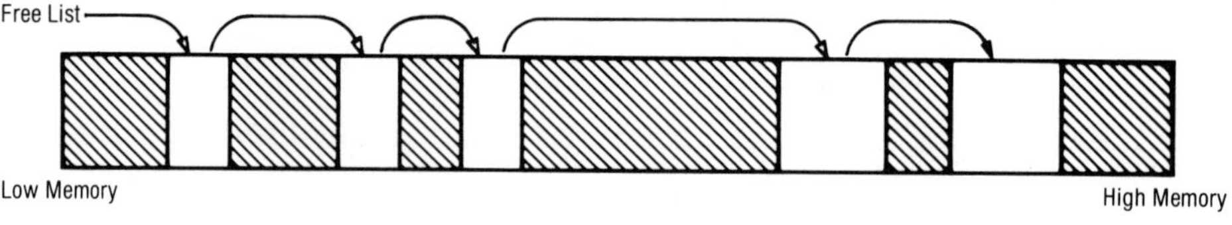

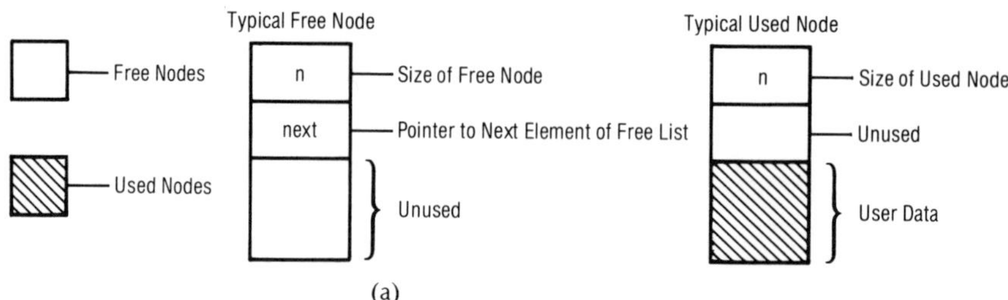

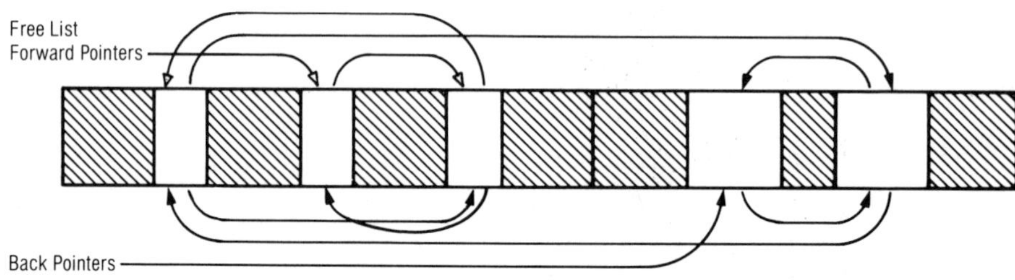

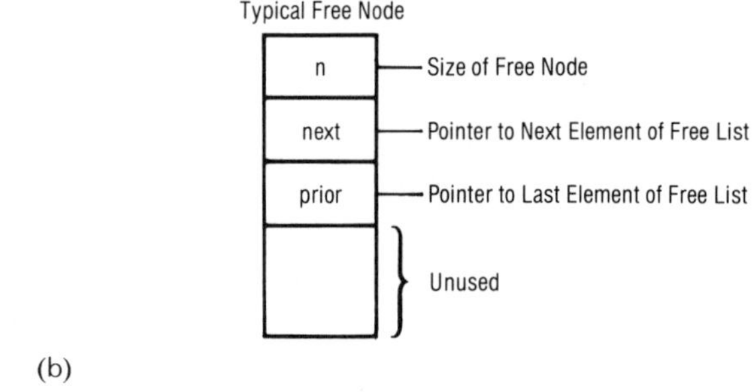

Fig. 1. The heap space. (a) Singly linked, ordered free list. (b) Doubly linked, unordered free list.

Deallocate(Old Node)
Initially, set the "current node" to be the first in the free list.
  1) Scan free list until address of current node is less than the address of Old Node, and the next node has a greater address than Old Node.
  2) If current node ends at beginning of Old Node, consolidate nodes.
  3) If next node begins at end of Old Node, consolidate nodes.
  4) Return with no error.

Algorithm 1. Deallocation of heap space.

Allocate(*n*)—*n* is size of desired block
Initially, set current node to head of free list.

  1) Loop:
  2)   If size of next node is = *n*
  3)   unlink next node from free list and return next node.
  4)   If size of next node is > *n*
  5)   free up excess at beginning of next node (if possible)
  6)   and allocate end of next node and return it.
  7)   If size of next node < *n* (Note: true, by exhaustion.)
  8)   set current node to next node and keep looping at Step 2).

At end, Return with error to report failure. (Note: no node of correct size had been returned.)

Algorithm 2.   Allocation of heap space.

To free a node, the free list is scanned from the beginning to the end, and the node is inserted into its proper place, depending upon its address; immediately adjacent free nodes are coalesced to form larger free nodes, if possible.

To allocate space, the free list is searched from its beginning; when a node of appropriate size is found, it is removed from the free list and returned. If the node is larger than necessary, an attempt is made to return part of that node to the free list, if there had been enough extra space; otherwise, the entire node, including the excess space, is allocated from the free list. If no space had been found, the allocation procedure returns with an error.

An alternative method for free node management would be to keep nodes in an *unordered*, doubly linked free list, and to coalesce memory only if no free node of adequate size is found upon attempted allocation, as illustrated next:

Deallocate(Old Node)

  1)   Place Old Node at beginning of free list.
  2)   Return with no error.

Algorithm 3.   Deallocation with doubly linked free nodes.

Allocate(*n*)—*n* is size of desired block
(Note: all steps through Step 8) are as in Algorithm 2.)

   9)   For each node *F* on free list:
 10)   If the next physical heap node is free and adjacent to *F*
 11)   coalesce *F* and its neighbor in the heap space;
 12)   If the resultant node is of size $\geq n$,
 13)   allocate and return it as in Steps 2) through 6);

At end, Return with error to report failure.

Algorithm 4.   Allocation with doubly linked free nodes.

In this method, to free a node, one would merely attach it to the free list, either at the beginning or at the end. To allocate memory, the free list would be scanned in the first method; if no node of appropriate size were found at this time, the free list again would be scanned, and successive free nodes would be coalesced. The extra link allows a free node to be easily pulled from its random place in the free list, so that it may be coalesced with its neighbor. (Alternatively, coalescing adjacent free nodes may be performed in conjunction with the original allocation attempt, as the free list is scanned.) This method represents a strategy of work only *upon demand;* that is, as little work as possible is done at any time, and more complicated processing occurs only as resources become scarce. This method may produce faster response for the user, but may cause the system to run slowly as resources are used up. The former method of memory management (based upon a singly linked sorted free list) amortizes the cost of allocation and deallocation over all operations, achieving a more stable response time.

Natural Order Recalculation

In a spreadsheet or database, the value of an element may be specified by a formula over constants and values of other elements; in a document, the position of footnotes, indices, page breaks, and the like are dependent upon positions of other elements in the document. The modification of the value of a element, by user input, for example, may require that the value of another element be calculated, to ensure consistency of the mathematical model described by the spreadsheet or database, or to ensure correct positioning of text in a document. For example, if the formula for the element in a spreadsheet's cell $B1$ were "$A1 + 2$," and if $A1$'s value were to change from three to seven, then the proper value of $B1$ would necessarily change from five to nine. *Recalculation* in a spreadsheet or database is the process in which formulas are evaluated and elements receive new values, as a consequence of a change in the value of some data element, due to user input. This process of recalculation is necessarily performed for the cells of a spreadsheet or the records of a database to contain logically consistent and mathematically correct information, or for the document to have correct placement of pages, paragraphs, etc.

Recalculated values are dependent upon the order in which elements are examined and their values recomputed; recalculation in the wrong order may lead to erroneous results. The first spreadsheet programs for microcomputers, such as *VisiCalc*, recalculated cell values in order of increasing row or column index: the user could choose *rowwise* recalculation order, in which all cells in a row would to be recalculated left to right, for each row (from top to bottom) in the spreadsheet; alternatively, the user could select *columnwise* recalculation order. Note that the recalculation order was completely independent of the formulas which defined the cell values; the cell's position relative to the upper left origin of the spreadsheet was the sole factor in determining the cell's place in the recalculation order.

In a spreadsheet (or database) program, there are two problems with a recalculation order which ignores the cells' (or fields') formulas. The first is the problem of the "forward reference": if the value of a cell $B2$ was dependent upon the value of another cell $C4$ that was to the right of and below cell $B2$, then the recalculated value of $B2$ would be incorrect, as it would be based upon the previous value of $C4$, and not its current value. For example, let the derivation of spreadsheet cell $B2$ be "$C4 + 2$," and let $C4$ be described by "$A1*2$." If the value of $A1$ were to change from three to four, $C4$ should change from six to eight, and $B2$ should change from eight to ten. However, with either rowwise or columnwise recalculation order, the evaluation of the formula for $B2$ would be based upon the previous value of $C4$, since $C4$ would not have as yet been recalculated under the ordering; $B2$ would hence remain unchanged, with an incorrect value.

Another problem with geometry-based recalculation order is that the user must be aware of the internal architecture of the software. The user of a spreadsheet wants the numbers to be calculated correctly, and that is *all* he or she desires. Being required to bother with recalculation order is, at best, a nuisance, and the user carries a strong suspicion that the program may not be capable of solving the problem for which it was developed.

The solution to these desiderata is a "natural order" recalculation schema, in which the recalculation order is derived from the formulas which define the cell values. As the physical geometry of the spreadsheet or database is ignored, there is no such thing as a "forward reference" problem, as all references (independent of direction) are handled in an identical fashion. This natural order method allows recalculation of elements' values with the great efficacy, relieving the user of the tedium of deciding which geometry of recalculation to use.

The basis for natural order recalculation is the *topological sort*. A topological sort fabricates a consistent total ordering on a set, given a list of partial orderings over elements of that set. By examining the dependencies as indicated in the formulas for the database or spreadsheet elements, natural order recalculation builds a total order for database or spreadsheet recalculation. That is, topologically sorting the implied element dependencies gives the proper recalculation order.

Consider that the value of a cell, say $C9$, is used in the formula for another cell, say $B1$. This implies that $B1$ is dependent upon $C9$ having the correct value: $C9$ is a *dependency* of $B1$. If the operator " < " is interpreted to mean "must be calculated before" or, equivalently, "is a dependency of," then one can write "$C9 < B1$." Topologically sorting the entire set of such statements for the spreadsheet will produce a consistent ordering for recalculation.

A topological sort can be thought of as creation of a proper "chaining" of partial orderings or preferences. For example, given the partial orderings, $C9 < B1$, $C11 < C9$, $C10 < C9$ the total orderings $C10 < C11 < C9 < B1$ and $C11 < C10 < C9 < B1$ are both acceptable total orderings given the three partial orderings; either could be the output of topologically sorting the first three inequalities. Note that there may be no one unique output from a topological sort, as many total orderings may be consistent with the input data (partial orderings), or that there may be no consistent total ordering (see Fig. 2). As another example, if one preferred candidate A to B, candidate B to C, and candidate B to D, one could vote in either of the orders A-B-C-D or A-B-D-C in a preferential ballot; one would perform a topological sort to create a total preferential order over the partial preferences.

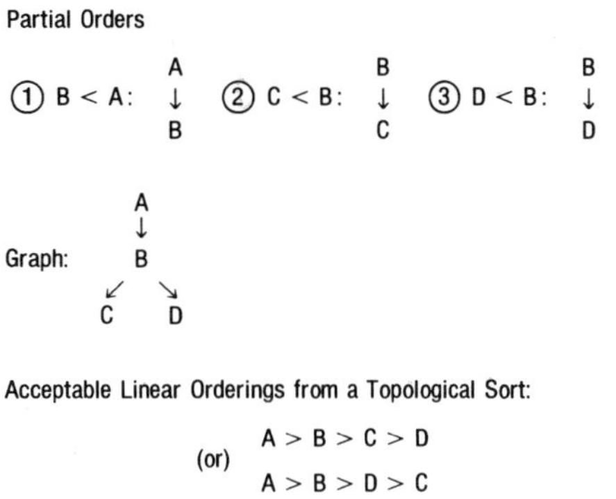

Partial Orders

$$\text{①}\ B < A:\quad \begin{matrix} A \\ \downarrow \\ B \end{matrix} \qquad \text{②}\ C < B:\quad \begin{matrix} B \\ \downarrow \\ C \end{matrix} \qquad \text{③}\ D < B:\quad \begin{matrix} B \\ \downarrow \\ D \end{matrix}$$

Graph:

$$\begin{matrix} & A & \\ & \downarrow & \\ & B & \\ \swarrow & & \searrow \\ C & & D \end{matrix}$$

Acceptable Linear Orderings from a Topological Sort:

$$\text{(or)}\quad \begin{matrix} A > B > C > D \\ A > B > D > C \end{matrix}$$

Fig. 2. Topological sort: An example.

As a specific example, consider the spreadsheet whose formulas are given in Fig. 3, which imply the partial orderings:

$$
\begin{aligned}
B1&: C9/C11 &\Rightarrow\quad & C9 < B1, C11 < B9; \\
C9&: C11\text{-}C10 &\Rightarrow\quad & C11 < C9, C10 < C9; \\
C10&: E6*C3 + E7 &\Rightarrow\quad & E6 < C10, C3 < C10, E7 < C10; \\
C11&: C3*E5 &\Rightarrow\quad & C3 < C11, E5 < C11.
\end{aligned}
$$

From these ordering, one can see that there are a multiplicity of appropriate orderings for recalculation, such as, e.g., $C3 < E5 < E6 < E7 < C10 < C11 < C9 < B1$ and $E5 < C3 < C11 < E7 < E6 < C10 < C9 < B1$. (Neither of these proper orders would be produced by either rowwise or columnwise recalculation, as $C9 < B1$ in both orders.)

This type of recalculation presents a serendipitous bonus: constants need never be reevaluated. In the above example, the order could be simplified by the reordering algorithm to be $C10 < C11 < C9 < B1$ or $C11 < C10 < C9 < B1$; presumably constant values, such as $C3$, $E5$, $E6$, and $E7$, need not be examined. (In geometrically based recalculation, these cells would be reexamined.) As many spreadsheet models contain a large percentage of constant values, this savings may be a great advantage (saving upwards of 75 percent of recalculation time in some instances).

An analogous database example is given in Fig. 4. The following dependencies may be derived by inspection. (Again, keep in mind that " < " specifies the order of calculation for an element, and not size of the value.)

$$
\begin{aligned}
\text{ROS} &= \text{Profit/Revenue} &\Rightarrow\quad & \text{Profit} < \text{ROS}, \text{Revenue} < \text{ROS}; \\
\text{Profit} &= \text{Revenue} - \text{Cost} &\Rightarrow\quad & \text{Revenue} < \text{Profit}, \text{Cost} < \text{Profit}; \\
\text{Cost} &= 5*\text{Sales} + 250 &\Rightarrow\quad & \text{Sales} < \text{Cost}; \\
\text{Revenue} &= \text{Sales}*10 &\Rightarrow\quad & \text{Sales} < \text{Revenue}.
\end{aligned}
$$

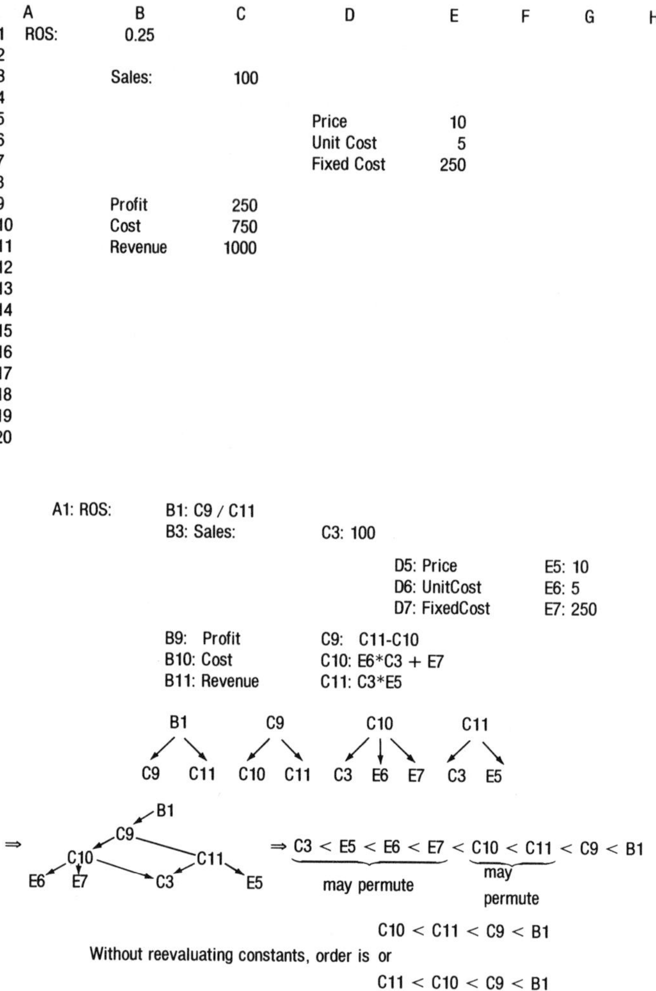

Fig. 3. Spreadsheet ordering: An example.

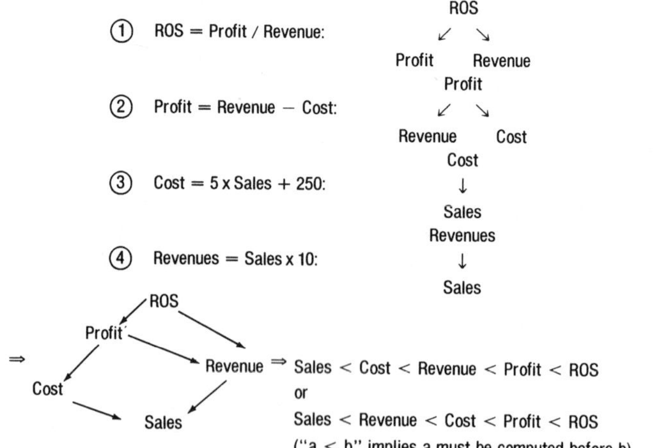

Fig. 4. Database recalculation order: An example.

Given the sales for a month, one should calculate the Revenue and Cost (in either order), then the monthly Profit, and finally the ROS; recalculation in any other order, as a response to the user changing the Sales figure, would give incorrect results.

The topological sort can be quickly generated from a given set of partial orders. The algorithms to follow assume that there are no loops, no "circular dependencies"; otherwise, there would be no proper topological sorting for the elements. The algorithms force all of an element's dependencies to be put in the order (outputted from the topological sort) prior to the element itself, thus ensuring that all values upon which the element depends are to be recalculated before the element is recalculated, and providing the correct recalculation order for a database or spreadsheet.

One method for generation of the recalculation order, described by the algorithm below, assumes that the list of partial orders are given in a table indexed by the successor element (i.e., the element to the right of the " < " comparison operator). This table is of similar structure to the lists given in either the database or the spreadsheet example above, and may be quickly constructed by examining the formulas which define the values of the elements. We assume there is a maximal element, Source, such that for all other elements E, $E <$ Source; let Source be the direct successor for each element which has no other successor (that is, put Source at the top of the tree).

TopSort(Element) (Note: call initially with TopSort(Source).)
    1)   For each of Element's dependencies, D,
    2)   If D has not yet been outputted
    3)   TopSort(D); (Note: recursively process predecessor in tree.)
    4)   Output Element at end of constructed order.

Recalc
    1)   For each element in constructed order,
    2)   Evaluate its formula and set its value.

Algorithm 5. Top-down topological sort and recalculation of elements.

The algorithm precedes by a "depth-first search" which starts at the Source element. As an element is examined, its predecessors are checked to guarantee that they have been previously outputted from the topological sort, and the algorithm recursively operates on each predecessor that has not been so placed; only after all of the element's predecessors have been put on the topologically sorted list may the element itself be placed there, thus ensuring correct operation according to the definition of a topological sort.

This algorithm would operate on the database example as follows. (See Fig. 5; note that the Source element has one predecessor, viz., ROS.)

Input Table of Partial Orders Indexed by Sucessor:

ROS	< Source
Profit, Revenue	< ROS
Cost, Revenue	< Profit
Sales	< Cost
Sales	< Revenue

    1)   The first and only predecessor (dependency) of Source, ROS, is examined.
    2)   As ROS has predecessors which have not been placed on the final total order, its first predecessor, Profit, is examined.
    3)   Similarly, Profit has untouched predecessors, and the first of these, Cost, is examined.
    4)   Cost's first (and only) predecessor, Sales, is examined; as Sales has no dependencies, it is placed on the final total order.
    5)   As all of Cost's dependencies have been outputted, it may now also be placed on the final total order.

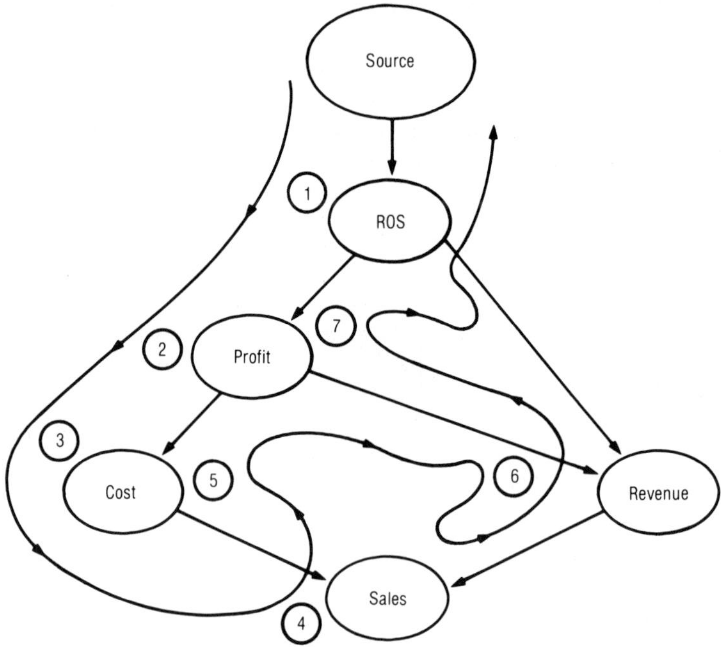

Fig. 5. Top-down reordering.

6) The algorithm returns to the Profit element, and examines its next predecessor, Revenue; all of Revenue's dependencies have previously been outputted, so Revenue is placed on the final order.

7) Profit may now be placed in the order; the algorithm returns to process the ROS element, which may now be put in order.

8) The processing finally returns to Source, all the dependencies of which have been placed in order, and so Source is placed at the end of the order (in theory; as this element is fictitious, this final action need not transpire).

It is seen that the algorithm, as in the example, looks at each partial order once.

An alternative method, given in Algorithm 6, starts at the bottom of all of the partial orders, and works towards the Source element. It is assumed there is an easily accessed table of partial orders that is indexed by the predecessor element in the order (on the left of the inequality), and that the table also includes the number of dependencies for each element. This table is created by inspection from the formulas. We further assume that there is a least element, Sink, such that for all other elements E, Sink $< E$; let Sink be the direct predecessor for each element which has no other predecessor (that is, put Sink at the bottom of the tree).

TopSort(Element) (Note: call initially with TopSort(Sink).)

1) Output Element at end of constructed order. (Note: all of Element's dependencies have been outputted previously.)

2) For each of Element's successors, S,

3) decrement the dependency count of S;

4) If this count for S became zero,

5) TopSort(S).

Algorithm 6. Bottom-up topological sort for recalculation of elements.

The algorithm proceeds by doing a type of depth-first search across the least elements in the set, beginning at the Sink: when an element is examined for the last time, all of its dependencies have previously been placed on the list, so the element may then join them, and its successors are examined. The processing continues exhaustively, until all elements have been placed on the total order. (This method is somewhat similar to the "breadth-first" method given by Knuth [3, pp. 258–268]. A topological sort of this type which builds the order in place of the partial orders, and hence uses no space (save a small constant amount), has been developed by the author [4].)

This algorithm would process the database example as follows.
(See Fig. 6; the Sink element has one successor, viz., Sales.)

Input Table of Partial Orders Indexed by Predecessor:

[0 dependencies]	Sink	< Sales
[1 dependency]	Sales	< Cost, Revenue
[1 dependency]	Cost	< Profit
[1 dependency]	Revenue	< ROS, Profit
[2 dependencies]	Profit	< ROS
[2 dependencies]	ROS	

1) Sink's only successor, Sales, is examined. Its dependency count is decremented to zero, so all of its dependencies are known to have been previously placed on the final total order. This element is therefore being examined for the final time: this element is placed onto the total order (i.e., is outputted from the topological sort at this time), and processing continues at this element.

2) The first of the successors of Sales, Cost, is examined. This is its final examination, so it is placed on the output order, and is immediately processed by the algorithm.

3) The only element of the successor list of Cost, Profit, has its dependency count decremented to one.

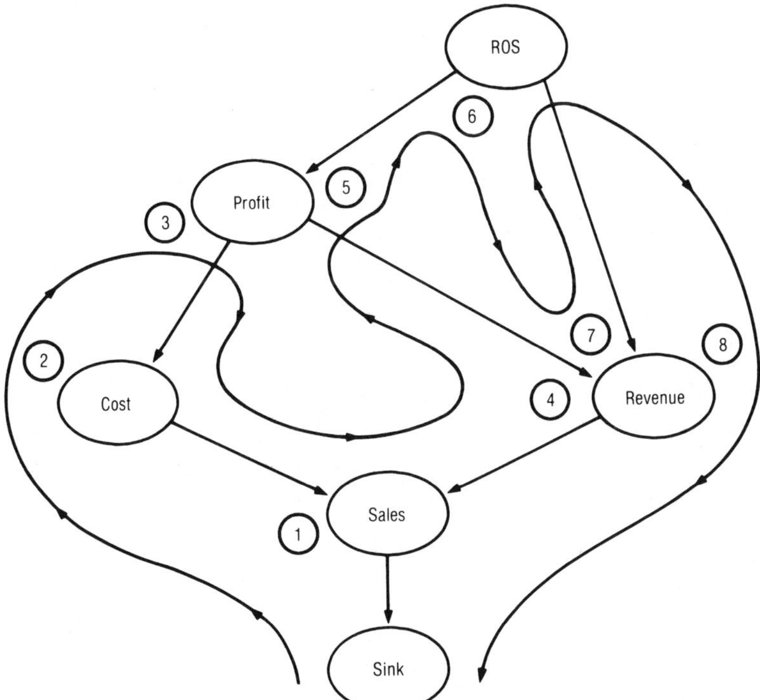

Fig. 6. Bottom-up reordering.

4) Back to Sales: its next and final successor, Revenue, is examined. Its dependency count goes to zero, so it is placed at the end of the total order, and will now be examined.

5) The successor list of Revenue is examined: the first element, Profit, is seen for the last time, and so is placed on the output order.

6) The single element from Profit's successor list, ROS, has its dependency count set to one.

7) Back to Revenue: the last element of its successor list, ROS, has its dependency count decremented to zero, and is placed on the total order. It would be examined, but it has no successors.

8) Revenue returns to Sales and the processing ends.

(Note that each partial order is examined at most once.)

For either of the above algorithms, the total processing time for creation of the total order on the elements is proportional to the total number of element references in the all the formulas of the database or spreadsheet, which equals the total number of dependencies or partial orders. The space requirement for the input table for either of the algorithms is also proportional to the total number of dependencies, as each partial order appears exactly once in the table. Both depth-first methods implicitly use space from the control stack of the program to remember which elements to return to for later processing. (This space for control may be borrowed from the space for the input table [4].)

Menu Processing

Commands are invoked in most professional personal computer programs by means of some sort of menu interface. Depending upon the specific menu interface design, the user may select the next command to perform by typing the first letter of a command, by typing a number corresponding to the command, or by positioning the cursor (or mouse pointer) above the command name and pressing the return key (or a mouse button). Activating a command frequently presents another level of menu interface to the user, who then selects a subcommand; this process continues until a function with no subcommands is invoked, at which time some procedure is actually performed. In many programs, any subcommand may be aborted by pressing a special key such as the "Escape" key, at which point the program returns to the previous menu.

As an example, the user may wish to add one column to a spreadsheet. The user would type a virgule ("/") to enter the menu-based command structure of 1-2-3 or VisiCalc. Next, the user of 1-2-3, for example, selects the "Worksheet" command from a choice of nine commands at the top level. Eight subcommands are presented, one of which is "Insert." After this is selected, the user is given the choice of "Row" or "Column" insertion; the latter is selected, and the user is asked to indicate the number of columns to insert, and the place in which they are to be inserted. Thus indicated, a final carriage return causes the column insertion to be carried out. (See Fig. 7.)

In a program such as 1-2-3, all commands are accessed via the menu command interface (or the IBM PC's function keys), which takes advantage of the IBM PC's built-in cursor motion keys. Such a consistent interface methodology allows novice users to learn most parts of the product quickly, while letting experienced users invoke commands relatively quickly. It relieves the user of the burden of memorizing arcane one-letter mnemonics for functions, at the cost of having to remember a possibly contrived menu structure. This command interface technique also hides little-used functions from the novice user.

Program commands may be visualized as residing in a graph structure. The menu command interface allows the user to traverse the graph structure; selecting a subcommand forces the program down one edge of the graph, to a level farther from the top-level root. At the fringe of the graph are commands with no subcommands; selection of one of these forces invocation of an actual procedure, and then the user is returned to the uppermost processing level of the program, ready to enter new program data. If each subcommand were to have exactly one

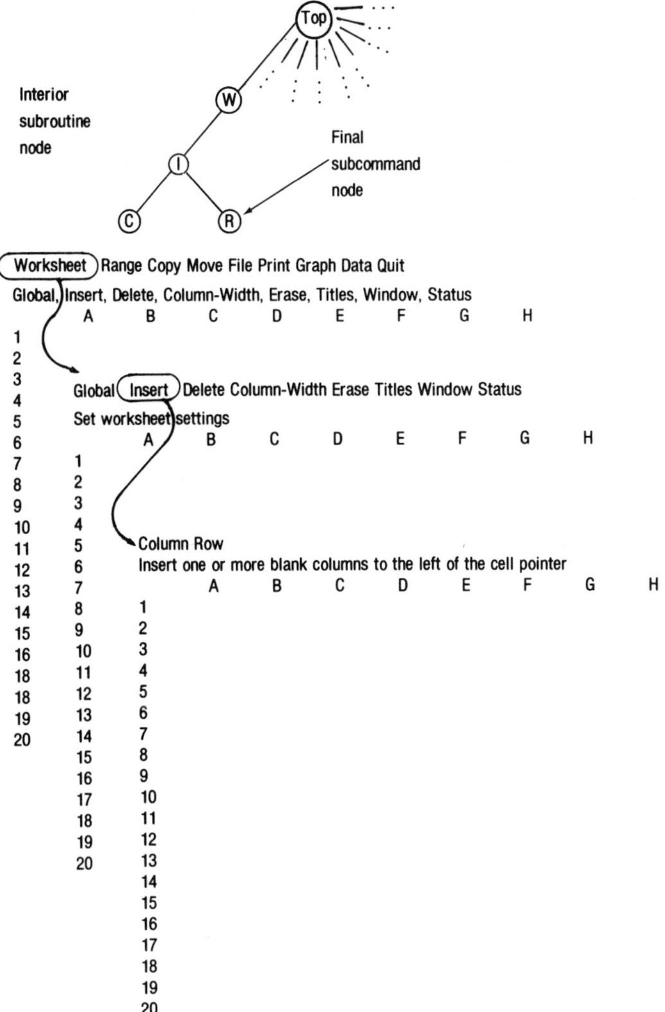

Fig. 7. Menu structure: An example.

(unique) predecessor, the graph structure of the program would be seen to be a tree, and not a general graph.

There are two major ways to control a menu system. The first, which employs a dynamic, programmatic menu control method, has the advantage of flexibility, as any graph structure may be supported, and the graph may be reconfigured dynamically; the cost of this method is inherent complexity. The second, employing a static, table-driven menu control method, is simpler, but only supports a tree-structures command set whose geometry is statistically defined at the time the program is written.

A set of algorithms that describes the dynamic menu control method is indicated next. Each subcommand of a menu actually corresponds to a subroutine in the program:

Top Level:
1) Set menu pointer to top level menu information structure.
2) Call menu processor.
3) Clear menu.
4) Continue program input processing.

Menu Processor:
  1)   Display menu.
  2)   Get user input.
  3)   If escape pressed,
  4)   return escape code to caller (subroutine);
  5)   If valid selection made,
  6)   call subroutine associated with selection.
  7)   If clear code returned,
  8)   return to caller (subroutine).
  9)   If escape code returned, (Note: only other possible case.)
10)   go back to Step 1).
11)   If invalid selection made,
12)   signal user (with beep)
13)   and go back to Step 1).

Generic Interior Subroutine (not a final command):
  1)   Set menu pointer to menu information structure.
  2)   Call menu processor.
  3)   Return code from menu processor to caller (menu processor).

Generic Final Subcommand:
  1)   Process request.
  2)   Return clear code to caller (menu processor).

Algorithm 7.   Program-Driven Menu System.

When a subcommand menu item is selected, its respective subroutine is called. For those subcommands which in turn have subcommands of their own, the subroutine merely calls the menu processing routine again with a pointer set to the new menu structure. The menu processing routine calls a new subroutine; this recursive menu-subcommand-menu invocation pattern is halted when a subcommand at the fringe of the graph is called, and some nontrivial action occurs (rather than another menu being displayed). After such action, the lowest level subcommand returns to the menu processing routine, which returns to the subroutine which invoked it, which returns to the menu routine, etc.; this continues until the control stack is unwound back to the top-level of the program. The reader may duly note how confusing this method may seem; it is indeed more complex to debug and modify than is the method to follow, but such is the cost of its flexibility.

This dynamic method supports any graph structure, as return points are kept on the stack. Let us assume there were many ways to reach some interior node of the graph. (An example of this flexibility would be if one were allowed to print a graph in 1-2-3 via either the Graph subcommands or the Print subcommands, a choice which one is *not* given.) The menu path that was actually taken by the user would be noted (as the address of each calling subroutine is pushed on the control stack), and the same path would be reversed for the final return from the interior subroutine. Note that as no menu structure is statically kept in a table, this inherent menu structure may be grown dynamically at its fringes, given some general menu-interface procedures.

A simpler method is given in Algorithm 8. This method only supports tree-structured menus, as each node may have only one predecessor. The menu structure is kept in a static table in memory, so that the menu geometry may not change (that is, not without dynamically rewriting the table, which is, of course, quite possible). This method is relatively straightforward to understand, and the menu structure may be easily modified by the programmer: to change this menu structure, merely the table need be changed; no extra subroutines need be written.

Top Level:
1)   Call menu processor.
2)   Continue spreadsheet input processing.

Menu Processor:
1)   Set menu pointer to information at top of menu table.
2)   Display menu.
3)   Get user input.
4)   If escape pressed,
5)   if there is predecessor menu information,
6)   set menu pointer to it,
7)   and go to Step 2).
8)   if there is no predecessor information,
9)   return to caller (top level).
10) If valid selection made,
11)   if selection is interior subroutine node of structure,
12)   set menu pointer to subroutine menu, and go to Step 2);
13)   if functional command invoked. (Note: only other case.)
14)   process command, clear menu, and return.
15) If invalid selection made,
16)   signal user (with beep)
17)   and go back to Step 2).

Algorithm 8.   Table-driven menu system.

This method presents each subcommand; as a selection is made, the corresponding menu is displayed. When a final command (at the fringe of the tree) is invoked, the menu processor merely calls the appropriate subroutine and then returns (one level) to its top-level caller. Processing is iterative, as the menu processor simply loops as it displays the menu choices; contrast this with the recursive processing nature of the previous method.

This latter method of menu control has the limitation that the menu structure must be a tree, and full graphs, in which a subcommand node may have two or more predecessors, are not supported. This limitation, however, may well be considered a *design feature* of the second method: it is poor (or naive) design practice to give the user more than one way to perform one unique operation. It may appear that a program with such flexibility is making it easier for the user to do what he or she wishes; what actually happens, however, is that the user invariably becomes confused. Therefore, in practice, the restriction of the menu structure to a tree is not a limitation at all, for most reasonable programs.

Tutorial Hooks

For many software products, the purchaser is provided with a tutorial program on a separate disk. This tutorial program attempts to teach the novice some of the important features of the program. The tutorial program requests specific keyboard actions from the user, and displays how the actual program would react under similar input keystrokes. A simple but effective architecture for such a tutorial system is described in this section.

The tutorial program may actually be a complete program with special programmatic "hooks" added as a dynamic interface with tutorial scripts. Assume that the standard program requests keystrokes from one keyboard handler subroutine, and keys are returned in a user input buffer; the tutorial hooks intercept these requests for keystrokes, thus "faking out" the full program, which is operating independently of the tutorial system. This architecture is depicted in Fig. 8.

When the tutorial program is executed, the full program (with trivial modifications) comes up, and requests keyboard input. The tutorial script driver now takes over, as described in Algorithm 9 on page 299.

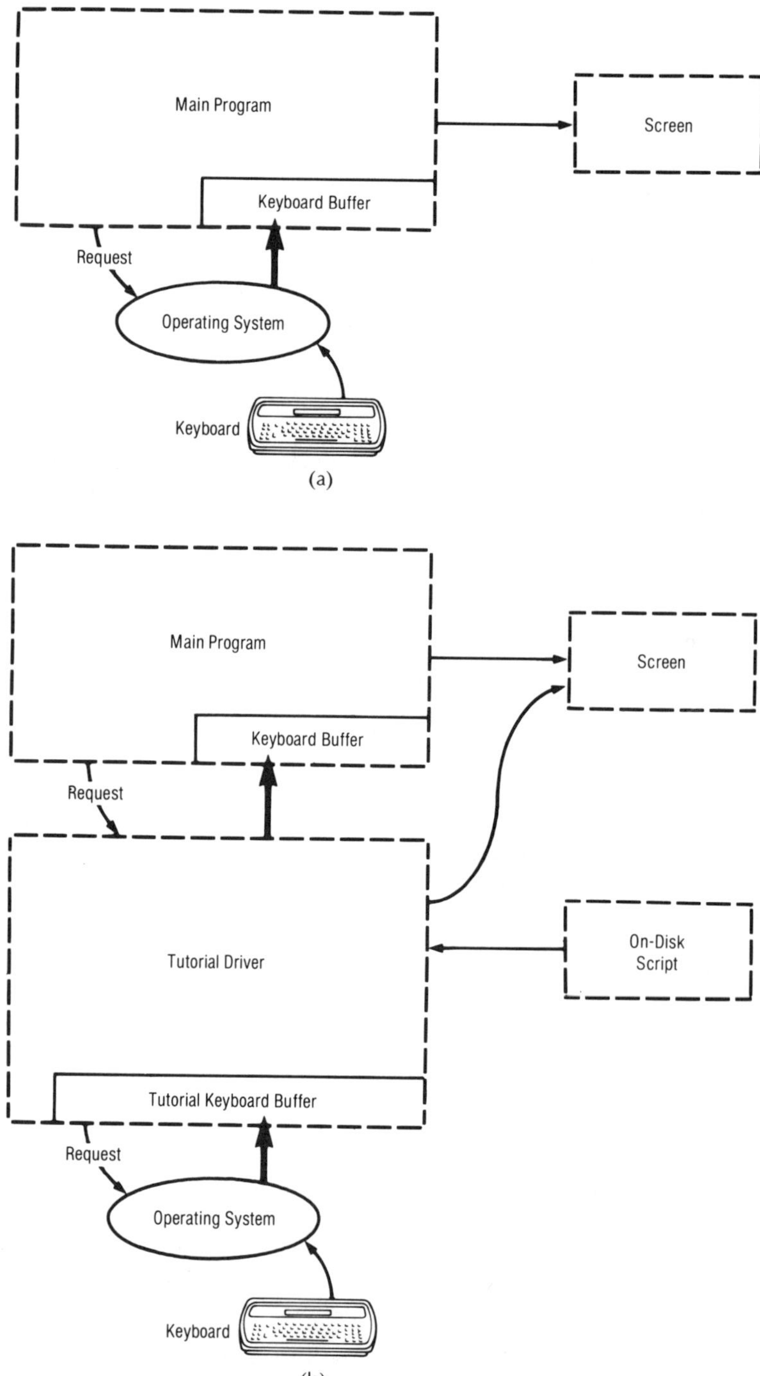

Fig. 8. Tutorial system architecture. (a) Standard program. (b) Program with tutorial hooks.

Tutor: (called by main program with request for keystrokes)

1) Read next script from disk.
2) Display message (from script) to user.
3) Wait for correct keystrokes (match keys indicated in script).
4) Highlight area of screen (indicated in script).
5) Fill main program keyboard buffer (with keys from script).
6) Return to main program.

Algorithm 9. Tutorial processing.

Instead of waiting for user input, as the actual program would, the tutorial driver reads a script off of the disk. The driver displays an informative message to the tutorial student (as indicated in the script), and waits for the correct keyboard response to match (again, the matching conditions are indicated in the script). Upon receiving the correct response, the tutorial system may highlight certain text, place keystrokes into the program's keyboard buffer and then returns to the main program; the latter processes the commands that have been placed into its buffer, and calls the tutorial driver again for further input.

This method of tutorial processing is obviously simple, but in practice it appears to be quite effective, for those who use the tutorial. The major aim of such a tutorial system is to give beginning users a minimal "feel" of how the product behaves; simplicity of the tutorial system need not be a major drawback in achieving this end. The given tutorial system's inherent behavioristic methodology is a by-product of the processing mode: a truly advanced "coaching" system which let the user play freely, and then told the user what he or she did correctly or incorrectly, is beyond the state of the art at this time.

III. CONCLUSION

The key features of any successful software product for the professional market (such as Lotus 1-2-3) result from the quality of its design and implementation, as is true for all software. The technical issues discussed in the preceding sections offer a good survey of the issues faced in the design of many business software products. To summarize the previous technical remarks:

1) Data structures should reflect the basic data processing interactions presented to the user, as seen in the tables for menu control and in recalculation processing.
2) Traditional problems and necessary chores of software products, such as memory management, still arise in the microcomputer applications development environment, and may be effectively solved by traditional methods.
3) Obvious, direct, and simple solutions to problems may offer necessary power and effectiveness (with the added bonus of being easily implemented), as seen in the tutorial system and in the second method of menu processing.
4) Subtle algorithms and data structures may greatly improve product performance, and decrease processing time, without a large investment in code or data space, and without adding great complexity to the product, as indicated by the recalculation ordering technique. (The algorithms may be implemented in just a page or two of code.)
5) Flexibility, generality, and complexity must be frequently traded off, as seen in the menu processors and recalculation method.
6) Processing costs may sometimes be amortized over the entire system, as seen in the memory management methods.

The above issues will appear time and time again during the course of development of future microcomputer software products, in a variety of areas and disguises.

As a side note, the most innovative aspect seen in recent successful software products is the quantity of resources spent on marketing, a trend most dramatically seen in the advent of 1-2-3: Lotus spent an unprecedented amount of over $1 million to market 1-2-3 during its first three months, while, in total, over $3 million was spent to market 1-2-3 during its first year of sales.

The real innovation in 1-2-3 was the understanding that software has entered the realm of consumer goods, and must be promoted as such.

In the future, user interface techniques will be more sophisticated [8]: application products will use a greater variety of input media, such as the touch-screen, mouse, light pen, and preprogrammed function keys, as well as the standard keyboard, numeric keypad, and cursor keys. Menu choices may be iconic, instead of textual, and menu structures will be simpler. Many claim that these features will make programs easier to use without detracting from product flexibility. Efficient support of these user interface techniques will present problems similar to those discussed above.

Future computational hardware will be faster and more powerful (permitting access to a greater volume of data) than current machines, of course, and disk drives and other peripheral storage devices (such as optical disks) will similarly be faster and of greater capacity. Software users will demand greater functionality at an increased rate of program response, and will require that the quantity of data effectively managed by the program be larger than in the past. Ironically, due to the increased user demands upon the hardware, the classic problem of allocating hardware resources to perform software functions will perhaps be exacerbated by faster machines, rather than be relieved.

The issues faced in the design of current products, and the lessons that may be gleaned from those experiences, will continue to confront designers of future products. Old methods may be the basis for new solutions, or entirely original techniques may be invented to overcome challenges. As the sophisticated user of the future (i.e., next year) places greater demands of creativity, integrity, and elegance upon the software productivity tool, traditional problems and traditional trade-offs will appear in many guises; creative technology will be the key to technical triumph, which, along with creative marketing efforts, will ensure product success.

ACKNOWLEDGMENT

The original problem of natural order of recalculation was presented to the author by the inimitable Mitch Kapor; the first solution was developed in telephone consultation with Jonathan Sachs. Some of the ideas in this article regarding appropriate user interface techniques evolved during discussions with Joanna K. Hoffman.

REFERENCES

[1] A. Aho, J. Hopcroft, and J. Ullman, *The Design and Analysis of Computer Algorithms.* Reading, MA: Addison-Wesley, 1983.
[2] Future Computing, Inc., *Office Personal Computer Software Market Report*, October 1983.
[3] D. Knuth, *The Art of Computer Programming Vol. 1: Fundamental Algorithms.* Reading, MA: Addison-Wesley, 1975, pp. 258–268.
[4] R. Ross, "A garbage-collecting associative memory for interactive database systems," in *Integrated Interactive Computing Systems*, P. Degano and E. Sandewall, Eds. New York: North-Holland, 1983.
[5] ______, "Venture capital and software innovation in the United States and Japan," unpublished draft of article, May 1984.
[6] *Softletter*, February 1984.
[7] T. Standish, *Data Structure Techniques.* Reading, MA: Addison-Wesley, 1980.
[8] H. D. Toong and A. Gupta, "Graphics—The new direction in personal computer software," in *Insights Into Personal Computers* (This Book). New York: IEEE PRESS, 1985, Ch. 13.

16
Expert Systems for Personal Computers: The TK!Solver Approach

MILOS KONOPASEK AND SUNDARESAN JAYARAMAN

The advancements in the fields of artificial intelligence (AI) and microcomputer technology are converging to a point where it is becoming feasible to implement some of the AI concepts in the inexpensive personal computer environment. One such example of a software package that makes the personal computer a more intelligent partner in the problem-solving and decision-making process is TK!Solver. Aside from being an expert system in its own right, TK!Solver can be used by noncomputer and non-AI professionals as a framework for building and tailoring personalized expert systems in disciplines with quantifiable knowledge bases.

The Editors

I. HISTORICAL NOTE

Early research in artificial intelligence (AI) was aimed at producing domain-independent reasoning techniques. As a classic example, GPS [35] could prove theorems, and solve a variety of problems and puzzles. However, it was inadequate for larger real-world problems. By the mid-1960s the research efforts had shifted to the building of expert systems with large stores of domain-specific knowledge, such as DENDRAL at Stanford University and MACSYMA at MIT. This marked the beginning of increased research interest in the development of applied AI systems, and the philosophy behind it is reviewed in literature [2], [4], [8], [20], [44]. Further interest in expert systems triggered by the proliferation of computing power is reflected in popular reviews by Duda and Gaschnig [17] and Nau [34].

The fundamental issue of problem representation [1] became more important in the context of these expert systems. Efforts were directed at determining proper structures for representing the knowledge applicable to the problem domain in an efficient manner, with the difficulty increasing as the domain broadened. Goldstein and Papert characterized these efforts as a paradigm shift in AI [23].

The knowledge bases for the expert systems were hand assembled—requiring many man-years of effort and mediation of a knowledge engineer. According to Feigenbaum, this was the principal bottleneck in the development of expert systems [20]. TEIRESIAS was the first step towards the elimination of this bottleneck [12]. Although it was limited to helping debug and fill out the knowledge base of MYCIN that had already been largely codified, it separated the two basic components of an expert system—the knowledge base and the problem-solving or inference part. This was also a step towards domain independence, i.e., realization of the idea of removing the current knowledge base and "plugging in" a different one [10].

The authors are with Software Arts Products Corp., 27 Mica Lane, Wellesley, MA 02181, USA.

More recently, because of the increasing cost of development of expert systems and experimentation with them, a trend towards the development of design tools for building expert systems is emerging. These tools also facilitate easy modifications of and experimentation with the constructed expert systems. EMYCIN [47], OPS [21], AGE [38], EXPERT [48], and HEARSAY III [3] are some examples of this trend.

TK!Solver (TK for Tool Kit) developed in 1981–1982, and commercially available since the spring of 1983, is one such framework for building and experimenting with expert systems in various fields of knowledge. It is a realization of many of the concepts expounded by research in AI, human–computer interface design, and problem solving by humans. The system has no built-in knowledge of any particular discipline, but provides a framework that makes it easy for the user to construct expert systems with such knowledge. The knowledge engineer—the bottleneck mentioned earlier—is eliminated.

There are strong links between the prehistory of TK!Solver and the developments in AI. Prior to elucidating these links we have to mention the efforts outside the mainstream of AI aimed at creating special purpose languages/frameworks for computer-assisted problem solving in specific areas. ICES for Civil Engineering [41], statistical package SPSS [37], and simulation package GPSS [24] are typical examples. These programs lacked "knowledge" in the AI sense and on the surface they just simplified the noncomputer professional's task of using computers. They naturally reflected the then state of the art in commercially available hardware and software. Yet, a large amount of domain-specific and mathematical knowledge went into the design of constituent subprograms and command structures. Running these programs is equivalent to accessing the embedded knowledge and using it for solving a variety of problems.

The development of these and scores of similar packages (for CAD, operations research, forecasting, etc.) was facilitated by application programmers' grasp of particular fields of expertise, coupled with experts' grasp of programming in high-level languages. The high utility of these packages, their complexity and their relative efficiency still present a challenge to AI techniques proper and to the methodology of expert system design.

In the late 1960s, Milos Konopasek, then at University of Manchester Institute of Science and Technology, was assigned the task of developing what in present terminology would be equivalent to an expert system for a textile professional. The knowledge base in question included (but was not limited to) components from mechanical, industrial, and chemical engineering. He faced a dilemma: on one hand the nature of the knowledge base did not justify or require the ICES/GPSS/SPSS approach; the AI approach, on the other hand, looked promising in principle, but unlikely to yield quick results because of lack of practical tools at that time.

Most of the knowledge under consideration dealt with relationships which could be described in terms of algebraic equations and empiric functions. This fact, and the desire to increase both quantitatively and qualitatively the computer's share in the problem-solving process, led to the idea of making the user communicate with the computer at the level of relationships (represented by equations) rather than at the level of sequential programs and assignment statements. In 1972, a "GPS," limited in scope but suitable for solving a large variety of real world problems inexpensively, was born. It was called "Question Answering System on mathematical models and related data bases" or QAS for short [27], [29]. It was implemented first on PDP-10 and other mainframe timesharing systems, and much later on microcomputers [28].

In QAS the expert sets up (i.e., types in or loads) the domain-specific knowledge as a "model" consisting of a set of relationships in the form of equalities

$$\langle expression \rangle = \langle expression \rangle$$

and empiric functions defined by lists of pairs

$$(\langle argument\ value \rangle, \langle function\ value \rangle).$$

He or she then assigns the values of any combination of variables as input, and lets the computer find its way of solving for the unknowns using either the consecutive substitution procedure or iteration.

Interestingly enough, the intended role of QAS as an expert system naturally brought about the separation of the knowledge base and control strategy—a key factor in the design of expert systems.

The strong points of QAS were fast response to any question, high power/resources ratio, and its knowledge-carrying potential. Its weak point, especially in the light of recent developments in human–computer interface, was the line-oriented dialogue.

This shortcoming is remedied in TK!Solver which represents a substantially enhanced implementation of the QAS ideas. This development was made possible by the rapid proliferation of inexpensive microcomputers with a direct memory to screen mapping which facilitates screen-oriented dialogues and results in an improved human–computer interface. Along another line of reasoning we may view TK!Solver as an answer to the need for easy-to-build and easy-to-use expert systems which would fit the mass-produced professional class personal computers.

II. OVERVIEW OF TK!SOLVER

Fig. 1 shows the architecture of TK!Solver. The domain specific knowledge responsible for the high performance of the system is contained in the knowledge base. The problem-solving tools embodying the control strategy—the *direct and iterative solvers*—utilize the knowledge base in the process of solving particular problems. For interaction (or I/O) TK!Solver provides "sheets" displayed through one or two windows on the screen.

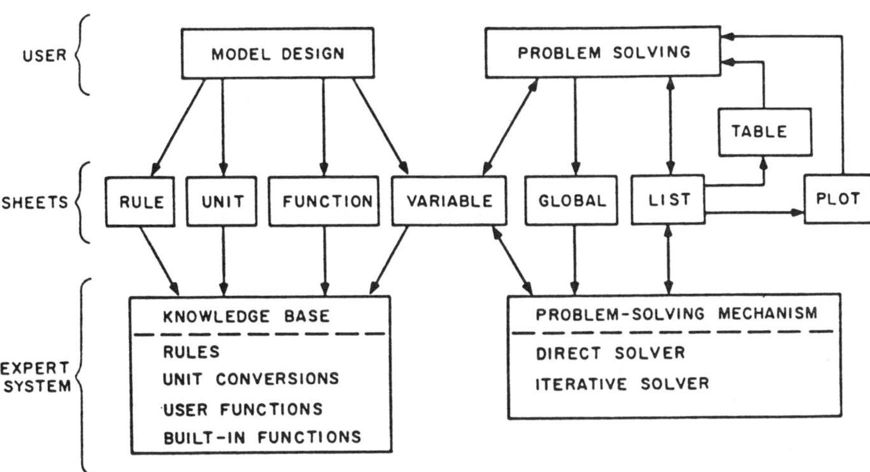

Fig. 1. Functional diagram of TK!Solver—user interface (the arrows indicate predominant flow of information, all links are actually bidirectional).

The main feature of the architecture is the explicit division between the knowledge base and the control strategy. Consequently, the expert/user deals only with issues of domain specific knowledge, and is insulated from the details of the implementation of the control strategy.

In the following paragraphs we describe the four components of the knowledge base, the characteristics of a model and the problem-solving mechanism. We will illustrate these concepts by examples for which we have chosen an oversimplified knowledge base that has information about Ohm's law, Joule's law, and resistivities of materials. Obviously, the kind of interaction shown here is not restricted to this particular knowledge base.

Rules

The rule is the basic component of the domain-specific knowledge. It expresses the underlying mathematical relationship in terms of the equality of left-hand and right-hand side expressions. Equations, constraints, or definitions may all be represented as rules. Fig. 2 shows the *rule sheet* with the set of rules in our sample knowledge base. The set of rules can be represented in the form of a network of relationships called the *R*-graph (for relationships graph) as shown in Fig. 3. A variable is represented by a node in the *R*-graph and each subgraph or polygon corresponds to a rule in the knowledge base.

```
===================== RULE SHEET =====
S Rule
- ----
    I = V / R            " Ohm's Law
    I^2 = P / R          " Joule's Law
    P = V * I
    U = P * t
    rho = fun(MC)
    R / rho = L / A
    A = pi()/4 * D^2
```

Fig. 2. "Laws of electricity..." knowledge base: rule sheet.

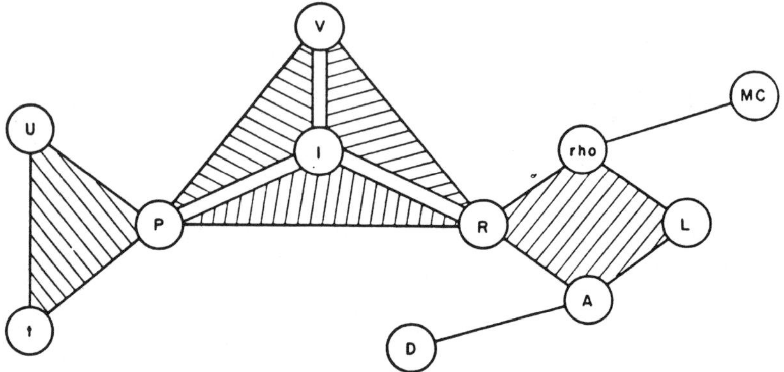

Fig. 3. *R*-graph for equations in Fig. 2.

Unit Conversions

Units of measurement are associated with most measurable quantities. Conversions between them are frequently encountered in problem solving and have to be defined in the knowledge base. Fig. 4 shows the *unit sheet* with the unit conversions in the knowledge base of our example.

```
===================== UNIT SHEET ===============
From          To          Multiply By  Add Offset
----          --          -----------  ----------
hour          min         60
min           sec         60
kW            W           1000
J             cal         .239
W             cal/sec     .239
kWh           J           3600000
hp            W           746
m             cm          100
m^2           cm^2        10000
```

Fig. 4. "Laws of electricity..." knowledge base: unit sheet.

Function Definitions

Empiric relationships between sets of values are expressed in the form of (user-defined) functions, and make up the third component of the knowledge base. Fig. 5 shows the *user function subsheet* relating the materials and their resistivities as a part of our knowledge base example.

```
==================== USER FUNCTION: fun =========
Comment:          Electrical Properties of Matter
Domain List:      material
Mapping:          Table
Range List:       resistivity
Element Domain        Range

-------- ------        -----

1         'aluminum    .0000000263
2         'copper      .0000000162
3         'gold        .0000000222
4         'iron        .00000011
5         'platinum    .000000111
6         'silver      .000000016
```

Fig. 5. "Laws of electricity..." knowledge base: user function subsheet.

Built-In Knowledge

Irrespective of the domain-specific knowledge, TK!Solver can solve problems involving basic arithmetic operations and a large variety of built-in mathematical functions. A standard variety of these is supplemented by a few special ones like "element" for retrieving list components or "apply" for associating empiric functions with arguments (it may, for instance, associate the function defining the stored load-deformation characteristics with a particular type of material).

Model

The model encompasses the first three components of the knowledge base in Fig. 1 (rules, unit conversions, user functions) as contained in the *rule, variable, unit,* and *user function* sheets. In more general terms, the model can be seen as a compact, high-level representation of structure, organization, and content of the domain knowledge. The composition of the model coupled with its elegant internal representation allow for a simple yet powerful control strategy. The model also serves as a user-friendly guide during the problem-solving process.

The model usually reflects a certain part of the knowledge base in a particular discipline. The models may be easily merged by the subsequent loading of some or all of the knowledge base components into TK!Solver, in order to create larger models capable of addressing more complicated problems. There is also the concept of TK!SolverPacks or sets of models from particular disciplines; these are available for mechanical engineering, financial analysis, building design, and other areas. Creating and using more comprehensive knowledge bases are within reach.

Problem-Solving Mechanism

The direct solver is the workhorse of the problem-solving mechanism. In it lies the grace and power of TK!Solver. It manipulates the equations depending on the problem formulation and solves for the unknowns. The solution process goes through the *R*-graph and "fires" all polygons with only one unknown node. It continues until as many unknowns as possible are evaluated. This "propagation of solution" strategy actually simulates the consecutive substitution procedure. If an inconsistency error or an illegal operand is detected, the solution process is terminated, and the rule causing the problem is flagged with the appropriate error message. Since the solution path depends on the problem formulation, the control strategy may be regarded as forward chaining or data-driven.

Whenever the direct solver cannot match the nature and complexity of a given problem, the iterative solver can be used. The heart of the iterative solver is a modified Newton–Raphson procedure which handles sets of simultaneous linear and nonlinear equations. It can be either explicitly invoked or automatically called when the direct solver fails to produce a solution.

A detailed account of the workings, features and applications of TK!Solver may be found in the book by Konopasek and Jayaraman [30].

Examples

Figs. 6 through 8 show the variable sheets with the formulations and solutions of a few problems concerning the sample knowledge base defined in Figs. 2–5. The so-called "calculation units" (i.e., units implied in rules in Fig. 2) are specified and used in Fig. 6 for all the variables except t. In the next two figures the units for U, D, and A were changed respectively to kWh, cm, and cm^2, and the values changed accordingly.

```
==================== VARIABLE SHEET ==============================

St Input        Name    Output    Unit        Comment
-- -----        ----    ------    ----        -------

   4            I                 amp         current
   110          V                 volt        voltage
                R       27.5      ohm         resistance
                P       440       W           power
                U       3168000   J           energy
   2            t                 hour        time
                MC                            material of conductor
                rho               ohm-m       resistivity of material
                L                 m           length of conductor
                D                 m           diameter of conductor
                A                 m^2         cross-sectional area
```

Fig. 6. Variable sheet with list of variables used in the rules in Fig. 2. It shows the solution of a problem concerning the energy supplied to a motor drawing 4 A from a 110 V line over a period of 2 h.

In Fig. 7 the user overconstrained the model by assigning $U = 1.25$ without releasing I from the set of input variables. The partial view of the variable and rule sheets shows the offending rule and related variables marked by $>$. Bringing the cursor over the $>$ mark in the rule sheet causes the error message "inconsistent" to be displayed in the status line.

The asterisks in front of the last three rules in Fig. 7 indicate that those rules were not used in the attempted solution. The solution of the problem in Fig. 8 involved all the rules, the function relating the type of material and resistivity, and the unit conversions.

The ease with which the knowledge base may be changed is demonstrated by the example in Fig. 9. In order to solve a few simple problems concerning the elements of a triangle (after finishing with electrical properties of matter), the user has to type /RA (for reset all) and load the "Triangle" model. To set up the problem in Fig. 9 and solve it is a trivial matter.

Somewhat more complicated situations are exemplified in Figs. 10–13. The results in Figs. 11 and 13 had to be arrived at using the iterative solver. Fig. 12 shows an impromptu modification of the knowledge base: the desire to solve for an isosceles triangle is expressed simply by adding the rule $a = b$ to the rule sheet.

In Fig. 14 the knowledge base is again changed for one dealing with simple projectile problems.

```
(3s) Status: > Inconsistent

==================== VARIABLE SHEET ===
  St Input        Name    Output    Unit
  -- -----        ----    ------    ----
      4            I                amp
     110           V                volt
                   R       27.5     ohm
   >               P       440      W
   > 1.25          U                kWh
   > 2             t                hour


==================== RULE SHEET =======
  S Rule
  - ----
    I = V / R
    I^2 = P / R
    P = V * I
  > U = P * t
  * rho = fun(MC)
  * R / rho = L / A
  * A = pi()/4 * D^2
```

Fig. 7. What must have been the current if, in the example in Fig. 6, the energy supplied was 1.25 kWh? (See text for the explanation of the inconsistency.) The solution, after removing the value of *I* from input, is *I* = 5.68 A, *R* = 19.36 Ω, and *P* = 625 W.

```
==================== VARIABLE SHEET =============================
  St Input      Name    Output    Unit    Comment
  -- -----      ----    ------    ----    -------
                I       10        amp     current
                V       1.5       volt    voltage
    .15         R                 ohm     resistance
    15          P                 W       power
                U       .0075     kWh     energy
    30          t                 min     time
    'copper     MC                        material of conductor
                rho     1.62E-8   ohm-m   resistivity of material
                L       7.2722052 m       length of conductor
    .1          D                 cm      diameter of conductor
                A       .00785398 cm^2    cross-sectional area
```

Fig. 8. Variable sheet with the solution of the following problem: What would be the current and the voltage across a 0.15 Ω copper resistor producing 15 W of heat? What is the energy supplied in 30 min if the wire diameter is 0.1 cm?

In short, the demonstrated power of TK!Solver comes from the ease with which a particular knowledge base may be set up or selected, problems formulated, assumptions varied, and results generated.

III. TK!Solver and Expert Systems

It follows from the previous section that TK!Solver by itself may be considered an expert system primarily in the area of numerical problem solving. As such it does the following:

1) parses entered algebraic equations and generates a list of variables;
2) solves sets of equations using consecutive substitution procedure (direct solver);

```
=================== VARIABLE SHEET ==============================
St Input     Name    Output    Unit      Comment
-- -----     ----    ------    ----      -------
             alpha   36.869898 deg       angle opposite to side a
             beta    53.130102 deg       angle opposite to side b
             gamma   90        deg       angle opposite to side c
   3         a                           side a
   4         b                           side b
   5         c                           side c
             P       12                  perimeter
             A       6                   area
==================== RULE SHEET ================================
S Rule

- ----

* alpha + beta + gamma = pi ()          " sum of angles equals pi
* a^2 = b^2 + c^2 - 2*b*c*cos(alpha)     " cosine theorem
* a / sin(alpha) = b / sin(beta)         " sine theorem
* P = a + b + c                          " perimeter
* A = a * b * sin(gamma)/2               " area
```

Fig. 9. The variable and rule sheets for the triangle model showing the solution of a right-angle triangle with sides 3, 4, and 5.

```
=================== VARIABLE SHEET ===
St Input     Name    Output    Unit
-- -----     ----    ------    ----
             alpha             deg
   55        beta              deg
             gamma             deg
G 3          a
G 4          b
   5         c
             P
   7         A
```

Fig. 10. What would be the elements of a triangle given angle $\beta = 55°$, side $c = 5$, and area $A = 7$? Direct solver failed. Partial variable sheet shows a and b set as guesses for iterative solver.

```
==================== VARIABLE SHEET ===
St Input     Name    Output    Unit
-- -----     ----    ------    ----
             alpha   42.652161 deg
   55        beta              deg
             gamma   82.347839 deg
             a       3.4181688
             b       4.1325618
   5         c
             P       12.550731
   7         A
```

Fig. 11. Solution of the problem in Fig. 10.

```
==================== VARIABLE SHEET ===
St  Input       Name      Output     Unit
--  -----       ----      ------     ----
                alpha     42.652161  deg
                beta                 deg
                gamma     82.347839  deg
    G 3.7753653 a
                b         4.1325618
      5         c
                P         12.550731
      7         A
==================== RULE SHEET =======
S Rule

- ----
* alpha + beta + gamma = pi()
* a^2 = b^2 + c^2 - 2*b*c*cos(alpha)
* a / sin(alpha) = b / sin(beta)
* P = a + b + c
* A = a * b * sin(gamma)/2
* a = b
```

Fig. 12. What would be the elements of an isosceles triangle with side c and area A as in Fig. 11 and no angle given? Constraint $a = b$ is added to the rule sheet. Guess value for a arrived at by typing in $(a + b)/2$ (rationale: expected value must lie between previous values of a and b). Values in output field left from previous solution do not count.

```
==================== VARIABLE SHEET ===
St  Input       Name      Output     Unit
--  -----       ----      ------     ----
                alpha     48.239700  deg
                beta      48.239700  deg
                gamma     83.520599  deg
                a         3.7536649
                b         3.7536649
      5         c
                P         12.507330
      7         A
```

Fig. 13. Solution of the problem in Fig. 12.

```
==================== VARIABLE SHEET ==============================
St  Input     Name    Output     Unit      Comment
--  -----     ----    ------     ----      -------
    100       V0                 m/sec     initial velocity
    30        alpha              deg       angle of departure
    32        a                  ft/sec^2  accln. due to gravity
              time    10.252625  sec       time taken
              maxht   128.15781  m         maximum height reached
              range   887.90334  m         horiz. dist. travelled

==================== RULE SHEET ==============================
S Rule

- ----
  maxht = V0^2 * sin(alpha)^2 / (2 * a)
  range = V0^2 * sin(2*alpha) / a
  time = sqrt(8 * maxht / a)
  (range/time)^2 = V0^2 - 2*maxht*a
```

Fig. 14. The variable and rule sheets for the projectile model with the solution of the following problem. A baseball is thrown with an initial velocity of 100 m/s at an angle of 30°. How far does it travel and how long does it take before it hits the ground?

   3) solves sets of simultaneous algebraic equations by a modified Newton–Raphson iterative procedure when consecutive substitution procedure fails (iterative solver);

   4) searches through tables of data and evaluates either unknown function values or arguments when required in the process of 2) or 3);

   5) performs unit conversions;

   6) detects inconsistencies in problem formulation and domain errors;

   7) generates series of solutions for lists of input data and displays results in tabular and graphical forms.

More importantly, however, TK!Solver with the above (and a few more) features and capabilities may be considered as a general framework for setting up expert systems in a whole class of disciplines; this class is defined by the heavy dependence of human experts on the use of mathematical and logical skills provided by TK!Solver and listed above.

We prove our point by reviewing the position of TK!Solver in the light of the attributes of expert systems as they evolved and as they have been discussed in literature. In the following paragraphs the typical or desired characteristics of expert systems are juxtaposed with current features of TK!Solver.

(1) The domain-specific knowledge (Knowledge Base) and problem solving methodology (Inference Engine) should be separated [8], [13], [17], [34], [36], [47].

TK!Solver: The domain specific knowledge is represented by relationships in terms of equations and optionally, domain-related empiric functions and unit conversion tables. Problem solving methodology is embodied in the direct and iterative solvers.

(2) The expert system should think the way the human expert does [20].

TK!Solver: The expert solving problems in the domain of his interest thinks in terms of relationships and constraints and in terms of "knowns" and "unknowns." This is exactly how TK!Solver handles the input information and generates results.

(3) Bias towards telling the computer "what" the problem is rather than "how" to solve it [19].

TK!Solver: The user tells the computer "what" by selecting a model and by typing in the values of known variables. The control strategy knows "how" to make use of the knowledge base in order to arrive at the response to the query.

(4) Dynamic knowledge base—should be expandable, modifiable, and should facilitate "plugging in" different knowledge modules [8], [10], [11], [13], [17], [20], [25], [47].

TK!Solver: The models consisting of rules, equations, constraints, empiric relations, etc. are easy to edit, amend, and merge. Different knowledge modules may be "plugged in" by simply loading another model or typing it in.

(5) Interactive knowledge transfer; minimize the time needed to transfer the expert's knowledge to the knowledge base [12], [32], [34].

TK!Solver: In the highly interactive environment resulting from the uniform internal representation of knowledge, and good human-engineered I/O, building and maintaining the knowledge base is fast and easy.

(6) Addition of a new rule results in a new competency for the system and, conversely, the absence of the rule marks the absence of the related ability [31].

TK!Solver: The addition or removal of rules is a major feature of the model design and problem solving process.

(7) Interaction in the language "natural" to the domain expert; allow the user to think in problem-oriented terms. System should adapt to the user and not the other way around. User should be insulated from the details of the implementation [7], [8], [12].

TK!Solver: Interaction in terms of mathematical relationships pertaining to the domain of interest represents a major advancement as compared to programming in conventional languages.

(8) The principal bottleneck in the transfer of expertise—knowledge engineer—should be eliminated [20].

TK!Solver: Expert communicates directly with TK!Solver; no need for knowledge engineer.

(9) Control strategy should be simple and user-transparent, the user should be able to understand and predict the effect of adding new items to the knowledge base. At the same time it should be powerful enough for solving complex problems. [8], [12], [16], [40].

TK!Solver: The direct and iterative solvers are easy to grasp because their design reflects the human problem solving strategy. At the same time TK!Solver allows for a level of complexity which makes manual approach impossible, and dedicated programming inefficient.

(10) Computationally fast and not demanding on the resources. Avoiding the situation when, according to Gerring *et al.*, interactive intelligent systems suffer from a basic conflict between their computationally intensive nature and the need for responsiveness to a user [22].

TK!Solver: Response ranges from immediate to a few seconds thanks to the thoughtful design of internal knowledge representation and control strategy.

(11) Inexpensive framework for building and experimenting with expert systems [8], [34], [47].

TK!Solver: The ease, with which the rules may be added or removed, and the distribution of the known and unknown variables changed prove to be of exceptional help in the building, verification, and use of the system.

(12) Human engineering aspects are important for making the system understandable, for keeping experts interested and for making users feel comfortable [8], [34].

TK!Solver: The command structure strikes a fine balance between simplicity and sophistication depending upon the individual user's needs. He can easily modify (tailor) the knowledge base to suit his changing interests.

(13) Provision for help and English language dialogue [8].

TK!Solver: On-line help facility provides information on features and commands as requested. No need for natural language communication, see (7).

(14) Display-oriented interface (e.g., INTERNIST [40], with additional advantage of window concept as in SMALLTALK [45].

TK!Solver: Exploits the direct memory-screen mapping for an instantaneous display-oriented interface. User communicates with the system via well laid-out information sheets displayed through windows (one or two at a time). Sheets can also be scrolled in the windows.

(15) Reasoning under conditions of uncertainty and insufficient information, and probabilistic reasoning [11], [16], [25], [43].

TK!Solver: generally not applicable; in particular situations, however, TK!Solver can be used for determinacy and dependency analyses. Also, probability measures may be easily attached to the rules and their components.

(16) System should be able to explain "why" a fact is needed to complete the line of reasoning and "how" a conclusion was arrived at [11], [20].

TK!Solver: Underlying laws of algebra make transparent both "why" and "how." In addition it points out "what" was responsible for the termination of solution under error conditions.

(17) Pragmatic systems are needed—should be robust, general, and efficient for routine use [8].

TK!Solver: Well debugged; meets other characteristics as well.

(18) Available for users in properly sized and properly packaged combinations of hardware and software; chronic absence of cumulation of AI techniques in the form of software packages that can achieve wide use [20]; proliferation should lead to expert systems at everyone's disposal [17].

TK!Solver: Available on affordable microcomputers and priced for mass consumption; supplemented with extensive documentation.

(19) Usefulness of the system, i.e., responsiveness to the practical needs of professional communities; real-world systems [8], [34].

TK!Solver: By virtue of the perfect match between adopted control strategy and most commonly used mathematical techniques, TK!Solver is gaining acceptance in a wide range of disciplines.

(20) Expert systems should be capable of learning from experience [11], [33].

TK!Solver: In a narrow sense, it "learns" from experience to the effect of speeding up repetitious solution processes. In a broader sense the symbiotic relationship between the user and TK!Solver results in extensive complementary "learning from experience."

It should be mentioned in addition to the above points that we experimented extensively with the use of TK!Solver for building expert systems in a variety of disciplines. We were able to quickly set up a large number of models and use them for solving, for instance, whole sets of problems in Schaum's Outline Series on physics, chemistry, finance, etc.

Several publishers are contemplating, or are in the process of converting reference literature and standard textbooks into the format of TK!Solver models. The first of them is McGraw-Hill's *TK!SolverPack to Accompany Hicks: Standard Handbook of Engineering Calculations,* by Ross [42].This is a practical example of knowledge representation in a framework that allows for utilization, and modification when necessary.

The TK!Solver concept also comes out extremely strong particularly when covering a whole body of well-structured knowledge as embodied, for example, in the classic engineering manual by Hudson [26] consisting of 1029 "chunks" of knowledge and 30 accompanying tables of empiric relationships, functions, constants, unit conversion factors, etc. (with the exclusion of about 10 percent of the text dealing with concepts beyond the scope of the control strategy of the current version of TK!Solver). This experience compares favorably with the domain limitations of systems like MECHO [9], [31] or NEWTON [15]; the latter also faced difficulties in interfacing the quantitative knowledge with the mathematical expertise provided by MAC-SYMA.

IV. Conclusion and Further Developments

It follows from the description of the TK!Solver design in Section II and from the comparison of its features with the widely accepted characteristics of expert systems in Section III that

TK!Solver in its present form provides a general framework for building expert systems in a wide class of scientific, engineering, and other disciplines. In that sense it falls in the category of knowledge representation languages like KRL [5], NETL [18], Klone [6], or Prolog [11], [25].

It may be argued that TK!Solver falls short of learning capabilities, analogical reasoning, reasoning under conditions of uncertainty, and some other features stipulated by the theoreticians of expert systems or proclaimed, for instance, in the grand design of the Japanese 5th generation computers [46]. There are other "standards" set for work in AI and for design of expert systems, which TK!Solver seems to ignore: natural language interface, restriction to problems which are "not algorithmic or totally understood" [8], and "representation of symbolic knowledge for use in machine inference" (Buchanan and Feigenbaum in [14]). Finally, there is the implicit notion of the need to use a list processing language for AI work (incidentally, TK!Solver is implemented in a LISP-like language; on the other hand, even if it had not been it would still have had all the attributes qualifying it as a meta-expert system).

In fact all these advanced attributes are present in TK!Solver to a small or embryonic extent, and it would serve no purpose to argue to what extent they have to be present in order to classify the system one way or another.

We would rather point to what TK!Solver can do in its present form (which is a lot!), and stress the fact that it provides a solid basis for implementing additional features and capabilities as the advances in hardware permit and as the mass user requires. In its further development TK!Solver should look two ways: first, at concepts and tools emerging from research in AI, and second at the time-proven "non-AI" program packages that have become a part of human experts' lives. TK!Solver will naturally continue to take maximum advantage of the state of the art in human–computer interface.

ACKNOWLEDGMENT

An adapted version of this chapter appeared in the May 1984 issue of *BYTE* magazine. The authors wish to thank McGraw-Hill, Inc. for permission to publish this full version.

REFERENCES

[1] S. Amarel, "On representation of problems of reasoning about actions," *Machine Intell.*, vol. 3, pp. 131–171, 1968.
[2] S. Amarel, B. G. Buchanan, C. Kulikowski, and H. Pople, "Reports of panel on applications of artificial intelligence," in *Proc. IJCAI-77*, pp. 994–1006.
[3] R. Balzer, L. Erman, P. London, and C. Williams, "HEARSAY—III: A domain independent framework for expert systems," in *Proc. 1980 AAAI Conf.*, Stanford, CA, 1980.
[4] A. Barr and E. A. Feigenbaum, *The Handbook of Artificial Intelligence*, Vol. 2. Los Altos, CA: Kaufmann, 1982.
[5] D. G. Bobrow and T. Winograd, "An overview of KRL, a knowledge representation language," *Cognitive Sci.*, vol. 1, pp. 3–46, 1976.
[6] R. J. Brachman, "On the epistemological status of semantic networks," in *Associative Networks: Representation and Use of Knowledge by Computer*, N. V. Findler, Ed. New York: Academic, 1979, pp. 3–50.
[7] R. J. Brachman and H. J. Levesque, "Competence in knowledge representation," in *Proc. 1982 AAAI Conf.*, Pittsburgh, 1982, pp. 189–192.
[8] B. G. Buchanan, "New research on expert systems," *Machine Intell.*, vol. 10, pp. 269–299, 1982.
[9] A. Bundy, L. Byrd, G. Luger, C. Mellish, and M. Palmer, "Solving mechanics problems using meta-level inference," in *Proc. IJCAI, 1977*, pp. 1017–1027.
[10] J. R. Carbonell and A. M. Collins, "Natural semantics in artificial intelligence," in *Proc. 3rd IJCAI*, 1973, pp. 344–351.
[11] K. L. Clark and F. G. McCabe, "PROLOG: A language for implementing expert systems," *Machine Intell.*, vol. 10, pp. 455–470, 1982.
[12] R. Davis, "Applications of meta-level knowledge to the construction, maintenance and use of large knowledge bases," Ph.D. dissertation, Stanford University, Stanford, CA, 1976.
[13] _____, "Interactive transfer of expertise: Acquisition of new inference rules," in *Proc. IJCAI-77*, pp. 321–328.

[14] R. Davis and D. B. Lenat, *Knowledge-Based Systems in Artificial Intelligence.* Hightstown, NJ: McGraw-Hill, 1982.

[15] J. de Kleer, "Multiple representations of knowledge in a mechanics problem-solver," in *Proc. IJCAI-77*, pp. 299–304.

[16] R. O. Duda, J. Gaschnig, P. E. Hart, K. Konolige, R. Reboh, P. Barrett, and J. Slocum, "Development of the PROSPECTOR consultation system for mineral exploration," Final report, SRI Projects 5821 and 6415, Artificial Intelligence Center, SRI International, Menlo Park, CA, 1978.

[17] R. O. Duda and J. G. Gaschnig, "Knowledge-based expert systems come of age," *BYTE*, pp. 238–281, Sept. 1981.

[18] S. E. Fahlman, *NETL: A System for Representing and Understanding Real-World Knowledge.* Cambridge, MA: MIT, 1979.

[19] E. A. Feigenbaum, "Artificial intelligence research: What is it? What has it achieved? Where is it going?"·(Invited paper), presented at Symp. on Artificial Intelligence, Canberra, Australia, 1974.

[20] ______, "The art of artificial intelligence: Themes and case studies of knowledge engineering," in *Proc. IJCAI-77*, pp. 1014–1029.

[21] C. Forgy and J. McDermott, "OPS, A domain-independent production system language," in *Proc. IJCAI-77*, pp. 933–939.

[22] P. E. Gerring, E. H. Shortliffe, and W. van Melle, "The interviewer/reasoner model: An approach to improving system responsiveness in interactive AI systems," *AI Magazine*, pp. 24–27, Fall 1982.

[23] I. Goldstein and S. Papert, "Artificial intelligence, language and the study of knowledge," *Cognitive Sci.*, vol. 1, 1977.

[24] G. Gordon, *System Simulation.* Englewood Cliffs, NJ: Prentice Hall, 1969.

[25] P. Hammond, "Appendix to PROLOG: A language for implementing expert systems," *Machine Intell.*, vol. 10, pp. 471–475, 1982.

[26] R. G. Hudson, *The Engineers' Manual*, 2nd ed. New York: Wiley, published originally in 1917.

[27] M. Konopasek, "An advanced question answering system on sets of algebraic equations," in *Proc. European Conf. on Interactive Syst.*, D. Lewin, Ed. Uxbridge, England: Online Publications, 1975.

[28] M. Konopasek and M. Kazmierczak, "A question answering system on mathematical models in microcomputer environments," in *Proc. First West Coast Computer Fair Conf.*, San Francisco, CA, 1977, pp. 182–186.

[29] M. Konopasek and C. Papaconstadopulus, "The question answering system on mathematical models (QAS): Description of the language," *Computer Languages*, pp. 145–155, 1978.

[30] M. Konopasek and S. Jayaraman, *The TK!Solver Book: A Guide to Problem-Solving in Science, Engineering, Business and Education.* Berkeley, CA: Osborne/Mc-Graw-Hill, 1984.

[31] G. F. Luger, "Mathematical model building in the solution of mechanics problems: Human protocol and the MECHO trace," *Cognitive Sci.*, vol. 5, pp. 55–77, 1981.

[32] W. S. Mark, "The reformulation approach to building expert systems," in *Proc. IJCAI-77*, pp. 329–335.

[33] R. S. Michalski, J. G. Carbonell, and T. M. Mitchell, *Machine Learning: An Artificial Intelligence Approach.* Palo Alto, CA: Tioga Publishing, 1983.

[34] D. S. Nau, "Expert Computer Systems," *Computer*, pp. 63–85, Feb. 1983.

[35] A. Newell and H. A. Simon, "GPS, A program that simulates human thought," in *Computers and Thought*, E. A. Feigenbaum and J. A. Feldman, Eds. New York: McGraw-Hill, 1963.

[36] ______, *Human Problem Solving.* Englewood Cliffs, NJ: Prentice Hall, 1972.

[37] N. H. Nie, C. H. Hull, J. G. Jenkins, K. Steinbrenner, and D. H. Bent, *Statistical Package for Social Sciences.* Hightstown, NJ: McGraw-Hill, 1975.

[38] H. P. Nii and N. Aiello, "AGE (attempt to generalize): A knowledge-based program for building knowledge-based programs," in *Proc. IJCAI, 1979*, pp. 645–655.

[39] G. S. Novak, "Representations of knowledge in a problem for solving physics problems," in *Proc. IJCAI-77*, pp. 286–291.

[40] H. E. Pople, "The formation of composite hypotheses in diagnostic problem solving and exercise in synthetic reasoning," in *Proc. IJCAI-77*, pp. 1030–1037.

[41] D. Ross, *ICES Systems Design.* Cambridge, MA: MIT, 1967.

[42] S. S. Ross, *McGraw-Hill's TK!SolverPack to Accompany Hicks: Standard Handbook of Engineering Calculations.* New York, McGraw-Hill, 1984.

[43] E. H. Shortliffe, *Computer-Based Medical Consultations: MYCIN.* New York: American Elsevier, 1976.

[44] M. Stefik, J. Aikin, R. Balzar, J. Benoit, L. Birnbaum, F. Hayes-Roth, and E. Sacerdoti, "The organization of expert systems: A tutorial," *Artificial Intell.*, vol. 18, pp. 135–173, 1982.

[45] L. Tesler, "The Smalltalk environment," *BYTE*, pp. 90–147, Aug. 1981.

[46] P. C. Treleaven and I. G. Lima, "Japan's fifth-generation computer systems," *Computer*, pp. 79–88, Aug. 1982.

[47] W. van Melle, "A domain independent system that aids in constructing knowledge based consultation programs," Ph.D. dissertation, Stanford University, Stanford, CA, 1980.

[48] S. Weiss and C. Kulikowski, "EXPERT: A system for developing consultation models," in *Proc. IJCAI-79*, pp. 942–947.

17
The Personal Computer in "C & C"

KOJI KOBAYASHI, KAZUYA WATANABE, RYOHEI ICHIKAWA, AND
AKIRA KATO

*Computer technology and communications technology are gradually merging together. The advent of
personal computer networks serves as a testimony to the growing need to equip personal computers with
the ability to communicate efficiently with other computers. Technological advances in the areas of
microelectronics, packaging, and improved machine intelligence are all contributing to enhancing the
quality of the man–machine interface. These issues are discussed in this chapter. In addition, an overview of
the Japanese computer market is presented. This chapter focuses on the design and architecture of the NEC
PC-100 personal computer.*

The Editors

I. INTRODUCTION

After a century of progress in electrotechnology, we have arrived at the remarkable and
exciting stage when Computer and Communications technologies are merging. To describe this
challenging trend, one of us (Kobayashi) coined the term "C & C" in 1977 [1]–[3].

In the field of communications, data communications and image communications have
become key supplements to conventional telephone-based audio communications. As *communications* technology has advanced from analog to digital, in terms of transmission and
switching, it has become compatible with digital-based computer technology. At the same
time, the focus in *computers* has evolved from data processing to information processing, and
from centralized processing to distributed processing. Computer systems and subsystems are
now linked via a network of communication lines, to compose a total system. This integration
of two preeminent areas of electrotechnology will continue to progress into the 21st century [4],
[5].

The invention of semiconductor devices has proved fundamental among the factors that have
encouraged the emergence of "C & C." In a relatively short period, we have seen transistors
give way to ICs, ICs to LSIs, and the development of VLSIs. The impact of these microelectronic
components can be seen in the increased miniaturization, lower power consumption, and faster
operating speeds. The industry is now approaching one million components on a tiny chip of
silicon. Thus integration and reliability have jumped while costs have plummeted. As a result,
the cost–performance ratio has improved at an annual rate of 30 percent. These ICs, LSIs, and
VLSIs are indispensable in the manufacture of both computers and communications equipment.
Moreover, with the rapid expansion of the capacity of memories and sophistication of the
functions of logic circuits, LSIs and VLSIs are now beginning to incorporate intelligence. Hence,
the systems built using these chips are becoming functionally closer to human beings.

K. Kobayashi is with NEC Corporation, 33-1, Shiba 5-Chome, Minato-ku, Tokyo 108, Japan.

K. Watanabe, R. Ichikawa, and A. Kato are with NEC Corporation, 210, Hisamoto, Takatsu-ku, Kawasaki,
Kanagawa 213, Japan.

A. Man–Machine Interface [6]–[8]

Conventionally, it has been necessary for people to adapt and to become closer to machines in order to use computers and communications equipment effectively. While the amount of effort required has reduced over the years, it is still necessary to put considerable work into approaching and using sophisticated systems. Our ideal is to arrive at a more fulfilling social and cultural life through the use of information systems that anyone, not only specialists, can use quickly and easily.

The field that demands most human effort is software. The so-called "software crisis" emphasizes that the world has been unable to keep up with the burgeoning need to develop necessary software. Fig. 1 shows that the reduction of human effort has been made possible by improvements in software, beginning with the use of higher level languages and continuing with advances in various terminal equipment. As we have seen, this change has been made possible by the addition of intelligence through the use of LSIs and VLSIs; in other words, by advances in the intelligence of the machines themselves.

A recent trend in the area of man–machine interface is in the design of personal computers which are able to recognize the user's voice and speak a specific natural language, instead of relying solely on input through the keyboard and output via the display screen. This operating method makes access to personal computers much easier for most users.

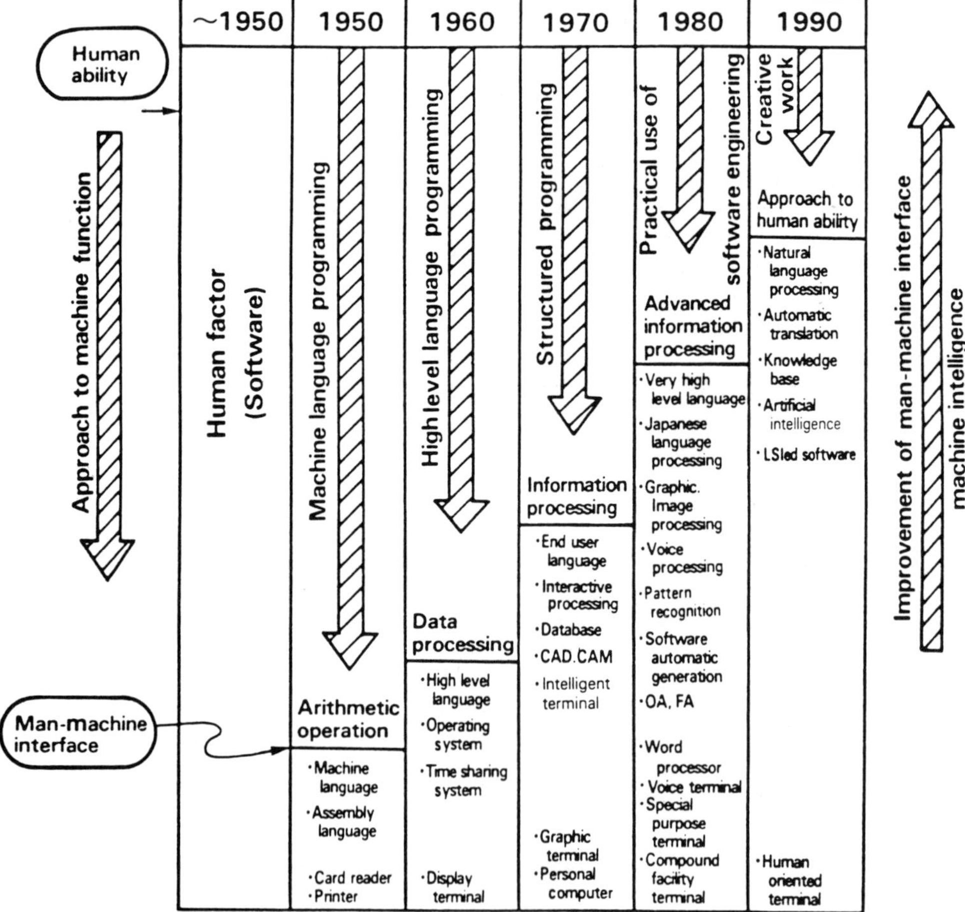

Fig. 1. Machine approaches man.

When personal computers are connected to international communication networks, information and messages enter in foreign languages. Therefore, a necessity arises for automatic translation functions to allow the user to receive information in his or her native tongue. This, in turn, leads to the challenge of automatic interpretation of incoming and outgoing messages in the future.

B. Role of Communications

Fig. 2 shows the role of personal computers in modern communications [9]. They appear in the home system and business system shown on the left-hand side of the illustration. A TV receiver, a telephone set, and a personal computer represent terminals in the home system. Telephone sets, workstations or personal computers, a local area network (LAN), and an office processor are representative elements of the business system. (Here, "office processor" is a general term for shared information equipment.) These home and business system terminals are connected to broadcast program centers, facsimile broadcast centers, and teletext centers via direct broadcast satellites or local broadcast stations through air or CATV cables. These terminals are also connected to videotex centers, electronic mail centers, and other intelligent information facilities through domestic networks and user-access systems. Incidentally, the recent development in bidirectional communications between the above terminals and some of the aforementioned intelligent information facilities is functionally close to the "telescreen" predicted in George Orwell's novel *1984*, though in the free world the TV cameras attached to the terminals are not intended to allow Big Brother to watch us.

By installing a modem to the telephone set and loading commercially available network communication software, a subscriber to a personal computer network service can access, by

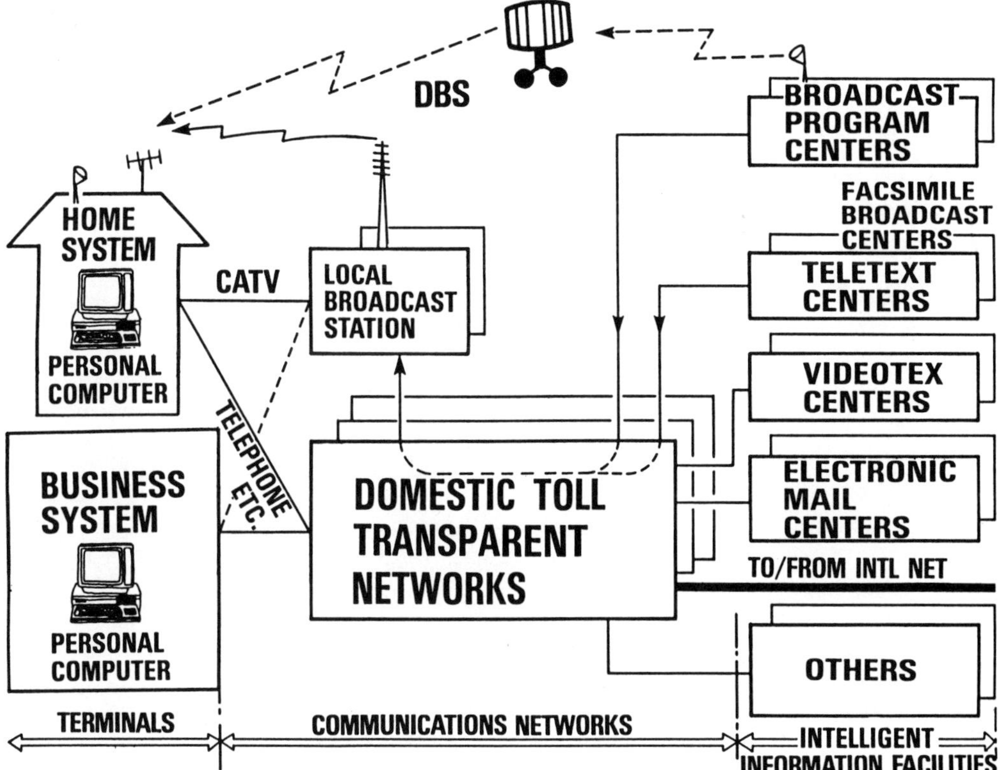

Fig. 2. Role of personal computers in modern communications.

password, travel guides, theater guides, encyclopedias, and other databases provided by one of the intelligent information facilities shown in Fig. 2. The advantage of this system is its accommodation of various types of personal computers, while the videotex system allows access to only its own terminals. However, its disadvantage is that it displays only letters and characters, whereas the videotex system can display color images as well.

Personal computer network systems can also be used for an electronic mail service among subscribers and for on-line and real-time conferences via display screens and keyboards among a multiple number of subscribers using a specific channel. In the near future, personal computer networks will be able to process color images as well, like the present videotex service, and will play a central role in the videotex system.

The advent of sophisticated communication networks allows office work to be done at home using personal computers, and the products to be transmitted to the office via communication networks. In the near future shopping and banking, too, will become possible through personal computers. By loading personal computers with the appropriate software or by connecting them to one of the intelligent information centers specializing in a particular field, these personal computers can serve educational needs. Also, they can function as the brain of home intrusion detection systems and fire detection and alarm systems. Gradually, personal computers will become the nucleus of home information systems.

The application of personal computers is rapidly increasing all over the world. At present, however, the level of intelligence of personal computers is still insufficient and there is room for further improvement in the man–machine interface. Over time, as personal computer usage increases at home, in business, and in government, they will become much more user-friendly. Accordingly, these personal computers will play a vital role and generate changes in the business community and in the wider society, as we move towards realization of the "C & C" world.

In the light of the above trends, NEC Corporation now offers three representative 16-bit personal computers in the world market. In this chapter we focus on the design of one of them, the PC-100.

II. PC-100 Specifications

The main functional specifications of the PC-100, introduced in October 1983, are summarized below:

  1) CPU: μPD8086 (8 MHz)

  2) Storage

        Main RAM: 128K bytes (standard)

                          can be extended up to 768K bytes

        Video RAM: 128K bytes (standard)

                          512K bytes when color board is installed

  3) Display

        Display system: full-bit map system

        Resolution: 720×512 dots (for horizontal installation of CRT)

                          512×720 dots (for vertical installation of CRT)

        Text: 90 characters $\times 32$ lines (for horizontal installation)

                          64 characters $\times 45$ lines (for vertical installation)

        Colors: 16 out of 512 colors can be displayed for each dot

                          palette function is provided to set colors

  4) Mouse: 2 select switches provided

                          resolution of 0.25 mm (1 pulse/ mm)

  5) FDD: 1 or 2 units of standard 5-1/ 4-in thin-type (360K bytes/drive unit)

  6) Printer interface: parallel interface in accordance with the Centronics' specifications

7) Serial interface: in accordance with the RS-232C standard 150 to 19 200 Bd (can be selected by software)

8) Calendar clock: year/ month/ day/ hour/ minute/ second (backed up by NiCd battery)

9) Number of slots: 4

10) Kanji
    Font: 16 × 16 dots/character
    Kinds: JIS first level (2965 characters) including approximately 700 characters other than Kanji

11) Keyboard: total of 91 keys: numeric pads, 5 function keys, control key, copy key, and cursor keys

12) Optional LSIs
    NDP: 8087 (8 MHz)
    DMAC: custom LSI.

The position of the PC-100 relative to other prominent Japanese personal computers is summarized in Table 1. The functionality of the PC-100 reflects emphasis on the following design goals.

a) Most of the software should run in the PC-100 minimum configuration. As the operating system functionality expands, so does its storage requirements. The MS-DOS Version 2.0 software employed in the PC-100 together with the BIOS occupy 60K bytes of storage. Our first

Table 1 Prominent Personal Computers Available in the Japanese Market

Maker Type	CPU	Main RAM (byte)	V-RAM (byte)	Max. Color Number	Max. Graphics Pixel	Mouse	FDD	Operating System	Basic
NEC									
PC-100	μPD-8086	128K	128K	16	720 × 512	O	$5\frac{1}{2}$ in	MSDOS	O
PC-9801E	μPD-8086	128K	198K	8	640 × 400	—	optional	—	O
PC-8801MKII	μPD780 (Z-80)	64K	48K	8	640 × 400	—	$5\frac{1}{2}$ in	—	O
PC-8201	8085	32K	3K	LCD monochrome	256 × 48	—	optional	—	O
PC-8001MKII	μPD780 (Z-80)	64K	16K	4	600 × 200	—	optional	—	O
PC-6601	μPD780	64K	16K	15	320 × 200	—	$3\frac{1}{2}$ in	—	O
Fujitsu									
FM-11EX	i8088	128K	192K	8	640 × 400	—	$5\frac{1}{2}$ in	CP/M-86	O
FM-7	6809	64K	48K	8	640 × 200	—	optional	—	O
F-9450-II	MN1613	256K	optional	optional	640 × 480	—	8 in	APCSIII	—
Toshiba									
PASOPIA-16	i8088	192K	128K	optional	640 × 500	—	$5\frac{1}{2}$ in	MSDOS	O
PASOPIA-7	Z-80	64K	48K	8	640 × 200	—	optional	—	O
Sharp									
MZ-5511	8086	128K	98K	8	640 × 400	optional	$5\frac{1}{2}$ in	CP/M-86	O
MZ-2200	Z-80	64K	48K	8	640 × 200	—	optional	—	O
MZ-700	Z-80	64K	—	8	optional	—	—	—	O
X1	Z-80A	64K	48K	8	640 × 200	—	—	—	O
PC-1500	custom	8.5	—	LCD monochrome	26 ch × 4 line	—	—	—	O
Hitachi									
MARK-5	6809	64K	80K	8	640 × 200	—	optional	—	O
Oki									
if-800/50	8086	256K	128K	8	640 × 475	—	8 in	MSDOS	O
Mitsubishi									
MULTI16	8088	192K		8	640 × 400	—	8 in	CP/M-86	O

goal was to realize an inexpensive entry system with only 128K bytes of main memory and capable of operating most of the application software in this limited storage space.

b) The PC-100 should offer high-resolution on a full-bit mapped color screen. This requirement comes from two points of view. One is, of course, the need for good graphics. The other is the need for displaying Kanji (Chinese characters used in Japanese writing), an objective unique to the Japanese market [15]. Being more complex to display than alphanumeric characters, the Kanji font generally cannot be displayed on a 9×7 dot matrix used for alphanumeric characters but requires at least a 16×16 dot matrix. This means that the number of Kanji characters that can be displayed on a CRT is about half that of alphanumeric characters. Increasing the number of dots on a screen is favorable to the users. We opted for 720×512 dots on a screen and to support color graphics, permitting selection and simultaneous display of 16 colors out of 512 possible colors.

c) The fine bit-map should be realized at low cost without sacrificing throughput. Since the use of CRT control LSIs or dual processors implies an expensive system and a limited number of buyers, we decided to design the PC-100 such that both main storage and video RAM can be accessed without bus arbitration.

d) The PC-100 should offer an improved user interface. The user interface may be divided into two areas: input and output. In the area of input, it was decided to employ a mouse, which was then attracting worldwide attention. In the area of output, it was decided to design the CRT such that it could be aligned either vertically or horizontally and to provide software for such processing [10].

e) The PC-100 should support Kanji. NEC decided to support Kanji at all levels: the operating system level [20], the language level (BASIC level) [21], and the applications software level in addition to support at the hardware level.

The PC-100 system is shown in Fig. 3. Its detailed system diagram is presented in the next section.

Fig. 3. External view of the PC-100 personal computer.

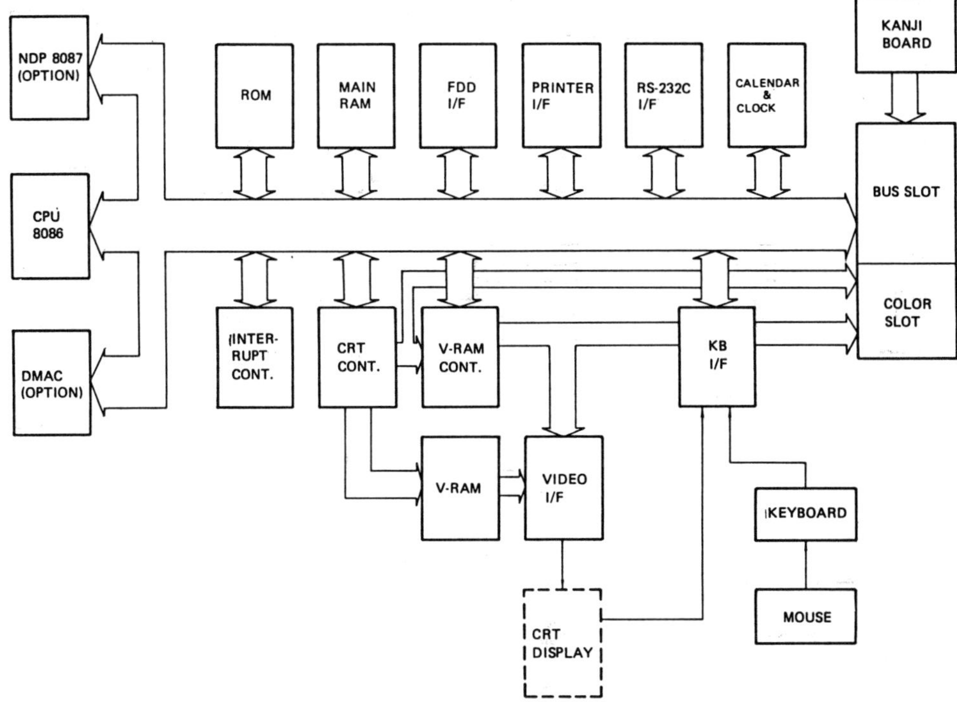

Fig. 4. PC-100 block diagram.

III. System Block Diagram

As shown in Fig. 4, the PC-100 uses an 8086 as its main CPU. In addition, a second CPU (8048) is mounted in the keyboard.

The main storage area is assigned addresses 00000 (hex) through BFFFF (hex). The video RAM (V-RAM) area is allocated 128K bytes from C0000 (hex) through DFFFF (hex). The allocation of 128K bytes for the V-RAM does not change even if a color board (3 planes, 384K bytes) is added to the system. The ROM area is assigned addresses F8000 (hex) through FFFFF (hex), the top part of the storage area [10]. The Kanji memory board stores about 128K bytes of Kanji data and presently supports about 3000 characters of the JIS first level Kanji [15]. To avoid a large part of the 8086 address space being occupied by Kanji characters, the Kanji data have been mapped in I/O addresses 0080 through 0086.

The V-RAM, unlike other storage devices, is connected to the address bus of a multiplexer controlled by the CRTC. The capacity of this V-RAM is 128K bytes, which is equivalent to 1024 × 1024 dots on a display. Since the CRT display has 720 × 512 dots, the actual display uses an arbitrary area of 720 × 512 dots from the virtual screen of 1024 × 1024 dots. The V-RAM output data signals, via the video interface, are of two types: i) monochrome: analog imaging signal (binary) and TTL-level synchronizing signal and ii) color:analog RGB (red, green, and blue) image signal (octal) and TTL-level synchronizing signal. The display signal frequency is 31 kHz. Moreover, the employment of an analog RGB system makes it possible to provide a display having 8 color shades for each bit of R (red), G (green), and B (blue).

Besides the common key code data, the PC-100 keyboard outputs 3-byte initial data and a 1-byte status datum. The 3-byte initial data comprise the keyboard's device ID (identification) code, self-diagnosis datum, and the keyboard ID. The keyboard ID permits the CPU to judge the version of the keyboard.

The status data, transmitted to the PC-100 every 20 ms, are comprised of mouse data and special-key data. These data permit the CPU to detect the location of the mouse and the

ON/OFF state of the mouse switch. The CPU also detects vertical/horizontal installation of CRT when the switch in the CRT display is connected to the input at the I/O controller.

IV. DETAILED DESCRIPTION OF DESIGN

A. ROM

The PC-100 is normally equipped with a 5-in flexible disk drive (FDD) of 360K bytes. In systems having FDDs, the ROM usually serves to store the software of the IPL (initial program loading) or the character generator. In the PC-100 the ROM also stores I/O handler routines such as the FDD control routine, the CRTC control routine, and the keyboard/mouse control routine. Although the I/O handler block is only 25K bytes long as compared to the 8086 address area of 1M byte, storage of these I/O handler routines in ROM, rather than in the main storage, serves to reduce storage requirements for the disk operating system (DOS).

B. Timing

Although an 8-MHz version of 8086 is used, the clock frequency is only 7 MHz. This is based on throughput considerations described below.

1) CRT Display Requirements: Fig. 5 shows the relationship between the horizontal scan speed for CRT display [17], the scanning time on display area, and the number of dots. At 31

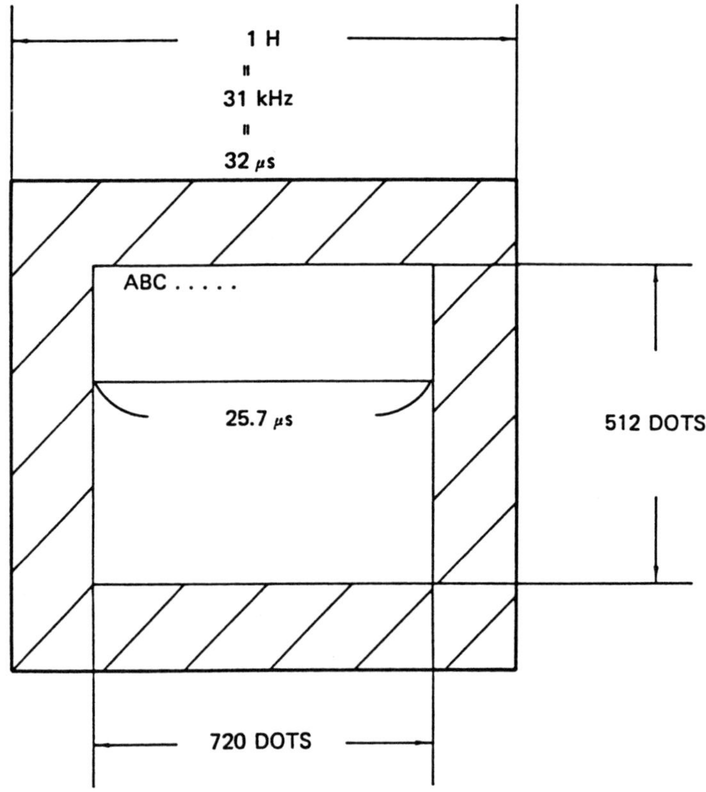

Fig. 5. CRT scanning speed.

kHz, the time required for a single horizontal scan is about 32 μs. The display area of 720 dots is the middle part of the CRT and the time required to scan this area is 25.7 μs. Therefore, the dot frequency at which each dot is to be scanned is

$$\frac{1}{25.7\,(\mu s)/720} = \frac{1}{35.7\,(ns)} = 28\ \text{MHz}.$$

This calculation shows the need for a 28-MHz clock frequency to provide a display of 720 $\times$ 512 dots.

2) CPU Access and CRTC Access: There are two ways of displaying data on a CRT which allow for access to the main storage during execution of jobs. One is by providing the system with a display CPU, thereby allocating the V-RAM in a different area from the main CPU area [16]. The other is by equipping each bus with a multiplexer, thereby permitting switching between the CPU access and the CRTC access (bus arbitration). The first method permits asynchronous operation of the main CPU and display CPU without interference between the two CPUs, and promises maximum possible throughput. This technique, however, involves extra cost for the support circuit. The other method, though with no extra cost, reduces throughput because the CPU must wait during the CRTC access. This happens because, if the CRTC access, which should be given top priority, is in a wait status, it cannot give a proper display.

3) Retaining High Throughput with Low-Cost Architecture: The low-cost second alternative described above was modified to support high throughput. Earlier we noted that the access to the V-RAM can be either: i) a CPU access, in which the CPU rewrites data into the V-RAM; or ii) a CRTC access, in which V-RAM outputs data to the CRT display. The two types of access are not allowed to occur simultaneously on the V-RAM, because the CRTC access is given priority for its real-time display on the CRT. When the CRTC seeks access to the V-RAM, the CPU must be made to wait temporarily. To do so, a wait signal must be generated and transmitted to the CPU. As shown in Fig. 6(a), the minimum bus cycle for the CPU (8086) is made up of four states (4 clocks). The 8086 specification says that the CPU uses the bus only during the $T2$ and $T3$ time intervals in the minimum bus cycle [11], [12]. If, therefore, the system is designed such that the CRTC can access V-RAM during the $T4$ and $T1$ states, that is, while the CPU is not using the bus, the V-RAM can be accessed from the CRTC without suspending the CPU operation. The

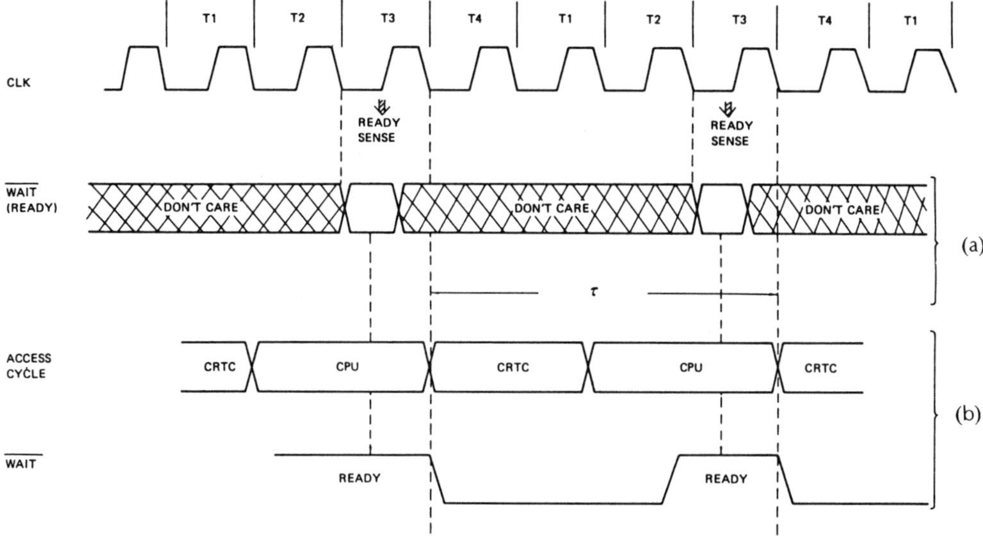

Fig. 6.   Timing chart for CPU access and CRTC access.

wait signals sent to the CPU due to the CRTC access of the V-RAM, should be active for the two clock cycles during the CRTC accessing and also for the succeeding clock cycle in order to avoid bus interference. Since the CPU can sense the wait signal only in state $T3$, if the CRTC accesses the V-RAM in the $T4$ and $T1$ states, the wait signal is active in the $T4$, $T1$, and $T2$ states (three clocks total) and inactive, that is, in the ready state, in $T3$ states (see Fig. 6(b)). This design ensures that the CPU can continue to execute without waiting [11], [12]. Thus τ (CRTC access period) = 4 clocks is ideal.

4) V-RAM Requirements and Synchronous Execution: The block diagram in Fig. 7 shows the sequence of operations from the occurrence of the V-RAM access signal to the transfer of data to CRTC. The V-RAM access signal, when input to the CRTC, causes the CRTC to switch the address selector, permitting the V-RAM to be accessed by the CRTC. The V-RAM accessed outputs 16-bit parallel data to the parallel/serial converter, which converts the data into serial data and inputs them to the video output controller. Finally, data are transferred to the CRT display as analog signals. The frequency of the signal output to the CRT display, as calculated above, should be 28 MHz. The required time (t) for CRT to display data (16 bits) from V-RAM for each access is

$$t = \frac{16 \text{ bits}}{28 \text{ MHz}} = 571 \text{ ns}.$$

If, therefore, the V-RAM access signal occurs every 571 ns, data can be displayed on a CRT without interference. This interference-free display can be obtained by making $\tau = t$. This condition can be satisfied by specifying $\tau = t = 571$ ns. Since the CPU clock frequency $f(c)$ is equal to the state frequency $f(T)$ and τ occupies four states in one bus cycle, $f(c)$ is

$$f(c) = f(T) = (571 \text{ ns}/4)^{-1} \doteqdot 7 \text{ (MHz)}.$$

In the PC-100, the CPU actually runs at a frequency of 6.9888 MHz. This architecture, however, is effective only when the CPU handles 4-state instructions. Instructions having five or more states cause disturbed synchronization, and the system remains in the wait state until the next cycle.

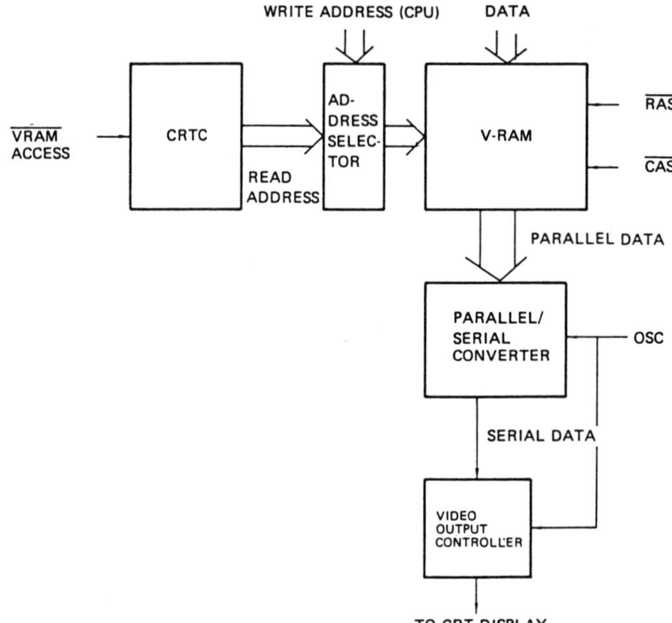

Fig. 7.   CRT control block diagram.

C. Graphics

The PC-100 uses a full-bit-map system capable of displaying graphics at any position on the CRT. In such full-bit-map systems, the display rate may be kept low, because the CPU must provide data to each bit. To solve this problem, a sophisticated graphics control LSI is relevent; however, such a chip is still not available.

To increase the display rate and to lighten the load on software, the PC-100 uses the concepts of bit shift and bit mask as shown in Fig. 8, where a part of the CRT display has been magnified. Each display element has been sectioned into rectangles of 16 bits × 1 bit. This is because one access permits the V-RAM data to output one word, that is, 16 bits at a time. Assume the heart mark in Fig. 8 to be an icon (graphics symbol) of application software. This icon is positioned between the vertical lines and can be displayed by directing the CPU to read out the icon data from the pattern area word (16 bits) by word and inputting the data to the V-RAM. Now, assume that the operator uses the mouse to move the icon to the position shown in Fig. 9.

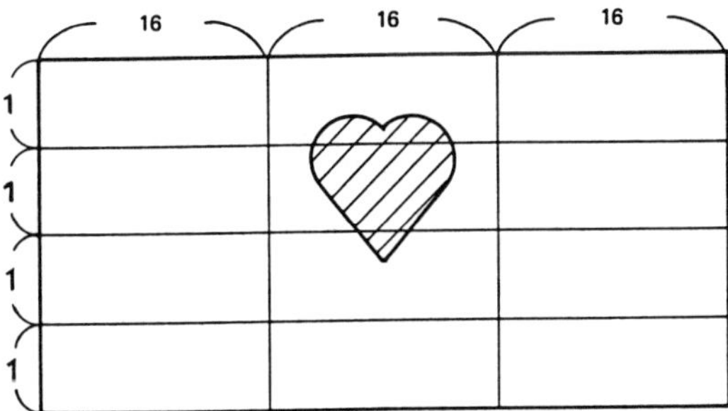

Fig. 8. An icon drawn within one word length.

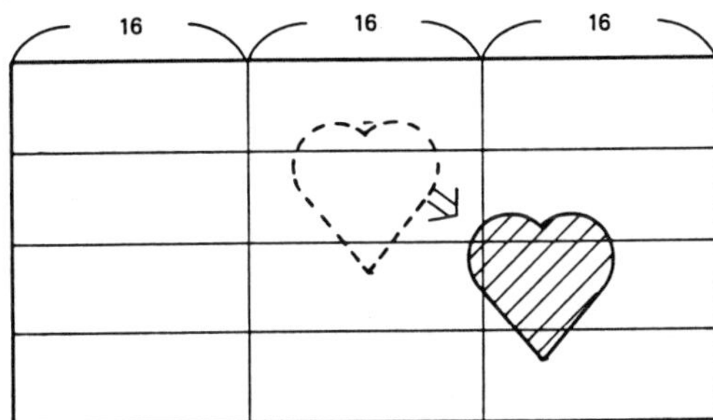

Fig. 9. An icon drawn across word boundary.

Since the icon overlaps a vertical line, two words are required. Moreover, the CPU must discriminate between the data on the left and right pairs of the vertical line and provide each of the two words with the respective data. If all these jobs are processed by software only, the burden on the CPU increases, resulting in a slower display rate [22]. To mitigate this problem, the PC-100 is equipped with two logic circuits (Fig. 10): i) the bit shift logic, which modifies input data to the V-RAM, and ii) the bit mask logic, which decides whether the input data should actually be written into the V-RAM or not.

The bit shift logic is comprised of 16 I/O addresses and is controlled by the OUT instructions. The bit shift logic has a shift register that stores 1-word (16-bit) image data sent from the CPU. When the OUT instruction is given to input shift data, the contents of the register is rotated to the right according to the number of bits specified by these shift data and the input to the V-RAM. The bit mask logic is controlled by the PPI 8255. Data sent by the OUT instruction to control the bit mask logic are converted and input to the WRITE ENABLE terminal of the 64K-bit dynamic RAM [13], which constitutes the V-RAM. The CPU judges whether or not to write the image data input to the V-RAM into the RAM.

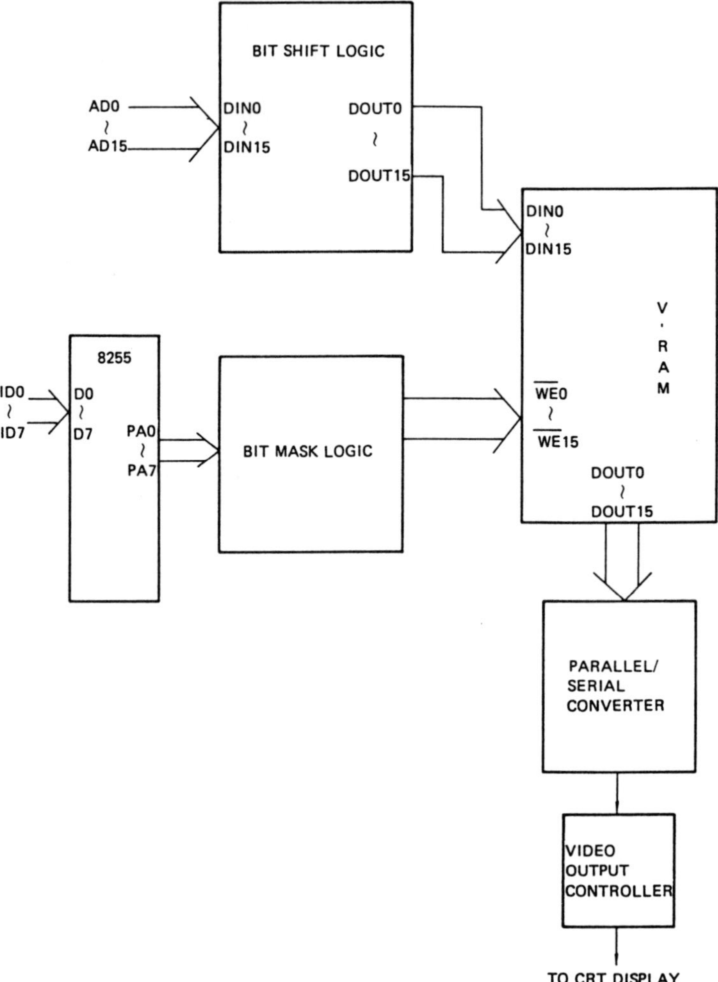

Fig. 10. Bit mask and bit shift logic block diagram.

The process by which the bit mask logic and bit shift logic actually produce the icon in Fig. 9 is shown in Fig. 11. The image input data from the CPU to the bit shift logic are contained in one word (16 bits) at stage (a) in Fig. 11. These data are subjected to a bit shift, resulting in image (b). The data at stage (b) have some undesirable shifted parts, which are subjected to bit mask, resulting in the final image (c). Overall this strategy enables graphics to be effectively displayed at any point on the CRT.

D. Colors

The PC-100 employs two techniques that NEC has never previously used in its personal computers: the palette gate array and the analog RGB output system [14], [17], [18]. The PC-100 color version has four planes of V-RAM. However, these four planes do not correspond directly to R (red), G (green), B (blue), and brightness, respectively. In other words, each plane stores a bit of the 4-bit data given to the palette gate array but does not store the color image data themselves.

The CPU transmits 4-bit color image data to the corresponding V-RAM, and to V-RAM0 through V-RAM3 (see Fig. 12). When a CRTC access occurs, the image data selected by the

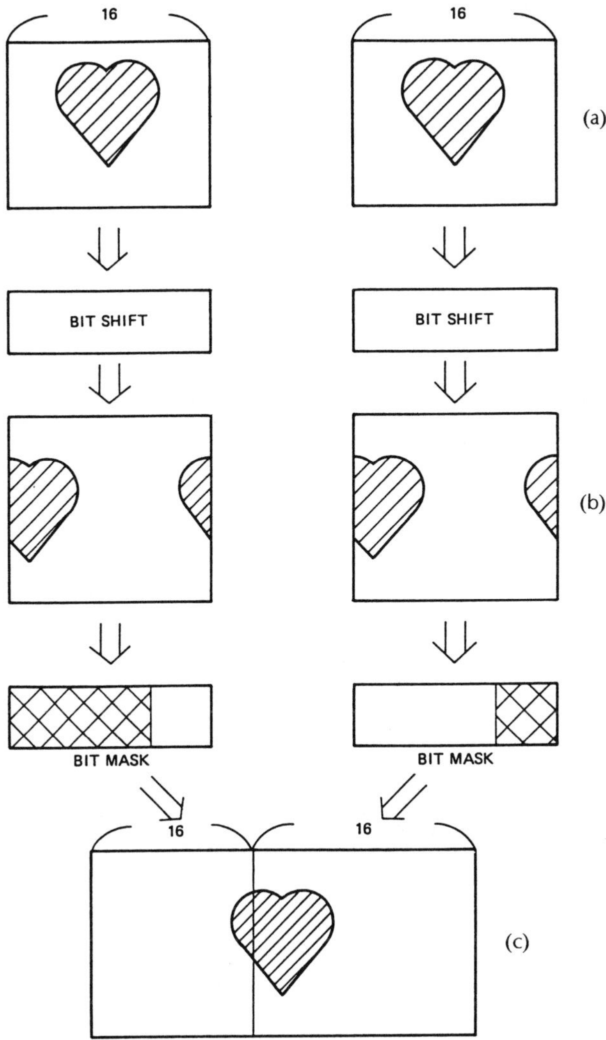

Fig. 11. Display method with bit shift and bit mask logics.

CRTC are transmitted from V-RAM0 through V-RAM3, via the video output controller, to the three gate arrays, GATE ARRAY0 through GATE ARRAY2. Four bits (one bit each from V-RAM0 through V-RAM3) are input to each gate array. As shown in Fig. 13, each gate array contains 16 3-bit registers, $R0$ through $R15$. The contents of each 3-bit register serve to store shade data, of which there are $8(=2^3)$. Each color can have eight different shades. The values of registers $R0$ through $R15$ are set by the OUT instruction; it specifies the I/O address of each register ($R0$ to $R15$), which is mapped in the I/O address, and then color shade data are input to the proper address. Finally, the 4-bit data input to GATE ARRAY0 through GATE ARRAY2 is decoded by a decoder in each gate array to select the register which is specified by the data. The contents of the registers selected are output to a ladder-type resister network and then input to the CRT display as analog signals. Since each gate array (GATE ARRAY0 through GATE ARRAY2) receives the same 4-bit data from the V-RAM, the register to be selected has the same number in each gate array. For example, if

$$V\text{-}RAM0 = 1$$
$$V\text{-}RAM1 = 1$$
$$V\text{-}RAM2 = 0$$

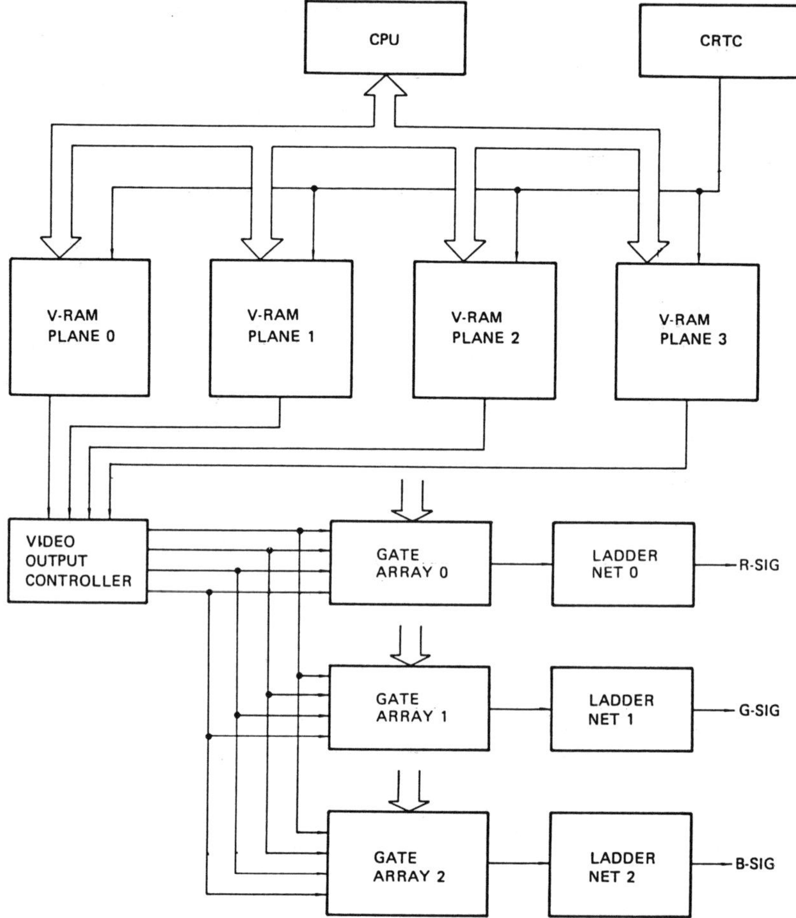

Fig. 12. Color control block diagram.

and

$$V\text{-}RAM3 = 0,$$

then each gate array receives a "3" (decimal), and the registers selected by these data are $R3$ registers.

In each palette gate array, every register independently receives shade data (palette DATA) from the CPU via the I/O port (see Fig. 13). The lower the number, the higher the brightness—a 0 implies maximum brightness, and an 8 implies the darkest level of shade. If in the previous example shade data are 0, 3, and 8, respectively, for each $R3$ register, then the actual color displayed on the screen is a mixture of bright red, fairly light green, and very dark blue. Since there are three sets (R, G, and B) of 16 registers in the color palette block, it is possible to realize up to 16 different combinations of primary colors on one frame without revising the shade DATA. Overall, the PC-100 can display $2^3 = 8$ individual shades of red, green, and blue giving a total of 512 combinations ($2^3 \times 2^3 \times 2^3$). Of these, 16 can be displayed simultaneously on the CRT.

V. Conclusion

The PC-100 was aimed at being an easy-to-use system. It has found wide application in fields such as office automation represented by spreadsheets and word processors, in computer

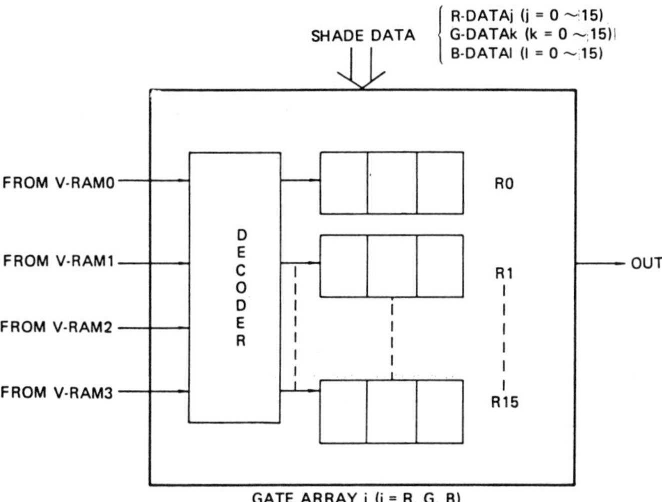

Fig. 13.   Color palette gate array block diagram.

graphics and computer-based education, as well as in entertainment through its ability to play sophisticated games. The goals set for the PC-100 have been mostly achieved. However, we believe that this personal computer is only a milestone in our endeavor towards a "C & C" world.

Several users feel that the user interface is still not very friendly. Also, there are complaints about software. The BASIC language, furnished as a standard language on personal computers, sometimes scares novice users. Although all these opinions are partly true, it should be remembered that no useful tool can ever be utilized without proper study and training; activities requiring intelligence, effort, and time. The adverse feeling towards computers arises not because of an application software concept or a logical process but because a personal computer is an electronics device with which many customers are still unfamiliar. In other words, an ideal personal computer is one that allows a user to concentrate his or her efforts to understand the logical structure of the application—not the program itself but rather its function.

Software is the key towards realizing this requirement. It is extremely uncomfortable for users to learn different operations and commands for the same function. In a word processor, control-X means file exchange. However, in spreadsheets it is necessary to press Function Key-2 to exchange a file, for example. Since a personal computer is supported by a variety of programs from different software firms, standardization of operations and commands must be taken very seriously [19].

In the software technology area, improvements in the "help" function will significantly contribute towards making the personal computer easy to handle. An advanced "help" function will tell the user the current phase of his or her job with regard to the application software and show every possible next process he or she can handle. In addition, it is mandatory that the "help" function is appreciated not only by novices but also by skilled, sophisticated users. Such advanced "help" functions involve database technology, pointing device technology, high-resolution CRT technology and, perhaps, voice technology.

Another improvement will be in the input process. Documentation already printed on paper should be treated in the same way as documentation stored in electronic or magnetic files. Image input system and pattern recognition technology will provide answers for this requirement.

Apart from the above, there are many areas in which no attempt has yet been made towards improving functions in such areas due to limitations in available technology and even limitations in man's imagination. The final objective always seems to be just beyond the horizon. When current problems are overcome and desired goals are accomplished, another horizon is always seen ahead, because technology keeps progressing and customers demand more nearly perfect products. The present century of innovations in communications and computer technology serves as evidence of this hypothesis. By performing more intelligent functions, and with lesser human intervention, personal computers of tomorrow will play a vital role in the "C & C" world!

REFERENCES

[1] K. Kobayashi, "Shaping a communications industry to meet the ever-changing needs of society," presented at INTELCOM 77, Atlanta, GA, Oct. 10, 1977.

[2] ______, "The Japanese computer industry: Its roots and development," presented at the 3rd U.S.A.–Japan Computer Conf., San Francisco, CA, Oct. 10, 1978.

[3] ______, "The Japanese telephone industry in the year 2000," presented at the Third World Telecommunication Forum 1979, Geneva, Switzerland, Sept. 19, 1979, issued in the *Proceedings*, pp. II. 6.1–6.7.

[4] ______, "A perspective on the information oriented age: 'C & C'," *NEC Res. Devel.*, no. 56, Jan. 1980.

[5] ______, "Telecommunications in the future," *IEEE Commun. Mag.*, June 1980.

[6] ______, "Computers, communications and Man: The integration of computers and communications with Man as an axis—The role of software," presented at the 23rd IEEE Comput. Soc. Int. Conf., Washington, DC, Sept. 16, 1981.

[7] ______, "Future role of 'C & C' in the home," presented at the Massachusetts Institute of Technology, Cambridge, MA, June 11, 1982.

[8] ______, "Man and 'C & C': Concept and perspectives," presented at the Int. Institute of Communications (IIC) Annual Conf., Helsinki, Finland, Sept. 6, 1982, also issued in concise form and entitled "Man and 'C & C': The long term view," *Intermedia*, vol. 10, no. 6, pp. 18–23, Nov. 1982.

[9] ______, "Strategic approaches to modern communications: 'C & C'," presented at the 4th World Telecommunication Forum, Geneva, Switzerland, Oct. 27, 1983, issued in the *Proceedings*, pp. III. 1.3.1–1.3.11.

[10] *PC-100 Technical Manual*, NEC Corp., Tokyo, Japan, 1983.

[11] *MULTIPROCESSOR DATA BOOK*, NEC Corp., Tokyo, Japan, 1983, pp. C-582–C-640.

[12] R. Rusell and G. Alexy, *The 8086 Book*.   New York: Osborne/McGraw-Hill, 1980, Ch. 7, pp. 364–388.

[13] *IC MEMORY HANDBOOK*, NEC Corp., Tokyo, Japan, 1983, pp. D-20–D-30.

[14] *TTL GATE ARRAY DESIGN MANUAL*, NEC Corp., Tokyo, Japan, 1982.

[15] H. Ishida, "Chinese character Input/Output and transmission in Japanese personal computer," in *Proc. CompCon, Fall '79*, pp. 402–409, 1979.

[16] S. Hamada, "16 bit personal computer, PC-9800 series," *NEC Tech. J.*, vol. 36, no. 5, pp. 1–9, 1982.

[17] W. Pratt, "A precision color raster-scan display for graphics application," *Hewlett-Packard J.*, pp. 19–24, Dec. 1980.

[18] K. Kanazu, "CRT display for personal computer," *NEC Tech. J.*, vol. 36, no. 5, pp. 50–55, 1982.

[19] "A fierce battle brews over the simplest software yet," *Business Week*, pp. 61–63, Nov. 21, 1983.

[20] *PC-100 MS-DOS Programmer's Manual*, NEC Corp., Tokyo, Japan, 1983, pp. 149–171.

[21] *N100-BASIC User's Guide*, NEC Corp., Tokyo, Japan, 1983, Ch. 5, pp. 65–74.

[22] J. D. Foley and A. Van Dam, *Fundamentals of Interactive Computer Graphics*.   Reading, MA: Addison-Wesley, 1982, Ch. 11, pp. 450–456.

18
Communications and Personal Computers

B. O. EVANS

Since the advent of the telegraph system and telephone technology in the nineteenth century, communication technology has continued to evolve. The invention of the electronic computer gave rise to integration of computer and communication technologies in the form of terminals and multiprocessor computer systems. Today communications technology plays an important role in the areas of personal computers and local area networks. Satellite communication facilities give a new dimension to the prophesied evolution of electronic cottages. This chapter presents an overview of communications technologies and their important role in the current personal computer revolution.

The Editors

I. INTRODUCTION

In 1844 Samuel F. B. Morse sent the world's first telegram a distance of 40 miles between a railroad station in Baltimore, Maryland, and the U.S. Supreme Court in Washington, DC. Samuel Morse's message "What hath God wrought!" marked the beginning of electrical communications. When Alexander Bell demonstrated his invention of the telephone in 1876, communications' reach and flexibility took another important step. Two decades later, Marchese Marconi sent the first message by wireless telegraph.

The application of electrical energy to computation occurred almost a century after the telegraph, for it was late in the 1930s when H. H. Aiken of Harvard University and G. R. Stibitz of the Bell Telephone Laboratories developed an automatic electric calculator using electromechanical relays. In 1946 John von Neumann and his associates at the Institute for Advanced Study in Princeton, New Jersey, developed a new theory and architecture for electronic computation. Maurice Wilkes, a member of the von Neumann group, returned to Cambridge University and in 1949 demonstrated a working model of the new theory— a stored program digital computer. Shortly thereafter the Institute for Advanced Study operated their stored program computer. Early electronic computers were produced using vacuum tubes and electromechanical relays. Subsequently, the advent of newer technologies and more efficient devices such as the transistor and the integrated circuit enabled computer processing performance to improve by a factor of 3000 (Fig. 1) [1], the cost of multiplication to decrease by a factor of 400 (Fig. 2) [1], and the magnetic disk storage capacity per dollar to improve by a factor of 300 (Fig. 3) [1]—all in less than 30 years!

Back in the 1950s users coded their own problems in each computer's unique instruction set. Striving to cope with the idiosyncrasies of the computers' designs was very difficult, e.g., "I

The author was with International Business Machines Corp.; he is with Hambrecht & Quist, San Francisco, CA, USA.

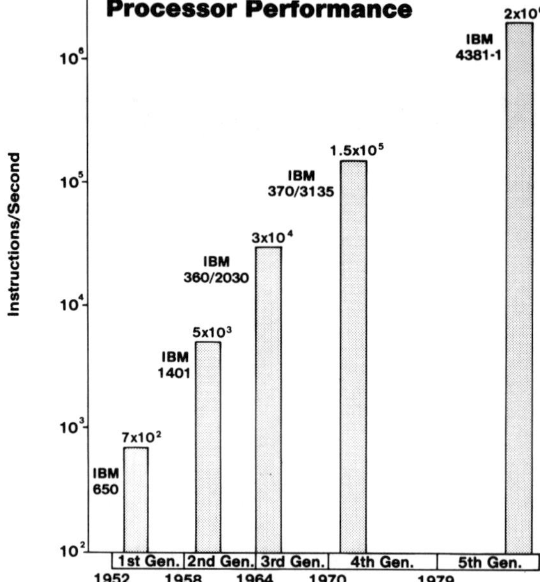

Fig. 1. Processor performance measured in terms of number of instructions executed every second.*

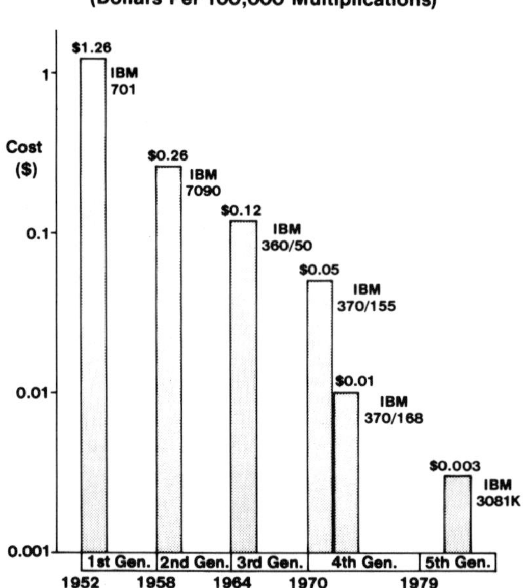

Fig. 2. Cost of performing 100 000 multiplications.

have 113.5 milliseconds between the PRINT instruction and the instant the data needs to be at the printer so I will squeeze in this table look-up subroutine. Now let's see, this instruction takes 36 microseconds, this one 54 microseconds . . . ." In those days computer rooms were organized with intermediaries operating the systems, sometimes even coding the users' problems. The user often had to wait days for the response from the computer. The limited power of

*Editors' Note: The definition of generations used by IBM is slightly different from the more widely accepted definition—see Table 1 in Chapter 2. This note will also apply to Figs. 2, 3, and 4.

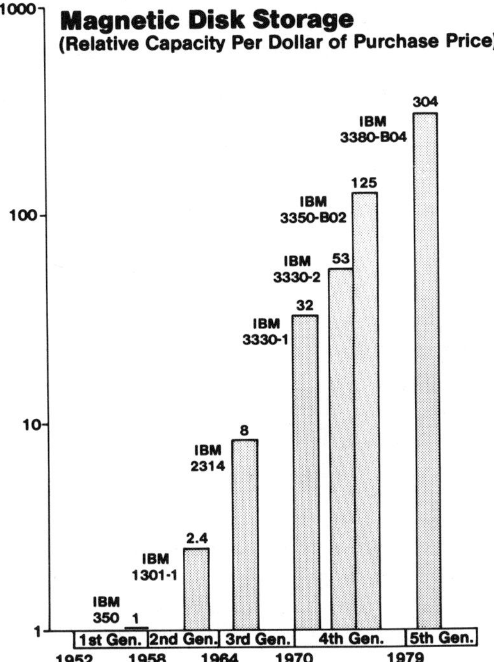

Fig. 3. Magnetic disk storage capacity per dollar.

the machine allowed only one job to be processed at a time. The advent of concepts such as multiprogramming and remote terminals enabled the computer to respond simultaneously to multiple users since the high speed of the computer allowed concurrent service, with each user perceiving as if the computer were dedicated to that user. Personal computers reflect the next logical stage in this progression. They have dramatically reduced the effort involved in interacting with computers. At another level they have dispensed with the notion of shared hardware—like the original computers, a personal computer operates exclusively for one individual at a time.

Although personal computers have been in existence for less than a decade, they have become a force in the information systems area. Indeed, personal computer sales worldwide exceeded minicomputers in 1982 and, some predict, will surpass large CPUs by 1986 [2]. The personal computer is rapidly becoming pervasive, not just in terms of volume, but also in more subtle ways, as personal computers are displacing more traditional controllers within digital computer systems as well as being the electronic intelligence in a number of new application areas such as teleconferencing control systems, electronics test equipment, instrumentation, graphic design systems, and campus computing networks. The growing number of personal computers and the inherent need for sharing information make it necessary to develop newer and more efficient mechanisms for supporting communications between computing resources.

Integration of Technologies

The first linking of computers and communications was indirect for, in the early 1950s, transceivers, operating independent of the computer, transmitted punched card images from one unit to another linked via low speed communications lines. Transmission efficiency was soon improved by using magnetic tape units capable of handling faster data rates. The direct connection between the user and computer did not occur until the advent of the key driven terminal. By the late 1950s various terminals and input–output devices were on-line to the computers—remotely linked to central computers through many types of communications facilities. Over the years the types and applications of terminals have increased steadily. Based on their power and functionality, the spectrum of terminals can be classified as follows [3], [4]:

a) Simple terminals with alphanumeric keyboard and printer
b) Programmable terminals with keyboard, printer, and user programmable processor
c) Portable terminals
d) Data entry terminals
e) On-line data entry terminals with interactive display facilities
f) Message switching terminals
g) Graphics terminals
h) Remote batch controllers
i) Interactive systems controllers
j) Automated banking teller terminals
k) Credit verification terminals
l) Point of sale terminals
m) Industrial data collection terminals
n) Optical character recognition terminals
o) Intelligent workstations.

In 1970, only one-fourth of the computer installations used terminals [5]. Now more than 90 percent of all the mini, midi, and large systems in use rely on terminals. In 1983 terminals accounted for almost 20 percent of the computer hardware purchased in the U.S. [6]. Before the end of this decade, terminals will account for over one-fourth of computer hardware sales. Even more significant is the continuing increase in computing power and functionality of these terminals. In a sense, personal computers can be viewed as the end product of the increasing sophistication of terminals. By serving as intelligent building blocks in a distributed computing network, as well as being useful when used independently of other hardware, personal computers offer an unprecedented level of flexibility for use in a diverse range of applications.

II. THE AGE OF PERSONAL COMPUTERS

In 1983 the U.S. information industry exceeded $75 billion not including expenditures on information services, copiers, value added data networks and data switching products [6]. The global figures are approximately twice the U.S. figures. The market will approach $400 billion worldwide by 1987 and is predicted to reach the trillion dollar level in the early 1990s. Whereas the annual compound growth rate in the value of installed computer systems was 13 percent during the period 1969–1974 and 15 percent during 1975–1983, it exceeds 20 percent today. The segment of personal computers shows even more spectacular growth rates. Including inexpensive home computers, there were more than one million personal computers, with a sales value of $5.8 billion, installed worldwide at the end of 1980. In three years the numbers increased to 13 million units with a sales value of $24 billion. This yields compound growth rates of 127 percent and 61 percent based on number of units and sales value, respectively [7].

The position of the personal computer has been superimposed on the performance history of the computer industry in Fig. 4 [1]. This figure illustrates that the personal computer offers performance comparable or superior to that of the mid-range mainframes of the mid-1960s. Fig. 5 uses the purchase price per million instructions per second (MIPS) of computing capability as a figure of merit [1]. The top curve plots the U.S. purchase price of IBM's largest general purpose processors. The figure of merit declined from $600000 per MIPS in 1978 to $300000 per MIPS in 1983. The lower curve illustrates the intermediate range of general purpose systems and shows that in 1983 the indicator was well under $200000. In the case of personal computers, the same figure of merit was $15000 in 1981 and decreased to under $10000 by 1984. One may argue that the problem solving ability of the various instruction sets is not equivalent. However, this difference should not account for more than a factor of two. Even with this normalization, a personal computer offers one MIPS for just $20000!

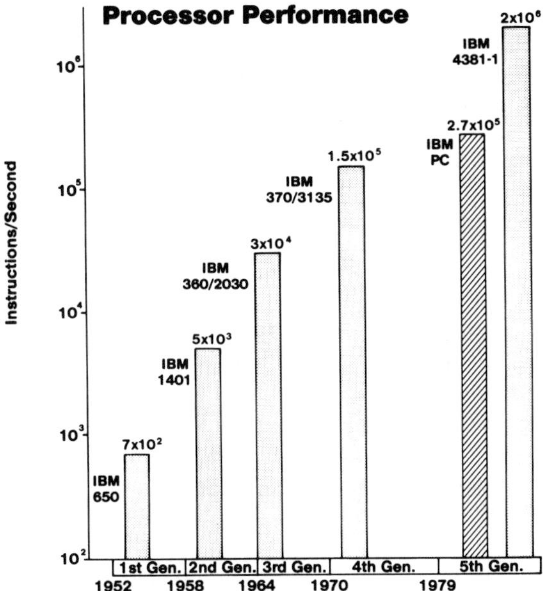

Fig. 4. Processor performance of the IBM Personal Computer in comparison to the performance of other IBM computers.

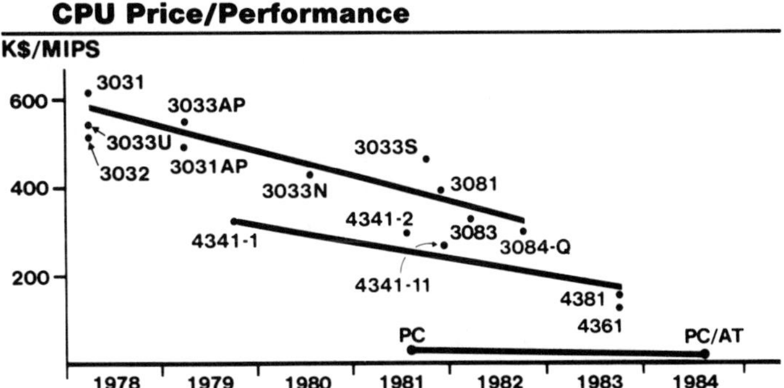

Fig. 5. Trends in price-performance ratios of personal computers and other computers.

Will microsystems eventually push traditional mini-, midi-, and maxi-systems aside? Many believe such domination by networks of interconnected personal computers is inevitable. Others feel that the abilities of the traditional systems will continue to improve as technology advances, and that personal computers will generate even greater needs for larger machines with broader problem solving abilities. Technology and inertia is certainly on the side of the microsystems, particularly as the problems of task segmentation, task scheduling, and task management are refined and strings of parallel microsystems can be brought to bear on strings of individual tasks. Networks of microsystems may eventually operate at speeds exceeding 10 000 MIPS—two orders of magnitude greater than the performance of contemporary super systems.

The range of personal computer application programs is already very broad. For example, there are literally hundreds of programming packages just for handling traditional BICARSA (billing-inventory control-accounts receivable-sales analysis) applications. Among the plethora of application packages, many are designed for esoteric applications which one would rarely contemplate automating using earlier generations of computers. For example, one application program can help keep track of names and addresses of church congregation members, their occupations, skills, anniversaries, pledges, and committee assignments; it also prints out contribution summaries, preparation of mailing labels and financial reports. Another program helps organize a legal case for trial, keeping track of the court, judge, opposing parties, opposing attorneys, witnesses, expert witnesses, documents, exhibits, pleadings, discovery, etc. By virtue of their low cost and wide applicability, personal computers are attracting the attention of persons from many diverse fields.

Computers have traditionally been marketed using a direct sales force. However, with the advent of low-priced personal computers, manufacturers could no longer depend upon dedicated sales forces for all of their marketing. Thus a wide variety of new distribution channels have opened. Major personal computer manufacturers are marketing products in their own stores, through established retailers such as Sears and J.C. Penney and through new specialized retailers such as Computerland. In addition, marketing is done through value added resellers, VARs, who produce specialized programming and equipment to add to particular products. These VARs also serve as the warranty and maintenance agency. Additionally, systems integrators assemble a compendium of manufacturers' equipment to perform a specialized function, provide programming assistance as required, test the assembled equipment, install it and oversee its operation.

Maintenance practices have changed. Previously, computers were serviced on-site by engineers resident at the customer's site or dispatched from a nearby maintenance office. Now, with tens of thousands of personal computers in an area, such directed service is no longer possible. The customer must transport or ship a malfunctioning unit to a service center where he or she can pick up the repaired unit on the following day. In many instances the customer receives a loan of equivalent equipment. In addition, low cost field replaceable subassemblies are fostering a "throw it away and replace it" philosophy.

As volumes move to thousands of units per day, manufacturers are modernizing plants relying heavily on tailored automation and robotic automation. New philosophies of "just in time" component and subassembly delivery are employed to minimize the work-in-process inventory costs. Also, manufacturing plants are being established in developing nations offering low cost labor such as South Korea, Taiwan, the Philippines, Singapore, and India, and already the effects of these electronic equipment shipments are showing in the balance of trade of these developing nations.

New Businesses

Another important aspect is the emergence of new businesses. A recent catalog of hardware and software [8] shows more than one thousand vendors. Of the 903 companies reporting their year of establishment, approximately 500 were established in the period January 1980 through March 1983 (see Fig. 6) [8]. Only two of the companies existed during the first decade of this century; four were established in the second decade, five in the third decade, four in the fourth decade, four in the fifth decade, nine in the sixth decade and only 51 of the companies providing such equipment were established in the period 1960–1969. An additional 51 commenced operation in the first half of the decade of the 1970s and all of the rest, 773 companies, commenced operation in 1975 or later. As an aside, many of the new companies have names such as "Data"-this-or-that, "Micro"-this-or-that, "Software"-this-or-that. Also, there are whimsical names, such as Aardvark Software, Aha Inc., Computer Coverup Inc., Computer Tamers, Kate's Komputers, Mighty Byte Computer, Inc., Once Begun Computations, PC Goodie Co. and, perhaps the epitomy of names, NBI, standing for "nothing but initials"! While there is humor in the names, the more important point is that there is a tide of new engineering and management talent moving into the expanding world of personal computers.

Concomitant with the rapid growth of personal computers comes the need to implement communication links to interconnect personal computers to each other peer-to-peer as well as

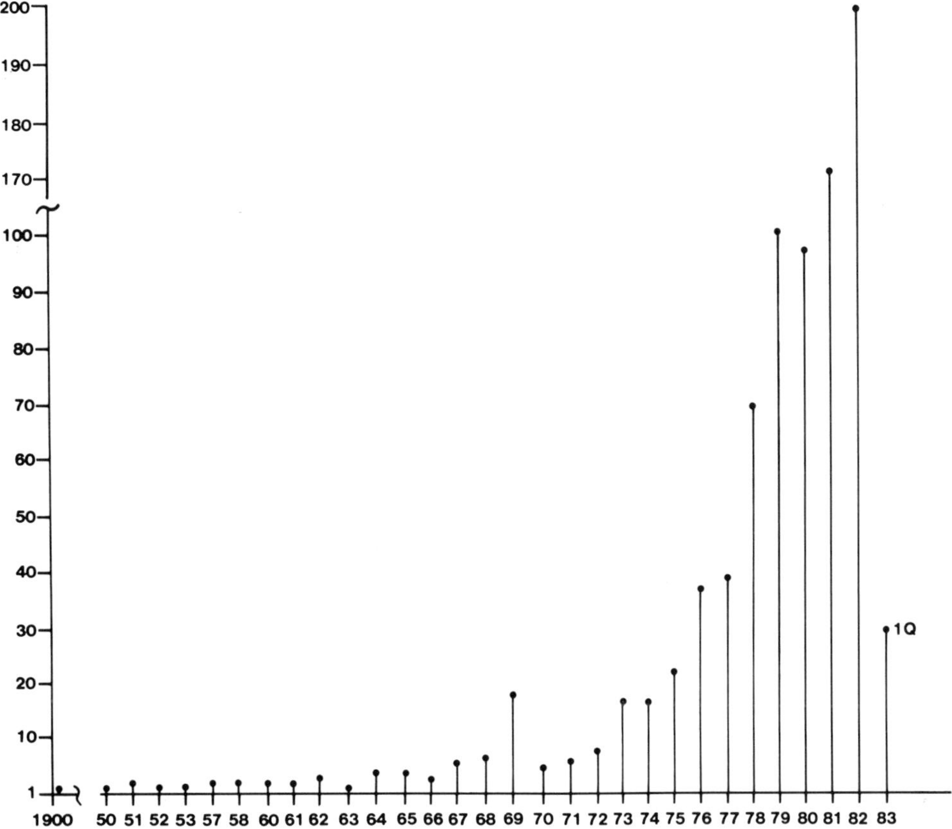

Fig. 6. New Vendors for IBM Personal Computer products: year estimated (903 out of 1100 vendors reported their year of establishment).

to host mini-, midi-, and maxi-processors. Such interconnections are essential to allow sharing of data and programs for commercial, scientific, and educational needs. A number of universities including MIT, Carnegie Mellon University, and Brown University are moving towards bringing "computational plenty" into the campuses through networks of personal computers installed in classrooms, laboratories, dormitories, libraries, and offices. Before analyzing the role of communications in the realm of personal computers, it is pertinent to discuss broader trends in the communication field.

III. COMMUNICATIONS FACILITIES

Most of the communications common-carrier facilities used for data transmission today were originally designed for voice communications. Although the global telephone system is very complex, most portions of it can be considered to be a single system since it is possible for more than 98 percent of the world's 400 million telephones to interconnect. Even though these facilities can be utilized for many data applications, it is unrealistic to expect voice communications facilities to be ideal for applications other than those for which they were designed.

Telecommunications services are forecast to grow steadily to exceed $100 billion in the U.S. early in the 1990s. Nonvoice is projected to grow at the fastest pace, with data comprising most of the nonvoice traffic (Fig. 7) [9]. The historical mix of different communication technologies is shown in Fig. 8 [10] illustrating AT & T's plant evolution. The present common-carrier network is built upon analog voice channels of 4 kHz nominal bandwidth suitable for transmitting either

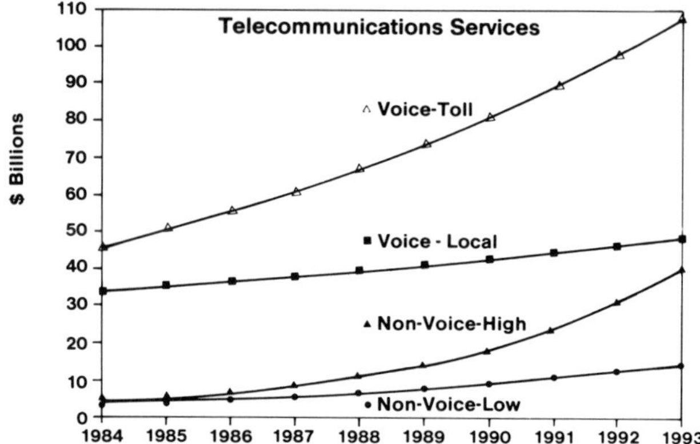

Fig. 7. Forecast growth rates.

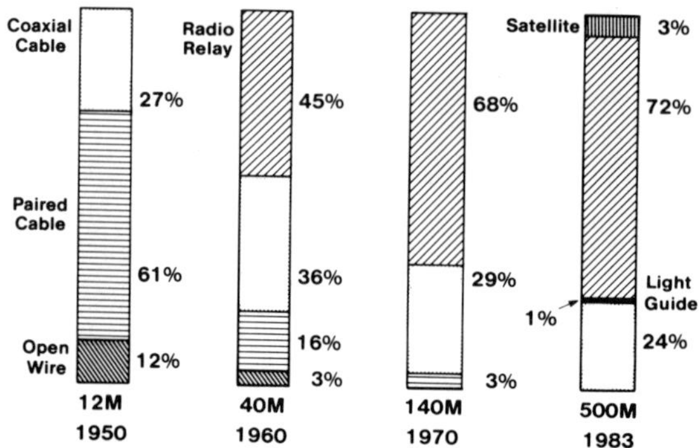

Fig. 8. AT & T message service circuit miles.

voice or data up to several thousand bits per second. Using either frequency-division or time-division multiplexing, voice-grade channels can be subdivided into a number of low-speed telegraph-grade channels. Frequency-division multiplexing is also used to combine multiple voice-grade channels into larger bandwidth blocks for transmission over long-distance carrier systems. A standard hierarchy of channels makes it possible to obtain broad-band channels for data transmission or other purposes. These channels are normally equivalent in size to 12, 60, or 240 voice-grade channels with new high-speed channels in service equivalent to 1200 voice-grade channels. Currently, the largest part of the voice telephone network is based on analog signal handling using frequency division multiplexing. Although digital techniques are being increasingly employed, analog facilities will remain predominant for several more years.

The two major classes of common-carrier services are private (leased) lines and switched services. Private-line service gives the user dedicated lines in the common-carrier system that pass through the switching centers with the necessary interconnections permanently wired or assigned. Private-line service is available in a wider variety of speeds and bandwidths than switched service, with transmission speeds such as 19.2 kbit/s and 230.4 kbit/s available only with private lines. Private-line characteristics are relatively stable since the same facilities are used for each connection. Variations do occur due to total system load, weather factors, etc.; however, it is much simpler to compensate for changing characteristics with private lines than with switched calls and it is possible to obtain line conditioning at an extra charge to extend the usable bandwidth and provide more ideal frequency characteristics. Thus, the superior and more stable frequency characteristics of private lines make it feasible to transmit data at higher rates than over switched lines, especially since they avoid some of the impulse noise originating from switching equipment.

Switched service is available, for example, on telegraph-grade lines, the standard dial network, the Western Union Telex and TWX offerings in the United States. The circuits obtained when using switched services vary in quality from call to call and, in some cases, the variations can be quite pronounced. These variations make it difficult to design data-transmission equipment which will operate satisfactorily over all circuits encountered. Either more narrow, compromised characteristics must be used in systems design, or expensive adaptive circuitry must be employed to automatically adjust to the changing line characteristics. Apart from information bearing signals, the switched system must exchange supervisory information for routing, "on hook" and "off hook" status information, network control information for seizing or disconnecting lines, and various types of ringing signals. Many of these signals are internal to the network and are of little concern to the user, except they do affect the network's data-handling capabilities, connection setup time, and the permissible energy spectrum that can be transmitted. Typical connection times for a direct dialed long-distance connection are shown in Table 1 [11]. Thus, where response time or higher speed transmission are important, dedicated communications facilities become necessary.

Table 1 Connect Time for Direct Distance Dialed Calls [11]

Airline Distance (Miles)	Connect Time (Seconds)	
	Mean	Standard Deviation
0–180	11.1	4.6
180–725	15.6	5.0
725–2900	17.6	6.6

With respect to most transmission facilities, there are three main components—the local loop, short-haul transmission systems, and long-haul transmission systems. The *local loop* is generally a twisted pair of copper wires between users and the local central office. Design of the local loops is influenced primarily by transmission requirements but additionally by economic parameters such as cost of right of way, installation costs, and future service projections. Economic parameters dictate that many multipair cables be channelized into as few routes as feasible. Such common routing for local loops can have adverse consequences on a high-availability data-processing system that uses duplex paths to insure availability, since redundant communication paths will not offer improved systems availability when an outage caused by a cut cable or a rain-storm-filled underground cable vault cripples several local loops simultaneously. Special arrangements to insure separate redundant paths are sometimes possible, but they, in turn, are quite costly.

The *short-haul system* is restricted to spanning distances no greater than 50–250 miles. Open wire pairs, coaxial cable, and microwave radio systems are used for different classes of short-haul systems. Short-haul systems handle multiple voice-grade systems—typically 12–24 channels, with either frequency- or time-division multiplexing used to distinguish among the different channels. Analog amplifiers are used to boost the signal level each time it has traveled a certain distance and, since these amplifiers boost noise levels as well, noise is introduced throughout the system. This becomes more limiting as transmission rates increase, thus requiring more comprehensive error detection, correction, and recovery capabilities in the computer hardware and programming.

Digital communications technologies promise lower power consumption, lower cost, small physical size, increased reliability and flexibility, and improved local-loop capacity. Also, they are more compatible with electronic switching in both central and in private exchanges, and provide a more direct interface to computer terminal equipment. In the T-1 system, for example, 24 voice channels and system signaling information are time-division multiplexed into a 1.544M-bit/s bit stream of data. A very low transmission error rate is obtained through the use of regenerative repeaters located approximately every mile. The newer T-1 systems do a better job of quantizing analog signals—62.667 bits/s voice channel versus 56 000 bits/s for the older system. The new systems, as they become more widely available, will become the preferred media for transmission of data.

Long-haul carrier systems are designed to be extremely efficient. Thousands of voice channels are combined in a multiplexing hierarchy for transmission over coaxial cable or microwave channels. The voice channels are assembled into groups (12 voice channels in a 48-kHz bandwidth), supergroups (5 groups in a 240-kHz bandwidth, and mastergroups (10 supergroups in approximately a 2.4-MHz bandwidth). These systems typically span distances of 250–400 miles. They are designed to exacting standards and usually contribute much less noise and distortion per unit per system than do short-haul systems. Most long-haul systems currently in use are analog in nature, using frequency-division multiplex techniques. An exception is the digital T-2 system with a capacity of four T-1 systems or 96 voice-grade channels and a range of approximately 500 miles.

Echo suppressors and echo cancellers are used to allow flow of energy in only one direction of the transmission system. To permit full-duplex data transmission, the echo control system must be disabled, which is accomplished with a special signal from the data modem. On half-duplex systems, where the channel is used first in one direction and then in the other, the echo-suppression activation and deactivation process consumes tens of milliseconds each time the transmission direction is reversed, often referred to as "turn-around time" of the channel.

Thus, there are many parameters and conditions within transmission facilities that add cost and complexity and sometimes reduce performance of computer communications systems.

Trends in the United States

The recent divestiture of AT & T is unleashing a new spectrum of opportunities for a rapidly widening circle of competitors although it is forcing communications users through a gauntlet of new complexities as the new entities settle into their new world of new markets, new competition, and independence from the former integrated system. Newcomers such as the specialized carriers offer alternative microwave channels and private-line service for voice, teleprinter, data, and facsimile. New packet carriers provide nationwide communication services and charge by volume rather than by miles or contact-time. The increased level of competition is resulting in lower communication costs. Also, services are being targetted towards specific communication needs. The current costs of voice-grade private lines (up to 14 400 bit/s) and terrestrial digital circuits (up to 1.544 million bit/s) are shown in Tables 2 and 3. Two examples are considered in Table 4. All these cost figures will reduce over time.

New communications protocol standards for local area networks are emerging. A collision sense, multiple access architecture is being implemented in many personal computer applications. The token ring architecture is another favorite. Low data-rate modems (up to 300 baud) and medium data-rate modems (300–1200 baud) are now widespread. The typical personal computer modem unit operates at 1200 baud (full duplex), has auto answer capabilities with automatic data-rate selection to match the sending device, and includes sophisticated dial tone detection and test mode equipment. Auxiliary hardware products include:

a) Multiplexors for networking many different communication protocols
b) Message processors for direct and automatic access to telex, TWX, and direct dialing networks
c) File converters for transferring files between different data architectures
d) Encryptors adhering to the U.S. Federal Data Encryption Standard for protection of data during transmission.

A user can now access the latest data from the *Wall Street Journal*, *Barrons*, and the Dow Jones

Table 2 Monthly Rates for Voice Grade Private-Line Service

Mileage	Interexchange Channel Rates
1–14	73.56 + 2.59/mi > 1
15–24	109.82 + 2.16/mi > 15
25–99	131.42 + 1.62/mi > 25
100–999	252.92 + 0.94/mi > 100
Over 1000	1098.92 + 0.58/mi > 1000
Station Terminal	26.05 each

Table 3 Monthly Rates for Terrestrial Digital Circuits

| | | Rates | |
Component	Mileage	Fixed	Variable Per Mile
Inter	1–16	$ 528	$48.35
Rate	17–50	$ 556	$46.60
Center			
Channel	51 +	$1386	$30.00
Local Rate Center Channel		$ 450	

Table 4 Comparison of Rates in the Two Cases

	Terrestrial Digital Circuit	Voice Grade Private-Line Service
Example 1		
Long Haul		
@150 miles	$1386.00 + ($30 × 150) = $5886.00	$ 252.92 + ($.94 × 50) = $299.92
Local Loop	2 × ($450.00) = $ 900.00	2 × ($36.05) = $ 72.10
TOTAL	$6786.00	$372.02
Example 2		
Long Haul		
@1000 miles	$1386.00 + ($30 × 1000) = $31386.00	$1098.92 + ($.58 × 0) = $1098.92
Local Loop	2 × ($450.00) = $ 900.00	2 × ($36.05) = $ 72.10
TOTAL	$32286.00	$1171.02

Newswire Service, and obtain quotes on stocks, bonds, and warrants using the *Dow Jones Reporter. The Source*, another on-line service, makes available a wide variety of data bases including airline schedules and hotel lists. These on-line services make it feasible to access information about many different alternatives on a virtually instantaneous basis.

International Differences

The data communications environment in each country is critical to the development of data-processing applications, time-sharing services and, eventually, international data-processing networks. However, the tariff structures for data, the attachment policies, and the regulatory environment vary from country to country.

The cost applicable in different countries for 1200 and 2400 bit/s leased telephone lines (excluding drop charges) as a function of distance is projected in Figs. 9 and 10 [12]. The U.S. tariff for a 1200 bit/s half-duplex line is the lowest. One conclusion is that a system in Germany or France, utilizing leased facilities, would have a larger percentage of communications costs, although both countries are decreasing long-distance charges while increasing local charges.

The economics of leased voice-grade versus public-switched networks vary by country. In the U.S., for applications that use the public switched network for approximately 1 to $1\frac{1}{2}$ hours per day for a 300 kilometer network, it would usually be just as economical to lease a line. In Europe the economic crossover point is usually around 4–7 hours per day even with the more

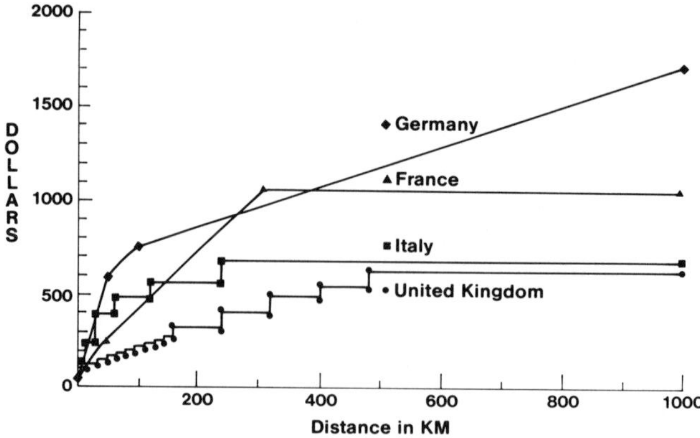

Fig. 9. Europe 2 wires leased lines at 1200 bit/s.

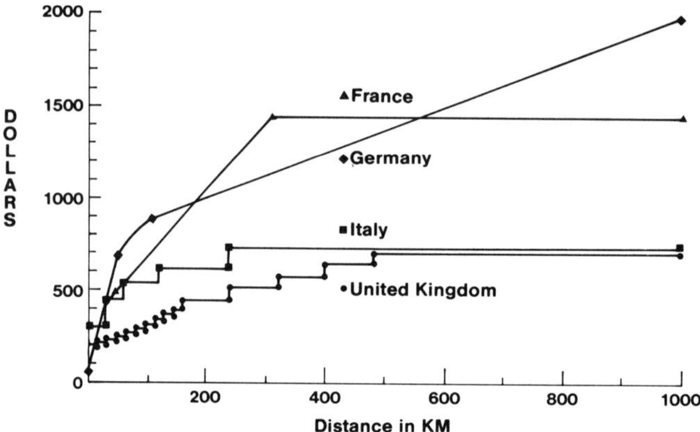

Fig. 10. Europe 4 wires leased lines at 2400 bit/s.

limited intracountry distances. This higher crossover point influences decisions of computer-network designers.

Attachment policies also vary by country. There are countries where the user can provide his or her own modulation–demodulation equipment to attach to the leased network and others where it is mandatory to use a carrier-supplied modem in the leased and/or switched network. At the extreme, acoustical coupling has not been allowed in Australia, Japan, Sweden, Spain, and many Latin American countries. Finally, the physical shape of the handsets limits the use of acoustical coupling devices in certain international systems.

Apart from issues of distance, rules, and practices of countries involved, it becomes necessary to analyze additional aspects such as line quality, time of day, peak and average transmission speeds required, facilities available, etc. Consider the hypothetical network in Fig. 11: 3200 kms in length with 12 terminals attached in six cities of variant distance from the computer. The base case assumes a low volume of only 67 500 characters per terminal transmitted per day at 300 bit/s lines. Also, the packet switched case assumes that each packet is fully utilized. The total costs of operating such a network (in 1981) under various scenarios and in different countries are summarized in Tables 5, 6, and 7. These tables also show the variations in rates if a) the packets hold an average of only 10 characters which is not unusual for many interactive applications; b) the transmission is accomplished at night when certain rates are lower; c) twenty times the data is transmitted daily assuming 4800 bit/s lines; and d) the 12-terminal network is only 800 km in length. Clearly the network designer must carefully evaluate a number of parameters in selecting transmission facilities and, most often, suboptimal compromises are necessary.

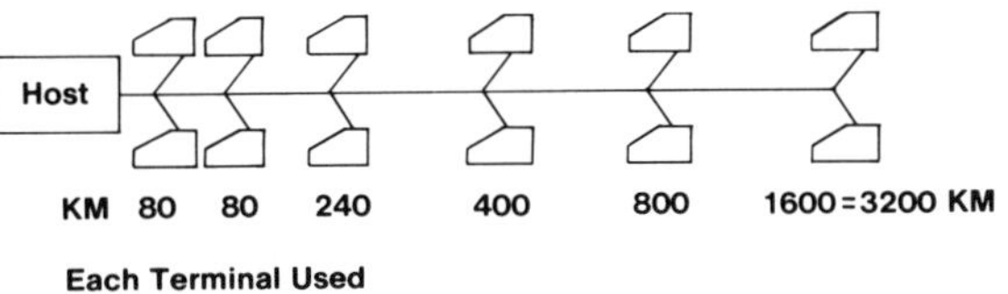

Fig. 11. A hypothetical network connecting 6 cities (two terminals in each city) and one host computer. Each terminal is used to transmit 67 500 characters per day (300 bit/s), 22 working days per month.

Table 5 Cost of Alternative Communication Options in the United States

United States

| | Leased | | Switched | | |
| | | | Public Switched Network | Wide Area Telephone Service | Packet (Telenet) |
3,200 KM Network	**Analog**	**Digital**			
Base, 128-Char. Packets	$2,540	$3,028	$3,211	$2,286	$1,466
10-Character Packets	$2,540	$3,028	$3,211	$2,286	$2,287
Night Rates	$2,540	$3,028	$1,651	$2,286	$1,466
20 x Data	$4,009	$4,009	$5,363	$3,755	$12,194
800 KM	$1,482	$1,970	$2,746	$2,261	$1,466

Table 6 Cost of Alternative Communication Options in Canada

Canada

| | Leased | | Info-Exchange Circuit Switched | Packet (Datapac) |
3200 KM Network	**Analog**	**Dataroute**		
Base, 128 Char. Packets	$6,478	$1,205	$1,853	$769
10-Character Packets	$6,478	$1,205	$1,853	$1,853
Night Rates	$6,478	$554	$1,853	$769
20 x Data	$8,974	$6,803	$4,771	$2,559
800 KM	$3,056	$918	$1,402	$746

Table 7 Cost of Alternative Communication Options in France

France

| | Leased | | Switched | Packet |
800 KM Network	**Analog (Multipoint)**	**Digital (Point to Point)**	**Caducee**	**(Transpac)**
Base, 128 Char. Packets	$10,300	$15,760	$24,650	$3,340
Small Packets (2)	$10,300	$15,760	$24,650	$3,480
Night Rates	$10,300	$15,760	$15,415	$2,970
20 x Data	$14,260	$16,330	$25,550	$9,945
200 KM	$4,660	$8,555	$12,960	$3,340

On the matter of standards, many exist today. Under the aegis of the International Consultative Committee for Telegraphy and Telephony (CCITT) and the International Standards Organization (ISO), the various carrier agencies are working to resolve standards and improve telecommunications with special attention to digital hierarchies.

Emerging Alternatives

Different media offer potential services for interconnection within and between computer systems. For example, light interconnection technology converts electrical signals to light using light-emitting diodes and lasers and provides for transmission over reliable and relatively economical groups of small fiber-optic bundles and reconverts light to electrical signals using photodiodes. *Light interconnection technology* (LIT) has some intrinsic advantages including nonmechanical signal connection since interconnection is accomplished with light-emitting diodes and photodiodes, devices that are made in area arrays. Therefore, LIT has the ability to communicate directly with the large scale integration chips in the computer subsystems, a characteristic that has important ramifications. Further, array LED and photodiode chips, like any other LSI component, can be fabricated at very high densities without concern for crosstalk. In addition, LIT offers electronic insulation as LIT is not affected by ordinary electrical interference and does not radiate energy that can be intercepted and decoded. Therefore, at least for short distances and perhaps in environments where electronic noise or security are very important, light interconnection technology will play a role in computer communications of the future.

In addition, potential sharing of CATV facilities will certainly be a consideration because, in 1983 for the U.S. alone, several million American households were connected to CATV. While there may be difficulties in adapting computers to the varying CATV implementations and additional equipment is required for two-way digital transmission, these networks do offer substantial bandwidth. With their spreading growth, especially in the larger cities, CATV seems destined to play a role in computer applications, particularly where home services develop.

Communications satellites are fascinating both to the computer designer and to the user because of their capabilities for wide-band, on-demand, switched, all-digital network service connecting the far-flung reaches of large geographical areas such as the contiguous United States. Urban, suburban, and rural areas are all connected alike. Besides offering high transmission capacities, the same network can be used for voice, data, and image transmissions unlike the case with terrestrial facilities. Capacity can be added or transferred between classes of traffic and allocated dynamically. Moreover, services from communications satellites are largely distance insensitive.

Most communications satellites operate in the 4–6 GHz frequency region, thus sharing frequency with terrestrial microwave facilities, which imposes limitations on radiated power and physical placement of the earth stations. This, in turn, has cost consequences because of the very large antennas and sensitive receivers required. Newer commercial oriented communications satellites are using reserved frequencies of 11–14 GHz, where there is no regulated limit on power radiated, and little terrestrial frequency congestion. However, these frequency transmissions are attenuated by intense rain droplets, and, as such, the placement of satellites over high-density rain environments is not suitable. This problem can be solved by either placement of selected redundant earth stations or by selective off-load to terrestrial communications facilities.

Communications satellites allow all stations in the antenna's earth coverage to simultaneously receive the transmitted information. Also, the cost is independent of distances between transmitting and receiving stations. For a satellite in synchronous orbit at 35 000 km, an interactive transaction involving a round trip through the satellite will require approximately one-half second. This fixed delay can simplify network programming when considering the satellite approach versus the variable delays encountered in a multinode terrestrial path, but the half-second delay also has the potential of reducing satellite applications where fractional-second response time is essential. Overall, satellite communications are expected to complement —rather than displace—conventional terrestrial communication techniques.

IV. OVERALL TRENDS

Contemporary computer systems have been steadily moving towards distributed intelligence and cooperative processing where job streams flow across a network and are handled in processors as well as in both local and remote terminal controllers. In more advanced configurations, front-end processors handle simple transactions at network nodes without having to transmit to the larger CPUs. In addition, whether computing is accomplished within micro, mini, or larger computers, enterprises have increasing operational needs for interrogation of remote data bases as well as for interchange of computational results and capacity. Hence, instead of microcomputers restricting the growth of communications in computing applications, the price-performance of microcomputers is motivating growth in new applications—thus strengthening the communications-computer relationship.

By 1990 we should see widespread high-bandwidth communication services, paced by both fiber optics and communications satellites for off-premises communications and a variety of wide-band interconnection offerings for on-premises communications. There will be pervasive computer power available, with a maturation of distributed intelligence, and cooperative processing utilizing general-purpose networking. Databases will be distributed throughout enterprise networks. Durable interfaces will increase across the computer industry; thus users will be able to mix or match from various vendors, and acceptance of the standards will help accelerate computer use.

Data, image, and voice terminals will be mass produced and will be quite flexible in their application and adaptability as manufacturers and users will select from a menu of subassembly alternatives to form the function and capacity required for each application (Table 8). Remote terminals and personal computers can be expected to apply to traditional billing, inventory

Table 8 End Use Terminal Primitives

INPUT	OUTPUT	
X	X	PAPER TAPE
X	X	CARD
X	X	MAG-CARD
X	X	MAG-TAPE
X	X	STYLUS
X	X	MICRO-FILM
X	X	TELEPHONE HAND-SET
X	X	VOICE
X	X	OTHER AUDIO
X	X	DISK
X		KEYBOARD
X		TABLET
X		MOUSE
X		WAND
X		OPTICAL CHARACTER RECOGNITION
X		MAGNETIC INK CHARACTER RECOGNITION
X		IMAGE SCANNER
X		SENSOR
X		LIGHT PEN/PROBE
X		SOUND PEN
X		TEMPLATE
X		TOGGLE SWITCH
	X	DISCRETE LIGHT
	X	PRINTER
	X	REPRODUCER
	X	PROCESS SIGNAL
	X	TV
	X	PLOTTER
	X	DISPLAYS (A/N–GRAPHIC–IMAGE–TEXT)

control, remote job entry, accounts receivable and sales analysis, purchasing, and remittance processing; plus a growing list of newer areas such as mass data entry, presentation preparation, discipline problem solving such as design automation, production procedures, plant floor automation, engineering and scientific calculations, administrative automation including internal mail, telephone logs, action files; image data file processing, copying and reproduction, and in-house publication including text processing.

V. Conclusion

Terminals and personal computers are the fastest growing products in the information industry; this growth is predicted to accelerate. By the end of 1987, there will be an installed base of 81.5 million personal computers of which 25.8 million will be in business use, 51.1 million in the home, 157 million in scientific applications and 2.4 million in education [7]!

New communications services, particularly those bringing more cost-effective wide-band communications, will cause further acceleration in the use of personal computers. With variable bandwidth communications and on-demand review, image input/output, and processing will increase, and cryptography as well as refined personal identification techniques will safeguard image and character data to better insure against misuse. Overall, the performance and the price of communications will continue to exert strong influence on the growth of electronic computers.

References

[1] IBM Corporation, submitted to the public record in the U.S. versus IBM antitrust proceedings, 1978, updated 1984, unpublished.
[2] International Data Corporation, 1982.
[3] *Electronic News*, supplement, March 8, 1976.
[4] B. O. Evans, "Computers and Communications," in *The Computer Age: A Twenty-Year View*, M. L. Dertouzoes and J. Moes, Eds.   Cambridge, MA: MIT Press, 1979, pp. 338–366.
[5] *Computerworld*, Jan. 10, 1973.
[6] *Electronics*, p. 124, Jan. 12, 1984.
[7] International Data Corporation, *Personal Computer Markets*, June 1983, pp. 4 and 8.
[8] *IBM Expansion and Software Guide*, third ed.   Que Corporation, 1983.
[9] Satellite Business Systems, private communication, April 4, 1984.
[10] Bell Telephone Laboratories, private communication, Feb. 19, 1984.
[11] Bell Telephone Laboratories, private communication, 1971.
[12] IBM, LaGaude, France Laboratory, April 2, 1984. Assumptions: (a) As the German service has mandatory modems, for comparison $600 and $1200, respectively, are added to the tariffs of other countries. (b) For 2 wires, normal quality is used; for 4 wires, rates are for special quality. (c) The exchange rates per U.S. dollar are France, 8.05FF; Germany, 2.62DM; Italy, 1623IL; and U.K., 0.6975BP.
[13] Carlotta Eaton, IBM, Raleigh, NC, April 11, 1984, unpublished report.

19

The Role of Venture Capital in the Growth of the Personal Computer Industry

STANLEY E. PRATT and ROUBINA KHOYLIAN

Among the nontechnical factors that have motivated the rapid growth of the personal computer industry, the principal factor has been the financial support provided by venture capitalists. During the cycle of growth from the initial conception of a new idea to the eventual operation of a major manufacturing company, venture capital provides a very effective mechanism to nucleate fast progress in an innovative industry. Venture capitalists provide seed money, start-up financing, first-stage financing, and subsequent rounds of financing to facilitate expansion of research and manufacturing capabilities. Historically, venture capitalists have preferred to concentrate in electronics and computer related areas. The current microelectronics and information revolution serves as a testimony to the role of new companies financed by such investors.

The Editors

I. INTRODUCTION

A little over a century ago Charles Babbage conceived the design of a mechanical computer. He spent several years trying to motivate the British government to finance the development of a working prototype. Even though the technical ideas were sound, the project was a failure because of delay and insufficiency in terms of financial support.

During the past century, innovations in financing mechanisms have reduced the level of dependence on governmental support. Banks, insurance companies, and public securities markets provide alternative channels of obtaining money to fund development activities. However, these channels are available primarily to companies that have already demonstrated the viability of their businesses. Venture capital, on the other hand, is targeted towards early-stage financing of new and young companies to enable them to grow at a rapid pace.

II. VENTURE CAPITAL

The venture capital industry covers a broad spectrum. Venture capitalists provide seed money, start-up financing and first-stage financing [1]; in addition, they fund the expansion of companies that have already demonstrated the viability of their businesses but do not yet have access to the public securities or to credit-oriented institutional funding sources such as banks or insurance companies. They also provide management/leveraged buy-out financing to assist

---

The authors are with Venture Economics, Inc., 16 Laurel Avenue, Wellesley Hills, MA 02181, USA

operating managements purchase and revitalize a division of a major corporation or an absentee-owned private company.

The success of companies financed by venture capitalists has attracted more entrepreneurs to bring about a myriad of venture investment opportunities. The dramatic expansion of the venture capital industry which began in 1978 under the impetus of the capital gains tax reduction program continues. With some $12.1 billion in committed capital, the industry has almost five times the resources available only six years ago [2]. In 1982 and 1983 venture capitalists disbursed an estimated $1.8 billion and $2.8 billion, respectively—more than the total aggregate disbursements of the prior four years [3]. It is a classic example of increased supply producing greater demand. Informal individual investors in venture developments have also reemerged, overcoming the strong risk aversion produced by the recession of 1974 and 1975. Even the public stock market has become an important factor with a massive increase in underwritings of companies with a net worth of $5 million or less from $619 million in 1982 to $3.7 billion in 1983 [4].

III. ROLE OF THE VENTURE CAPITALIST

Value-added involvement to assist entrepreneurs and long-term investment orientation are the factors that differentiate venture capital from other investment disciplines [5]. Venture capital should be referred to as "the business of developing businesses," rather than as just an investment business. The relationship between the entrepreneurial management team and the venture capitalist can be best viewed as a partnership. It works best as a long-term peer relationship based upon mutual trust and understanding. The practical experience of the venture capitalist in business development complements the management and technical skills of the entrepreneurs enabling the company to develop faster and more efficiently than without such involvement. This is of particular value in areas, such as personal computers, where product development cycles are relatively short. Apart from financing, the venture capitalist's supportive role includes:

a) providing assistance in finding and selecting key management team members;
b) making customer and supplier introductions;
c) providing assistance with long-range planning, financing, and marketing; and
d) providing a young company increased credibility with potential customers, suppliers, and bankers.

Given the potential value of a venture capitalist's nonmonetary contributions, many successful entrepreneurs emphasize the importance of sources for funding, rather than how much capital and at what price.

Professional venture capitalists enable businesses to develop through successive rounds of financing. This has advantages for both the entrepreneur and the venture capitalist. For the entrepreneur, raising capital is more feasible if investors are able to see reduced business risks prior to the commitment of large amounts of capital. Further, since successive rounds of financing are often made at higher prices to new investors, there is less equity dilution for the entrepreneurial management team in the future. Since professional venture capitalists operate from a committed pool of capital and are locked into their private investments, entrepreneurs who meet their objectives are reasonably certain of receiving future rounds of financing. In general, venture investors prefer to provide capital requirements on a staged basis rather than "up front" before they are able to realistically judge a company's strengths and weaknesses. They normally anticipate future financing rounds for early-stage investments and seek compatible investors with whom they can share lead, as well as participating, roles. The timing and structure of future capital needs, as well as the availability of capital, are major considerations in the venture capitalist's decision process.

Entrepreneurs who receive venture capital funding to start a company have made it over one hurdle. However, they are aware that within a year or two they will probably need additional financing and thus they must perform credibly in order to make the company attractive for the next round of financing. Subsequent investment decisions are made on an objective basis that evaluates past performance, future opportunity, and the apparent risks and rewards. Performing exactly as planned is not as critical as the reaction to plan deviations. One key determinant in future financing rounds is whether the business can adapt to unforeseen difficulties and opportunities, and thereby demonstrate credibility, progress, and promise.

IV. Venture Capital Investment Criteria

The single most important factor behind a venture capitalist's investment decision is judgment of the character and quality of the management team that intends to develop the new business. It is often said that real estate investors concentrate upon three factors: *location, location, location.* Venture capitalists, in much the same way, look for a solid management team as indicated by these five criteria:

1) *Management*
2) *Management*
3) *Management*
4) *Market Niche*
5) *Product or Service.*

Most successful entrepreneurs have some background of management experience, often at the divisional or departmental level of a larger corporation. It is important that they understand how to commercialize a product or service in order to build a new business. As General Georges Doriot, the founding father of the U.S. venture capital industry, observed, "We can back a first rate management team with a second rate product and have success; but if we back a first rate product with a second rate management team we can seldom achieve our objectives."

The competence of the management team is judged by their capability of defining a clear market opportunity and how their product or service will be sold within that market. A new business must address a clear market need that is too small to be of interest to major potential competitors, or a niche that will enable the company to survive its initial development. This niche, however, must be in a market area that promises exceptional growth within three to five years so that the new business can establish itself as a significant factor within that time period. Within five to seven years the market must be potentially large enough so that reasonable market penetration could lead to enough interest for a possible public stock offering or for acquisition by a larger corporation. Venture capitalists must have an exit vehicle for realizing a gain on their investment. While the initial objective may be an independent publicly traded company, the market growth must be great enough to stimulate the acquisition interests of large corporations.

While the particular product or service is important, this factor is often overemphasized by entrepreneurs seeking financing. Venture capitalists avoid products in search of a market; they seek markets in search of a product. A proprietary position in a rapidly growing market can offset errors in judgment of the original management team since the expanding demand for the products or services will attract new managers capable of carrying out the business plan. The product must have a sufficient gross profit margin to provide initial cash flow before the entry of major competitors into the market. Adequate profit margins must be maintained even after aggressive competitor pricing enters into the picture. A high gross margin is a measure of the value-added to the product or service offered for which the customers are willing to pay.

V. Investment Patterns by Industry

Historically, venture capital investments have been concentrated in computer and electronics related areas. The level of investment in various industry sectors in 1983 is shown in Table 1 [6]. Although many view venture capitalists as "high technology" investors, the real emphasis of

Table 1 1983 Venture Capital Investment Activity

Industry	Percent of Investment Activity	
	Number of Companies	Amount Invested
Computer Hardware Systems	28%	39%
Software & Services	12	7
Medical/Health Care Related	11	9
Electronics Components, Equipment and Instrumentation	10	10
Telephone and Data Communications	9	11
Consumer Related	7	7
Genetic Engineering	3	3
Energy Related	3	3
Commercial Communications	3	2
Industrial Automation	3	2
Industrial Machinery and Products	3	2
Other Products and Services	8	5
	100%	100%

venture capital investment is on the application of technology developments to productivity improvement in commercially viable markets [7], and not for the support of new scientific and technological breakthroughs. This is evident from the list of areas in which venture capitalists have been actively investing, as shown:

- Personal computers
- Computer software and peripherals
- Computer graphics, CAD/CAM, and CAE
- Office automation
- Telephone and data communications
- Robotics and vision systems
- Health care delivery and medical products.

Clusters of venture capital financings often precede a take-off in industry sales by three to five years as in the classic case of the semiconductor industry [8], [9]. Venture capitalists have been involved in the financing of such computer industry pioneers as Digital Equipment Corporation, Intel, Prime Computer, Storage Technology, and, more recently, Apple Computer and Apollo Computer. Because of this early involvement, patterns of venture capital investment often form a leading indicator for identification of future growth industries and promising business opportunities. In the personal computer industry, venture-backed companies helped to create and build a market segment to the level where it was large enough to attract the interest of major corporations.

VI. Personal Computer Industry

Venture capital involvement with the personal computer industry really started more than fifteen years ago with the financing of Intel which pioneered the development of the microprocessor. Venture investment in personal computer companies surged after the initial financings of Durango Systems in 1977 and Apple Computer in 1978. The growth of the personal computer market was then spurred by venture capitalists investing in application software companies. A number of venture-backed software companies including Context, Lotus, and VisiCorp benefited from early stage financing. On the other hand, Digital Research and Microsoft did not have venture capital involvement until the expansion stage. During 1983 the emphasis was more towards software (see Fig. 1). In all, over $250 million has already been committed to almost 90 software companies. On the hardware side, more than 50 personal computer manufacturers have so far received financing from the venture capital community

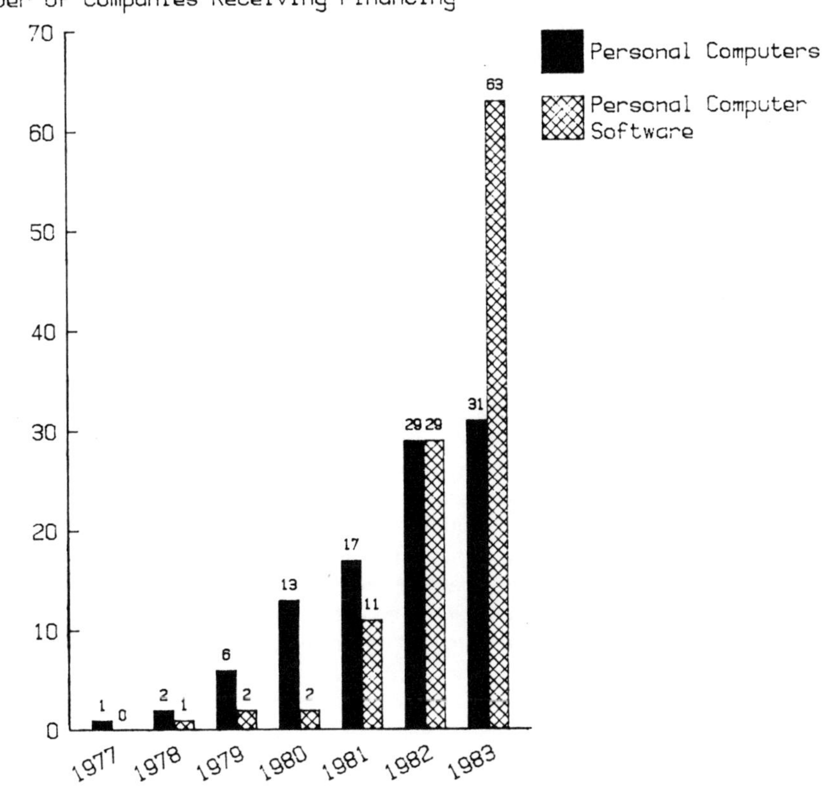

Fig. 1. Venture capital investment in personal computers and software.

totaling to about $410 million. Among the early recipients of venture capital financing, such as Convergent Technologies, Durango Systems, Ithaca Intersystems, Momentum Computer Systems, and Onyx Systems, more than a dozen have already received three or more rounds of financing.

Most of the recently financed companies are targeting specialized market niches. As the overall market has expanded, producing just another personal computer is no longer a market niche. At one end, companies like Compaq, Creative Communications Systems, Gavilan Computer, Grid Systems, Hicomp Technology, Otrona, and Sunrise Systems are targeting towards portable computers. As in any growing market, not all of the entrants can be successful. Findex and Osborne Computer are two venture-backed companies in the portable market that have had difficulties. At the other end of the market spectrum are multiuser systems. In this area, Apollo Computer has succeeded while Fortune Systems has been having trouble. While most of the venture-backed firms offer innovative products, some must be classified as "me-too" companies imitating products of other manufacturers. Venture capitalists have supported some of the "me-too" companies in order to gain a participation in the personal computer market. As increasing competition forces prices down, however, these companies may experience major difficulties as independent entities.

VII. EXPECTED FUTURE DEVELOPMENTS

Although this industry will continue to experience high growth rates and new companies will continue to be financed, the venture capitalists will spend more time and capital supporting their current portfolio of companies and in helping these companies develop and survive in less favorable market conditions. With increased competition, profit margins for hardware companies and now for software companies as well have been diminishing. In the case of personal computer hardware, almost all recent venture capital investments have been follow-on financings of existing companies. In the software area, new companies are still receiving financing although the rate of growth in investments has dropped off in 1984.

The personal computer hardware companies financed to date have received an average of $7.9 million while the software companies have only averaged $2.9 million. Because of the lower capital requirements and the superior growth potential for software companies, more investments will be made in the software sector. Growing competition will also cause increasing acquisition activity. Many ventures produce successful products but do not become successful independent companies. Some products do not provide enough of a base from which to build a growth company, but are very suitable for a larger company to develop as part of a broader product line. As software is more easily transportable than hardware, software companies will be more susceptible to acquisition by larger companies.

Venture capitalists are also investing in companies such as Businessland and Entre Computer Stores which are expanding distribution channels and seeking to educate and train potential users. Also increasing are investments in networking and data communications related to personal computers. The original investments by venture capitalists were instrumental in the development of the personal computer industry. These markets in turn are nucleating a new crop of investment opportunities. This regenerating interrelationship will continue to catalyze the rapid evolution of the personal computer market in the foreseeable future. Overall, venture capital has provided a major ingredient to sustain this revolution.

References

[1] S. E. Pratt and J. K. Morris, *Pratt's Guide to Venture Capital Sources.* Wellesley Hills, MA: Venture Economics, 1984.
[2] "Venture capital industry resources," *Venture Capital J.*, vol. 24, no. 7, pp. 4–6, July 1984.
[3] *Venture Capital Investment—1983.* Wellesley Hills, MA: Venture Economics, 1984.
[4] "New issue barometer," *Venture Capital J.*, vol. 24, no. 1, pp. 24–25, Jan. 1984.
[5] J. A. Timmons, "Venture capital: More than money?" in *Pratt's Guide to Venture Capital Sources*, S. E. Pratt and J. K. Morris, Eds. Wellesley Hills, MA: Venture Economics, 1984.
[6] "Venture capitalists invest $2.8 billion in 1983," *Venture Capital J.*, vol. 24, no. 5, pp. 7–11, May 1984.
[7] *Government-Industry Cooperation Can Enhance the Venture Capital Process.* Washington, DC: U.S. General Accounting Office, Aug. 1982.
[8] N. D. Fast, "Venture watching," *Planning Rev.*, vol. 9, no. 6, Nov. 1981.
[9] N. D. Fast and R. S. Mellberg, "Identifying new business opportunities," in *SRI International Guidelines*, no. 1053, 1980.

20
Epilogue

AMAR GUPTA AND HOO-MIN D. TOONG

Within a decade of their birth, personal computers have become ubiquitous aids to mankind. Concomitantly, the task of selecting a personal computer has become increasingly complex. This chapter provides frameworks to analyze four important issues: a) potential personal computer applications; b) configuration of hardware; c) directions in software; and d) vendor strengths and long-term viability. By analyzing the potential set of applications in some detail and relating them to the technical specifications, one can identify the subset of systems that can meet the needs. In making the final decision, it is necessary to consider both technical and nontechnical issues.

I. INTRODUCTION

Mainframe computers and minicomputers were harbingers of contemporary personal computers. In terms of basic computing power, the mainframes of the 1960s, the minicomputers of the 1970s, and the contemporary personal computers are all in the same performance bracket. Now for the first time the crucial questions of "What to buy?" and "When to buy?" must be addressed directly by the individual who is going to use the computing equipment. The process of selecting and configuring one's own personal computer system has become increasingly complex because of several factors: the rapid pace of technology, the large number of companies on the market with their myriad of pricing strategies, the diversity of applications possible with this technology, and the lack of any easy method of matching user needs with specifications of available systems. We begin by examining some of the motivations for buying a personal computer.

User Requirements

In any business environment, the potential users of personal computers come from several different disciplines—Personnel, Accounting, Management, Manufacturing, Research, Sales. This makes it difficult to develop a representative functional scenario. For example, Research and Personnel have very dissimilar computing requirements. Even within a particular department, there are many diverse applications. For example, the personnel department may run personnel files and database applications on a regular basis; in addition, they may want to examine the impact of personnel policies on manpower planning for manufacturing, or the financial impact of hiring people, or the evaluation of incremental revenue benefits of increased sales personnel. The computing support required for such *ad hoc* applications varies significantly with the individual personality of the actual user. Thus, it is virtually impossible to define a uniform customer profile.

There are, however, broad categories of end-user requirements that hold across the organizations spectrum, e.g., the need for calculation and the need for typed copies. Organizations

The authors are with the Sloan School of Management, Massachusetts Institute of Technology, Cambridge, MA 02139, USA.

generally justify the acquisition of personal computers for the following reasons:

a) To perform general word processing and office automation tasks that have traditionally been handled by dedicated units such as typewriters, word processors, calculators, and photocopying devices;
b) To mitigate the heavy workload on the central computer facility; and
c) To increase the productivity of white collar workers by assisting them to manage and spot trends in data pertinent to their job functions.

These broad justifications reflect a second-order attempt to define the general end-user requirements. The experience in many organizations indicates that instead of serving existing applications, the personal computer creates and fills completely new application needs, or complements existing applications. For instance, a personal computer is initially installed to serve as an intelligent terminal for access to the main computer facility. In the process of retrieving data from the main computer to run application programs locally, users find that the memory and processing capabilities of the personal computer are too limited. Users also find that tools like VisiCalc, 1-2-3, dBase II, and Framework are sufficiently powerful to enable rudimentary modeling and planning. As a complementary application, they often extend their models and databases to evaluate alternative business strategies and to answer "What...if...?" type questions on an instantaneous basis. Frequently, the original application for which the personal computer was purchased becomes a secondary application as compared to the use of modeling and elementary database tools available in the personal computer environment. The availability of good software packages and the sizes of these packages determine the lower limit of the computing speed and the memory capacity of the initial hardware configuration.

II. HARDWARE

Central Processing Unit

The computing power of a personal computer is determined to a large extent by the microprocessor used for performing the calculations. The Intel 8088 microprocessor family is one of the more popular building blocks in the personal computer industry. It is used in the IBM Personal Computer, the IBM PC/XT, the IBM PCjr, the TI Professional Computer, the Fujitsu FM-11 EX, the Toshiba PASOPIA-16, and in many others. The Intel 8088 microprocessor has 16-bit wide internal data paths but only 8-bit wide external data paths. Larger external paths require the chip package to have a large number of pins, which increases the total packaging and production costs. The disadvantage of using smaller external paths is the need for multiplexing signal lines which degrades performance. The true 16-bit version of the Intel 8088 is the Intel 8086 microprocessor. By using the latter chip, personal computers such as the Data General Model 10, the AT&T Personal Computer, and the Wang Professional Image Computer are able to offer higher performance than the basic IBM Personal Computer.

The Intel 8086 microprocessor was introduced in 1978. The first personal computer to make use of this technology was introduced three years later. This time lag can be attributed to several factors: software development for microprocessors, availability of development systems, system development time, product design, actual manufacturing, and marketing related delays. As superior 16-bit microprocessors have become available, they have been incorporated into newer families of personal computers. The IBM Personal Computer-Advanced Technology (AT) uses the Intel 80286 (see Chapter 11) which is a higher capability version of the Intel 8086. By using more recent technology, the new chip offers roughly six times the speed of the old chip. If the auxiliary circuits can cope with the increased speed of the microprocessor, personal computers embodying the Intel 80286 can offer superior performance, by similar factors, as compared to personal computers using the earlier microprocessor.

The Motorola 68000 is the second-most popular family of microprocessors used in personal computers. Microprocessors from this family are used in the Apple Lisa, the Apple MacIntosh, the HP-200, and the IBM System 9000. As seen in Chapter 10, the Motorola 68000 is architecturally superior to the Intel 8086. It is therefore natural that for many applications these computers offer faster computing speeds than the basic IBM Personal Computer. The philosophy of Apple has been towards providing an easier user interface and a display of high resolution.

High performance 32-bit microprocessors have so far been used in workstations too costly to be classified as personal computers. The HP-9000 series computers use the HP 32-bit microprocessor described in Chapter 10. The AT&T 3B2 computer system relies on the Bellmac-32A, also known as the Western Electric 32000. With its full 32-bit data paths and its support of the Unix System V operating system, the 3B2 possesses both excellent hardware and excellent software.

There is a growing trend towards using more than one microprocessor in one personal computer. Coprocessors, attached processors, and auxiliary processors are used to handle specific subfunctions with speed and efficiency. In many cases, the task of decoding keyboard depressions is entrusted to a dedicated 8-bit processor. Another motivation is compatibility. The DEC Rainbow personal computer contains an Intel 8088 microprocessor and a Z-80A 8-bit microprocessor. Similarly, the DECmate II contains a custom designed CMOS 6120 12-bit microprocessor in conjunction with a higher performance 16/32-bit microprocessor which allows a user to execute existing application programs as well as to benefit from the architectural sophistication of newer technology.

Because of their limited physical size, portable computers often lag behind desktop models in terms of computing power. Portable computers use CMOS devices since they consume less power. For example, the Radio Shack TRS-80 Model 10 uses an OKI 80C85, the CMOS equivalent to the Intel 8085 microprocessor. The limited address space available on some of the portable computers is not always sufficient to efficiently run fourth-generation application software.

Memory

There are several different types of memory available. User programs and data reside in RAM. ROMs, PROMs, and EPROMs are used to hold special programs that are hardwired into the microcomputer and, in contrast to RAM, will not be lost when power is shut off. For example, the BASIC Language Interpreter is frequently available in ROM (permanent storage). The size of memory refers to the amount of RAM installed in the computer. There are two constraints that determine the upper limit. The first constraint deals with the memory address space of the particular microprocessor used in the personal computer. Most 8-bit microprocessor-based personal computers have a native address space of 64K bytes (a 16-bit address). Although this address space can be increased using memory mapping techniques, performance degrades. Personal computers using 16-bit microprocessors have native address spaces of 1M-byte or even more. For instance, the Intel 8086/8088 microprocessor has a 20-bit address yielding a 1M-byte address space. Personal computers based on the Motorola 68000 utilize a 24-bit address to yield a 16M-byte native address space. The second constraint comes from physical packaging limitations. To create a memory capacity of 1M-byte, it is necessary to use either 128 chips each of 64K-bit RAM, or 32 chips each of 265K-bit RAM. In addition, support chips are needed. In either case, the memory takes up substantial room inside the personal computer. These packaging constraints will shift by a factor of four with the availability of the 1M-bit RAM in 1986–1987.

At present most personal computers are purchased with an initial memory capacity of between 64K bytes to 256K bytes. However, not all of this memory is available for user programs. System programs such as the operating system, system utilities (e.g., print routines), and others which are not resident in ROM must reside in RAM during the application program execution. The operating system and auxiliary entities such as the system stack, input and output buffers, monitor vector locations, display buffers all use part of the RAM. The amount of physical memory listed in the manufacturer's software manual can be deceptive. Often application programs will not operate in the memory size available with the base configuration of the machine. Instead of buying a system with just enough memory, it is often preferable to get an initial RAM size roughly twice the size of the largest application program. As sophisticated modeling packages, larger database systems, and graphics processing programs are adopted, memory will need to be augmented to 1M byte or even more. As in the case of large computer systems, the personal computer environment, too, testifies to the fact that "No matter how large the size of memory, the user will eventually find some way of consuming it and then asking for more!"

Secondary Storage

The floppy disk has become the ubiquitous storage mechanism for personal computers by virtue of its low cost and the ease of media interchange offered by it. Originally, single-sided disks of 8-inch or $5\frac{1}{4}$-inch size were used. Now double-sided, double-density $5\frac{1}{4}$-inch floppy disks (capacity up to 5M bytes) have become the preferred version with a smaller size of $3\frac{1}{2}$ inches starting to gain significant usage. This does not imply, however, that one can take a floppy disk from an Apple computer and use it in conjunction with an IBM Personal Computer. Because the drive electronics, sectoring, and formating conventions differ between manufacturers, floppy drives and their interface electronics are customized for each personal computer model. Also, different floppy drives reflect different levels of technological sophistication. Aside from increasing the number of tracks on each side of the disk and reducing the distance between two adjacent bits on a track, new innovative techniques are evolving for increasing storage capacities. Usually, all tracks on a disk are of equal capacity even though the physical size of each track is different—tracks near the center of the disk are much shorter than the tracks farther from the center. Thus, as one moves from the center of the disk to its periphery, one finds that an increasing amount of the track space is not utilized. By allowing each track to be optimized independently for the total number of bits on the track, it is feasible to increase disk capacity. This innovation is equally applicable to Winchester disks. Also, it is possible to enhance performance by locating the disk directory (or file allocation table) on the middle track rather than on the innermost track (or outermost track). Obviously a disk with a directory on the middle track cannot be read using a drive which assumes that the directory is on the innermost track. Finally, the technique of vertical recording of data has the potential of enhancing storage capacity several fold.

Another question to ask in considering floppy drives is the number of units configured. Many software application programs are written to make use of two drives. With a one-drive system a great deal of disk swapping is required to do simple operations such as back up, compiling, and editing. Consequently, it is best to configure systems with at least two drive units. Floppy disks offer low throughput rates, and the average access times are typically between 200–500 ms. A single access in itself is not very long in duration; however, if an application program is working with a database or makes frequent retrievals from the disk, processing times can easily escalate to minutes and sometimes to hours in a floppy disk environment. Where better performance is required, a Winchester disk is the best alternative. Typically, a Winchester offers ten times the storage capacity and one-tenth the access time as that in the case of a floppy disk. However, a Winchester disk costs significantly more. Also, in a Winchester disk environment normal back-up procedure involves the use of many floppy disks or the use of a "streaming tape." Both these techniques are rather cumbersome.

With the advent of the optical disk, the situation will change significantly. Capable of storing hundreds of megabytes on a single $5\frac{1}{4}$-inch disk and costing $50 or less, first-generation optical disk units with their write-once capability are most suited for two distinct sets of applications. First, as a permanent storage media for financial, educational, medical, and legal records. Second, as a low-cost media for widespread distribution of databases containing information that is updated regularly, e.g., for distributing stock prices and airline timetables. Until the second generation of optical disks with their full read and write capabilities become available, floppy disks and Winchester disks will be the two best media for storing and retrieving user programs.

Input–Output Devices

In spite of increasing competition, the ubiquitous keyboard continues along. In fact, newer keyboards are being designed with more intelligence to act as interfaces for mice and as interpreters to do voice recognition. Until fairly recently each computer manufacturer had its own version of a keyboard. In the summer of 1983 IBM announced its willingness to sell its personal computer keyboard. Later the same year, it equipped the IBM PCjr with a keyboard manufactured by Advanced Input Devices. The updated PCjr keyboard released in 1984 is from the same manufacturer.

The mouse has become a popular input device; it couples the screen cursor to a mechanical or optical rolling device on the tabletop. Tablets are also available for absolute positioning of inputs from a stylus on a grated surface. The Hewlett-Packard 150 computer system has pioneered the use of touch screens in the domain of personal computers. The interruption caused by the user's hand is detected by sensors along the two sides of the screen using beams of infrared light.

Displays are of two types: video and flat screen. Flat screen displays are primarily used for portable personal computers and are built in, or are configured with the unit by the manufacturer. Consequently, for the desktop environment, the user must select and configure units from the different options available with video technology. The television display, though inexpensive, cannot accommodate the 80-character column widths used in business word processing with enough resolution to be easily read by the human eye. The choice of user displays for business applications is limited to the following video monitor characteristics:

a) Color versus monochrome (monochrome is usually white/black, green/black or orange/black).
b) Degree of resolution capable of being displayed by the monitor. For instance, a normal medium-resolution monitor can display approximately 600 × 400 pixels where a pixel is one dot on the screen. High-resolution monitors can display upwards of 1000 × 1000 distinct pixels on a screen.

Hard copy output can be generated using four alternative devices: thermal printers, impact dot matrix printers, letter quality printers, and laser printers. Prices continue to drop in all categories. A laser printer, for example, can now be purchased for under $4000. Color printers, too, can now be purchased at affordable prices. Four sets of halftone dots are printed. In addition to the three primary colors, black is printed separately as combinations of the primary colors are unable to generate a deep black color. Different color dots are printed very close to each other, and the human eye spatially integrates the picture to present a continuous colored appearance. More colors can be printed at the expense of resolution. As memory costs diminish, and as color hard copy technology becomes progressively cheaper, color printers will eventually replace the present generation of black-and-white printers just as color photography has virtually replaced black-and-white photography.

The IDS Prism color and the Xerox Diablo inkjet color printers have both been designed specifically for use in conjunction with personal computers. Although performing the same function, these two printers differ in terms of the print quality, the number of colors supported, the size of the print buffer, and the level of control possible through software. In some cases the aspect ratio of the printed picture is different from the displayed version. In spite of such minor irritants, the use of color printers is gaining widespread acceptance.

III. SOFTWARE

The choice of software to configure with a personal computer system can be broken down into two categories: programming languages and their development tools, and user application packages. Because of the astronomical costs for software program development in terms of programmer time, documentation, maintenance, and field support, the option of configuring languages and program development tools with a personal computer system is normally considered only for specialized applications for which programs are not available commercially. The vast majority of application needs can be satisfied with off-the-shelf application programs or through the use of "fourth-generation languages," such as spreadsheets, DBMS systems and DSS packages. Unlike previous generation languages (BASIC, Pascal, and Fortran) which offered little support for transferring information between alternative programming environments, fourth-generation languages support such exchange through the concept of "windows." These windows, which are simply separate areas or boxes on the display screen, are used to facilitate the simultaneous display of multiple programs on a personal computer and to enable information to be interchanged between such programs.

The concept of "windows" as an effective user interface was pioneered by the Smalltalk system developed at the Xerox Palo Alto Research Center. This graphics oriented interface presents images of several overlapping pieces of paper on a grey electronic desktop. Each piece of paper, or window, represents an activity which can proceed independently of all others. A "mouse" is used to select a window, to operate a scrolling mechanism that brings the desired data into view in the window, and to invoke commands from menus. The Apple Lisa uses this window concept, as well as the concept of a menu bar containing up to twelve different menu titles. The concept of visual *icons*, which originated in the Xerox Star user interface, has been used in systems such as the Apple Lisa/MacIntosh and the $200 Commodore 64 computer. Instead of using words, the menu uses pictures of objects. For example, to type, one points to the typewriter; to erase, one points to the trash basket; and so on.

The above concepts have been refined and implemented in commercial software products by several companies. Prominent examples are Visi-On (VisiCorp), MS-Windows (Microsoft), Concurrent DOS (Digital Research), Window Master (Structured Systems Group), DesQ (Quarterdeck), In View (Graphicon Software), and Concept VP (Scientia Inc.). However, the concept of windows is not standardized across software vendors. Microsoft Windows have a tiled structure. The size of each tile is dependent on the number of windows being displayed at a given time. Creating a new window shrinks all existing windows and deleting a window causes all other windows to expand to make use of all the space on the screen. In contrast, Visi-On and Concurrent DOS use an overlapped window structure resembling a pile of papers lying on the table. Except for the top window, all other windows are at least partially obscured from view. Any of these windows can be uncovered instantly by bringing it to the top of the heap.

Visi-On takes an all encompassing viewpoint by requiring that a new set of application programs (such as Visi-On Calc, Visi-On Word, Visi-On Graph, Visi-On Query) be used. This implies that no application program developed by another software house can be used under such an environment. On the positive side, such an approach implies a consistent command structure and maximum possible level of data exchange between programs. In sharp contrast, DesQ has been designed to integrate stand-alone application programs. Because of the great diversity between different programs, one must use different commands under different operating environments to perform the same function. MS-Windows has opted to take the safer middle ground, permitting existing programs to be run along with newer application programs that provide a more consistent and powerful operating environment.

The windowing software developed by the big three software houses (VisiCorp, Microsoft, and Digital Research) uses a bit-mapped structure. As opposed to the character-based structure used in some other packages, this strategy permits both text and graphical information to be exchanged and displayed readily. The data-exchange protocol allows for the data to be transferred in context rather than simply as numbers or text. By passing contextual information, it is feasible to use a spreadsheet program and a graphic program together so that any updates are automatically recalculated and regraphed. Obviously, the context information is relevant only under certain conditions. For example, a word processing program has little use for the formulas used by the spreadsheet program. Visi-On, MS-Windows, and Concept-VP are three programs that offer facilities to transfer some level of contextual information aside from the raw data.

VisiCorp is going directly after end customers. Microsoft, instead, is concentrating on personal computer manufacturers. The hardware manufacturers will sell machine-specific versions of the product just as they sell versions of the MS-DOS operating system. Also, leading software companies have agreed to modify their programs to run under an MS-Windows environment.

Two integrated packages that make heavy use of windows are Symphony (Lotus Development Corporation) and Framework (Ashton-Tate). Both of these packages offer spreadsheet, word processing, graphics, database and telecommunication capabilities. Because of this wide functionality, the concept of windows has been employed to allow users the capability to work on different activities without requiring them to complete one activity before taking up another.

When the Symphony program is loaded, a spreadsheet window called Main is displayed. Additional windows, overlapping each other like a stack of papers, can then be created with the active window on the top. Alternatively, the Window Pane command can be used to split one window into two or four tiled windows. The Window Layout command is used to move the window around the screen and to change the size of a window. At any instant, the Zoom function allows a given window to be expanded to occupy the full screen. Symphony employs a strategy of a unified data structure. No matter what the application, information entered in a particular cell will invariably appear the same, irrespective of which "window" it is viewed through. Thus, if the data is altered using a particular window or "context," for example database, the change would also occur in a different window (for example, spreadsheet) which is showing the same data cell. This strategy, however, rules out the possibility of having two distinct spreadsheets be active simultaneously. As in the case of Lotus 1-2-3, a separate Print Graph program must be loaded to generate a hard copy. The versatility of the package is itself somewhat of a drawback—even for persons familiar with Lotus 1-2-3, it requires several hours of initial effort to learn how to create and manipulate the windows and their contents.

When the Framework program is loaded, a one-line menu appears on the screen. The options are: Disk, Create, Edit, Locate, Frames, Words, Numbers, Graphs, and Print. Selecting one of these options brings the relevant menu to the screen. Each window, or "frame" in Framework parlance, is treated as a discrete unit and is stored as a separate disk file. Thus, unlike Symphony, an alteration of data is not automatically replicated in other windows. In order to cause update of data in a different frame, the two frames must be interlocked by inserting a reference to the second frame in the first frame. However, Framework offers the advantage of being able to print text and graphics together. A highlight of Framework is its Undo command which allows the adverse impact of erroneous commands (even another Undo!) to be easily erased. One particular frame, called DOS Access frame, is used to execute other PC-DOS application programs without leaving the Framework environment. However, such flexibility is of little relevance to new users. Overall, Symphony is more suited for applications involving numbers, and Framework is more suited for word processing applications.

One long-term benefit of the windowing environment is that the user will be insulated from hardware idiosyncracies. Today when a user migrates from a computer of one make to a computer of another make, he or she must go through a relearning exercise even if the same application program is being run in both cases. Now software such as Visi-On and MS-Windows control all of the interfaces of the computer and present a "virtual-machine" environment to the user. If the translation of the virtual-machine to the real machine is implemented correctly, then the "virtual-machine" environment can be made to appear identical to a user even if he or she shifts from one piece of physical hardware to another. Thus, users can migrate to newer hardware without having to redevelop software. Further, such virtual environments provide the ability to use information developed by other individuals on different personal computers.

Conversion Issues

Conversion of mainframe and minicomputer software to a personal computer environment represents an interesting development. The limited capabilities of the personal computer do not, in general, allow for a mainframe software package to be transported in its entirety to a personal computer. Also, because of large centralized databases it is not always desirable to move the entire mainframe package. Most likely, the original mainframe software is partially hosted to different degrees on both machines with communications between them. The personal computer provides terminal emulation, screen handling and query preprocessing and postprocessing capabilities. The mainframe retains responsibility for its principal task of database access, security, and query response. Thus a large number of tasks previously handled by the mainframe alone are now split between the personal computer and the host. A system such as the IBM PC-XT/370 offers facilities for better interfacing to the mainframe and for executing the original programs with little or no modification. Depending on the make of the mainframe or the minicomputer which is currently being used in an organization, there are some advantages in using a personal computer of the same make or, alternatively, a personal computer which offers facilities for emulation of instruction sets of the mainframe computer.

Graphics

The use of pictorial information in the realm of personal computers was initially spearheaded by the myriad of game packages on home computers. In such packages the entire picture was designed in advance, and the user was given no flexibility to alter the picture displayed. Then came business oriented packages like VisiPlot, 1-2-3, Chartmaster, and Chartman which allowed data to be displayed in the form of line diagrams, bar charts, pie charts, and histograms. Currently, we are witnessing the era of presentation graphics packages with emphasis on creating pictures for meetings and presentations. Whereas a two-dimensional representation suffices for business applications, many engineering applications in the CAD/CAM areas need three-dimensional graphics with shading and real-time simulation capabilities. Currently such facilities are provided on systems which are too costly to be classified as personal computers. As seen in Chapter 13, graphics represent the new direction in personal computer software, and virtually all personal computers now offer some level of support for graphics.

IV. VENDOR CONSIDERATIONS

The entry of vendors such as IBM and DEC into the personal computer arena set in motion enormous competitive pressures that are causing a shake out in the personal computer hardware industry. In order to maintain presence as a viable manufacturer in this industry, a market share of approximately 8 percent must be achieved. Only a few major vendors will remain viable in the long run. Several vendor considerations deserve mention here:

a) *Breadth of Product Line*—The manufacturer must offer a broad base of products in the personal computer area. This includes both the "CPU mainframe" as well as peripherals such as disks, displays, printers, and communication interfaces. It is preferable to select a vendor who supports a family of personal computer systems, that is, multiple models with various levels of performance. This allows a user flexibility in choosing an appropriate initial machine as well as providing a potential upgrade path for his or her future needs.

b) *Upward Compatibility*—At least some of the software should run on different hardware models. Radio Shack, for example, offers several models ranging from hand-held units upwards to a multiuser, 16-bit microprocessor system, but users cannot easily transport programs or data between various models. Similarly, the Apple Lisa is not compatible with the Apple IIe or the Apple III, making it very difficult for users with Apple IIs to upgrade directly and transport their software base upwards to the Lisa machine. In these examples additional investment is required to migrate to the new system.

c) *Plug Compatible Suppliers*—The strength of a vendor can be measured by the quantity of fully compatible hardware or software modules that are available for its machine. An example of plug compatibility is a disk drive for the IBM system that is manufactured by a separate vendor but which can plug-in with no modifications into the IBM system. The plug compatible vendor has lower costs than IBM and can pass on these savings to the customer. This concept is similar to the mainframe environment where the plug compatible suppliers are referred to as PCMs (plug compatible manufacturers). Generally, plug compatible suppliers offer price advantages of 10–30 percent off the original equipment manufacturer's price.

d) *Add-On Market*—Further strengths of a vendor can be ascertained by examining the size of the personal computer add-on market. These are devices or software modules which can be added on to the original equipment and are not offered by the original manufacturer. For instance, graphics processing modules to allow higher resolution color graphics on the IBM Personal Computer became available first from manufacturers other than IBM.

e) *Delivery, Service, and Documentation*—Final considerations relating to vendor strengths include the ability to deliver promptly, to provide competent service, and to supply good documentation to allow novice users to operate the nonsupported personal computer system. These characteristics are often lacking from current personal computer vendors as compared to traditional mainframe service and documentation standards. A counterbalancing force is that current personal computer users are often more tolerant of poorer service and documentation than traditional mainframe users.

Vendor Growth and Compatibility

When configuring a personal computer system one must identify a growth path in terms of both hardware and software to avoid the need to transport software between incompatible machines. Several factors are important:

a) *Architectural Obsolescence*—Architectures of personal computer systems have migrated from 8-bit microprocessors upwards to 16-bit and now to 32-bit microprocessors. Although it is possible to maintain upward software compatibility, in many cases vendors will not provide such an upwards growth path when transitioning between an 8-bit machine and a 16-bit machine, or between a 16-bit machine and a 32-bit machine. Some manufacturers are trying to maintain compatibility by incorporating the older 8-bit microprocessor in new 16/32-bit systems enabling the old software based on the 8-bit machine to be executed while developing new application programs in the 16/32-bit environment.

b) *Compatibility Among Nonhomogeneous Systems*—In virtually all large organizations, several different makes of personal computers are appearing. As with calculators, it is almost impossible to legislate through decree, policy, or coercion the purchase and use of only one manufacturer's unit for the entire organization. As a result most organizations will face the problem of integrating nonhomogeneous systems (e.g., Apples and IBMs) in the future. The nonhomogeneity of personal computer systems within an organization encourages selection of personal computers that can also execute programs designed for other personal computers.

c) *System Upgrade Path*—It is important to establish a continuous upgrade path within the family offered by a particular vendor. Starting out with a medium capability personal computer should not prevent the user from trading upwards at a future time to a more powerful machine with no loss in software functionality, but rather a gain in hardware and software capabilities. This implies upwards compatible systems and the ability for the user to easily transfer to the new technology as it becomes available.

V. CONCLUSION

Personal computer technology continues to evolve at a spectacular rate. At the dawn of the personal computer revolution one could have scarcely visualized that within a single decade personal computers would become so widespread. The rapid pace of evolution makes it difficult to make accurate predictions about future numbers of personal computers and their exact role in society. Each individual is finding it hard to identify the optimal time to buy a personal computer and the system appropriate to his or her needs. At present, advances in personal computer technology are occurring in several dimensions: advances in microprocessors, advances in input–output, advances in software, and advances in graphics. Undoubtedly, the next generation of personal computers will be even more impressive than the computers of today.

The personal computer field is an exciting and dynamic area with potential benefit for all individuals. Although the task of deciding on a system and its configuration may often be confusing and difficult, it is better to proceed with some choices, however arrived at and however *ad hoc*, than not to take any action at all. Opportunity costs of taking no action are too high. *The personal computer revolution is for everyone, with potential benefits for all.*

Authors' Biographies

Wallace W. Anderson is with Texas Instruments, Dallas. Currently he is working in the Speech Systems group of the Corporate Engineering Center. He developed the 2400 bit/s analysis/synthesis software for the TMS320 in the Speech Command board and is working on additional speech capabilities for the TI Professional Computer. At TI he was also in charge of software development for the on-board minicomputer of the HARM missile. Before joining TI in 1976, he worked at the Naval Underwater Systems Center, Newport, RI, in the area of torpedo and remotely piloted vehicle control systems.

Dr. Anderson received the B.S. degree in Mechanical Engineering from Iowa State University, Ames, and the S.M. and Sc.D. degrees in Mechanical Engineering from MIT, Cambridge, MA. He is a member of the IEEE.

David J. Bradley is the Manager of Personal Systems Architecture for the IBM Personal Computer. He has worked for IBM since 1975 on products such as the Series/1, the System/23 Datamaster, and the IBM Personal Computer XT. He is the author of a book on assembly language programming.

Dr. Bradley received the B.E.E. degree in Electrical Engineering from the University of Dayton, OH, and the M.S.E.E. and Ph.D. degrees in Electrical Engineering from Purdue University, Lafayette, IN.

J. Fred Bucy is President and Chief Executive Officer of Texas Instruments, Dallas. He was a founding member of the Technology Assessment Advisory Council of the Office of Technology Assessment of the Congress of the United States.

He is a member of the Council of Foreign Relations, a member of the Comptroller General's Consultant Panel, as well as the National Academy of Engineering, Sigma Pi Sigma, and Tau Beta Pi. Mr. Bucy is a Fellow of the IEEE. He has served several times as Chairman of the Board of Regents for Texas Tech University and Texas Tech University School of Medicine.

Mr. Bucy received the Bachelors degree in Physics from Texas Tech University, Lubbock, and the Masters degree in Physics from the University of Texas at Austin.

Robert E. Childs, Jr., is with Intel Corporation, Santa Clara, CA. His current assignment is as Senior Technical Marketing Manager with Special Programs, Corporate Marketing. He was Chief Architect of the iAPX 286 and the K286 operating kernel. His prior experience includes serving as Manager of Advanced Development of an ECL mainframe, architect of a special-purpose minicomputer, and architect of both a communications store and forward system and an interactive graphics system.

Mr. Childs received the B.S.E.E. and B.S. degrees in Engineering Mathematics from the University of Michigan, Ann Arbor. He is a member of the Association for Computing Machinery and the IEEE.

John D. Clarke is Engineering Group Manager at Digital Equipment Corporation, Maynard, MA, for DECmate series personal computers. He has been engaged in hardware and firmware engineering for word processing systems since joining Digital in 1971. Before working for Digital he designed the power system for MIT Lincoln Laboratory's TX-0, which was the first transistorized computer. He was also in charge of magnetic recording development at RCA's Computer Systems Division.

Mr. Clarke received the B.E.E. degree in Electrical Engineering from Rennselaer Polytechnic Institute, Troy, NY.

John Crawford is the architect of the 80386 microprocessor, and manages the microcode and diagnostics development team at Intel Corporation, Santa Clara, CA. He has also participated in the definition of microprocessor architectures and the development of software products.

Mr. Crawford received the B.S. degree in Computer Science from Brown University, Providence, RI, and the M.S. degree in Computer Science from the University of North Carolina, Raleigh.

Bruce Daniels has been a key member of the management team of the Lisa project at Apple Computer Inc., Cupertino, CA, from its inception five years ago. He served as the Lisa Software Manager with overall responsibility for all the Lisa software. He has also served as a leader of the Software Advanced Development Group for Lisa where he was responsible for software architecture, integration, performance, and reliability. Previously, he served as the first software project leader and system architect for the Apple III. He was the codesigner of the Apple III Sophisticated Operating System (SOS). Before joining Apple Computer, he was at Hewlett-Packard in the General Systems Division where he was responsible for development systems.

Mr. Daniels received the B.S. and M.S. degrees in Computer Science from MIT, Cambridge. He also worked in the Ph.D. program in the areas of programming languages and compilers.

Ahmed H. M. El-Sherbini is a Senior Engineer at Wang Laboratories, Inc., Lowell, MA, where he is doing research on image processing issues such as data compression, interpolation, document analysis, and symbol matching. He has also worked on digital signal processing and pattern recognition applications at Case Western Reserve University, Cleveland, OH.

Dr. El-Sherbini received the B.Sc. degree with honors in Electrical Engineering and the M.Sc. degree in Communications Engineering from Cairo University, Egypt. He received the Ph.D. degree in Electrical Engineering from Case Western Reserve University. He is a member of the Egyptian Engineering Society and the IEEE.

Philip D. Estridge is President of the Entry Systems Division at IBM. This new division combines entry systems activities in Boca Raton, FL, and office workstation product activities in Austin, TX. Mr. Estridge is responsible for worldwide development and product management, and the US manufacturing for IBM's general-purpose, low-cost, personal-use computer systems. He has also worked on the development of a Series/1 integrated product.

Mr. Estridge received the B.Sc. degree in Electrical Engineering from the University of Florida, Gainesville.

Bob O. Evans retired as IBM Vice President of Engineering, Programming, and Technology on July 1, 1984. He is now Senior Investment Partner at Hambrecht & Quist, San Francisco, CA. At his most recent job with IBM he was responsible for IBM's worldwide engineering, programming, and technology activities. In addition, he was a member of the Partner's and Executive Committee of Satellite Business Systems, a partnership involving Aetna, Comsat General, and IBM. He was responsible for coordinating IBM's involvement in this communications satellite-based company.

He was awarded Iowa State's Professional Achievement Citation in Engineering in 1971. He is a Fellow of the IEEE, a member of the National Academy of Engineering, served on the Defense Science Board, is a member of the Board of Trustees of Rensselaer Polytechnic Institute, a member of the MIT Visiting Committee for the Department of Electrical Engineering and Computer Science, a public member of the Charles Stark Draper Laboratory, a member of the Board of Trustees of the New York Public Library, and a consultant to the Science and Technology Advisory Group of the Executive Yuan, Republic of China.

Mr. Evans received the B.S. degree in Electrical Engineering from Iowa State University and has done graduate work at Syracuse University.

Barry James Folsom is Engineering Group Manager at Digital Equipment Corporation, Maynard, MA, for the Rainbow series of personal computers. Previously, he was New Products Program Manager for Incoterm.

Mr. Folsom received the B.S. degree in Electrical Engineering and the M.S. degree in Information and Computer Science from Georgia Institute of Technology, Atlanta.

Stan Fry is Department Manager in Research and Development at Wang Laboratories, Inc., Lowell, MA, where he directs efforts in database systems, image processing, voice applications, tools, and communications. He has also directed the software development and has been a key contributor to the design of the Professional Image Computer.

Mr. Fry studied at Pennsylvania State University, State College. He is a member of the Association for Computing Machinery.

Amar Gupta (Coeditor) is Principal Research Scientist at the Sloan School of Management, Massachusetts Institute of Technology, Cambridge. His interests include multiprocessor architectures, performance measurement, decision support systems, analytic modeling, office automation, and internation technology transfer. He has been involved in research on tightly coupled SIMD and MIMD machines. Before joining Sloan School of Management, he worked for the Department of Electronics, Government of India, and was responsible for evaluation and procurement of imported computers into India. He has also worked as a Systems Designer in the Indian Embassy in London, England.

He was awarded the Rotary Fellowship for International Understanding in 1979 and the Brooks Prize (honorable mention) in 1980. He is an Associate Editor of *IEEE Transactions on Industrial Electronics* and an Assistant Chairman for IECON, 1985. He is the Editor of *Advanced Microprocessors* (IEEE PRESS, 1983) and Coeditor of *Personal Computers* (and books, 1983). Recently, he acquired a U.S. permanent-resident status.

Dr. Gupta received the B. Tech. degree in Electrical Engineering from the Indian Institute of Technology, Kanpur, the S.M. degree in Management from the Massachusetts Institute of Technology, Cambridge, and the Ph.D. degree in Computer Technology from the Indian Institute of Technology, Delhi.

Ronald J. Ham is Engineering Group Manager at Digital Equipment Corporation, Maynard, MA, for the Professional 300 series personal computers. Previously, he managed a variety of software projects for Honeywell. Mr. Ham has been Chairman of the CODASYL Program Language Committee responsible for developing the industry-standard COBOL language. He has also been a speaker and instructor in software management for AMR Inc., and currently teaches in the Computer Sciences Department at Northeastern University, Boston, MA.

Mr. Ham received the B.S. degree in Mathematics from Villanova University, Villanova, PA.

William R. Hewlett is the cofounder of the Hewlett-Packard Company, which started in 1939 in Palo Alto, CA. His current title is Vice-Chairman, Board of Directors. He is the recipient of many awards and honorary degrees. Some of his awards include California Manufacturer of the Year (1969), West Coast Electronic Manufacturers Association Medal of Achievement (1971), and the Herbert Hoover Medal for Distinguished Service from Stanford University (1977). Together with David Packard, he has received the IEEE Founders Medal (1973), Vermilye Medal from the Franklin Institute (1976), and many others.

He is a member of the National Academy of Engineering and the National Academy of Sciences. He is also a Fellow of the American Academy of Arts and Sciences. Mr. Hewlett is a Life Fellow of the IEEE.

Mr. Hewlett received the B.A. and E.E. degree from Stanford University, Stanford, CA. He received the M.S. degree from the Massachusetts Institute of Technology, Cambridge.

David L. House is the Vice President and General Manager of Intel's Microcomputer Group, reporting to Intel's President, Andy Grove. The Microcomputer Group includes the Microprocessor Operation, Peripheral Controller Operation, and the Development Systems Operations in Hillsboro, OR, and Santa Clara, CA. Previously, while working for Honeywell, Mr. House received the

Harold W. Sweat Engineer Scientist Award for outstanding engineering contribution to minicomputer architecture and design. He is a member of the IEEE.

Meichun Hsu is an Assistant Professor of Computer Science at the Division of Applied Sciences at Harvard University, Cambridge, where she teaches courses in operating systems and database systems. Her primary research interests are in synchronization and distributed control algorithms for database systems and transaction processing systems, especially those algorithms related to the multiprocessor implementation of such systems for purposes of performance, reliability, and cost-effectiveness. She has also consulted for government and industry on issues of system architecture and performance.

She is a member of the Association for Computing and Machinery and the IEEE Computer Society.

Dr. Hsu received the B.A. degree from the National Taiwan University, the M.S.B.A. degree from the University of Massachusetts at Amherst, and the Ph.D. degree in Management Information Systems from the Massachusetts Institute of Technology, Cambridge.

Ryohei Ichikawa is an Engineering Manager in the Personal Computer Development Division, NEC Corporation, Kawasakishi, Kanagawa, Japan. He has also worked in the Integrated Circuit Division at NEC.

Mr. Ichikawa received the B.E. degree in Mechanical Engineering from Yokohama National University, Yokohama, Kanagawa, Japan.

Sundaresan Jayaraman is a Project Manager at Software Arts Products Corporation, Wellesley, MA. His research interests are in the areas of applied artificial intelligence, design of very high level computer languages, and enhancing the role of computers in the problem-solving and decisionmaking processes.

He has coauthored *The TK!Solver Book: A Guide to Problem-Solving in Science, Engineering, Business and Education* (Osborne/McGraw-Hill, Berkeley, CA, 1984).

Dr. Jayaraman received the B. Tech. and M. Tech. degrees in Textile Technology from the University of Madras, India, and the Ph.D. degree from North Carolina State University at Raleigh.

Akira Kato is with the Personal Computer Engineering Department of NEC Corporation, Kawasakishi, Kanagawa, Japan. His major works have been in the PC-8000 series and the PC-8800 series which are both best selling machines in the Japanese market.

Mr. Kato received the B.E. degree from Saitama University, Saitama, Japan.

Roubina Khoylian is Manager of Research Services at Venture Economics, Wellesley Hills, MA. In this capacity she is responsible for the company's proprietary databases related to the venture capital industry and companies financed by venture capitalists, and coordinates Venture Economics' research activities.

Ms. Khoylian received the Sc.B. degree in Applied Mathematics and Economics from Brown University, Providence, RI.

Koji Kobayashi is Chairman of the Board and Chief Executive Officer of NEC Corporation, Tokyo, Japan. He heads a company devoted to the manufacture of telecommunications, computers, and electronic systems and equipment, including satellite communications systems and equipment, as well as electronic devices.

He is affiliated with many industrial, professional, and government organizations. His many honors include the First Class Order of the Sacred Treasure as well as the Purple and Blue Ribbons awarded by His Majesty the Emperor of Japan. He has also received the Frederik Philips Award and the Founders Medal from the IEEE and decorations from the governments of Brazil, Egypt, Jordan, Paraguay, Peru, Poland, Thailand, and Madagascar. Dr. Kobayashi is a Fellow of the IEEE.

Dr. Kobayashi graduated from Tokyo Imperial University in 1929 and received the

Doctor of Engineering degree from the same university in 1939. He holds honorary doctorates from Monmouth College, the Polytechnic Institute of New York, and the Autonomous University of Guadalajara, Mexico.

Milos Konopasek is a Senior Scientist at Software Arts Products Corporation, Wellesley, MA. He also holds a visiting faculty position at the Massachusetts Institute of Technology, Cambridge, Department of Mechanical Engineering. Previously, he has held a number of management, research, and teaching positions in Czechoslovakia, U.K. and the U.S., most recently at Georgia Institute of Technology, Atlanta, and at North Carolina State University, Raleigh. The bulk of his research interests and contributions have been in textile engineering, applied mechanics, operations research and computer language design, in areas as diverse as CAD/CAM, large deflection analysis of slender bodies, pattern packing, and topology of line structures. During his stay at the University of Manchester Institute of Science and Technology, he conceptualized and developed the first working version of QAS, which later served as a springboard for the development of TK!Solver at Software Arts.

Dr. Konopasek graduated from Leningrad Textile Institute and received the Ph.D. and D.Sc. degrees from the University of Manchester, England.

David A. Kummer is with IBM. He was the lead engineer on the design of the IBM PCjr. He has also worked on the design of the IBM Personal Computer and the IBM Personal Computer XT. When he first joined IBM he worked on the IBM System/23 Datamaster.

Mr. Kummer received the B.S. degree in Electrical Engineering from Florida Atlantic University, Boca Raton. He is a member of the IEEE.

Steven W. Leininger is the Director of Strategic Planning for Tandy Electronics, the manufacturing division of Tandy Corporation, Fort Worth, TX. Previously, he was the primary hardware and software designer for the Radio Shack TRS-80 Microcomputer.

Mr. Leininger received the B.S.E.E. and M.S.E.E. degrees from Purdue University, Lafayette, IN. He is a member of the IEEE.

Stuart E. Madnick is Associate Professor of Management Science at the Sloan School of Management at MIT where he is also a member of the Center for Information Systems Research and affiliate member of the Laboratory for Computer Science. At MIT he is Principal Investigator of the INFOPLEX Database Computer project, the Composite Information Systems project, and the Systematic Design Methodology project. He has also been active in industry as a consultant to several corporations. In addition, he was cofounder of MITROL, Inc. (currently a subsidiary of GE's Information Systems Co.) and is currently Vice-Chairman of Knoware, Inc., a developer of personal computer software.

He is a member of Sigma Xi, the Association for Computing Machinery, and the IEEE. He is an Associate Editor of the *ACM Transactions on Database Systems*, founding member of the IEEE Technical Committee on Database Engineering, and former member of the IEEE Computer Society Board of Governors. He has coauthored the textbooks *Operating Systems* and *Computer Security*.

Dr. Madnick received the B.S. degree in Electrical Engineering, the M.S. degree in Management and also in Electrical Engineering, and the Ph.D. degree in Computer Science, all from the Massachusetts Institute of Technology, Cambridge.

Michael L. McMahan is a Senior Member of the Technical Staff at Texas Instruments, Dallas. He is currently working in TI's Corporate Engineering Center, with responsibility for DSP-based speech system development for the TI Professional Computer. Previously, he has worked in the area of secure voice communications, speech synthesis, and speech recognition.

Mr. McMahan received the S.B. degree in Electrical Engineering from MIT, Cambridge, and the M.S. degree in Computer Science from the University of Illinois, Urbana. He is a member of the IEEE.

Robert C. Miller is Senior Vice President, Business Division, at Data General Corporation, Westboro, MA, where he is responsible for overall management for the company's Information Systems Division, Desktop Division, and Technical Products Division, as well as the Systems Development Division. Prior to joining Data General Corporation he was Director of the Boulder, CO, Laboratories for IBM General Business Group.

He is a Registered Professional Engineer in the State of New York, a member of the National Society of Professional Engineers, and is on the Board of Directors for the Massachusetts Technology Park Corporation. He is a Senior Member of the IEEE.

Mr. Miller received the B.S. degree in Mechanical Engineering from Bucknell University, Lewisburg, PA, and the M.S. degree from Stanford University, Stanford, CA.

Gerald E. Nelson is Software R&D Manager for the Fort Collins Systems Division of Hewlett-Packard Company in Fort Collins, CO. He is responsible for all system software for the 9000 Series 200 and 500 computers. He has also worked on the development of frequency synthesizers, network analyzers, digital voltmeters, data acquisition systems, circuit test systems, and desktop computers.

He is one of the inventors of the IEEE-488 Standard Digital Interface for Programmable Instrumentation. He shared the Society Award from the IEEE Instrumentation and Measurement Society for this work.

Mr. Nelson received the B.S.E.E. degree from the University of Denver and the M.S.E.E. degree from Colorado State University, Fort Collins.

Robert N. Noyce cofounded Fairchild Semiconductor in 1957 and Intel Corporation in 1968. Currently, he is Vice Chairman of the Board of Directors of Intel Corporation, Santa Clara, CA.

He is coinventor of the integrated circuit with Jack Kilby. They have jointly received the Ballantine Medal of the Franklin Institute and Cledo Brunetti Award of the IEEE for this work. With Gordon Moore, cofounder of Intel Corp., he has received the AFIPS Harry Goode Award for leadership in computer science. He was awarded the National Medal of Science and the I.E.E. Faraday Medal in 1979, and IEEE Medal of Honor in 1978. He is a member of the National Academy of Science, the National Academy of Engineering, the American Academy of Arts and Sciences, and Phi Beta Kappa. Dr. Noyce is a Fellow of the IEEE.

Dr. Noyce received the B.A. degree from Grinnell College, Grinnell, IA, and the Ph.D. degree in Physical Electronics from the Massachusetts Institute of Technology, Cambridge.

Kenneth H. Olsen founded the Digital Equipment Corporation, Maynard, MA, in 1957 and has served as its President since that time. Prior to 1957, he was on staff at MIT's Digital Computer Laboratory, where he served as leader of the section which designed and built the MTC computer used in the SAGE Air Defense Computer design program. He also supervised the building of the high-performance, transistorized digital computers, the TX-0 and TX-2.

He has served on the Computer Science and Engineering Board of the National Academy of Sciences, Washington, DC, and the President's Science Advisory Committee. He is the recipient of many awards and honors, among others the "Young Electrical Engineer of the Year" (1960) from Eta Kappa Nu and the Franklin Institute's Vermilye Medal (1980). He is a Fellow of the American Academy of Arts and Sciences and a member of the National Academy of Engineering. Mr. Olsen is a Fellow of the IEEE.

Mr. Olsen received the B.S. and M.S. degrees in Electrical Engineering from the Massachusetts Institute of Technology, Cambridge.

Stanley E. Pratt is President of Venture Economics, Wellesley Hills, MA, Editor and Publisher of *Venture Capital Journal*, which has been reporting on and analyzing business development investing since 1961, and Editor of the eighth edition of *Pratt's Guide to Venture Capital Sources*. He is a noted consultant and spokesman for the venture capital industry, providing data and consultation for international clients as well as background for the media. He spent seven years in investment banking and brokerage and fourteen years with two private venture capital firms prior to purchasing Venture Economics in 1977.

Mr. Pratt received the A.B. degree in English from Brown University, Providence, RI.

John V. Roach is the Chairman of the Board, President, and Chief Executive Officer of Tandy Corporation, Fort Worth, TX. As Vice President of Radio Shack Manufacturing from 1975 to 1978, he was the key executive behind Radio Shack's initial entry into the computer marketplace.

He was elected *Financial World's* Chief Executive Officer of the Year in 1981. In 1981, he was also given the ADL Man of the Year Award. He received the Distinguished Lecturer Award in 1983 from the Delta Phi National Honorary Business Education Fraternity. He serves on President Reagan's Advisory Council on Private Sector Industry and Governor White's Science and Technology Council.

Mr. Roach received the B.A. degree in Physics and Mathematics and the M.B.A. degree from Texas Christian University, Fort Worth.

Richard A. Ross is the founder of Metatron, a firm dedicated to the development of effective, new generation software. He received the S.B. and S.M. degrees in Computer Science from MIT, and is currently on leave from the Ph.D. program there. He holds Certificate de Cuisine from the Cordon Bleu Ecole de Cuisine, Paris.

Mr. Ross has worked at Lotus Development Corp., Cambridge, MA, and Analytica Corporation, Freemont, CA, on database-modeling-recalculation systems, business graphics, and systems executive. Among his varied pursuits, he is interested in problems of political economy and public policy in high technology industries.

Mike Smutek is with Wang Laboratories, Inc., Lowell, MA, where he is Section Manager for developing software and has been a key contributor to the development of the Professional Image Computer. Previously, as Director of Systems Engineering, he was active in the development of an electronic picture-processing camera interfaced to minicomputers. Before joining Wang Laboratories, Inc., he helped develop a second-generation machine based on laser scanners, contributing the character recognition software. He also worked on the development of a multiterminal editing system for newspaper use.

Mr. Smutek received the B.S. degree in Electrical Engineering from the Massachusetts Institute of Technology, Cambridge. He is a member of the Association for Computing Machinery and the IEEE.

Richard T. Tarrant is a Senior Member of the Technical Staff in Texas Instruments' Corporate Engineering Center, Dallas. His interests include design of microprocessor-based computer systems and computer peripherals. While at Texas Instruments, he has also served as Project Manager for development of the TIPC Speech Command hardware, runtime utilities, and application software.

He is a member of Tau Beta Pi, Eta Kappa Nu, the IEEE Computer Society, and the IEEE. He is a Registered Professional Engineer in the State of Texas.

Mr. Tarrant received the B.S.E.E. degree from Texas Tech University, Lubbock, and the M.S.E.E. degree from the University of Texas at Austin.

Harry R. Tennant is the Manager of Artificial Intelligence Research in Texas Instruments' Computer Science Laboratory, Dallas. His branch is involved with many aspects of artificial intelligence and user interfaces. His own research has centered on natural language understanding, both building and evaluating natural language interfaces, and on aspects of human–computer interaction environments.

He is the author of the book, *Natural Language Processing: An Introduction to an*

Emerging Technology. He is also the author of a commercial version of Lisp. He is a member of the IEEE.

Dr. Tennant received the B.S. degree in Information Engineering and Computer Science and the M.S. degree in Information Engineering from the University of Illinois at Chicago Circle. He received the Ph.D. degree in Computer Science from the University of Illinois at Urbana-Champaign.

Hoo-min D. Toong (Coeditor) is with Sloan School of Management at MIT, and is the Founder and Chairman of Visual Communications Network, Inc. His research deals with advanced architectures, incorporating concurrent multiprocessor systems. He is investigating issues of synchronization, fault tolerance, nonstop computing, mechanisms for distributed control, and multiprocessor operating systems. He has also conducted research on the organizational impact of the microcomputer technology. His teaching focuses on microprocessors and microcomputer systems, personal computers, and business applications of the microcomputer technology. He has won several awards for excellence in teaching. He has directed several large projects for transfer of technology to Asia and Europe.

He is a member of Tau Beta Pi, Eta Kappa Nu, Sigma Xi, the Association for Computing Machinery, and the IEEE. He has authored *Personal Computers* (and books, 1983), and coedited *Advanced Microprocessors* (IEEE PRESS, 1983).

Dr. Toong received the B.S., S.M., and E.E. degrees from MIT, Cambridge. He also received the Ph.D. degree in Electrical Engineering and Computer Science from MIT.

Donald A. Wade is a Project Leader for Central Processor Development of Data General Corporation's System Development Division, Westboro, MA. Before joining Data General Corporation, he was at the MIT's Biomedical Engineering Center.

Mr. Wade received the B.S.E.E. and M.S.E.E. degrees from the Massachusetts Institute of Technology, Cambridge.

Christine Wallis is a Software Program Manager for Desktop Systems within Data General Corporation's Systems Development Division. Prior to that she was Software Marketing Manager for the company's Technical Products Division. Before joining Data General Corp. She was Manager of Operating Systems in Varian Associate's Instrument Division.

Ms. Wallis received the B.A. degree in Computer Science from the University of California at Berkeley.

William T. Walters is the Product Manager for the TRS-80 Model 100 computer at Tandy Corporation, Fort Worth, TX. He was deeply involved in the development of the final design specification for the Model 100 computer.

Mr. Walters received the B.B.A. degree from the University of Texas at Arlington and the M.B.A. degree from Chapman College, Orange, CA.

Frederick A. Wang is Executive Vice-President and Chief Development Officer of Wang Laboratories, Inc., Lowell, MA. Additionally, he is a member of the Executive Operations Committee, and a Director of the corporation. He oversees the efforts of 2000 scientists, engineers, and technical specialists in Wang's research and development organization.

He is a director of BayBank/Middlesex, a corporator at The Museum of Science, Boston, and a trustee of Brown University.

Mr. Wang received the B.Sci. degree in Applied Mathematics with a specialization in Computer Science from Brown University, Providence, RI, and is a graduate of Harvard University's Program for Management Development.

Kazuya Watanabe is Vice-President in charge of the personal computer business for NEC Corporation, Kawasaki, Kanagawa, Japan. He is also Chairman of the committee for coordination of personal computers in the Japan Industry Development Association.

Mr. Watanabe graduated from Yamanashi University, Yamanashi, Japan, with a degree in Electronics Communication Engineering.

Nancy Webb joined Wang Laboratories, Inc., Lowell, MA, in 1980 to work on the word processing editor or the Wangwriter. Previously, she worked on hardware device drivers, file management systems, disc drivers, and classified ad applications. Her current interests involve integration of images for word processing applications and image access methods.

Ms. Webb received the B.A. degree in Psychology from the University of New Hampshire, Durham. She is a member of Phi Beta Kappa.

Author Index

A

W. W. Anderson, 55

B

D. J. Bradley, 135
J. F. Bucy, 55

C

R. E. Childs, Jr., 201
J. D. Clarke, 78
J. Crawford, 201

D

B. Daniels, 266

E

A. H. M. El-Sherbini, 103
P. D. Estridge, 135
B. O. Evans, 331

F

B. J. Folsom, 78
S. Fry, 103

G

A. Gupta, 1, 17, 167, 247, 353

H

R. J. Ham, 78
W. R. Hewlett, 37
D. L. House, 201
M. Hsu, 222

I

R. Ichikawa, 315

J

S. Jayaraman, 301

K

A. Kato, 315
R. Khoylian, 347
K. Kobayashi, 315
M. Konopasek, 301
D. A. Kummer, 135

L

S. W. Leininger, 150

M

S. E. Madnick, 222
M. L. McMahan, 55
R. C. Miller, 120

N

G. E. Nelson, 37
R. N. Noyce, 201

O

K. H. Olsen, 78

P

S. E. Pratt, 347

R

J. V. Roach, 150
R. A. Ross, 282

S

M. Smutek, 103

T

R. T. Tarrant, 55
H. R. Tennant, 55
H. D. Toong, 1, 17, 167, 247, 353

W

D. A. Wade, 120
C. Wallis, 120
W. T. Walters, 150
F. A. Wang, 103
K. Watanabe, 315
N. Webb, 103

Subject Index

A

Aardvark Software, 336
Accumulator, 7, 9
ACM Society for Graphics, 253
Acoustical coupling, 342
Ada, 181, 182, 188, 192
Address. *See* Storage location
Advanced Input Devices, 357
Advanced Micro Devices, 170
Aha Inc., 336
Aiken, H. H., 331
Algorithms, 286, 287, 291, 295
Altair 8800, 18, 38
Alto personal computer, 17, 30
ALUs. *See* 16-bit ALU
AMI 29500 signal processor, 195
Apollo Computer, 350, 351
Apple Computer Inc., 10, 18, 266, 350
Apple Personal Computers, 31; Apple II,
     30, 120; Apple IIe, 360; Apple III, 360;
     Lisa. *See* Lisa personal computer
Application programs, 9, 51, 86
Artificial intelligence, 9
Ashton-Tate, 359
Assemblers, 8
Atari Inc., 11
AT&T, 11, 337, 340; Bell Laboratories, 27,
     28, 180, 191, 237, 331; study by, 251,
     3B computer system, 237; 3B2 computer
     system, 355; personal computer, 354
Attachment policies, 342
Audio magnetic-tape cassette, 2, 5, 19

B

Babbage, Charles, 347
Barrons, 340
BASIC, 3, 9, 18, 29, 47, 48, 55, 192, 329,
     358
BCD words. *See* Binary-coded decimal
     words
Bell, Alexander, 331
Bell Laboratories. *See* AT&T: Bell
     Laboratories
Bellmac-32A, 170, 180, 182, 186, 187, 189,
     355
Bell 103 compatible modem, 153
Bell 212A 1200-Bd modem, 85

B (continued)

Berkeley UNIX 51
BICARSA applications, 335
Binary-coded-decimal words, 169
Bit-map video controller, 83
Bit-sliced organization, 170
BPC microprocessor, 38, 42
Bricklin, Daniel, 29
Brown University, 337
Buchanen, B. G., 313
Burroughs B5000, 205
Burroughs Corp., 10
Burroughs 5000, 181
Bus. *See* Computing terminal interconnect
     bus; Intel multibus
Businessland Stores, 352
Byte, 3, 4

C

Cache memories, 169
CAD, 253
CAD/CAM, 262, 360
CAM, 253
Carnegie-Mellon University, 337
Carrier-sense multiple access with
     collision detection, 14
Cassette Tapes. *See* Audio magnetic tape
     cassettes
Cathode-ray tubes, 3, 5, 24
CATV, 344
CBS (Columbia Broadcasting System), 11
C&C (computers and communications).
     See Communications
Central processing unit, 2, 19, 30, 354
Character generator, 5
Chartman program, 10
C language, 29
Clocks. *See* Electronic clocks
CMOS technology, 168
COBOL, 3, 10, 18, 55, 192, 249
Coca Cola, 11
Coherent operating system, 191
Color printers, 357
Command language processors, 224, 231.
     See also SHELL command language
     processors
Command languages, 229, 236
Commodore Business Machines, 10, 18

Commodore Business Machines, 10, 18
Commodore 64 computer, 358
Common carrier services, 338
Communications, and Computers,
    315–346; economics, 341, 342, 343;
    facilities, 337–340; linking with
    computers, 333–334; role of personal
    computer in, 317; role in personal
    computing, 340–346
Communications register unit, 172
Communications satellites, 344
Compaq, 351
Compliers, 9. See also PASCAL compilers
Computer-aided design. See CAD;
    CAD/CAM
Computer-aided manufacturing. See
    CAD/CAM; CAM
Computer Coverup Inc., 336
Computer-generated outputs, 25
Computer graphics, 51, 247–265;
    acceptable output, 256; business
    graphics, 252, 256; home graphics, 252;
    image data, 256; penetration graphics,
    253; three-dimensional, 360;
    user-friendly interface, 255;
    workstation/engineering graphics, 253
Computer industry, evolution of, 10
Computerland, 336
Computer languages. See Ada, BASIC;
    C language; COBOL; DATATRIEVE;
    Fortran; High-level languages; HP
    Standard Pascal; LISP; Machine
    language; PASCAL; PL/M
Computer logic. See Logic
Computer memories. See Memories
Computer networks, 51, 215. See also
    Carrier-sense multiple access with
    collision detection; Ethernet; Local area
    networks; Protocols
Computers, general-purpose. See
    General-purpose computers
Computer Tamers, 336
Computing systems, classes of, 262
Concurrent access, 235, 241
Concurrent CP/M, 243–245
Context, 350
Control programs, 27, 28, 191
Convergent Technologies, 351
Core graphics, 86
CP/M (Control Program for
    Microprocessors), 222, 235, 236. See
    also Concurrent CP/M
CPUs. See Central processing units
Creative Communications Systems, 351
Cromix operating system, 191
CRT. See Cathode-ray tubes
CSMA/CD. See Carrier-sense multiple
    access with collision detection
Computing terminal interconnect bus, 80

D

Daisy-wheel printer, 6
Databases, 287, 288, 290, 291, 292, 345.
    See also DBMS; Dow Jones
    News/Retrieval
Data General Desktop Generation Model
    10: 120–133, 354; console color monitor,
    126; design alternatives, 122; generation
    program, 131; model 10, 132; office
    automation and decision support
    markets, 121; packaging, 130; product
    and system OEM markets, 121; small
    business system markets, 121; software
    architecture, 127; system processing
    unit, 124
Data General Eclipse, 179
Data General MicroEclipse, 20, 122, 123,
    124, 125, 127; software, 128
Data terminals, 345
DATATRIEVE, 86
dBase II, 354
DBMS (Data Base Management Systems),
    358
Debugging, 27
DEC J-11, 80
DECmate II, 78, 79, 94, 355; basic
    configuration of, 96; CP/M-80
    operating system, 95; floppy disk sizes,
    94; keyboard, 100; monitors, 99; power
    supply, 97; radio frequency interference
    protection, 97; system units, 96; Z80A
    auxiliary processor, 95
DEC Professional 300 series, bit-map
    video controller, 83; bus structure, 80;
    communications, 86; computer
    graphics, 84, 92; CPU selection, 80;
    diagnostics, 90, 91; hardware
    architecture, 79, 86, 87; loopback
    testing, 91; option modules, 81;
    software, 85, 86, 93; telephone
    management system, 84; terminal
    control program, 84; video data
    processor, 83
DEC Rainbow series, 30, 78, 79, 86–88,
    98, 130
DEC VAX 11/780, 86, 188, 259, 263
Department of Defense, 181
Desktop Generation Model 10. See Data
    General Desktop Generation Model 10
Device Management, 226, 234
Diagnostics firmware, 82
Design automation. See CAD; CAD/CAM
Digital Equipment Corporation, 10, 18,
    22, 30, 78, 350, 360. See also DEC
Digital Research, 27, 28, 191, 222, 283,
    350, 358
Disk drives, 10

Disk memories, 3, 4, 7. *See also* Floppy
  disks; Hard disk; Optical disks;
  Winchester disks
Displays, 24, 84, 345. *See also* Cathode-ray
  tubes; Flat-panel displays; Liquid-crystal
  displays; Video displays
Distribution channels, 11
Direct memory access, 80
DOS 2.0 operating system, 243–245
Dot matrix printers, 5, 6, 357
Dow Jones News/Retrieval, 59, 62
Dow Jones Newswire Service, 340
Dow Jones Reporter, 341
DSS packages, 358
Duda, R. O., 301
Dual-ported memories, 31
Durango Systems, 350, 351

E

Easywriter program, 10
Eclipse. *See* Data General Eclipse
8-bit microprocessor, 171
Electronic clocks, 4
Electronic worksheets, 29
EMACS editor, 52
Entre Computer Stires, 352
Epson, 150
Ethernet, 57
ExecuVision. *See* VCN Execuvision
Expert systems, 301–313

F

Fairchild 9440, 168
Feigenbaum, E. A., 301, 313
Feiner, S., 259
File directory, 239
File management, 227, 234
File security, 235, 240
Firmware. *See* Diagnostics firmware
Flat panel displays, 5, 24, 357
Floating-point arithmetic, 51, 169
Floppy disks, 4, 19, 21, 30
Fortran, 3, 9, 10, 18, 29, 55, 192, 249, 358
4-bit microprocessors, 171
Framework, 354
Frankston, Robert, 29
Fujitsu, 179
Fujitsu FM-11 EX, 354
Future directions, 219

G

Gasching, J., 301
Gavilan Computers, 351
General Data Processor System, 181
General purpose computers, 1
Gold, B., 69
Goldstein, I., 301
Graphicon Software, 358
Graphics. *See* Computer graphics
Goodie Co., PC, 336
Grid Systems, 351

H

Hansen, P. M. *et al.*, 188
Hard copy output. *See* printers
Hard disk, 33
Hardware implementation, 215
Hewlett-Packard, Inc., 10, 17, 168, 180,
  181, 182, 185, 189. *See also* HP
Hewlett-Packard 32-bit microprocessor,
  169, 183, 186, 187
Hicomp Technology, 351
High-bandwidth communication services,
  345
High-level languages, 8, 17
Hitachi, 150
HP Interface Bus, 38
HP 150 system, 337
HP Series 80, 52, 53
HP Series 100, 52
HP Series 200, 30, 40–42, 44, 47, 48, 50,
  51, 53, 355, memory map, 43; HP 216,
  42; HP 226, 41; HP 236, 42; HP 236C, 42
HP Series 9000, 20, 169, 355; HP 9100, 17;
  HP 9100A, 17, 37; HP 9820A, 38, HP
  9830A, 38; HP 9920, 42
HP Standard Pascal, 50
HP-UX operating system, 44, 50
Hudson, R. G., 312

I

iAPX 432. *See* Intel iAPX
IBM Corp, 10, 11, 18, 20, 334, 360, 361
IBM Display Writer, 263
IBM mainframes, 202; IBM 3033, 243; IBM
  370, 180; IBM 37048, 189
IBM PC, 30, 31, 120, 130, 132, 133, 192,
  201, 258, 259, 284, 294, 354, 356
IBM PC/AT, 237, 243

IBM PCjr, 11, 24, 27, 135–149, 357; Basic Input/Output System, 145; color graphics, 139; component selection, 145; direct memory access, 145; diskette, 143; Disk Operating System 2.1, 144; display, 146; hardware architecture, 136, 139; infrared link, 143; internal modem, 144; keyboard, 142, 147; processing, 144, 145; ROM and cartridges, 40, 141; sound sources, 141; system board I/O, 142; system description, 136
IBM PC/XT, 132, 133, 135, 243, 354
IBM PC-XT/370, 135, 360
IBM System 9000, 355
IBM 3270, 135
IDRIS operating system, 85, 191
IEEE Standard 802, 192; Standard 488, 80; Standard P754, 170; Standard P796, 192
IEEE 488, 80
iMAX microprocessor, 192
IMSAI Manufacturing Corp., 10
Information storage. See Memories
Input/output, 19, 23, 357; buffer management, 226, 237; device management, 223
Integrated circuits, 2, 10, 201, 315, 316
Intel Corp., 10, 172, 350
Intel microprocessors, 2920 analog processor, 195; Intel 4004, 19, 167; Intel 8080, 38, 91; Intel 8085, 168; Intel 8086, 124–126, 172, 173, 191, 354; Intel 8086/8088, 202, 203, 205, 355; Intel 8087, 174; Intel 8088, 171, 174, 201, 354; Intel 80186, 174; Intel 80186, 174; Intel 80280, 168; Intel 80286, 175, 201–208, 210, 211, 212, 213, 215, 217–220; Intel 80386, 219, 220; Intel 80287, 204; iAPX 32, 180; Intel iAPX 86 family, 201–206, 208, 210, 212, 215, 219, 220; Intel iAPX 432, 181–183, 185, 186, 188, 189, 193; Intel iAPX 43201, 181; Intel iAPX 43202, 181, 183; Intel iAPX 43203, 181, 183, 194
Intel multibus, 192
Intel System Builder, 208
Interactive Systems Corp., 243
Interconnecting computer systems, 14
Interconnection standards, 192. See also ISO Open Systems Interconnection Reference Model
Interfaces, 3, 345. See also Jobcard interfaces, man–machine interfaces, parallel interfaces; program interfaces; RS-232 interfaces; windows
International Consultative Committee for Telegraphy and Telephony (CCITT), 344

International Standards Organization (ISO) 192, 344
Interpreters, 9
I/O. See Input/Output
ISO Open Systems Interconnection Reference Model, 13, 192, 204
ISO standards, 50
Itakura time registration technique, 72
Ithaca Intersystems, 351

J

Jobcard interfaces, 60

K

Kanji characters, 320, 321
Kate's Komputers, 336
Keyboards, 2, 3, 10, 23
Kilobits, 4
Knuth, D., 293
Kobayashi, K., 315
Konopasek, Milos, 302
Kyocera, 150

L

Language processors. See Command language processors; Compilers
Languages. See Ada; BASIC; Cobol; C language; Command languages; DATATRIEVE; Fortran; High-level languages; HP Standard Pascal; LISP; Machine language; Modcal language; Modula; PASCAL; PL/M
LANS. See Local area networks
Laser printers, 357
Letter-quality printers, 357
Light interconnection technology, 344
Light pen, 24
Linear predictive coding, 26
Liquid-crystal displays, 171
Lisa personal computer, 30, 266–280, 354, 358, 360; Charter 266; design goals 267; desktop manager, 279, 280; display, 269, 270; hardware, 267; hardware bus 271; memory management unit 268, 269; operating system 271; processor 267; software 271; software library, 277–279; user interface, 274–276;

LISP, 52
Local-area networks, 3, 19, 27, 193, 317,
    340. *See also* Ethernet; Token passing
    local area networks
Local loop, 339
Logic, 1, 2, 17. *See also* TTL NANDgate
LOGO, 30
Long-haul carrier systems, 340
Lotus Development Corp., 283, 350, 359
Lotus 1-2-3, 55, 250, 252, 294, 299
LSI. *See* Integrated circuits
LSI-11, 191

M

Machine language, 8
MacIntosh. *See* Apple personal
    computers: MacIntosh
Magnetic media, 5
Magnetic tapes, 2. *See also* Audio
    Magnetic-tape Cassette
Mainframe computers, 1, 18, 26, 29, 353,
    360. *See also* IBM mainframes
Man–machine interfaces, 316
Manufacturing automation. *See*
    CAD/CAM; CAM
Maps/PRO, 86
Marconi, Marchese, 331
Mark Williams Co., 191
Market segments, 12
Massachusets Institute of Technology,
    30, 52, 78, 301, 337
Megabyte, 4
Memories, 5, 7, 17, 19, 23, 24, 51, 355. *See
    also* Cache memories; Disk memories;
    Hard disks; Optical disks; Primary
    memories; RAMs; ROMs; Secondary
    memories; Winchester disks
Memory management, 223, 225, 232, 235,
    241
Microcomputer Applications Associates,
    27, 91
Microcontrollers, 167
MicroEclipse. *See* Data General
    MicroEclipse Computer
Microprocessors, 2, 4, 7, 10, 17–21, 25,
    27, 28, 167–197. *See also* Bellmac-32A;
    BPC microprocessor; Burroughs B5000;
    DEC F-11; DEC J-11; DEC VAX 11/780;
    8-bit microprocessors; Fairchild 9440;
    4-bit microprocessors; General Data
    Processor System; iAPX; iMAX, 192;
    LSI-11; Motorola 6809; Motorola 68000;
    Motorola 68010; Motorola 68020;
    National Semiconductor 16032;
    National Semiconductor 32032; Philips

Data Systems SP 16C/10; 16-bit
    microprocessors; TMS 320; Zilog Z-8;
    Zilog Z-80; Zilog Z-8000
Microprogramming, 168
Microsoft Corp., 27, 28, 132, 150, 191, 243,
    283, 350, 358, 359
Mighty Byte Computer Inc., 336
Minicomputers, 1, 2, 9, 17, 18, 20, 26, 27,
    29, 78, 333, 353. *See also* PDP-11/70
Mits Inc., 10, 18, 38
Modcal language, 50
Modems, 2, 19, 317. *See also* Bell 103
    compatible modem; Bell 212A 1200-Bd
    modem
Modula, 48
Modulator–Demodulator. See Modems
Momentum Computer Systems, 351
Moore, G. E., 169
Morse, Samuel F. B., 331
MOS technology, 167, 168
Motorola 6809, 171
Motorola 68000, 20, 30, 42–44, 168, 170,
    172, 176, 177, 191, 268, 273, 354, 355
Motorola 68010, 172, 177
Motorola 68020, 177, 178, 180
Mouse, 24, 357
MP/M operating system, 28, 191
MS-DOS operating system, 359
Multics Honeywell, 645, 205, 213
Multiplan Electronic Worksheet, 132
Multiple-window interface, 202
Multiprocessing, 194

N

Nagy, S., 259
National Science Foundation, 38
National Semiconductor, 172, 179
National Semiconductor 16032, 168, 169,
    178, 188
National Semiconductor 32032, 180
NaturalLink software, 55, 59, 61–64, 75
Nau, D. S. 301
NBI, 336
NCR Corp., 169
NEC. *See* Nippon Electric Corporation
NEC PC-100, 318–330; design description,
    322–328; role in office automation,
    328; system block diagram, 321
Newtown-Raphson procedure, 306; *1984*,
    317
Nippon Electric Corporation, 11, 31, 195.
    See also NEC PC-100
NMOS technology, 168
NPL Information Management, 86

O

Olivetti, 11
Once Begun Computations, 336
1-2-3. *See* Lotus 1-2-3
Onyx Systems, 351
Operating Systems, 222–245. *See also*
  Assemblers; Berkeley UNIX, Coherent
  operating system; Command language
  processors; Compilers; Control
  programs; CP/M Cromix operating
  system; DOS 2.0 operating system;
  HP-UX operating systems; Interpreters;
  MP/M operating system; MS-DOS
  operating system; UCSD *p*-system;
  ULTRIX, UNIX, VAX/VMS operating
  systems; VENIX; XENIX operating
  system
Optical disks, 22, 356
Optrex, 150
Osborne computer, 351
Otrona, 351
Output. *See* Computer-generated output
Output devices. *See also* Printers

P

PACE microprocessor, 172
Papert, S., 301
Parallel interface, 3
PASCAL, 9, 29, 55, 192, 358. *See also* HP
  Standard Pascal; UCSD Pascal
PASCAL compiler, 50
PASCAL workstation, 48, 49
PC/IX, Unix version, 243
PDP-7, 27
PDP-8, 79
PDP-11, 79, 80, 83, 85, 86, 179, 191
PDP-11/70, 80
J. C. Penney, 336
Personal computers. *See* Apple personal
  computers; Commodore 64 computer;
  Fujitsu FM-11 EX, 354; DECmate II; DEC
  Rainbow series; DEC Professional 300
  series; IBM PC; IBM PC/AT; IBM
  PC-XT/370; IBM System 9000; IBM
  3270; PDP-7; PDP-8; PDP-11; Radio
  Shack TRS Model 100; Radio Shack
  TRS-80 Model 10; Toshiba Pasopia-16;
  Wang Professional Image Computer;
  Whirlwind computer; Xerox Star; Age
  of, 334–336; Future trend, 51; Markets,
  32–34
Philips Data Systems SP 16C/10, 179
Phillips, 22
Pixels, 24
PL/M, 191

PMOS technology, 168
Primary memory, 2, 3, 4, 7, 9, 20
Prime Computer, 350
Printers, 25, 357. *See also* Color printers;
  Daisy-wheel printers; Dot matrix
  printers; Laser printers; Thermal printers
Process creation, 233, 238
Processor management, 223, 226, 233,
  238
Process scheduling, 238
Process synchronization, 233, 239
Processor Technology Corp., 10
Program assemblers. *See* Assemblers
Program compilers. *See* Compilers
Program interfaces, 18
Program interpreters. *See* Interpreters
Programs. *See* Application programs;
  Chartman program; Control programs;
  DATATRIEVE; dBase II; Debugging;
  VCN EXECUVision; Framework;
  Computer graphics; LOGO; Lotus 1-2-3;
  Multiplan Electronic Worksheet; System
  programs; Terminal control program;
  VisiCalc; Visiplot; Wordstar
Program storage. *See* Memories
Protocols. *See also* Carrier sense multiple
  access with collision detection
Prudential Insurance Co., 11

Q

Quarterdeck, 358

R

Rabiner, L. R., 69
Radio Shack, 10, 18, 360
Radio Shack TRS-80 Model 100, 150–166;
  software, 152–154; hardware, 154–165
Radio Shack TRS-80 Model 10, 355
RAMs, 4, 20, 21
Random Access Memory. *See* RAMs
RCA Corp., 168
Read Only Memories. *See* ROMs
Read/Write Memories, 4
Record management and buffering, 234,
  240
Reference Model. *See* ISO Open Systems
  Interconnection Reference Model
Remote terminals, 345, 346
Resource management, 223, 225, 232
RGB Cartesian coordinate system, 253
Rockwell International, 168, 172
ROMs, 4, 5, 20

Ross, Richard A., 293
Ross, S. S., 312
RS-232 interface, 88
RSX-11M software, 86
RSX-11M-Plus, 85, 86

S

Schaum's Outline Series, 312
Schell, R. R., 215
Scientia Inc., 358
Screen, 2
Sears Roebuck, 61, 336
Secondary Memories, 2, 4–6, 21, 235, 241,
  356
Secure systems, 215
Serial interface information, 3
Sharp, 22
SHELL command language processor, 241
Short-haul systems, 339
SIGGRAPH. *See* ACM Society for Graphics
Signal processor. See AMI 29500 signal
  processor
Silicon chips, 2
Single-chip microcomputers, 170
SINGRAPH, 86
16-bit ALU, 173
16-bit microprocessors, 173, 179
Smalltalk system, 274
Software, 7, 282–300, 357, 358, 359. *See
  also* Application programs; Chartman
  program; Control programs;
  DATATRIEVE; dBase II; Debugging;
  VCN ExecuVision; Framework;
  Computer graphics; LOGO; Lotus 1-2-3;
  Multiplan Electronic Worksheet;
  Operating systems; RSX-11M; Software
  RSX-11M plus; System programs;
  Terminal control program; Visicalc;
  VisiPlot; Wordstar
The Source, 341
Speech Command, 55, 57, 59, 68–70, 74
Speech synthesis, 25, 26
Spreadsheets, 288, 289, 290
Standards. *See* IEEE standards;
  Interconnection standards; ISO
  standards; U.S. Federal Data Encryption
  Standard
Stanford University, 301
Stibitz, G. R., 331
Storage devices. *See* Memories
Storage Technology, 350
Structured Systems Group, 358
Sunrise Systems, 351
Supercomm-20 Communications, 86
Swapping, 238

Switched service, 339
System architecture, 230, 243
System programs, 4

T

Tablets, 24
Tandon Corp., 10
Tandy Corp., 150
Task sharing, in floppy-based system, 89;
  in Rainbow, 100
Tektronics HLS color model, 253
Telephone management system, 84
Terminal control program, 84
Terminals. *See* Data Terminals; Voice
  terminals; Remote terminals
Texas Instruments; 55, 169, 171, 172, 173,
  195. *See also* TI 9900; TI professional
  Computer
Thermal printers, 6, 357
32-bit microprocessors, 180. *See also*
  Hewlett-Packard 32-bit microprocessor
Thompson, Kenneth, 191
THOMSON/CSF, 22
Time-Life, 11
TI 9900, 172, 177
TI Professional Computer, 55–75, 354;
  design, 55; keyboard, 56; speech
  command system, 64, 65, 75; system
  architecture, 57; TMS 320 architecture,
  66
Time-sharing, 17
TK!Solver, 86, 301–313
TMS controller module, 85
TMS 320, 195
Token-passing local area network, 14
Toshiba Corp., 22
Toshiba Pasopia-16, 354
TTL NAND gate, 171
Touch screens, 24
TWX, 339

U

UCSD *p*-system, 28
University of California at Berkeley, 237
ULTRIX, 85
University of California at San Diego, 49,
  191
University of Southern California, 38
UNIX, 79, 85, 191, 227, 237, 243–245, 272;
  advantages of, 50; contributions of,
  50; shell of, 27, 28

UNIX SYSTEM V, 237, 239, 355
U.S. Federal Data Encryption Standard, 340
U.S. information industry, 334

V

Van Dam, A., 259
VAX-11/780. *See* DEC VAX 11/780
VAX/VMS operating systems, 86
VCN ExecuVision, 10, 30, 256, 259, 262
VENIX, 85
Venture Capital, 347; areas of active investment, 350; computer industry, 350; investment patterns, 349; role of, 347, 348; expected future developments, 351
Video data processor, 83
Video displays, 357
Video games, 25
VisiCalc, 9, 10, 15, 29, 120, 249, 250, 284, 288, 294, 354
Visicorp, 283, 350, 358, 359
VisiPlot, 250, 252
VLSI. *See* Integrated circuits
Voice recognition, 25. *See also* Speech command
Voice Terminals, 345
von Neumann, John, 331

W

Wall Street Journal, 340
Wang Laboratories, 30

Wang Professional Computer, 103–118, 354; hardware, 106, 107–111; software, 106, 111–117
Western Electric 32000. *See* Bellmac-32A
Western Union Telex, 339
Whirlwind Computer, 78
Wilkes, Maurice, 331
Winchester-based system, 265
Winchester disks, 22, 26, 356
Windows, 358
Word processor, 2
Word size, 4
Wordstar, 10, 55
Worksheets. *See* Electronic Worksheets
Work stations, 1, 202. *See also* PASACAL work station

X

XENIX, 191
XENIX operating system, 243
Xerox Alto. *See* Alto personal computer
Xerox Corp., 11, 17, 274, 358
Xerox Star, 202

Z

Zero insertion force connectors, 82, 96
Zilog, 172
Zilog Z-8, 171
Zilog Z-8000, 175, 191
Zilog Z-80, 171, 191
Zilog Z80A, 87